AMERICAN GREATNESS

AMERICAN GREATNESS

People and Events that
Made America a Great Nation

John Peter Dunnell, Ed.D.

To order additional copies of this book, contact:
Xlibris Corporation
1-888-795-4274
www.Xlibris.com
Orders@Xlibris.com
50946

CONTENTS

Ours is the land of the free because it is the home of the brave. America's future will always be great because our nation will always be strong. And our nation will be strong because our people will be free. And our people will be free because we will be united, one people under God, with liberty and justice for all.

—RONALD REAGAN
November 4, 1984

DEDICATION

To my wife, June Louise Eckhardt Dunnell. We met in 1951 when we were both teachers. We fell in love that fall and were married the next summer on August 16, 1952. We had the perfect marriage—love, admiration, and respect for each other. She encouraged me to finish my thesis and receive my master's degree. She brought two wonderful children into the world, Scott and Amy, and they have been a pride and joy.

When I gave thought to making an application to Illinois State University to seek a doctor's degree, she helped me in many ways. It took me seven and a half years, but she encouraged me in every step of the way—preparing for the entrance exams, the course work, the comprehensive exams, and the most trying part, the dissertation. I could not have done it without her.

We had fifty-five years and eighty-eight days of true wedded bliss. I lost my true love on November 11, 2007. This book is a living tribute to a great person, a wonderful wife, a devoted mother and greatly loved grandmother.

INTRODUCTION

T housands of laborers built the Pyramids of Egypt over 4,900 years ago for the express purpose of creating burial chambers for their king and his queen. The pyramids are a marvel of unbelievable engineering.

The Parthenon in Greece was built around 440 BC. Today it stands in ruins, but the Greeks gave the world its first peek at democracy.

The Coliseum in Rome was built so that Roman emperors could watch gladiators kill each other. Rome's true contribution was the establishment of a universally recognized legal system.

The Great Wall of China took over 270 years to complete with the purpose of keeping out the barbarians in the north. Its 1,400 miles is something to behold. Other Chinese contributions include the invention of gun powder and the discovery of paper.

What does the United States of America have to be proud of? Not one structure to compare with those ancient ruins—unless you count the four presidents on Mount Rushmore. Instead it has two valuable pieces of paper—the Declaration of Independence and the United States of America's Constitution. They stand as living documents to the world that the *freedom* and *liberty* that we enjoy, are a lasting tribute to the men and women who came to this country 400 years ago. They settled the land, tilled the soil, fought off starvation, hardships and unfriendly Indians.

The seeds of democracy were planted when 102 people seeking religious freedom risked their lives to come across the Atlantic Ocean from England in a small sailing ship. They wanted to determine their own future. They agreed to be obedient to laws, ordinances, and acts passed for the good of the colony *they* established in 1620 in a village they named Plymouth.

Over the next 112 years, thirteen English colonies were established. From 1619 to 1775, different leaders in these colonies not only showed dissatisfaction with decisions made by England but showed a growing desire for independence. The determining factor was a combination of many decisions on both sides of the Atlantic. Many of the first generations of colonists felt some loyalty to their mother country, but as the years went by, more colonists thought of themselves as American and not so beholden to Britain. It is interesting to note that two men from Britain—one an Englishman, John Locke, and the other, Adam Smith from Scotland—may have contributed as much as anyone to the growing idea that the divine right of kings is to be not only questioned but seriously considered as an affront to men seeking their destiny.

Locke's *Essay on Human Understanding* and his *Two Treaties on Government* helped lay the groundwork for men to think that there must be a better way to govern. Adam Smith's *Wealth of Nations* lay to rest the idea that mercantilism was the answer for nations, and he showed that it had outlived its purpose to increase the monetary wealth of a nation by strict governmental regulations of the entire national economy.

What made up the character of these people who believed they should be free to select their own leaders and choose their own style of government? Nothing like that had ever been thought of before, let alone tried. What makeup and experience helped to mold a new land of people who wanted nothing but their own lives and the lives of their offspring to be influenced by no one but themselves? When and where and with whom did it start? Was it the Pilgrims whose original number of 102 dwindled to 50 after the first long winter, who buried their dead and flattened the graves so that the Indians would not know how many had died, and in the spring planted seeds of grain to cover them?

Or was it George Washington's determination to fight the greatest army in the world at that time in an unconventional manner? He may well have learned how in fighting the Indians and the French as a colonial officer in the British army. His strategy as commander of the Continental army was to harass the British at every turn and then retreat to fight another day. His other generals like Ethan Allen, Francis Marion, Nathanael Greene, Daniel Morgan, and Horatio Gates applied similar tactics with surprising results.

Men who wanted their freedom were willing to go to great lengths to make that dream a reality—and women too. Mary Ludwig Hays, wife of a private from Pennsylvania, won immortal fame in her service of carrying water to the parched soldiers in the Battle of Monmouth. She was given the rank of sergeant and forever after would be known as Molly Pitcher. Nathan Hale had only one regret—that he had but one life to give. John Paul Jones's reply to his adversary's request to quit in a sea battle was, "I have not yet begun to fight."

Where do people like that come from? None was of noble birth. Many had little education. But they learned to adjust, adapt, and yes, sacrifice, to make sure that what they believed would endure.

The purpose of this book is to show the world what made America great. The many, many people who were, some say, at the right place at the right time or others say who were common people rising to uncommon challenges, preserved the spirit that made the United States of America not only free but destined to become a great nation. What they said and accomplished should be preserved for all future generations to know and appreciate. What they said and accomplished has already been chronicled in numerous ways but bears repeating. As philosopher John Dewey said in 1916, "Democracy must be reborn in each generation, and education is the midwife."

John P. Dunnell, Ed.D.

PREFACE

If someone were to ask me, how is America different from every other country on earth? and told me to describe my answer in one word, I would think that the answer would have to be *diversity*.

No other nation can claim to be as diverse as the United States of America. The first colonies in America were settled mostly by the English, but some were settled by the Dutch and Swedes. Over the course of four hundred years (1607-2007), people from every conceivable part of the world have come to America. Some, such as the slaves from Africa, had no choice; but all others sought, as their destination, a place to earn a living wage, a chance to own a farm or start a business, and also to worship in their own way to their own supreme being. Some dreamed of finding streets paved with gold, but most just wanted a chance to live productive lives for themselves and their future generations.

Some of the earliest emigrants from England came as indentured servants—binding one person to work for another for a given period. In the eighteenth century, that method of getting to the New World was replaced by the Irish and Germans. These people were willing to be free servants just so they could go and stay in America.

The potato famine brought many from Ireland beginning in the 1840s. They dug the canals—the Erie and the Illinois and Michigan canals—and helped build the Union Pacific Railroad after the Civil War. Later, these Irish became a large part of the police forces in New York City and Chicago as well as other places.

The Chinese came to America following the gold discovery in 1848. When they were denied mining rights, they helped build the Central Pacific Railroad.

During the industrial boom beginning in the 1870s, many new immigrants found their own neighborhoods in and around the big cities. Italians, Germans, Poles, and Jews found their own kind, worked in crowded factories, and sweated, but survived. In cities like San Francisco and Chicago, the Chinese lived and worked together, and today are famous for their Chinatowns.

From the time of Texas's annexation, many Mexicans stayed and worked the fields and other jobs that no one else wanted to tackle. Today, the Hispanic population is the largest minority in the United States.

Another unique thing happened in America that did not happen in any other part of the world. Mixed marriages became the norm rather than the exception. Englishmen chose brides that came from other countries. Scotch mixed with Irish; Germans mixed with all of them. Jews even married Gentiles. Nowhere on Earth could this have happened, let alone work.

Thanks to two relatives, I have documented proof of my American ancestors. My mother is mentioned in the genealogical section of a book written by Phoebe Strong Cowen titled *The Herkimers and Schuylers. An Historical Sketch of Two Families.* It was published in Albany, New York by Joel Munsell's Sons in 1903.

On my father's side, my cousin Mary Dunnell Peters did extensive research in the State of Maine where she found proof of our early ancestor, Henry Donnell, coming from Scotland to America. I am greatly indebted to both of them.

I come from a mixture of Scotch, German, Dutch, and Irish. On my father's side, my great-great-great-great-great-great-great-grandfather Henry Donnell came from Scotland about 1634. My great-grandfather was Mark Hill Dunnell. He served in Congress and helped to found the Republican Party in the State of Maine. He moved to Owatonna, Minnesota, where his home is located in the Village of Yesteryear.

On my mother's side, my great-great-great-great-great-great-great-grandfather Jurgh (George) Herkimer came from the Palatinates in present-day Germany in 1721. He and his wife, Madeline, had one child, Johann. Johann and his wife had thirteen children. Their second child is my great-great-great-great-great-grandfather Henry Herkimer. Henry's older brother, Nicholas, was general in charge at the Battle of Oriskany in 1777. In that battle, he was mortally wounded. My great-great-grandmother Kathleen Herkimer married Peter Schyler from the prominent Schylers of New York, a fine Dutch family. My grandfather Harry Strong married an Irish lassie about 1880.

These nine generations of my ancestors are something to be proud of, but not to dwell on. What has happened since has more of a meaning to me. When I was ten years of age—1935—I was watching a Memorial Day parade. There were soldiers from the Great War (later called World War I), marching in uniform. There were also some veterans from the Spanish-American War. But the biggest applause and cheering was reserved for the few Civil War veterans who were riding in open cars. They were somewhere in their 90s, and at the time I wondered if, when they were ten years old, they watched a parade of veterans that represented the war with Mexico, the War of 1812, and even a few in their middle 90s who were veterans of the War of Independence. It gave me something to think about.

That was my earliest recollection of the importance of history. There were many other factors that led to my interest in the story of our country. My social studies teacher in junior high school, Mable Crabtree, made history come alive. I entered high school in January 1939. That September, Germany invaded Poland, and Great Britain and France responded with a declaration of war. A course in world history in my sophomore year took on added meaning, and as a junior, we all had to take American history. Our teacher, Reid Stephens, held lively discussions; and we became well-informed of the progress of the war.

The Congress lowered the minimum draft age from twenty-one to eighteen in November 1942, and in 1943, I was drafted into the army; and instead of reading about the war, took a small part in it serving in the custodian of codes, part of the Signal Corps, in New Guinea and the Philippines.

After the war, blessed with the GI Bill, I followed my dream and majored in history—political science as well as education at Millikin University in Decatur, Illinois. Following graduation in 1950, I attended Illinois State University, majoring in social studies. With that preparation, I joined the teaching world and thoroughly enjoyed imparting my knowledge and passion for history.

In 1955, I received a master of science in education degree, having written a thesis titled *The Illinois and Michigan Canal and the Old Northwest*. I have Professor Helen Cavanaugh of Illinois State University to thank for her inspiration and love of American history that kept me interested in the story of our remarkable country. When I matriculated back to ISU in the early 1960s to work on my doctorate in educational administration, Dr. Cavanaugh said that we needed more administrators with an appreciation for American history.

Many history books go into great detail, and while important, it sometimes leads to turning off the reader. My attempt is to chronicle the story of America in a more concise, and for the most part, positive narrative of our country.

It starts with Columbus, and I try to show a connection with the many and various events that took place over the more-than-five-hundred years since that historic voyage. It covers all of the presidents, from George Washington to Ronald Reagan. The only living president included in that group is Jimmy Carter.

Throughout my story of our great country, I have included thirty poems that help to show, in another way, the many different and important events that took place. It is my earnest hope that a greater appreciation of the United States and its struggles and successes can be realized by reading *American Greatness: People and Events that Made America a Great Nation*.

John P. Dunnell
River Forest, IL

ACKNOWLEDGEMENTS

No author of a history book, with the exceptions of Herodotus (484-432 BC) and Thucydides (471-400 BC), can claim that his or her book is the work of only one person.

Many people, either directly or indirectly, contributed to my final project. The first person that deserves a great deal of credit in bringing my book to fruition is a freelance writer whose sharp eyes and subtle suggestions made it possible to not only have the manuscript edited but she brought timely ideas that helped to make the story clearer in meaning. I am forever grateful to Julia Roberts.

Other people have helped me in a variety of ways. The staff of the River Forest Public Library in River Forest, Illinois, was most helpful, and I appreciate their guidance. Rene Scharli, a graphic designer and high school classmate, suggested and designed the cover for my book. It helps to convey the tone of my story, and I greatly appreciate his help.

The technical aspects of putting my book together was made possible by a number of knowledgeable computer experts, including Ed Miller and Mike Hansen who own and operate www.thatcomputershop.net in Oak Park, Illinois. Scott Plesnicar, computer technician at *Best Buy* in Melrose Park, Illinois, was also very helpful. I also received a great deal of help from Henry Sutton, a Triton College professor. I learned many things about computers in his classes. Triton College in River Grove, Illinois, has not only an up-to-date computer lab but makes also available knowledgeable tutors, like Jason Smetters and especially Carolyn Righeimer who guided me through techniques that were unheard of when I wrote my master's thesis in 1955 and my doctoral dissertation in 1970 on a portable Royal typewriter.

Every author, I'm sure, has favorite sources. I am no exception. Certain authors or editors were indispensible in the writing of my book. Stephen Ambrose, John Bartlett, Henry Steele Commager, Robert Dallek, Dean Dorrell, William Langer, Roger Matuz and Bill Harris, Allan Nevins, Ronald Reagan, and Richard Webster contributed in many ways that I deeply appreciate. The women include Nancy

Anderson, Jill Canon, Page Smith, and Sally Bedell Smith. There were, of course, many others as my bibliography clearly shows. I am indebted to all of them.

I am also indebted to not only the authors but also the publishers of the many books on history. They include some of the most respected names in the publishing world. Some are no longer with us, but it does not take away their importance.

The publishers include Harper and Row; Simon and Schuster; Viking; Alfred A. Knopf; Little, Brown and Company; Thomas Y. Crowell Company; the National Geographic Society; Bellerphone Book; Harvard University Press; Bantam Books; Pantheon Books; Prentice Hall, D. Appleton Century, University Press of America Inc.; One World Book Co.; William Marrow and Company Inc.; Houghton Mifflin Company; Grolier Publishing Company; Encyclopædia Britannica Inc.; Garden City Publishing Co.; Franklin Watts; King Library Press; Doubleday; G. & C. Merriam Company; Dover Publications Inc.; G.P. Putnam's Sons; Willett Clark and Company; Louisiana State University Press; Scott Fetzer Company; Fairfax Press; Naval Institute Press; Black Dog & Leventhal Publishers Inc.; John Wiley and Sons, Inc.; Charles Scribner's Sons; Buechler Publishing in Bellville, Illinois; Adams and Bishop Publishers; McGraw-Hill Book Company; Random House; Pocket Books; Burrow Brothers; the Third World Press; Joseph Okpaku Publishing Company, Inc.; the Heritage Press; Educator Association; HarperCollins; the New York Times Company; the International Herald Tribune, and a special thanks to the *Chicago Tribune* that faithfully put an accurate and helpful almanac in their *Metro Section* that I used many, many times.

The maps that I have used throughout my book were compiled by H. George Stoll, Hammond Incorporated, 1967 and rev. by U.S. Geological Survey, 1970. They are part of the Perry-Castaneda Library Map Collection made available from the University of Texas at Austin, Texas. These maps help to show the growth and expansion of our country.

Thank you one and all.

Last, but certainly not least, is the Xlibris Corporation, a strategic partner of Random House Ventures with home offices in Philadelphia, Pennsylvania. Their entire staff has been most helpful in bringing my book to fruition.

PART A

FROM DISCOVERY TO INDEPENDENCE 1492-1781

When Columbus left Spain on August 3, 1492, no one could imagine how the world would change. His discovery of a small island set off a chain of events like nothing the world had ever seen.

Spain sent others to explore this new world, mostly in what became Mexico, but also parts of what would some day be called Florida as well as the southwest part of the United States.

France's explorations took place along the Atlantic coast and up the Saint Lawrence River. Later the French would explore inland along the Great Lakes and down the Mississippi River.

Early English explorations included Nova Scotia and even farther north, seeking the illusive Northwest Passage—a shortcut to China.

Spain and France explored and exploited their respective areas—Spain seeking and taking back the gold and France taking back furs to their respective countries. England attempted to start colonies starting in 1584. After two failures, they succeeded in 1607, with the first permanent settlement named after their king, and called it Jamestown.

This was the beginning of more and more colonies being established along the Atlantic coast—some by Dutch and Swedes but eventually controlled by the English. The last colony, Georgia, was not established until 1731, nearly 150 years since the first attempt on Roanoke Island.

Over that same period, there was growing dissatisfaction with the mother country—England. Through the years of the ten reigns from Elizabeth I to George III, the colonists felt less and less loyalty to these monarchs and resented their intrusion on what they considered their freedom.

When England defeated the French in 1759, they sought financial assistance in the manner of many different types of taxes. The colonists rebelled and this led to the Revolutionary War. From 1775 to 1781, a period of six and a half years, the under-strengthened Continental army fought the well-equipped British and frequently lost. Finally, with the help of France, Washington was able to corner Cornwallis at the tip of a Virginia Peninsula, and the war was over.

In 290 years, America had been discovered, explored, settled, and fought over. With victory at Yorktown, a new country began with a hope to grow like none other had ever done before.

CHAPTER I

DISCOVERIES AND EXPLORATIONS
1492-1578

CHRISTOPHER COLUMBUS
1451-1506

Born in Genoa, Italy, Columbus traveled extensively in the then-known world. His interests in seeking a water route to the land that was called Cathay (China) undoubtedly came from reading what Marco Polo had written about China while in prison in 1298. But the route that Marco Polo took was shut down when the Turks captured Constantinople, and the Ottoman Empire made it impossible to travel east overland to China.

Columbus had access to maps and charts and was keenly interested in foreign countries. One of the few men of that day that believed the earth was round, he dreamed of sailing west by ship to reach the east.

He first sought funds from his native Genoa, but when turned down, he appealed to King John II of Portugal without luck. Next he appealed to Henry VII of England and to the dukes of Medina Sedona and Medinaceli who suggested that he contact the monarchs of Spain. After seven years of waiting, on April 17, 1492, King Ferdinand and Queen Isabella of Spain agreed to finance Christopher Columbus's voyage to seek a western ocean passage to Asia. Almost four months later, Columbus set sail from Spain on August 3, 1492, with three small ships. They sailed into the unknown for seventy days before sighting land[1]

At two hours after midnight appeared the land, at a distance of two leagues. They handed all sails, and set the *treo*, which is the mainsail without bonnets, and lay-to-waiting for daylight Friday, when they arrived at an island of the Bahamas that was called in the Indians' tongue Guanahaul. (San Salvador)

Journal of Columbus's First Voyage, October 12, 1492.[2]

This spirit of determination by Columbus, who never faltered in his belief that he would succeed, is best expressed by the poem written by Joaquin Miller.

COLUMBUS[3]

Behind him lay the gray Azores,
Behind the Gates of Hercules:
Before him not the ghost of shores,
Before him only shoreless seas.
The good mate said: "Now must we pray,
For lo! The very stars are gone.
Brave Admiral, speak, what shall I say?"
Why, say 'Sail on! Sail on! And on!'"

"My men grown mutinous day by day;
My men grown ghastly wan, and weak."
The stout mate thought of home; a spray
Of salt wave washed his swarthy cheek.
"What shall I say, brave Admiral, say,
If we sight naught but sea at dawn?"
"Why you shall say at break of day:
'Sail on! Sail on! Sail on! And on!'"

They sailed and sailed, as winds might blow,
Until at last the blanched mate said:
"Why, now not even God would know
Should I and all my men fall dead.
These very winds forget their way,
For God from these dread seas is gone.
Now speak, brave Admiral, speak and say"—
He said: "Sail on! Sail on! And on!"

They sailed. They sailed. Then spake the mate:
"This mad sea shows his teeth to-night.
He lifts his lips, he lies in wait,
With lifted teeth, as if to bite!
"Brave Admiral, say but one good word,
What shall we do when hope is gone?"
The words leapt like a leaping sword:
"Sail on! Sail on! Sail on! And on!"

Then, pale and worn, he kept his deck,
And peered through darkness. Ah, that night
Of all dark nights! And then a speck—
A light! A light! A light! A light!
It grew, a starlit flag unfurled!
It grew to be Time's burst of dawn.
He gained a world: he gave that world
Its grandest lesson: "On, sail on!"

Columbus made a total of four voyages to the New World, the last one in 1503. He returned to Spain in 1504, worn-out. He died May 20, 1506 at the age of fifty-five.

John Cabot, a Genoese, sailed for Henry VII of England and found Nova Scotia in 1497. Other explorers soon followed. Ponce de Leon, who had been with Columbus on his second voyage and had become governor of Puerto Rico in 1509, set sail on his own in 1512 and landed in Florida. Balboa crossed the Isthmus of Panama in 1513 to be the first European to see the Pacific Ocean. Hernandez de Cordova discovered Yucatan, and Juan de Grijalva found Veracruz. Hernando Cortéz conquered Mexico in 1519 and claimed the country and its gold for Spain. [4]

Magellan's ships were the first to circumnavigate the globe between 1520 and 1522. Between 1540 and 1542, Coronado explored much of the southwestern area that is today Arizona and New Mexico, and De Soto went westward from Florida and found the Mississippi River. [5]

France began her exploration in 1524 when Verrazano explored the Atlantic coast and entered New York Bay. Between 1514 and 1542, Jacques Cartier discovered and named the St. Lawrence River, followed it inland to a small Indian village, and named it Mont Real, which is Montreal today. He claimed this northern territory in the name of France. [6]

England continued to explore the new lands, and sent Sir Martin Frobisher, between 1576 and 1578, west to seek the illusive Northwest Passage to India. Instead, he found Frobisher Bay in South Baffin Island and entered Hudson Strait. [7]

In 1577, with Queen Elizabeth's secret approval, Sir Francis Drake sailed through the Straits of Magellan and raided Spanish towns along the Pacific coast, plundered Pacific settlements, and claimed the California coast in the name of Queen Elizabeth. [8]

Ten years later, England was at war with Spain. Drake had destroyed the Spanish fleet at Cadiz, Spain. This and King Philips's displeasure with constant raids on his treasure ships coming back from Mexico led to building a large fleet called the Invincible Armada, which had over 130 vessels.

The armada sailed for England in July 1588. In a battle with the English, led by Drake, Hawkins, and Howard, plus a storm, the Spanish Armada was destroyed.

In 1609, Henry Hudson, and an Englishman employed by the Dutch East India Company, sailed to North America and entered Chesapeake Bay, Delaware Bay, and the river that bears his name. A year later, in an English ship, he explored Hudson Bay where he died being marooned by mutineers.[9]

AMERICA DISCOVERED

The age of discovery had taken place over a period of a little over one hundred years. No other period of history so changed the face of the earth. Three great powers of Europe—Spain, France, and England—would determine how the New World would be divided and ruled.

All three nations would establish settlement of a sort. Spain was first, but limited her choices. France was next, but stopped after establishing Quebec and a few outposts in the interior. England took a different approach. They avoided the mistakes of the other two.

CHAPTER II

SPANISH AND FRENCH MISTAKES

And so the stage was set to determine who would establish permanent settlements and thus controls this new and bountiful land. The three great powers of Europe in the sixteenth century were Spain, France, and England with the Netherlands and Sweden playing minor roles. Portugal confined her exploration to South America. Spain claimed Florida and established the oldest city in North America, St. Augustine, in 1565. Samuel de Champlain founded the settlement of Quebec on July 1, 1608, and from there sent explorers to the Great Lakes and beyond. Jean Nicollet got as far as Green Bay, and Robert de La Salle established Fort Crevecoeur near present-day Peoria, Illinois. Others went down the Mississippi River to the Gulf of Mexico where a settlement was made in present-day Louisiana in 1699.

But both of those powers made the same mistake that other empires had made. Egypt's dynasties included conquering Libya, Syria, and Palestine. Alexander the Great's conquests included as far south as Egypt and as far east as India. The Roman Empire extended to Gaul in 58 BC and Britain in 54 BC. Charles the Great—Charlemagne—created an empire that went out from France and took part of Italy and much of what is Germany, Austria, Czech, Slovenia, and Romania from 747 to 814. The Mongol Empire was started by Genghis Khan in 1206 with the capture of China and continued with Kublai Khan who got as far West as Poland and Hungary; but he died in 1294, and the empire fell apart. The Ottoman Empire began in 1300 and included what is today Turkey, Greece, Albania, Bulgaria, Macedonia, and Bosnia. That empire lasted until 1481 when Mohammed II died.

What did these empires have in common? They conquered land and subjugated its people. They ruled with an iron hand and did not allow for any dissention from its people. Spain followed the same formula in the conquest of their newfound land. They wanted the gold and killed thousands to get it.

France, on the other hand, developed a working relationship with the American Natives in the area they explored. But their main interests were exploration, Christianizing the natives, and putting into practice the idea mercantilism with rich furs that were to be found, trapped, and sent back to Europe where the demand was great.

France lost their share of America because of corruption and an inability to govern between three factions. The governor, intendants (administrative officials), and the Catholic church—all appointed by the king of France—each jealously guarded their own turf. The king only allowed Catholics to settle in the few settlements. [1] This all came together in the French and Indian War when the British won on the Plains of Abraham, where Quebec is located, in 1759.

England was the last of these countries to establish settlements in the new world. But they did it in a different way. They sent people to settle the land, and if possible become friendly with the American Natives. They did what no other people had ever done—move to a foreign land and not only survive but eventually prosper. No one told them it could not be done, so they did it and became a cohesive group that worked together for the common good.

The thirteen English colonies did not all come into being at the same time. The period of settlement took almost 150 years.

TERRITORIAL GROWTH

COLONIAL PERIOD: 1775

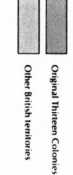

Original Thirteen Colonies

Other British territories

UNITED STATES: 1790–1920

States

State claims

Special status areas

Territories

Unorganized territories

Claimed areas

Foreign areas

1803 Dates of territorial acquisitions
1805 Dates of initial territorial organization
(1809) Dates of latest change within given time period
1812 Dates of admission to the Union

Map scale 1:34,000,000

Compiled by H. George Stoll, Hammond Incorporated, 1967;
rev. by U.S. Geological Survey, 1970

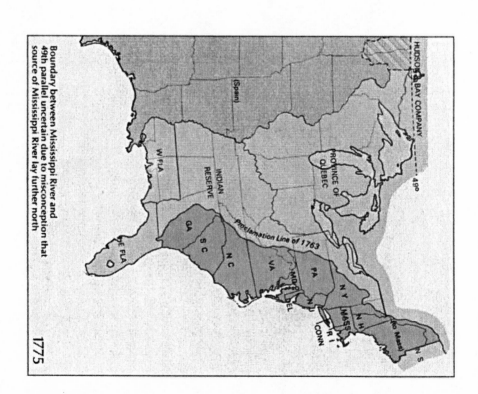

HUDSON BAY COMPANY

49°

[Spain]

PROVINCE OF QUEBEC

W FLA

INDIAN RESERVE

Proclamation Line of 1763

E FLA

GA

S C

N C

VA

PA

MD

DEL

N Y

N J

MASS

N H

R I

CONN

(to Mass)

N S

Boundary between Mississippi River and
49th parallel uncertain due to misconception that
source of Mississippi River lay further north

1775

CHAPTER III

ENGLISH COLONIZATION AND GROWING DISSATISFACTION 1584-1759

In 1584, Sir Walter Raleigh provided for an expedition to what became Virginia, named for Queen Elizabeth I, the Virgin Queen. The small group of a little over one hundred colonists landed on Roanoke Island but stayed only a year before being rescued by Sir Francis Drake. Undaunted, Raleigh sent a second group to the same island in 1587 where Virginia Dare, the first English child, was born on August 18, 1587. But when supply ships came back from England in 1591, they found no one.[1]

1607 JAMESTOWN, VIRGINA

Undaunted, King James I, who succeeded Queen Elizabeth's forty-five year reign in 1603, established a permanent colony in Jamestown in 1607, which survived, thanks to John Smith's courage; and after two years of hardships, more colonists came. These new arrivals decided not to stay when they heard of the tales of hunger and set sail for England but were met by Lord De La Warr at the mouth of the James River. He was bringing more colonists and enough supplies to make do, and so they stayed, and Virginia survived.[2]

Just as the settlements of the colonies took almost a century and a half to achieve, so the idea of self-government took root early and grew with dissatisfaction over a period of years.

In 1619, the Virginia House of Burgesses came about as a result of colonists requesting a voice in government after they were forced, in military fashion, to work for the Virginia Colony. This was the first representative assembly in the colonies, and it planted a seed of discontent that would grow over the years.[3]

In 1620, the band of separatists, referred to by Governor Bradford as pilgrims and strangers, sailed from Plymouth, England, and before leaving their small vessel on the shores of Massachusetts, drew and signed a compact, which took for granted that the people were to "combine ourselves together into a civil body politic . . . to enact, constitute, and frame such just and equal laws . . . for the general good of the Colony." [4]

In 1699, Williamsburg became the capital of the Virginia Colony. Here future leaders like George Washington, Thomas Jefferson, Patrick Henry, and other Virginia patriots helped frame a new government. In the last days of May 1765, ten years before the Revolution started, Patrick Henry would deliver his "Caesar-Brutus" speech. George Washington would introduce the Virginia Resolves against the Townshend Acts on May 16, 1769. The House of Burgesses adopted Virginia's Resolution for Independence on May 15, 1776, which led to the Declaration of Independence. The Virginia Declaration of Rights, an antecedent to the federal Bill of Rights, was produced by George Mason on June 12, 1776. It was in Williamsburg that Thomas Jefferson introduced his Statute for Religious Freedom, a beacon for the First Amendment freedom of conscience. [5]

Today, this birthplace of freedom can be seen as it was in the eighteenth century, thanks to John D. Rockefeller, Jr. Many of the buildings are reproductions in the colonial style. The Capitol, the Governor's Palace, the Raleigh Tavern, and Bruton Parish Church and many private dwellings makes one believe, when they visit this wonderful place, they are back in those times. The parish church and the original main building of the College of William and Mary survive from the colonial period. [6]

1620 MASSACHUSETTS

The second permanent settlement, and the first in New England, was this group of 102 men, women, and children who left Plymouth, England, in September, seeking freedom to worship as they pleased. They landed in Massachusetts in November of that year, and 50 survived the harsh winter. More settlers came the following year, and the small colony eventually thrived. They wrote:

THE MAYFLOWER COMPACT[7]

In the Name of God, Amen. We, whose names are underwritten, the Loyal Subjects of our dread Sovereign Lord King James, by the Grace of God, of Great Britain, France, and Ireland, King, *Defender of the Faith, Etc.* having undertaken for the Glory of God, and Advancement of the Christian Faith, and the Honour of our King and Country, a voyage to plant the first colony in the northern part of Virginia; Do by these Presents, solemnly and mutually in the Presence of God and one another, covenant and combine ourselves together not a civil Body Politick, for our better ordering and Preservation, and Furtherance of the Ends aforesaid; and by the Virtue hereof to enact. Constitute, and frame, such just and equal Laws, Ordinances, Acts, Constitutions, and Offices, from time to time, as shall be though most meet and convenient for the general Good of the Colony; Unto which we promise all due Submission and Obedience. In WITNESS whereof we have hereunto subscribed our names at *Cape Cod* the eleventh of November, the reign of our Sovereign Lord King James of England, France and Ireland, the eighteenth and of Scotland, the fifth-fourth, *Anno Domini*, 1620.

Mr. John Carver	Mr. Stephen Hopkins
Mr. William Bradford	Digery Priest

1620 THE LANDING OF THE PILGRIM FATHERS[8]

Felicia Dorthea Hemaus

The breaking waves dashed high
        On a stern and rock-bound coast,
And the woods, against a stormy sky,
        Their giant branches tossed;

And the heavy night hung dark
        The hills and water o'er,
When a band of exiles moored their bark
        On a wild New England shore

Not as the conqueror comes,
        They, the true-hearted, came:
Not with the roll of stirring drum,
        And the trumpet that sings of fame;

Not as the flying come,
        In silence and in fear,-
They shook the depths of desert's gloom
        With their hymns of lofty cheer.

Amidst the storm they sang,
        And the stars heard, and the seas;
And the sounding aisles of the dim woods rang
        To the anthem of the free!

The ocean-eagle soared
From his nest by the white wave's foam,
And the rocking pines of the forest roared;
This was their welcome home!

There were men with hoary hair
Amidst that pilgrim band;
Why had they come to wither there,
Away from their childhood's home?

There was a woman's fearless eye,
Lit by her deep love's truth;
There was manhood's brow serenely high,
And the fiery heart of youth.

What sought they thus afar?
Bright jewels of the mind?
The wealth of seas, the spoils of war?-
They sought a faith's pure shrine;

Aye, call it holy ground,
The soil where first they trod!
They have left unstained what there they found-
Freedom to worship God!

1623 NEW HAMPSHIRE

Permanent settlements were made at Rye and Dover, New Hampshire, as early as 1623, but it was not named until 1629 when John Mason received the land between the Merrimac and the Piscataquis rivers from the crown and named it New Hampshire.[9]

1623 NEW JERSEY

The Dutch made settlements in New Jersey in 1623 on the Delaware and Hudson rivers, where Gloucester and Hoboken now stand. The English took over this small settlement and named it New Jersey after the Channel Islands in 1664.[10]

1624 NEW YORK

New Netherland was first settled by thirty Dutch families in 1624. Charles I became England's king in 1625. In 1664, English ship appeared in the harbor of

12

New Amsterdam and demanded the colony, which was transferred to the English on September 9, 1664, and renamed New York. [11]

1629 AND 1729 NORTH AND SOUTH CAROLINA

A large parcel of land south of Virginia was granted by Charles I to Sir Robert Heath in 1629, but was not settled until 1660. Charles II gave the land to the Duke of Albemarle and seven nobles designated as proprietors. The colonists were at cross-purposes with the proprietors for unjust and severe taxation, a problem that was to be one of the cornerstones of independence. By 1729, the territory was divided into North and South Carolina.[12]

1631 DELAWARE

Delaware was first settled by the Dutch in 1631; but Sweden took over in 1643, only to lose it to the English in 1664, the same year England claimed New York.[13]

1634 CONNECTICUT

In 1634, some one hundred discontented settlers left Massachusetts Bay Colony and formed a new government in what became Connecticut. The Fundamental Orders of Connecticut differed from the Massachusetts government in one respect. A man's right to citizenship was not based on religious creed. This document mentioned neither England nor her King[14] Sixty-seven years later, in 1701, the Collegiate School of Connecticut was charted in New Haven. Today it is called Yale University.

1636 RHODE ISLAND

Roger Williams left the Massachusetts Bay Colony in 1636 to settle in Rhode Island, being dissatisfied with the dictates of the Puritans. Harvard College was found that year. Others followed in 1638 and settled Portsmouth and Newport in 1639. [15]

Between 1643 and 1684, four colonies—Massachusetts Bay, New Plymouth, Connecticut, and New Haven—formed the New England Confederation to give them combined strength in their defense against the Indians, the Dutch, and the French. [16]

1664 MARYLAND

In 1649, Lord Baltimore proposed the Maryland Toleration Act, the first attempt at religious toleration in America. Cecil Calvert, the second Lord Baltimore brought out the first colonists, mostly Roman Catholics, from England. [17]

1649 THE MARYLAND TOLERATION ACT[18]

APRIL 1649

This was actually the cornerstone of religious freedom in the United States

And whereas the enforcing of the conscience in matters of religion hath frequently fallen out to be of dangerous consequence in those commonwealths where it has been practiced . . .

Be it therefore . . . enacted . . . That no person or persons whatsoever within this province, or the islands, ports, harbors, creeks, or havens thereunto belonging professing to believe in Jesus Christ, shall from henceforth be any ways troubled, molested or discountenanced for or in respect of his or her religion nor in the free exercise thereof within this province of the islands thereunto belonging nor any way compelled to the belief or exercise of any other religion against his or her consent.

In 1676, Nathanial Bacon, a member of Virginia's Governor Berkeley's council, led a revolt against the governor's oppressive rule, including excessive taxes, unfairness in qualifying voters and injustice in laying tobacco duties. [19]

1682 PENNSYLVANIA

William Penn, a wealthy English Quaker, was owed sixteen thousand pounds by then King Charles II, and asked for a "tract of land in America, north of Maryland, west of Delaware and northward as far as plantable." Penn sailed with one hundred colonists, landing at present-day Chester on October 29, 1682. Penn wrote the constitution for the new colony and founded Philadelphia. [20]

1688 THE EARLIEST PROTEST AGAINST SLAVERY

Slavery came to the English colonies in 1619. The first protest against slavery came from the Mennonites of Germantown, Pennsylvania.

These are the reasons why we are against the traffic of men-body, as followed: In there any that would be done or handled at this manner? Viz, to be sold or made a slave for all the time of his life?[21]

14

1732 GEORGIA

Fifty years later the thirteenth colony, Georgia, was founded to serve as a buffer between South Carolina and the Spanish. James Oglethorpe obtained a charter from George II, which they named Georgia. [22]

1735 JOHN PETER ZENGER

John Peter Zenger, the editor and the printer of the *New York Weekly Journal*, was found in opposition to the Governor William Cosby, who had him arrested for printing the following:

> We see men's deeds destroyed, judges arbitrarily displaced, new courts erected, without consent of the legislature, by which it seems to me, trials by jury are taken away when a governor please.[23]

He was put in prison for ten months before his case came up for trial. Andrew Hamilton, the most prominent lawyer of the day, surprised the justices, and he won the day with a stirring argument.

> I should think it my duty, if required, to go to the utmost part of the land, where my service could be of any use in assisting to quench the flame of prosecution upon information, set on foot by the government, to deprive a people of the right of remonstrating (and complaining too) of the arbitrary attempts of men in power. Men who injure and oppress the people under their administration provoke them to cry out and complain; and then make that very complaint the foundation for a new oppression and prosecution. I wish I could say there were no instances of this kind. But to conclude; the question before the court and you, gentlemen of the jury, is not of small nor private concern, it is not the cause of a poor printer, nor on New York alone, which you are now trying. No! It may in its consequence affect every freeman that lives under a British government on the main of America. It is the best cause. It is the cause of liberty; and I make no doubt but your upright conduct, this day, will not only entitle you to the love and esteem of your fellow-citizens, but every man, who prefers freedom to a life of slavery, will bless and honour you, as men who have battled the attempt of tyranny; and by an impartial and uncorrupt verdict, have laid a noble foundation for securing to ourselves, our posterity, and our

neighbors, that to which nature and the laws of our country have given us a right—the liberty—both of exposing arbitrary power (in these parts of the world, at least) by speaking and writing truth.

Mr. Chief Justice: "Gentlemen of the jury. The great pains Mr. Hamilton has taken to show how little regard juries are to pay to the opinions of the judges; and his insisting so much upon the conduct of some judges in trials of this kind is done, no doubt, with design that you should take but very little notice of what I may say upon this occasion."

The jury withdrew, and in a small time returned, and being asked by the clerk, whether they were agreed of their verdict, and whether, John Peter Zenger was guilty of printing and publishing the libels in the information mentioned. They answered by Thomas Bunt, their Foreman, Not Guilty. Upon which there were three Huzzas in the hall which was crowded with people, and the next day I was discharged from my imprisonment.[24]

The significance of this trial might well have laid the groundwork that resulted in freedom of the press and part of the First Amendment to the United States Constitution fifty-seven years later in 1791.

In 1754, the Albany Plan of Union was approved by all the colonies except Delaware and Georgia. It contained the beginning of an answer to the problem of imperial order that would eventually be solved by the Federal Constitution of the United States.[25]

1754 FIRST CARTOON IN AMERICAN NEWSPAPERS

On May 9, 1754, Benjamin Franklin's *Pennsylvania Gazette* depicted a snake cut into sections, representing the Thirteen Colonies, with the caption, "Join or die."[26]

In 1759, the Virginia Parsons' Cause was a protest of underpaid clergy. This brought Patrick Henry's daring assertion that class favoring laws branded the king a tyrant who "forfeits all rights in obedience."[27]

A GLANCE BACK AND A LOOK AHEAD

From the founding of Jamestown in 1607 to 1759 is a span of 152 years—approximately five generations. Many who lived in the 1700s felt little loyalty to the former "Mother Country"—Great Britain. From the Virginia House of Burgess in 1619, when the colonists showed their dissatisfaction, to the John Peter Zenger trial that allowed a freedom of expression to prevail to the Virginia

Parsons' case where Patrick Henry brazenly spoke of the king as a tyrant "who forfeits all rights to obedience," a growing feeling of self-determination was planted and took root. Would it grow? Were there men who would not only speak out but take action that would change the course of history? The next sixteen years would tell the story.

CHAPTER IV

STEPS TO REBELLION
1759-1775

1759 FRENCH AND INDIAN WAR'S LAST BATTLE

One of the decisive battles of the world was fought at Quebec in 1759, where the destiny of the North American continent was at stake. The British, under the command of General James Wolfe, drew up the forces on the Plains of Abraham where the battle with the French, under General Louis Montcalm was waged. There are deep undertones of personal sentiment in the following ballad, which depicts that Wolfe and Montcalm had been close friends. Wolfe was a young man of thirty-two, recently betrothed in England where he was never to return. Montcalm also died in this battle.

MONTCALM AND WOLFE[1]
John Galusha

Bad new has come to town, bad news is carried,
Some say my love is dead, some say he's married.
As I was a-pondering on this, I took to weeping,
They stole my love away whilst I was sleeping.

"Love, here' a ring of gold, long years I've kept it,
Madame, it's for your sake, will you accept it?
When you the posy read, pray think on the giver,
Madame, remember me, for I'm undone forever."

Then away went this brave youth, embarked on the ocean,
To free America was his intention;

He landed in Quebec with all his party,
The city to attack, being brave and hearty.

He drew his army up in lines so pretty
On the Plains of Abraham, back to the city,
At a distance from the town where the French would meet him
In double numbers who resolved to beat him.

Montcalm and this brave youth together walked,
Between two armies they like brothers talked,
Till each one took his post and did retire,
It was then these numerous hosts commenced their fire.

Little did he think death was so near him,
Oh, little did he think death was so near him,
When shot down from his horse was this our hero,
We'll long lament his loss in tears of sorrow.

He raised up his head where the cannon did rattle,
And to his aide he said, "How goes the battle?"
His aide-de-camp replied, "It's ended in our favor."
Then says this brave youth. "I quit this earth with pleasure."

With the conclusion of the French and Indian War in 1763, the English parliament believed the American colonies should help pay for this victory over France. They first imposed a tax from the Sugar Act, followed by the Stamp Act, passed by the House of Lords on March 8, 1765, which taxed fifty-five different items, including all legal documents [2]

In 1764, a secret group known as the Sons of Liberty, helped bring on by fanning the flame of rebellion against taxation. [3]

The Stamp Act Congress of 1765, representing nine of the Thirteen Colonies, was the first indignation meeting against English Policy, and they adopted their own *Declaration of Rights*.[4]

1765 PATRICK HENRY (1736-1799)

Caesar had his Brutus; Charles I his Cromwell; and George III ("Treason!" cried the Speaker)—*may profit by their example.* If *this* be treason, make the most of it.

Speech on the Stamp Act, House of Burgess,
Williamsburg, Virginia—May 29, 1765[5]

Between 1765 and 1776, on organization known as the Regulator Movement, composed of thousands of North Carolina farmers, took up arms against taxation and extortion.

1765 JOHN ADAMS (1735-1826)

> Liberty cannot be preserved without a general knowledge among the people, who have a right . . . and a desire to know; but besides this, they have a right, an indisputable, unalienable, indefeasible, divine right to that most dreaded and envied kind of knowledge. I mean of the characters and conduct of their rulers.
>
> *A Dissertation on the Canon and Feudal Law 1765* [6]

The Townshend Acts of 1767 gave England the right to collect duty on glass, lead, paper, pepper, and tea which was brought to the colonies from England. The Americans were so incensed, it resulted in rioting in the streets of Boston. English soldiers, sent to keep the peace and enforce the tax, resulted in four people being shot down in one of the outbreaks. This became a rallying cry and was referred to as the Boston Massacre. [7]

England repealed all duties except the one on tea, and this led to a group of citizens, dressed as Indians, boarding three vessels on the night of December 16, 1773 and throwing chest after chest of imported tea into the harbor.

THE BOSTON TEA PARTY—DECEMBER 18, 1773
From *The Letters of John Andrews, Esq.*

> For my part, I went contentedly home and finish's my tea, but soon inform'd what was going forward; but still not crediting it without ocular demonstration, I went and was satisfied. They muster'd, I'm told, upon Fort Hill, to number of about two hundred, and proceeded, two by two, to Griffin's wharf, where Hall, Bruce, and Coffin lay, each with 114 chests ill-fated articles on board; the two former with only that article, but the latter arrived at the wharf only the day before, was freighted with a large quantity of other goods, which they took the greatest care not to injure in the least, and before nine o'clock in the evening, every chest from on board the three vessels was knock'd to pieces and flung over the sides. They say the actors were Indians from Narragansett. Whether they were or not, to a transient observer they appeared as such, being cloth'd in Blankets with heads muffled, and copper color'd countenances, being each arm'd with a hatchet or axe, and a pair of pistols, nor was their dialect different from what I conceived theses geniuses to speak, as their jargon was unintelligible to all but themselves.

1773 JOHN ADAMS ON THE BOSTON TEA PARTY

John Adams was born in Braintree, later named Quincy, Massachusetts. He was a young and early advocate of American Independence and used any opportunity to advance the cause. He was selected as one of the three to present a memorial against the Stamp Act of 1765. When he heard about the tea incident, he was so delighted that he wrote in his diary.[9]

DECEMBER 17, 1773 DIARY ON THE BOSTON TEA PARTY[10]

This is the most magnificent movement of all! There is a dignity, a majesty, a sublimity in this last effort of the patriots that I greatly admire. The people would never rise without doing something to be remembered—something notable and striking. This destruction of the tea is so bold, so daring, so firm, intrepid and inflexible, and it must have some important consequences, and so lasting, that I can't but consider it as an epoch in history.

England retaliated with the Boston Port Bill in 1774, closing the harbor until the tea would be paid for. By punishing Massachusetts, it became a rallying cry and resulted in the First Continental Congress where the colonies agreed not to import any English goods or export their own to England.[11]

In addition, the British parliament passed the Quebec Act in 1774, expanding the predominantly French province in Canada into lands claimed by the seaboard colonies. This effectively barred settlement beyond the Ohio valley, and helped fuel the desire for independence.

PATRICK HENRY (1736-1799)

Born a year after John Adams in Hanover County, Virginia, to Scottish and Welsh parents, he failed as a farmer and merchant and took up the study of law in 1760. He soon became famous for his oratory, speaking in defense as the counsel for the defendants in the Parson's Cause. Elected to the legislature in the House of Burgess in Williamsburg, he was an early advocate in taking up the struggle against Britain. He was governor of Virginia from 1776 to 1779 and served in the state legislature until 1784. He was again governor of Virginia from 1784 to 1786.[12]

His famous speech came March 23, 1775. Less than a month later, the farmers and merchants of two small towns near Boston stopped the British from taking their stores of arms and powder. If there were turning points in deciding the fate of the colonies, his speech must rank as one of the most important deciding factors.

AMERICA'S DUTY TO RESIST [13]
Patrick Henry
From his speech to the Virginia legislators urging armed resistance to British policy.

The battle, Sir, is not to the strong alone; it is to the vigilant, the active, the brave . . . There is no retreat but in submission and slavery. Our chains are forged—their clanking may be heard on the plains of Boston. The war is inevitable; and let it come!

The gentlemen may cry peace! Peace! But there is no peace. The war is actually begun! The next gale that sweeps from the north will bring to our ears the clash of resounding arms! What is that the gentlemen wish? What would they have? Is life so dear, or peace so sweet, as to be purchased at the price of chains and slavery? Forbid it Almighty God! I know not what course others may take; but as for me, give me liberty or give me death!

SIXTEEN FATEFUL YEARS

England had fought three other wars prior to the French and Indian War. There was the King William's War with France from 1689 to 1697 then Queen Anne's War from 1702 to 1713—again against France, and finally King George's War from 1743 to 1748, also against France. With all these expenses for war, the English parliament made a grievous error. It had passed the Molasses Act in 1733, which placed prohibitive duties on sugar and molasses imported into the colonies from other British possessions.

The colonists had gotten around this by smuggling and illicit trade during both King George's War and the French and Indian War. When the British decided that further revenue was needed, it passed the Sugar Act in 1764 followed by the Stamp Act the next year. That same year, the Quartering Act was passed that provided that British troops could be quartered in public hostelries.

On October 18, 1767, the boundary between Pennsylvania and Maryland was settled based on computations by English astronomers Charles Mason and Jeremiah Dixon. It would be known as the Mason-Dixon Line.[14] No one could realize the implications this line would have in the history of the United States.

The Townshend Acts of 1767 was probably the straw that broke the camel's back, placing duty tax on glass, lead, paper, pepper, and tea. British soldiers arrived in Boston in October 1768, and the town refused to provide quarters. In 1770, the Boston Massacre took place.

When all parts of the Townshend Act were repealed except the part on tea, this led to more than talk. The Boston Tea Party in December 1773 was the first overt act and the last step toward any chance to reconcile the differences. On September 4, 1775, the First Continental Congress met in Philadelphia. Six months later, Patrick Henry chose his course and the course for a new nation—"give me liberty or give me death!"

CHAPTER V

THE WAR FOR INDEPENDENCE
1775-1781

1775 PAUL REVERE (1735-1818)

Revere was born in Boston, and became an engraver by trade and was one of the finest silversmiths of his day. He had been an active member in the Sons of Liberty and had taken an active part in the Boston Tea Party. But he is most famous for the ride that he and his compatriot, William Dawes, never completed. On the night of April 18, 1775, Revere started out from Boston after getting the prearranged signal from the North Church. Revere reached Lexington first, awakened John Hancock and Samuel Adams then, with Dawes, rode toward Concord. They were joined by Dr. Samuel Prescott, whose aid they sought in a chance meeting along the road. Captured by the British, Dawes got away. Then Dr. Prescott escaped and brought word to Concord.

PAUL REVERE'S RIDE[1]
Henry Wadsworth Longfellow

Listen, my children, and you shall hear
Of the midnight ride of Paul Revere,
On the eighteenth of April, in seventy-five;
Hardly a man is now alive
Who remembers that famous day and year.

He said to his friend, "If the British march
By land or sea from the town to-night,
Hang a lantern aloft in the belfry arch
Of the North Church tower as a signal light,—

One, if by land, and two if by sea;
And I on the opposite shore will be,
Ready to ride and spread the alarm
Through every Middlesex village and farm,
For the country folk to be and to arm."

Then he said, "Good night!" and with muffled oar
Silently rowed to the Charlestown shore,
Just as the moon rose over the bay,
Where swinging wide at mooring lay
The Somerset, British man-of-war;
A phantom ship, with each mast and spar
Across the moon like prison bar,
And a huge black hulk, that was magnified
By its own reflection in the tide.

Meanwhile, his friend, through alley and street,
Wanders and watches with eager ears,
Till in the silence around him he hears
The muster of men at the barrack door,
The sound of arms, the tramp of feet,
And the measured tread of the grenadiers,
Marching down to their boats on the shore.

Then he climbed the tower of the Old North Church
By the wooden stairs, with stealth tread,
To the belfry-chamber overhead,
And startled the pigeons from their perch
On the somber rafters, that round him made
Masses and moving shapes of shade,—
By the trembling ladder, steep and tall
To the highest window in the wall,
Where he paused to listen and look down
A moment on the root of the town,
And the moonlight flowing over all.

Beneath in the churchyard, lay the dead,
In their night-encampment on the hill,
Wrapped in silence sop deep and still
That he could hear, like a sentinel's tread,
The watchful night-wind, as it went
Creeping along from tent to tent.

And seeming to whisper, "All is well"
A moment only he feels the spell
Of the place and hour, and the secret dread
Of the lonely belfry and the dead;
For suddenly all thoughts are bent
On a shadowy something far away.
Where the river widens to meet the bay,—
A line of black that bends and floats
On the rising tide, like a bridge of boats.

Meanwhile, impatient to mount and ride,
Booted and spurred, with a heavy stride
On the opposite shore walked Paul Revere.
Now he patted his horse' side,
Now gazed at the landscaped far and near,
Then, impetuous, stamped the earth,
And turned and tightened his saddle-girth;
But mostly he watched the eager search
The belfry-tower of the Old North Church,
And it rose above the graves on the hill,

Lonely and spectral and somber and still.
An lo! As he looks, on the belfry's height
A glimmer, and then a gleam of light!
He springs to the saddle, the bridle he turns,
But lingers and gazes, till full on his sight
A second lamp in the belfry burn!

A hurry of hoofs in a village street,
A shape in the moonlight, a bulk in the dark,
And beneath, from the pebbles, in passing, a spark
Struck out by a steed flying fearless and fleet;
That was all! And yet, through the gloom and the light,
The fate of a nation was riding that night;
And the spark struck out by the seed, in his flight
Kindled the land into flame with its heat.

He has left the village and mounted the steep,
And beneath him, tranquil and broad and deep,
In the Mystic, meeting the ocean tides;

And under the alders that skirt its edge,
Now soft on the sand, now loud on the ledge,
Is heard the tramp of his steed as he rides.

It was twelve by the village clock,
When he crossed the bridge into Medford town.
He heard the crowing of the cock,
And the barking of the farmer's dog,
And felt the damp of the river fog,
That rises after the sun goes down.

It was one by the village clock,
When galloped into Lexington.
He saw the gilded weathercock
Swim in the moonlight as he passed,
And the meeting-house windows, bland and bare,
Gaze at him with a spectral glare,
As if they already stood aghast
At the bloody work they would look upon.

It was two by the village clock,
When he came to the bridge in Concord town.
He heard the bleating of the flock,
And the twitter of birds among the trees,
He felt the breath of the morning breeze
Blowing over the meadows brown.

And one was safe and asleep in his bed
Who at the bridge would be first to fall,
Who that day would be lying dead,
Pierced by a British musket-ball.

You know the rest. In the books you have read,
How the British Regulars fired and fled,—
How the farmers gave them ball for ball,
From behind each fence and farmyard wall,
Chasing the red-coats down the lane,
Then crossing the field to emerge again
Under the trees at the turn of the road,
And only pausing to fire and load.

So through the night rode Paul Revere'
And so through the night went his cry of alarm
To every Middlesex village and farm,—
A cry of defiance and not of fear,
A voice in the darkness, a knock at the door,
And a word that shall echo forevermore!
For, borne on the night-wind of the Past,
Through all our history, to the last,
In the hour of darkness and peril and need,
The people will waken and listen and hear
The hurrying hoof-beats of that steed,
And the midnight message of Paul Revere.

The next day, April 19, farmers and other colonial settlers took up arms early in the day, awaiting the British sent to take their gunpowder. They stood in various parts of the road and at the bridge. They did not want the British to make a decision that affected their lives and future. They were willing to make any sacrifice to preserve their long sought freedoms.

At Lexington, Captain John Parker cautioned the minutemen not to fire unless fired upon, but said, "If they mean to have a war, let it begin here." [2]

The following was sung at the completion of the Battle Monument, July 4, 1837.

CONCORD HYMN [3]
Ralph Waldo Emerson

By the rude bridge that arched the flood,
    Their flag to April's breeze unfurled,
Here once the embattled farmers stood
    And fired the shot heard around the world.

The foe long since in silence slep'
    Alike the conqueror silent sleeps;
And Time the ruined bridge has swept
    Down the dark stream which seaward creeps.

On this green bank, by this soft stream,
    We set today a votive stone;
That memory may their deed redeem,
    When, like our sires, our sons are gone.

> Spirit, that made those heroes dare
> To die, and leave their children free,
> Bid Time and Nature gently spare
> The shaft we raise to them and thee.

Emerson was born in Boston, Massachusetts, in 1803. He was an essayist, poet, and philosopher. He is best remembered for the poem he wrote to commemorate the monument to the Minutemen who stood their ground and "fired the shot heard round the world."

In May 1775, one month after Revere's ride and the battle at Lexington and Concord, the Second Continental Congress met. All the colonies were represented, and they were to be in session for six years. George Washington was appointed commander in chief of the colonial armies in June. The Battle of Bunker Hill, on June 17, 1775 showed the Americans had courage. The English claimed a victory, but the Americans' confidence grew.

"Don't one of you fire until you see the whites of their eyes" was the order given to the colonists by William Prescott at the top of Bunker Hill. [4]

Washington was able to drive the British troops out of Boston in March of 1776. Still, some colonists thought a compromise could be sought with Britain. But the Continental Congress moved toward independence by appointing a committee to draft a declaration. The committee was appointed on June 11, 1776.

Five people were chosen: John Adams of Massachusetts, Benjamin Franklin of Pennsylvania, Robert Livingston of New York, Roger Sherman of Connecticut, and Thomas Jefferson of Virginia.

The committee selected John Adams and Thomas Jefferson to prepare a draft, but John Adams persuaded Jefferson to write the draft. When he asked Adams why, Adams gave three reasons: " . . . First, you are a Virginian . . . Second, I am obnoxious, suspected, and unpopular. Third, you can write ten times better than I can." "Well," said Jefferson, "If you are decided, I will do as well as I can."[5]

Jefferson alone wrote the main body of the declaration, and the Committee of Five made some changes. Jefferson was a well-read person and used ideas from different sources, not an uncommon practice in those days. They include John Lock's *Second Treatise of Government*; Britain's own *Declaration of Rights* which formally ended the reign of James II and inaugurated the reign of William and Mary; and parts of the preamble and Constitution of Virginia.[6] Jefferson's greatest gift was his ability to put into words the basic ideas that we cherish to this day.

Jefferson must have been aware of the House of Burgesses' decision to have its own representative assembly in 1619. He no doubt had read the Mayflower Compact of 1620 that first dealt with the freedom of worship or Connecticut's idea that citizenship not be based on religion or Maryland Toleration Act of 1649 that prohibited any discrimination.

As early as 1660, colonists had shown their disgust for "severe taxation"; and a hundred years before Jefferson sat down to write, Nathanial Bacon had led a rebellion against Virginia's Governor Berkeley for excessive taxes and paid for it with his life. Jefferson must have been moved when he read about the abuses of the King from the Parsons' case where Patrick Henry had ruled the King a tyrant and not deserving of obedience in 1759.

The Sugar Act of 1764, the Stamp Act of 1765, and the Townshend Act of 1767 fueled the flame that led to the Boston Massacre in 1770; and the Boston Tea Party in December of 1773 was undoubtedly the result of the Tea Act of 1773. Some colonists referred to these as Intolerable Acts, and rightly so in the eyes of the members of the First Continental Congress who met to coordinate their opposition in 1774. When the British marched on Lexington and Concord in April 1775, the Second Continental Congress met one month later. They carefully and fully deliberated what had to be done and then finally decided to declare their intentions in writing. In June 1776, it was resolved "that these united colonies are and of right ought to be free and independent states." The next step belonged to Thomas Jefferson, and he came through.

The declaration is a truly remarkable document, and was and still is the basis of our great country. It is almost unbelievable that Thomas Jefferson was appointed no earlier than June 12, 1776, and completed it before July 4, 1776. *Three weeks to write the greatest document in American history!*

The document has four paragraphs. The first two paragraphs set the tone of justifying why we should be free, a concept that was wholly foreign to anyone at that time. The second part lists twenty-seven separate and devastating reasons for the grievances they had with King George III. The last part was the formal declaration to be free and independent of Great Britain, "and for the support of the Declaration, with a firm reliance on the protection of Divine Providence," they pledged to each other their lives, their fortunes and their sacred honor.

THE DECLARATION OF INDEPENDENCE [7]
In CONGRESS, JULY 4, 1776

THE UNANIMOUS DECLARATION OF THE THIRTEEN UNITED STATES OF AMERICA

When in the course of human events it becomes necessary for one people to dissolve the political bands which have connected the with another, and to assume among the powers of the earth, the separate and equal station to which the Laws of Nature and of Nature's God entitle them, a decent respect to the opinions of mankind requires that they should declare the causes which impel them to the separation.

We hold these truths to be self evident, that all men are created equal, that they are endowed by their Creator with certain unalienable Rights, that among these are life, Liberty and the pursuit of Happiness—That to secure these rights, governments are instituted among Men, deriving their just powers from the consent of the governed,—That whenever any Form of Government becomes destructive of these ends, it is the Right of the People to alter or to abolish it, and to institute new Government, laying its foundation on such principles, organizing its powers in such form as to them shall seem most likely to effect their Safety and Happiness. Prudence indeed, will dictate that Governments long established should not be changed for light and transient causes; and accordingly all experience hath shown that mankind are more disposed to suffer, while evils are sufferable, than to right themselves by abolishing the forms to which they are accustomed. But when a long train of abuses and usurpations, pursing invariable the same Object evinces a design to reduce them under absolute Despotism, it is their right, it is their duty to throw off such Government, and to provide new Guards for their future security—Such has been the patient sufferance of these Colonies; and such is now the necessity which constrains them to alter their former Systems of Government. The history of the present King of Great Britain is a history of repeated injuries and usurpations, all having in direct object, the establishment of an absolute Tyranny over these States. To prove this, let Facts be submitted to a candid world.

He has refused his Assent to Laws, the most wholesome and necessary for the public good. He has forbidden his governors to pass Laws of immediate and pressing importance, unless suspended in their operation till his Assent should be obtained; and when so suspended, he has utterly neglected to attend to them.

He has refused to pass other Laws for the accommodation of large districts of people, unless those people would relinquish the right of Representation in the Legislature, a right inestimable to them and formidable to tyrants only.

He has called together legislative bodies at places unusual, uncomfortable, and distant from the depository of their public Records for the sole purpose of fatiguing them into compliance with his measures.

He has dissolved Representative Houses repeatedly, for opposing with manly firmness his invasions on the rights of the people.

He has refused for a long time after such dissolutions to cause others to be elected; where by the Legislative powers, incapable of Annihilation, have returned to the People at large for their exercise; the State remaining in the meantime exposed to all the dangers of invasion from without, and the convulsion within.

He has endeavored to prevent the population of these States; for that purpose, obstructing the Laws for Naturalization of Foreigners; refusing to pass others to encourage their migration hither, and raising the conditions of a new Appropriation of Lands.

He has obstructed the Administration of Justice, by refusing his Assent to Laws for establishing Judiciary powers.

He has made Judges dependent on his Will alone, for the tenure of their offices, and the amount and payment of their salaries.

He has erected a multitude of New Offices, and sent hither swarms of Officers to harass our people, and eat out their substance.

He has kept among us, in times of peace, Standing Armies without the Consent of our legislatures.

He has effected to render the Military independent of and superior to the Civil power.

He has combined with others to subject us to a jurisdiction foreign to our constitution, and unacknowledged by our law; giving his Assent to their Acts of pretended Legislation:

— For quartering large bodies of armed troops among us:
— For protecting them, by a Mock Trial, for punishment for any Murders which they should commit on the Inhabitants of these States:
— For cutting off our Trade with all parts of the world:
— For depriving us in many cases of the benefits of Trial by jury:
— For transporting us beyond Seas to be tried for pretended offenses:
— For abolishing the free System of English Laws in a neighboring Province, establishing therein an Arbitrary government and enlarging its Boundaries, so as to render it as once an example and fit instrument for introducing the same absolute rule into these Colonies:
— For taking away our Charter, abolishing our most valuable Laws, and altering fundamentally the forms of our Governments:
— For suspending our own Legislature, and declaring themselves invested with power to legislate for us all cases whatsoever.

He has abdicated Government here, by declaring us out of his protection and waging War against us.

He has plundered our seas, ravaged our Coasts, burnt our town, and destroyed the lives of our people.

He is, at this time transporting large Armies of foreign Mercenaries to complete the works of death, desolation and tyranny, already begun with circumstances of Cruelty & perfidy scarcely paralleled in the most barbarous ages, and totally unworthy the Head of a civilized nation.

He has constrained our fellow citizens taken Captive on the high Seas to bear Arms against their Country, to become executioners of their friends and Brethren, or to fall themselves by their Hands.

He has excited domestic insurrections amongst us, and has endeavored to bring on the inhabitants of our frontier; the merciless Indian Savages, whose known rule of warfare is undistinguished destruction of all ages, sexes and conditions.

In every stage of these Oppressions, we have Petitioned for Redress, in the most humble terms; Our repeated petitions have been answered by repeated injury. A Prince, whose character is thus marked by every act which may defile a Tyrant, is unfit to be the ruler of a free people. Nor have we been wanting in attention to our British brethren. We have warned them, from time to time, of attempts by their legislature to extend an unwarrantable jurisdiction over us. We have reminded them of the circumstances of our emigration and settlement here. We have appealed to their native justice and magnanimity, and we have conjured them, by ties of our common kindred, to disavow these usurpations, which would inevitably interrupt our connections and correspondence. They too have been deaf to the voices of justice and of consanguinity. We must, therefore, acquiesce in the necessity, which denounces our Separation, and hold them, as we hold the rest of mankind, Enemies in War, in Peace Friends.

WE, THEREFORE, THE REPRESENTATIVES OF THE UNITED STATES OF AMERICA, in General Congress, Assembled, appealing to the Supreme Judge of the World for the rectitude our intention, DO, in the Name, and by authority of the good People of these Colonies, solemnly publish and declare, That these United Colonies are, and of Right ought to be FREE AND INDEPENDENT STATES; that they are absolved from all Allegiance to the British Crown, and that all political connection between them and the State of Great Britain, is and ought to be, totally dissolved; and that as FREE AND INDEPENDENT States, they have full power to levy war, conclude peace, contract alliances, establish commerce, and do all other acts and things which independent states may of right do. And for the support of this Declaration, with a firm reliance on the protection of Divine Providence, we mutually pledge to each other our Lives, our Fortunes, and our sacred Honor.

Signed by 56 Brave Men

BENJAMIN FRANKLIN (1706-1790)

On signing the Declaration of Independence said, "We must all hang together, or assuredly we shall all hang separately."[8]

GEORGE WASHINGTON (1732-1799)

Washington addressed the Continental army before the Battle of Long Island on August 27, 1776. No one realized it at the time, and how prophetic were his words.

The time is now near at hand which must probably determine whether Americans are to be freemen or slaves; whether they are to have any property they can call their own; whether their houses and farms are pillaged and destroyed, and themselves consigned to a state of wretchedness from which no human effort will deliver them. The fate of unborn millions will now depend, under God, on the courage and conduct of this army. Our cruel and unrelenting enemy leaves us only the choice of brave resistance, or the most abject submission. We have, therefore, to resolve to conquer or die.[9]

NATHAN HALE (1755-1776)

"I only regret that I have but one life to lose for my country." [10]
Last words before being hanged
by the British as a spy—September 22, 1776

On September 9, 1776, the Second Continental Congress ruled that the term "United States" was official, replacing United Colonies. On October 10 of that historic year, Thaddeus Kosciusko, a Pole, arrived in the colonies. He was recommended by Benjamin Franklin to Congress, and they appointed him a colonel of engineers.

The year 1776 drew to a close with an article that would help to change the minds of many who were still undecided or were still considering making a truce with Britain. Thomas Paine was born in England and came to the colonies in November 1774, and where he, the writer, joined the *Pennsylvania Magazine* staff. His writings preceded the Declaration of Independence, but his "Call to Arms" article is his most famous.

A CALL TO ARMS[11]
From *The Crisis*, December 23, 1776—Thomas Paine

These are the times that try men's souls. The summer soldier and the sunshine patriot will, in this crisis, shrink from the service of their country; but he that stands it *now*, deserves the love and thanks of men and women. Tyranny, like hell, is not easily conquered; yet we have this consolation with us, that the harder the conflict, the more glorious the triumph . . . . It is the only object of war that makes it honorable. And if there was ever a just war since the world began, it is this in which America is now engaged . . . .

We fight not to enslave, but to set a country free, and to make room upon the earth for honest men to live in.

In December 1776, Washington had retreated from New York across New Jersey to Pennsylvania. But in a bold and dangerous move, he led six thousand of his men across the Delaware River on Christmas night. Surprising the Hessian mercenaries under the command of Colonel Rail at Trenton, Washington's troops captured much needed supplies and one thousand enemy soldiers who were celebrating the holiday.

The year 1777 was a decisive year. The British attempted to split the colonies. British General Howe was successful at the battles of Bennington and Germantown. But reinforcement failed to show due to the Battle of Oriskany when General Herkimer's small forces stopped British Colonel St. Leger's forces from joining with British General Burgoyne.

In October of that year, Burgoyne was decisively defeated by General Horatio Gates at the Battle of Saratoga, considered by many the turning point of the war. [12]

On July 27, 1777, Ms. Jane McCrea was captured by the Indians who had been employed by the British. Word came down by way of Thomas Paine "to the people of New England that she has been shot and scalped. Thousands of New Englanders—farmers, shopkeepers, and artisans—take up the cry to go against Burgoyne, the British general."

July 31, 1777 Lafayette, who volunteered his services, is appointed a major general by Washington. Lafayette was twenty years old!

RESOLUTION OF THE CONTINENTAL CONGRESS OF THE UNITED STATES FLAG[13]

That the flag of the thirteen United States be thirteen stripes, alternate red and white; that the union be thirteen stars, white in a field of blue, representing a new constellation.

June 14, 1777

Betsy (Elizabeth) Ross (1752-1836) was a Philadelphian seamstress who, according to legend, made the first American flag at the request of George Washington.

There were many battles fought between Britain and the Colonies from April 1775 to September 1781. Washington had both success and losses and he had able generals who helped win independence.

ETHAN ALLEN (1737-1789)

Allen is remembered as a very colorful character. On May 10, 1775, he captured Fort Ticonderoga with the stirring command to surrender "in the name of the great Jehovah and the Continental Congress."[14]

COUNT CASIMIR PULASKI (1746-1779)

A Polish soldier, who joined the Colonial army and distinguished himself at the Battle of Brandywine, received a brigade of cavalry, which he commanded until 1778. When he refused to serve under General Anthony Wayne, he resigned and organized his own independent cavalry unit. He was mortally wounded in 1779. [15]

HORATIO GATES (1728-1806)

Gates was born in England, and came to the colonies in 1755. He took part in the French and Indian War, but at the beginning of the Revolutionary War in 1775, he left his farm in Virginia. He was in command of the Northern Continental Army, and took the surrender of Burgoyne at Saratoga on October 17, 1777. When given the command in the South in 1780, he was defeated by Cornwallis at Camden, South Carolina. He was suspended and superseded by General Greene, and in 1782 was reinstated. [16]

NATHANAEL GREENE (1742-1786)

He was regarded by many as second only to Washington in ability among the generals. Born in Potowomut, Rhode Island, he enlisted as a private in 1774. He was appointed in command of the Rhode Island division in 1775. He showed brilliant qualities of leadership at the battles of Trenton and Princeton. Appointed to replace Gates in the South, he reorganized the dispirited forces and began a campaign to harass the British and force them into costly battles. His tactics forced Cornwallis north to Virginia in 1781. [17]

DANIEL MORGAN (1736-1802)

Colonel Morgan and his Virginia riflemen were key players. His men were mainly frontier sharpshooters and were important in the Battle of Saratoga. Benedict Arnold was also a contributor in the same battle, but the animosity between Gates and Arnold contributed to Arnold's turning traitor at West Point.

Daniel Morgan refused to join Gates's intrigues against Washington in the Conway Cobal, which Washington survived. The plot was named after Thomas Conway who allegedly led a group to remove George Washington as commander and replace him with Horatio Gates. The plot not only failed but strengthened Washington's position. Following an investigation, it was discovered that Conway was unfairly accused. [18]

HENRY KNOX (1750-1806)

Born in Boston, Knox joined the army after the Battle of Lexington, and fought in the Battle of Bunker Hill. Commissioned brigadier general of artillery in 1775, he showed distinguished service in battles from Princeton to Yorktown and was promoted to major general. He was appointed first secretary of war in 1785 and served in that capacity under Washington from 1789 to 1795. [19]

MARY LUDWIG HAYS (1754-1832)

Commissioned a sergeant by General Washington for bravery at the Battle of Monmouth where she won fame for her service in carrying water to the parched colonial troops during the battle. She was dubbed Molly Pitcher. [20]

TWO IMPORTANT EVENTS

The winter of 1778-1779 saw two important events take place. One was the terrible winter at Valley Forge where Washington's soldiers starved and some died, but with endurance and courage, most survived. Baron Frederick von Steuben joined Washington in February 1778 and helped train the men for the future battles. The other event took place a thousand miles west.

GEORGE ROGERS CLARK (1752-1818)

During the American Revolutionary War there was an obscure battle in the western part that is hardly recognized as important as those fought in the colonies along the Atlantic shores. Detroit and Chicago were forts held by the British in the summer of 1778. Vincennes and Kaskaskia were settlements along the Wabash and Mississippi rivers, respectively.

Lieutenant Governor Henry Hamilton of Britain was able to recapture the post at Vincennes, but winter arrived, and Hamilton decided to wait until the spring of 1779 before trying to recapture the settlement at Kaskaskia.

George Rogers Clark decided to attempt to retake Vincennes in the middle of winter. With only a handful of men, Clark made the long march in February and bluffed the British and captured Vincennes as well as Hamilton. Though Clark was never able to fulfill the dream of capturing Detroit, his stubborn grip on this region was the principal factor in securing the Old Northwest as well as the land that extended to the Mississippi River for the United States in the negotiations which resulted in the Treaty of Peace with Great Britain, September 3, 1783. [21]

JOHN PAUL JONES (1747-1833)

"I have not yet begun to fight." Aboard the *Bonhomme Richard* when engaged with the British frigate, *Serapis,* which he captured off Flamborough Head, east Yorkshire, September 23, 1779. [22]

FRANCIS MARION (1732-1795)

Marion was born near Germantown, South Carolina. He formed the *Marion's Brigade,* made up of volunteer mountain men and hunters from his colony. Nicknamed the Swamp Fox, they harassed the British who had come south in 1780. [23]

The year, 1781, was to be decisive. Daniel Morgan defeated the British at Cowpens, North Carolina. Nathanael Greene harassed the British continuously, and so decimated Cornwallis's forces. He retreated north to Virginia, awaiting help that never came.

TO THE MEMORY OF THE BRAVE AMERICANS [24]
Philip Freneau

Under General Nathanael Greene in South Carolina in the action of September 8, 1781

At Eutaw Springs the valiant died;
 Their limbs with dust are covered o'er-
Weep on ye spring, your tearful tide;
 How many heroes are no more;

If in this wreck of ruin, they
 Can yet be thought to claim a tear,
O smite you gentle breast, and say;
 The friends of freedom slumber here;

Thou, who shalt trace this bloody plain,
 If goodness rule thy generous breast,
Sigh for the wasted rural reign;
 Sigh for the shepherd, sunk to rest;

Stranger, their humble graves adorn;
 You too may fail, and ask a tear;
"Tis not the beauty of the morn
 That proves the evening shall be clear.

They saw their injured country's woe;
　　The flaming town, the wasted field;
Then rushed to meet the insulting foe,
　　They took the spear—but left the shield

Led by the conquering genius, Green,
　　The Britons they compelled to fly;
When distant few the fatal plain,
　　None grieved, in such a cause to die-

But, like the Parthian, famed of old,
　　Who flying, still their Arrows threw,
These routed Briton, full as bold,
　　Retreated, and retreating slew.

Now rest in peace, our patriot band;
　　Though far from nature's limits thrown,
We trust they find a happier land,
　　A brighter sunshine of their own.

Born in 1752, in New York City, Philip Freneau was captured during the American Revolution. After his release, he wrote about the heinous practices of British prison ships. He is best known as the author of lyrics to "The Indian Burying-Ground," "The Wild Honeysuckle," and "The Rising Glory of America."

OCTOBER 19, 1781 YORKTOWN

The victory at Yorktown may well have started on September 5, 1781 when Admiral Count Francoise de Grasse sailed from France in the summer to the West Indies and then to the waters outside Chesapeake Bay. Here he defeated the British fleet, sailed into the Bay, and disembarked three thousand soldiers that joined Lafayette.

Washington and General Comte de Rochambeau brought their respected armies from New York during September and, with a combined army of sixteen thousand soldiers, surrounded Yorktown.

The siege lasted from September 28 to October 19, 1781. When Cornwallis realized there was no escape by land or sea, he proposed to capitulate. The British and Germans marched out to lay down their arms while the British band played "The World Turned Upside Down."

A WAR WON AND THE GREATEST CHALLENGE
YET TO COME

England had never lost a war to a foreign power. Only Cromwell's reign from 1653 to 1660, when England was not a monarchy, marred a perfect record from 1066, when William the Conqueror defeated King Harold at the Battle of Hastings.

The English had defeated France on three occasions. The English navy had stopped the Spanish Armada in 1588. How could a small inexperienced militia hope to succeed against the greatest power at that time on the face of the earth?

The upstart nation had a few things in their favor. They were fighting on their own soil, for their own soil. England had to transport, not only its troops, but all its supplies. There were American leaders who knew how to fight, when to fight, and where to fight. And they had a cause that they knew was just. They were willing to die, and many did.

BUT THEY WON!

James Russell Lowell graduated from Harvard in 1838, distinguishing himself in literature. He was professor of modern languages at Harvard from 1855 to 1877, succeeding Henry Wadsworth Longfellow.

OUR FATHERS FOUGHT FOR LIBERTY[25]
James Russell Lowell (1819-1891)

Our fathers fought for liberty,
They struggled long and well,
History of their deeds can tell-
But did they leave us free?

Are we free to speak our thought,
To be happy and be poor,
Free to enter Heaven's door,
To live and labor as we ought?

Are we then made free at last
From the fear of what men say.
Free to reverence today,
Free from the slavery of the past?

Our fathers fought for liberty,
They struggled long and well,
History of their deeds can tell-
But *ourselves* must set us free.

TERRITORIAL GROWTH

COLONIAL PERIOD: 1775

 Original Thirteen Colonies

 Other British territories

UNITED STATES: 1790–1920

Map scale 1:34,000,000

States

State claims

Special status areas

Territories

Unorganized territories

Claimed areas

Foreign areas

1803   Dates of territorial acquisitions
1805   Dates of initial territorial organization
(*1809*)   Dates of latest change within given time period
1812   Dates of admission to the Union

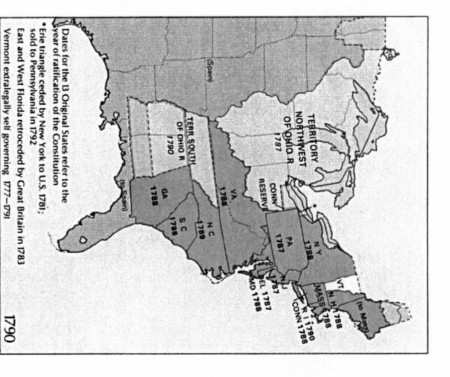

Dates for the 13 Original States refer to the
year of ratification of the Constitution

* Erie triangle ceded by New York to U.S. 1781;
sold to Pennsylvania in 1792

East and West Florida retroceded by Great Britain in 1783

Vermont extralegally self governing, 1777–1791

TERRITORY NORTHWEST OF OHIO R. 1787

TERR. SOUTH OF OHIO R. 1790

CONN. RESERVE

VA. 1788

GA. 1788

S C 1788

N C 1789

PA. 1787

N Y 1788

N J 1787

DEL. 1787

MD 1788

VT

N. H. 1788

R. I. 1790

MASS 1788

CONN 1788

(Spain)

(to Spain)

(to Map)

1790

Compiled by H. George Stoll, Hammond Incorporated, 1967;
rev. by U.S. Geological Survey, 1970

PART B

AN EXPANDING AND GROWING NATION 1781-1860

Over the next eighty years, the United States grew to its present size, except for the Hawaiian Islands and Alaska.

Before this expansion could take place, the founding fathers realized they had to establish a government that would be by the people and work for the people. This was accomplished in a relatively short period. The first attempt was the Articles of Confederation, drafted in 1776, which tried to bring the separate colonies into a consolidated confederation. Ratified in March 1781, the different leaders realized the Articles of Confederation did not answer or solve the important questions, and many problems remained. The articles stated that each state could maintain its "sovereignty, freedom, and independence." Congress would be hampered in many ways.

Beginning in 1785, different points of view were expressed in a variety of attempts to satisfy the needs of all. Finally, in the latter part of May 1787, a committee worked through the summer to the middle of September, signed and submitted a document that would be the guiding light for a new country—something never before tried.

This document provided for three separate, but equal branches of government. The legislative branch, composed of two separate bodies—the House of Representatives and the Senate—gave the individual states representation based on both population as well as equal representation for all states. The executive branch would have the responsibility for governing; and a series of checks and balance, including the judicial branch, would assure that no one part of the government would have more power or control over the other parts. In addition to this marvelous structure, the new and untried Constitution provided for opportunities to add, by amendments, the needed laws for a growing and changing country.

Other nations had expanded their borders or added colonies to their empires, mostly by wars. The United States took an entirely different approach. Following the Paris Peace Treaty of 1783, the new nation—twenty years later—purchased the Louisiana Territory for $15 million. Two year later, a small band of men, led by Lewis and Clark, explored and claimed this new acquisition. In 1819, Florida was purchased from Spain for $5 million. And the Oregon treaty of 1846 settled the boundary between the United States and British Canada.

When forced into a war with Mexico, the United States first won the war, and then paid for what they had conquered in 1848. The price of $15 million gave the United States territory that would one day become Texas, California, New Mexico, Arizona, and Utah.

The smallest territory acquired was the Gadsden Purchase, which settled a dispute with Mexico in 1853, for $10 million. This forty-five-thousand-square-mile area south of Arizona and New Mexico assured the United States of a having a clear southern route to the Pacific for a future southern transcontinental railroad.

There was one major flaw in the new United States. The major problem of slavery was a serious one. The first slaves were brought from Africa in 1619. The first official protest against slavery did not come until seventy years later, in 1688.

When Thomas Jefferson wrote the Declaration of Independence, he failed to bring the topic up. The United States Constitution recognized slavery only by giving the states with slaves three-fifths of a person in the population count. An act prohibiting the importation of slaves was finally passed and became effective January 1, 1808. Nothing further would be done until the Emancipation Proclamation was issued fifty-five years later, in 1863.

When people in the North wanted to abolish the slavery in the South, resentment grew into hatred, and any attempt to reconcile their differences failed.

In the election of 1860, a split vote between Democrats made it possible for the country to choose a leader with an impossible task. Talks had failed, compromises had failed, and every attempt to preserve the union was tried, but to no avail.

CHAPTER VI

STARTING A NEW NATION
1781-1800

ARTICLES OF CONFEDERATION

Even before the declaration was approved, the Continental Congress appointed a committee in June 1776 to draft plans for a confederation of the separate colonies. It was a first, but ultimately futile attempt to consolidate the colonies into a working union. It had some good points, but was weak in many other ways. There was little recognition of a national union; states claimed territory from the Atlantic coast to the Mississippi River. Maryland refused to ratify the articles until several states ceded the territory to the west. The Articles of Confederation were agreed to by Congress in November 1777 and ratified March 1, 1781.

The nine Articles of Confederation, among other things, acknowledged that Britain recognize the new United States and set the boundaries that gave the young country land west, from the Atlantic Ocean to the Mississippi River, thanks to George Rogers Clark, and from the Great Lakes south to the line along the 31° north latitude, which is the northern boundary of Florida.

1783 TREATY OF PEACE WITH GREAT BRITAIN

A little more than four months after Cornwallis surrendered at Yorktown, the King of England urged the House of Commons to end the war. The motion passed on February 27, 1782, and both sides entered into negotiations for definitive peace.

The United States Congress appointed five well-known Americans to conduct the negotiations: John Adams, Benjamin Franklin, John Jay, Henry Laurens and

Thomas Jefferson. The main burden fell upon Franklin, and the treaty is a tribute to the seventy-six-year-old greatly respected statesman. He had concluded the Treaty of France in 1778, and that helped turn the tide in the Revolution and he was widely known and admired in both France and England.

1787 NORTHWEST ORDINANCE

While the various states met and discussed ways of resolving the many problems connected with the Articles of Confederation, the federal Congress did adopt one measure with far-reaching implications: *An Ordinance for the Government of the Territory of the United States Northwest of the River Ohio.* The ordinance stated that regions should become self-governing as quickly as the population warranted and be eligible for statehood when the population of a given territory reached sixty thousand. Most important, slavery was forbidden. The ordinance was adopted July 13, 1787. [1]

1786 THE ANNPOLIS CONVENTION

There was growing dissatisfaction with the Articles of Confederation after they had been ratified in March 1781. And with the victory at Yorktown, the various states demanded that the articles be revised. In 1785, George Washington invited men from Virginia and Pennsylvania to his home at Mount Vernon to discuss the problem.

James Madison got a resolution passed through the Virginia legislature appointing a commission to meet with others to take into consideration the problems that all agreed must be studied and improved. They met at Annapolis in September 1786. They made a recommendation that the commissioners meet in May in Philadelphia to "take into consideration the situation of the United States, to devise such further provisions as shall appear to them necessary to render the constitution of the federal government adequate to the exigencies of the Union."[2]

1787 THREE OTHER PLANS[3]

In late May, the Virginia or Randolph plan suggested a new plan rather than a revision of the Articles of Confederation. On June 15, 1787, the Paterson or New Jersey Plan resolved that the articles be revised. Three days later, Alexander Hamilton presented his Plan of Union. Each of these plans had something to offer, and each would be seriously considered.

1787 THE WRITING OF THE UNITED STATES OF AMERICA'S CONSTITUTION

As decided at the Annapolis Convention, the delegates met on the second Monday in May, but there was a not a quorum until May 25, 1787. They worked through the summer months and, on September 17, 1787, signed the document and submitted it to Congress. In turn, the Congress submitted the constitution to be ratified by the thirteen states. The first Federalist Papers, a series of essays calling for its ratification was published in a New York newspaper. By June 21, 1788, the ninth state, New Hampshire, ratified the Constitution; and according to Article VII, that was "sufficient for the establishment of this Constitution between the states to ratify the same".[4] The last state to ratify was Rhode Island who finally did so on May 29, 1799.

At the conclusion of the Constitutional convention, Benjamin Franklin was asked, "What have you wrought?" He answered, "A Republic, if you can keep it."[5]

The Webster dictionary says, "a preamble is an introductory statement, *specifically* the introductory part of a constitution or statute that usually states the reasons for and intent of the law".[6] The preamble of the Constitution of the United States certainly does that.

PREAMBLE[7]

WE THE PEOPLE of the United States, in order to form a more perfect Union, establish Justice, insure domestic Tranquility, provide for the common defense, promote the general Welfare, and secure the Blessings of Liberty to ourselves and our Posterity, do ordain and establish this Constitution for the United States of America.

From the end of May to the middle of September 1787—*a little less than four months*—a document like no other had been written to guide this new nation. It is remarkable in its clarity and outstanding in the fact that it solved so many problems that had plagued the colonies early in their history and even some of the problems that would arise later.

"The Declaration of Independence was the promise; the Constitution was the fulfillment," stated the first chief justice of the United States Supreme Court, John Jay.[8] Thomas Jefferson had, in the Declaration of Independence, enumerated the twenty-seven "injuries and usurpations, all having in direct object the establishment of an absolute Tyranny over these States."

The colonies did not want any one person to have that much power and so devised a system of checks and balances that has worked effectively ever since. A legislative body would have the responsibility to make policy judgments and write laws to govern any aspect that the constitution did not cover. The executive branch would have the power to implement and enforce the legislation and propose new initiatives. As its duty, the Supreme Court would resolve disputes as well as render interpretations of laws that had been made by the legislative and approved by the executive branches.

Two other vastly important points were incorporated into this marvelous document. There had been bitter arguments about how the representatives from each state would be allocated. Virginia and other large states favored representation in proportion to the population. The smaller states held out for an equal representation of states. With this division of thought, it looked like the Constitutional convention might fail.

But Connecticut saved the day with a proposal that would satisfy both large and small states. They proposed two houses of Congress. A House of Representatives based on the population, giving larger states more representatives, and a Senate "composed of two senators from each state, chosen by the Legislature"[9] of each state. This latter solution was further revised by the Seventeenth Amendment which stated, "The Senate of the United States shall be composed of two senators from each state, *elected by the people thereof.*"[10]

The other important point that made the Constitution a truly *Living Document,* was Article V. "The Congress, whenever two thirds of both houses shall deem it necessary, shall propose Amendments to this Constitution . . ."[11] This made it possible to amend or add to the basic Constitution as the need became clear and obvious.

On September 25, 1789, almost exactly two years since Congress had signed the Constitution, the same Congress submitted twelve amendments to the state legislatures. Ten were adopted and declared in force on December 15, 1791, and would become known for evermore as our *Bill of Rights.* They were the first, but not the last ones to be adopted. As the need arose, more amendments would be added, the latest being the XXVII Amendment *proposed September 27, 1789, and finally adopted May 7, 1992!*

BILL OF RIGHTS [12]

ARTICLE I

Congress shall make no law respecting an establishment of religion, or prohibiting the free exercise thereof; or abridging the freedom of speech, or of the press; or the right of the people peaceably to assemble, and to petition the government for a redress of grievances.

ARTICLE II

A well regulated militia, being necessary to the security of a free State, the right of the people keep and bear arms, shall not be infringed.

ARTICLE III

No soldier shall, in time of peace be quartered in any house, without the consent of the owner, nor in time of war, but in a manner to be proscribed by law.

ARTICLE IV

The right of the people to be secure to their person, houses, papers, and effects, against unreasonable searches and seizures, shall not be violated, and no warrants shall issue, but upon probable cause, supported by oath or affirmation, and particularly describing the place to be searched, and the persons or things to be seized.

ARTICLE V

No person shall be held to answer for a capital, or otherwise infamous crime, unless on a presentment or indictment of a grand jury, except in cases arising in the land or naval forces, or in the militia, when in actual service in time of war or public danger; nor shall any person be subject for the same offense to be twice put in jeopardy of life or limb; nor shall be compelled in any criminal case to be a witness against himself, nor be deprived of life, liberty, or property, without due process of law; nor shall private property be taken for public use, without just compensation.

ARTICLE VI

In all criminal prosecutions, the accused shall enjoy the right to a speedy and public trial, by an impartial jury of the state, and district wherein the crime shall have been committed, which district shall have been previously ascertained by law, and to be informed of the nature and cause of the accusation; to be confronted with the witnesses against him; to have compulsory process of obtaining witnesses in his favor, and to have the assistance of counsel for his defense.

ARTICLE VII

In suits of common law, where the value in controversy shall exceed twenty dollars, the right of trial by jury shall be preserved, and no fact tried by a jury shall be otherwise reexamined in any court of the Untied States, than according to the rules of the common law.

ARTICLE VIII

Excessive bail shall not be required, nor excessive fines imposed, nor cruel and unusual punishment inflicted.

ARTICLE IX

The enumeration in the Constitution, of certain rights, shall not be construed to deny or disparage others retained by the people.

ARTICLE X

The powers not delegated to the United States by the Constitution, nor prohibited by it to the States, are reserved to the States respectively, or to the people.

1789 GEORGE WASHINGTON INAUGURATED AS THE FIRST PRESIDENT

Congress, on April 6, 1789, counted the electoral votes which were unanimous for Washington. He was notified on April 14, 1789, and set out two days later from Mount Vernon for New York, the capital. On April 30, 1789 George Washington gave the first ever inaugural address to the "Fellow-Citizens of the Senate and of the House of Representatives".

He reminded the Congress that he renounced any pecuniary compensation when he had been appointed commander in chief of the Continental army, and now that he was president, he refused any compensation except "to be limited to such actual expenditures as the public good may be thought to require."[13]

In compliance with the Constitution, Washington gave the first State of the Union address to both houses of Congress on January 8, 1790. His advice included, "To be prepared for war is one of the most effectual means of preserving the peace."[14]

1789-97 ACCOMPISHMENTS DURING GEORGE WASHINGTON'S PRESIDENCY

During Washington's first four years, much was accomplished. Congress created a national bank and a United States Mint. It took over states' debts and pressured North Carolina and Rhode Island to ratify the Constitution. It submitted the first ten amendments to the Constitution. Washington's proclamation on neutrality came about as a result of the war between France and Britain, Austria, Prussia, and Sardinia. Congress created three executive departments: State, Treasury, and War. Washington selected Thomas Jefferson for secretary of state, Alexander Hamilton for secretary of the treasury, and Henry Knox as secretary of war. Knox had had a distinguishing military career during the Revolutionary War, taking part in the battles of Bunker Hill, Princeton, and Yorktown. The other two selections, Jefferson and Hamilton, were also excellent choices.

On August 9, 1790, the American ship the *Columbia* returned to Boston harbor after a three-year voyage, becoming the first vessel to carry the American flag around the world.

Over the next few years, three new states joined the Union. Vermont, in 1791, had been part of New Hampshire. Kentucky was part of Virginia until 1792; and in 1796, Tennessee, which had been part of North Carolina, joined the Union.

TWO IMPORTANT EVENTS

Two important events took place in 1793. George Washington laid the cornerstone for the new national capital on the site he had selected in 1791. The other far-reaching event was the beginning of the Industrial Revolution. Eli Whitney invented the cotton gin which greatly stimulated cotton production. Whitney is also credited with being the father of mass production as he introduced the method of interchangeable parts.

Even though the treaty of peace with Great Britain had ceded the Northwest Territory to the United States, the British gave no indication of surrendering this region and wanted to retain control of both the Indians and the great fur trade.

Expeditions by General Harmer in 1790 and General St. Clair in 1791 were unsuccessful. But General Anthony Wayne, a brilliant general during the Revolutionary War, decisively defeated the Indians at the Battle of Fallen Timbers on August 20, 1794. This resulted in the Treaty of Greenville, whereby the Indians ceded all of Ohio, except the northwest quarter, making it possible for increased settlements, which led to early admission of Ohio as the first to come from the Northwest Territory.

The first amendment to be ratified after the Bill of Rights was to limit the judicial powers of the United States. It was ratified February 7, 1795.

TERRITORIAL GROWTH

COLONIAL PERIOD: 1775

 Original Thirteen Colonies

 Other British territories

UNITED STATES: 1790–1920

 States

State claims

Special status areas

Territories

Unorganized territories

Claimed areas

Foreign areas

1803 Dates of territorial acquisitions
1805 Dates of initial territorial organization
(1809) Dates of latest change within given time period
1812 Dates of admission to the Union

Map scale 1:34,000,000

Compiled by H. George Stoll, Hammond Incorporated, 1967;
rev. by U.S. Geological Survey, 1970

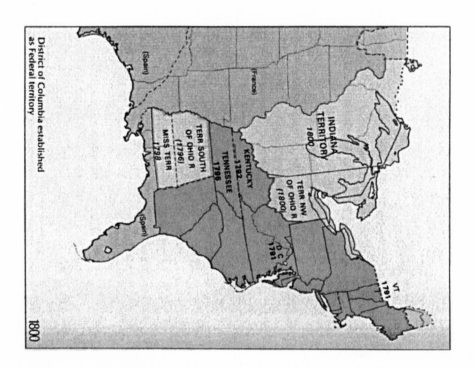

District of Columbia established
as Federal territory

1800

AMENDMENT XI[15]

The judicial powers of the United States shall not be construed to extend to any suit in law or equity, commenced or prosecuted against one of the United States by citizens of another State, or by citizens or subjects of any Foreign State.

The Jay Treaty, ratified on June 24, 1795, forced the British to "withdraw all his troops and garrisons from all posts and places with the boundary lines assigned by the Treaty of Peace to the United States".[16] They had until June 1, 1796 to accomplish this directive. The Pinckney Treaty with Spain, on October 25, 1795, gave the United States navigation rights of the lower Mississippi River. Washington refused to accept a third term and gave his farewell address on September 17, 1796.

FROM GEORGE WASHINGTON'S FAREWELL ADDRESS

Observe good faith and justice towards all nations; cultivate peace and harmony with all. Religion and morality enjoin the conduct; and can it be that good policy does not equally enjoin it? It will be worthy of a free, enlightened, and at no distant period, a great nation, to give to mankind the magnanimous and too novel example of a people always guided by an exalted justice and benevolence.[17]

He warned of "permanent alliances with any portion of the foreign world, so far, I mean, as we are now at liberty to do it."[18]

On March 4, 1797, John Adams assumed the presidency, with Thomas Jefferson as the vice president. That same year, Charles Newbold of New Jersey received a patent for a cast-iron plow. This would have a great impact on the agricultural community and made farming not only easier, but to some extent profitable.

George Washington retired to his beloved Mount Vernon and enjoyed his remaining years in a quiet life. He passed away on December 14, 1799. He was loved and admired by his fellow countrymen and was rightly deserving of the resolution presented to the House of Representatives by Henry Lee (father of Robert E. Lee). "To the memory of the Man, first in war, first in peace, and first in the hearts of his countrymen." [19]

MOUNT VERNON
Stephen Jenks[20]

What solemn sound the ear invades,
What wraps the land in sorrow's shade?
From heaven the awful mandate flies,
The Father of his country dies.

Where shall our country turn its eye,
What help remains beneath the sky?
Our friend, protector, strength, and trust,
Lies low and mould'ring in the dust.

1797-1801 JOHN ADAMS SECOND PRESIDENT

John Adams was elected with 71 electoral votes while Thomas Jefferson received 68 electoral votes. Adams was declared president and Jefferson vice president even though they belonged to different political parties. This method of selecting the president and vice president was changed in 1804 with the Twelfth Amendment.

In Adams's first year, on October 21, 1797, the United States frigate *Constitution* was launched. It would have a noble history in its future and would earn the nickname *Old Ironsides.*

During his four years, Adams averted war with France who had broken off diplomatic relations with the United States following the Jay Treaty. Adams sent Charles Pinckney, Elbridge Gerry, and John Marshall to reestablish peace when France privateers attacked and took American ships. Talleyrand, France's foreign minister, refused, to see the Americans but sent three men to demand huge sums of money for a peaceful settlement. Pinckney is reported to have said, "Millions for defense, but not one cent for tribute."[21] This was the so-called XYZ affair. There was a loud cry for war from America, and Washington was called from Mount Vernon to take command of the army. Fortunately, war was avoided. Napoleon became the first counsel of France, and a treaty was signed in 1800.

In November 1800, Congress moved from Philadelphia to its permanent home in the new city of Washington. The presidential election of 1800 was not only a striking change in national politics but a test of the Constitution's Article II, Section 1, which states that the House of Representatives would determine who would be president if no one had a majority of the electoral votes. Adams received sixty-five votes; Thomas Jefferson and Aaron Burr each received seventy-three electoral votes. The House selected Jefferson for president and Burr for vice president.

THE END OF AN ERA

The end of the 1700s was the end of an era of change. Men and women had come to America for freedom of many sorts. They had strived to make their colonies not only successful but peaceful and acceptable to all. It was not to be and slowly they took on the task of declaring their desire to rule themselves.

In a long and bitter struggle, they won their independence and liberty to not only worship as they pleased but to govern themselves in a manner never before considered in the history of mankind. They stumbled and struggled in attempt to put down on paper ideas that would govern all citizens equally and fairly. What they came up with was *not* perfect, but they knew that. They did their best and elected their best to lead them in this new adventure that would become a beacon to the world.

They closed the century with a hope and a dream and a determination to succeed in whatever they undertook. Someone thought there ought to be a record of their accomplishments of the past and preserved for future generations yet unborn. And so the Library of Congress was established with a fund of $5,000, and Thomas Jefferson gave his entire private library.

Benjamin Franklin was born a few years after the beginning of the eighteenth century—in 1706. George Washington died just a year before the end of the century—in 1799. Nearly one-hundred years spanned the lifetime of two great leaders and statesmen. Many others had contributed to the success that had been so difficult to obtain.

Would the next hundred years prove to be as fruitful? Would there be people who would come forward at the right time to solve problems, make difficult decisions, and lead the country so that *all* would benefit and have for *all* the blessings of life, liberty, and the pursuit of happiness? Only time would tell.

TERRITORIAL GROWTH

COLONIAL PERIOD: 1775

Original Thirteen Colonies

Other British territories

UNITED STATES: 1790–1920

States

State claims

Special status areas

Territories

Unorganized territories

Claimed areas

Foreign areas

1803 Dates of territorial acquisitions
1805 Dates of initial territorial organization
(1809) Dates of latest change within given time period
1812 Dates of admission to the Union

Map scale 1:34,000,000

Compiled by H. George Stoll, Hammond Incorporated, 1967;
rev. by U.S. Geological Survey, 1970

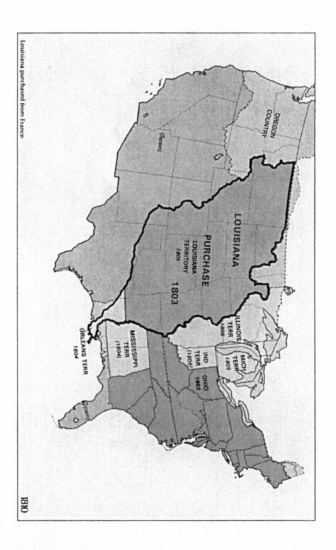

Louisiana purchased from France

1810

CHAPTER VII

EXPANSION AND GROWTH
1791-1848

The next election is sometimes called the Revolution of 1800. John Adams, a Federalist, was not reelected. Thomas Jefferson, a Republican, succeeded him. Of the electoral votes, John Adams received sixty-five, Jefferson and Aaron Burr each received seventy-three and, with no majority, the election was decided by the House of Representatives, according to Article II, Section 1 of the relatively new and untried Constitution. Ten states voted for Jefferson, four for Burr, and two states did not record their votes. Jefferson became president and Burr his vice president, though they were from different political parties.

This resulted in the passage of the Twelfth Amendment, which changed part of Article II, Section 1 of the Constitution. It was ratified on June 15, 1804, in time for the next election, as well as future elections if the problem ever arose again.

1801-1809 THOMAS JEFFERSON THIRD PRESIDENT

Jefferson assumed the office of president when he was fifty-eight years old, one year older than Washington was when he became president and four years younger than John Adams. He had a vision of limiting the power of the federal government and giving more power to the states. One example was reducing the size of the army and navy, but this proved to be a mistake, and they would have to build more ships between 1802 and 1805 to attack the pirates of the Barbary Coast in North Africa who had been preying on American shipping.

Napoleon wanted to reestablish a French colonial empire in America. The land west of the mouth of the Mississippi River had been ceded to Spain in 1762 but secretly returned to France in 1800. Jefferson sent Robert Livingston, the United States minister to France, to seek a solution. Napoleon was very tied up in Europe with wars and had no success in his attempt to recapture Santo Domingo. He began to lose interest in his American empire dream.

President Jefferson sent James Monroe to aid Livingston and, with Congress's approval, offered Napoleon $2,000,000 for New Orleans and the entrance to the Mississippi River.

Napoleon countered the offer by offering all of the Louisiana territory for $15,000,000. Though Jefferson did not have Congressional approval for such a transaction, Jefferson *boldly* accepted the offer and got the United States Senate to approve. [1]

Fourteen states would eventually be admitted to the Union from this purchase, and it's estimated that the land cost about four cents an acre. *The greatest real estate bargain ever!* The cession of Louisiana from France went into effect on April 30, 1803.

States in New England were concerned that this purchase would lessen their influence and formed a Northeastern Confederacy, composed of the states that made up New England, along with New York. To entice New York, they approached Aaron Burr, vice president, to run for the New York governorship. He lost the election and blamed Alexander Hamilton and then challenged him to a duel. Burr killed Hamilton, finished his term as vice president, but was replaced for Jefferson's second term by George Clinton. [2]

Jefferson ordered a fort to be built at the southern part of Lake Michigan. Captain John Whistler and his family left Detroit on July 14, 1803 by boat and met Lieutenant James Strode Swearingen and his troops of sixty-seven men who had come overland from Detroit. They arrived at the Chicago River August 17 and erected a fort on the banks of the river where it emptied into Lake Michigan. Named for the secretary of war, Fort Dearborn served as an outpost until it was destroyed following the massacre during the War of 1812. [3]

The state of Ohio, the first state from the Northwest Territory, was admitted into the Union in 1803. The United States was expanding and growing. Jefferson's next step would make it expand even further.

President Jefferson's interest in the territory between the Mississippi River and the Pacific Ocean went back to the early 1780s. A few weeks after the end of the Revolutionary War, Jefferson approached General George Rogers Clark, the hero who had won the Northwest Territory, about exploring the west with an army. Clark suggested a small force of three or four young men. [4]

In January 1793, with the backing of the American Philosophical Society of Philadelphia, whose members included George Washington, Robert Morris, and Alexander Hamilton, Jefferson proposed an overland expedition. A young eighteen-year-old by the name of Meriwether Lewis volunteered to lead the expedition, but Jefferson felt he was too young and too inexperienced. [5]

Nine years later, in 1802, a year *before* the Louisiana Purchase was consummated, Jefferson informed Captain Meriwether Lewis that he was to command the expedition to the Pacific. Jefferson wanted to know, once and for all, if there was a northwest passage that had been discussed and sought since the time of Columbus.

58

1803-1806 MERIWETHER LEWIS AND WILLIAM CLARK'S EXPEDITION

Explorers starting with Columbus sought a shortcut to the Far East. John Cabot searched for the western passage in 1497. Between 1534 and 1542, Jacques Cartier went up the St. Lawrence River, seeking a shorter way to the east. Though Balboa had seen the Pacific Ocean in 1513, and Magellan had sailed around the southern tip of South America on his voyage that would take his ship around the world about 1520, there were still those who believed there was a shortcut that came to be called the *Northwest Passage*.

Henry Hudson, an Englishman employed by the Dutch, explored the great river that bears his name in 1609, and a year later sought the Northwest Passage by exploring the Hudson Bay. Champlain, who founded Quebec in 1608, selected and trained Jean Nicolet to explore the great waters beyond where Champlain had trekked from 1609 to 1615. When Nicolet stepped ashore from his canoe about 1640, dressed in a damask robe hoping to make a grand entrance into the capital of the Great Kahn, he was disappointed to find Winnebago Indians at the place we now call Green Bay. More of the Great Lakes had been explored, and the dream of finding a route to the Western sea was slowly crumbling. [6]

From January to the middle of March 1803, Lewis went to school. He learned map making and how to make scientific observations, including celestial observations. He planned how large a boat would be needed, the size of the expedition, and what supplies to take, including things to trade with the Indians. He also realized he needed another leader. [7]

Meriwether Lewis selected William Clark, younger brother of George Rogers Clark. Lewis and Clark had campaigned together at the Battle of Fallen Timber in 1794 under General Anthony Wayne. The two men were good friends, and Clark had much to offer. He was a veteran of the army, a great judge of men, and was not afraid to make tough decisions.

The expedition made its way down the Ohio River to the Mississippi River and up to Saint Louis where they arrived in November 1803. They spent the winter there and in May 1804 started their journey up the Missouri River. The travel was slow but steady, and by November, they had reached the central part of what would become North Dakota. There they set up winter camp and, in April 1805, set out again up the Missouri until they were forced to leave their vessel and march up the mountain. [8]

August 12, 1805

"At the Continental Divide. This morning . . . Captain Lewis . . . wound along the foot of the mountains to the southwest approaching obliquely the main stream he had left yesterday, the road was still plain, and as it led then directly on towards the mountain stream gradually became smaller, till after going two miles it had so greatly diminished in width that one of the men in a fit of enthusiasm, with one foot on each side of the river, thanked God that he had lived to bestride the Missouri." [9]

Almost three months later, they neared the Pacific Ocean.

November 7, 1805

"The morning was rainy and the fog so thick that we could not see across the (Columbia) river . . .

"At a distance of twenty miles from our camp we hailed at a village . . . Behind two small marsh islands . . . . Opposite to these islands the hills on the left retire, and the river widens into a kink of bay crowded with low islands, subject to be overflowed occasionally by the tide. We had not gone far from this village when the fog cleared off, and we enjoyed the delightful prospect of the ocean; that ocean, the object of all our labours, the reward of all our anxieties. This cheering view exhilarated the spirits of all the party, who were still more delighted on hearing the distant roar of the breakers. [10]"

The return trip was much easier, and they arrived back in St. Louis on September 22, 1806. Much had been accomplished. Lewis and Clark had found the source of the Missouri River and established for all time that the only Northwest Passage was *overland*. Their discoveries in the field of botany, ethnology, geography, and zoology were of extreme value. The first white men and the first black man, York, brought back stories that would thrill the new nation. And it gave the United States a claim on the Oregon Territory.[11]

The United States of America was growing. People were moving West and finding a new life on the prairies. Soon they would expand and reach farther West, but first they would have to fight another war.

1807 Robert Fulton's steamship, the *Clermont*, made its first successful voyage. Two important pieces of legislation passed that year. In March, *An act to prohibit the importation of slaves* was passed and became effective on January 1, 1808. In June 1807, the American ship *Chesapeake* was fired on by the British ship *Leonard*, demanding to be searched for escaped English deserters. This led to the ill-fated *Embargo Act* passed in December 1807. It was a ban on all foreign trade, including not bringing trade to American ports. It failed in its purpose and was repealed and replace by the *Non-intercourse Act* in March 1809, which forbade trade with England and France only. It was replaced a year later with the *Macon Bill 2*, which gave the president power to renew non-intercourse against one nation the minute another lifted its restrictions against American shipping.[12]

1809 JAMES MADISON FOURTH PRESIDENT

Madison's presidency started with nothing but trouble. American grievances against England increased. English impressments of American seamen continued. The western frontier accused the British of stirring up Indian warfare against them. Both the French and the British continued their blockade, violating the three-mile limit.

The midterm election of 1810 found many older members of Congress defeated and replaced by younger men; many coming from the new states. Men like Henry Clay of Kentucky and John C. Calhoun from South Carolina were dubbed *War Hawks* for their desire to engage the English.

William Henry Harrison had been appointed governor of the Indiana Territory and was successful in securing land cession from the Indians. He was also the hero of the Battle of Tippecanoe in 1811. Later he would defeat both the British and the Indians at the Battle of Thames. In 1813, he was appointed a major general.

On June 1, 1812, Madison was persuaded to ask Congress for a declaration of war, the reasons being impressments of American sailors, the English blockade, and the British incitement of Indian wars in the northwest.[13] In 1812, Louisiana became the eighteenth state to join the Union.

The war on land did not go well for the new nation. Two attempts to take Canada ended in failure. The Fort Dearborn massacre took place in August 1812, and the British burned the new Capitol building and then the executive mansion called the president's home.

After the English departed, it was discovered that the walls of the mansion had not suffered as much as first thought. A heavy coat of white paint was used to hide the damage—from then on it was known as the *White House.*

The British were repulsed at Baltimore in September 1814, whereupon the British launched attacks against the State of Maine and also prepared to capture New Orleans.

The war at sea was a different matter. The American privateers captured three hundred British vessels and outmaneuvered the British fleet at every turn. One startling example was the American ship *Constitution*'s victory over the British ship the *Guerriere.*

Early in the war, Captain Isaac Hull put out to sea in the *Constitution* from Boston Harbor and met the British frigate *Guerriere* off the coast of Halifax on August 19, 1812. In battle lasting twenty-five minutes, the forty-four-gun *Constitution* reduced the thirty-eight-gun *Guerriere* to a complete wreck. The ship was totally dismasted and her hull so riddled that she was not thought worth towing into port and was blown up.[14] The *Constitution* had been made from oak trees, and when fired upon, the British shots bounced off her side; and she was nicknamed *Old Ironsides.*

1812 THE CONSTITUTION AND THE GUERRIERE[15]

D.P. Horton

It oftimes has been told, that the British seaman bold
Could flog the tars of France so near and handy, oh!
But they never found their match, till the Yankees did them catch,
Oh, the Yankee boys for fighting are the dandy, oh!

The *Guerriere*, a frigate bold, on the foaming ocean rolled,
Commanded by proud Dacres the grandee, oh!
With a choice of British crew, as a rammer ever drew,
Could flog the Frenchmen two to one so handy, oh!

When this frigate hove in vies, says proud Dacres to his crew,
"Come clear ship for action and be handy, oh!
"To weather gauge, boys, get he, and to make his men fight better,
Gave them drink, gunpowder mixed with brandy, oh!"

Then Dacres loudly cries, "Make this Yankee ship your prize,
You can in thirty minutes, neat and handy, oh!
Twenty-five's enough, I'm sure, and if you'll do it in a score,
I'll treat you to a double share of brandy, oh!"

The British shot flew hot which the Yankees answered not,
Till they got within the distance they call handy, oh!
"Now," says Hull unto his crew, "Boys, let's see what you can do
If we take this boasting Briton we're the dandy, oh!"

The first broadside we poured carried her mainmast by the board.
Which made this lofty frigate looked abandoned, oh!
Then Dacres shook his head and to his officers said,
"Lord! I didn't think those Yankees were so handy, oh!"

Our second told so well that their fore and mizzen fell,
Which dous'd the Royal ensign neat and handy, oh!
By George!" says he, "we're done," and they fired a lee gun,
While the Yankees struck up Yankee Doodle Dandy, oh!

Then Dacres came on board to deliver up his sword,
Tho'loth was he to part with it, it was so handy, oh!
"Oh! Keep your sword," says Hull, "For it only makes you dull,
Cheer up, and let have a little brandy, oh!"

Now fill your glasses full and we'll drink to Captain Hull,
And so merrily we'll push about the brandy, oh!
John Bull may toast his fill, but let the world say what they will,
The Yankee boys for fighting are the dandy, oh!

1813 OLIVER HAZARD PERRY (1787-1819)

Perry commanded Commodore Chauncey on the Great Lakes. On September 10, 1813, he defeated the British fleet and sent the following message to General Harrison. "We have met the enemy, and they are ours."[16]

Other naval victories included the *Essex* capturing the *Alert*, the *Constitution* capturing the *Java;* the *Wasp* capturing the *Frolic;* the *United States* capturing the *Macedonia;* the *Hornet* took the *Peacock;* and the *Enterprise* captured the *Boxer.* [17]

1814 FRANCIS SCOTT KEY (1780-1843)

During the War of 1812, Dr. William Beames of Baltimore, and a close friend of Key, was captured by the British and brought to the flagship to be tried and possibly hung from the yardarm. Key asked President Madison for credentials and took a sailboat to their flagship under a flag of truce. He arrived at the very moment the British were going to bombard Baltimore, and then attack the fort guarding the entrance to Baltimore. The British were not about to let Key go ashore with this knowledge and so he was kept on board during the British bombardment of Fort McHenry.

One of the British officers said to Francis Scott Key, "Listen, American, you had better have a good look at that flag of yours over there. Tomorrow morning, you will no longer be able to see it."

Key watched the battle throughout the night, and on the morning of September 14, 1814, peered out at dawn to see that the American flag was still flying over the fort. Moved by what he had witnessed, he wrote the famous poem that became our national anthem. He called it "Bombardment of Fort McHenry."[18]

THE STAR-SPANGLED BANNER

Oh say can you see by the dawn's early light,
What so proudly we hail'd at the twilight's last gleaming;
Whose broad stripes and bright stars thro' the perilous fight,
O'er the ramparts we watch'd, were so gallantly streaming?
And the rocket' red glare, the bombs bursting in air,
Gave proof thro' the night that our flag was still there.
REFRAIN
Oh, say does that Star-Spangled Banner yet wave,
O'er the land of the free, and the home of the brave?

On the shore dimly seen, thro' the mist of the deep,
    Where the foe's haughty hosts in dread silence reposes,
What is that which the breeze o'er the towering steep,
    As it fitfully blows, half conceals, half discloses?
Now it catches the gleam of the morning's first beam,
    In full glory reflected now shines on the stream.
REFRAIN
    "Tis the star-spangled banner, oh long may it wave,
    O'er the land of the free and the home of the brave.

And where is the band who so vauntingly swore
    That the havoc of war and the battle's confusion
A home and a country would leave no more?
    Their blood has washed out their foul footsteps' pollution
No refuge could save the hireling and slave
    From the terror of flight or the gloom of the grave!
REFRAIN
    And the Star-Spangled Banner in triumph doth wave
    O'er the land of the free and the home of the brave.

O! thus be it ever when freemen shall stand
    Between their loved homes and the foe's desolation;
Bless'd with victory and peace, may our Heaven-rescued land
    Praise the Power that have made and preserved us a nation.
Then conquer we must, for our cause it is just-
    And this be our motto—"In God is our trust!"
REFRAIN
    And the Star-Spangled Banner in triumph shall wave
    O'er the land of the free and the home of the brave.

In no time at all, the poem was set to music of an eighteenth-century English tune which was originally called "Anacreon in Heaven." One hundred and seventeen years later, March 3rd 1931, President Herbert Hoover signed the Act of Congress which made "The Star-Spangled Banner" the national anthem. [19]

By December, America was ready to end the war and the Treaty of Ghent, Belgium, was signed on December 24, 1814. It restored the *status quo ante*—the existing state of affairs prior to the war—and provided for joint commissions to determine the disputed boundaries.

Unfortunately, word of the treaty did not reach America before the British landed at New Orleans with 10,000 soldiers. On January 8, 1815, Andrew Jackson defeated the British forces with only 5,000 American soldiers.

1815 THE BATTLE OF NEW ORLEANS[20]

Martin G. Fowler

On January 8, 1815, the British forces under General Edward Packenham attacked the hastily entrenched forces of General Andrew Jackson in an attempt to capture New Orleans. "The Battle of New Orleans" is a contemporary, realistic piece describing the engagement.

"Twas on the eighth of January, just the dawn of the day.
    We spied those British officers all dress'd in bat'l array,
Old Jackson then gave orders, "Each man to keep his post,
    And form a line from right to left, and let not time be lost."

With rockets and with bombshells, like comets we let fly;
    Like lions they advance us, the fate of war to try.
Large streams of fiery vengeance upon them we let pour
    While many a brave Commander lay withering in his gore.

Thrice they marched up to the charge, and thrice they gave up ground
    We fought them full three hours, then bugle horns did sound.
    Great heaps of human pyramids lay strewn before our eyes;
We blew the horns and rang the bells to drown their dying cries.

Come all you British noblemen, and listen unto me;
    Our Frontiersmen has proved to you America is free.
But tell your Royal Master when you return back home
    That out of thirty-thousand men but few of you returned.

The nation was growing by leaps and bounds. Indiana was admitted into the Union in 1816. The next five years were to see five new states join the Union.

In1809, Nancy Hanks Lincoln gave birth to a boy on February 12. This was in Kentucky where the Lincoln clan had emigrated with Daniel Boone. Tom Lincoln and his family moved to Indiana in 1816, and two years later, Abraham Lincoln's mother died.

TERRITORIAL GROWTH

COLONIAL PERIOD: 1775

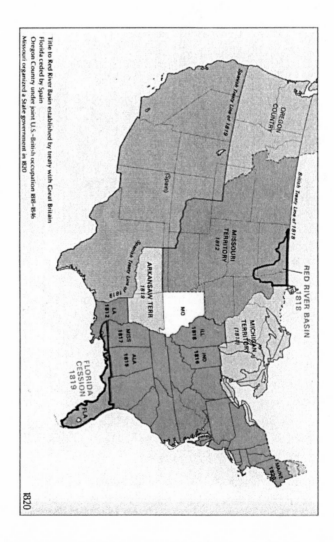

Original Thirteen Colonies

Other British territories

UNITED STATES: 1790–1920

States

State claims

Special status areas

Territories

Unorganized territories

Claimed areas

Foreign areas

1803 Dates of territorial acquisitions
1805 Dates of initial territorial organization
(1809) Dates of latest change within given time period
1812 Dates of admission to the Union

Map scale 1:34,000,000

Compiled by H. George Stoll, Hammond Incorporated, 1967; rev. by U.S. Geological Survey, 1970

OREGON COUNTRY

(Spain)

Spanish Treaty Line of 1819

MISSOURI TERRITORY
1812

British Treaty Line of 1818

RED RIVER BASIN
1818

Spanish Treaty Line of 1819

ARKANSAW TERR.
1819

MO

LA
1812

MISS
1817

ALA
1819

ILL
1818

IND
1816

MICHIGAN TERRITORY
(1818)

MAINE
1820

FLORIDA
FLA
CESSION
1819

Title to Red River Basin established by treaty with Great Britain
Florida ceded by Spain
Oregon Country under joint U.S.–British occupation 1818–1846
Missouri organized a State government in 1820

1820

EULOGY FOR NANCY HANKS [21]
Dean Dorrell February 10, 2002

"God bless my mother, all that I am or ever hope to be I owe to her." These are Abraham Lincoln's own words, describing his "angel mother," Nancy Hanks Lincoln.

The question then became "What exactly did she give him, and why?" Nancy Lincoln had no way of knowing who Abe would become. The idea that he would become President, let alone the greatest President the union has known, would have been laughable during her lifetime.

Lincoln himself apparently believed that he *inherited* from her, ambition, mental alertness, and a power of analysis that were lacking in the rest of the family. These traits were important to the man he would become, but they were not necessarily the most important traits.

What was much more important though, to whom Abe became, were the lessons she taught him as a very young boy. We know that she taught him his letters, even though she could not write much, if at all. She sent him to ABC schools, where he learned to read, and learned the power of reading. We know that as an infant he listened to his mother's voice, reciting verses from the Bible as she worked. We know he learned from her the great power of language, which he used so effectively in his years as a politician and president. He maybe even have learned on some level from her to take complex ideas, even ideas like freedom and democracy, and using stories and illustrations, put these ideas in a form understandable to everyone.

We know that most of a child's sense of right and wrong is instilled within the first few years of his life. From this we can be confident that Abe gained from Nancy and Tom Lincoln his honesty, integrity, and sense of moral purpose that served him—and the nation—so well during his later years.

We know that Tom and Nancy belonged to a church that taught in no uncertain terms that slavery was wrong. We can be sure he learned from her at least the roots of that great single moral truth that drove him throughout his life and his political career: to believe *above all else,* that "all men are created equal; that they are endowed by their creator with certain unalienable rights, that among these are life, liberty, and the pursuit of happiness" as Jefferson so eloquently put it. Abe came to believe in those words even more than the founding fathers who wrote them.

But why? At the time of Nancy Lincoln's death, Abe was only nine. He was not Honest Abe, the Great Emancipator, the man who saved the Union, and perhaps even democracy and freedom as we know it. He was not even the successful lawyer in Illinois. He was Abe, the young boy on the frontier, who would more than likely grow up to become a farmer and carpenter like his father, struggling to make a decent living, if he grew up at all.

She taught him without knowing what he would become. She taught him these things because she had faith that this child should know his letters—should be able to read—should believe in the equality of men, whether his destiny was to become a humble farmer or carpenter, or even president of the United States. And she did all of this on faith and faith alone, that what she taught him mattered. That whatever he became, he would be good, and kind, and honest.

And it was because she taught him these things that he went on to be Honest Abe, the Great Emancipator, the Savior of the Union, and to produce that New Birth of Freedom, of which he spoke so eloquently.

Abraham Lincoln's mother died when Abe was only nine years of age. The following poem asks the question, "What if Nancy Hanks had come back?"

1818 NANCY HANKS[22]

Rosemary Benet

If Nancy Hanks
Came back as a ghost,
Seeking news
Of what she loved most,
She'd ask first
"Where's my son?
What happened to Abe?
What's he done?"

"Poor little Abe,
Left all alone
Except for Tom,
Who's a rolling stone;
He was only nine
The year I died.
I still remember
How hard he cried

"Scraping along
In a little shack
With hardly a shirt
To cover his back
And a prairie wind
To blow him down,
Or pinching times
If he went to town.

"You wouldn't know
About my son?
Did he grow tall?
Did he have fun?
Did he learn to read?
Did he get to town?
Do you know his name?
Did he get on?"

Julius Silberger wrote a poem in response to Rosemary Benet's poem about Nancy Hanks:

A REPLY TO NANCY HANKS[23]

Yes, Nancy Hanks,
The news we will tell
Of your Abe
Of whom you loved so well.
You asked first,
"Where's my son?"
He lives in the heart
Of everyone.

1817-1825 JAMES MONROE FIFTH PRESIDENT

This time was referred to as the Era of Good Feeling and with just cause. The settlers moved West in ever growing numbers. Roads were built, and on July 4, 1817, work began on the Erie Canal. And Mississippi came into the Union in 1817.

Illinois's population was mostly in the southern part of the territory. Fort Dearborn had been rebuilt starting in 1816. The northern boundary of the territory had been set by the Northwest Ordinance in 1787, which stated, "That, if Congress shall hereafter find it expedient, they shall have the authority to form one or two States in that part of the said territory which lies north of an east and west line drawn through the southerly bend or extreme of the Lake Michigan." [24]

Illinois Congressional-delegate Nathanial Pope presented a petition to Congress for admission, but also asked that the northern boundary be changed from 41°39' to 42°30', approximately forty miles north of the east-west line. The object of the amendment was for the purpose of gaining a coast on Lake Michigan that "would afford additional security to the perpetuity of the Union." [25]

In addition to gaining a port for Chicago, it would also afford a port for "a canal between Lake Michigan and the Illinois River." This passage had been envisioned by Joliet and Marquette back in 1673. The bill passed and Illinois became a state on April 18, 1818. Alabama would join the Union in 1819.

Andrew Jackson, the hero of New Orleans, in 1817 and 1818 invaded Florida to stop the raids against settlements in Georgia and Alabama by the Seminole Indians. John Quincy Adams, Secretary of State demanded that Spain keep order or cede Florida to the United States, Spain chose the latter and the United States paid Spain $5,000,000. Spain also had to give up any claim to the area in the Louisiana Purchase Pacific north of the forty-second parallel. The Florida Treaty was signed February 27, 1819. [26]

In 1820, Missouri applied for statehood, having been settled by people mainly from the South. It was intended as a slave state and this caused a problem, since the Senate was evenly divided in terms of free and slave states. A compromise was reached when Maine was admitted as a free state in 1820; Missouri was admitted in 1821, but no state could be a slave state north of the 36°30' parallel.

The reelection of Monroe was overwhelming. He received 231 out of 235 electoral votes. The good feeling continued. The United States had been an independent country since 1787—a short thirty-three years. And the idea of independence had spread—first to France and then the European colonies in the Western Hemisphere. Europe was ready to use force to hold on to its colonies. England proposed to the United States that the two join to prevent Spain, Portugal, or France from annexing territory on this side of the Atlantic, but Monroe distrusted England.

In 1823, James Monroe's message to Congress enunciated the famous doctrine that bears his name.

THE MONROE DOCTRINE[27]
James Monroe

> We owe it, therefore, to candor and to the amicable relations existing between the United States and these (European) powers to declare that we should consider any attempt on their part to extend their system to any portion of this hemisphere as dangerous to our peace and safety. With the existing colonies or dependencies of any European power, we have not interfered and shall not interfere.

What audacity! Here was a young nation less than forty years in existence, fighting two wars with Britain and coming out the winner, and now telling Europe, *HANDS OFF!* It was a spirit of determination that had been born during the Revolutionary War, and in some cases before, that gave Americans the courage to stand up for what they believed was not only right, but also the prudent direction that this new nation was going. If ever a country was writing its own destiny, the Monroe Doctrine was the opening chapter.

1824 LAFAYETTE VISITS AMERICA

The United States Congress invited Marquis Lafayette to the country he had helped liberate. They voted him a grant of $200,000 and a township of land to show their appreciation for what he had done.

1825-1829 JOHN QUINCY ADAMS SIXTH PRESIDENT

The election of 1824 was between four candidates: John Quincy Adams, son of the second president, John Adams; Andrew Jackson; Henry Clay; and W. H. Crawford. None received a majority of the electoral votes. Jackson was awarded 99 electoral votes; Adams received 84 votes; Clay 37, and Crawford 41. Once again, the election was decided by Article II of the Constitution, and the House of Representatives voted and declared Adams the new President. It was the first time that a count had been made of the popular vote. Adams received 108,740 votes, while Jackson received 153,544 votes. Clay and Crawford each received less than 48,000 votes. The outcome was not received well by the Jacksonian people, and they worked hard for the next four years to change the outcome.

In 1825 the Erie Canal was completed, connecting the Great Lakes with the Hudson River, near Albany. This assured that New York would have a very important port, and the canal would allow easier access to the land in the west.

A year later, the Quincy tramway, sometimes called the first railroad in the United States, was built between Quincy, Massachusetts, and the tide water, a distance of three miles. The first railroad of any significance was the Baltimore and Ohio, where construction started on July 4, 1828. [28]

While New England states became more industrialized, the south depended on an agricultural economy, aided by slaves. To protect American industry against the cheaper products from Europe, a Tariff Bill was passed. The South opposed this and passed a protest called the *South Carolina protest against the Tariff of 1828.* This asserted her right to nullify the tariff within her jurisdiction. The South took up the cry of nullification, and this was the beginning of states in the South thinking they could act independently.

In the election of 1828, Adams received only 83 electoral votes, while Andrew Jackson received the remaining 178 electoral votes. For a second time, an Adams had only served one term as president. But that would be the rule rather than the exception. After Jackson, Lincoln, and Grant would be the only presidents in the nineteenth century to be elected twice. [29]

1829-1837 ANDREW JACKSON SEVENTH PRESIDENT

Jackson's election was a triumph for those who made up the west of the young country. The previous six presidents had come from either Virginia or Massachusetts.

Other parts of the country felt they had a leader that was not only a hero, but represented the frontier part of the country, Jackson coming from Tennessee.

Although previous presidents had appointed their friends to serve various posts, Andrew Jackson perfected the *spoils system*. Jackson seldom met with his appointed cabinet and instead, made decisions with advice form his close friends. It became known as the *Kitchen Cabinet*.

In 1829, the process of manufacturing galvanized iron was perfected. By coating the iron with zinc, it prevented rust, and was a big boom for the many uses of iron. In 1831, William Lloyd Garrison established the newspaper *Liberator* in Boston, and this marked the beginning of the abolitionist movement. [30]

1832 found problems in the south and out west. Another Tariff Bill really upset South Carolina which passed a nullification bill. This caused great debate, but Henry Clay got a compromise bill passed that would reduce the tariff over a ten-year period. This satisfied South Carolina and the talk of nullification subsided. Out west, the Indian Chief Black Hawk was in insurrection against the settlers for encroaching on Indian tribal lands.

As a result of the Black Hawk War, which included Abraham Lincoln and Zachary Taylor's participation, the Indian title to Northern Illinois and much of Wisconsin was yielded. This rich region was thrown open to settlement, and returning troops made known the attractiveness of this area to those in the east.

Also in 1832, a canal connecting Lake Erie with the Ohio River was opened. The election of 1832 reelected Jackson, but Vice President John C. Calhoun was replaced with Martin Van Buren. On August 5, 1833, Chicago would be incorporated as a village with a population of two hundred. Fifteen years later, on the completion of the Illinois and Michigan Canal, Chicago's population would be 20,023. In 1834, Cyrus McCormick invented the reaping machine, which would revolutionize the agricultural world.

In 1835, a Frenchman by the name of Alexis De Tocqueville made the following observation about America:

> America is a land of wonders, in which everything is in constant motion and every change seems an improvement. The idea of novelty is their indissolubly connected with the idea of amelioration. No natural boundary seems to be set to the efforts of man; and in his eyes what is not yet done is only what he has yet attempted to do.[31]

1835 SAMUEL FINLEY BREESE MORSE

Morse first demonstrated a working model of the telegraph in 1835. With $35,000 appropriated by Congress in 1843, he built an experimental line between Baltimore and Washington, D.C. Finally completed, he sent a message over the wire on May 24, 1844, "What hath God Wrought?" [32]

In 1835, Samuel Colt secured the first patent of a revolving breech pistol but was unable to manufacture it profitably until 1847.

1836 FALL OF THE ALAMO

With over twenty thousand Americans making their homes in Texas by the middle of the 1830s, Santa Anna the new dictator of Mexico, opposed the independent attitude of these new settlers and started a war in 1835. With three thousand Mexican troops, he attacked the Alamo mission in San Antonio on March 6, 1836, which was defended by 187 Americans, including Davy Crockett, William Bowie, and commanded by Colonel Barret Travis who offered to surrender on the condition that his men's lives be spared.

But the answer was that they must surrender without any guarantee of life. All of the Americans in the garrison were killed except for an old woman and a Negro slave. The Mexicans lost over three hundred. News of the slaughter reached Sam Houston and with Texas volunteers, defeated Santa Anna in the Battle of San Jacinto, on April 21, 1836.[33] No doubt someone used the phrase, *Remember the Alamo*. The Republic of Texas was established March 2, 1836. Arkansas was admitted into the Union that same year.

1836 also saw the invention of the screw propeller that was perfected by 1838.[34] This would change forever the method by which ships, both large and small, would be propelled through the water. In 1837, John Deere introduced the steel plow.

The USS *Constitution* had won in a battle with the British ship *Guerriere* in the War of 1812. Upon preparation for dismantling her in the 1830s, Oliver Wendell Holmes's poem saved her, and she resides in the Navy yard of Charleston, Massachusetts.

OLD IRONSIDES[35]

Ay, tear her tattered ensign down!
Long has it waved on high,
And many an eye had danced to see
That banner in the sky;
Beneath it rung the battle shout,
And burst the cannon's roar;
The meteor of the ocean air
Shall sweep the clouds no more.

Her deck, once red with heroes' blood,
Where knelt the vanquished foe,
When winds were hurrying o'er the flood,
And waves were white below,
No more shall feel the victor's tread,
Or know the conquered knee;
The harpies of the shore shall pluck
The eagle of the sea!

TERRITORIAL GROWTH

COLONIAL PERIOD: 1775

Original Thirteen Colonies

Other British territories

UNITED STATES: 1790–1920

States

State claims

Special status areas

Territories

Unorganized territories

Claimed areas

Foreign areas

1803 Dates of territorial acquisitions
1805 Dates of initial territorial organization
(1809) Dates of latest change within given time period
1812 Dates of admission to the Union

Map scale 1:34,000,000

Compiled by H. George Stoll, Hammond Incorporated, 1967;
rev. by U.S. Geological Survey, 1970

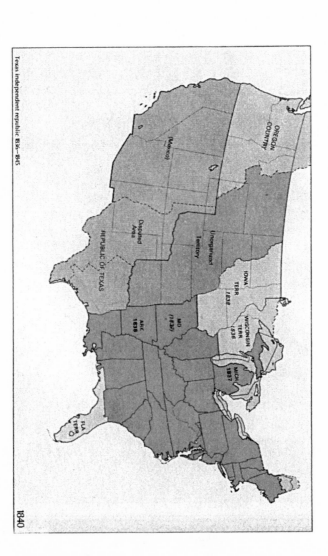

OREGON COUNTRY

(Mexico)

Disputed Area

Unorganized Territory

REPUBLIC OF TEXAS

IOWA TERR. *1838*

WISCONSIN TERR. *1836*

MO. *(1821)*

ARK. 1836

MICH. 1837

FLA. TERR.

Texas independent republic 1836–1845

1840

Oh, better that her shattered hulk
Should sink beneath the waves;
Her thunders shook the mighty deep,
And there should be her grave;
Nail to the mast her holy flag,
Set every threadbare sail,
And give her to the god of storms,
The lightning and the gale!
Oliver Wendell Holmes (1809-1894)

1837-1841 MARTIN VAN BUREN EIGHTH PRESIDENT

About the only good thing that happened the first year of Van Buren's presidency was the admission of Michigan into the Union. Misfortune marked the greater part of Van Buren's term in office, and most of it was not of his making. The Panic of 1837, the first financial crisis of the United States, came about mainly because of the speculation and reckless expansion that had started in 1833. Failure of certain business houses in Britain, poor crops in the west in 1835, and again in 1837, plus Jackson's Special Circular of July 11, 1836, requiring that public lands be paid for in hard money, all contributed to the bank failures throughout the country.

Other problems included the *Caroline Affair*, when Canadian militia seized an American steamer on the American side of the Niagara River. This was resolved in January 1838 by a letter from President Van Buren. A dispute between the State of Maine and of New Brunswick of Canada resulted in the Aroostook County War which lasted from 1838 to 1839, and was finally resolved in August 1842, with the Webster-Ashburton Treaty.[36]

The abolitionist movement that came into being back in the early 1830s kept expanding. The New England Antislavery Society was founded in 1832, and the American Antislavery Society in 1833. In 1835, a Boston mob broke up an antislavery meeting and dragged William Lloyd Garrison, publisher of the *Liberator* through the streets. In 1837, Elijah Lovejoy, an abolitionist, was murdered in front of his newspaper office in Alton, Illinois. In 1838, the Underground Railroad was organized to safely "transport" escaped slaves to the northern free states. Feelings were high in both the North and the South, and it appeared that the day of reckoning was not too far in the future.

The Whig Party, which had been founded in 1832 and made up of different factions in both the North and South, had a common bond—hatred and distrust of Andrew Jackson. By 1840, they were big enough to nominate William Henry Harrison to oppose the attempted reelection of Martin Van Buren. With all the bad things that had happened during Van Buren's first term, there was not much chance for a second one. Harrison was the first candidate to receive over 1,000,000 popular votes, and he won with 234 electoral votes to Van Buren's 60 electoral votes. [37]

1841 WILLIAM HENRY HARRISON NINTH PRESIDENT

Harrison was from Ohio, and his vice president, John Tyler, was from Virginia. Their campaign slogan had been Tippecanoe and Tyler Too. Tippecanoe was a river feeding into the Wabash River, where Harrison had won a battle against the Indians and had secured land cession from them. He was administered the oath of office on March 4, 1841. On April 4, 1841, Harrison died of pneumonia. President Harrison was the first president to die in office, but not the last.

Zachary Taylor had served with Abraham Lincoln in the Black Hawk War, and also served with distinction in the War with Mexico, but died July 9, 1850, from physical strain only sixteen months after taking office. Warren Harding went on a nationwide tour, and in Seattle became very ill. He died in office on August 2, 1923. The fourth president to die in office was President Franklin Delano Roosevelt. He was in Warm Spring, Georgia, one of his favorite vacation spots, and complained of a headache and died two hours later.

Four presidents were assassinated while in office, and there were attempts on others. Lincoln, elected in 1860 and again in 1864, was assassinated as was Garfield who was elected in 1880, and McKinley who was elected in 1896. John F. Kennedy was elected in 1960 and was assassinated in November 1963. An attempt on President Truman was stopped, but a Secret Service agent was killed. Two attempted assassination were thwarted during Gerald Ford's short term in office, and an attempted assassination was prevented when Ronald Reagan was shot but recovered in 1985, having been elected in 1980.

In war, you expect and accept casualties. When eight leaders gave their lives and three nearly so, while on duty as president of the United States, it was the ultimate sacrifice that was paid by great men. But the smooth transition that was accomplished following these tragedies was living proof that liberty and freedom would continue for the United States of America, a country founded by brave courageous and farsighted men, but governed, not by men, but by the rule of laws that they had proposed, written, agreed upon, but most important, lived up to.

1841-1845 JOHN TYLER TENTH PRESIDENT

Tyler was from Virginia, and had admired Jefferson, and was more of a states' right man than a nationalist. He antagonized Congress by twice vetoing bills that would provide for a new United States Bank and various branches. Frustrated by his action, the entire Cabinet resigned, except for Daniel Webster, who waited until he completed the Webster-Ashburton Treaty that fixed the boundary between Maine and Canada, and then walked out, leaving Tyler alone.[38]

About the only good thing that happened to President John Tyler during his nearly four-year term was that he married Julie Gardiner in New York City on June 26, 1844. Texas applied for admission into the Union in 1844, but the Senate rejected the treaty, and that became an issue in the 1844 election. Henry Clay, running for president on the Whig ticket, wrote a letter opposing Texas annexation. The Democrats nominated James K. Polk from Tennessee as their candidate, who favored annexation. When New York threw its weight by voting for the Liberty Party candidate, James G. Birney, an antislavery proponent, James Polk received 170 electoral votes and Clay 105 electoral votes. [39]

1845-1849 JAMES K. POLK ELEVENTH PRESIDENT

One of Congress's first acts in the new administration was to declare that all national elections would be held on the first Tuesday, after the first Monday, of November.

During Polk's one and only term, more territory was added to the United States than in any other time, except for the Louisiana Purchase by Thomas Jefferson.

The Oregon Treaty settled the boundary between the Oregon territory and British Canada at the forty-ninth parallel and was signed June 15, 1846. [40]

Florida was admitted into the Union as the twenty-seventh state in 1845. That same year, *petroleum* was discovered near Pittsburgh, Pennsylvania. Iowa would join the Union in 1846. On September 30, 1846, *ether* was used as an anesthetic for the first time by Boston dentist William Morton.

1846 SMITHSONIAN INSTITUTE ESTABLISHED

John Quincy Adams, the sixth president of the United States, was asked to speak at the opening of this great institution. He said, "To furnish the means of acquiring knowledge is . . . the greatest benefit that can be conferred upon mankind. It prolongs life itself and enlarges the sphere of existence." [41]

1845-1848 WAR WITH MEXICO

Texas was annexed by a joint resolution of Congress and passed on March 1, 1845. Texas claimed the Rio Grande River as its southwestern boundary, which Mexico disputed. In May 1845, General Zachary Taylor was sent to the border and was attacked by Mexico in April 1846 by a superior force. Taylor defeated the Mexicans in two different battles, Palo Alto on May 8 and Resaca de la Palmas on May 9, 1846.

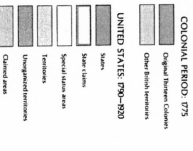

TERRITORIAL GROWTH

COLONIAL PERIOD: 1775

Original Thirteen Colonies

Other British territories

UNITED STATES: 1790–1920

States

State claims

Special status areas

Territories

Unorganized territories

Claimed areas

Foreign areas

1803 Dates of territorial acquisitions
1805 Dates of initial territorial organization
(1809) Dates of latest change within given time period
1812 Dates of admission to the Union

Map scale 1:34,000,000

Compiled by H. George Stoll, Hammond Incorporated, 1967;
rev. by U.S. Geological Survey, 1970

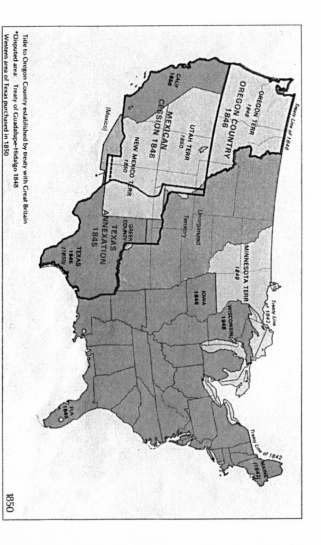

Title to Oregon Country established by treaty with Great Britain
*Disputed area: Treaty of Guadalupe-Hidalgo 1848
Western area of Texas purchased in 1850

1850

Congress declared war on Mexico on May 13 and Mexico declared war on the United States on May 23. Four different moves under separate leaders were planned. Taylor was to hold the Rio Grande; Winfield Scott was to advance on Mexico City from Vera Cruz; Colonel Stephen Kearney was to take and hold New Mexico, and then go to California and join Captain John C. Fremont.

Following his two victories in May, Taylor captured Matamoras; and in September, he captured Monterey. He then sent ten thousand men to reinforce General Scott's march toward Mexico City. General Santa Anna met Taylor's remaining force of four thousand men while Santa Anna had twenty thousand men and demanded Taylor's surrender.

Zachary Taylor's reply was: *"TELL HIM TO GO TO HELL!"* [42]

The two-day battle in February 1847 was hard fought. But the Americans sent the Mexicans in full retreat and made Taylor a hero. Two graduates of the West Point Academy served under Taylor but would not formally meet for another twenty years. One was Robert E. Lee and the other was Ulysses S. Grant.

Captain Stephen Kearney's trip to New Mexico was successful. He then proceeded to California to aid Captain Fremont and Commodore Stockton's Pacific Fleet which captured San Diego and Los Angeles.

The Treaty of Guadalupe Hidalgo was signed on February 2, 1848—ten days after the discovery of gold at Coloma, California. Mexico gave up its claim to the Rio Grande. She also ceded the territory now occupied by California, New Mexico, Arizona, and Utah, for which the United States paid Mexico $15,000,000.

In 1846 Elias Howe was credited with inventing the lockstitch sewing machine. Isaac Singer invented the first practical domestic sewing machine five years later. In 1847, Richard Hoe invented the rotary printing press.

THE IRISH CONTRIBUTIONS

In 1846 and 1847, the potato crops of Ireland, which were a staple of the peasants, failed, causing widespread starvation while hundreds and then thousands of people immigrated to the United States. It is estimated that 1,700,000 Irish—a little less than a quarter of the population of Ireland when the famine began—emigrated during the 1840s and 1850s. [43]

Many went to New York and Boston; and others found work near Chicago, digging the canal that would connect Lake Michigan with the Illinois River, which flows into the Mississippi River.

Wisconsin joined the Union as the thirtieth state in 1848. April 19, 1848 saw the opening of the Illinois and Michigan Canal, with a width of 60 feet at the water level. This was a big improvement over the Erie Canal, thanks to Chief Engineer William Gooding, who had worked on the Erie Canal and saw the limitations

In 1836, when the canal was started with much pomp and ceremony in Chicago on July 4, the orator of the day, Colonel Richard J. Hamilton, predicted that there were men living that would see Chicago with a population of fifty thousand.[44] On that day in 1836, Chicago had only 3,820 people. In 1860, twenty-four years later, the population of Chicago was over *one hundred thousand!* Two great bodies of water had been joined and the land around the Great Lakes had another outlet for its growing resources.[45]

On July 19, 1848 the First Women's Rights Convention was held in Seneca, New York. It was the first of its kind in the world and brought women like Lucretia Mott, Elizabeth Cady Stanton and the Grimke sisters, Sarah and Angelina, who would become famous for the fight to have women's equality recognized.[46] On August 14, 1848, the Oregon Territory was established. Also in 1848, Horace Mann gave his Report on Education that he quoted in his *Common School Journal.*

> The only sphere, then left open for our patriotism is the improvement of our children—not the few, but many, not a part of them, but all. This is but one field of exertion, but it opens an infinite career, for the capacities of mankind can go on developing, improving, perfecting, as long as the cycles of eternity revolve. For the improvement of the race, a high, a generous, an expansive education is the true and efficient means.[47]

Horace Mann was the president of the Massachusetts Senate in 1837, when he signed a bill creating a state board of education. He believed in a nonsectarian, free education of all designed to make better citizens.

In 1848, political storms swept across Europe. There was an abdication in Austria, a revolution in Italy and another in Germany, and in Sicily an uprising against the King of Naples. This would start a movement that would be the largest immigration the world had ever seen. Between 1821 and 1935, about *36 MILLION* people sought their freedom by coming to the United States.[48]

NEARLY A HALF CENTURY OF GREATNESS

Nearly fifty years had elapsed since the beginning of the nineteenth century. Men had come forward to carry the torch that had been passed by the founding fathers. The flame grew brighter as Thomas Jefferson had the great insight to purchase the Louisiana Territory and then had Lewis and Clark successfully explore it.

James Madison, considered by many the author of the Constitution, successfully saw the War of 1812 once again turn back the British. James Monroe had the courage to tell Europe that the Western Hemisphere was off limits to them. Andrew Jackson, the hero of New Orleans, brought in an era of the common man. James K. Polk expanded the country so that it stretched from sea to sea, and secured boundaries in the North and the South.

Transportation on land and water had been greatly improved with canals, roads, and the start of railroads, and improved shipping vessels with Fulton's steamship and later the invention of the screw propeller. Communication, once limited to messengers, got its start with tremendous improvement in the telegraph. Newspapers would see remarkable change with the rotary printing press that would have made Benjamin Franklin proud. The *Chicago Tribune* was first published on June 10, 1847, with a circulation of four hundred. The American Medical Association was founded in Philadelphia on May 7, 1847.

The industrial revolution saw the process of galvanized iron perfected; DuPont established a powder mill in Wilmington, Delaware; petroleum was found in Pennsylvania; and Sam Colt's pistol would help tame the west. The agricultural boom would be aided by Cyrus McCormick's reaper, and John Deere's steel plow.

Word of the discovery of gold on January 24, 1848, would take the better part of the year to get back to the east. This would be the cause of the greatest migration in the country's history—the California gold rush which got its start in 1849.

Women's work would be eased with the sewing machine, thanks to Elias Howe and Isaac Singer. And women would take up the cause of equal rights that would finally reach its goal on August 18, 1920 with the Nineteenth Amendment to the Constitution. *Seventy-two years* after the First Women's Rights Convention. Sometimes democracy moved with speed of glaciers, but move it did.

American education for all citizens took a large leap forward with the help of Horace Mann.

What would the future years bring? Were there leaders to take up causes for the good of all? Would the United States continue to grow and improve life for all of it citizens, regardless of race? Would leaders with the eloquence of Thomas Jefferson or the tenacity of John Adams (both of whom died on July 4, 1826), come forth to carry the torch of freedom? Would there be military leaders like George Washington, John Paul Jones, Andrew Jackson, William Henry Harrison, and Zachary Taylor to win battle if the need arose? Again, only time could answer those questions.

CHAPTER VIII

ATTEMPTS AT RECONCILIATION
AND THE ROAD TO WAR
1848-1861

J ohn Quincy Adams had been elected by the House of Representatives in 1824 when there was not a clear electoral majority. Zachary Taylor, the hero of the Mexican War, was elected because a third party—the Free Soil Party—nominated Martin Van Buren from New York who took away votes in that important state from Taylor's opponent, Lewis Case, a Democrat.

1849-1850 ZACHARY TAYLOR TWELFTH PRESIDENT

Taylor took the oath of office on March 5, 1849 as March 4 was a Sunday. By then, many had heard of the gold discovery in California and prepared to head that way either by land or water.

1849 THE CALIFORNIAN

Jesse Hutchinson

When news of the gold rush reached New England, one of the companies sailing from Massachusetts was the Salem and California Mining and Trading Company. The original members of the company purchased the barge *La Grange* and changed the name of their group to the La Grange Company. It was from members of this company that the *Society of Californian Pioneers of New England* afterward came into being. The *La Grange* sailed from the Phillips Wharf, Salem, on March 17, 1849. The wharf was crowded with hundreds of relatives, friends, and observers; and before the vessel pulled out, the members of the company sang "The Californian," the words for which were written by Jesse Hutchinson of the famous New England family troupe. The ship took 184 days to reach San Francisco.

> We've formed our band and are well manned
> To journey afar to the promised land,
> Where the golden ore is rich in store
> On the banks of the Sacramento shore.
> Then ho! Boys, ho! Who to California go,
> For the mountain cold are covered with gold,
> Along the banks of the Sacramento.
> Ho! Ho! Away we go, digging up gold in Francisco.
> Oh, the gold is there, most anywhere,
> And they did it out with an iron bar,
> And when it's thick with spade and pick,
> They've taken out lumps as big as bricks.
> Oh, don't cry or heave a sign.
> We'll come back again by and by,
> Don't breathe a fear or shed a tear,
> But patiently wait about two year
> We expect our share of the coarsest fare,
> And sometimes to sleep in the open air,
> Upon the cold around we shall all sleep sound
> Except when the wolves are howling 'round.
> As off we roam over the dark sea foam,
> We'll never forget our friends at home,
> For memories kind will bring to mind
> The thought of those we leave behind.
> In the days of old, the Prophets told
> Of the City to come, all framed in gold;
> Peradventure they foresaw the day
> Now dawning in Californi—a.

Also in 1849, Samuel Colt and Elisha Root developed a practical way to manufacture Colt's revolver by using interchangeable parts. [2]

In early 1850, California had enough of a population to seek admission into the Union. On January 29, 1850, Henry Clay introduced a resolution that would forever be known as the Compromise of 1850. It was debated all spring and summer by such famous Americans as Henry Clay, Daniel Webster, John C. Calhoun, Jefferson Davis, William Henry Seward, and Salmon Chase. When it finally passed on September 9, 1850, California became the thirty-first state and a free state, in terms of slavery. Some other factors in the resolution included the abolishment of slavery in the District of Columbia, and an improved fugitive slave law. [3]

On June 3, 1850, nine southern states met in Nashville, Tennessee, and demanded the extension of the 36° 30' line, separating the slave states from the free states that had been agreed upon in the Missouri Compromise of 1820.[4] Also that year, Congress gave land grants to railways, one of the first uses of the eminent domain—power of the government to appropriate private property for public use of the public good.

During that summer, Zachary Taylor died on July 9, 1850 and Vice President Millard Fillmore from the state of New York was sworn in the next day.

1850-1853 MILLARD FILLMORE THIRTEENTH PRESIDENT

When Fillmore signed the Fugitive Slave Act on September 18, 1850, as demanded by the Southern states, he felt he was taking the only possible course to preserve the Union, but he weakened his leadership with the rest of the country. He desired the nomination for a second term, but lost out to Winfield Scott. In the election of 1852, Winfield Scott was defeated by the Democratic candidate Franklin Pierce from the state of New Hampshire.[5]

On June 2, 1851, the State of Maine became the first state to prohibit the manufacture or sale of alcoholic beverages. In 1852 Harriet Beecher Stowe's *Uncle Tom's Cabin* caused the North to be more solidified against slavery. Stowe had heard about slavery from her older brother who had worked in New Orleans.

1853-1857 FRANKLIN PIERCE FOURTEENTH PRESIDENT

Pierce's one and only term as president was filled with mostly bitter feelings, violent debate, and actual bloodshed over the slavery issue. But there were some positive events that took place.

A dispute with Mexico was settled on December 30, 1853, by James Gadsden, the United States minister to Mexico. A little over forty-five thousand square miles of land that bordered New Mexico and Arizona, was purchased for $10,000,000.[6] This purchase rounded out and completed the boundaries of the United States that would not change until the purchase of Alaska in 1867.

That same year a trial was held in Virginia, charging Mrs. Douglas "for teaching colored children to read." The slave codes of most Southern states forbade the teaching of reading or writing to slaves. Mrs. Douglas was found guilty and sentenced to one month in jail.[7]

Also in 1853, surveys were initiated for a proposed railway to the Pacific. Jefferson Davis, from Mississippi, was Pierce's secretary of war. He sent out four teams of surveyors to explore various routes. Naturally Davis favored a Southern route; the final decision would be years away. If a Northern route was selected, more settlers would take up land along the route chosen. This alarmed the southern states since easier transportation would encourage settlement west of Missouri and north of the demarcation line. This would bring in free states and upset the balance of power in Congress.[8]

If one measure precipitated open rebellion that would lead to the Civil War, it may well have been the Kansas-Nebraska Act, passed May 30, 1854. Proposed by Stephen A. Douglas, senator from Illinois, it provided for the repeal of the Compromise of 1820, undid the section truce of 1850, opened the Kansas-Nebraska territory to settlement with the provision of settlers choosing the slavery question. This was known as Popular sovereignty by some and squatters sovereignty by others.[9] When the act was still in the bill state, six independent Democrats wrote an appeal.

JANUARY 19, 1854 APPEAL OF THE INDEPENDENT DEMOCRATS[10]

We arraign this bill as a gross violation of a sacred pledge; as a criminal betrayal of precious rights; as part and parcel of an atrocious plot to exclude from a vast unoccupied region immigrant from the Old World and free laborers from our own States, and convert it into a dreary region of despotism, inhabited by master and slaves.

Take your maps, fellow citizens, we entreat you, and see what country it is this bill gratuitously and recklessly propose to open to slavery.

We appeal to the people. We warn you that the dearest interest of freedom and the Union are in imminent peril. Demagogues may tell you that the Union can be maintained only by submitting to the demands of slavery. We tell you that the Union can only be maintained by the full recognition of the just claims of freedom and man. The Union was formed to establish justice and secure the blessing of liberty. When it fails to accomplish these ends it will be worthless, and when it becomes worthless it cannot endure.

We entreat you to be mindful of the fundamental maxim of Democracy—EQUAL RIGHTS AND EXACT JUSTICE FOR ALL MEN.

The appeal had a great effect. It was reprinted in all of the important newspapers in the country, and was partly responsible for the organization of the Republican Party.

With the passage of the Kansas-Nebraska Act, settlers from both free and slave states rushed to Kansas, and the New England Emigrant Aid Society was formed in April 1854 to send free soilers to Kansas. This aroused proslavery people, and they attacked Lawrence, Kansas. In return, John Brown attacked Pottawatomie Creek; and further pillage, burning, and murder prevailed until 1858, earning the name of Bleeding Kansas.[11] That same year, Minnesota was admitted into the Union, and Commodore Matthew Perry negotiated a treaty with Japan, opening the country to commerce with the United States. The young United States, only eighty-two years away from declaring its independence, was feeling its power its yet in another way.

The year 1855 found the development of the turret lathe by American machine toolmakers; the opening of the Soo Canal between Lake Superior and Lake Huron provided cheap transportation for the iron ore, which was a major reason for the rapid development of the steel industry. Also in 1855, John Roebling completed a wire cable bridge at Niagara, and his son, W. A. Roebling, used the same technique when he constructed the Brooklyn Bridge in 1883. This method became the standard construction technique for all great expansion bridges. [12]

The year 1856 was the year that Henry Bessemer perfected the technique for converting pig iron into steel by directing an air blast upon the molten metal.

1857-1861 JAMES BUCHANAN FIFTEENTH PRESIDENT

The election of 1856 found the new Republican Party nominating John C. Fremont of California. The Democrats dumped Franklin Pierce and nominated James Buchanan of Pennsylvania. Millard Fillmore, the thirteenth president, ran on the American Party ticket but did not affect the outcome. James Buchanan won with 174 electoral votes, Fremont got 114, and Fillmore only 8 votes. [13]

If anyone was prepared to take on the tough job that the nation faced, it was James Buchanan. He was born in 1791, and would be the last Democrat president until 1884, when Grover Cleveland was elected. Buchanan was a lawyer for nine years before being elected to Congress for five terms from 1821 to 1831.

Andrew Jackson had appointed Buchanan Minister to Russia, and he was twice elected to the United States Senate. Under President Polk, he had served as secretary of state where he settled the Oregon boundary controversy. He was also minister to Great Britain. [14]

The seven previous Presidents had served only one term or less. Buchanan would be the eighth president to serve one term, but much of the reasons for this were not his fault.

MARCH 7, 1857 DRED SCOTT DECISION

Dred Scott was born into slavery about 1795 in Virginia. Taken to St. Louis, Missouri—another slave state—he was sold to Dr. John Emerson, an army surgeon. As a servant, he was taken to Rock Island, Illinois, and then to Fort Snelling in the Wisconsin Territory from 1834 to 1838. On Dr. Emerson's death, Scott was transferred to his widow, who later remarried a Massachusetts physician, who in due course was elected to two terms of Congress, making ownership of Dred Scott an embarrassment.

Neither Mrs. Chaffee (nee Emerson) or her brother, John Sanford, wanted him and when Dred Scott and his wife brought suit in 1846 for his freedom, on grounds that he had become free when taken to the free State of Illinois and the Wisconsin Territory, he had the support of Henry Taylor Blow, one of the sons of the original owner who lent his assistance.

The decision went through Missouri's state courts, an appeal court, and eventually came before the United States Supreme Court. Three major questions were involved: one, was Scott a citizen of Missouri; two, had he been set free when taken to a free state and territory; and three, was the Missouri Compromise constitutional?

The court ruled that Scott was not a citizen of Missouri or the United States and therefore not qualified to sue in the federal courts. It also found the Missouri Compromise of 1820 unconstitutional.[15]

When the makeup of the highest court in the land is known—five Southerners and four Northerners—the outcome of the *Dred Scott* case is not surprising. It was a black mark that would be only partially erased on January 1, 1863, with the Emancipation Proclamation, and permanently eliminated when the Thirteenth Amendment was ratified on December 6, 1865. Even then, bitter feelings prevailed, and to this day there is still a feeling of animosity.

AMENDMENT XIII[16]

Section 1. Neither slavery nor involuntary servitude, except as a punishment for crime whereof the party shall have been duly convicted, shall exist within the United States, or any place subject to their jurisdiction.

Section 2. Congress shall have power to enforce this article by appropriate legislation.

1857 FREDERICK DOUGLASS (1818-1895)

Frederick Douglass, born a slave, was sent to Baltimore to work as a laborer in the shipyards. He taught himself to read and write and, in 1838, escaped to the North where he became famous as a lecturer, newspaper editor, and writer. He spoke at many gatherings and, on July 4, 1852, spoke these words.

Fellow Citizens: Pardon me, and allow me to ask, why I am called upon to speak here today? What have I or those I represent to do with your national independence? Are the great principles of political freedom and of natural justice, embodied in that Declaration of Independence extended to us?

What to the American slave is your Fourth of July? I answer, a day that reveals to him more than all other days of the year, the gross injustice and cruelty to which he is the constant victim. To him your celebration is a sham; your boosted liberty an unholy license; your national greatness, swelling vanity; your sounds of rejoicing are empty and heartless; your denunciation of tyrants, brass-fronted impudence; your shouts of liberty and equality, a hollow mockery; your prayers and hymns, your sermons and thanksgiving, with all your religious parade and solemnity, are to him mere bombast, fraud, deception, impiety, and hypocrisy—a thin veil to cover up crimes which would disgrace a nation of savages.[17]

Five years later in a speech at Canandaigua, New York, August 3, 1857, Douglass said:

The whole history of progress of human liberty shows that all concessions yet made to her august claims have been born of earnest struggle . . . If there is no struggle, there is no progress. Those who profess to favor freedom and yet depreciate agitation, are men who want crops without plowing up the ground, they want rain without thunder and lightning. They want the ocean without the awful roar of its many waters. The struggle may be a moral one; or it may be a physical one; or it may be both moral and physical, but it must be a struggle. Power concedes nothing without a demand. It never did and it never will.[18]

In spite of the eloquence, Negroes could do little but till the fields of the Southern plantations. Uprisings as early as 1800 by Gabriel Prosser, Denmark Vesey in 1822, and the most famous uprising by Nat Turner in 1831, did nothing but cause growing resentment—by the slaves in the South, as well as those in the North seeking to end slavery and looking for ways to solve this terrible mark on the United States. Some would attempt to do it through persuasive and political means. Others would take a more violent approach to the problem.

ABRAHAM LINCOLN (1809-1865)

Living in Indiana, Nancy Hanks Lincoln, Abe's mother, passed away in 1818, two years after the family had moved from Kentucky. There, with his sister Sarah and his father Tom, Abe lived in squalor in coarse clothing, shoeless and with ill-cooked food.

That changed when Thomas Lincoln's new wife, Sarah (Sally) Johnson Lincoln, took charge. She washed the children, combed and fed them, brightened the cabin, and encouraged them both to read. Abe's first books were the Bible, *Pike's Arithmetic; Noah Webster's Spelling Book, Robinson Crusoe, The Pilgrims Progress, Aesop's Fables,* Grimshaw's *History of the United States,* and William Scott's *Lessons in Elocution.* Later came *The Revised Laws of Indiana* and William Shakespeare's marvelous works.

Abe helped to clear the land in Indiana, and when he was twenty-one, the family moved to Illinois—first to Decatur and then to New Salem. He worked as a stock driver, ferry hand, and twice journeyed to New Orleans by river boat with pork, meal, and other produce. In the South, he witnessed for himself the treatment of the slaves and must have formed a strong opinion that would later serve him well.

In 1832 he volunteered for service in the Black Hawk War. He tried his hand at surveying and storekeeping. In 1834, he was elected to the Illinois legislature, and reelected three times. After serious study of a few law books, he was admitted to the bar in 1836. In 1841, Lincoln became law partners with Judge Stephen Logan and, in 1844, with William Herndon.

He built his reputation as an attorney on hard work, a grasp of the principle of equality, and the ability to present issues so clearly that the dullest juror could understand.

In 1846, Lincoln was elected to the United States House of Representatives where he voted with the antislavery party. When the Republican Party was formed to prevent any extension of the slave-holding states, Lincoln soon became its leader in Illinois.[19]

In a speech at Peoria, Illinois, Lincoln made his first of many speeches that contained his philosophy concerning slavery.

> No man is good enough to govern another man without that other's consent.[20]

As a lawyer he defended the newly built railroads. He represented banks, insurance companies, merchants and a gas light enterprise. He appeared in all the State and Federal courts of the area. He dealt with constitutional law, admiralty law, patent law and common law.

A month before he was nominated for the candidacy of senator, he conducted the defense of Duff Armstrong, son of a friend and benefactor. He obtained an acquittal of the murder case with logic, aided by the almanac which proved that a witness could not have seen the act he swore he had seen by moonlight since the moon had not risen at the time of the murder.[21]

At the Republican State Convention, Lincoln delivered a very carefully prepared speech whose text was widely reprinted in the newspapers throughout the State of Illinois. In a masterful way, it reviewed the crisis that confronted the nation; and the most memorable part was, in fact, unconsciously borrowed from Edmund Quincy, but originally from the Bible.[22]

> "A house divided against itself can not stand." I believe this government cannot endure permanently half slave and half free. I do not expect the Union to be dissolved; I do not expect the house to fall; but I do expect it will cease to be divided. It will become all one thing, or all the other.

Either the opponents of slavery will arrest the further spread of it, and place it where the public mind shall rest in the belief that it is in the course of ultimate extinction, or its advocates will push it forward till it shall become alike lawful in all the States, old as well as new, North as well as South.

JANUARY 17, 1858 REPUBLICAN STATE CONVENTION— SPRINGFIELD, ILLINOIS.[23]

Nominated for the candidacy of senator on July 24, 1858, Lincoln challenged Senator Stephen A. Douglas to a series of joint debates, between August 21 and October 15. The challenge was accepted, and seven cities were selected: Ottawa, Freeport, Jonesboro, Charleston, Galesburg, Quincy, and Alton.

Besides the cities chosen for the debates, both Douglas and Lincoln campaigned in many other locations. Senator Douglas spoke at Beardstown on August 11, Havana on August 13, and Lewiston and Peoria following that. Even during the debates, Douglas spoke in between dates, as did Lincoln. Douglas spoke at Hennepin, Henry, Pekin, Oquawka, Burlington, and Monmouth. They both campaigned in Sullivan, Danville, and Urbana. Lincoln campaigned at Carlinville, Bloomington, Monticello, and Paris. [24]

In August 1858, Lincoln said, "As I would not be a slave, so I would not be a master. This expresses my idea of democracy. What differs from this, is to the extent of the difference, no democracy." [25] On September 2, Lincoln said, "You can fool all of the people some of the time, and some of the people all of the time, but you cannot fool all of the people all the time." [26] When they debated, it was not short answer posed by some neutral party. One man would speak for an hour, and the other would reply for an hour and a half. Then the first would have a thirty-minute rejoinder.

Large crowds packed five of the seven towns, ranging from twelve thousand in Charleston and Quincy to fifteen thousand in Ottawa and Freeport to twenty thousand in Galesburg. [27]

Most experts agree that the second debate, held at Freeport, was the most decisive. Lincoln proposed four questions to Douglas, the second question being:

Can the people of a United States Territory, in any lawful way, against the wish of any citizen of the United States, exclude slavery from its limits prior to the formation of a State constitution? [28]

In effect, Lincoln was asking Douglas if he could reconcile popular sovereignty with the *Dred Scott* decision. Douglas did not hesitate to reply to the question.

I answer emphatically, as Mr. Lincoln has heard me answer a hundred times from every stump in Illinois that in my opinion the people of a

Territory can, by lawful means, exclude slavery from their limits prior to the formation of a State constitution. [29]

Though it was the correct answer, the debate had caught the attention of the entire nation, including the South. It was to have a great impact on the election for president two years later.

Lincoln won the popular vote for the senate seat, polling 125,275 votes to Douglas's 121,090 votes. [30] But the Constitution of the United States at that time stated:

> Article 1, Section 3. "The Senate of the United States shall be composed of two Senators from each State, *chosen by the Legislature thereof,* for six years, and each Senator shall have one vote." (Revised April 8, 1913 by Amendment XVII)

Since the Democrats controlled the Illinois Legislature, Stephen Douglas was elected. If the Seventeenth Amendment had been ratified earlier, then Abraham Lincoln would have been the senator from Illinois during the Civil War. As it was, he was not, but he gained a lot of attention nationally, and that was to be in his favor. Douglas would be adversative when he returned to the Senate and was most critical in the early stages of the war. [31] Stephen Douglas died at the early age of forty-eight on June 3, 1861. In 1858, Minnesota joined the Union; and Oregon did the same in 1859.

1859 LINCOLN BEGINS THE RUN FOR NOMINATION FOR PRESIDENT

On August 13, 1859, he gave a speech in Concert Hall in Council Bluffs, Iowa. In the audience was Grenville M. Dodge, a twenty-eight-year-old well-known railroad engineer. The next day, Lincoln met with Dodge and immediately asked, "What's the best route for the Pacific railroad to the West?" Dodge replied, "From this town out the Platte Valley." Lincoln asked why, and Dodge gave his reasons. Lincoln was thinking ahead, as he did with many problems, and Dodge was impressed with Lincoln. Dodge would live (1831-1916) to see the transcontinental railroad completed, using his recommendation for the route following the Platte River. [32]

1859 JOHN BROWN (1800-1859)

A descendent of the Mayflower Pilgrims, John Brown was born in Connecticut. His father was a strong religious man and a respected man of the community in Ohio. John Brown's mother, like her mother, died insane.

TERRITORIAL GROWTH

COLONIAL PERIOD: 1775

Original Thirteen Colonies

Other British territories

UNITED STATES: 1790–1920

States

State claims

Special status areas

Territories

Unorganized territories

Claimed areas

Foreign areas

1803 Dates of territorial acquisitions
1805 Dates of initial territorial organization
(1809) Dates of latest change within given time period
1812 Dates of admission to the Union

Map scale 1:34,000,000

Compiled by H. George Stoll, Hammond Incorporated, 1967; rev. by U.S. Geological Survey, 1970

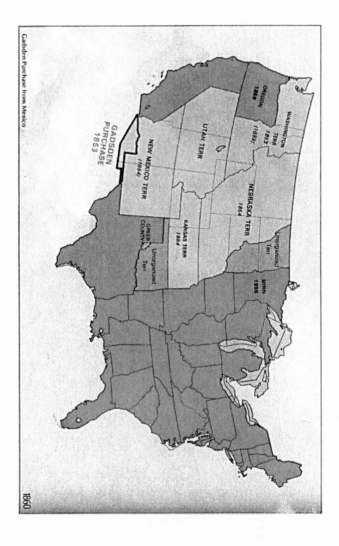

OREGON
1859

WASHINGTON
TERR
1853

UTAH TERR
(1859)

NEBRASKA TERR
1854

GADSDEN
PURCHASE
1853

NEW MEXICO TERR
1854

KANSAS TERR
1854

Unorganized
Terr

Unorganized
Terr

GREER
COUNTY

Unorganized
Terr

MINN
1858

Gadsden Purchase from Mexico

1860

Brown had little schooling and moved from Ohio to Pennsylvania, back to Ohio, then to Virginia, then to Massachusetts, and then to New York. He had seven children by his first wife and thirteen by his second wife.

At first a moderate abolitionist, he became more active and then violent. In 1856, he murdered five men in Pottawatomie Creek in Kansas. On July 3, 1859, John Brown with his two sons and a friend came to Harper's Ferry, Virginia, as base of their operation. Located on the border of Maryland on the banks of the Potomac River, Harper's Ferry was eighty miles from Baltimore and only sixty miles from Washington. The town housed an arsenal, an armory, and rifle works which had several million dollars' worth of arms and ammunition.

On October 16, 1859, John Brown and his small band seized the federal property and took Colonel Lewis W. Washington—great-grandnephew of the first president—as a hostage. When word spread of the takeover, both Maryland and Virginia had their militia prepare. President Buchanan heard of the trouble and dispatched Brevet Colonel Robert E. Lee of the Second Cavalry and Lieutenant J. E. B. Stuart of the First Cavalry. Both would serve with distinction in the Confederate army during the Civil War,

After careful planning, Lee succeeded in putting down the attempted revolt within thirty-six hours. Brown was captured, but his two sons, Oliver and Watson, were mortally wounded. A trial was begun on October 25, 1859, and on November 2, Judge Richard Parker asked the jury for their verdict. He was found guilty on all three counts. Then Judge Parker asked Brown if he had anything to say. Almost as a prophesy, he stated:

> Now, if it deemed necessary that I should forfeit my life for the furtherance of justice, and mingle my blood further with the blood of my children and with millions in this slave country, whose rights are disregarded by wicked, cruel, and unjust enactments, I say, let it be done.

John Brown was hung on December 2nd 1859.[33]

1860 CAMPAIGNS FOR THE NOMINATION OF PRESIDENT

Lincoln was invited to New York to debate the popular William Seward at Cooper Union Hall in New York City on February 27, 1860. It was there that Lincoln said,

> Let us have faith that right makes might, and in that faith let us to the end dare to do our duty as we understand it.[34]

The Democrat Party held its convention in Charleston, South Carolina, the last part of April 1860. There were a number of candidates; the biggest and most important one was Stephen Douglas from Illinois. Many Southerners were not happy with Senator Douglas because of his stand on the *Dred Scott* issue that had been brought up in the debate with Lincoln at Freeport. They wanted someone who would favor the South's position on slavery. Guthrie came from Kentucky, and Andrew Johnson came from Tennessee. It is interesting that Andrew Johnson would become Lincoln's vice president in Lincoln's second term and consequently become president.

On the first ballot taken, where 202 votes were needed for the nomination, Douglas received 145½, Guthrie received 36½, Hunter 42, and 30 votes were spread among others. Twelve different ballots were taken that day, and 45 more ballots the next day with no results, and the convention adjourned. This split the Democrat Party, and the Northern Democrats nominated Stephen Douglas while the Southern Democrats nominated John C. Breckinridge of Kentucky, who was John Buchanan's vice president. John Bell from Tennessee would run on the Union Party ticket. With so many candidates from the former Democrat Party, it almost assured a Republican victory in the fall election. [35]

The Republican Convention was held at the Wigwam in Chicago during the last half of May 1860. There were a number of men seeking the nomination—many were "favorite sons" of different states like Chase from Ohio. The leading candidate coming into the convention was William Seward from New York. He was certain of nominating votes from New York, Michigan, Wisconsin, and Minnesota with a good chance of taking Iowa, California, and a good part of New England.

On May 19, the first poll was taken. Seward received 177½ votes; Lincoln 102 votes; and the other votes were spread out between Cameron, Chase, Bates, Collamer, and Dayton. The total was 466, with 233½ needed for the nomination. On the second ballot, Cameron's and Collamer's votes went to Lincoln, as did Chase's and McLean's. The new total showed Seward with 184½ votes; Lincoln with 181; Bates 35; and a scattering of 41 votes.

On the third ballot, Massachusetts changed four votes from Seward to Lincoln; Rhode Island gave Lincoln two votes, New Jersey gave him eight votes, Pennsylvania gave him four more and nine from Maryland. When the totals were made, it showed Seward had dropped to 180 votes, and Lincoln had 231½. At that point, Ohio switched four votes from Chase to Lincoln, and he became the Republican Candidate for the president of the United States of America. [36]

NOVEMBER 6, 1860 ELECTION OF ABRAHAM LINCOLN

There were thirty-three states in the Union on election day. Lincoln won in twenty of the states, all in the North, plus California and Oregon in the West. Breckinridge won in nine states: Texas, Arkansas, Louisiana, Mississippi, Alabama, Georgia, Florida, and North and South Carolina—all in the South. Douglas only took Missouri. Bell took the remaining three states: Kentucky, Tennessee, and

Virginia. The totals show an interesting set of facts, with respect to electoral votes and the popular votes.

Candidates	Party	Electoral Votes	Popular Votes [37]
Abraham Lincoln	Republican	180	1,866,452
Stephen Douglas	Union Democrat	12	1,376,957
J. C. Breckinridge	Democrat	72	849,781
John Bell	American	39	588,879

Had the Democrats selected only one candidate, they would have had a total of 2,815,617 popular votes and 123 electoral votes. There is no telling what that would have created.

SECESSION LEADS TO WAR

November 30, 1860 was the date of the first actual step of a state considering seceding from the Union. Mississippi passed a resolution that stated:

> *Be it resolved by the Legislators of the State of Mississippi*, that in the opinion of those who now constitute the said Legislature, the secession of each aggrieved State is the proper remedy for those injuries.[38]

President Buchanan, in his last message to Congress three days later on December 3, 1860, made the statement:

> The question fairly stated is, Has the Constitution delegated to Congress the power to coerce a State into submission which is attempting to withdraw or has actually withdrawn from the Confederacy? If answered in the affirmative, it must be on the principle that the power has been conferred upon Congress to declare and to make war against the State. After much serious reflection I have arrived at the conclusion that no such power has been delegated to Congress or to any other department of the Federal Government.[39]

One last attempt to resolve the problem was the Crittenden Peace Resolution of December 18, 1869, proposed by Senator Crittenden of Kentucky. It was rejected by Congress, and the last hope for a peaceful solution went for naught.

South Carolina seceded on December 20, 1860. Mississippi made its formal secession shortly after, and nine other states soon followed: Florida, Alabama, Georgia, Louisiana, Texas, Virginia, Arkansas, Tennessee, and North Carolina.

On February 4, 1861, seven states met in Montgomery, Alabama and formed a provisional government, taking the name of Confederate States of America. Four days later Jefferson Davis was elected president, with Alexander H. Stephens as vice president. [40]

1861-1865 ABRAHAM LINCOLN SIXTEENTH PRESIDENT

In his inaugural address on March 4, 1861, Lincoln stated:

> I do not but quote from one of those speeches when I declare that "I have no purpose directly or indirectly, to interfere with the institution of slavery in the States where it exists. I believe I have no lawful right to do so, and I have no inclination to do so."

> In your hands, my dissatisfied fellow-countrymen, and not in mine, is the momentous issue of civil war. The government will not assail you. You can have no conflict without being yourselves the aggressors.

> You have no oath registered in heaven to destroy the government, while I have the most solemn one to "preserve, protect and defend it."

> I am loath to close. We are not enemies, bur friends. We must not be enemies. Though passion may have strained, it must not break, our bonds of affection. The mystic chords of memory, stretching from every battle-field and patriot grave to every living heart and hearthstone, all over this broad land, will yet swell the chorus of the Union, when again touched as surely they will be, by the better angels of our nature.[41]

The last paragraph was written by William Seward, soon-to-be Lincoln's secretary of state. Lincoln's attempts to be conciliatory failed, and when Major John Anderson wrote Lincoln that he desperately needed supplies at Fort Sumter in Charleston, South Carolina's harbor, Lincoln told him to hold out and that an expedition would be on its way to relieve the situation.

Three small ships were to transport troops and supplies. The first left on April 8; a second one on the ninth; and the last one on the tenth. When General Pierre Beauregard of the Confederacy heard that relief was near, he asked Major Anderson for unconditional surrender. When he refused, Beauregard's batteries fired on Fort Sumter, and the Civil War—as most would call it—started. [42]

THIRTEEN YEARS OF HIGHS AND LOWS

The second half of the nineteenth century began with high hopes. The gold rush to California in 1849 was so great that it became a state a year later. Three other states would take a little longer: Minnesota in 1858, Oregon in 1859, and Kansas in 1861.

Inventions like the turret lathe, the Bessemer process for making steel, the building of suspension bridges, the purchase by James Gadsden of more territory, the opening of the Soo Canal, and Commodore Perry's visit to Japan to open trade would be of great help in making America an industrial power that would be recognized world wide in the years to come. In 1861, the first message was sent over the transcontinental telegraph line. It would have a great impact on the conduct of the Civil War.

On the debit side of the ledger, the problems seemed to start when nine Southern states sought to extend the line dividing free and slave states to the west coat. The Fugitive Slave Law satisfied the South but made the abolitionists more antagonistic than ever. Mrs. Douglas spent a month in jail for teaching slaves to read. The passage of the Kansas-Nebraska Act brought not only bitter feelings but also bloodshed. The *Dred Scott* decision was the wrong decision, and it would be another factor in leading the country to split. John Brown would become the best-known abolitionist and a martyr to many. Frederick Douglass, a former slave, would prick the conscience of the nonbelievers with his many lectures and his book.

In 1834, at the age of twenty-five, a young man would win a seat in the Illinois Legislature. He would serve three more terms there and then serve a term in the House of Representatives. He would then run for the United States Senate, debate the well known and well-respected Stephen Douglas, gain more votes, but lose the election. By gaining national recognition, this tall, lanky, thoughtful, and perceptive man would win an election when the country was ready to divide—at any cost.

Lincoln tried to placate the South and failed. His greatest challenge was before him. Could he lead a split nation in a war to preserve the Union? Would he find generals who could lead men in battle and win those battles? Would he show resolve when the going got tough? Would he show compassion for friend and foe alike? And would he make fair and equitable plans for the reconstruction of a worn and battered nation? Could any *one* man do all this?

If any one man could possibly do all this, it was Abraham Lincoln.

PART C

TWO MOMENTEOUS EVENTS 1830-1869

The two great events that paralleled each other were the Civil War and the building of the transcontinental railroad. Both had their start in the late 1820s and early 1830s.

STEPS TO THE CIVIL WAR

A tariff bill in 1828 to protect the industrial North brought protests from South Carolina. This Southern nullification was the first step in a state declaring it rights above that of the nation.

The abolitionist movement in the North expanded and resulted in the early death of William Lloyd Garrison, publisher of the abolitionist newspaper, *Liberator*, in 1835, and the murder of Elijah Lovejoy, editor from Alton, Illinois, in 1837.

The 1840s were taken up with the War with Mexico, but the 1850s generated bitter feelings on both sides. Nine Southern states demanded an extension of the 36°30' line separating slave states from the free states. The book, *Uncle Tom's Cabin*, and the South charging a Virginia woman with teaching a colored child to read were two additional factors.

The Kansas Nebraska Act in 1856 allowed settlers in this territory and after as states, to choose slavery or free choice, and both sides rushed their people there to make the decisions. Further action brought burnings and killing. John Brown's raid on Harper's Ferry in Maryland in 1859, brought federal troops, and led by Colonel Robert E. Lee.

November 1860 saw Mississippi pass a resolution that secession was a proper remedy. Shortly after that nine more Southern States would secede. Lincoln's attempts to placate the South failed, and he had no choice but to *preserve, protect, and defend* the government.

BEGINNING OF A RAILROAD

The first railroad between Liverpool and Manchester, England, opened in 1830. America's first railroad was started shortly thereafter, and in four years had 762 miles of track. Twenty years later, in 1854, the United States would have over 15,000 miles of track.

Leadership and financial support were the first requirements if the transcontinental railroad was to succeed. Later, men would be needed to build it. Four men came to California from the East between 1849 and 1852. These four—Charles Crocker,

Collin Huntington, Mark Hopkins, and Leland Stanford—formed a working partnership and hired Ted Judah, a railroad engineer. This would become the Central Pacific Railroad, starting from Sacramento, California. Judah made numerous trips back East to convince the federal government to finance the endeavor. A bill was passed and signed on July 1, 1862, by Abraham Lincoln.

The Union Pacific Railroad owed its beginning to one man—Grenville Dodge. Educated at Norwich University, he gained practical experience working for the Rock Island and Illinois Central Railroads. In the early 1850s, he made surveys across Iowa and then along the Platte River in the Nebraska Territory.

In 1859, in a chance meeting with Abraham Lincoln, Dodge convinced Lincoln of the best route west from Council Bluffs. When the Civil War started, Dodge volunteered. He was wounded in battle in March 1862 and, when he recovered, built and repaired railroads for General Grant. Called to Washington, Dodge told Lincoln that the Pacific Railroad Act of 1862 left much to be done to make it work. Lincoln agreed but told Dodge that he had a war to win first.

THE CIVIL WAR

The first shots were fired on April 12, 1861, when Union Major John Anderson refused to surrender Fort Sumter in Charleston Harbor to Confederate General Beauregard. The first battle was three months later at Bull Run.

In the next four years, there were numerous battles or skirmishes in all parts of the country but mainly in the East. Other locations include Kentucky, Tennessee, and Mississippi where Ulysses S. Grant would emerge as a winning general. Other skirmishes took place in the Dakotas, New Mexico, and Texas. Sea battles included the famous *Monitor and the Merrimac* exchange in the East, and Admiral Farragut's success in Mobile Bay.

Leaders came forward from both sides. Robert E. Lee and Thomas "Stonewall" Jackson from the South; Ulysses S. Grant and William Tecumseh Sherman from the North. In addition, women and even girls would become involved on both sides as heroines—some as spies and others such as Dorthea Dix and Clara Barton, organizing relief for the wounded.

The final battle was the longest and most costly in terms of casualties. It finally came to an end on April 9, 1865 when Robert E. Lee realized further fighting was useless and surrendered to Ulysses S. Grant.

Over *six hundred thousand* men from both sides died, fighting for what they believed. The final casualty—Abraham Lincoln—died on April 15, 1865.

CHAPTER IX

THE FATE OF A NATION
1861

Fifteen presidents had preceded Abraham Lincoln. Each had challenges during their term of office. Washington had the unenviable task of setting many precedents. He established a national bank and a national mint. He saw the Bill of Rights approved, selected outstanding men for his cabinet—including, among others, Thomas Jefferson, Alexander Hamilton, John Jay, and Henry Knox. He saw three new states added to the Union and laid the cornerstone for the new national capital.

John Adams's term of office was only four years long, but his biggest accomplishment was averting a war with France. Thomas Jefferson is best remembered for writing the Declaration of Independence, the Louisiana Purchase, and initiating the Lewis and Clark expedition. He also saw the first state from the Northwest Territory—Ohio—join the Union. James Madison saw the War of 1812 brought to a successful conclusion and Louisiana and Indiana join the Union.

James Monroe enjoyed the Era of Good Feeling and proclaimed the *Monroe Doctrine* that made the Western Hemisphere safe from interference from European countries. He also saw five new states added to the Union: Mississippi (1817), Illinois (1818), Alabama (1819), Maine (1820), and Missouri (1821). John Quincy Adams was limited to four years but saw the Erie Canal completed that opened the Midwest to the growing population. Railroads that were to be the new way of the future in terms of transportation began during his one term. Unfortunately the Tariff Bill that was passed brought ill-feelings from the Southern states that would lead to bigger problems with the South voting for nullification of the bill.

Andrew Jackson saw the rise of the Abolitionist Movement, the success of the Black Hawk War that opened more territory for the eager settlers, the importance of the McCormick reaper, and the beginning of rapid communication with the introduction of the telegraph. During the latter part of his administration, Arkansas joined the Union in 1836, the same year the Alamo was attacked and Texans slaughtered. They would be vindicated with the win at the Battle of San Jacinto, and ten years later, Texas would join the Union.

Martin Van Buren was unfortunate to have the Panic of 1837, and the *Caroline* affair which was caused when British Canada seized an American ship, but the problem was resolved, as was the dispute between the State of Maine and New Brunswick of Canada. The expansion of the Abolitionist Movement resulted in violence in Boston and murder in Illinois, as well as the beginning of the "underground railroad". Michigan joining the Union was the good news.

William Henry Harrison was only president for a month before he died from pneumonia. His vice president, John Tyler, caused many of his own problems with antagonizing Congress as well as his cabinet. James K. Polk was more fortunate. He saw the Oregon Treaty signed, the successful completion of the War with Mexico, which gave the United States still more territory. Four new states joined the Union: Florida (1845), Texas (1845), Iowa (1846), and Wisconsin (1846).

The Irish immigrants would help dig the canal connecting Lake Michigan with the Illinois River, and later they would help build the Union Pacific Railroad from Nebraska to Utah. Women would begin their quest for equality with the first ever meeting in Seneca, New York. Education would take a step forward with the help of Horace Mann, and the Smithsonian Institute would be opened. Polk would die within three months of leaving the presidency after only one term.

Zachary Taylor, the hero of the War with Mexico, died in office one year and four months after being sworn in. His vice president, Millard Fillmore, signed the Fugitive Slave Law. which helped alienate the Southern states. Harriet Beecher Stowe's *Uncle Tom's Cabin* incited strong feelings and brought further resentment from the South and more fuel for the North. California became the thirty-first state to join the Union.

Franklin Pierce served only one term mainly because of the Kansas-Nebraska Act, which would be a big reason for the War Between the States as the South would call it. The only good news was the Gadsden Purchase on December 30, 1853 to settle a dispute with Mexico for $10,000,000.

James Buchanan was well prepared for the job and was there when the *Dred Scott* decision came down but refused to do anything when Mississippi ceded from the Union. On the plus side, three new states were added to the Union: Minnesota (1858), Oregon (1859), and Kansas (1861).

All previous holders of the highest office had their challenges and problems, some more than others. But *none* faced the dilemma that confronted Abraham Lincoln on March 4, 1861.

He faced almost-insurmountable tasks. The Union army had only sixteen thousand officers and men in *total*. When Lincoln offered the office of general in chief to Robert E. Lee, Lee turned him down. The general in chief (today it is called the chief of staff) was Winfield Scott, a seventy-five-year old veteran of the War of

1812 and the Mexican War. He was so overweight that he could not mount a horse or even walk a distance without pain. [1]

There were not any officers in that first year that were capable of administering, let alone leading a large army. Winfield Scott's experiences had been limited to a relatively small force. West Point had not taught the history or theory of war but instead had educated the young men in the knowledge of engineering, fortifications, and mathematics. Only a small part of the curriculum was devoted to strategy, but none to staff work—administrative problems and formulating war plans. Only those who could read French or went abroad learned anything about what the army was really all about. [2]

Four of Lincoln's cabinet members had been at the Republican Convention, hoping to be the presidential nominee. Seward became secretary of state; Chase, the secretary of the treasury; Cameron, the secretary of war; and Bates, the secretary of justice (today the attorney general). They argued among themselves and did little to support President Lincoln.

Lincoln was *not* supported by the extreme wing of the abolitionists who could not understand his tolerance. He was *not* supported by the conservatives who blamed Lincoln for not compromising and for bringing on the war. Even the people were against him when he failed to send an unprepared army into immediate action.[3]

Eleven states seceded from the Union from December 1860 to May 1861. Soon Kentucky and Missouri would join the Confederacy. Lincoln took literally his oath of office "to the best of my ability, preserve, protect and defend the Constitution of the United States"[4]

Fort Sumter, under the command of Major John Anderson, surrendered on April 14, 1861, after two days of bombardment by Confederate General Beauregard. (Exactly four years later, Lincoln would be fatally shot.) The next day, Lincoln declared war and asked for seventy-five thousand volunteers for a three-month enlistment. The answer was that ninety thousand men enlisted and still more came. By December of 1861, the Union had six hundred thousand men under arms.

A COMPARISON

The twenty-three Union states had a total population of **23,000,000** people, a working railroad system between East and West, and manufacturing facilities that would enable the North to clothe and arm its men. The commander in chief—Abraham Lincoln—had a very limited military stint with the Illinois militia during the Black Hawk War, and he knew next to nothing about the military or how to give orders. [5]

The South had a total population of whites over **5,000,000** and cotton-growing as its main industry. The call for volunteers brought thousands to the army of the Confederacy. It had one advantage—many graduates of West Point had come from the Southern states, and most of them resigned to join the Confederacy. Two examples were Thomas Jackson and Robert Edward Lee—both would play important roles in the war. [6]

TERRITORIAL GROWTH

COLONIAL PERIOD: 1775

- Original Thirteen Colonies
- Other British territories

UNITED STATES: 1790–1920

- States
- State claims
- Special status areas
- Territories
- Unorganized territories
- Claimed areas
- Foreign areas

1803 Dates of territorial acquisitions
1805 Dates of initial territorial organization
(1809) Dates of latest change within given time period
1812 Dates of admission to the Union

Map scale 1:34,000,000

Compiled by H. George Stoll, Hammond Incorporated, 1967; rev. by U.S. Geological Survey, 1970

Alaska purchased from Russia
Red band encloses Confederate States 1861–1865;
dates underlined refer to readmission to the Union

1870

Jefferson Davis, who had been elected president of the Confederate States of America on February 8, 1861, was not only a graduate of West Point, but had seen service in the army on the northwestern frontier of Iowa. He retired from the army but served as a colonel from Mississippi Volunteers during the War with Mexico and saw action both at Monterey and Buena Vista. Following that, he represented Mississippi in the U.S. Senate then ran for governor of Mississippi but lost by a small margin. After that, he served as secretary of state under President Pierce, showing great ability as an organizer and executive. [7]

How was Lincoln to cope with those shortcomings that put him at such a great disadvantage no one could possibly see any chance of success? He must have been born with an innate ability, along with his wide range of experiences dealing with people in all walks of life, and his knowledge that had been been gained by reading and traveling to all parts of the country from the east coast west through the prairie of Indiana and Illinois to the frontier in Iowa, and from the forests of Wisconsin to the slave states along the Mississippi.

Lincoln had the genius to not only see the big picture, but he was very likely a born strategist. He realized from the beginning what the task was—to restore the Union. To do so, the Union would have to take the offensive; and with the advantage of both natural resources as well as numbers, Lincoln knew, given time, the North would succeed and the Union prevails. But there were battles to be fought, generals dismissed, and others to take their place, and decisions to be made—and most of them would fall to Abraham Lincoln.

One of Lincoln's first acts, five days after Fort Sumter was forced to surrender, was to order a blockade of all Southern ports on April 19, 1861. [8]

In May, Lincoln put troops on the south bank of the Potomac River to guard the capital. He put Brigadier General Irvin McDowell, who had recently only been a major in charge of the army of the Potomac. McDowell was well liked by the politicians; he had an impeccable military background and possessed more knowledge or military theory than many others. He had to train an army from the volunteers, and formulate a plan for a campaign to invade the Confederacy. [9]

On July 3, 1861, the federal government created a Western Department that included Illinois, Kentucky, and all the territories between the Mississippi River and the Rocky Mountains. Lincoln selected John C. Fremont to head the department. Fremont was well known for his exploring expeditions. While in California, he became involved in the Mexican War, resigned from the military in 1848, was elected a senator from California in 1850, and was named the Republican nominee for president in 1856, but was defeated by James Buchanan. [10]

With limited military experience Fremont had to rely on professionals. One such person was Henry Halleck, a graduate of West Point, who had been appointed major general in the Missouri Department by Lincoln. This was an administrative post, and he did an excellent job of organizing and preparing the way for eventual victories in the west.

THE PONY EXPRESS

The Pony Express, a mail delivery system, ran from St. Joseph, Missouri to the capital of California, Sacramento and operated for just a little over a year. The overland telegraph put the express out of business, but not before Mark Twain (Samuel Langhorne Clemens) witnessed it from an overland coach. He noted that each rider covered a distance of fifty miles or more, but the horses were changed about every fifteen miles. [11]

This two-thousand-mile express service was started by William Russell, who called it the Central Overland California & Pikes Peak Express Company. It began April 14, 1860 with seventy-five to a hundred different riders, five hundred horses, and four hundred relay stations. A trip usually took ten days, but a copy of Lincoln's inaugural address was delivered in seven days and seventeen hours. [12]

On July 4, 1861, Lincoln called a special session of Congress to plan for the war. He asked for five hundred thousand more volunteers, requested a $500,000,000 loan, made new and higher tariff duties, and proclaimed the property of the states in rebellion subject to confiscation.[13]

Since the North was going to be manned by volunteers, many of the brigades and even divisions came from the various states as a group. New York had its divisions as did Massachusetts and other states. Formed as state units, men knew each other, and this helped in both the training and when they went into battle.

In Illinois, the adjutant general was responsible for organizing the many troops that showed up in Springfield. With no military experience, chaos reigned. When Governor Yates saw the confusion, he sought help. A friend of Yates suggested a thirty-nine-year old man with military experience who had just arrived from Jo Davies County with volunteers from that area. Yates immediately sent for him and made him his mustering officer. [14]

And so began a second chance for a military career—this time in the Civil War—of a man who would rise to the highest position in the military, and later become the commander in chief. But for now, in the late summer of 1860, Captain Sam Grant would begin duties as a glorified clerk, working busily all day, making out muster rolls, writing orders, filing papers, and bringing order out of chaos.

Governor Yates was so impressed with Ulysses S. Grant he offered him a promotion to Colonel and a regiment. On June 15, 1861, he accepted and moved his new command to the Mississippi River. Promoted to Brigadier General, Fremont gave him command of southeastern Missouri and southern Illinois with headquarters in Cairo, Illinois, at the confluence of the Ohio River with the Mississippi. [15]

More would be heard from this quiet and gentle man who had graduated from West Point in 1843, being first in horsemanship. After faithful service in the Mexican War as a captain, he resigned in 1854—partially due to depression and partly to alcoholism. He tried and failed at farming and real estate and was working in a family-owned harness shop when he got the call that would save his life and eventually the Union.

The people were clamoring for action, and even though Lincoln knew the new troops were ill-prepared for battle, he believed the Confederates were in the same boat. He encouraged McDowell to plan for battle, and this was one of McDowell's strengths—organization and planning. But more would be needed than good plans if the North was to succeed.

TWO GREAT EVENTS

Two great momentous events took place from 1861 to 1869. One was the Civil War. It didn't just start with the bombardment of Fort Sumter. Some historians would say that the Civil War came about because of factors going back to the 1820s, when Missouri was admitted into the Union as a "slave" state, only to be offset by admitting Maine as "free" state. The year 1828 saw the Tariff Act opposed by South Carolina declaring it was a "sectional benefit." This was followed by the Tariff Bill of 1832 that really upset the State of South Carolina and declared the tariff null within its state.

The abolitionist movement came in the early 1830s with the Anti-Slavery Society and William Garrison's abolitionist paper the *Liberator*, plus Elijah Lovejoy's murder in front of his newspaper's office in Alton, Illinois, only added fuel to the flame for rebellion. By 1850 feelings were very strong in both the North and the South. The Compromise of 1850 introduced in January and finally passed in September of that year abolished slavery in the District of Columbia and revised the Fugitive Slave Law. In retaliation, the South demanded the extension of the 36° 30' line agreed upon in 1820.

The Kansas-Nebraska Act of 1854 was probably the "straw that broke the camel's back," along with the *Dred Scott* decision in 1857. The Lincoln-Douglas debates were another reason for the ill feeling on both sides; and John Brown's raid on Harper's Ferry in October of 1859 was the first overt act of aggression. With Lincoln's election in 1860, Southern states began seceding, and Lincoln had no choice but to attempt to preserve the Union.

The other major event of this time was the railroad. Conceived in 1830, it quickly gained favor with those who wanted it as well as those who would enjoy the benefits of this new and modern means of transportation. When the gold rush of 1849 brought California into the Union the very next year, it was inevitable that a railroad would be built to join the East with the West.

These two events were entwined with one another in many ways, but each is so great in importance to the history of the United States, that each event can stand alone.

Both stories deserve to be told so they can be appreciated.

CHAPTER X

THE TRANSCONTINENTAL RAILROAD—
ONE OF THE GREATEST CHALLENGES
THE FIRST PHASE:
1830-1862

T he history of transportation is the progressive story of moving from one place to another in a faster and safer manner. Over the centuries, man has attempted to conquer both time and distance, and later space.

Magellan's ships took two years to circumnavigate the earth. Columbus took *seventy* days to reach the "New World." George Washington took two days to travel by horseback from Mount Vernon, Virginia, to New York City, where he would be sworn in as the first president.

Lewis and Clark started their historic journey in April 1804 and took two years and five months to reach the Pacific Ocean and return to St. Louis. Pioneers in the 1830s, 1840s, 1850s, and most of the 1860s took six months or more to travel over the Overland, Oregon, or Santa Fe trails to the West Coast. Those who went by ship around South America took even longer.

The transcontinental railroad, when completed, would shorten that travel time to less than a week!

OVERCOMING OBSTACLES

The history of the United States could be viewed as a series of overcoming obstacles. From weathering the first bleak winter in 1620, where half of the pilgrims perished, to the winter of 1777-1778 where some of Washington's men died and others survived to train and learn to fight and win their independence. These were some of the first obstacles overcome. There were others.

The Declaration of Independence was just the first of many documents that overcame the opposition to the country's desire to be left alone and be free. The Constitution overcame the obstacles that the Articles of Confederation had not answered. The Monroe Doctrine overcame the obstacle of European interference in the Western Hemisphere.

Less than forty years after the United States became a sovereign nation, the first obstacle of connecting the East with the West was overcome with the completion of the Erie Canal in 1825. Twenty-three years later, the opening of the Illinois and Michigan Canal overcame the obstacle of connecting the Great Lakes with the heart of America—something that Joliet and Marquette had only dreamed about when they saw the possibility in 1673.

The Emancipation Proclamation was the beginning of overcoming the obstacle of slavery, although it would take a Civil War and thousands of lives to make it come true.

Another great challenge was the many obstacles that had to be confronted and overcome in connecting the east with the west by rail. There were men who had dreamed of this connection since the 1830s, but some would do more than dream. They would plan, organize, and work until the dream became a reality.

The story of the building of the Union Pacific and the Central Pacific to make this remarkable accomplishment a reality is exceptionally well done in the late Stephen Ambrose's book *Nothing Like It in the World*. [1] It is a *must* read for serious historians.

THE START OF THE RAILROAD THAT CHANGED THE FACE OF A NATION

George Stephenson was born in 1781 in Northumberland, England. At the age of fourteen he worked as a fireman in a colliery—a coal mine and its connected buildings—where he gained valuable and practical knowledge of mechanics. In 1821, he constructed the Stockton and Darlington Railway. A completed railway system was opened in 1830 between Liverpool and Manchester, England. [2]

The first American train, the Best Friend of Charleston, was built in South Carolina in 1830. By 1834, there were 762 miles of track in the United States. Ten years later, the mileage of track had increased to 4,311 and by 1854 to 15,675 miles of track. By 1864, the total miles of track in the United States were nearly 34,000. [3]

The building of this railroad to connect the East with the West would require three important factors: one, leadership; two, finance; and three, men not afraid to leave home—if they had one—and work in all kinds of weather and under trying conditions to build, not with machines, but *by hand*, the longest railroad ever completed at that time.

LEADERSHIP

George Washington did not win the War for Independence by himself. He had help, like Ethan Allen who captured Fort Ticonderoga, Casmir Pulaski who was important at the Battle of Brandywine, Horatio Gates who won the decisive Battle of Saratoga, George Rogers Clark who secured the western part of the colonies that gave the United States territory from the Atlantic to the Mississippi River, John Paul Jones who didn't know the meaning of surrender, Francis Marion who harassed the British in the Southern colonies, and Nathanael Greene who rose in the ranks from private to general and took part in many decisive battles. And of course the thousands of patriots who fought under them.

Thomas Jefferson wrote the major part of the Declaration of Independence, but he also had the assistance of the Continental Congress. Meriwether Lewis selected William Clark to assist in their historic journey. James Madison is credited with being the father of the Constitution, but he had help. Andrew Jackson, the hero of the Battle of New Orleans, inspired an outnumbered group of Americans, and they won a major victory. Zachary Taylor was hailed as the hero of the War with Mexico, but he had the assistance of Winfield Scott, Stephen Kearney, John Fremont, Commodore Stockton, and thousands of loyal soldiers.

Leaders can not always predict how well their chosen subordinates will perform, but if they have the courage to recognize failure and replace those responsible, that in itself is a sign of good leadership.

Abraham Lincoln selected Irvin McDowell, who failed at the first Battle of Bull Run and was replaced with George McClellan. When McClellan lost the Battle of Mechanicsville, Lincoln replaced him with Henry Halleck, who selected John Pope—who lost the Second Battle of Bull Run. Lincoln gave McClellan a second chance, but it was not to be. McClellan had twice the number of troops at the Battle of Antietam Creek, but the battle ended in a draw. Lincoln replaced McClellan with Ambrose Burnside, who lost the Battle of Fredericksburg, and was replaced by Joseph Hooker, who in turn lost the Battle of Chancellorsville and was replaced by Gordon Meade. Meade barely won the Battle of Gettysburg but hesitated about pursuing Lee's tattered forces. Finally Lincoln selected Ulysses S. Grant who had given the Union its victories at Shiloh and at Vicksburg.

Leadership entails many factors. Among them are the ability to inspire, select good people to assist the leader, as well as the courage to change and replace those who do not live up to the task. Such leaders helped build the transcontinental railroad.

LEADER OF THE CENTRAL PACIFIC RAILROAD

Six men who came to California were to be instrumental in building the Central Pacific Railroad. The first was Lieutenant William Tecumseh Sherman, born in 1820 in Ohio, who was a West Point graduate in 1840. He was sent to California via a ship that left July 14, 1846 that went around Cape Horn, South America, and arrived January 26, 1847—a voyage of 202 days. [4]

Charles Crocker was born in 1822 in Troy, New York. He did not go beyond the eighth grade in school but was a sharp businessman. In 1849, he and his two brothers wanted to get to the California gold fields. They traveled overland, taking almost a half a year. [5]

Charles Huntington was born in October 1821 in Connecticut. When he was twenty-one, he went to work in New York and did very well in business ventures. He set out for California in January 1849 aboard ship, as did eight thousand others in ninety ships. Huntington got off at Panama and crossed the Isthmus, taking another ship north to San Francisco Bay and arrived August 30 with more money than when he left. [6]

Mark Hopkins was born on the shores of Lake Ontario in September 1814. He worked as a storekeeper and later a bookkeeper in New York City. In January 1849, he and his partners set sail for California and arrived 196 days later. [7]

The next of the six to come west was Leland Stanford, born in 1824. He came to California in 1852, became a merchant and later would become governor of California from 1861-1862 and then a United States senator from 1885 to 1893. He would give a large sum of money for the founding of Stanford University as a memorial to his son. [8]

Hopkins and Huntington had stores next to one another. When a fire destroyed both stores, they combined their talents and became close friends. Crocker was also a storekeeper after trying his hand at seeking gold. The bond of similar interests was to be the glue that formed a friendship and later a business interest that would bring them together to form the basis of the railway that was to stretch from Sacramento, California, to Promontory Summit, Utah.

In 1849, Sherman, now a Captain was ordered to look for a passage through the Sierra Nevada range. In 1852, a group of Californians, including Sherman, wanted to build a railroad north and east of Sacramento. They formed the Sacramento Valley Railroad with no railroad equipment. Sherman resigned from the army the next year and became a banker in San Francisco and vice president of the "railroad" company. Realizing that a railroad engineer was needed, the president of the company went east to see the governor of New York, Horatio Seymour, and Seymour's brother who recommended Theodore Judah, a railroad engineer.[9] Judah would be the last of the six important people.

Theodore "Ted" D. Judah was born in Bridgeport, Connecticut on March 4, 1826. He graduated form Rensselaer Polytechnic Institute with a degree in engineering. In 1844 Ted Judah began planning and working on the construction of railroads. He married Anna Pierce, an artist and writer with a charming personality. He worked on a number of railroads and was engaged with the Erie Railroad system when he got a telegram from Governor Seymour's brother. After traveling to New York City, Judah met for three days and then telegraphed his wife, "Be home tonight; we sail for California April (1854) second." [10]

They took a ship to Nicaragua, disembarked and went across that country to the Pacific Ocean and arrived in San Francisco the middle of May where Judah went to work for the Sacramento Valley Railroad. By the end of the month, he reported to the owners that the possibility of running a railroad from Sacramento to the western edge of the sierra range was very good. He had determined the best route, the need for grading, and the approximate cost. By February of 1855, actual grading began; and in August of that year, a railroad extended from Sacramento to Folsom, California, less than twenty miles.[11]

Ted and his wife, Anna, returned to Washington on three different occasions, but with only one thought in mind—convincing the federal government to finance the transcontinental railroad. He also felt a complete survey of the route selected was needed to show elevation, grading or ascent, practicality of routes and estimated costs.[12]

Congress listened and asked Judah questions, but did little else. President Buchanan favored the southern route and would veto any other route selected.[13]

In April 1859, the California legislature passed a resolution calling for a convention to consider the Pacific railroad. The convention met in September and adopted a resolution showing a preference for a central route to Sacramento. This was the first time that the term *central* had been used to designate the railroad route.[14]

The California convention sent Judah back to Washington to convey its memorial to Congress, a typical move in those days. Ted Judah and Anna arrived in Washington late in 1859. He met with President Buchanan who was now in favor of a railroad to the Pacific, regardless of the route. Samuel Curtis of Iowa proposed a transcontinental railroad from Iowa. Representatives from the South added an amendment for a Pacific route in the southwest as Jefferson Davis had wanted. The bill was finally debated in December 1860, but did not pass.[15]

When Judah failed to get the financial backing in Washington, he returned to Sacramento determined to find financial backers. He knew he had to have convincing evidence and went out to make a survey. He received a letter from a druggist, Daniel Strong, who wanted to show Judah the best possible route. Strong showed Judah a pass that would be best—the Donner Pass.[16]

Judah convinced Charles Crocker, Collis Huntington, Mark Hopkins and Leland Stanford to finance a survey to the Sierra Nevada range. On June 28, 1861, the Central Pacific Railroad of California was started with Stanford as president; Huntington, vice president; Hopkins, treasurer; James Bailey, secretary; and Judah, chief engineer. They would make up the board of directors, plus Daniel Strong and Charles Marsh.[17]

Convinced that Judah had all the information needed to persuade Congress for appropriation of Land and United States bonds to aid in the construction of the railroad, the Central Pacific directors sent him back to Washington. A bill was introduced by Aaron Sargent, a Representative from California on January 1862.[18]

The Senate passed the bill on June 20, 1862 and sent it to Abraham Lincoln for his signature, which he signed on July 1. The railroad would receive financial aid. They would also get the right-of-way of two hundred feet on both sides of the roadbed as well as land for stations, machine shops, and sidings. The Central Pacific had to complete fifty miles of track within two years and fifty miles each year after. The entire railroad was to be competed by July 1, 1876, three days before the centennial of the nation.[19]

Ted Judah was so pleased with the passage of the bill he had fought for that he wired those in California on the newly established telegraph, "We have drawn the elephant. Now let us see if we can harness him."[20]

LEADER OF THE UNION PACIFIC RAILROAD

While Ted Judah was mainly responsible for getting the Central Pacific Railroad started, with the help of Collis Huntington, Charles Crocker, Mark Hopkins, and Leland Stanford, the Union Pacific Railroad's start can be credited to only one man.

Grenville Dodge was born in Massachusetts on April 21, 1831. At the age of fourteen, he began working as a surveyor under the direction of Frederick Lander who encouraged Dodge to go to Norwich University to learn engineering.[21]

Dodge went to Norwich University and then went to work for the Rock Island Railroad and then the Illinois Central Railroad. When he found that the Rock Island was planning to cross the Mississippi River and build to the Missouri River, Dodge came back to the Rock Island. All this happened between 1848 and 1852.[22]

During 1853, Dodge, with a party of fourteen, surveyed across the state of Iowa to Council Bluffs. After crossing the Missouri River, he went west along the Platte River valley to the first major tributary, the Elkhorn River. He took a leave, returned to Illinois to marry Anne Brown in May 1854, then came back to build a cabin on his claim along the Elkhorn where his brother and father joined him in 1855.[23]

Dodge began farming a fertile land, and in the summer of 1855, he was reunited with his mentor, Frederick Lander who had been surveying for the government out in the Washington Territory. They both agreed that the best route for a railroad west was from the Missouri River along the Platte Valley to the Rocky Mountains. In 1856, Dodge made a survey along the Platte and reported this information to two of the financiers—Dr. Thomas Durant and Henry Farnam. On the basis of Dodge's information, they chose Council Bluffs as the eastern terminus of the Rock Island Railroad and the beginning of the Union Pacific Railroad. The Panic of 1857 slowed down further activities.[24]

Grenville and Anne Dodge built a home in Council Bluffs in 1858, where he went into a number of businesses, including banking, milling, merchandising, contracting, and real estate. In the spring of 1858, Dodge did another survey of the Platte Valley and returned August 11, 1859, the day before Abraham Lincoln was to be in Council Bluffs where he was campaigning for the presidency of the

United States. On August 13, Abe Lincoln and Dodge met, and this association was to make the difference in starting the Union Pacific.[25]

Dodge and other influential men in Iowa went to Chicago, where the Republican convention would be held in May 1860. These men used their influence on the convention delegates to help nominate Lincoln. Then Dodge returned to his earlier ambition, the planning of the transcontinental railroad.

When Lincoln took office in March 1861, war was close at hand. When Fort Sumter was fired upon the next month, Dodge put aside his dream and joined the army. The transcontinental railroad would be delayed, but not forgotten.

Grenville Dodge was a General in 1862 when he was wounded at the Battle of Pea Ridge in Arkansas between March 6 and March 8, 1862. A month later, Ulysses S. Grant won the costly Battle of Shiloh in April 1862. While Dodge was in the hospital, men interested in the Pacific Railroad tried to convince Dodge to leave the army.

"I have enlisted for the period of the war," was Dodge's reply.[26]

By June Dodge was out of the hospital and repairing and building railroads for General Grant between Shiloh and Corinth. He did an excellent job, and Grant took notice of this hardworking man. Dodge even used slaves who had walked off the plantations. In the spring of 1863, Dodge received orders from General Grant to report to President Lincoln in Washington.[27]

Dodge and Lincoln discussed the transcontinental railroad; the best route which Dodge reiterated was the Platte Valley route and the terminus at Omaha, Nebraska, across the Missouri River from Council Bluffs. Dodge also told Lincoln that the Pacific Railroad Act of 1862 left a lot to be desired, including the raising of capital. Lincoln agreed and showed a real desire to see the railroad built across the nation but told Dodge he had a war to wage and win before any consideration could be given to this great endeavor.[28]

THE CIVIL WAR INTERRUPTS THE BUILDING OF THE TRANCONTINENTAL

The American Civil War was the bloodiest conflict in the history of the United States. There were skirmishes in many different states. Dodge was wounded in one of the minor battles. George McClellan was promoted to general in chief because of a minor battle that he was credited with winning.

The major battles were devastating in the brutality and extent of casualties. No one can be anything but horrified at the loss of so many good men on both sides, but it is a part of our history and can only be understood by telling the truth of what happened.

CHAPTER XI

THE BATTLES BEGIN
1861-1865

FIRST BATTLE OF BULL RUN JULY 21, 1861

M cDowell had an army of 35,000 men made up of five divisions, and each division had three brigades. Two of the brigades were commanded by Colonel William T. Sherman and Colonel Ambrose E. Burnside. Both were to have a future in which they distinguished themselves. Of the 35,000, only 18,500 were actually engaged in the battle.

The Confederate army composed of Beauregard's Army of the Potomac and Johnson's army of the Shenandoah totaled about 32,500, but only 18,000 were actually engaged in the battle.

McDowell's plan was to have aged General Robert Patterson, who was a veteran of the War of 1812, hold Confederate General Johnson's forces in check near Harper's Ferry while McDowell attacked Beauregard at the town of Manassas Junction, which was split by the Bull Run River. But Winfield Scott's order to General Patterson was so vague that the check was not accomplished. Part of Johnson's army under Brigadier Thomas Jackson was able to slip away, by the use of a railroad no less, join Beauregard at Bull Run; and after much fighting, the South prevailed and sent the Union army in full retreat, stopping outside of Washington. The Confederates were too exhausted to pursue the Union's shattered forces and waited near Bull Run for the next Union move. [1]

Four important outcomes of the battle were noted. One, the telegraph was used for the first time in a war. Two, with the South's victory, they assumed the war had ended, and many went home. Three, most Northerners recognized that it would be a long war and made plans accordingly. The fourth outcome happened during an important phase of the battle. Brigadier General Bee, one of Johnson's

Confederate brigade commanders, reported to Brigadier General Thomas Jackson that "General, they are beating us back."

General Jackson's reply was, "Sir, we will give them the bayonet." Hearing this, Bee rode back to his brigade, stood tall in the saddle, and exclaimed, "Form! Form! There stands Jackson like a stone wall! Rally behind the Virginians!" [2]

After that, Thomas Jackson would forever be known as *Stonewall* Jackson. He would serve with distinction until May 1863 when he was accidentally shot by his own men.

The casualties of the North totaled 2,900 killed, wounded, or captured. The South lost 2,000 killed, wounded, or captured. [3]

These were nearly 5,000 American that had died, were wounded, or captured, but a small number compared to what was to be in the next four years.

The thousands of Union soldiers that had fled back to Washington gathered in groups around campfires to cook their food. Julia Ward Howe was visiting the military camps and was inspired to write a poem that made her famous. She gave the poem to the editor of the *Atlantic Monthly,* James T. Field, who printed it in April 1862, giving it the title, "The Battle Hymn of the Republic." It was soon set to the music of a campground song that had mocked John Brown. [4]

THE BATTLE HYMN OF THE REPUBLIC

Mine eyes have seen the glory of the coming of the Lord;
He is trampling out the vintage where the grapes of wrath are stored;
He hath loosed the fateful lightning of His terrible swift sword;
His truth is marching on.

CHORUS
Glory, glory! Hallelujah!
Glory, glory! Hallelujah!
Glory, glory! Hallelujah!
His truth is marching on.

I have seen Him in the watch fires of a hundred circling camps;
They have builded Him an altar in the evening dews and damps;
I can read His righteous sentence by the dim and flaring lamps;
    His day is marching on.

I have read a fiery gospel writ in burnished rows of steel;
"As ye deal with condemners, so with you my grace shall deal;"
Let the Hero born of woman crush the serpent with his heel,
    Since God is marching on.

He has sounded forth the trumpet that shall never call retreat;
He is sifting out the hearts of men before his judgment seat;
O, be swift, my soul, to answer him! Be jubilant, my feet!
    Our God is marching on.

In the beauty of the lilies Christ was born across the sea;
With the glory in his bosom that transfigures you and me;
As He died to make men holy, let us die to make men free,
    While God is marching on.

Following the defeat, Lincoln knew that he needed a general who could deliver. He sent for George McClellan, a commander of the Ohio Volunteers who gained some success in a battle in the western part of Virginia that was only modest in size, but a success nevertheless. He asked McClellan to reorganize the army. McClellan had served on General Winfield Scott's staff during the Mexican War and had been sent to observe the Crimean War in Europe in the 1850s.[5]

In August 1861, joint naval and military expeditions were sent out to capture key places along the coast. Fort Clark and Hatteras in North Carolina were taken.[6] Also in August, the United States levied an income tax for the first time. Incomes of more than $800 were taxed at the rate of 3 percent.[7]

Lincoln decided that Winfield Scott had to be replaced, and Scott himself felt that he was no longer effective. On November 1, 1861, Lincoln appointed George McClellan as general in chief. McClellan was an 1846 graduate of West Point and had served under Scott during the Mexican War. He resigned from the army in 1857, but when the Civil War broke out, he was commissioned as major general of the Ohio Volunteers. He was a superb man for administering and organizing the ragtag army that that suffered a defeat at Bull Run as well as training the thousands of new volunteers that joined the Union army. But he was egotistical and seemed to take credit for others' accomplishments and dismissed criticism of his own shortcomings. He had other failings that would become evident later in 1862.[8]

In February 1862, the federal forces captured Roanoke Island and Elizabeth City, Virginia. In March they captured Amelia Island and Jacksonville, both in Florida, and New Bern, North Carolina, which forced the Confederates to keep an army nearby to protect their capital at Richmond.[9]

THE NAVAL WAR

On March 8, 1862, the Confederate ship, the ironclad *Merrimac,* appeared in part at Hampton Roads, Virginia—a small body of water off the mouth of the James River—and sank the Union ship, *Cumberland.* The next day the Union ironclad

Monitor engaged the *Merrimac* in a battle which ended in a draw, but also an epoch making development in naval warfare. [10]

In April, Flag Officer (later Admiral) David Farragut and General Benjamin Butler, with a force of twenty-seven ships and fifteen thousand, troops bombarded the fort and captured the city of New Orleans. [11] On July 1, 1862, Congress established the Bureau of Internal Revenue, partly to fund the war.

PREPARATION FOR WAR IN THE WEST

Jefferson Davis, president of the Confederate States of America, appointed General Albert Johnston to head up the western part of the Confederacy, stretching from the Cumberland Gap on the Virginia border to the Mississippi River. To do this, Johnston only had forty-five thousand men. [12]

Major General Halleck, commanding general of the Missouri Department for the Union forces had three armies under him. Major General Buell's army was stationed at Louisville, Kentucky. Major General Pope's army operated in Missouri. In between, Brigadier General Grant's army was based at Cairo, Illinois. There was also a flotilla of shallow-draft gunboats commanded by Flag Officer A. H. Foote, stationed at Cairo where they could operate jointly with Grant. The total strength of Halleck's combined forces was over sixty-five thousand officers and men.

General Halleck was ambitious and at the same time timid when it came to military matters. General Buell was a courageous soldier, but also a plodder, hesitant to take any chances. Grant, on the other hand, was not afraid to take risks, and captured Paducah, Kentucky, not far from Cairo. With that as a base, Grant could attack Fort Henry and Fort Donelson in Kentucky and imperil the Confederacy. [13]

Halleck was opposed to Grant's idea, but allowed him a limited expedition to take Fort Henry, which fell on February 6, 1862, with the help of Foote's gunboats. Grant, on his own, decided to move on Fort Donelson, and again with Foote's help, a savage battle ensued. The fight, the bloodiest to that time, saw Grant lose three thousand men while the Confederates lost two thousand. When Confederate General Buckner asked Grant what were the terms of surrender, Grant's reply was, "No terms except an unconditional and immediate surrender can be accepted." [14] Grant would be known from then on as Unconditional Surrender Grant, a fine tribute to Ulysses Simpson Grant.

Halleck claimed the victory at Fort Donelson for himself and accused Grant of neglect of duty, inefficiency, and drunkenness. Halleck wired General in Chief McClellan of the accusations he had made of Grant and asked about a court-martial. General McClellan's reply was, "If the good of the service requires it." Halleck appointed Brigadier C. F. Smith, one of Grant's division commanders, to take Grant's place. Grant was relieved, but not court-martialed.[15]

General Polk's Confederate army had retreated from Columbus, Kentucky, to Corinth, Tennessee. Confederate Major General Bragg had brought ten thousand troops from the gulf to Corinth. General Johnson had given up Nashville and joined Polk and Bragg at Corinth. Their total was sixty thousand men.

In March, Brigadier General William T. Sherman of the Union army discovered on one of his raids a place called Pittsburg Landing, close to a church called Shiloh. General Smith, who had taken Grant's place, injured his leg and contracted a tetanus infection which proved fatal. Halleck, desperate for a leader, restored Ulysses S. Grant to command.[16]

THE BATTLE OF SHILOH
April 6-7, 1862

The Confederate armies of Johnson were made up of three corps: Major General Polk, Bragg, and Hardee. Brigadier General Breckinridge commanded a reserve corps. He was the previous vice president of the United States with James Buchanan from 1857 to 1861.

Johnson had them line up in four columns, one behind the other, much in the same fashion that Caesar's legions lined up for battle. The Union forces had forty-eight thousand men to fight against Johnson's forty thousand.[17] Buell's army of eighteen thousand had yet to arrive from Kentucky. Johnson took the initiative and attacked.

The South took the North by surprise, and the battle raged all-day long. The bullets were flying so thick and fast that the area was referred to as the Hornet's Nest. The end of the day saw Bragg wanting to launch one last effort, but Beauregard, who had taken Johnson's command when Johnson was fatally wounded, stopped Bragg. Some claim that Beauregard "snatched defeat from the jaws of victory." That evening, Grant was reinforced with Buell's army as well as General Lew Wallace's division that had been camped five miles from the day's battle. Lew Wallace would later author the book *Ben Hur.*[18]

April 6 belonged to the South, but April 7 was the Union's day. By 2:30 p.m. the Confederates had retreated, and the Union had prevailed. It was the bloodiest battle up to that time; the South suffered nearly 11,000 casualties—1,700 killed; 8,000 wounded, and 1,000 captured. The North lost 13,000-1,750 killed, 8,400 wounded, and 2,850 captured.[19]

In view of the near defeat of the Union forces at Shiloh, there were many who wanted Grant relieved of command. But Lincoln could not be persuaded and said, "I can't spare the man, he fights."[20]

SHILOH[21]

Herman Melville

Skimming lightly, wheeling still,
    The swallows fly low
Over the field in clouded days,
    The forest-field of Shiloh-
Over the field where April rain
So laced the parched ones stretched in pain
Through the pause of nigh
That followed the Sunday fight
    Around the church Shiloh-
The church so long, the log-built one,
That echoed to many a parting groan
    And natural prayer
Of dying foemen mingle there-
Foeman at morn, but friends at eve-
    Fame or country least their care;
(What like a bullet can undeceive!)
    But now they lie low,
While over them the swallows skim,
    And all is hushed at Shiloh.

Born in 1819 in New York City, Melville is best known as the author of *Moby Dick*, published in 1851. An experienced sailor for years, Melville's book *White Jacket*, published in 1850, helped to end flogging in the United States Navy.

BATTLES AND SKIRMISHES IN THE WEST

Christopher "Kit" Carson was born the same year as Abraham Lincoln, 1809. Born also in Kentucky, he became a legend as a hunter, trapper, and explorer's guide. He guided John C. Fremont during his exploration and then became an Indian agent.

In the spring of 1861, Kit Carson resigned his government job and joined the Union army as lieutenant colonel to command the First Mexico Volunteers Infantry Regiment. His hometown was Taos, in the New Mexico territory where Southern sympathizers pulled down the American flag and put up a Confederate flag. Outraged, Carson ordered it hauled down, and the Union flag hoisted. He declared that his town was Union since the Mexican War and would stay Union.[22]

In the early 1860s, the West was any land west of the Missouri River. California, admitted in 1850, Oregon in 1859, Texas in 1845, and Kansas in 1861 were the only Western states in the Union. The rest of the West was territories.

In late January 1861, Lieutenant Colonel Robert E. Lee commanded the Second United States Cavalry on the Texas frontier. Ordered to Washington for reassignment, he gave a great deal of thought about the secessionist crisis. He left San Antonio February 19, 1861, to meet General in Chief Winfield Scott, having made the decision to stand with his native Virginia and resign his army commission.[23]

From 1861 to the end of the war, there were numerous skirmishes with Indians in central Minnesota as well as in the Dakota Territory. There were battles in Texas, Arkansas, and Louisiana, between Union and Confederate forces, but the most important battle in the West took place in the New Mexico Territory.

In February 1862, Confederate Major General Henry Hopkins Sibley took his regiment from Fort Bliss, located on the Texas-New Mexico border, up the Rio Grande River to attack Fort Craig which was located halfway between the Texas border and Albuquerque.[24]

The Union commander, Brigadier General Edward Canby, with a mixture of regulars, and Kit Carson's New Mexico Volunteers, battled Sibley between February 16 and 21. The rebels won a victory of sorts. When Sibley demanded surrender of the fort, Canby refused. Not wanting to attack a well-fortified fort, Sibley left a small detachment and moved up the Rio Grande, capturing Albuquerque, and prepared to battle the federal troops that were sure to come. [25]

In the meantime, Union Colonel John P. Slough was ordered by acting governor of the Colorado Territory, Lewis Weld, to march to New Mexico. They marched across plains and mountains filled with snow in freezing weather, arriving March 25 at a ranch on the Santa Fe Trail. [26]

Battling Sibley's forces in a skirmish on March 26, the main battle took place March 28, when part of Slough's forces led by Union Major John M. Chivington, a huge Methodist minister, crossed sixteen miles of mountain wilderness to discover eighty wagons of Confederate supplies, five hundred horses and some federal prisoners. Releasing the prisoners and horses and destroying the supplies, Chivington returned to the ranch on the Santa Fe Trail where they had ample supplies and water. [27]

The Sibley Texans had no other choice but to withdraw. The Battle of Glorieta Pass would become known as the *Gettysburg of the West*. Thus ended the hopes of the Confederates conquering the Southwest. [28]

It is conjectured by some historians that had the Confederates been successful in their effort to win the Southwest and procure the gold so necessary to winning the war, the Europeans might have given speedy recognition to the Confederacy. [29]

TWO HISTORIC ACTS BY CONGRESS

Two acts by Congress in the late spring and early summer of 1862 would have far-reaching effects for the nation in both the near and distant future.

THE HOMESTEAD ACT

This act was passed by both houses of Congress in 1859, but vetoed by President Buchanan. With a Republican Congress and president, the act passed and was signed into law on Mary 20 1862.

An ACT to secure homesteads to actual settlers on the public domain.

Be it enacted, That any person who is head of a family or who had arrived at the age of twenty-one years, and is a citizen of the United States . . . and who never borne arms against the United States Government or given aid and comfort to its enemies, shall from and after the first of January, eighteen hundred and sixty-three, be entitled to enter one quarter-section or less quantity of unappropriated public lands, upon which said person may have filed a pre-emption claim, or which may, at the time the application is made, be subject to pre-emption at one dollar and twenty-five cents, or less, per acre.[30]

This made it possible for men who wanted a farm of their own to be able to acquire land at a very reasonable cost. The United States—only eighty-six years in existence—was largely an agricultural nation, and this act was very well received and used.

THE MORRILL LAND GRANT ACT

A little over a month later, July 2, 1862, Congress passed the Morrill Land Grant Act proposed by Congressman Justin Morrill of Vermont. This act granted each *loyal* state thirty thousand acres for each senator and representative for the purpose of endowing at least one state agricultural college. [31]

It made possible the great state universities that we have today. The next great act for education would come eighty-two years later, with the *Servicemen's Readjustment Act of 1944,* better known as the GI Bill of Rights.

WAITING AND THE WAR IN THE EASTERN THEATER

General in Chief George McClellan had taken command on November 1, 1861. He eventually had over one hundred thousand troops at his disposal. Yet he hesitated time and again to move his troops toward the South.

Lincoln had more trouble with McClellan than any other general during the entire war. A conservative Democrat, McClellan had a poor opinion of Lincoln and would, at times, make disparaging remarks about him. He looked for excuses not to go into battle and asked Pinkerton, who operated an intelligence service, to find out the strength of the Confederates. Pinkerton told him the South had more troops that they really had, and McClellan used that information to delay any action.

By April 1862, McClellan had a force of 130,000 men. He moved most of them by boat down the Potomac River to the Chesapeake Bay and from there to Fort Monroe. He brought with him 300 cannons and other heavy weapons. His plan was to lay siege and then capture Yorktown, move up the river, and bombard Richmond. This would be supported by the navy's gunboats and ironclads. [32]

CAMPAIGN OF THE PENINSULA

When McClellan entered Yorktown on May 2, he found the fort deserted. He quickly pursued the Rebel forces to the outskirts of Richmond, but there he stopped. Even though McClellan had twice as many men as General Johnston, he hesitated to attack. Johnston was equally hesitant until May 30, when Jefferson Davis prodded Johnston into action.

The Battle of Seven Pines, also called Fair Oaks, was badly managed. Johnston lost eleven thousand men and was wounded himself. Davis appointed Robert E. Lee to take charge of what looked like a hopeless cause.

McClellan hesitated, and this gave Lee time to organize and instill a spirit in his smaller army. The battle of Mechanicsville began on June 26, 1862. When it was over, the Confederates had defeated the Union forces, thanks to Lee's brilliance and "Stonewall" Jackson's timely arrival. The North lost fifteen thousand, and the South lost twenty thousand. With Richmond safe for the time being, Lee pursued McClellan who put up a stiff resistance. The Peninsular Campaign of Seven Pines was over, the bloodiest battle thus far.[33]

LOOKING FOR LEADERS

Both presidents—Jefferson Davis of the Confederate States of America, and Abraham Lincoln, president of the United States—knew that they needed a leader who could plan *and* execute battle plans. Davis knew that he did not have the resources that the North possessed, so he was looking for someone who could outmaneuver the enemy that had greater numbers. The Peninsular Campaign was successful at the last moment because of Robert E. Lee. Had Davis found his general? Future battles would answer his question.

Lincoln's first choice was Lee who turned him down and joined the Confederacy. Then he selected McDowell for the first battle that turned out to be a disaster for the Union. McDowell was never used again. Lincoln replaced the ailing and aging Winfield Scott with a young West Point graduate, George McClellan. McClellan's ability was in organizing and training men, and he did an excellent job of that. His men admired him, and he was hesitant to put them into harm's way. When forced to go into battle he balked, chose to use the tactic of siege, and almost cried when he saw the wounded and dead on the battlefield. He lost the Battle of Seven Pines even though he had more men and equipment.[34]

The only success that the Union had was at Shiloh in Tennessee under the command of Brigadier General Ulysses S. Grant. Was this the man Lincoln was looking for? What were the characters of these two men—Lee and Grant? Their backgrounds are worthy of a close examination.

ROBERT EDWARD LEE

He was born January 19, 1807, one of five children, who's mother was Ann Hill Carter, from one of the wealthiest families in the country. His father was Henry Lee who had been nicknamed Light Horse Harry and was famous for his eulogy of George Washington when he stated, "First in war, first in peace, and first in the hearts of his countrymen." What were not so famous were Henry Lee's faults.

His first marriage was to his cousin Matilda Lee who had considerable land and money. Henry invested much of the money in ill-advised ventures and left the family destitute. When Matilda died at an early age, she left two children: Henry and Lucy. Henry Lee then sought a second wife and found Ann Hill Carter. He wasted much of her money, and the year after Robert E. Lee's birth, he tried to leave the country and the next year went to debtors' prison. In 1813, when Robert E. was only six years old, Henry left for the West Indies and did not return for five years and then died on his way home.

Ann Hill Carter Lee took charge of her family and especially her youngest son Robert. He was enrolled in Mrs. Leary's Academy in Alexandria where he did well in both class and in deportment. In 1824, Lafayette came back to America, and the Lees were invited to the reception. When Robert E. reached the age seventeen, the family had to decide on a career for him. With little money, college was out of the question. Robert's older brother, Smith, had joined the navy, so it was decided to have Robert apply for admission into West Point, the military academy that had been established in 1802 with ten cadets. Letters of recommendation were required, and his family connections brought letters signed by five senators and three members of the House. Robert was introduced to Senator Andrew Jackson and Secretary of War John C. Calhoun. If Robert's father was next to useless, at least his eulogy of Washington had served a purpose.

Robert E. Lee did extremely well both academically and otherwise at West Point. He did so well in mathematics that he was asked to teach it his third year. At the end of his third Year, he was selected adjutant of the corps, making him the most prestigious cadet at the academy. He graduated second in his class and had no demerits during his entire time at West Point. Given a choice of branches in the army, he chose the engineers; the most looked-up-to branch.

He married Mary Custis, a great-granddaughter of Martha Custis Washington, four years after graduation in 1831. Lee would serve faithfully in the United States Army for thirty more years. He distinguished himself in the War with Mexico and was responsible for the capture of the Abolitionist John Brown at Harper's Ferry in October 1859. On April 20, 1861, after declining the offer to lead the Union army, Robert E. Lee tendered his resignation. [35]

ULYSSES SIMPSON GRANT

Ulysses Grant's father, Jesse Root Grant, was born in 1794, the second of five children to Rachel Kelly Grant and Noah Grant. The family moved to Ohio in 1804 and a year later Ulysses's grandmother, Rachel, died. The Grants were so poor, the family was broken up, and Jesse was apprenticed to the tanning business. He learned the business well, worked hard, and was to a certain extent, a successful entrepreneur. When he was twenty-seven, Jesse married Hannah Simpson, and they had a modest but attractive house on the Ohio River. A year later, on April 27, 1822, their first child was born. He was named Hiram Ulysses Grant.

A year and a half later, the family moved to a new town, Georgetown, Ohio, where Ulysses grew up, went to school, and did all the chores expected of him. In 1836, he stayed with relatives in Maysville, Kentucky, where he spent a year at an academy. The next year he studied in Ripley, Ohio. His best subject was arithmetic, but what he really loved was horses.

In 1839, Ulysses entered West Point, thanks to his father who had sought an appointment for his son from Congressman Thomas Harmer. Always called Ulysses, his middle name, he registered as U. H. Grant at the hotel where he would stay until enrolled. When he registered at West Point, there were two Grants on the rolls, Elihu Grant from New York and U. S. Grant from Ohio. When Congress Harmer had sent his recommendation for appointment, he was not sure of Ulysses's middle name, but knew his mother's maiden name was Simpson, and so the letter sent from Harmer was addressed with the initials, U. S. Grant.

When Grant entered West Point, he was only five feet one inch and 117 pounds at the age of seventeen. With the initials U. S., the upperclassmen nicknamed him Uncle Sam. Four years later, he was five feet seven inches tall but still not very heavy. He had no trouble with the entrance exams or with any of the course work. One course that he did enjoy and did quite well was art. He excelled at horsemanship, and upon graduation in 1843 was disappointed that he was not selected for the cavalry. His roommate during his fourth year was Frederick Dent, and upon graduation, they were both assigned to Jefferson Barracks outside St. Louis, Missouri, a slave state. This was not far from Fred Dent's hometown and, when he took Grant with him for a visit, Grant was introduced to his sister, Julia Dent.

Both Ulysses and Julia loved to ride horses, and before long they fell in love. But they would have to wait until after the War with Mexico to get married. Grant was in Mexico, but most of his service was spent as a quartermaster where he proved to be very useful. He was in one skirmish and acquitted himself well. Grant had the opportunity to observe General Zachary Taylor and General Winfield Scott and may well have picked up some pointers on both their action as well as their dress. Taylor never wore a uniform, dressing for comfort while Scott was the opposite, dressing in full uniform. Grant's duty as quartermaster was to help him later, but he did not realize it at the time.

Ulysses and Julia were married in August 1848, and Julia went wherever Grant was posted except between 1852 and 1854 when Grant was stationed on the West Coast. Missing Julia, he resigned from the army July 31, 1854. He and Julia tried their hands at farming for four years but had to give it up, partly due to the Panic of 1857. Ulysses even tried selling firewood on the streets of St. Louis during the winter months. He applied for a job as county engineer, for which he was well qualified, but it was a political assignment and he lost out on it.

Grant even tried his hand at rent collecting, working for a cousin of his wife, Julia. Grant hated the job, and they decided to seek help from Ulysses's father who had a successful harness business in Galena, Illinois. It was April 1861, and Fort Sumter had fallen. Grant was asked by Congressman Washburne to take charge of enlisting volunteers from Galena. Then he was responsible for taking them to Camp Yates in Springfield for drilling. With thousands of volunteers reaching Springfield, Governor Yates sought help. Washburne suggested Grant, and he was immediately given a commission. [36]

Here were two men, Robert E. Lee and Ulysses S. Grant. Eighteen years apart in age; one was coming from a Southern family with a historic background. Lee hated slavery, had great credentials, and proud service for his country. The other came from humble beginnings and a family that knew what hard work was and not afraid to do it. Grant went to West Point also but did not enjoy it. He served faithfully during the Mexican War, but resigned when he missed his wife too much. He tried farming, with slave help, but failed at that. He finally sought help from his father and went to work in a harness shop until he was asked to sign up and train recruits for the coming war. Would these two ever meet, and if so, under what circumstances? History would record that these two men, each in their own way, would leave a mark that would determine the destiny of the United States.

LETTER TO HORACE GREELEY

In Lincoln's inaugural address on March 4, 1861, he had stated, "I have no purpose directly or indirectly, to interfere with the institution of slavery in the States where it exists." On August 22, 1862 he wrote to the editor of the *New York Daily Tribune*:

My paramount object in this struggle is to save the Union, and is not either to save or destroy slavery. If I could save the Union without freeing the slaves, I would do it; and if I could save it by freeing the slaves, I would do it; and if I could do it by freeing some and leaving others alone, I would also do that.[37]

Lincoln was a shrewd politician as well as a good judge of men. He realized that it would be a long war, and an impetus was needed if the focus of the war was to be maintained. What was needed was a battle victory to be able to announce the end of slavery. The North would have a purpose to continue the fighting other than preserving the Union.

BATTLES AND CHANGES OF GENERALS

Following the defeat of the Northern troops at the Battle of Mechanicsville in June 1862 and their retreat from Pennsylvania, Lincoln chose Major General Henry Halleck who was in charge of the Western Department, to replace McClellan. Halleck selected General John Pope for the next battle which took place at Bull Run the last days of August 1862 where the first battle of Bull Run earlier in the war had taken place.

Pope was outgeneraled by Lee and Stonewall Jackson, and the Union forces retreated back to Washington. Lincoln sacked Pope and reinstated McClellan who acted quickly to restore the equipment that had been lost in the Peninsula Campaign and the Second Battle of Bull Run. This was McClellan's strength, and he had the better part of seventy thousand men, mostly veterans, ready within four days.

On September 5, 1862, General Lee moved across the Potomac River while his regimental band played "Maryland, My Maryland." Lee had written orders delivered to his corps commanders, but one was lost and later discovered by two men of the Twenty-seventh Indiana. The note was delivered to McClellan, and he boasted, "Here is a paper with which, if I cannot whip Bobbie Lee, I will be willing to go home."

The Battle of Antietam Creek took place on September 17, 1862, near the town of Sharpsburg, only forty miles from Washington. McClellan had 195 infantry regiments, 14 cavalry regiments, and 63 batteries of artillery, totaling 87,000 men. Lee had 186 regiments of infantry, 15 cavalry regiments, and only 3 batteries of horse artillery, totaling about 40,000 men.

After the bloodiest battle yet in the war, the Union forces lost nearly **28,000** men killed, wounded, or captured. The Confederates lost close to **14,000** men killed, wounded, or captured. Though Lee returned back across the Potomac with half the losses incurred by the Union forces, the battle was indecisive.[38]

"The Ballad of Antietam Creek" was recorded by Sidney Robertson Cowell from the singing of Warde H. Ford at Central Valley, California in 1939.

THE BALLAD OF ANTIETAM CREEK[39]

'Twas on the field of Antietam where many's the soldier fell,
Is where occurred the story which now to you I'll tell;
The dead lay all around me we all together lay,
For we had had a fearful fight upon the field that day.

And as I lay there musing upon the damp cold ground,
My knapsack for a pillow, my blankets wrapped around,
And as I lay there musing, I heard a bitter cry,
It was "Lord Jesus, save me, take me home to die!

"I was the oldest brother, just three years ago
I left my home and kindred for the State of Ohio;
Not finding any other work to which I might apply,
I bound myself apprentice, my fortune for to try.

"I did not like my master, he did not use me well,
So I fixed a resolution not long with him to dwell,
And with this resolution from him I ran away,
I started then for New Orleans and cursed be the day.

"Twas there I was conscripted and sent into the field,
Not having any other hope but I must die or yield,
And so with many another boy I marched away that night
And this had been the tenth time that I have been in fights.

"I thought the boy who shot me had a familiar face,
But in the battle's fury 'twas difficult to trace;
I thought it was my brother Jay, if him I could but see,
I'd kiss him and forgive him and lay me down to die."

I quickly ran into him and heard his story o'er,
It was my long-lost brother who lay weltering in his gore;
As I spoke of our loved ones left behind and soothed his fevered brow,
He whispered, "My dear brother, I can die happy now."

Then quickly as a slumbering babe in fluttering eyelids closed,
I saw him sink with shortening breath to death's long last repose;
And with many a tear and sad farewell, I scooped a narrow grave,
And there he sleeps beneath the sod of Antietam's rippling creek.

While the Battle of Antietam Creek was not an overwhelming victory, Lincoln decided that now was the time to issue his proclamation, which he had had since July. On September 22, 1862, he made his proclamation to become effective January 1, 1863.

THE EMANCIPATION PROCLAMATION[40]

Whereas, on the twenty-second day of September, in the year of our Lord one-thousand eight-hundred and sixty-two a proclamation was issued by the President of the United States, containing among other things, the following to wit:

That on the first day of January, in the year of Lord one-thousand eight-hundred and sixty-three, all persons held as slaves within any State, or designated part of a State, the people whereof shall then be in rebellion and forever free; and the Executive Government of the United States, including the military and naval authority thereof, will recognize and maintain the freedom of such persons, and will do no act or acts to repress such persons, or any of the them, in any effort they make for their actual freedom.

November 5, 1862, Abraham Lincoln relieved George McClellan for the second and last time. When Lee heard that his old adversary had been dismissed, he remarked, "We always understood each other so well. I fear they may continue to make these changes till they find someone whom I don't understand." McClellan was replaced by General Burnside who had been at Antietam Creek but had not been defeated.

General Burnside decided to march his Union army south to Richmond, Virginia, the South's capital, engaging Lee wherever he found him. Forty miles north of Richmond is the town of Fredericksburg, Maryland, and here the last battle of 1862 took place.

The Union lost twelve thousand men at the battle of Fredericksburg.[41] Burnside was replaced by Major General Joseph Hooker who had commanded the First Corps at the Battle of Antietam Creek

On seeing a federal charge repulsed at Fredericksburg, General Robert E. Lee stated, "It is well that war is so terrible, or we should get too fond of it."[42]

The following poem recounts an incident during that battle. Barbara Frietchie refused to lower the Union flag, and when Confederate General Stonewall Jackson entered Frederick, Maryland, he would not allow any of his soldiers to fire and/or molest her.

BARBARA FRIETCHIE[43]
John Greenleaf Whittier

Up from the meadows rich with corn,
Clear in the cool September morn,
The clustered spires of Frederick stand
Green-walled by the hills of Maryland.

Round about them orchard sweep,
Apples and peach trees fruited deep,
Fair as the garden of the Lord
To the eyes of the famished rebel horde.

On that pleasant morn of the early fall
When Lee marched over the mountain wall;
Over the mountains winding down,
Horse and foot, into Frederick town.

Forty flags with silver stars.
Forty flags with crimson bars,
Flapped in the morning wind, the sun
Of noon looked down and saw not one.

Up rose old Barbara Frietchie then,
Bowed from fourscore years and ten;
Bravest of all in Frederick town
She took up the flag the men hauled down;

In her attic window the staff she set,
To show that one heart was loyal yet.
Up the street came the rebel tread,
Stonewall Jackson riding ahead.

Under his slouched hat left and right
He glanced; the old flag met his sight.
"Halt"—the dust-brown ranks stood fast.
"Fire!"—out blazed the rifle blast.

It shivered the window, pane and sash;
It rent the banner with seam and gash.
Quick, as it fell, from the broken staff
Dame Barbara snatched the silken scarf.

She leaned far out on the window-sill,
And shook it forth with a royal will.
"Shoot, if you must, this old gray head
But spare your country's flag," she said.

A shade of sadness, a blush of shame,
Over the face of the leader came;
The nobler nature within him stirred
To life at the woman's deed and word;

"Who touches a hair on yon gray head
Dies like a dog! March on!" he said.
All day long through Frederick Street
Sounded the tread of marching feet;

All day long that free flag tost
Over the heads of the Rebel host.
Ever it torn folds rose and fell
On the loyal winds that loved it well;

And through the hill-gaps sunset light
Shone over it with a warm good-night.
Barbara Frietchies's work is o'er,
And the Rebel rides on his raids no more.

Honor to her! And let a tear
Fall, for her sake on Stonewall's bier.
Over Barbara Frietchie's grave,
Flag of Freedom and Union, wave!

Peace and order and beauty draw
Round the symbol of light and law;
And ever the stars above look down
On the stars below in Frederick town!

CIVIL WAR HEROINES

Barbara Frietchie was not the only heroine during the Civil War. Women and sometimes even girls did much to help their cause on both sides of the conflict. There are over fifty females whose contributions are documented.[44]

On the Union side, five documented reports of women, acting as spies, did daring deeds. Probably the most famous one was Harriet Tubman, an escaped slave whose daring career started well before the war began. She made nineteen trips to the South to smuggle out over *three hundred* of her fellow slaves through a network of sympathizers called the *Underground Railroad*. When the Civil War started, she became a Union scout, spy, and nurse. She gathered valuable information from slaves about the Confederate troops—their position and supply source. She never got caught. [45]

Rebecca Wright, a young Quaker schoolteacher in Winchester, Virginia, lost her teaching job because of her opposition to slavery. She helped Major General Philip Sheridan by giving him information that he needed in winning the Third Battle of Winchester in August 1864. [46]

Elizabeth Van Lew was known as *Crazy Bet* in Richmond, Virginia. While singing and muttering to herself while publicly declaring her Union sympathies, she passed on needed information in code and invisible ink to federal officers. [47]

Pauline Cushman, a well-known actress, was bribed by two Confederates to toast the South during her performance in Louisville, Kentucky, a Union-held town with many rebel sympathizers. She gave a toast to Jeff Davis and the Southern Confederacy. As a result, she was able to gather important information for advancing Union forces. When caught with information, Confederate General Braxton Bragg ordered her to be tried, and the court sentenced her to hang as a spy. Before the court could carry out the hanging, the Union troops attacked and the rebels abandoned her. [48]

Mrs. E. H. Baker gathered needed information about a new machine capable of moving underwater to attack the Union blockage fleet. Returning to Richmond, her previous home, she recorded information, hid it in her bonnet, and delivered it to the North who used it to discover and disable the newfangled submarine. [49]

On the South's side of the war, Rose O'Neal Greenhow lived in Washington, D.C., where she ran a spy ring. She helped Confederate General P. T. G. Beauregard with coded information that helped him in the First Battle of Bull Run in 1861. [50]

Charlotte "Lottie" Moon was at the altar as a bride to Ambrose Burnside. When asked if she took this man for her husband, she said, "No siree-bob" and made a quick exit.

Her spying career started in 1862 when she relayed messages to the Confederates in Lexington, Kentucky. Dressed as an old woman, she was able to get past Union sentinels and carried messages to the South.

In 1863, Lottie appeared in General Burnside's office, pretending to be a tourist from Britain. Burnside recognized her from thirteen years before when he was left at the altar. He had her arrested, but later softened and let her go. [51]

Emmeline Piggott from Beaufort, North Carolina, lost her sweetheart at the Battle of Gettysburg and decided to take up secret service work as a spy and smuggler. Hiding dispatches in large pockets under her skirt, she carried them between Union lines. Nearly captured many times, she was finally caught but managed to chew and swallow the important message. The Yankees imprisoned her, but finally released her without a trial and sent her home.[52]

Nancy Hart was a strong mountain woman who never attended school. She would stay around isolated federal outposts and report their strength, population, and vulnerability to General Stonewall Jackson. Then she would guide his men through the mountains for their attack. When caught by the Union troops, she stole a guard's musket, killed a Yankee colonel, and escaped on horseback.[53]

Belle Boyd was only eighteen years old and very pretty when she shot a Union soldier who insulted her mother. When Union forces used her aunt's home in Front Royal, Virginia, Belle would eavesdrop from an upstairs closet and listen through a hole in the floor. She delivered the information to General Stonewall Jackson.

By the time she was twenty-one, Belle had been arrested six or seven times and imprisoned twice. While in prison in Washington, D.C., she passed information from fellow imprisoned rebels to admirers by putting the information inside rubber balls that she tossed through the prison bars.[54]

There were other brave women on both sides that helped whenever and wherever they could. There were at least five women who became soldiers during the Civil War. One well-known lady was Jennie Hodgers. She came to the Untied States from Ireland by stowing away on a ship in 1844.

When war started, Jennie dressed herself as a man and enlisted in the Illinois Volunteer Infantry. She called herself Albert D.J. Cashier and took part in campaigns with the army of Tennessee, fighting Nathan Forrest's southern cavalry in battles in Northern Mississippi.

She broke her leg at the age of sixty-six. The doctor discovered her true identity, but she still collected her soldier's pension until she died in 1913.[55]

Of all the women who served in the various capacities, two stand out. One was Dorothea Dix. She was already well known for reforming insane asylums. Though sixty years of age, she took on the enormous task of organizing and managing all women nurses for the Union armies. Nothing like it had ever been done before.

She worked without pay, improving the appalling conditions of hospitals, creating new hospitals, organizing public drives of dried fruit and preserves for the wounded, and inspecting hospitals throughout the North. She demanded better diets for the wounded and wanted doctors found drunk on duty to be court-martialed. Though despised by the doctors as well as the surgeon general, she was loved by the wounded that brought her baskets of fruit and flowers.

The secretary of war joined the list of critics and had her transferred with her duties to the surgeon general. Dorothea Dix swallowed her pride and continued working until the war ended, and then she returned to her first love of helping the emotionally disturbed. [56]

The other woman who did so much was Clarissa "Clara" Barton. She was a clerk in Washington, D.C., in 1861. When a Union regiment arrived in Washington, D.C., bloodied by a group of Southern sympathizers in Baltimore, she started a new career. She gave the soldiers towels and bandages and got friends to donate food and clothes.

She took in the wounded into her home; when it was filled, she rented space in a nearby warehouse. After the Battle of Cedar Mountain, she arrived with a mule team loaded with supplies just as the hospital was running low on dressings. She worked for five days and five nights with little sleep, handing out supplies and carrying food and water to men lying in the field. James Dunn, the brigade surgeon said, "She was like an angel, an angel of the battlefield."

For the next three years, she followed army operations in Virginia and South Carolina. After one of the bloodiest battles at Antietam Creek, surgeons ran out of dressings for the wounds of the men, and they began using corn husks until Clara Barton arrived with bandages.

Later she organized a program for locating men missing in action. By the end of the Civil War, Clara Barton had done many of the tasks that were later incorporated into the organization that became the American Red Cross, which she founded in 1881. [57]

LINCOLN CONTINUES TO LOOK FOR THE RIGHT GENERAL

Lincoln was desperate for a general who would give him a victory. The selection of Major General Joseph Hooker was based on two things. He had, as a divisional commander, engaged in all of the major engagements so far. The other factor was that Joe Hooker's fighting reputation had been based on a typing error in a dispatch which changed from "still fighting—Joe Hooker" to "fighting Joe Hooker." A drunk and debaucher so well known, his name became a popular synonym for prostitute. [58]

On the positive side, Hooker improved the sanitary, dietary, and social aspects of the camp he took over. He also had the advantage of accurate intelligence when Pinkerton was replaced with Colonel Sharp who had a network of scouts, spies, and informants working for him. Hooker also formed a corps of experienced cavalrymen, numbering 12,000. Hooker's total force amounted to over 130,000 men. [59]

STONEWALL JACKSON SHOT BY HIS OWN MEN

The Battle of Chancellorsville, some ten miles west of Fredericksburg, took place the first four days of May 1863. Even though Lee had only half the force of Hooker, Lee defeated him with brilliant moves. The Union forces suffered over

17,000 casualties while the South lost 12,000 men and one of the finest generals either side would ever see—Major General Thomas "Stonewall" Jackson.

On the night of May 2, 1863, Jackson and some of his staff went to scout the Union positions. There was a full moon, and when he returned to his own lines, he was shot at by a group of North Carolina infantry. It did not appear to be a fatal wound, and he seemed likely to recover. Jackson had his right arm amputated, and he lapsed into a fever and died on Sunday, May 12, 1863. Robert E. Lee was devastated. He had lost his best general, and he knew it. It was a loss that the South could never replace. Some military critics claim that if Jackson had lived, Lee would have succeeded at the next battle that took place two months later near a small Pennsylvania town. [60]

THE TURNING POINT OF THE WAR

On May 28, 1863 the North's first black regiment left Boston to fight in the Civil War. They would serve with distinction.

General Robert E. Lee had had great success with his style of warfare. With Stonewall Jackson as his *right arm*, Lee was able to defeat his opponents who had larger numbers of men, sometimes outmanned two to one. He and Jackson had won battles because they could maneuver with Jackson's and Jeb Stuart's cavalry harassing the Yankees.

Now he had lost Jackson, and his next in command was Lieutenant General James Longstreet, a West Point graduate whose ambition before the war was to be chief of the army Paymaster's Department. Longstreet believed in fighting a defensive war, which was unsuited to Lee's reckless way of fighting.

Lee planned to invade the North to draw the Union forces away from the South's capital, Richmond. He wanted to force Lincoln to recall all of his armies from everywhere—from the Carolinas to the Mississippi—in a final battle. Lee believed his army was invincible.

Lee had his army march north from Fredericksburg in the early part of June 1863. He used Jeb Stuart to hide the move north, but a Northern general, Alfred Pleasanton, discovered the plot and engaged Stuart in a battle near Brandy Station, Virginia. The Yankees gave a good account of themselves, but Pleasanton was forced to withdraw. [61]

Another battle took place at Winchester on June 14 where Confederate General Richard Ewell decisively defeated General Schenck, capturing five thousand Northern troops, twenty-three canons and two hundred rounds of small-arms ammunition.

On the 27 of June 1863, Union General Joseph Hooker was replaced by General Gordon Meade. Lincoln told his cabinet that he did so because Hooker refused to carry out orders and kept asking for more troops. This sounded like McClellan and Lincoln couldn't be bothered. On June 20, West Virginia was admitted into the Union.

During the Battle of Fredericksburg, Meade's Pennsylvania reservists had broken through Stonewall Jackson's lines—the only good thing that the North did. Meade was well regarded by his men, but not offensive minded. He relied on his subordinates for accurate information as well as their analysis of any given situation. Major General Meade had one other good quality—his attention to detail and caution was to pay big dividends, at least on the last day of the battle.

Brigadier General John Buford, part of Major General Pleasanton's cavalry corps engaged the Confederates in a skirmish on the outskirts of Gettysburg. Meade had planned to fight a defensive battle in and around the small town of Pipe Creek in Maryland.

When one of Meade's corps commanders, Major General John Reynolds, reported that the terrain at Gettysburg was more suitable for a defensive battle than Pipe Creek, General Meade changed his mind and had his troops head towards Gettysburg. He had guessed correctly of Lee's intentions and prepared to fight a defensive battle. [62]

THE BATTLE OF GETTYSBURG

July 1 and July 2 belonged to the Confederates. Lee had used his infantry and cavalry in maneuvers that gained him some of the land around Gettysburg. Meade had used various parts of the land to his best advantage. Cemetery Hill, Cemetery Ridge, Little Round Top, and Big Round top would become famous for the decisive battles that were waged those first three days of July. Meade had a council of war with his generals. They decided to sit and defend for one more day. Meade thought that Lee would attempt to charge the center of Meade's forces and prepared for what was to come.

Lee *did* decide to attack the center of Meade's defense. Lee's second in command, Lieutenant General James Longstreet, did not share Lee's decision and told Lee so. But Robert E. Lee had faith in his rebels, based on previous successes. Major General George Pickett—last in his class at West Point—was to line up his division and charge after an initial bombardment by over 150 canons that the South had prepared.

The North had 77 canons, and when the bombardment started at 1:00 p.m. on July 3, 1863, both sides traded shells for almost two hours. During that time, Union Brigadier General Alexander Hays had his men of the Third Division collect all the stray guns they could lay their hands on. Some ended up with as many as four rifles, cleaned and loaded.

The 15,000 men of Pickett's division were cut down as they moved across the field. Only 5,000 were able to stagger back to their lines. Robert E. Lee had witnessed the battle from Seminary Ridge and rode out to meet them when they retreated. He praised their courage and begged their forgiveness. He told Pickett to place his men into line for a possible counterattack.

Pickett replied, *"General, I have no division."*

Lee took the blame for the defeat at Gettysburg. Both sides were exhausted, and the next day faced each other, but neither took any action. Lee took what remained of his army back to Virginia. Meade followed Lee but did not engage him even when Lee reached the Potomac River which had high water and prevented him from crossing.

The North had lost 23,094 men killed, wounded, captured, or missing. The South had lost 27,000 men killed, wounded, captured, or missing. It was the bloodiest battle that the Americans had engaged in up to that time. [63]

VICTORY AT VICKSBURG

Lincoln was disappointed that Meade had not engaged Lee when he had the chance. On July 7, 1863, Lincoln received word that Vicksburg had finally fallen after many months of maneuvers and a siege by Ulysses S. Grant.

But Grant had to fight more than the Southern forces. He had to fight jealous generals as well as politicians who wanted Grant removed. But Lincoln had believed in Grant ever since the Battle of Shiloh. To satisfy Grant's critics, Lincoln had sent Charles Dana as an observer. Supposedly, Dana was sent to investigate the paymaster service.

Charles A. Dana had been a reporter for the *New York Daily Tribune* whose editor was Horace Greeley. Dana was to send daily reports to the War Department. He had come west from Washington in March 1863 and stayed until July. His daily dispatches were well written, and nearly every dispatch was highly favorable to Grant.

Others came to judge Grant, including Lincoln's adjutant general Edward Bates, Lorenzo Thomas, Congressman Washburne, and Governor Yates from Illinois. All got a favorable impression of how Grant handled himself. His siege of Vicksburg was a long-drawn-out affair, but in the end he was successful. [64]

On July 5, 1863, two days *before* Lincoln had received word of Grant's victory at Vicksburg, Lincoln answered critics of Grant, including members of Congress and some in the press who wanted Grant removed.

> I rather like the man, I think I'll try him a little longer. He doesn't worry and bother me. He isn't shrieking for reinforcements all the time. He takes what troops we can safely give him . . . and does the best he can with what he has got . . . . If Grant took Vicksburg, why Grant is my man and I am his for the rest of the war.[65]

When Robert E. Lee had to retreat back to Virginia, and Meade refused to pursue him, the Southern army was far from broken. The fall of Vicksburg had virtually sealed off the Mississippi River to the Confederates. Memphis had fallen earlier as had New Orleans.

What was left? The center of the Confederacy—all of Alabama, Georgia, North and South Carolina, Virginia, and most of Mississippi—the heart and soul of the South.

BATTLE FOR TENNESSEE

The next battles were partly in Tennessee and partly in northwest Georgia. Major General William Rosecrans, a graduate of West Point and a native of Ohio, had been with McClellan when the Union had won a small victory in what would become West Virginia, the thirty-fifth state on June 20, 1863.

In June 1863, Rosecrans moved his fifty-thousand-man Army of the Cumberland from Murfreesboro, Tennessee, and captured Tullahoma, Tennessee. This exposed Chattanooga, an important Confederate rail center. General Braxton Bragg, commander of the Confederate army of Tennessee had to retreat, evacuating Chattanooga.

Edwin Stanton, the Union's secretary of war who had replaced Simon Cameron, was so delighted with the news of Rosecrans's success, he wired him "Vicksburg is surrendered to Grant on the 4 of July. Lee's army overthrown, Grant victorious. You and your noble army now have the chance to give the finishing blow to the rebellion. Will you neglect the chance?" [66]

Both armies moved south where the Battle of Chickamauga took place on September 19 and 20. Rosecrans had a chance to win, but hesitated. Longstreet had come from the east to reinforce Bragg. Longstreet planned carefully and his attack was devastating. Rosecrans was forced to withdraw to Chattanooga where they were under siege until relieved by Grant's men. The North had lost sixteen thousand killed, wounded, captured, or missing, but the South had lost nearly eighteen thousand killed, wounded, captured, or missing. [67]

A CEMETERY IS DEDICATED

The Battle of Gettysburg, considered by many historians as the decisive battle of the American Civil War, lasted three days—July 1, 2, and 3, 1863, and claimed over forty thousand soldiers' lives on both sides. A cemetery was erected, and a decision to dedicate the cemetery was made. Edward Everett was selected as the orator of the day, and he spoke for more than an hour. The committee, at the last moment, asked Lincoln to say a few appropriate remarks following Everett. He spoke his short address of 267 words.

Brief, eloquent, and moving, Mr. Everett is said to have told Lincoln that his short speech of two minutes better expressed the true sentiments of the day than his long speech.

THE GETTYSBURG ADDRESS[68]
Delivered at Gettysburg, Pennsylvania, November 19, 1863

Fourscore and seven years ago our fathers brought forth on this continent a new nation, conceived in liberty, and dedicated to the proposition that all men are created equal.

Now we are engaged in a great civil war, testing whether that nation or any nation so conceived and so dedicated, can long endure.

We are met on a great battlefield of that war. We have come to dedicate a portion of that field as a final resting place for those who here gave their lives that that nation might live.

It is altogether fitting and proper that we should do this.

But in a larger sense we cannot dedicate, we cannot consecrate, we cannot hallow this ground. The brave men, living and dead, who struggled here, have consecrated it far above our poor power to add or detract.

The world will little note, nor long remember, what we say here; but it can never forget what they did here.

It is for us, the living, rather to be dedicated here to the unfinished work which they who fought here have thus far so nobly advanced. It is rather for us to be here dedicated to the great task remaining before us, that from these honored dead we take increased devotion to that cause for which they gave the last full measure of devotion; that we here highly resolve that these dead shall not have died in vain; that this nation, under God, shall have a new birth of freedom, and that government of the people, by the people, and for the people shall not perish from the earth.

This address stands by itself in all literature for its simplicity, diction, perfection of pattern, and cogent utterance.

ULYSSES SIMPSON GRANT, APPOINTED GENERAL IN CHIEF

After Lincoln returned to Washington, much thought was given to changing the method of command. Congress and Lincoln worked together to bring about a structure to the military command that met the needs of a modern army. In the meantime, Grant submitted his grand strategy for fighting the war. He wanted to move his armies to Mobile, Alabama, and invade the Confederacy from the south. His plan was rejected, but in February 1864, Congress revived the rank of lieutenant general that previously had been held by only George Washington and Winfield Scott. In March, Ulysses S. Grant was offered the command of all United States forces and the rank to go with it. [69]

How had Grant achieved this pinnacle of military success? He was only five feet eight inches tall and not at all distinguishing looking. When he came to Washington with his son, Fred, for his new assignment, this ordinary-looking man asked for a room at the Willard Hotel. Told that there were only rooms available at the top floor, he signed the register U. S. Grant and son, Galena, Illinois. When the clerk recognized the name, he immediately changed the room to one that had been reserved for him on the second floor.

Grant's success had come about slowly but surely. He had started as a captain, working first as a mustering officer in Springfield. When he proved so successful, he was promoted to colonel and given command of a small unit. During his service in the Mexican War, Grant had shown his value in the Quartermaster Corps and knew well how logistics worked and could win battle. He knew the importance of ammunition supplies as well as transporting them to the battlefield. He learned about staff work at the regimental level, a necessary evil. He saw the benefits of using an offense at Fort Henry and Fort Donelson. He also saw the dangers that he encountered at Shiloh. He gained much of his knowledge of warfare from experience as well as from his subordinate officers. With his new appointment as general in chief, Grant was well trained and experienced for the position.

GRANT MAKES PLANS TO BRING THE WAR TO A CLOSE

The first thing Grant did was select known leaders for the different commands. He assigned William Tecumseh Sherman to the Western Command. Sherman was courageous and determined in battle. He was also loyal to Grant. He said, "Grant stood by me when I was crazy, and I stood by him when he was drunk." [70]

He replaced Albert Pleasanton with Phil Sheridan—only five feet four inches—to head up the cavalry. He made Halleck, who had been general in chief, his chief of staff. One thing that Grant did not want was to be desk bound. He took over the Union Army of the Potomac with Meade as his second in command. To Meade's credit, he accepted his role graciously. There were 860,000 men on the rolls when Grant took charge, but only 533,000 were available for duty, including those who were in backwater departments, garrisoned for supply duty, or assigned to artillery to guard the Capitol; Grant immediately ordered 6,000 to field duty. Grant's experience and determination were beginning to pay off. [71]

Grant had to deal with politically appointed generals who were anything but leaders. Ben Butler was a prominent Democrat, and in an election year, it was important to keep all the allies one could. Franz Siegel was a Prussian émigré who was the leader of a German community and took it upon himself to communicate with the War Department through congressmen. General Grant soon straightened Siegel out and put a trusted officer, Baldy Smith to join Butler.

Grant had given himself eight weeks to prepare for two campaigns at once. He ordered General Sherman to advance from Chattanooga and "move against Johnston's army, to break it up, and to get into the interior of the enemy's country as far as you can, inflicting all the damage you can." Sherman prepared his hundred thousand Army of the Cumberland and would begin his campaign on May 3, 1864.

Grant's instructions to General Meade's Army of the Potomac were, "Wherever Lee's army goes, you will go also." Grant knew that constant pressure would prevent Lee from moving one of his units to aid another, something that Lee had been so successful with in the past. [72]

GRANT BATTLES LEE

Grant headed for Richmond, and when Lee sought to cut him off, the Battle of Wilderness took place on May 5 and 6. After two days, Grant reported a loss of 17,600 out of 102,000 while Lee probably lost 8,000 out of his 60,000, including General James Longstreet, Lee's best commander. Ironically, Longstreet was shot by his own men. The South thought they had won the battle and expected the North to retreat as they had done in past battles. Men in the ranks of the North thought they would do that also, as they had with McDowell, Pope, Burnside, and Hooker. But Grant thought differently.[73]

He ordered his army to head for the Spotsylvania Court House, some fifteen miles southwest. When Grant's men discovered that they were advancing and not retreating, their spirits rose. The Battle of Spotsylvania lasted from May 8 to May 19. Grant lost 18,000 killed, wounded, captured, or missing. Lee lost about 10,000, mainly because they had taken up defensive positions during the twelve-day battle.[74]

Lee did not know what Grant's next move would be, but he feared for the capital, Richmond. Grant and Lee fought two more battles almost immediately after Spotsylvania. One was at North Anna River from May 21 to May 31. The next was at Cold Harbor from June 1 to June 3, 1864.

SHERMAN BATTLES JOHNSTON

Sherman left Chattanooga May 3, 1864 with three armies: his own Army of the Cumberland, commanded by Major General George Thomas; the Army of the Tennessee, commanded by Major General James McPherson; and the Army of the Ohio, under Major General John Schofield. Their total was about 100,000 men.

Confederate General Joseph Johnston had only 40,000 soldiers to battle Sherman's Union forces. An 1839 graduate of West Point, Johnston was a very cunning leader who saw the need for a different strategy with the South's lack of men and resources. His experiences at the Battle of Bull Run and the Peninsula Campaign served him well in his present position.[75]

Jefferson Davis wanted Johnston to reoccupy Tennessee, but Johnston knew that would be a waste. What he intended to do was to retreat slowly, harassing Sherman in the mountains between Chattanooga and Atlanta. The one hundred miles between Chattanooga and Atlanta would cost Sherman dearly from May 3 to July 17, 1864, when the Battle of Atlanta would last from July 20 to September 2, 1864.

With the one-hundred-mile retreat and the Battle of Atlanta, Sherman lost nearly 32,000 killed, wounded, captured, or missing. During the same period, Johnston lost nearly 35,000 men killed, wounded, captured or missing.[76]

The two leaders—Sherman and Johnston—had great respect for one another, even after the war. When Sherman died in the winter of 1891, Johnston was one of the honorary pallbearers. When the coffin passed, Johnston, out of respect, took off his hat. "General," an officer said, "please put on your hat—you'll get sick in this weather." Johnston replied, "If I were in there, he'd have his hat off." Johnston died five weeks later of pneumonia. [77]

PACIFIC RAILWAY ACT OF 1864

All of Congress knew that the Railway Act of 1862 would have to be revised. In May, a bill was introduced. It passed both houses of Congress and was signed into law July 2, 1864. It allowed three important factors. One, the Union Pacific and the Central Pacific directors were to issue their own first mortgagee bonds, putting the government bonds in a status of second mortgage. Two, the companies were given the rights to coal and iron and other minerals in their land grants. Three, the act allowed the Central Pacific to build up to 150 miles east of the California-Nevada border and limited the Union Pacific to building no more than three hundred miles west of Salt Lake City.[78] Even though the building would not start until after the war, a beginning had been made that Lincoln and others had dreamed about since railroads first became practical.

DAMN THE TORPEDOES: FULL SPEED AHEAD

From April 1862 to August 1864, David Farragut wanted to capture Mobile, Alabama. As flag officer, he was in command of the Western Gulf Blockading Squadron where he assisted on the Mississippi Gulf, capturing New Orleans, Galveston, Corpus Christi, Sabine Pass, and Port Hudson. Finally given the chance, Farragut defeated Admiral Franklin Buchanan in the Battle of Mobile Bay in August 1864. During the battle, Farragut, with forty-nine years of uninterrupted service, in the middle of the battle exclaimed his famous order, "Damn the torpedoes. Full speed ahead." [79] He won the battle, but Mobile, farther up the river, never surrendered. Two months later, Nevada joined the Union, October 31, 1864.

ELECTION OF 1864

There were many dissatisfied with the progress of the war and blamed Lincoln. Farragut's naval battle victory at Mobile Bay in August and the capture of Atlanta in September helped Lincoln win reelection. His vice president was Andrew Johnson, a Democrat. The Democrats nominated George McClellan, the general that Lincoln had fired twice early in the war. Lincoln received 2,213,635 popular votes; McClellan got 1,805,237 votes. Lincoln received 212 electoral votes and McClellan only 21.

THE BATTLE FOR NASHVILLE

The last battle of 1864 started when Confederate General John Hood left Atlanta on September 1 and headed for Tuscumbia, Alabama. He arrived on October 31 and awaited General Bedford Forrest's cavalry. They moved north and battled General Schofield at Columbia, Tennessee. After that, Hood moved farther north and fought another battle near Franklin, Tennessee. He then attempted to take Nashville but was beaten badly by Major General George Thomas, a Virginian who graduated from West Point in 1840, fought in the Seminole Wars as well as in the Mexican War. Thomas lost a little over three thousand men in the engagement while Hood lost approximately six thousand men.[80]

SHERMAN'S MARCH TO THE SEA

After the fall of Atlanta in early September, Sherman took two months to rest and rebuild his army. Then on November 9, 1864, he began his march to the sea. With two corps on either side, numbering fifty thousand men, Sherman moved on a fifty-mile wide swath, destroying everything in his path on a three-hundred-mile march, reaching the Atlantic Ocean December 12 and taking Savannah on December 20. On December 22, General Sherman sent a message to Lincoln. "I beg to present you a Christmas gift, the city of Savannah." He then turned north and captured Columbia, South Carolina, on February 17, 1865. A federal fleet took Charleston the next day.

Major John Anderson, who had to capitulate at Fort Sumter at the opening of the war in April 1861, had finally been vindicated.

Sherman moved north and took Goldsboro, North Carolina, on March 19. It looked like only a matter of time before Sherman would meet up with Grant, and together they would take on Lee's remaining army.[81]

LINCOLN INAUGURATED FOR HIS SECOND TERM

On March 4, 1865 Lincoln took the oath of office for the second time. Lincoln knew that the war was near its end. How would the end be approached? What would be the terms of surrender? How should the South be treated? Would the Congress approve of his ideas for reconstruction?

Lincoln, in his most eloquent speech since the Gettysburg Address, said among other things:

> With malice towards none, with charity for all, with firmness in the right as
> God gave us to see the right, let us strive on to finish the work we are in,
> to bind up the nation's wounds, to care for him who shall have borne the

battle and for his widow and his orphans, to do all which may achieve and cherish a just and lasting peace among ourselves and with all nations.[82]

THE SIEGE AND BATTLE OF PETERSBURG

The battle in and around Petersburg was not only the longest of the war, but the most costly in terms of casualties. The Union casualties: *eighty-nine thousand,* the South: *twenty-eight thousand.*

General Grant moved his forces from the area of Cold Harbor to the town of Petersburg with a population of eighteen thousand—only twenty-three miles south of Richmond. Here Grant hoped to either conduct a siege of Lee's Army of North Virginia into starvation or force him to come out and fight.

The siege and series of battles lasted from June 15, 1864 to April 6, 1865, nearly ten months. This length of time was due to a number of factors. Lee had less troops, but he had been in that situation many times. His only mistake was at Gettysburg, but he had learned a profitable lesson.

Grant knew he had a superiority of numbers and was not afraid to fight a war of attrition. But other factors came into the picture that would prolong the struggle: weather, inept leaders, luck, and ideas that backfired.

Grant had crossed the James River and headed for Petersburg, much to Lee's surprise. He had sent Major General William F. Smith (Ol' Baldy), as an advance force with three divisions including a newly formed division of Negroes. When Smith's corps arrived at Petersburg, he decided to make a reconnaissance of the Confederate lines before attacking Beauregard's much-smaller forces. When Smith decided to finally attack, he found out that the artillery was not in place because no one had told them of the attack. The Confederates, outnumbered and outgunned, retreated; but Smith, typical of other Union generals in the past battles, did not pursue.

Next, Union General Hancock brought his corps of four divisions but did not attack. But Union Generals Burnside and Warren did attack but were thrown back. When General Meade ordered Burnside to attack, they took two hills and then stopped when a support division did not advance because Union General James Ledlie was asleep. Beauregard retreated to a more defensible position; and Meade, mad with rage, ordered them forward. They charged against the Confederate earthworks and were repulsed. Grant called off the slaughter. This was typical of what happened time and again.

The next month, July, someone in the Forty-eighth Pennsylvania Regiment made up largely of coal miners from the Schuylkill County coal fields made the comment that "We could blow that damned fort out of existence if we could run a mine shaft under it". When given the go-ahead, they dug a tunnel five hundred feet long and loaded the end with four *tons of powder.* The colored division, as it was referred to at that time, would be given the honor of being the first troops to charge the open area created by the explosion. Brigadier General Edward Ferrero, who commanded the colored division, prepared his men who were eager to lead the attack that might end the war.

Ulysses Grant did not think it was a good idea. "If we put the colored troops in front, and it should prove a failure, it would be then said, and very properly, that we were shoving these people ahead to get killed because we do not care anything about them. But that could not be said if we put white troops in front." [83]

The explosion was set and went off early on the morning of July 30. It blew a gap 170 feet long, 60 feet wide and created a crater 30 feet deep. The Union soldiers went through the gap but had to go down into the crater before they could charge the Confederate lines. The white troops and the colored were both cut down as they tried to come up the crater. The crowding, the heat, and the lack of water made it a place like hell. The crater attack was a dismal failure. Union Brigadier Generals Ledlie and Ferrero were both drunk in a dugout.

Other Union failures took placer in August, September, and October. The only Union success in October was Phil Sheridan's defeat of Jubal Early's division at Cedar Creek. The months of November and December were relatively quiet, but with Sherman coming up from North Carolina and Sheridan coming to join Grant, Lee would be outmanned. In March, Lee decided to evacuate Richmond, and moved what remained of his fifty-seven thousand Confederates west along the Appomattox Road in early April. On April 1, Sheridan in his victory over some of Lee's forces at Five Forks took six thousand prisoners and cut the last supply lines of the Confederacy.

After battling superior forces, Lee saw that it was useless to continue, and rather than fighting to the last man, Lee accepted Grant's conditions and surrendered on April 9, 1865. [84]

"The war is over—the rebels are our countrymen again", Grant said upon stopping his men from cheering after Lee's surrender at the Appomattox Court House on April 9, 1865. [85]

Confederate General Joseph Johnston surrendered to Major General William Tecumseh Sherman on April 26. The last to surrender was General Kirby Smith at Shreveport, Louisiana, on May 26, 1865. President Jefferson Davis fled to Georgia but was captured May 10, 1865.

The greatest calamity in American history was over! *Six hundred thousand*—2 percent of the nation's total population—had been lost. It would take years for both sides to recover, emotionally as well as other ways. What was needed was a start for reconciliation. Lincoln had said on March 4, 1865, "With malice towards none, with charity for all . . . let us strive . . . to bind up the nation's wounds . . . to do all which may achieve and cherish a just and lasting peace among ourselves and with all nations." Would General in Chief Ulysses S. Grant take up Lincoln's challenge? In his own words, Grant remembers:

THE SURRENDER OF ROBERT E. LEE[86]
1865

(From the Personal Memoirs of Ulysses S. Grant)

I found him (Lee) at the house of a Mr. McLean, at Appomattox Court House with Colonel Marshall, one his staff officers, awaiting my arrival.

I had known General Lee in the old Army, and had served with him in the Mexican War, but did not suppose, owing to the difference in our age and rank, that he would remember me, while I would naturally remember him distinctly, because he was the Chief-of-Staff of General Scott in the Mexican War.

General Lee was dressed in a full uniform which was entirely new, and was wearing a sword of considerable value, very likely the sword which had been presented by the State of Virginia; at all events, it was an entirely different sword from the one that would ordinarily be worn in the field. In my rough traveling suit, the uniform of a private with the straps of a lieutenant-general, I must have contrasted very strangely with a man so handsomely dressed, six feet high and of faultless form. But this was not a matter that I thought of until afterwards.

I then said to him that I thought this would be about the last battle of the war—I sincerely hoped so; and I said further I took it that most of the men in the ranks were small farmers. The whole country had been so raided by the two armies that it would be doubtful whether they would be able to put in a crop to carry themselves and their families through the next winter without the aid of the horses they were riding. The United States did not want them, and I would therefore, instruct the officers I left behind to receive the paroles of his troops to every man of the Confederate Army who claimed to own a horse or mule take the animal to his home. Lee remarked again that would have a happy effect.

General Lee, after all was completed and before taking his leave, remarked that his army was in a very bad condition for want of food, and that they were without forage; that his men had been living for some days on parched corn exclusively and that he would have to ask me for rations and forage. I told him "certainly" and asked for how many men he wanted rations. His answer was "about twenty-five thousand," and I authorized him to send his own commissary and quartermaster to Appomattox Station, two or three miles away, where he could have, out of the trains we had stopped, all the provisions he wanted. As for forage, we had ourselves depended almost entirely upon the country for that . . . Lee and I then separated as cordially as we had met, he returning to his own lines, and all went into bivouac for the night at Appomattox.

As early as 1867, the women of Columbus, Mississippi, decorated the graves of both Union and Confederate soldiers. Such action spread and helped to slowly erase the bitterness of that great struggle.

THE BLUE AND THE GRAY[87]
Francis Miles Finch

By the flow of the inland river,
    Whence the fleets of iron have fled,
Where the blades of the grave-grass quivers.
    Asleep are the ranks of the dead:—
Under the sod and the dew,
    Waiting the Judgment Day:-
Under the one, the Blue;
    Under the other, the Gray.

These in the robins of glory,
    Those in the gloom of defeat,
All with the battle-blood gory,
    In the dusk of eternity meet:-
Under the sod and the dew,
    Waiting the Judgment Day:-
Under the laurel, the Blue;
    Under the willow, the Gray.

From the silence of sorrowful hours
    The desolate mourners go,
Lovingly laden with flower,
    Alike for the friend and the foe:-
Under the sod and the dew,
    Waiting the Judgment Day:-
Under the roses, the Blue;
    Under the lilies, the Gray.

So, with an equal splendor
    The morning sun-rays fall,
With a tough impartially tender,
    On the blossoms blowing for all:-

Under the sod and the dew,
    Waiting the Judgment Day:-
Bordered with gold, the Blue;
    Mellowed with gold, the Gray.

So, when the summer calleth,
    On forest and field of grain,
With an equal murmur falleth
    The cooling drip of the rain:-
Under the sod and the dew,
    Waiting the Judgment Day;
Wet with the rain, the Blue;
    Wet with the rain, the Gray.

Sadly, but not with upbraiding,
    The generous deed was done,
In the storm of the years that are fading
    No braver battle was won:-
Under the sod and the dew,
    Waiting the Judgment Day;
Under the blossoms, the Blue;
    Under the garlands, the Gray.

No more shall the war cry sever,
    Or the winding rivers be red;
They banish the anger forever
    When they laurel the graves of our dead;
Under the sod and the dew,
    Waiting the Judgment Day;-
Love and tears for the Blue;
    Tears and love for the Gray.

Lincoln had spent from March 23 to April 7, 1865 at Grant's headquarters at City Point, Virginia, where Lincoln's son, Robert, had been serving. When he realized that the war was all but over, Lincoln returned to Washington. On 14 of April, Lincoln had breakfast with his son, lunched with his wife, Mary, and late in the afternoon they took a drive to the Navy Yard. On returning to the White House, he found Governor Dick Oglesby of Illinois and a few friends. [88]

Something needed Lincoln's attention, and he went to the Cipher Room of the War Department. There he spoke to Thomas Eckert who had organized and run the telegraph system during the war. Lincoln invited the Eckerts to join him and his wife at the Ford Theater that evening where he was looking forward to seeing the play, *Our American Cousin*. Thomas Eckert declined the kind invitation, pleading that he had work to do for Secretary Stanton.

When the Lincolns attended the play, Southerner John Wilkes Booth shot the man who saved the Union. Lincoln died the next day, April 15, 1865. On the death of Lincoln, Secretary of War Edwin Stanton said, "*Now he belongs to the ages.*"[89]

What more could be said of this great man who "gave the last full measure of devotion . . . that this nation, under God, shall have a new birth of freedom". Maybe Walt Whitman and William Cullen Bryant said it best.

Walt Whitman, one of America's greatest poets, is best known for his many editions of his *Leaves of Grass*. During the Civil War, he volunteered his services in military hospitals and wrote accounts of his experiences with the wounded. On the death of Lincoln, Whitman is best remembered for his poem.

O CAPTAIN! MY CAPTAIN![90]
Walt Whitman (1819-1892)

O Captain! My Captain! Our fearful trip is done,
The ship has weather'd every rack, the prize we sought is won
The port is near, the bells I hear, the people all exalting,
While follow eyes the steady keel, the vessel grim and darling;

But O heart! heart! heart!
O the bleeding drops of red,
Where on the deck my Captain lies,
Fallen cold and dead.

O Captain! My Captain! Rise up and hear the bells;
Rise up—for you the flag is flung—for you the bugle trills,
For you the bouquets and ribbon wreath—for you the shores are crowding,
For you they call, the swaying mass, their eager faces turning

Here Captain! dear father!
The arm beneath your head!
It is some dream that on the deck,
You've fallen cold and dead.

Born in 1794, William Cullen Bryant wrote most of his poems before he was forty. He was the distinguished editor of the *New York Evening Post* for fifty years.

THE DEATH OF LINCOLN[91]
William Cullen Bryant (1794-1878)

Oh, slow to smite and swift to spare,
Gentle and merciful and just!
Who, in the fear of God, didst bear
The sword of power, a nation's trust!

In sorrow by the bier we stand,
Amid the awe that hushes all,
And speak the anguish of a land
That shook with horror at thy fall.

The task is done; the bonds are free;
We bear thee to an honored grave,
Whose proudest monument shall be
The broken fetters of the slave.

Pure was thy life: its bloody close
Hath placed thee with the sons of light,
Among the noble host of these
Who perished in the cause of Right.

Late in April Abraham Lincoln's body was put aboard a special train. On May 2, 1865, the sixteenth president of the United States arrived in Chicago to lie in state. He was buried in Springfield, Illinois, where thousands every year pay their respects to this great man.

AMERICAN LITERARY WRITERS AND POETS

During the first 65 years of the nineteenth-century America produced many fine writers and poets that best expressed the positive side of this great nation. It started with Washington Irving (1783-1859) whose most famous story was *The Legend of Sleepy Hollow.* James Fennimore Cooper (1789-1851) gave us *The Last of the Mohicans.* William Cullen Bryant's *Thanatopsis* was written when he was only eighteen. Ralph Waldo Emerson (1803-1880) is best remembered for the *Concord Hymn.* Nathaniel Hawthorne (1804-1866) gave us many stories, but *The Scarlet Letter* is his most famous. Poet Henry Wadsworth Longfellow (1807-1882) wrote the famous "Evangeline" as well as "The Village Blacksmith" and of course, "Paul Revere's Ride."

John Greenleaf Whittier (1807-1892) gave us such delightful poems as "Snowbound" and "The Barefoot Boy." Edgar Allan Poe (1809-1849) lived only forty years but wrote many stories and poems, including "The Raven" and "Annabel Lee." Oliver Wendell Holmes (1809-1894) is remembered for saving the naval ship USS Constitution with his poem "Old Ironsides." Henry David Thoreau (1817-1862) wrote *Walden, or Life in the Woods* which is noted for its natural descriptions.

Julia Ward Howe (1819-1910) gave us "The Battle Hymn of the Republic" and James Russell Lowell (1819-1891) gave us the humorous *Biglow Papers*. Walt Whitman (1819-1892) wrote a book of poems, *Leaves of Grass* as well as "O Captain! My Captain!" Stephen Foster (1826-1864) wrote about 125 songs, both words and music. His most famous were "My Old Kentucky Home" and "Oh! Susanna." Mark Twain—Samuel Langhorne Clemens—(1835-1910) wrote about the Pony Express, but his best works were to come later, as was Louisa May Alcott (1832-1888) with her famous *Little Women* in 1869.

PROMISES AND PROBLEMS IN THE FUTURE

The rest of the nineteenth century from 1865 to 1900 was to have its share of problems but also an opportunity for great steps forward during the heart of the Industrial Revolution. Men with brilliant minds would bring about inventions that would change not only the United States but would change the world as well.

Few political figures would emerge that could compare to those who had founded and expanded the nation or saved the Union. Men and women, of many nationalities not afraid of work or danger, would connect the East and West with ribbons of steel, and tens of thousands would migrate and would fill in the new states and make America a breadbasket for the world.

Lincoln's death brought many problems. Andrew Johnson would try to implement the reconstruction efforts that Lincoln had planned and in some cases had started. But selfish men who wanted the power for themselves would do all they could to discard the plans that Lincoln had foreseen as a way of bringing the divided parts of the nation together.

Later, in the twentieth century, great men would come forward to lead America in many ways. More than one would become a world leader and help to make America truly great.

PART D

IMPEACHEMENT, COMPLETING THE TRANSCONTINENTAL RAILROAD, AND THE FIRST MAJOR SCANDAL 1865-1877

Lincoln's untimely death created a host of problems. Certain men in Congress rejected Lincoln's plans for a just and honorable reconstruction. When President Johnson attempted to put the plans into effect, he was met with strong resistance.

The Thirteenth Amendment eliminated slavery, but it meant more representation in the House of Representatives for the Southern states, and congressmen from the North resented this. The Civil Rights Act of 1866 led to the Fourteenth Amendment, which defined citizenship and gave protection to life, liberty, and property, which could not be deprived without due process.

The year 1867 saw Nebraska admitted into the Union and Alaska purchased for $7,200,000. Also that year the Reconstruction Act and the Tenure of Office Act was passed over President Johnson's vetoes. The latter act would be the reason for bringing impeachment proceedings against the president. The trial took place on May 16, 1868 and lasted ten days. Thirty-five senators voted guilty and nineteen voted not guilty. The Constitution required two-thirds for conviction, so Johnson was acquitted by a *single* vote.

The Central Pacific Railroad had its start on October 26, 1863, when the first spike was driven into the first tie. By June 1864, thirty-six miles had been laid from Sacramento. The shortage of manpower was caused by the war and by men working a short time only to leave to try and find gold or silver.

In 1865, the superintendent of construction for the Central Pacific, James Strobridge, after a trial period, had been convinced that Chinese laborers could do the work and hired seven thousand to do the grading, blasting, felling of trees, and the drilling of holes when and where tunnels would be needed. By December 1865, fifty-four miles of track stretched east from Sacramento.

That same year, Grenville Dodge was still in the army until the war ended in April. When Dodge was released, and veterans from the North and South as well as men from Ireland became available, work began in earnest on the Union Pacific. Survey, grading, and laying of track brought the end of track forty miles west of Omaha by the end of 1865.

The Railway Act of 1864 required that the entire transcontinental railroad be complete by July 1, 1876. The entire distance between Omaha; Nebraska; and Sacramento, California, was 1,776 miles. Some believed it was an impossible task, but others were determined to meet the goal.

During Ulysses Grant's first year in office, 1869, the railroad that would bind the East with the West was completed. In his last year, 1876, the Centennial Celebration of the United States took place. Between these times, numerous scandals occurred.

Raid on the gold market created financial ruin. Fraud was discovered in dealings with the transcontinental railroad that included men in leading financial positions as well as members of Congress. Another setback during Grant's administration was the Panic of 1873.

Stealing over $100,000,000 from the New York Treasury, taking kickbacks from whiskey distillers by officers of the internal revenue department, and illegal selling of army supply contracts and appointments by Grant's secretary of war were three more black marks.

On June 25, 1876, George Armstrong Custer made his last stand.

The positive side of these times included the ratification of the Fifteenth Amendment, which gave the right to vote to all males. Alexander Graham Bell's invention of the telephone, introduced at the centennial celebration, would eventually change not just the United States but also the world.

It was a period of great joy and, in many ways, great sorrow.

CHAPTER XII

ATTEMPTS AT RECONSTRUCTION
1865-1868

T he Civil War's national debt had increased from \$64,842,287 to \$2,777,236,173.[1] But that was the least of President Andrew Johnson's problems.

Just prior to Lincoln's death, the Freedom Bureau was established on March 3, 1865. The purpose of the act was to care for the freed slaves and their families as well as the supervision and management of abandoned land. It was limited to one year but could be renewed if approved by Congress and signed by the president. [2]

ANDREW JOHNSON SEVENTEENTH PRESIDENT (1865-1869)

Johnson was sworn in on April 15, 1865. On May 28, he issued a Proclamation of Amnesty, granting a pardon to all who participated in the rebellion and were willing to take an oath of allegiance. It was almost identical to Lincoln's proclamation of December 8, 1863. [3]

On June 30, 1865 President Johnson issued the Proclamation of Reconstruction for South Carolina. Since Lincoln had already established provisional governments for Louisiana, Tennessee, Arkansas, and Virginia, only six states remained; but within two months, the other six states were to receive proclamations.

The Proclamation of June 30, 1865 had some very important provisions.[4]

1. The Fourth Section of the Fourth Article of the United States Constitution stated: "The United States shall guarantee to every State of this Union a Republican Form of Government." [5]
2. The President made Commander-in-Chief by the Constitution shall have the authority to carry out the necessary directives, including the appointment of a Provisional Governor.

3. It is provided for the loyal citizens to organize a state government.

4. It allowed for the election of those who had taken the oath of amnesty.

The Thirteenth Amendment, ratified December 18, 1865, was the first change in the Constitution since 1804. It was short and to the point.

AMENDMENT XIII[6]

Section 1. Neither slavery nor involuntary servitude, except as a punishment of crime whereof the party shall have been duly convicted, shall exist within the United States or any other place subject to their jurisdiction.

Section 2. Congress shall have power to enforce this article by appropriate legislation.

This Amendment did more than guarantee the freedom of slaves. It changed part of the Constitution. Article I, Section 2, had restricted southern states with slaves to counting them as only three-fifths of a person, in terms of electing members of the House of Representatives.

Now the Southern states would have greater representation in the House of Representatives, and this worried the Northern congressmen who were bent on revenge and taking advantage of Lincoln's death and President Johnson's hesitation to make a strong stand for the reconstruction plans that Lincoln had outlined prior to his untimely death.

The Thirteenth Amendment also eliminated part of Section 2 of Article IV, which had dealt with returning escaped slaves to their rightful owner.

When the Freedmen Bureau Act came up for renewal in February 1866, additions were made that enlarged its powers and was vetoed by President Johnson. The Congress passed the bill over the president's veto as allowed in Article I, Section 7 of the United States Constitution. This was the beginning of *open warfare* between the radicals of Congress and President Johnson.[7]

The next confrontation between Congress and President Johnson came when the Civil Rights Bill was passed by Congress on March 12, 1866, but was vetoed by the president on March 27. This act conferred citizenship upon the Negroes, superseding the *Dred Scott* decision where the Supreme Court had ruled that Dred Scott was not a citizen of the United States or the State of Missouri.

An April 9, the Congress overrode Johnson's veto. There was some doubt about the constitutionality of the act, which induced Congress to begin proceeding to enact most of its provisions into the Fourteenth Amendment, which eventually became part of the United States Constitution when it was ratified on July 8, 1868.[8]

AMEMDMENT XIV[9]

Section 1. All persons born or naturalized in the United States, and subject to the jurisdiction thereof, are citizens of the United States and of the State wherein they reside. No State shall make or enforce any law which shall abridge the privileges or immunities of citizens of the United States, nor shall any State deprive any person of life, liberty, or property, without due process of law; nor deny to any person within the jurisdiction the equal protection of the laws.

Section 2. Representatives shall be apportioned among the several States according to their respective numbers, counting the whole numbers of person in each state, excluding Indians not taxed. But when the right to vote at any election for the choice of electors for President and Vice President of the United States, Representatives in Congress, the Executive and Judicial officers of a State, or members of the Legislature thereof, is denied to any of the male inhabitants of such State, being twenty-one years of age, and citizens of the United States; or in any way abridged. Except for participation in rebellion, or other crime, the basis of representation therein shall be reduced in the proportion which the number of such male citizens shall bear to the whole number of male citizens twenty-one years of age in such State.

Section 3. No person shall be a Senator or Representative in Congress, or elector of President and Vice President, or hold any office, civil or military, under the United States, or under any State, who having previously taken an oath, as a member of Congress, or as an officer of the United States, or as a member of any State legislature, or as an executive or judicial officer of any State, to support the Constitution of the United States, shall have engaged in insurrection or rebellion against the same, or given aid or comfort to the enemies thereof. But Congress may by a vote of two-thirds of each House, remove such disability.

Section 4. The validity of the public debt of the United States, authorized by law, including debt incurred for payment of pensions and bounties for services in suppressing insurrection or rebellion, shall not be questioned. But neither the United States nor any State shall assume or pay any debt or obligation incurred in aid of insurrection or rebellion against the United States, or give claim for the loss or emancipation of any slave, but all such debts, obligations and claims shall be held illegal and void.

Section 5. The Congress shall have power to enforce, by appropriate legislation, the provisions of this article.

For the first time, citizenship was defined, and the federal government threw its protection around rights that might be invaded by the state governments. The first part of this amendment gave rise to more adjudication than any other part of the Constitution. [10]

A great injustice had been corrected. The male Negroes had the citizenship as did every male citizen. But there would be some who would deny them their full rights, including the right to vote by such devices as literary tests and property qualifications, as well as a poll tax.

Over the next ninety years, Negroes would wait patiently for their equal rights. Then in 1955, the struggle would take on added meaning when a small black lady would refuse to give up her seat to a white person on a bus in a Southern town. But there were many years of fear by the Negroes, and some of it started right after the Civil War.

The Ku Klux Klan, founded in 1865 in Pulaski, Tennessee, was one example of how some in the South tried to scare the Negroes and, in some cases, used lawlessness and violence to keep them subservient. [11]

The price that Southern states would have to pay to be readmitted into the Union was their ratifying the Fourteenth Amendment. The proud states of the South would vote against ratification, except Tennessee who was readmitted and restored to statehood. Their representatives came to Congress on July 24, 1866. [12]

There was some good news to report as 1865 gave way to 1866. James Nason of Franklin, Massachusetts, patented the coffee percolator. The first successful cable was laid across the floor of the Atlantic Ocean. Salmon canning on the Columbia River began bringing that delivery within reach of those who lived in the middle of the country, and Massachusetts passed a law limiting the hours for a child laborer to eight hours. [13]

The bad news was the midterm election of 1866, where Johnson was hoping to gain support for his ideas on reconstruction. But the opposite happened, and the new Congress came in even more anti-Johnson.

During the Civil War, France took the opportunity to establish a monarch in Mexico. First it sent French troops to occupy Mexico City in June 1863, and then Napoleon III sent Maximillian, an Austrian archduke, in 1864 at the request of the Mexican royalists. The United States was too busy to do much about this, but they verbally opposed this move and, when the war was over, demanded withdrawal of the French troops in keeping with the Monroe Doctrine. Napoleon III withdrew his troops; Maximillian was captured and then executed by the forces of Mexicans led by Juarez. Benito Juarez restored order and was elected president of Mexico in December 1867. [14]

The year 1867 saw Nebraska admitted into the Union on March 2. Also the passage of the Reconstruction Act as well as the Tenure in Office Act, both of which were vetoed by Johnson, and then passed over his veto. The Tenure of Office Act prevented the president from removing anyone from administration offices, such as cabinet officers, without the consent of the Senate. When Johnson removed Secretary of War Stanton, the Congress reinstated him. When Johnson removed him a second time, the Congress said it was illegal, and the House of Representatives proceeded to consider impeachment against President Johnson, as permitted by Article I, Section 3 of the Constitution. [15]

In the meantime, Alaska was being considered for purchase from Russia. As early as 1855, Russia was prepared to sell her territory so that the British could not claim it during the Crimean War. In 1859, California Senator William McKendree Gwin offered Russia $5,000,000. The Civil War brought a halt to the negotiations, but in December 1866, the Russian ambassador, Baron Eduard de Stoeckl, broached the possibility of the sale to Secretary of State Seward. They agreed on a price of $7,200,000, and it was approved on March 30, 1867. Nearly six hundred thousand square miles in size, it was larger than Texas and California *combined!* [16]

In December of 1867, Congress considered impeachment proceedings against President Johnson but did not have the votes. When Johnson tried to forcibly replace Stanton with General Lorenzo Thomas, the Congress reconvened; and on February 22, 1868, the House of Representatives voted 126 to 47 for impeachment of Johnson. [17] How ironic that the date that the first president to be impeached happened on the birthday of the first president of the United States, George Washington.

The trial of President Johnson on eleven articles of impeachment began on May 16, 1868. It ended ten days later on May 26, 1868. There were fifty-four senators present for the trial, some so sick they had to be carried into the Senate chamber. On all eleven articles, thirty-five senators voted guilty while nineteen voted not guilty. Since the Constitution required two-thirds for conviction, (thirty-six votes would be needed), Johnson was declared not guilty by *one vote* by the United States Supreme Court Chief Justice Salmon Chase who presided at the trial as required by Article I, Section 3 of the United States Constitution. [18]

One other president would be impeached and then tried 130 years later. President William Clinton was impeached by the House of Representatives and tried by the Senate in 1998. He was also acquitted.

The remainder of Johnson's presidency was a sad time for the country that had been divided with four years of war and now was being torn apart by those in the North and South that had no scruples about taking revenge instead of devoting their efforts to reconstruction. New terms came into use—scalawags: unprincipled Southerners who turned Republican for self interest, and carpetbaggers: Northerners going to the South and taking advantage of the *Reconstruction Act* for private gain.

LOOKING AHEAD AND BUILDING FOR THE FUTURE

In spite of the sad era that still divided the nation and had lasted far too long, the nation was anxious to see the completion of the railroad that would bring the East and the West so much closer.

There were also encouraging signs. Men with a conscience would step forward to preserve and protect the beauty of this bountiful land. Still others would fight for the dignity of the working men and women who stood to be exploited in the growing and crowded cities by selfish industrialists. It would be an era of vast changes, remarkable improvements, and necessary challenges.

Many of the changes would be due to the building, the completion, and the use of the railroad that would go from Omaha, Nebraska, to Sacramento, California.

CHAPTER XIII

BUILDING AND COMPLETING
THE TRANSCONTINENTAL RAILROAD
1862-1869

FROM WAR TO RAILROADS

With the conclusion of the Civil War in April 1865, the nation turned its attention to healing its wounds. There were those who wanted to profit from the victory by the Union forces and some in the United States Congress who wanted to be harsh on the South for attempting to leave the Union. But many wanted to go home, if they had one to go to, and start life anew and look for work wherever possible. So the third ingredient, after leadership and sufficient finances, to building a transcontinental railroad was made available—men and more men.

There were leaders for both the Union Pacific and the Central Pacific railroads that had been planning in many ways during the Civil War struggle. The Pacific Railway Act of 1864 had provided for the beginning of financing this tremendous endeavor, though money would have to come from other sources as well. Now what was needed were men to do the work in many different capacities, and those who were willing to do so would be hired to build—almost entirely by *hand*—the longest railroad the world had ever seen.

Shortly after Lincoln won reelection in 1864, he gave his Annual Message to Congress. While the war was the major topic, Lincoln also spoke of the transcontinental railroad, referring to it as the great enterprise. He said it:

> Has been entered upon with a vigor that gives assurance of success, notwithstanding the embarrassments arising from the prevailing high prices of material and labor. The route of the main line of the road has been definitely located for one-hundred miles westward from the initial point

161

of Omaha, Nebraska, and a preliminary location of the Pacific Railroad of California has been made from Sacramento, eastward, to the great bend of the Truckee River in Nevada.[1]

TWO RAILROADS—ONE GOAL

The Union Pacific and the Central Pacific faced entirely different problems. The Union Pacific had flat land that made it easier to survey, grade, and lay track, but had no wood for ties. They would have to use cottonwood trees, but they were too soft unless treated. They also had the Indians to face as they went farther West, away from *civilization*.

The Central Pacific had different problems. One was getting enough men to stay and help build the line from Sacramento, east, instead of leaving to seek their fortunes in the streams of California and the mountains of Nevada. While they didn't have to worry about lack of wood or danger from Indians, they had the almost-insurmountable task of going up and over or *through* the Sierra Mountains, which many said was impossible.

All the important needed equipment—tools, supplies, rails, even spikes, and other fittings, not to mention the locomotives and cars—had to be sent by ships around the southern tip of South America at tremendous expense.

The Pacific Railway Act of 1864 laid down certain conditions, including how money would be distributed to the two lines. The two lines had to meet certain conditions to be eligible for their money, including laying a certain amount of track by a certain date—June 27, 1866.

STARTING THE UNION PACIFIC

Before a mile of track could be laid, someone had to plan the exact route that would connect the East and the West. These were the surveyors. They had to know that in the nineteenth-century, locomotives could not run up or down an incline of more than a 2-percent grade. They followed the general route that Grenville Dodge and Peter Dey had agreed was the best possible way from Omaha—on the north side of the Platte River.[2]

But Dodge and Dey were not the first to see that route as the best possible way west. Indians and the buffalo had used it for many years. After that came the mountain men, fur traders, and eventually the travelers and emigrants as early as 1841; then by the Mormons in 1846; and finally the gold seekers from 1849 and later. They and others would use it for the next twenty years.[3]

The surveyors had to take into account hills and ridges that would have to be cut through and ravines that would have to be filled in. They looked for a route as straight as possible, avoiding major lakes and rivers. Through most of Nebraska, it would be a much easier task where it was relatively flat. The more difficult challenges would come later in the foothills and more so in the mountains.

One important consideration was the requirement that the railroad had to be near water where water stations could be built for the steam locomotive. The Platte River would provide that, but wood for the ties would be another problem, especially through Nebraska where there was little wood for over two hundred miles.

Using surveying equipment of the same vintage that George Washington had used a hundred years previously, the surveyors of the railroads did a remarkable job. A hundred years after they did their job, when surveyors had modern equipment to plan Interstate I-80, they could do no better and followed the same route that the railroad surveyors had made.[4]

While surveyors like Arthur Ferguson and his group, in the summer of 1865, surveyed the route from Columbus, Nebraska, west along the Platte River for the next 150 miles, Dodge and Dey were working their way farther west, looking for ways to cross the first of a series of mountains. Peter Dey found three possible routes west of Julesburg, Colorado. One would go over the Black Hills through the Cheyenne Pass, a second would divert to Denver; but the best route found was just south of the Black Hills also called the Laramie Mountains.[5]

STARTING THE CENTRAL PACIFIC

While the Union Pacific got started after the Civil War, the Central Pacific was started much earlier, thanks to Ted Judah. When he came West in 1854, he immediately began looking for the best possible route from Sacramento eastward. He personally surveyed the area from Sacramento to the Sierra Mountains, following a number of trips he had to make back to Washington, D.C., and with the help of Daniel Strong, found the route that would be most feasible in 1860, the Donner Pass.

On September 4, 1861, Leland Stanford had been elected governor of California. Three weeks later, Ted Judah completed a very extensive report on the problems to be faced, including the elevations to be conquered, the rivers and deep gorges to be crossed, the snow problems to be faced, and the necessary tunnels to be dug and blasted. So complete was his report that Huntington, Stanford, Crocker, and Hopkins sent Judah back to Washington; and the Pacific Railway Act of 1862 was passed and signed by President Lincoln on July 1, 1862.[6]

Judah had many arguments with the Big Four of the Central Pacific (Governor Stanford, Collis Huntington, Charles Crocker, and Mark Hopkins), but he had done much to keep the Central Pacific from going broke and being disbanded. But in October of 1863, Ted Judah and his wife, Anna, started back to the East by way of the steamer, *St. Louis*, to meet Cornelius Vanderbilt. On the way, Judah got caught in a rainstorm helping women and children on board. He contacted yellow fever and died on November 3, 1863. The week prior to his death, October 26, Charlie Crocker spiked the first rails to their ties.[7]

Judah's replacement was Samuel Montague, an engineer that Judah had hired and trained, along with Lewis Clements, a Canadian canal engineer that Judah also trained well.[8]

More financial problems caused the CP (Central Pacific) to almost go under. But the Railway Act of 1864 saved them. By June of 1864, Crocker's men had laid track from Sacramento to Newcastle, a distance of only thirty-six miles, at a cost of $3,000,000![9]

By the end of 1864, much had been accomplished; but the Central Pacific was almost broke, and the expenses needed to build the railroad were getting larger. The Railway Bill of 1864 required that only U.S. iron could be used. The cost of rails went up dramatically, plus the cost of transporting all the materials and the locomotives around South America. Until 1865, the CP operated for the most part on the Big Four's money and loans.[10]

With Ted Judah's untimely death, others like Montague and Clements would step forward to take his place. The next four years, 1865 through 1869, would bring more challenges to be met and unforeseen problems. But the determination to bring the East together with the West was so strong, nothing could hold back the American spirit to succeed in this noble dream. Tocqueville said it best in 1835, when he stated, "what is not yet done, is only what he (the American) has yet attempted to do."[11]

1865 SERIOUS PROGRESS

Central Pacific: James Harvey Strobridge, a big, six-foot Irishman had worked on railroads in the East then came to California to work for Charles Crocker. He worked well and was promoted to the position of superintendent of construction.[12] Hiring and retaining men to work for the CP were a problem. Men would work for a short time to get enough money to stake themselves for a chance to seek their fortune in gold or silver. By the winter of 1864-65, the workforce was down to only five hundred men.[13]

In January 1865 Strobridge placed an ad in the *Sacramento Union:*

> Wanted, 5,000 laborers for constant and permanent work, also experienced foreman. Apply to J. H. Strobridge, Superintendent.

Many applied for the $3-a-day wages—some two thousand. After a week of work, only about a hundred were left.

In spite of the small workforce, construction continued; and by spring 1865, they had graded and tracked to Auburn, a distance of about forty miles. Huntington received $1,258,000 in United States Bonds that helped to pay off the loans that had been required to keep the work going. By June, the CP had reached Clipper Gap, forty-three miles from Sacramento. But the problem was having enough workers to assault the Sierra Nevada Mountains.[14]

Crocker proposed to Strobridge that he hire Chinese—there were some sixty thousand in California. They had come for the same reason as everyone else—*gold!* But California passed so many laws against the Chinese who wanted to mine gold that many of them ended up as cooks, laundrymen, gardeners, and errand boys for a little as $3 a *week.*[15]

Strobridge was dead set against the use of Chinese for labor on the railroad. They were too small he complained. *"They built the Great Wall of China, didn't they?"* said Crocker to Strobridge.

Still skeptical, Strobridge agreed to try out fifty of them for a month under white supervision.[16] After the trial period, Strobridge admitted that the Chinese worked extremely well. Working in teams, they took few breaks, learned quickly, stayed healthy, and most important stayed on the job. They began to hire more and more of them, paying them $28 a month at first but later $31. By the end of 1865, there were seven thousand Chinese working on the CP line. The Chinese did the grading, cutting, blasting (they had invented gun powder), felling trees, drilling holes as well as putting the black powder in to blast and help make the tunnels.[17] By the end of 1865, the Central Pacific had laid fifty-four miles of track from Sacramento. Not a great distance, but it was a start.

Governor Leland Stanford, who had referred to the Chinese as the *dregs of Asia,* won votes to become governor. When he wrote to President Andrew Johnson later he said, "As a class, they are quiet, peaceable, patient, industrious, and economical. Without the Chinese, it would have been impossible to complete the western portion of this great national highway."[18]

Union Pacific: Granville Dodge was still in the army when General U. S. Grant appointed Dodge to command the Department of the Missouri, which meant all the land between the Missouri River and the Rocky Mountains. On January 15, 1865 President Lincoln ordered Dodge to watch the State of Missouri, which had those loyal to either the South or North and could cause trouble.[19]

The main problem in the plains of Nebraska was the Indians, and both Grant and Dodge felt this problem would have to be confronted before any track could be laid. Dodge attacked the Indian problems like he did everything else—with great vigor and determination. He had the soldiers everywhere looking for those that caused trouble and forcing them north and south of the Platte River valley.

Durant wanted Dodge so badly that he promised to keep the job of chief engineer open until the war ended, and he was willing to pay him $10,000 a year—a very large wage for those times. In addition, Durant offered stock in the Crédit Mobilier. This was the company that Doc Durant and George Train had renamed from the Pennsylvania Fiscal Agency they had purchased in March 1864.[20] But Dodge told them nothing could be done until the Indian problem was solved.

When the Civil War ended, thousands of veterans from both the North and the South became available. The surveyors worked in all kinds of weather and detailed a route along the river as far as Columbus, Nebraska, by August 2, 1865. They had come some sixty miles west of Omaha, and it was time for the graders to get involved.[21]

The graders were an interesting mix of men from various parts of the country. Some from the East, others were those who had just arrived from Europe, especially Ireland. The majority were veterans from both sides of the war, anxious to make the $2 or $3 a day. They worked all day, except for an hour when they were well fed. The men worked with shovels, picks, and wheel barrows. They plowed the ground, made fills, and made the grade-two feet or more above the ground so that the track would not be flooded during the rainy season.[22]

At night, after they had eaten supper, the men played cards or sang. Some of the songs were "Poor Paddy He Works on the Railroad" or "*The Great Pacific railway for California hail, bring on the locomotive, lay down the iron rail.*" Others were *Pat Malloy; Whoop Along Lima Jane* and *I'm a rambling rake of poverty, the son of a gamboleer.* The only musical instruments were an occasional Jew's harp or harmonica.[23]

By the middle of October 1865, the *Omaha Weekly Herald* reported that the graders had reached Columbus, and the first major river was ready to be crossed with a 1,500 foot trestle that had been made in Chicago according to specifications made by the surveyors and ready to be erected in the spring of 1866.[24]

Behind the graders came the laying of ties and track. They covered only forty miles to the Elkhorn River where Dodge had first built a cabin in 1854 after marrying Anne Brown in May. But it was a beginning, and much had been learned in this first year for the Union Pacific. Almost everyone could hardly wait for the snows to melt so that work would continue in 1866.

1866 STEADY PROGRESS

Union Pacific: Omaha, the eastern terminus of the UP, grew and benefited as few towns had done. By 1865 it had doubled in size to fifteen thousand people, and would grow even more in 1866.[25] The amount of materials and supplies that had to be shipped by way of the Missouri River boats from St. Louis was staggering. By April 1866, more than one hundred thousand ties and twelve hundred tons of rails were piled up in Omaha. Workers waiting for the weather to break so they could begin grading and laying track, found employment unloading the boats as well as work in the many shops, making the needed items like flatcars, or building the needed storage places to house the equipment that would be used, including the Burnettizer, an ingenious invention which treated the cottonwood ties by extracting the water out of the lumber and putting a zinc solution in it place.[26]

In April 1866, Grenville Dodge wrote General Sherman, requesting leave to work on the UP. May 1, General Sherman approved with these encouraging words. "I consent to your going to begin what I trust will be the real beginning of the great road."[27] Dodge refused to accept Durant's offer as chief engineer unless given complete control of the operation. His military experience had convinced him that that was the only way that building the UP could succeed.[28]

So Dodge put the job of building the Union Pacific on a military basis. Since nearly all of Dodge's chief subordinates had been in the Union army, and almost all of the men who would do the grading and track laying had served in the Union or Confederate armies, they were ready to obey and carry out the orders given them. Without this, the chances of the UP being built was very small indeed.[29]

The Indians, who did not want to see the railroad built, were a problem that Dodge quickly solved, at least temporarily. Each worker was given a rifle to keep handy. This doomed the Indians' way of life and diminished the herd of buffalo that would not cross the tracks that had been laid.[30]

When spring arrived and the Missouri River rose enough to accommodate the river traffic, the Casement brothers, Jack and Dan, who had been appointed by Durant to be in charge of laying track, went to work. By early June 1866, the track extended a hundred miles from Omaha, satisfying one of the requirements stated in the Railway Act of 1864.

By late July, they reached Grand Island, 153 miles from the home base. News of this fast-moving construction was heralded by the editor of a Massachusetts newspaper, Samuel Bowles as well as by Bayard Taylor, a well-known travel writer. The *Cincinnati Gazette* said, "There is nothing connected with the Union Pacific Railroad that is not wonderful. In one sense, the road is as great an achievement as the war and as grand a triumph."[31]

In August, *The New York Times* wrote that the new town of Kearney was "small, but vigorous and promising," predicting that "she will be a rich and busy city someday."[32] Many of the problems had been worked out over the first six months of 1866. Workers came on their own from hearing of the steady work available, the good food served on a regular basis, and relatively cheap room and board for $5.00 a week while being paid from $2.50 to $4.00 per day, depending on the type of work they did.[33]

There were added inducements like fresh tobacco for every mile of track or more laid in one day. If they laid two miles a day, Dan Casement offered double wages.[34] By the end of August, the end of track was fifteen miles beyond Kearney, a total distance of 205 miles from Omaha.[35] On October 6, the end of track was 247 miles from Omaha, and Doc Durant invited many notable people, including five senators and twelve representatives and others including Robert Todd Lincoln, Abe's son, to accompany him in grand style. He had ordered for himself, from the Pullman Palace Car Company, a very fancy car with extravagant specifications—a director's car.

Other fancy cars were added for the reporters and guests, including the *Lincoln Car* which had been built for the president but had only been used for his funeral back to Illinois.[36]

By November 30, the Union Pacific had 305 miles of track from Omaha to ten miles past North Platte, Nebraska. It had been a good year with seven times more track laid than in the previous year.[37] Just as important, the surveyors had found the best route westward: first to Julesburg on the Colorado-Nebraska border then through Nebraska to Wyoming, below the Laramie Mountains and up the valley to cross the Medicine Bow Mountains and to head almost straight west to the Rocky Mountains.[38]

By 1866, the Union Pacific was employing as many as eight thousand men, one thousand of them working on the end of track. Of those men, some three hundred freed slaves also worked.[39] Supplying this large a group required four locomotives, with ten cars to a locomotive, to haul the rails, ties, bridging, fastenings, fuel, food, and supplies.[40] But it worked well.

When the settlers first came to the colonies, they thought that the only good land to grow things was where the trees grew. They worked hard to cut down the trees that they used to build their houses and worked even harder to remove the stumps so they could begin planting. When they moved west over the Allegheny Mountains after they had won their independence, they found groves of trees but also large areas of prairie where the ground was fertile but almost impossible to plow.

As early as 1819, Jethro Wood had developed a cast-iron plow, and John Lane introduced a steel-bladed plow-share—a part of a plow that cuts the furrow—in 1833. But the most popular and most used steel plow was introduced in 1837 by John Deere.[41] The farmers of Indiana and Illinois proved that the tough but fertile soil of their states could be plowed and used to grow many types of crops. The same was true in Iowa and Missouri. When the Homestead Act of 1862 passed, families could purchase a quarter section of land at the very reasonable price of $1.25 per acre.

Men who wanted to farm for themselves rushed to Nebraska as the Union Pacific was being built. So many came to that state that by 1867, there were enough people for Nebraska to become a state long before it was expected to be. When there was no wood to build houses, they improvised and made sod homes.

Central Pacific: While the Union Pacific was able to build over three hundred miles of track by the end of 1866, the Central Pacific had the challenge of laying track continuously up a grade that would be almost impossible. In spite of that, Collis Huntington wanted to change the Pacific Railway Act of 1864 so that the Central Pacific would not be limited to 150 miles east of the California-Nevada border as the farthest it could build.[42]

To accomplish this, Huntington hired Richard Franchot, an ex-congressman and former Union general to represent the Central Pacific's interest in Congress. He was the first paid lobbyist but would not be the last to spread money to influence votes of members of the House of Representatives as well as senators. What Huntington wanted was a chance to compete with the Union Pacific. The directors of the Union Pacific did not fight this attempt as they did not think that the Central Pacific could get to the California-Nevada border before they could. The amendment to the railroad bill was approved overwhelmingly and signed by President Johnson on July 3, 1866.[43]

The winter of 1865-1866 was the wettest on record. There was five feet of snow on New Year's Day, and in March more sleet and snow; and the storms lasted until the end of May 1866.[44]

By the spring of 1866, Crocker and Strobridge had hired over ten thousand workers, with eight thousand being Chinese. The biggest challenge was the Summit Tunnel, the longest of the twelve tunnels that would have to be blasted to make the route passable for the locomotives and the trains they would be pulling. The summit tunnel was 1,659 feet long, over a third of mile, and as much as 124 feet below the surface of the mountain it was to go through.

Montague made the decision to drill a shaft down the middle from the top of the mountain so that the Chinese could drill and blast in four different directions—from each end and from the middle outward in both directions. They took a cannibalized locomotive and *dragged* it to the top to serve as a hoist for pulling up the blasted granite and lowering the timber to be used to shore up the blasted tunnel. The drilling from the top of the summit to where the workers could begin drilling the tunnel took six weeks, and the job of actually drilling and blasting the tunnel started December 19, 1866.

When Crocker decided to hire more experienced miners, he hired Cornish men from Virginia City, Nevada. Crocker pitted the Chinese against the Cornish miners, and the Chinese outworked the Cornish men who quit after a week.[45]

The Chinese were using great amounts of black powder, so Crocker and Strobridge decided to try nitroglycerin, which had been invented in Italy in 1847 and refined in the 1860s by Alfred Nobel of Sweden. Though five times more powerful than black powder, it was too dangerous and caused too many accidents.[46]

The decision to begin surveying beyond the Summit Tunnel even while they were drilling was to keep men employed and working, but also they wanted to get to Nevada and go east as far and as fast as they could. The first survey was through a very desolate part of Nevada east of Reno. Samuel Bowles, the editor from Massachusetts who had praised the Union Pacific, had crossed the continent and found a route that paralleled the Humboldt River where the land was fertile with both wood and water. He championed this route, and Crocker chose it.[47]

Butler Ives surveyed two approaches from the source of the Humboldt River in the Ruby Mountains and selected the north route around the Great Salt Lake, across Bear River, then south along the base of the Wasatch Range to Weber Canyon.[48]

By November 5, the end of track reached Emigrant Gap, only eight miles west of Cisco, California, and twenty-one miles from the summit. On December 31, the Central Pacific ran from Sacramento to Cisco, a distance of ninety-two miles. Work continued on the tunnels during the winter months by three shifts of men, some eight thousand—mostly Chinese. A large group of men had been working three hundred miles beyond the end of track. Twelve tunnels would be completed by the spring of 1867, except the Summit Tunnel. That would be finished by September 1867.[49] Truly, a miracle had been accomplished, but there was still further work to be done the next year.

1867 CHALLENGING PROGRESS

Union Pacific: If the winter of 1865-66 was one of the wettest for the Central Pacific Railroad, the winter of 1866-67 was one of the coldest in the nineteenth century.[50] The construction crews headed by the Casement brothers wanted to begin in February, but everything was frozen, including the Missouri River. There were severe storms in March, and in early April, the heavy rains destroyed over twenty miles of track east of Grand Island and damaged track up and down the line from North Platte back to Fremont.[51]

Finally in May, surveyor Arthur Ferguson tried to begin work but was stopped when the wagons became mired in the mud, and then the Indians began attacking the men and running off the livestock. Dodge pleaded with General Sherman for protection by the military, but Sherman could not promise much in that way because enlistments were down.[52]

In spite of the weather and Indian problems, construction started in mid-April and continued. The track was to run to Julesburg, Colorado, then break away from the Platte River they had been following from Omaha and follow the Lodgepole Creek, a tributary of the North Platte River in Wyoming.[53]

With better than a year's experience, the graders and track layers moved efficiently. Construction trains were *twenty miles long.* The laying of track was down to a science.

A wagon with rails would be emptied by carrying them to a place that would be the next connection. Right behind them came the gaugers to make sure the rails were exactly four feet eight and a half inches apart, the exact width decided by Lincoln much earlier, and then the spikers and bolter to connect the rails with one another with fishplates.[54] Maury Klein, the author of *Union Pacific,* a history of the railroad, probably said it best in describing the cooperation the men showed for the project and for each other:

> What unites them all is a fierce determination not to let down those coming behind. Every party is bent on holding up its end. The men will not be outstripped by those pushing on ahead or chasing from behind. No one will know the names of thousands who provided the brawn, but the greatest accomplishment of all will be theirs: they built the railroad.[55]

The attacks by Indians continued. In June, L. L. Hills, one of Dodge's surveyors was caught by a band of Arapahos and shot with arrows. J. M. Eddy, a young, nineteen-year old helper, rallied the men and drove off the Indians. Hills died, but when Dodge heard what Eddy had done and that he had served under Dodge in the Civil War at the age of sixteen, Dodge promoted him and he became Dodge's assistant. Eddy stayed with the UP and eventually became the general manager of the Union Pacific.[56]

A month later, Percy Brown, another of Dodge's surveyors, was in western Nebraska, looking for the Continental Divide. Caught by the Sioux, Brown was wounded in the abdomen. When he fell, he begged his assistant to shoot him before they rode off. But his men did not leave; instead, they released their horses, and the Indians chased after the horses. The men made a litter with their carbines and carried Brown to a stage station where he died peacefully without complaint.[57]

As the building of the railroad reached farther west, they had to pause in the middle of winter. When they stopped at North Platte, men increased the population from almost nothing to five thousand. Crafty men from Chicago invested in tents and lumber. They provided gambling dens, prostitution, taverns, music halls, hastily erected hotels, and occasionally a restaurant.[58]

The railroad workers were only too glad to spend their hard-earned money on these vices. Some unknown person gave this enterprise the name of *Hell on Wheels*. When the weather permitted the rebuilding of the railroad and reached Julesburg, some sixty miles farther west, the *Hell on Wheels* moved there also. But when Dodge found they had taken up land that belonged to the UP, he sent Jack Casement, a teetotaler, to remove them. When the gamblers refused to pay or move, Casement ordered his two hundred men to open fire. When Dodge came into town, he asked what happened, and Casement took him to a nearby hill that had become the town's cemetery. He said, "General, they all died but bought peace. Julesburg has been quiet since."[59]

Dodge had the authority to establish townsites and selected a place about forty miles west of the Nebraska-Wyoming border. In honor of the major tribe of the region, he named it Cheyenne. It was where the plains first met the mountains at an elevation of just over six thousand feet. So ideal was its location that years later, trains would run north to Montana and south to Denver, and Interstate Highways I-80 and I-25 today parallel these railroad routes.[60]

Dodge went on to Fort Sanders and shortly after laid out another town that was called Laramie. Meanwhile there were still raids by the Indians, and President Johnson appointed a Peace Commission, headed by General Sherman, to hold a big conference in North Platte with as many tribes as wanted to parley in September. Sherman made a speech. He told the Indians:

> This railroad will be built, and if you are damaged [by it] we must pay you in full, and if your young men will interfere, the Great Father, who out of love for you, withheld his soldiers, will let loose his young men and you will be swept away . . . We will build iron roads, and you cannot stop the

locomotives any more than you can stop the sun or the moon, and you must submit, and do the best you can.[61]

Pawnee Killer, the chief of the Cheyenne, walked out of the council in a rage. Casement and his track layers were almost to the Nebraska-Wyoming border, and by the beginning of November, they were within a few miles of Cheyenne.[62]

On November 16, 1867, the lead article of the *Chicago Tribune* read, "Dated Cheyenne 11/14/67; Yesterday at 5 o'clock in the afternoon, track-laying on the UP was completed to the city of Cheyenne."[63] Casement went into winter camp, pleased that the Union Pacific stretched from Omaha, Nebraska, to Cheyenne, Wyoming, a distance of nearly five hundred miles.

Interesting also was the fact that Mrs. Elizabeth Cady Stanton and Ms. Susan B. Anthony had come by train to Omaha where they gave lectures in favor of women suffrage, according to the same *Chicago Tribune* of November 14.[64] America was starting to grow in many ways.

Central Pacific: In 1867, the CP was still struggling to get through the Sierra Mountains and therefore not collecting any money from the government as the UP was doing for each mile of completed track.[65]

The Chinese were working in eight-hour shifts every day, drilling into the mountain face, stopping only for tea or when the holes were deep enough—eighteen inches or better—to place powder and light a fuse. Then after the explosion, they would repeat the process until it was necessary to remove the blasted rock away. The progress was between six and twelve *inches* a day.[66]

There were over forty storms that winter, but the most severe was the one that lasted from February 18 to February 22, when six more feet of snow fell, followed by five days of raging wind. Then another snowstorm from February 27 to March 2 dumped four more feet of snow. Twenty Chinese disappeared when a snow slide swept them away, their bodies found in the spring. Nineteen were killed on the east side of the summit, and many others simply vanished.[67]

Keeping the route free of snow was not only a problem, it was expensive. Stanford suggested to Crocker that building snowsheds over the track in the vulnerable places would, in the end, save time and money. Lewis Clements, one of the men who replaced Ted Judah, designed the snowsheds that eventually covered nearly fifty miles of track.[68]

In spite of that, the pace was too slow, and Crocker again considered using nitroglycerin. They hired a Scottish chemist to mix the ingredients—nitric acid, glycerin and sulfuric acid—that was brought up the mountain separately. It was much cheaper, and the Chinese slowly became accustomed to using it but later became careless. It was eight times more powerful than black powder, increasing the distance blasted through the long mountain each day from one foot or less to over four feet each day.[69]

While eight-thousand Chinese worked on the tunnels, another three-thousand were grading and laying track east of the summit. The surveyors, in the meantime, were as far east as the Great Salt Lake. By the spring, they were meeting up with the surveyors from the Union Pacific.[70]

Both the UP and the CP sent *spies* to find out how each other was doing. The CP tried to convince the UP that going through the mountains would be another two years, hoping that Durant would not be in such a hurry building the Union Pacific west. But when Durant found out that the CP was laying track beyond the summit, Durant said he would put an injunction on the CP to prevent any dodging of the summit that was to be completed first. Crocker commented that "this was ridiculous." The CP sent *spies* to find out what was being done in the UP's company office. It was obvious that the Union Pacific was winning the race, and Crocker felt like resigning.[71]

As if the Central Pacific did not have enough to worry about, in May, the Chinese went on strike, asking for $40 a month though they had been given a raise shortly before that from $31 to $35 a month. The CP tried to recruit freedmen, but that was not possible. When the Chinese raised their demand to $45, Crocker cut off their provisions. They suffered, and on July 1, 1867, the Chinese went back to work. When the Chinese leaders wanted a reduction in hours and a 25¢ per month more, Crocker said no.[72]

In August 1867 E. B. Crocker, Charles Crocker's brother sent a telegram to Huntington, "Summit Tunnel broke through at 4 P.M. Toot your horn."[73] It was only a single light in a small hole, but the breakthrough had been made. Drilling and digging from opposite ends, the summit had been breached, and Clement had done the impossible—over seven thousand feet above sea level—the two facing had met in the middle of the summit and were off by only *two inches*. It came out exactly where Ted Judah had said it should be done. It had taken almost a year of drilling, blasting and digging by thousands of Chinese and their foremen without the aid of any kind of mechanical or electrical device. Some had predicted it was a three-year job, but they were proved wrong. It was truly a great moment in American history![74]

The Central Pacific had only built thirty mile of track in 1867, but what miles they were! Stephen Ambrose said it best:

> They have transported all their material around South America or through
> Central America. They have overcome lawsuits, opposition, ridicule, evil
> prophecies, monetary uncertainty, and losses. They had organized a vast
> laboring force, drilled long tunnels, shoveled away snow, set up sawmills,
> hauled locomotives and cars and twenty tons of iron over the mountains by
> ox team. Nothing came easy. But they have done what other capitalists and
> politicians and ordinary folks thought impossible, drilled tunnels through
> the Sierra Nevada, most of all the tunnel at the summit.[75]

1868 ACCELERATED PROGRESS

Union Pacific: Progress was accelerated in the year 1868. Former General Dodge set his sights on building five hundred miles to Salt Lake City then still farther west to Ogden, then hopefully to Humbolt Wells in the northeastern corner of Nevada where he hoped to meet the Central Pacific.

Everything began to fall into place. Dodge had surveyed through Wyoming, Utah, and Nevada. The Chicago and Northwestern Railroad had reached Council Bluff, and a temporary bridge over the Missouri River made it possible to bring all the needed supplies that the Casement brothers were waiting for with sufficient men; all of whom were waiting for the weather to clear.[76] In the Black Hills was sufficient good timber to supply the needed ties and bridges that would have to be built.

Even the financing was a positive factor. From Omaha to Cheyenne, the UP had received from the Railway Act of 1864, $16,000 worth of government bonds for every mile of completed track. But as the track layers entered the mountains, they received $40,000 in bonds for every mile of track.[77]

The telegraph made it possible to not only relay progress daily from Sam Reed, construction superintendent, back to Omaha but also put in the needed orders for the anticipated supplies.

The weather broke in early April, and the tracklayers reached Sherman Summit, the highest point on the entire transcontinental railroad—8,242 feet above sea level—on April 7.[78]

About ten miles beyond Sherman Summit was a small creek called Dale Creek. It was down in a valley, and a bridge like none other would have to be constructed. The bridge would have to be 126 feet *above* the creek bed, and be seven hundred feet long. It would have to be able to carry a locomotive, its tender, and either passenger cars or freight cars while crossing the bridge with the Wyoming winds blowing. It was one of the greatest engineering feats of the century.[79]

The next hurdle was a bridge across the North Platte River. This was the branch of the Platte River that people had followed who made the trek of the Oregon Trail as early as 1841. The trail went up to what is now Casper, Wyoming, where there was fresh water. The bridge over the north branch was finished July 15.[80]

Not everything went perfectly. There were frequent accidents during the construction and even when track was laid. The other problem was the Indians. They would attack different groups of workers—surveyors, graders, and tracklayers. They had muzzle-loading rifles, and the problem grew serious until the Springfield rifle, invented in 1867, was supplied to the army and the workers. This major modification of the rifle was that it was loaded in the breech rather than the muzzle—the method used by the earliest colonist and the soldiers during the Revolutionary War, the War of 1812, the Mexican War as well as in the Civil War. It was the greatest improvement since the rifle had been invented.[81]

In the summer of 1868, a herd of eight hundred Texas cattle were brought by trail near the town of North Platte. Two years later, there were seven thousand cattle and even some sheep.[82] The first cattle town had been established, and the West was beginning to be tamed.

The route planned by the surveyors went west through the Wyoming desert from Rawlins to Green River. Rawlins had been named for General John Rawlins, General Grant's aide during the war. The bad water found in the desert caused boiler malfunctions in the locomotives until the UP learned how to apply a chemical process to the water that made it safe to use.[83]

Thomas "Doc" Durant was probably the most unscrupulous person connected with the Union Pacific. To make money, he took the profits from the government bonds for himself and his fellow trustees. He not only wanted to be rich as Rockefeller, Carnegie, and Vanderbilt but he wanted the power and a place in history.

He knew his biggest competition for being remembered was Grenville Dodge. Durant had hired Dodge with the stipulation that Dodge would have complete control of everything—surveying, grading, tracklaying, and overall construction. But Durant hired Silas Seymour, brother of Governor Horatio Seymour. The brothers had recommended Ted Judah to the Big Four of the CP back in 1853. Durant issued a general order that Consulting Engineer Silas Seymour's orders were to be obeyed, not Dodge's. Seymour made surveys different from Dodge's.

When General U. S. Grant, the Republican nominee for the presidency, along with General Sherman and Sheridan, visited Fort Sanders—a fort halfway between Laramie and Dale Creek—Dodge was in Salt Lake City. When Dodge was summoned by telegraph to join them, he charted a stagecoach to the end of track and arrived in Laramie for the meeting.[84]

At the meeting, Durant attacked Dodge on his choice of route for the UP and registered other complaints. Grant, who had remembered Dodge for his excellent work during the war at Shiloh and Corinth, asked Dodge, "What will you do about it?" Dodge replied, "If Durant or anybody connected with the Union Pacific or anybody connected with the government changes my line, I'll quit the road." With that, Durant withdrew all of his objections to Dodge.[85]

In August, the track was thirty miles past the North Platte River bridge, and on September 21, they reached the Green River. By early November, the end of track was nearly nine hundred miles from Omaha. A new town sprang up—Bear River City—just short of the Wyoming-Utah border, and with it another *Hell on Wheels*.[86]

The Mormons. Joseph Smith, founder of the Mormons (Church of the Latter-Day Saints of Jesus Christ) at Fayette, New York, in 1830, moved his flock to Nauvoo, Illinois, along the Mississippi River. When Joseph Smith and his brother were killed while they were in Carthage, Brigham Young became their leader and took the Mormons first to Council Bluffs in 1846 and then on a most difficult journey ending in Utah where he proclaimed, "This is the place." The year was 1847, and Salt Lake City was founded.

Brigham Young had an early interest in having a railroad reach his beloved town and played a large role in seeing it come true. During the Civil War, Doc Durant of the Union Pacific contacted Young about the best route to the West. Young sent his son, Joseph, to survey the land in eastern Utah and selected the same one later chosen by Grenville Dodge—Echo Creek and Weber Canyon. When UP surveyor Samuel Reed saw the route in 1864, he confirmed that it was the most favorable route from Bear Creek, Wyoming.[87]

Two factors came together in the spring of 1868. Durant needed graders well ahead of the tracklayers who had reached the Utah-Wyoming border. The Mormons had men looking for work due to the plague of grasshoppers that had destroyed the newly planted crops. Silas Seymour and Sam Reed negotiated a contract with Brigham Young. By the end of May 1868, Reed requested tools for five thousand willing workers. They came not only from the devastated fields but from as far away as England where converts to the Mormon religion made their way first to New York and then to Salt Lake City. Over three thousand new Mormons came ready to work.[88]

In the early summer, Dodge came to Salt Lake City and informed Young that the Union Pacific was going to go north of the Salt Lake and not go through Salt Lake City and around the south end of the lake. Young approached the Central Pacific, but to no avail as their surveyor, Butler Ives, had already decided the north route was best.[89]

In spite of this decision not to go through Salt Lake City, the Mormons kept their word and did as good a job as the Chinese in grading the land they had been assigned. In addition to grading and building bridges, they had to dig tunnels—a total of four. The longest was 772 feet long; the other three were 508 feet, 297 feet, and 215 feet in length. The total length of the four tunnels, 1,792 feet, was slightly longer than the Summit Tunnel that the CP had to dig through in the Sierra Nevada Mountains—1,659 feet.[90] But the Summit Tunnel was only one of *twelve* tunnels that the Central Pacific had to blast and dig out.

Central Pacific: Charles Crocker, in charge of construction, promised Stanford, Huntington, and Hopkins he would build a mile of track a day.[91]

In the middle of April, Construction Superintendent Strobridge moved thousands of Chinese from their grading job in Nevada back to the snowbound region above Donner Lake where removal of snow was necessary before track could be laid. Snow as deep as thirty feet required picks and shovels as well as blasting powder.[92] When the snow melted enough, plus the shoveling and blasting, work could begin on covering the track with the snowsheds. It would require thirty-seven total miles of sheds at a cost of over $2 million.[93]

The amendment to the Railway Act of 1864 allowed both the UP and the CP to grade three hundred miles ahead of the end of track and, upon completion of acceptable grade, to collect two-thirds of the subsidy government bonds before the track was laid. But most important, before either could be done, there had to be a continuous track—not a problem for the Union Pacific, but a big one for the Central Pacific.[94] The snow removal and shed building would be a top priority for the CP.

Once the graders were out of the mountains, track could be laid at the rate of a mile a day even though it had to go through the Nevada desert. Just inside the Nevada border, Crocker named a town after a Civil War general that was killed at the Battle of South Mountain in September of 1862. His name was Jesse Lee Reno.[95]

On May 1, the CP completed the track lying between Truckee, California, and Reno, Nevada, but the gap between Cisco and the tunnel number 12, the last link to be completed between Sacramento and the end of track in Nevada, was still to be finished. This gap was closed a month and a half later on June 15, 1868, and Crocker sent a telegram to Huntington, "The track is connected across the mountains. We have 167 continuous miles laid.[96]

At Truckee, the fresh and abundant meadows had provided sufficient feed for the earlier pioneers' cattle and horses. This was good news. Crocker didn't hesitate—he sent five carloads of supplies with ten cars in each train. When unloaded, they quickly returned to Sacramento for additional loads.[97]

After Truckee, the Central Pacific had to cross one-hundred miles of Nevada desert. Water for horses, men, and the locomotives had to come from the Truckee River—and carried in semiconical wooden vats on the flat cars.[98] One good thing about the desert was that it was flat with very little grade to overcome. During July and August, the tracklayers were able to lay down forty-six miles of additional track.[99] By September 3, the total miles of track from Sacramento were 307 miles.[100] By the end of October, the Central Pacific had reached Winnemucca, Nevada. By December 3, the CP had a total of 445 miles from Sacramento.[101] The total for the year was 362 miles, almost exactly what Crocker had promised.[102]

The Union Pacific had lain nearly 900 miles of track, and the Central Pacific had laid half of that, *but what a half it was.*

On November 9, 1868, Leland Stanford bargained with Brigham Young and got him to agree to work on the route from Ogden to Monument Point, north of the Great Salt Lake. The Mormons worked literally night and day but had to cease in December when the weather was so cold, the frozen earth could not be graded.[103]

Dodge had brought the Union Pacific clear across Wyoming when work had to cease in November 1868 due to the cold. Crocker had to stop his construction for the same reason. The year 1869 was going to be a year that both lines—the CP and the UP—would race to get as much complete mileage as possible before the historic meeting.

RAILROAD IMPROVEMENTS

In 1867, steel rails, rather than iron, were beginning to be manufactured, which would prolong the life of railroad tracks. They were first used in 1870. In 1868, George Westinghouse invented a movable device for switching a train from one track to another. In the same year, he invented an air brake for railway cars, which acted automatically in case of accidents. It was quickly adopted by nearly all railways worldwide. He received a patent for this lifesaving device in 1872.[104]

OTHER IMPROVEMENTS AND CHANGES

Ground wood pulp was first used in making paper in 1867. On May 30, 1868, John A. Logan, national commander of the Grand Army of the Republic chose that date as Decoration Day, when the cemeteries would be decorated to honor those who had fallen during the Civil War. On June 23, 1868, Christopher Latham Sholes, a Wisconsin journalist, received a patent for an invention he called the typewriter. On June 25, 1868, North and South Carolina, Georgia, Florida, Alabama, and Louisiana were readmitted into the Union. In a way, it was a small step in the needed reconciliation for the nation that was not yet one hundred years old.

On October 11, 1868, Thomas Alva Edison filed papers for his first invention, an electrical voice recorder to speed tabulation of votes in Congress. It was rejected.

The November election of 1868 was not even close. The Republicans had chosen Ulysses S. Grant, the hero of the Civil War. The Democrats selected Horatio Seymour of New York. It was Seymour and his brother who had been instrumental in getting Ted Judah to go to California to start the Central Pacific. Grant was well liked and well known. When the ballots had been counted, Grant had 3,012,833 votes to Seymour's 2,703,249. Grant won 214 electoral votes, while Seymour could only muster 80.[105]

1869 EVER THE TRAINS SHALL MEET

Mark Twain (Samuel Langhorne Clemens) was at the same conference as was Englishman Rudyard Kipling around the turn of the century. Kipling authored such famous stories as *The Light that Failed, Barrack-Room Ballad, Jungle Book, Captains Courageous,* and for the Diamond Jubilee for Queen Victoria, he wrote the hymn "The Recessional."[106]

When Kipling came to the podium to speak, there was a folded note handed to him on which the front of the note said, "Not true." Inside the note was the first line of a ten-verse ballad that Kipling had written in 1890:

"Oh, East is East, and West is West, and never the twain shall meet."[107]

The year 1869 would be a watermark year for the United States. There were many improvements politically, socially, and most certainly in the field of transportation. But there were also problems.

The Fifteenth Amendment to the Constitution was adopted by Congress on February 26, 1868. It would be sent to the states for ratification and become law February 3, 1870, after three-fourths of the states had ratified it, according to

Article V of the U.S. Constitution. Virginia, Texas, Mississippi, and Georgia were forced to ratify this amendment as a condition of restoration to the Union. It gave the right to vote to all citizens regardless of race, color, or previous servitude. It did *not* give women the right to vote. They would have to wait over *fifty years,* until 1920 for their right to vote with the ratification of the Nineteenth Amendment on August 18, 1920. But they did not sit still till then. Women suffrage was established in Wyoming in 1869, and on November 24, 1869, women from twenty-one states met in Cleveland, Ohio, to draft plans for the organization of the American Woman Suffrage Association. They did more than just meet, they planned. In the next presidential election on November 5, 1872, Suffragette Susan B. Anthony was fined $100 for attempting to vote in a presidential election.[108]

Also in 1869, the National Prohibition Party was organized at a convention held in Chicago. This group would grow over the years, and fifty years later would persuade the Congress to adopt the Eighteenth Amendment on January 16, 1919, which prohibited the manufacture, sale, or transportation of intoxicating liquors with the United States. It would be repealed fourteen years later with the Twenty-first amendment on December 5, 1933.

Congress passed the eight-hour work day for federal employees. On June 8, 1869, Ives McGaffey of Chicago obtained a patent for the first vacuum cleaner. It was the start of making life a little easier for the women. The first intercollegiate football game was played between Princeton and Rutgers on November 6, 1869. Rutgers won 6 to 4.

The invention of the refrigerator car on January 16, 1868 by William Davis of Detroit, Michigan, would be a big boom to transporting perishable goods across the country.[109]

But first the transcontinental railroad had to be completed.

PROBLEMS, PROBLEMS, AND MORE PROBLEMS

In the last year of construction, there were more and different problems that would slow the construction of the last miles. They included financial problems, lack of materials, costly laying of track, weather, the CP and UP working alongside each other in a wasted effort, strikes, bosses arguing among themselves, and even politics. President Johnson had favored the CP but would be leaving office on March 4, when Grant would be sworn in as the eighteenth president, and he knew well the men who had been with the Union Pacific from its beginning, especially Grenville Dodge. Grant would certainly give them every benefit he could.[110]

By the middle of February 1869, the CP had laid continuous track from Sacramento to twenty miles past Wells, Nevada. The UP was twenty miles past Ogden, Utah, but had not finished its longest tunnel of 772 feet. While they continued to blast the tunnel with over one thousand kegs of black powder, they temporarily bypassed the tunnel with a flimsy temporary track over the ridge.[111]

On April 9, Huntington and Dodge met in Washington, D.C. Huntington made the initial offer to buy the Union Pacific track between Promontory Summit and Ogden for $4,000,000. Dodge accepted, and it was agreed that the two lines would meet at the basin at Promontory Summit. Both lines would stop grading or laying track past that point.[112]

By April 23, the two lines were less than fifty miles apart. Crocker wanted to beat the UP's claim of laying eight miles of track in a single day. They planned with extensive preparations, and Crocker bet Durant that the CP could lay ten miles offtrack in a single day. Durant accepted, and after a day's delay due to a locomotive running off the track, the CP started at 7:15 a.m.—sunrise, April 28, 1869. The leaders of the UP—Durant, Dodge, Reed, and Seymour—came to watch. Nearly twelve hours later, at 7:00 p.m., the Central Pacific had laid ten miles and fifty-six feet of track. That record has stood and would never be matched.[113]

Two days later, April 30, the Central Pacific had reached Promontory Summit, 690 miles from Sacramento. The Union Pacific had to build a tremendous trestle over eighty-five feet high and four hundred feet long, and the work went slowly.[114]

The Big Four of the CP and the board of directors for the UP agreed that the day for the momentous meeting of the two lines would be May 8. Each line sent its dignitaries on May 6 toward Promontory Summit for the historic meeting. The UP made it almost to Piedmont, just east of the Wyoming-Utah border, when shots rang out, and the train had to halt due to ties piled up on the track. A mob of three hundred or so men, all workers for the UP, uncoupled the engine from the officials' car and had the engineer pull ahead after the track was cleared.

Durant came out and demanded to know what they wanted. The spokesman said they wanted their backpay, which was months overdue and something that Durant was noted for doing—not paying. He was taken to a telegraph station where he wired Oakes Ames in Boston to send $200,000. The money arrived and was distributed among the men. Dodge, always suspicious of Durant as well as Oakes Ames, really believed the whole incident was a setup.[115]

The CP had left Sacramento with two trains, the second being Stanford's special train carrying Stanford, the chief justice of California, the governor of Arizona, and other guests. They also carried the last spike—made of gold—and the last tie. As they proceeded up one of the summits, the train had to stop abruptly. Chinese were cutting timber, and after the first train went by, not knowing about the second train, felled a log that tumbled down and lay across the track. The engine was damaged, so word was sent by telegraph to hold the first train until Stanford's fancy coach could be attached. They arrived at Promontory on Friday, May 7. The UP train was held up by heavy rains that damaged the Devil's Gate Bridge, and they wouldn't arrive until May 10.[116]

Since May 8 was to be the day of joining the two lines, Sacramento and San Francisco held their celebrations after they were informed of the delay. There were bands, canons firing, and long parades in both cities. The celebration lasted three days, Saturday through Monday, May 8, 9, and 10.[117]

Both Crocker of the CP and Dodge of the UP has the same idea. If they built a track siding, they could claim terminal rights. Crocker, always one to carefully plan an operation, got all the equipment needed—rails, ties, spikes, bolts, and fishplates ready to go with the Chinese worker. Planning to start work on the siding early Monday morning before the celebration that was scheduled for 11:00 a.m., Crocker found that Dodge had already completed the job, working through the night of Sunday and the early hours of Monday. Dodge's men, led by Casement, were there to greet Crocker's Chinese.[118]

Stephen Ambrose in his book, *Nothing Like It in the World*, said it best in describing how the world would hear and know that the two Pacific railroads had been joined:

> Some decisions on what to do had been made earlier, including the two most important ones. One was to have a telegraph wire attached to the Golden Spike, with another to the sledgehammer. When the Golden Spike was tapped in, the telegraph lines would send the message all around the country.
>
> If everything worked, this would be a wholly new event in the world. People from New York, Philadelphia, Boston, Charleston, and all across the East Coast, people in Chicago, St. Louis, Milwaukee, New Orleans and all across the midsection of the country, people in San Francisco, Sacramento, Seattle, Los Angeles, all across the West Coast, even people in Montreal, Halifax, Nova Scotia, and London, England would participate, by listening, in the same event. What people of the radio and later the television age came to take for granted was here taking place for the first time. At the moment it happened it would be known, simultaneously, everywhere in the United States, Canada, and England.
>
> The second decision was to have Hart, Russell, and Colonel Savage of Salt Lake City free to roam, take whatever pictures they liked, ordering men to get into this or that pose . . . Thanks to that arrangement, some of the most famous photographs in American History were taken.[119]

Another interesting and authoritative account is described in F.E. Shearer's book, *The Pacific Tourist*. An illustrated Guide to the Pacific R.R. and California, and Pleasure Resorts Across the Continent:

DRIVING THE LAST SPIKE AT PROMONTORY POINT
The Great Railroad Wedding—Driving the Last Spike

American history, in its triumph of skill, labor, and genius, knows no event of greater thrilling interest, than the scene which attended the driving of the last spike, which united the East and West with bands of iron. First of great enterprises since the world's known history began—that gigantic task of joining the two great oceans with bands of steel, over which thousands of iron monsters are destined to labor for unnumbered years, bearing to this young country continued wealth and prosperity. The completion of a project so grand in conception, so successful in execution, and likely to prove so fruitful and rich in promise, was worthy of world wide celebrity.

Upon the 10 of May, 1869, the rival roads approached each other, and the two lengths of rails were lifted for the day's work. At 8:00 a.m., the spectators began to arrive; at quarter to 9:00 a.m., the whistle of the Central Pacific Railroad is heard, and the first train arrives, bringing a large number of passengers. Then two additional trains arrive on the Union Pacific Railroad, from the East. At a quarter of 11:00 a.m., the Chinese workmen commence leveling the bed of the road, with picks and shovels, preparatory to placing the ties. At a quarter past eleven the Governor's train (Governor Stanford) arrived. The engine was gaily decorated with little flags and ribbons-red, white and blue. The last tie is put in place—eight feet long, eight inches wide and six inches thick. It was made of California laurel, finely polished, and ornamented with silver escutcheon, bearing the following inscription:

"The last tie laid on the Pacific Railroad, May 10ᵗʰ 1869."

Then follow the names of the directors and officers of the Central Pacific Company, and the presenters of the tie.

The exact point of contact of the road was 1,085.8 miles west from Omaha, which allowed 690 miles to the Central Pacific Railroad, for Sacramento, for their portion of the work. The engine Jupiter, of the Central Pacific Railroad, and the engine 119 of the Union Pacific Railroad, moved up to within thirty feet of each other.

Just before noon the announcement was sent to Washington, that the driving of the *last spike* of the railroad which connected the Atlantic and the Pacific, would be communicated to all the telegraph offices in the country the instant the work was done, and instantly a large crowd gathered around the offices of the Western Union Telegraph Company to receive the welcome news.

The manager of the company placed a magnetic ball in a conspicuous position, where all present could witness the performance, and connected the same with the main lines, notifying the various offices of the country that he was ready. New Orleans, New York and Boston instantly answered "Ready".

In San Francisco, the wires were connected with the fire-alarm in the tower, where the heavy ring of the ball might spread the news immediately over the city, as quick as the event was completed.

Waiting for some time in impatience, at last came this message from Promontory Point, at 2:27 p.m.

"Almost ready, hats off, prayer is being offered."

A silence for the prayer ensued; at 2:40 p.m., the bell tapped again, and the officer at Promontory said:

"We have got done praying, the spike is about to be presented"

Chicago replied. *"We understand, all are ready in the East."*
From Promontory Point, *"All is ready now; the spike will soon be driven. The signal will be three dots for the commencement of the blows."*

For a moment the instrument was silent, and then the hammer of the magnet tapped the bell, *one, two, three,* the signal. Another pause of a few seconds, and the lightning came flashing eastward, 2,400 miles to Washington; and the blows of the hammer on the spike were repeated instantly in telegraphic accents upon the bell of the Capitol. At 2:47 p.m., Promontory Point gave the signal, *Done;* and the great American continent was successfully spanned. Immediately thereafter, flashed over the line the following official announcement to the Associated Press:

"Promontory Summit, Utah, May 10th. THE LAST RAIL IS LAID!
THE LAST SPIKE IS DRIVEN! THE PACIFIC RAILROAD IS
COMPLETED! *The point of junction is 1,086 miles west of Missouri
River, and 690 miles east of Sacramento City.'*
Leland Stanford
Central Pacific Railroad.

T.C. Durant
Sidney Dillon
John Duff   Union Pacific Railroad

A curious incident, connected with the laying of the last rails, has been little noticed hitherto. Two lengths of rails, 56 feet, had been omitted. The Union Pacific people brought up their pair of rails, and the work of placing them was done by Europeans. The Central Pacific people then laid their pair of rails, the labor being performed by Mongolians. The foremen, in both cases, were Americans. Here, near the center of the great American Continent, were representatives of Asia, Europe, and America—America directing and controlling.[120]

Professor Guy B. Johnson, author of *John Henry: Tracking Down a Negro Legend* (Chapel Hill, 1929), wrote:

I prefer to believe that (1) there was a Negro steel driver named John Henry at Big Bend Tunnel, that (2) he competed with a steam drill in a test of practicability of the device, and that (3) he probably died soon after the contest, perhaps from fever.

The Big Bend Tunnel on the Chesapeake and Ohio Railroad, nine miles east of Hinton, West Virginia, was under construction from 1870 to 1872.

JOHN HENRY[121]

When John Henry was a little babe,
    A-holding his mama's hand,
Says, "If I live till I'm twenty-one
    I'm going to make a steel-driving, man my babe,
    I'm going to make a steel-driving man.

When John Henry was a little boy,
    A-sitting on his father's knee.
Says, "This Big Bend Tunnel on the C. & O. Road
    Is going to be the death of me, my babe,
    Is going to be the death of me."

John he made a steel-driving man,
  They took him to the tunnel to drive;
He drove so hard he broke his heart,
  He laid down his hammer and died, my babe.
  He laid down his hammer and died.

O now John Henry is a steel-driving man,
  He belongs to a steel-driving crew,
And every time his hammer comes down,
  You can see the steel walking through, my babe,
  You can see the steel walking through.

The steel drill standing on the right-hand side,
  John Henry standing on the left;
He says, "I'll beat that steam drill down,
  Or I'll die with my hammer in my breast, my babe,
  Or I'll die with my hammer in my breast.

He places his drill on the top of the rock,
  The steam drill standing close at hand;
He beat it down one inch and a half
  And laid down this hammer like a man, my babe,
  And laid down his hammer like a man.
Johnny looked up to his boss-man and said,
  "O boss-man, how can it be?

AMERICA SHOWS THE WORLD WHAT IT CAN ACCOMPLISH

With the Civil War horrors slowly fading, the United States began to realize the potential it possessed. When the transcontinental railroad was first conceived, there were many who thought it could not be done. When given the go ahead by President Lincoln and the Congress, a deadline was set for its completion—July 1, 1876—three days before the hundredth anniversary of the country. It was accomplished seven years and two months before that deadline. From 1861 to 1869, Americans could be proud. The same could not be said for the next eight years—1869 to 1877.

CHAPTER XIV

FOR THE MOST PART, A SORRY CHAPTER IN OUR HISTORY
1869-1877

ULYSSES S. GRANT EIGHTEENTH PRESIDENT

Two momentous events bookended Grant's two terms in office. One was the opening of the transcontinental railroad on May 10, 1869, and the other was the Centennial Exposition held in Philadelphia in the summer of 1876 to mark the one hundredth anniversary of the United States.

In between those two events, there were many acts of violence, ill-conceived federal acts, corruption, financial panic, and scandals. President Grant, with no political background or savvy, was too honest and too trusting to suspect the financial and political corruption in any way. His real character of honesty and trust had been displayed in many ways since he had graduated from West Point in 1843.

He served faithfully, if not conspicuously, in the Mexican War from 1846 to 1848. Married to the love of his life, Julia Dent, Grant took her everywhere he was stationed, but when ordered to California in 1852, he missed her so badly that he resigned in 1854.

Together they tried their hand at farming in Missouri. When that failed, Grant was not too proud to try selling wood in winter on the streets of St. Louis. When all else failed, he was not ashamed of asking his father for a job in his harness shop in Galena, Illinois.

In 1861, Grant was asked to take charge of enlistments that came into Galena and took them to the capital, Springfield, where Governor Yates needed someone to bring order out of chaos. He took the job seriously and was recognized for his diligence and given command of troops and promoted, first to colonel and then brigadier general. When he was successful in capturing Fort Henry and Fort

Donelson in Kentucky, it was one of the few victories the North could claim in the first year of the war.

His superior, Major General Halleck, claimed the victories as his own, accusing Grant of inefficiency and drunkenness, and relieved him. When his replacement injured his leg, Grant was returned to command and won two successful battles at Corinth and Shiloh. Lincoln's answer to Grant's critics who wanted him relieved was, "I can't spare the man, he fights." [1]

In March of 1863, to satisfy the many critics of Grant, Lincoln sent a number of people to observe Grant's generalship. They included a former newspaper reporter, Illinois adjutant general, a congressman, and a governor. None could find fault with Grant and gave a favorable assessment of Grant's abilities to a pleased President Lincoln.

After many failed to bring decisive victories to the Union in the east, Lincoln selected Grant after his victory at Vicksburg. Given the opportunity of being the general in chief, Grant wasted no time in decisive and important decisions. He replaced Halleck who had wanted him court-martialed in the early years of the war. Grant made Halleck his chief of staff as an indication of how Grant dealt with those who were opposed to his view on the war.

Taking over the army of the Potomac from General Meade, Grant put him as his second in command. He also dealt with politically appointed generals who left a lot to be desired as far as generalship was concerned. Grant appointed known leaders and friends to high posts, including William T. Sherman in charge of the Western campaign, and Phil Sheridan to head the union cavalry.

When Robert E. Lee accepted Grant's conditions for surrender on April 9, 1865, Ulysses S. Grant's magnanimous attitude came through when he stopped his troops from cheering with his order, "The war is over—the rebels are our countrymen again."[2]

When he met with General Lee, Grant was most gracious and permitted Lee's soldiers to keep their horses or mules for the farming they would need to survive. When General Lee remarked that his troops had not had any food, Grant did not hesitate; and when Lee said he needed food for twenty-five *thousand* starving men, Grant immediately authorized that food be made available.[3]

In the fall of 1865, after the Civil War ended, then-president Andrew Johnson asked five well-respected men, including Grant, to make observations of the conditions in the South. Grant's response was an honest and forthright appraisal of what he observed.[4]

In the fall of 1868, Grant was elected with an overwhelming majority in both the popular vote as well as the Electoral College. On March 4, 1869, President Grant gave his inaugural address. Once again, the honest attitude came through when he said:

> I have taken this oath without mental reservation and with the determination to do the best of my ability all that is required of me. The

responsibilities of the position I feel, but accept them without fear. The office has come to me unsought; I commence its duties untrammeled, I bring to it a conscious desire and determination to fill it to the best of my ability to the satisfaction of the people.[5]

It was not the last time Grant would express himself with such sincerity, but until that time, there was much that went wrong during his presidency that was not his fault.

On May 10, 1869 the Union Pacific and Central Pacific were joined at Promontory Summit in north Central Utah. Two weeks after that great event, President Grant made it very clear that he wanted Doc Durant forced off the board of directors of the Union Pacific, and it was done.[6]

As early as 1868, Durant and his fellow trustees began handing out profits from their Crédit Mobilier to themselves. In January of that year, the dividend was 80 percent of their stock. In June, they made three distributions to stock holders, totaling nearly $5 million to themselves and other stockholders.[7]

Granville Dodge must have known of this and probably alerted President Grant with whom he had a genuine relationship. But that was just the tip of the iceberg, which would come to light in 1872.

On September 24, 1869, two financiers—Jay Gould and James Fisk—brought on the famous *Black Friday* panic when they put a raid on the gold market. It resulted in financial ruin for hundreds, if not thousands.[8]

The year 1870 saw some important events take place. Women in the Utah Territory gained the right to vote on February 14. On February 23, Mississippi was formally readmitted into the Union. In May, the Senate turned down Grant's request to annex Santo Domingo. On July 15, Georgia became the last of the Confederate states to be readmitted to the Union. On July 24, the first railroad car from the Pacific coast reached New York City, ushering in transcontinental train service. December 12 saw Joseph Rainey, of South Carolina, become the first black to be sworn into the U.S. House of Representatives, undoubtedly as a result of the Fifteenth Amendment ratified the early part of 1870.

The Fifteenth Amendment was adopted by Congress on February 26, 1868, eight months before Grant's election, and a little more than a year before he took office. The ratification by three-fourths of the states took until February 3, 1870. It forced four Southern states—Texas, Virginia, Mississippi, and Georgia—to ratify the amendment as a condition of being restored to the Union.[9]

AMENDMENT XV[10]

Section 1. The right of citizens of the United States to vote shall not be denied or abridged by the United States or any State on account of race, color, or previous servitude.

Section 2. The Congress shall have the power to enforce this article by appropriate legislation.

The Fifteenth Amendment made it possible for the Negro to vote, and this resulted in the New Republican party in the Southern states. The state legislatures were filled with Negroes, carpetbaggers, and renegade Southern whites.

But the amendment also created serious problems. The many Southern states found themselves in their own civil war, which brought greater violence and corruption and, to make matters worse, was supported and sustained by the Forces Act of 1870 and 1871.

On October 8, 1871, the Chicago fire took place, killing 250 residents. It received a great amount of publicity, but the same was not true of the fire in Peshtigo, Wisconsin, on the *same* date that killed 1,192. That same year, the National Rifle Association was incorporated.

The South's answer to all theses problems was the establishment of the Ku Klux Klan to protect the innocent and cope with the disorder. Unfortunately, it got out of hand and soon became such a despicable group of fanatics that the federal government passed the Ku Klux Klan Act of 1871 and 1872 to suppress the Klan's activities, but the act did not really accomplish much. [11]

One bright spot in 1872 was President Grant signing legislation authorizing the creation of Yellowstone National Park—the country's first national park. The first of twenty-six national parks, Yellowstone's 3,426 square *miles* is larger than either the states of Delaware (2,370 sq. mi.) or Rhode Island (1,248 sq. mi).[12]

By 1872—seven years after the Civil War—the problems of the South were becoming a repeated old story and when the federal scandal broke, it helped to restore responsible government to the South, which also was aided by the Amnesty Act of 1872. [13]

The *New York Sun*'s headline on September 4, 1872 read:

THE KING OF FRAUDS
How the Credit Mobilier bought
Its Way Through Congress
COLOSSAL BRIBERY
Congressmen who Have Robbed
People, and who now Support
The National Robber
HOW SOME MEN GET FORTUNES[14]

This earthshaking news became the biggest scandal of the century. It would damage the reputation of the Union Pacific that would take years to be restored to some semblance of respectability. The Central Pacific did not escape the scandal, and officials of both the UP and CP were required to testify at hearings held by the House of Representatives. The hearings last a full six months.[15] Because of the length of the hearings, the scandal did not affect the election of 1872, except that Grant's vice president was not Schuyler Colfax.

The election was held on November 5, 1872. Suffragist Susan B. Anthony was fined $100 for attempting to vote in the election. Many Republicans did not think that Grant could be reelected due to the corruption with the railroads and Grant's harsh treatment of the South regarding reconstruction. Some broke away and nominated Horace Greeley, whom the Democrats also nominated.[16]

When the votes were counted, Grant received 3,597,132 popular votes, over 500,000 more votes than he received in 1868. Greeley received 2,834,125 votes. Shortly after the election, Horace Greeley died, and the Democrats nominated Thomas Hendricks before the Electoral College met. Grant received 185 electoral votes, and Hendricks received 42 with a scattering of 21 votes and 17 votes not even counted.[17]

Some very prominent people were involved and found to be part of defrauding the U.S. government. While the railroads could never have been built without the government's financial backing, which included land grants and loans in the form of bonds, men took advantage without any thought of remorse.

Oakes Ames, president of the Union Pacific and a member of Congress, had distributed Crédit Mobilier stock to such men as Representative James Garfield, a future president; James G. Blaine, another Representative who would become a presidential candidate against Grover Cleveland in the election of 1881; Representative James Brooks; and Schuyler Colfax, the vice president under Grant.

After half a year, the House of Representatives passed two very weak resolutions of censure. One was against Oakes Ames and the other against James brooks. Brooks died on May 1, 1873 and Oakes Ames died of shame a week later, May 8.

The Big Four of the Central Pacific became very rich from their deals in building the railroad but were never penalized in any way due to the fact that all their financial books had been burned, either accidentally or deliberately.[18]

If the corruption and scandal of the railroads was bad, even worse was the Panic of 1873. Overexpansion in industry, overinvestment in railroads and new lands, unstable currency, and overexpansion of credit accounted for the failures in banking, railroads, and private businesses. The Panic resulted in thousands of workers being let go.[19]

Also in 1873, the *Salary Grab Act* increased the salaries of all three branches of the federal government—executive, legislative, and judicial. The act provided for the salary increases in the term of the congressmen who were presently serving. There was such an outcry by the newspapers and its readers that Congress returned the pay increases and reduced their raises they had proposed.[20]

This problem would finally be corrected. Originally proposed as part of the Bill of Rights in 1791, it became the Twenty-seventh Amendment to the Constitution when it was ratified on May 7, 1992! Two hundred years to make things right!

AMENDMENT XXVII[21]

No law, varying the compensation for the services of the Senators and Representatives, shall take effect, until an election of Representatives shall have intervened.

In 1874, the Republican Party was symbolized by an elephant in a cartoon by Thomas Nast in *Harper's Weekly* magazine. The year 1874 saw the manufacturing of barbed wire begin.

Three other serious problems evolved during Grant's second term in which Grant had no connection. The first involved a group of New York City political crooks under the leadership of William Tweed, better known as *Boss* Tweed. He organized some politicians that were bent on plundering the New York treasury. From 1869 to 1871, he and his followers stole over $100,000,000. Exposed, Tweed was sentenced to twelve years in prison. Released on legal technicalities then rearrested, he escaped first to Cuba and then to Spain. Again captured, he was imprisoned in the United States in 1876 and died two years later.[22]

On January 26, 1875, George F. Green of Kalamazoo, Michigan, patented the electric dental drill. On March 1, Congress passed the Civil Rights Act of 1873. "All Americans, regardless of race, color of skin, or persuasion" have equal access to public facilities. The United States Supreme Court declared it *unconstitutional!*

The second problem in 1875 dealt with what became the *Whiskey Ring*. It was an agreement between distillers and officers of the internal revenue to rob the government of tax on whiskey. Some suspected Grant's private secretary, Babcock, as one of the ring leaders, but it was never proven. [23]

The third fraud involved Grant's secretary of war, William Belknap. He was impeached on the charge of selling army supply contracts and appointments to frontier trading posts. He resigned to escape trial, but it was another black mark in Grant's administration. [24]

On the plus side, 1876 found Colorado joining the Union. It would be known as the Centennial State.

THREE HISTORIC EVENTS

From May to November 1876, the first *World's Fair* was held in a suburb of Philadelphia. Titled the International Centennial Exhibition of 1876, it cost $11,000,000. It officially commemorated the one hundredth anniversary of the issuing of the Declaration of Independence. The exhibit emphasized mining and manufacturing.[25]

On March 10, 1876, Alexander Graham Bell uttered the first intelligent words transmitted over his invention, when he said, "Mr. Watson, come here, I want you."

TERRITORIAL GROWTH

COLONIAL PERIOD: 1775

Original Thirteen Colonies

Other British territories

UNITED STATES: 1790–1920

States

State claims

Special status areas

Territories

Unorganized territories

Claimed areas

Foreign areas

1803 Dates of territorial acquisitions
1805 Dates of initial territorial organization
(1809) Dates of latest change within given time period
1812 Dates of admission to the Union

Map scale 1:34,000,000

Compiled by H. George Stoll, Hammond Incorporated, 1967;
rev. by U.S. Geological Survey, 1970

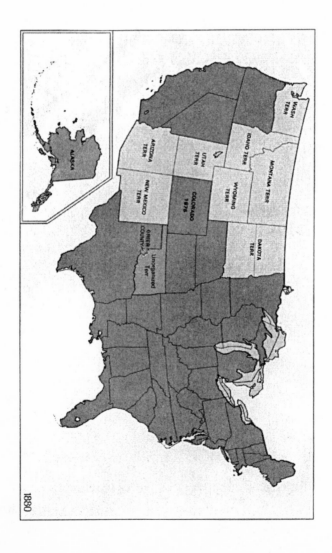

1880

WASH. TERR

IDAHO TERR

MONTANA TERR

ARIZONA TERR

UTAH TERR

WYOMING TERR

NEW MEXICO TERR

COLORADO 1876

DAKOTA TERR

GREER COUNTY

Unorganized Terr.

ALASKA

At the Centennial Exposition, this young inventor, aged twenty-nine who was born in Scotland and became a U.S. citizen, demonstrated his invention of the transmission of sound by electricity. He called it the telephone. It was considered little more than a toy.

The next year, 1877, Alexander Graham Bell founded the Bell Telephone Company.[26] It was, no doubt, one of the most important inventions of the nineteenth century. Today, millions of adults and children carry with them a portable *cell phone* that not only transmits voices throughout the country, and even the world, but also can transmit pictures at the same time.

The third historic event happened on June 25, 1876. George Armstrong Custer was the last in his class at West Point when he graduated in 1861. He distinguished himself in the Civil War, rising to the rank of major general. After the war, he was returned to a lower rank. Sent West to fight Indians, he was later sent to round up hostile Sioux and Cheyenne. His attempted surprise attack on a much-larger Indian force was unsuccessful. The 2,500 Indians, led by Chiefs Sitting Bull and Crazy Horse massacred Custer's 266 officers and men at the Battle of Little Big Horn in the Montana Territory.[27]

What is undoubtedly unique to Americans is their ability to take a tragedy like Custer's and turn it into a heroic effort. They did it with Nathan Hale's last words, "I only regret that I have but one life to lose for my country." John Paul Jones's famous "I have not yet begun to fight" inspired his ship to win the battle against the British frigate *Serapis* on September 23, 1779. The Battle of the Alamo resulted in the killing of all 187 Americans by the Mexicans but brought the battle cry, "Remember the Alamo," and the victory over the Mexicans at the Battle of San Jacinto on April 21, 1836. Ten years later, in the Mexican-American War, Zachary Taylor was outnumbered twenty thousand to four thousand. When Santa Anna asked for his surrender, Taylor's reply, "Tell him to go to hell," inspired an American victory.

GRANT'S FINAL ACT

Grant finished his two terms with a message to Congress, given on December 5, 1876.

> In submitting my eighth and last annual message to Congress, it seems proper that I refer to and to some degree recapitulate the events and official acts of the past eight years.

> Mistakes have been made, as all can see and I admit, but it seem to me oftener in the selection made of the assistants appointed to and in carrying out the various duties of administering the government—in nearly every case selected without a personal acquaintance with the appointee, but upon

recommendation of the representatives chosen directly by the people. It is impossible, where so many trusts are to be allotted that the right parties should be chosen in every instance. History shows that no administration from the time of Washington to the present has been free from these mistakes. But I leave comparisons to history, claiming only that I have acted in every instance from a conscientious desire to do what was right, constitutional, within the law, and for the very best interests of the whole people. Failures have been errors of judgment, not of intent.[28]

No other president, before or since, ever made such a magnanimous apology for acts of which he had no direct connection. One accomplishment that could not be taken away from Ulysses S. Grant was that he served two full terms. He was the first to do so since Andrew Jackson served from 1829 to 1837. The next president to serve two full terms was from 1913 to 1921 when Woodrow Wilson was president of the United States.

PART E

PRESIDENTS FACE PROBLEMS AND CHALLENGES: AMERICA MOVES TOWARD BECOMING A WORLD POWER 1877-1913

The colonists were so determined in their quest for independence that they fought a war to achieve it. Lincoln had no choice but to declare war to preserve the Union. The longest period of peace was from April 9, 1865 to April 21, 1898—a period of thirty-three years with no major wars.

Yet during that time, another group of Americans would *fight* for their rights. These rights, fought for by American workers, included the right to organize, bargain, protest, and if necessary, strike for recognition a living wage and job security. Later would come demands for health benefits.

While workers made their wishes known as early as 1834, and the first labor union was formed in 1845, it was the Panic of 1857 that caused a shutdown of shoe manufacturing. The first nationwide strike was in 1877, during Rutherford B. Hayes's one and only term as president. During Hayes's term, Thomas Edison would invent the light bulb.

James Garfield replaced Hayes, but only served four months before being assassinated. Vice President Chester Arthur, when he became president, worked to continue the civil service reform that Hayes had started. While Arthur was president, the Brooklyn Bridge was completed as was the Northern Pacific Railroad. Chicago saw the first *skyscraper* built (it was ten stories), and the cornerstone of the Statue of Liberty was laid in New York.

Nine months after Grover Cleveland became president, his vice president Thomas Hendricks died. This prompted the Presidential Succession Act of 1896.

Strikes would become a weapon that organized labor used when all else failed. The first large and effective union was the American Federation of Labor, founded in 1886. The railway workers throughout the country were demanding an eight-hour day. It would be the first large strike, involving one hundred thousand workers. Over the years, there would be many such strikes. This strike eventually led to the Haymarket riot in Chicago.

The year 1886 saw the Apache Indian chief Geronimo surrender and the Statue of Liberty unveiled. In 1888, the National Geographic Society was incorporated, the first roll-film camera patented, and the Washington Monument opened to the public.

When Benjamin Harrison became president in 1889, he got the Sherman Antitrust Act passed in July 1890. The act received support from both parties, but was not rigidly enforced. It would be strengthened and used by President Theodore Roosevelt many times before the end of his term in 1909.

Not all the union protests were successful. The steel strike in 1892 was over wages, but ended with the steel workers union being destroyed. The Pullman strike in 1894 was led by Eugene Debs. That same year, New York tailors protested the sweatshops they worked in. In 1897, coal miners would strike for an eight-hour work day. When the coal miners pay was cut in 1902, President Theodore Roosevelt intervened.

On June 4, 1896 Henry Ford made a successful run of his first automobile. In 1908, he brought out the Model T.

1898 was the start of the Spanish-American War, the shortest war in American history. With the turn of the century, America began taking a leading role in world activities. The Boxer Rebellion took place in August 1890. An attempted revolt in the Philippines was finally ended in 1901. In September of 1901, William McKinley was assassinated, and Theodore Roosevelt became the twenty-sixth president of the United States.

Important and positive events included the World's Columbian Exposition in Chicago in 1903. A visitor to that fair, Katharine Lee Bates, went farther West and composed "America the Beautiful." That same year, a treaty with Columbia would be the start of the Panama Canal. On December 17, 1903, two brothers made a successful first flight of a heavier-than-air machine, carrying one person.

William Howard Taft became president in 1909. He is best remembered for breaking up the giant Standard Oil Trust. The year 1912 saw Arizona and New Mexico become the forty-seventh and forty-eighth states. Henry Ford introduced the first assembly line in the manufacture of automobiles. The year 1913 saw two amendments added to the U.S. Constitution.

America had come of age and was recognized worldwide. No one could predict what the rest of the twentieth century would bring.

CHAPTER XV

HAYES, GARFIELD, ARTHUR, CLEVELAND, HARRISON AND CLEVELAND AGAIN 1877-1898

CLOSE ELECTIONS

P resident John Adams was elected president in 1796 with a very narrow majority of electoral votes—71 for Adams and 69 for Jefferson. Four years later Jefferson received 73 electoral votes, the same number as Aaron Burr, but the House of Representatives voted for Jefferson as president and Burr as vice president. There were no further complications in presidential elections until 1824 when John Quincy Adams, Andrew Jackson, Henry Clay, and W. H. Crawford split the total of 262 votes of the Electoral College, and no one received more than 50 percent of the Electoral College votes.

Once again the House of Representatives selected an Adams, even though Jackson had won the popular vote with 153,544 votes, while Adams had only 108,740 votes. That was the first election that counted the popular votes, but the Constitution specified that the determining factor was the electoral votes, according to Article II, Section 1 of the U.S. Constitution. [1]

There were no other close elections until 1876 when Rutherford B. Hayes ran against Samuel Tilden, both governors of their respective states, Hayes from Ohio and Tilden from New York. The popular vote went to Tilden by nearly 300,000 votes out of 8,336,798 total votes, but four states' electoral votes were in dispute. A very partial electoral commission awarded all the disputed votes to Hayes, and that gave him 185 electoral votes to Tilden's 184.

1877-1881 RUTHERFORD B. HAYES NINETEENTH PRESIDENT

Hayes grew up in Ohio, went to Kenyon College and then Harvard. At first a member of the Whig political party, he was an early supporter of the new Republican Party. During the Civil War, he entered as a major in the Twenty-third Ohio Regiment in 1861 and rose to the rank of major general by 1865, distinguishing himself as a leader and being wounded on four different occasions. He served in the House of Representatives for twelve years and then governor of Ohio for three terms. [2]

It might be said that the Compromise of 1877 helped to make him president. This agreement between four Southern states, whose electoral votes were in dispute, were awarded to Hayes in exchange for withdrawing all federal troops from Louisiana and South Carolina, the last two states still under *reconstruction*. This resulted in the Southern states electing all Democrat governors and senators, creating the *Solid South* that existed far into the twentieth century.[3] Federal troops left New Orleans April 24, 1877.

President Hayes's greatest contribution was reforming the civil service bureaucracy, which was needed. He issued an order in June of 1877 prohibiting government officials from taking part in management of political organizations. Those who disobeyed this order were suspended. The New York Customs House collector was Chester A. Arthur, who would later become the twenty-first president, was stripped of his responsibilities for his continued political dealings after the presidential order. Certain segments of the Republican Party were not at all pleased with his courageous move, and he was not renominated for the presidency in 1880.

The Panic of 1873 was still in effect in 1877, and businesses were stagnating. Thousands of laborers were out of work or only working part-time. The railroad workers of the Baltimore and Ohio Railroad went on strike when their pay was cut, and this affected other railway lines. But it was not the first strike ever called in the country.

THE GROWTH OF LABOR UNIONS

Labor unions had their beginning during the Jacksonian presidency. A citywide *trades' union,* composed of mechanics and women's shoe binders in and around Boston, declared their desire for equality in living conditions and schooling in 1834.

The Panic of 1837 brought forth more discontent among the working class. This stimulated the formation of the Federal Labor Reform Association in Lowell, Massachusetts, in 1845. [5]

In 1857, enough unrest among workers during the panic brought the shoe business to a standstill. After the Civil War, a movement for an eight-hour day was aided by the formation of the first national federation of unions, the National Labor Union. A three-month strike by one hundred thousand workers in New York was successful. [6]

In 1877, the railroad workers on the Baltimore and Ohio Railroad went on strike, determined to fight the wage cut from $1.75 a day for brakemen working twelve-hour days. The strike spread to Pittsburg, New York, Chicago, and St. Louis. [7]

Over one hundred thousand men were involved with strikes and riots everywhere in the country. State militia was ineffective, and federal troops were required to maintain order.[8] The railroads made some concessions, withdrawing the wage cuts; but more important, the strike had brought laborers from all over the country together in a common bond. It led to some important railroad legislation and was probably responsible for the creation of the American Federation of Labor as well as the labor-farmer parties that came about in the next two decades. [9]

SIGNIFICANT EVENTS IN THE 1870S

During the decade of the 1870s some very significant events took place. Henry Stanley, a well-respected newspaperman was sent to Central Africa to locate a missing physician-missionary. On November 10, Stanley found *his man* with the ever-famous statement, "Dr. Livingston, I presume." [10]

The year after the 1871 Chicago fire—a fire destroyed nearly one thousand buildings in Boston, Massachusetts on November 9, 1872. August 1, 1873 saw Andrew Hallidie successfully test a cable car he had designed for San Francisco's hills

On July 31, 1877 Thomas Edison took out a patent leading to the development of the phonograph. It was granted February 19, 1878. Later that year, on August 21, 1878, the American Bar Association was founded in Saratoga, New York.

William Tecumseh Sherman, the famous Civil War hero, stated in his graduation address to the Michigan Military Academy on June 19, 1879:

> I am tired and sick of war. Its glory is all moonshine. It is only those who neither fired a shot nor heard the shrieks and groans of the wounded who cry aloud for blood, more vengeance, and more dissolution. War is hell.[11]

1879 THOMAS ALVA EDISON 1847-1931

Thomas Edison had over one thousand patents, including ones for the first phonograph and the movie camera, but will always be remembered for the incandescent electric light.

How fortunate we are to have Edison's own description of the historic event that would change the world forever.

> We sent out and bought some cotton thread and carbonized it and made the first filament . . . We built the lamp and lighted it; it lit up, and in the

first few breathless minutes we measured its resistance quickly and found it was 275 ohm—all we wanted.

Then we sat down and looked at the lamp; we wanted to see how long it would burn. There was a problem solved—if the filament would last. The day was—let me see October 21, 1879. We sat and looked and the lamp continued to burn and the longer it burned the more fascinated we were. None of us could go to bed and there was no sleep for over forty hours; we sat and just watched it with anxiety growing into elation. It lasted about forty-five hours and then I said, "If it will burn forty hours now I know I can make it burn a hundred." (Thomas A. Edison, October 21, 1879)[12]

Three months later, on January 22, 1880, Thomas Edison received a patent for his electric incandescent lamp.

The significance of Edison's invention can only be appreciated when one considers what this brought about. Once it was shown that electricity could be changed into light, it eventually brought about a host of other uses of this marvelous source of energy. Electricity could be changed not only into light, but also sound, mechanical power, and heat as well as cooling. Edison could be credited with fundamentally changing the way people lived. Imagine a world without electric power—no refrigerators or freezers, no radio or television, no phonographs, no DVD or CD players, no movies, no air conditioners, and no computers. How dull life must have been before Edison came along. Alexander Graham Bell and Thomas Alva Edison—two great Americans—gave the world sound and light.

PRESIDENT HAYES'S LAST ACT

In President Hayes's last year, 1880, he gained approval from Congress to have a French business begin construction on the Panama Canal in spite of the Monroe Doctrine. Hayes was able to convince Congress to back the idea that had its beginning ten years before. President Grant's secretary of navy, George Robeson, sent a letter on January 10, 1870 to Commander Thomas Selfridge "to command an expedition to make a survey of the Isthmus of Darien to ascertain the point at which to cut a canal from the Atlantic to the Pacific Ocean.[13] The French, under the supervision of Ferdinand de Lesseps, had built and completed the Suez Canal in 1869.

Unfortunately, the French could not make it work, and it would take another two decades before construction would be underway.

On November 4, 1880, James and John Ritty of Dayton, Ohio, received a patent for their invention of a cash register. The year 1881 would see some important events. Kansas became the first state to adopt Prohibition, banning all alcoholic beverages. On May 21, Clara Barton founded the American Red Cross; and on July 20, Sioux

Indian leader Sitting Bull surrendered to the federal authorities. On August 31, the first US Open was played at Newport, Rhode Island.

1881 JAMES A. GARFIELD TWENTIETH PRESIDENT

Garfield was born in a log cabin near Cleveland, Ohio, on November 19, 1831. Contacting what appeared to be malaria, he recovered and then attended first Western Reserve Eclectic Institute and then William College in Massachusetts. He became an excellent public speaker, serving first as a preacher and then became a teacher at Western Reserve, which had been renamed Hiram College.

Extremely popular, Garfield became president of Hiram College at the age of twenty-six. With a fine reputation, he was elected to the Ohio State Senate two years later and then became an attorney in 1861. When the Civil War started, Garfield was appointed a colonel in the Forty-second Ohio Volunteer Infantry, and many of his former students followed him. Garfield displayed his heroic leadership in skirmishes and battles like Shiloh and Chickamauga.

Elected to the House of Representatives during the war, Lincoln encouraged Garfield to take his seat. He served for seventeen years. As chairman of the Military Affairs Committee, he established the Reserve Officer Training Corps (ROTC). In 1876, he served on the Electoral Commission that would determine who would receive the disputed electoral votes. He was instrumental in the investigation that led to Rutherford Hayes's election.

When Hayes decided not to run for reelection in 1880, three different factions of the Republican Party vied for the nomination. One wanted former President Ulysses Grant; another backed a well-known legislator from the State of Maine, James Blaine. The third was John Sherman who was President Hayes's secretary of treasury. James Garfield served as Sherman's campaign manger and gave a rousing nominating speech. At the convention, there were thirty-five ballots taken with no one gaining enough votes for the nomination. Finally, Blaine and Sherman both dropped out in favor of Garfield. To satisfy the people from New York, Chester Arthur, the Customs House collector that Hayes had fired during his term, was nominated for the vice presidency.

Garfield won the electoral vote by a significant margin: 214 to 155 for Winfield Scott Hancock. The popular vote was very close with Garfield winning by less than 10,000 votes out of nearly nine million total votes. Garfield selected James Blaine for secretary of state, and he served for four years before running for president against Cleveland in 1884.

Between March 4, 1881 and July 2, 1881, Garfield accomplished one important thing that would have a lasting effect. He appointed James Blaine for secretary of state. He needed approval of the Senate, according to Article II, Section 2 of the U.S. Constitution. Certain factions of the Republican Party did not approve, but Blaine was confirmed. This was the first step in reforming the patronage system and was further pursued by Garfield's successor that eventually led to the Civil Service Commission where appointments were made on merit rather than political favor.

A SECOND ASSASSINATION OF AN AMERICAN PRESIDENT

President Garfield was planning a trip to New England, and on July 2, 1881, while waiting in the Washington train station, Charles Guiteau, a fanatic, shot Garfield twice. The president was returned to the White House where a metal detector, invented by Alexander Graham Bell, located one of the bullets. The other could not be located because of interference with the metal bedsprings. This bullet caused infection and eventually death for President Garfield who died on September 19, 1881, ten weeks after he was shot.

Guiteau was convicted and hung for his crime, claiming that the Lord made him do it. His last words as he climbed the scaffold were, "I am going to the Lordy, I am so glad." [14]

1881-1885 CHESTER A. ARTHUR TWENTY-FIRST PRESIDENT

When Chester Arthur became president he was a widower. His wife, Ellen Herndon, an accomplished singer, had died of pneumonia in January 1880 at the age of forty-two. They had three children, the first only living to the age of two.

The day Garfield died, Chester Arthur took up the task that Garfield had started in fighting the spoils system. The National Civil Service Reform League was organized in 1881, and a law was passed in 1883. The Pendleton Act established a merit system for the national administration. It provided for all government employees to be placed in classified lists. Appointments were be made by competitive examination and forbidding recommendations to be made by congressmen. [15]

Another important, but unfair piece of legislation was the Chinese Exclusion Act of May 6, 1882, which provided that Chinese laborers would be excluded from entering the United States for a period of ten years. [16]

That same year, Thomas Edison built an electric power station on Pearl Street in New York City, and it went into operation on September 4, 1882.

The year 1883 saw the Brooklyn Bridge linking Manhattan with Brooklyn open on May 24. In September, the construction of the Northern Pacific Railroad across the northern part of the United States was completed with the driving of the last spike near Garrison, Montana, on September 8.

The world's first structure of ten stories was built in Chicago, Illinois, and completed May 1, 1884. It was called a skyscraper. That year, Alaska was organized as a territory.

In 1884, the Republicans were seeking a candidate other than Arthur who wanted the nomination for himself. They approached Civil War hero General William

T. Sherman who told the Republican Convention, "I will not accept if nominated and will not serve if elected." [17]

On August 5, 1884, the cornerstone of the Statue of Liberty was laid on Bedloe (now Liberty) Island at the entrance of the New York harbor. On December 6, army engineers completed construction of the Washington Monument.

Arthur supported appropriations for building new naval ships which improved the U.S. Navy to the extent that, a decade later, it was one of the world's most impressive naval forces.

One of Arthur's final acts was to dedicate the newly completed Washington Monument on February 27, 1885, five days before Grover Cleveland became president.

1885-1889 GROVER CLEVELAND TWENTY-SECOND PRESIDENT

Grover Cleveland had the distinction of being the only president to serve two nonconsecutive terms. He was born in 1837 in New Jersey, but the family moved to New York where his father, a Presbyterian minister, died in 1853. The family of nine children was in such bad straits that Grover gave up plans to go to college. Looking for work as he taught at a school for the blind, he went to Buffalo where he began working for his uncle.

With only a high school education, he studied and passed his bar examination in 1859. When the Civil War broke out two years later, Grover was caught in the military draft, but paid another man to take his place, which was legal under the Federal Conscription Act because he was supporting his family.

In 1870, he was elected county sheriff and did so well he was elected mayor of Buffalo in 1881. His record for honesty and efficiency brought him the nomination for governor of New York in 1882. In 1884 in Chicago, he won the nomination of his Democratic Party for president and was elected with 219 electoral votes against 182 electoral votes for the Republican nominee, James Blaine, who had been secretary of state for both President Garfield and President Arthur. The popular vote was very close with Cleveland polling 4,874,986 votes to Blaine's 4,851,981, a margin of only 23,005 votes out of 9,726,967.

President Cleveland took the oath of office as a bachelor. Later in his first term, he married Frances Folsom, a twenty-two-year old beauty, who was twenty-seven years younger than Cleveland. They were married in the White House, another first. American composer, John Philip Sousa, conducted the U.S. Marine band at the wedding reception.

Cleveland entered his first term with a great reputation and championed a civil service reform that did not seem to satisfy his democratic friends. During his first term, the Tenure of Office Act that had given President Johnson so much trouble was repealed.

The summer of 1885 saw the Statue of Liberty, a gift from the people of France to commemorate the United States' centennial, arrived in New York City aboard the French ship *Isère*. It had been designed by Frédéric A. Bartholdi, and the frame was designed by Alexandre Gustave Eiffel, who would design the tower in Paris in 1889. After the statue was constructed, it was then disassembled and brought to the United States. [18]

Former President Ulysses S. Grant died on July 23, 1885. He had been encouraged by Mark Twain to write his *Memoirs,* and he completed them a few weeks before his death. It became a best seller and made it possible for his widow, Julia, to live with financial security until her death in 1902.

The death of Cleveland's vice president, Thomas Hendricks, nine months after the inauguration, prompted the Presidential Succession Act of 1896. The law of 1792 regarding succession placed the president pro tempore and the Speaker of the House in line of succession. The 1886 law removed them from the line of succession and put members of the president's cabinet in line, after the vice president, starting with the secretary of state, the treasury followed by the secretary of war, attorney general, secretary of the navy and finally the secretary of interior. [19]

That remained the law of succession until the Twenty-fifth Amendment was ratified in 1967, where the president would nominate a vice president who would take the office after confirmation by both Houses of Congress. [20]

Strikes and lockouts continued in greater number, and on May 4, 1886, in what became known as the Haymarket riot in Chicago, at least ten Chicago police officers and labor demonstrators were killed when a bomb exploded in Haymarket Square during a rally for an eight-hour day.

On August 19, 1886, eight men were found guilty of murder in connection with the riot. Seven were sentenced to death and the eighth was sent to prison. Four were hanged, one committed suicide, and three were pardoned in 1893.

On September 4, 1886 Apache Indians, led by Geronimo surrendered to General Nelson Miles at Skelton Canyon, Arizona.

On October 28, the Statue of Liberty, a gift from the people of France, was unveiled in New York Harbor by President Cleveland. It had taken a year and four months to assemble on Bedloe Island. One hundred and fifty-one-feet high, it faced the ocean from where so many had come to America, and millions more would come to those same shores.

A Jewish girl, Emma Lazarus, who had been born in New York City in 1848, wanted to assist a national campaign for funds to construct the pedestal for the statue in 1883. She wrote her famous sonnet, "The New Colossus":

> Not like the brazen giant of Greek fame,
> With conquering limbs astride from land to land;
> Here at our sea-washed, sunset gates shall stand
> A mighty woman with a torch, whose flame
> Is the imprisoned lightning, and her name

Mother of Exiles. From her beacon-hand,
Glows world-wide welcome; her mild eyes command
The air-bridged harbor that twin cities frame.

"Keep, ancient land, your stories pomp" cries she
With silent lips,

"Give me your tired, your poor,
Your huddled masses yearning to free,
The wretched refuse of your teaming shore.
Send these the homeless, tempest-tossed to me:
I lift my lamp beside the golden door." [21]

These last five lines were inscribed on the book that the statue held in her hand.

On November 18, 1886, Chester Arthur, the twenty-first president, died in New York City. He was only fifty-six years old. That same year the American Federation of Labor (AFL) was founded in Columbus, Ohio. It would grow both in size and influence and be a great boon to millions of laborers.

After the Civil War, veterans were receiving pensions even if they had not seen any action or had even been dishonorably discharged. Cleveland vetoed over 230 private pension bills and picked up the nickname Veto President. [22]

In 1887, there was a surplus of $140,000,000 in the United States Treasury. Cleveland decided to lower the high protective tariff rates. His desire to reduce the unneeded revenue resulted in the Mills Bill, passed in 1888, providing for the reduction of protective duties.[23] These two events, the pension vetoes and the Mills Bill, was Cleveland's undoing, and he lost the 1888 election even though he received nearly 96,000 more votes than Benjamin Harrison. Again, the Constitution dictated that the Electoral College vote would determine the winner, and Harrison claimed the presidency with 233 electoral votes to Cleveland's 168. The next time a nominee won the presidency with fewer popular votes but had more electoral votes was the 2000 election between George W. Bush and Albert Gore.

The National Geographic Society was incorporated on January 27, 1888. It would be a great institution both in its publication and it explorations, and is still operating today. On September 4, 1888, George Eastman patented a roll-film camera and registered his *Kodak* trademark. On October 9 of that year, the Washington Monument was opened to the public.

1889-1893 BENJAMIN HARRISON TWENTY-THIRD PRESIDENT

Benjamin Harrison came from a very long line of famous Americans. His great-grandfather was one of the signers of the Declaration of Independence. His grandfather was William Henry Harrison, the ninth president of the United States, and his father served in Congress. With this background, Benjamin Harrison had much to live up to.

Born in Ohio in 1833, he graduated from the University of Miami in Ohio, where he met his wife, Caroline Lavinia Scott. A deeply religious man, he first considered the ministry but then chose law; and when they were married, they moved to Indiana where he opened a law practice in 1854. A very successful law practice also included his interests in politics where he campaigned for John Fremont in 1856 and Abraham Lincoln in 1860.

He became the city attorney for Indianapolis and later became secretary of the Republican State Central Committee. When the Civil War came, he was commissioned a colonel and put in charge of recruiting and training soldiers. Later in the war, he served under General William T. Sherman and distinguished himself in the Battle of Atlanta, eventually acquiring the rank of brigadier general.

After the war, he returned to Indiana and had further success as a lawyer, but lost in several elections until elected to the U.S. Senate by the Indiana Legislature in 1881 where he served until 1887. His famous name helped to get him the nomination for president.

He campaigned against Grover Cleveland on two issues. One was Harrison favored high tariffs to protect American business, and the other was that he was looked upon with favor by the Civil War veterans. Cleveland was the only president in the latter part of the nineteenth century not to have served in the Civil War.

Harrison was very effective, if not dynamic, as a president. He worked well with the Congress and had some very important legislation passed in his one term. The most significant piece of legislation was the Sherman Antitrust Act, passed on July 2, 1890. With the growth of corporations and trusts, and some very shady dealing within big business, there was a large demand for reform.

The government's first attempt to regulate trust and monopolies was vague, but it did help temporarily to slow the growing power of companies that were more concerned with profits than with people. [24]

The law was to penalize big monopolies that interfered with interstate or international commerce. The monopolies that were of major concern were the Sugar Trust, the Standard Oil Trust, and Armour's meatpacking company. Though the act passed with bipartisan support of Congress, it was not rigidly enforced, and the trusts soon found loopholes that let them reduce competition. [25]

A second piece of legislation that Harrison had promised in his campaign resulted in the McKinley Tariff Act, which placed duties on many imported items. In support of the Civil War veterans he authorized government funds for disabled veterans even if their injuries occurred after the war.

Harrison also faced a number of crises with international flavor. A conflict with Great Britain over fishing rights in the Bering Sea was settled by arbitration. An attack on American sailors in Chile brought an apology and reparations from the Chileans.

Harrison also had to deal with Italy when violence broke out in New Orleans where a policeman's death led to eleven Italians being murdered by an angry mob. Harrison denounced the killings and explained to the Italian government that wanted Harrison to intervene on the federal level that it was a matter for the State of Louisiana as required by the U.S. Constitution.

Harrison continued to expand the navy that President Arthur had initiated with sufficient appropriations. When a revolt broke out in Hawaii, Harrison signed a treaty with Queen Liliuokalani. He hoped to annex Hawaii as a navy base, but his successor, Grover Cleveland, withdrew the treaty of annexation. [26]

The Northern Pacific Railroad that had been completed in 1883 brought enough immigrants and emigrants to fill up four new states that were admitted the same year, 1889, and two more the following year. They were North and South Dakota, Montana and Washington first followed by Idaho and Wyoming the next year.

America was growing in both size and population. In the census of 1870, there were 39,818,449 people within the borders. In 1880, the population increased to 50,189,209. By 1890, there were 62,979,766 Americans. [27]

When Harrison became president in 1889, there were thirty-eight states. When he left office four years later there were forty-four states. More states were added during his one term than during any other presidents even those who served two terms.

IMPORTANT EVENTS DURING HARRISON'S PRESIDENCY

A number of events took place during Harrison's four years. Three months after his inauguration, the famous Johnstown, Pennsylvania, flood took the lives of 2,900 people after a dam collapsed. On August 13, 1889, William Gray of Herford, Connecticut, was granted a patent for the coin-operated telephone. The first jukebox made its debut in San Francisco on November 23, 1889.

On December 6, 1889, Jefferson Davis former president of the Confederate States of America, died at the age of eighty-one in New Orleans. Nearly a quarter of a century had passed since the end of the Civil War. No doubt many Southerners mourned his passing.

In 1890, Congress established the Sequoia National Park, and the Daughters of the American Revolution were founded in Washington. But an unforgivable tragedy occurred in December of that year. In North Dakota, Sitting Bull was shot down by agents of the United States Army. Shortly after his assassination, Chief Big Foot attempted to lead his people, mostly women and children, to safety on the Pine Ridge Reservation.

Twenty miles short of their destination, the federal troops corralled the Indians on a field at Wounded Knee Creek, South Dakota. In the last major conflict between Indians and troops of the U.S. Seventh Cavalry, three hundred Sioux Indians and thirty soldiers were killed. The Seventh Cavalry was the same unit that Sitting Bull and Crazy Horse had defeated at Little Big Horn back in 1876.

TERRITORIAL GROWTH

COLONIAL PERIOD: 1775

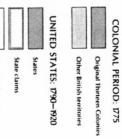

Original Thirteen Colonies

Other British territories

UNITED STATES: 1790–1920

States

State claims

Special status areas

Territories

Unorganized territories

Claimed areas

Foreign areas

1803 Dates of territorial acquisitions
1805 Dates of initial territorial organization
(1809) Dates of latest change within given time period
1812 Dates of admission to the Union

Map scale 1:34,000,000

Compiled by H. George Stoll, Hammond Incorporated, 1967;
rev. by U.S. Geological Survey, 1970

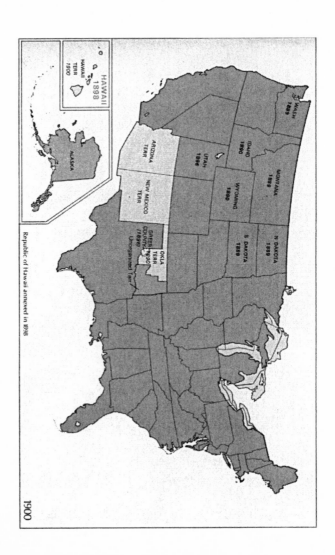

1900

Republic of Hawaii annexed in 1898

Labor problems started in 1892 when steel workers for the Carnegie Steel Company went on strike over a wage scale. Pinkerton detectives and, later, federal troops were used to put down violence and protect the Carnegie property. The Union that had called the strike, the Amalgamated Association of Iron and Steel Workers, was destroyed. The need for reform to help the workers was a ways off. [28]

On May 5, 1892, Congress passed the Chinese Exclusion Act, requiring Chinese in the United States to register or be deported. May 28 saw the Sierra Club organized in San Francisco and was incorporated June 4, 1892. On October 1, the University of Chicago opened its doors, and the first long-distance commercial telephone line was opened between New York and Chicago.

PROGRESS IN TRANSPORTATION AND GREAT INVENTIONS ARE A BEGINNING OF THINGS TO COME

The *early* part of the nineteenth century saw the federal government's internal improvement legislation help create a closer-knit nation with the building of canals like the Erie Canal in the East and the Illinois and Michigan Canal in the Midwest. The railroads, built after the Civil War, connected both coasts that would let many thousands travel the continent in less that a week, as well as transport them to fill in the new states.

The great invention of lighting by Edison sparked the nation to greater and greater ideas that would have a lasting effect. The telephone of 1876 was improved in a short fifteen-year period where people could talk halfway across the country. What waited were inventions, improvements, and changes that would make America a truly great nation.

Yes, there would be problems—big problems—to overcome. Women could not yet vote, laborers were not being paid what they were worth, and minorities were still being treated as second-class citizens. But given time, the right leaders, and a Congress with a conscience, most problems would be studied, debated, and eventually solved.

ELECTION OF 1892

The campaign of 1892 was not really a campaign at all. President Harrison's wife, Caroline was very ill, and Harrison stayed by her side, refusing to campaign. Out of respect, Grover Cleveland, the Democrat candidate, refused to campaign also. Caroline Harrison died October 25, 1892, a couple of weeks before the November election.

A third candidate, James Weaver, ran as a Populist Party candidate, representing many unhappy farmers and settlers. Cleveland won the election with 277 electoral votes to Harrison's 149 electoral votes. James Weaver was able to garner 22 electoral votes, but this had no direct effect on the outcome. Cleveland's popular vote was

5,556,918 while Harrison received 5,176,108 and Weaver's votes totaled 1,041,028. Cleveland's vice president was Adlai E. Stevenson, whose grandson would be the Democrat Party's presidential candidate twice against Dwight Eisenhower in 1952 and again in 1956.

1893-1897 GROVER CLEVELAND TWENTY-FOURTH PRESIDENT

Cleveland's second term as chief executive was filled with mostly problems that had started during Harrison's administration. The Panic of 1893 was a result of many factors, but chief among them was the problem with gold and silver.

Gold reserves were too low, and Cleveland called a special session of Congress to repeal the Silver Purchase Act of 1890, which had favored the purchase of practically the entire output of silver, a concession in return for Western support of the McKinley Tariff Act of 1890. The repeal was passed, but no legislation was initiated to protect the reserve of gold in any way. People began to horde their gold, businesses failed, banks closed, and silver mines were closed. [29]

THE 1893 PANIC BROUGHT ON UNEMPLOYMENT AND STIKES

By the winter of 1893-94, thousands were out of work; and in the spring of 1894, Jacob Coxey proposed to end the depression by federal relief through government-financed public work programs. (Sound familiar? Wait till 1933.) He led a group of five hundred to Washington., D.C., but was arrested for trespassing on the Capitol lawn. [30]

Workers in the Pullman Company went on strike in 1894 against pay cuts, and the strike spread to twenty-seven states, involving twenty-three railroads. There was much damage to railroad property: trains were stopped and the mails obstructed. Eugene Debs, born in Terre Haute, Indiana, became a fireman on the railway at the age of sixteen. He was responsible for organizing the men to form the American Railway Union in 1893 and led the strike in the Pullman workers' cause to improve working conditions as well as pay. He would be arrested and spend six months in jail for violating the ordinance that resulted in stopping the mails. Much more would be heard from this man in the years to come. Governor Altgeld of Illinois was sympathetic to the strikers and would not get involved, so Cleveland sent federal troops to stop the violence. This would cost him in the next election. [31]

On September 4, 1894, about twelve thousand New York tailors went on strike to protest the city's sweatshops.

In foreign affairs in 1893, Cleveland withdrew the Treaty for Annexation of Hawaii that President Harrison had proposed. In a dispute with Great Britain over a boundary argument between Venezuela and British Guinea, Cleveland invoked the Monroe Doctrine twice, and Britain finally conceded to arbitration. But Cleveland would not interfere with Cuba's struggle for independence from Spain. [32]

When the United States Treasury's gold reserve became very low, Cleveland sought help from wealthy industrialist, John Pierpont Morgan. He and a group of American and European bankers loaned the federal government the gold it need, and a tragedy was averted. [33]

Cleveland's wife, Frances Folsom Cleveland, gave birth to five children. Ruth, born in 1891, had a candy bar named after her—Baby Ruth. Esther, Marion, and Richard Cleveland were all born between 1893 and 1897, the first children to be born in the White House. Frances, the fifth child, was born in 1903 and lived to 1995. [34]

There were a few good things that happened during Cleveland's last term. On May 1, 1893, President Grover Cleveland opened the World's Columbian Exposition in Chicago.

Katharine Lee Bates, a professor of English at Wellesley College visited the World's Fair. She continued her travels and went to the Pacific coast and even ascended Pikes Peak with the aid of a mule cart. She was so taken with what she saw that she wrote a poem to show what a grand view she beheld. [35]

AMERICA THE BEAUTIFUL
Katharine Lee Bates

O beautiful for spacious skies,
    For amber waves of grain,
For purple mountains majesties
    Above the fruited plain.
America! America!
    God shed His grace on thee,
And crown thy good with brotherhood,
    From sea to shining sea.

O beautiful for pilgrim feet
    Whose stern impassioned stress,
A thorough-fare for freedom beat,
    Across the wilderness
America! America!
    God mend thine ev'ry flaw,
Confirm thy soul in self-control,
    Thy liberty in law!

O beautiful for heroes proved
    In liberating strife,
Who more than self their country loved,
    And mercy more than life!

America! America!
      May God thy gold refine,
Till all success be nobleness
      And every gain divine!

O beautiful for patriot dream
      That sees beyond the years
Thine alabaster cities gleam
      Undimmed by human tears!
America! America!
      God shed his grace on thee.
And crown thy good with brotherhood
      From sea to shining sea!

It was set to music by Samuel A. Ward, whose tune "Materna" made the song one of the great American hymns to be sung by adults and children alike. [36]

On July 18, 1893, the country's first eighteen-hole golf course opened in Wheaton, Illinois. On June 28, 1894 Congress made Labor Day a holiday, designating the first Monday in September. The Congress established the Bureau of Immigration on August 18, 1895.

On June 4, 1896, Henry Ford made a successful predawn test run of his horseless carriage, called a quadricyle, in Detroit. It would have an impact on transportation and all related factors that *no one* in the closing years of the nineteenth century could imagine. That same year, Utah was admitted into the Union as the forty-fifth state.

LITERARY AND ARTISTIC GREATS
THE LAST PART OF THE CENTURY

The last thirty-five years of the nineteenth century produced some of America's most-loved authors, poets, and artists. Mark Twain (1835-1910) is best remembered for his *Adventures of Tom Sawyer* and *Adventures of Huckleberry Finn,* but he wrote many others. (Francis) Bret Hart (1836-1902) gave us *Outcast of Poker Flat* and many others. Henry James (1847-1916) wrote *Daisy Miller* and Joel Harris (1848-1908) delighted us with his *Uncle Remus: His Songs and Sayings.* William Dean Howells was a prolific writer as well as editor of the *Atlantic Monthly.*

Great American artists include Winslow Homer (1836-1910) who gave us such beautiful paintings as *The Gulf Stream.* James Whistler's (1834-1903) most famous painting is of his mother; and Frederic Remington is best remembered for his paintings of cowboys and scenes of the American West.

In the field of music, Victor Herbert (1859-1924), was only thirty-four when he wrote his first light opera, *The Wizard of the Nile,* but his more famous works would come in the twentieth century. [37]

CLEVELAND'S LEGACY BROUGHT LEADERSHIP BACK TO THE EXECUTIVE BRANCH

Grover Cleveland's stand against high tariffs, radical economic policies, and his honesty brought much credit to him and helped the nation in a time of deep trouble. His leadership would be a beacon for the presidents that would follow.

For too long, the Congress had usurped the leadership role; but that was about to change, thanks to Cleveland. McKinley, Cleveland's successor, had very impressive credentials as did those who followed McKinley into the twentieth century.

FUTURE LEADERS AND THEIR QUALIFICATIONS

William McKinley, the last Civil War veteran to be president was also a congressman as well as governor of Ohio. In his second term, the vice president was Theodore Roosevelt who had many accomplishments to his credit. A Spanish-American War hero, author of over thirty books, police commissioner of New York City, assistant secretary of the navy, New York governor, and vice president of the United States made him well prepared for the most important job of his lifetime.

William Howard Taft would serve as U.S. solicitor general, governor of the Philippines, and secretary of war. After his presidency, he would serve as chief justice of the U.S. Supreme Court until his death in 1930. No other president achieved that high honor.

Woodrow Wilson, the first Democrat president since Cleveland, was a university president and the governor of New Jersey before being nominated on the forty-sixth ballot. His victory was due in part to there being three candidates for the office of president: Wilson, incumbent Taft, and former President Theodore Roosevelt.

These men not only had strong credentials but made bold and wise decisions that would bring credit to their country as well as themselves and would help make the United States one of the world powers.

CHAPTER XVI

STEPS TO BECOMING A WORLD POWER
1896-1909

ELECTION OF 1896

T wo new men came on the scene for the 1896 election. William McKinley was born in Niles, Ohio, in 1843, the seventh of nine children. He went to Allegheny College in Pennsylvania for a while, but illness made him return home where he worked as a postal clerk and part-time schoolteacher to make money.

When the Civil War started, he enlisted with the Twenty-third Voluntary Ohio Regiment. He served under Rutherford B. Hayes and rose through the ranks, attaining the rank of brevet major by the end of the war. He distinguished himself in several battles.

After the war, he attended Albany College and passed the bar exam in 1867. He married Ida Saxton in 1871, and their first child, Katherine, was born in December that same year. When his wife Ida became pregnant in 1873, their second daughter was born prematurely and died four months later. Two years later, their first daughter came down with typhoid fever and died a few weeks later. Most men would have been devastated, but McKinley worked even harder to cope with their loss.

William McKinley became an outstanding speaker and was elected to the House of Representatives in 1876. He was reelected each term through 1890, except for one term. While in Congress, he was responsible for the McKinley Tariff Act, which brought him national prominence. He next served as Ohio's governor from 1893 to 1897. His brilliant speaking skills at the 1892 Republican Convention brought many to consider him as a future candidate. His mentor, millionaire Mark Hanna, played a major role in getting him the nomination four years later[1].

The election was mostly about gold and silver. McKinley favored what was referred to as bimetallism—both gold and silver—but soon changed to just the gold standard. This brought him backing from the business community, and his stand on high tariffs offered a cautious approach to regaining prosperity. "Vote for McKinley and go back to work" was their campaign slogan. [2]

William Jennings Bryan was born in 1860 on the family farm near Salem, Illinois. He was educated at Illinois College in Jacksonville, Illinois, and in 1881 entered Chicago's Union College of Law. He became an excellent speaker and debater. He married Mary Baird in 1884, and the couple would have two children. They moved to Lincoln, Nebraska, where Bryan ran for Congress and won in 1891 and served until 1895. When he ran for the Senate, the mostly Republican Nebraska legislature would not confirm him. [3]

As an alternate delegate to the Democrat National Convention in Chicago, he gave a speech that so electrified the convention that he was nominated as their presidential candidate. His speech on July 8, 1896 ended with this statement:

> Having behind us the producing masses of this nation and the world, supported by the commercial interests, the laboring interests, and the toilers everywhere, we will answer their demand for a gold standard by saying to them: You shall not press down upon them the brow of labor their crown of thorns, you shall not crucify mankind upon a cross of gold.[4]

Bryan was also nominated by the Populist Party which represented people in the West and South who were faced with the Depression and the fear of powerful banking interests.

William McKinley won the election with 271 electoral votes to William Jennings Bryan getting 176 electoral votes. The popular vote was 7,104,799 for McKinley to 6,509,052 for Bryan.

1897-1901 WILLIAM MCKINLEY TWENTY-FIFTH PRESIDENT

McKinley and the Congress had selective high tariffs put on certain goods to help America's growing industries. Raw materials such as iron ore were not taxed, and this helped the growing steel industry.

America's ability to produce more efficiently agricultural products such as cotton, wheat, and tobacco allowed surpluses to be shipped overseas. Oil became a big export item in the 1880s and 1890s, and Standard Oil, controlled by the Rockefellers, accounted for 70 percent of the world oil production. [5]

He encouraged business by not attempting to control the growing monopolies, and with the gold rush of 1896 in the Klondike area of Alaska providing the necessary gold for backing the U.S. currency, prosperity returned for many, but not for all.

Immigrants poured into the country, and the population in 1890 of 62,979,766 climbed in ten years to 76,212,168, an increase of over 13,000,000.

Cities were not only overpopulated, but health concerns were a real problem for the millions of inhabitants that were crowded into tenement sections of the cities like New York and Chicago.

Workers were still not getting fair treatment. On September 11, 1897, a strike of coal miners in Pennsylvania, Ohio, and West Virginia ended with the miners winning an eight-hour day. That would set the stage for many others to seek the same.

YES, VIRGINIA . . .

The story goes that an eight-year-old girl by the name of Virginia O'Hanlon asked her father if there was a Santa Claus. Here was a question that had been asked of parents down through the ages. Virginia's father took an approach to the question that would go down in history. He told her to write the newspaper *New York Sun,* and if they said so, then it was true.

She wrote the *New York Sun* and pleaded. "Please tell me the truth, is there a Santa Claus?"

On September 21, 1897, the *New York Sun* published its famous editorial in which Francis P. Church answered eight-year-old Virginia O'Hanlon's question, "Is there a Santa Clause?"

> Yes, Virginia, there is a Santa Claus . . . Thank God! He lives forever. A thousand years from now, Virginia, nay, ten times ten thousand years from now, he will continue to make glad the hearts of children.[6]

When former President Cleveland withdrew the senate treaty of 1893, providing for the annexation of Hawaii, he denounced the method by which the Hawaiian revolution had been brought about. The Republic of Hawaii was established in July 1894 and was recognized by the United States. There was a request from Hawaii for annexation, and a treaty was concluded in 1897. While it was being debated in the United States Senate, as was necessary according to Article II, Section 2 of the U.S. Constitution, war broke out between the United States and Spain. The Hawaiian Islands were then annexed by joint resolution on July 7, 1898.[7] A formal treaty of sovereignty took place on August 12.

SPANISH-AMERICAN WAR

Cuba was discovered by Columbus on his first voyage to the new world, just after he discovered San Salvador. Spain controlled Cuba through the years, and when Spain declared war against Britain in 1762 in the Seven Years' War, also called the French and Indian War in America, Spain ceded Florida to England but retained Cuba as a colony.

Spain's inhumane treatment of the Cubans and enrichment for herself at the expense of Cuba's agriculture led to insurrection. The Ten Year's War—1868-1878—gained some concessions from Spain, but again in 1895, Spanish troops allowed inhumane treatment to prevail.

Cleveland had hesitated to invoke the Monroe Doctrine, but when McKinley became president, other events happened that would change the necessity to do more than just protest the treatment of Cuban inhabitants. A letter from the Spanish minister to a Cuban friend, mentioning McKinley in insulting terms, was published on February 9, 1898. Six days later, on February 15, the U.S. battleship *Maine* was blown up in Havana harbor, and 266 American sailors were killed.[8]

And then a relatively new phenomenon took place that would change everyone's mind. *Yellow journalism* came into existence. This sensational and jingoist approach by the Hearst newspapers came about as a scaring tactic in articles about the *yellow peril,* a scare originally raised by Germany about the increasing population of Japan and China. Others claim the term came about because of the illusion of the color of papers used by cheap newspapers.[9]

What resulted was a clamor by the American people for a war against Spain. Though European powers tried to prevent intervention by the United States, Congress passed a resolution on April 19, 1898, declaring that Cuba was free and independent and demanding that Spain relinquish any claim to the island. Spain's answer to this demand was to declare war against the United States on April 24. On April 25, the United States resolved that a state of war had existed since April 21, 1898.[10]

What became the shortest war the United States had ever fought lasted only four months. When President Arthur proposed appropriations to expand and modernize the navy in 1884, and President Harrison continued the expansion, it was to pay big dividends.

Captain William Samson, in charge of the North Atlantic squadron, was ordered to blockade Cuba and head off the Spanish fleet coming from the Cape Verde islands. Commodore George Dewey, commanding the Pacific squadron, was ordered by Theodore Roosevelt, assistant secretary of the navy to the Philippines. Dewey arrived April 30, 1898, in Manila Bay and confronted another part of Spain's navy. He gave the command, "You may fire when you are ready, Gridley."

The bombardment began at 5:00 a.m., and by 12:30, Dewey had destroyed the Spanish fleet. Sampson, in the meantime, found the Spanish fleet at Santiago, Cuba, in May; and when the fleet attempted to leave the harbor, Samson destroyed it.[11]

On land, General W. R. Shafter had seventeen thousand troops, which included the famous Rough Riders, led by Theodore Roosevelt. On July 1, the Rough Riders stormed and captured San Juan Hill. With Spanish fleets destroyed and Santiago bombarded, the city surrendered on July 17.[12]

An armistice was signed on August 12, and a treaty was signed in Paris on December 10, 1898. Spain gave up all claims to Cuba, Puerto Rico, and Guam. The United States paid Spain $20,000,000 for the Philippines. [13]

For the first time, the United States had expanded beyond its shores, and McKinley gave this expansion strong support by claiming the United States had a *Manifest Destiny*. He also supported international trade, and when different European powers attempted to take over parts of China, he sent his secretary of state, John Hay, to negotiate a treaty to guarantee open trade.

The Boxer Rebellion took place when groups of Chinese attempted to rid China of foreign influence. American marines and some European countries put down the revolt in August of 1900, shortly before the presidential election of 1900.

McKinley also sent fifty thousand troops to put down a revolt in the Philippines, where the Filipinos were rebelling, as they did not want to be ruled by the United States any more than they had been ruled by Spain. It took longer to deal with this problem, and the revolt was finally subdued in March 1901. [14]

Samuel Gompers (1850-1924) was born in England of Jewish ancestry. His family immigrated to the United States in 1863. He worked in a cigar-making factory and helped organize a cigar workers' union. Later he would become president of the American Federation of Labor, a post he held for over forty years. In 1898, he gave a speech that included these words:

> The trade unions are the legitimate outgrowth of modern societary and industrial conditions . . . . They were born of necessity of workers to protect and defend themselves from encroachment, injustice and wrong. [15]

This summed up the plight of the many workers, and much more would be heard of from this famous American labor leader.

March 2, 1899, saw the Congress establish Mt. Rainer National Park in Washington State. In December, George Grant received a patent for the golf tee.

A little over one hundred years after ratifying the Constitution of the United States, this young country could be counted as one of the great powers on the planet. McKinley brought the United States into the modern age and gained respect at home and abroad. It helped him win a second term in the election of 1898. He chose, as his vice president, Theodore Roosevelt since his vice president Garret Hobart had died just before McKinley's first term ended.

William Jennings Bryan was once again the Democrat nominee who criticized McKinley of imperialism and expansion beyond its shores. McKinley won by a large margin in the electoral vote, 292 to 155 and also won the popular vote by nearly 850,000.

Vice President Theodore Roosevelt gave a speech at the Minnesota State Fair on September 2, 1901. Part of the speech would become world famous:

> There is a homely adage that runs, "Speak softly, but carry a big stick; you will go far." If the American nation will speak softly and yet build and keep at a pitch of the highest training a thoroughly efficient navy, the Monroe Doctrine will go far.[16]

Five days later, tragedy would once again come to the United States. For the third time in the country's young history, an assassin would take the life of a United States of America's president.

PRESIDENT MCKINLEY'S SHORT-LIVED SECOND TERM

After his election McKinley decided to tour the country in a six-week trip to see and hear from Americans. While he was in California, his wife Ida, who never fully recovered from the deaths of their two daughters nearly thirty years before, became very ill. McKinley came back East.

In September, McKinley attended the Pan American Exposition in Buffalo, New York. On September 7, 1901, after giving a speech, he stood in line to greet and meet the people. Leon Czolgosz, a mentally disturbed man, shot President McKinley. He was rushed to the emergency hospital on the exposition's grounds. He seemed to be recovering, but on September 14, he died.

His body was taken to Washington for a State funeral, and then to Canton, Ohio, to be buried. Thousands lined the route to say farewell to the much-loved leader. He had brought the country into the twentieth century and made it recognized and respected throughout the world. He led the way for those who would follow. [17]

A COMPARISON OF CHARACTER TRAITS

Thrust upon the scene with no warning, Theodore Roosevelt would use all of his God-given skills. He had the tenacity and determination that Lincoln had exhibited and that Harry Truman would show when he was thrust upon the job that Franklin Delano Roosevelt had held much longer than any other president.

In the nearly eight years as president, Theodore Roosevelt would display the charm and charisma that John F. Kennedy and Ronald Reagan would bring to the presidency.

And last, but certainly not least, President Theodore Roosevelt would use his brain and strong personality to direct the country in a direction that would serve him and the country well and could very likely be compared to Thomas Jefferson for the vision that both men saw as a way of making the United States not only great but also a powerful and respected country.

EARLY INFLUENCES

Theodore Roosevelt was born in New York City on October 27, 1858. Suffering from asthma as a child, he began a physical training program for himself, learning to swim, box, play sports, ride horses, and hike and camp in the outdoors. He developed into a healthy and robust man.

Though nearsighted, he learned to read at an early age and became well-read in American history and literature. He so loved the outdoors that he wrote books about birds and would later purchase a ranch in the Dakota Territory where he enjoyed the West as rancher for two years.

His extensive travels in Europe, Africa, and the Middle East in his early teens gave him a greater appreciation for the world and its many complexities. This would serve him well later. He entered Harvard University in 1876, graduating four years later. Starting law school at Columbia University, he preferred research and writing, publishing *History of the Naval War of 1812,* which later became required reading at Annapolis Naval Academy.

In 1878, he met and married Alice Hathaway Lee. In 1884, they had one child, a daughter, named Alice Lee, named for her mother who died of kidney failure following the birth of Alice. [18]

POLITICAL PREPARATION

While in law school, Roosevelt decided to run for the New York legislature. He was elected and immediately discovered corruption with judges and supported laws to regulate sweatshops that hired children all the while learning to work with members of both political parties.

With the death of his wife Alice in 1884, Roosevelt went out West for two years to operate his ranch and write books on history of the American West, while his sister, Anna, took care of infant Alice. When he returned to New York for a visit, he met and fell in love with Edith Kermit Carow, whom he had known for many years. He ran for mayor of New York City, but lost badly. He then took Edith to Europe in 1886, and they were married in London on December 2 of that year.

Returning to the States, Roosevelt supported Benjamin Harrison in the election of 1888. He was rewarded with an appointment to the U.S. Civil Service Commission in Washington. While there, he uncovered a patronage system that employed people who had no qualifications for the position. His writing skills were used to rewrite the civil service exam to make them fair, and that opened up positions for women, something almost unheard of at that time.

In 1895, he resigned the position in Washington to accept the job of one of four police commissioners of New York City. Here he exposed police corruption and had landlords prosecuted that treated tenants unfairly. While he made enemies, the newspaper made him a hero to the common man.

When William McKinley was elected, Roosevelt sought an appointment as assistant secretary of navy, and when approved, Roosevelt began preparing the navy for a possible war with Spain. When the battleship *Maine* blew up in Havana harbor in 1898, Roosevelt ordered Commodore Dewey to the Far East and to prepare for war.

When Congress voted for a declaration of war, Roosevelt, who had served in the National Guard, resigned to serve as commander of a unit he organized himself, called the Rough Riders. His famous charge up San Juan Hill made the newspapers and made him a national hero. He returned after the war of four months and accepted the nomination to run for governor of New York.

He won in a close election and immediately began making changes and taking on large corporations. He improved the civil service that was a patronage system like he found in Washington. He attacked large corporations for excessive profits, supported prolabor legislation, helped to increase teachers' salaries, fought to eliminate racial discrimination in schools, and sought to preserve the New York State forests and wildlife.

While he was popular with the people for all that he tried to do, and in many cases succeeded, there were some politicians and businessmen in New York who did not like his campaign to take on big business as well as corrupt politicians in both political parties. New York Senator Thomas Platt convinced the Republican Party to support Roosevelt for the vice presidential nomination, a job of no consequence at that time, to replace vice president Hobart who had died toward the end of McKinley's first term. [19]

1901-1909 THEODORE ROOSEVELT TWENTY-SIXTH PRESIDENT

Roosevelt traveled to Buffalo when he received the word of the shooting of President McKinley on September 7, 1901. He arrived before McKinley passed away on September 14, and then was immediately sworn into office.

It was not too long into Roosevelt's term when he would be faced with a number of challenges. The Pennsylvania anthracite coal mines were in the hands of coal-carrying railroads. They cut wages of the miners, raised the price of coal, and concealed profits. A strike in May 1902 left 150,000 miners out of work; and cities, schools, and hospitals would suffer with the coming of winter. People clamored for help from the president.

Roosevelt first appealed to the owners and workers to come to Washington to settle their differences. The owners refused arbitration, and Roosevelt threatened to take over the mines in the form of "government receivership" to keep them open and working. This was the first—an American president intervening on a grand scale and backing the labor movement. The owners were forced to come to terms, and the miners went back to work in the spring of 1903. [20]

That same year, 1902, civil government was established in the Philippines. William Howard Taft had been appointed as civil governor of the Philippines in 1900 by McKinley.

Roosevelt nominated Oliver Wendell Holmes, Jr., to the United States Supreme Court. Holmes was the son of Oliver Wendell Holmes, the famous American author who wrote many books and also the poem "Old Ironsides" in 1830, in protest against an order to destroy the frigate, *Constitution*. His son would become a great justice of that august body. Another positive move in 1902 was to authorize the reclamation of arid lands in the southwest. [21]

On August 2, 1902 President Roosevelt became the first president to ride in an automobile. Later he would be the first president to fly in an airplane. On October 5, 1902, Ray Kroc, founder of McDonald's fast-food chain, was born in Oak Park, Illinois. Later, his idea of fast foods would change America's eating habits.

The year 1903 was to be an eventful year. In January the Hay-Herran Treaty between the United States and Columbia called for a strip of land, six miles wide across the isthmus, where a canal would be built. Ratified by the U.S. Senate, it was rejected by Columbia.

The Panamanians, who wanted the canal, rebelled against Columbia and established an independent republic, thanks to Roosevelt's assistance and approval. The U.S. Navy protected the new country from Columbia, and the United States recognized Panama within *three days*. A treaty was drawn up that gave the United States a ten-mile wide strip across Panama for $10,000,000 down and an annuity in perpetuity of $250,000. [22]

When Jimmy Carter was president, he asked the U.S. Senate to ratify a treaty that would turn over the Panama Canal to Panama. The Democrat-controlled Senate approved, and the canal was turned over to them on December 31, 1999. Many questioned this move, but a second treaty gave the United States the right to defend the canal's neutrality.

Also in 1903, a cable was strung from San Francisco to Manila in the Philippines. On August 31, a Packard automobile reached New York after a fifty-two-day trip from San Francisco, a first. Also in that year, President Roosevelt brought suit against the National Securities Company, a holding company that controlled three railroads. Later in 1904, the Supreme Court declared the combination illegal. [23]

But the most significant accomplishment occurred on December 17, 1903. Two brothers from Dayton, Ohio, went into the business of bicycles. They were natural mechanics and became interested in aviation as early as 1896. They built their first glider in 1900 and tested it at Kitty Hawk, North Carolina. After two years of many glider flights, they designed and built their own gasoline engine. They installed it and took their new device back to Kitty Hawk and made the first successful man-carrying flight. After three more flights, they sent a telegram to Reverend Milton Wright:

> Success/ four flights Thursday morning/ all against twenty-one mile wind/ started from level with engine power alone/ average speed through air thirty-one mile/ longest fifty-nine seconds/ inform press/ home Christmas. Orville and Wilbur.[24]

GREAT INVENTIONS BY AMERICANS

The telegraph came first in 1835, thanks to Samuel F. B. Morse. A little over forty years later, in 1876, Alexander Graham Bell brought the world the telephone. Three years later, Edison gave the world artificial light, and seventeen years after Edison's first light bulb came Henry Ford's success with the first automobile. With the success of the Wright brothers in 1903, sound, light, time, and distance had been conquered. Improvements and modification rapidly expanded in those areas of discovery. The final frontier was yet to be explored—space. That would take a little longer.

THE GROWTH OF THE PRESIDENT'S CABINET

When George Washington became president, he appointed five men to his cabinet: secretary of state, secretary of treasury, secretary of war, attorney general, and postmaster general. In 1798, John Adams created the secretary of the navy position. As the country grew and expanded, it was necessary to add other position.

Though Zachary Taylor was only president for a little more than a year, he created the post of secretary of the interior to handle the growing nation and its public lands as well as the problem with Indian affairs. The position also covered the patent office and the government pension system. Not until 1889 was the office of secretary of agriculture created.

When Roosevelt became president, there were many problems with the management of business and with labor. In 1903, Roosevelt saw the need and created the post of secretary of commerce and labor. Woodrow Wilson, in 1913, separated the two into secretary of commerce and secretary of labor. No further additions were made until after World War II.

The year 1904 saw Roosevelt intervene when Germany, Italy, and France attempted to force Venezuela and Santo Domingo to pay debts that were owed. Roosevelt was able to secure arbitration on the matter at the Hague Tribunal. The tribunal found the debts valid, and Venezuela agreed to pay. Roosevelt declared the right to police all international problems in the Western Hemisphere, and it became known as the *Big Stick* policy by those who opposed Roosevelt's stand. [25]

The election of 1904 was between Theodore Roosevelt and Judge Alton Parker. Mark Hanna, the capitalist who had been McKinley's mentor, hoped to start a movement to replace Roosevelt because of his reforms. The results were one sided with Roosevelt getting 60 percent majority of the popular vote, something that had never been done since popular votes were counted, beginning in 1824. Roosevelt won 336 electoral votes to Parker's 140. The popular vote count was 7,623,486 to 5,077,911—a difference of over 2,500,000 votes. Roosevelt had a mandate, and used it for the good of the country.

By the end of Roosevelt's second term, forty-four prosecutions against trusts were decided in favor of the government. The Hepburn Rate Bill was passed in 1906, giving the Commerce Commission power to regulate railroad rates, and those found guilty of rebating rates were convicted. Three famous trusts were *busted* in 1906 and 1907. The Standard Oil Company was convicted of granting rebates and ordered dissolved. Then the American Tobacco Company met the same fate, but it took until 1911 to do so. The third trust was the New York Central and Hudson River Railroad which was convicted of granting rebates in 1906. [26]

The newly created Department of Commerce and Labor had the authority, after a law was passed, to inspect the meat-packing plants, something that was badly needed to protect the public from tainted meats. This problems was experienced during the Spanish-American War in Cuba by Roosevelt himself, but Upton Sinclair's book, *The Jungle*, also exposed the unsanitary conditions in that industry. [27]

Russia and Japan went to war against one another in 1904, and it continued until 1905 with Japan defeating the Russians in Manchuria and winning the war. Roosevelt induced the negotiators to come to Portsmouth, New Hampshire, so that he could mediate a treaty. Japan readily agreed, and Roosevelt received the Nobel Peace Prize in 1906 for his effort.

In 1906, San Francisco sustained an earthquake that killed over seven hundred and left two hundred thousand homeless. Property damage exceeded over $500,000,000. That was the negative experience of the year. On the positive side, Roosevelt was responsible for appointing Colonel George Goethals of the United States Army Engineers to take over construction of the Panama Canal that had bogged down since 1904. Work began in earnest in 1907, and it would take until 1914 for the completion, but it was Roosevelt who deserved the credit for it inception and credit for seeing that the right man was put in charge to finish the job. [28]

On September 24, 1906 President Roosevelt signed a bill making Devils Tower in Wyoming the first national monument. But he did more than that in the way of conservation. One of his key advisors, Gifford Pinchot, was a naturalist who believed in the scientific management of undeveloped land. With Roosevelt's power and the 1891 Forest Preserve Act, Federal Reserve land increased from forty million acres to over two hundred million acres. He appointed Pinchot to head the new U.S. Forest Service, and together they brought forth many dam projects as well as much-needed irrigation projects. He also put forests, seashore, and wilderness areas under government control. Truly, Roosevelt's legacy had to include this great man's far-seeing and far-reaching goal to preserve the land and environment for future generations to see and appreciate. [29]

Roosevelt never hesitated to use showmanship in everything he did. This ardor made him the most charismatic president we ever had. He even used this in an international way, when he ordered an around-the-world cruise of the Unites States Navy in 1907. The cruise would take two years, and every country took notice. [30]

In 1907, Oklahoma became the forty-sixth state on November 16. Boys Town was founded outside of Omaha, Nebraska on December 12, 1907 by Reverend Ed Flanagan.

In 1908, the nation's first Mothers' Day observance was held in Philadelphia, Pennsylvania, and Grafton, West Virginia, on May 16. On October 1, 1908, Henry Ford introduced his Model T automobile that came off the assembly line. Each car cost $825.

LEISURE TIME INTRODUCED A VARIETY OF PLEASURES

In terms of leisure, the Pittsburg Pirates baseball team defeated the hometown team Boston Pilgrims, 7-3, in the first World Series game. It would become the national pastime. The International Olympics opened in St. Louis, Missouri, on May 14, 1904, the first to be held in the United States. The Nickelodeon, the first theater devoted to showing motion pictures, opened in Pittsburg on June 10, 1905. A new form of music was introduced called *blues*. New Orleans became the cradle of jazz as ragtime bands took up improvisation and developed *the sound*.

AMERICA TAKES ITS PLACE AS A WORLD POWER

America was growing in many ways. By 1908, the population was over 85,000,000. Prosperity had returned in many areas, and businesses were beginning to accept their responsibility for more than just making money. Leaders had come forth that made life just a little bit easier with inventions that changed everyone's lives. McKinley had started making the United States recognized and respected throughout the world. Roosevelt had expanded those concepts, and other countries turned to the United States for counsel and guidance.

CHAPTER XVII

WILLIAM HOWARD TAFT—TRUST BUSTER
1900-1913

BACKGROUND OF WILLIAM HOWARD TAFT

Taft was born in Cincinnati, Ohio, in 1857. He came from a very distinguished family—his father was secretary of war and also attorney general under President Grant as well as a diplomat under President Chester Arthur.

William Howard Taft was educated first at Yale and then returned to Ohio to get his law degree from Cincinnati Law School. After practicing law for several years, he was first appointed and then elected to the Superior Court of Cincinnati. He resigned when President Harrison offered him the position of solicitor general—the chief assistant to the attorney general. His next appointment by Harrison was in 1892 as a circuit judge, which he held during the Spanish-American War. After the war, President McKinley appointed him civil governor of the Philippines, which he held from 1901 to 1904. President Roosevelt selected him for the position of secretary of war and he served for two terms. [1]

Roosevelt vowed not to run in the 1908 election and persuaded the Republican Party to nominate William Howard Taft, whose friendship he enjoyed. Taft was reluctant to run, but his wife was very instrumental in persuading him. His opponent was William Jennings Bryan who was running for the third time. The results of the election were not close, as Taft received 321 electoral votes to Bryan's 162. Taft received 7,678,908 popular votes to Bryan's 6,409,104 popular votes.

Following President Taft's inauguration on March 4, 1909, Roosevelt left on an African safari, sponsored by the Smithsonian Institute. He would not return until June 10, 1909, over three months since the inauguration.

1909-1913 WILLIAM HOWARD TAFT TWENTY-SEVENTH PRESIDENT

Taft had many things going for him as he started his presidency. He had Roosevelt's backing, a growing economy, a valuable background of governmental experience both at home and abroad, and the good will of the people.

Following Roosevelt's lead, Taft pursued the anti-trust activities. He called a special session of Congress and got the Payne-Aldrich Tariff Act passed by August 1909. Of the 2,000 duty rates, 650 were reduced, but 220 rates were raised and 1,130 remained the same.

The people felt betrayed and it was the start of a decline of Taft's popularity. He toured the Midwestern States to allay the growing dissatisfaction. At Winona, Minnesota, Taft declared that the tariff bill was the best that the Republicans had ever passed. This provoked much criticism and would be another black mark against him. [2]

The second grievous error that President Taft made concerned the controversy between Richard Ballinger, secretary of interior, and Clifford Pinchot who President Roosevelt had appointed as head of the U.S. Forest Service. Pinchot accused Richard Ballinger of reentering for private ownership the coalfields in Alaska. Taft backed Ballinger and dismissed Pinchot. Roosevelt, who had returned to the United States by then, was outraged and this went further to make Taft's administration less workable. [3]

There were some good things during Taft's four years. In 1909, the NAACP was founded. In 1910 the Elkins Act enlarged the power of the Interstate Commerce Commission as well as regulated the railroad commerce. Postal savings banks were established and the White-Slave Traffic Act was passed. [4] On June 17, 1910, Father's Day was celebrated for the first time in Spokane, Washington.

In 1911, President Taft went after the biggest trust of all—Standard Oil. His attorney general, George Wickersham, brought suit against the John D. Rockefeller conglomerate and was successful in breaking up the giant trust. Also in 1911, Glacier National Park was established in Montana.

In 1911, both Arizona and New Mexico sought admission into the Union as the forty-seventh and forty-eighth states. Taft vetoed the Arizona Enabling Act on August 22, 1911, because of the clause in the Arizona Constitution providing for the recall of judges. Taft objected to this, and Arizona changed its constitution to conform to Taft's objections. After being admitted in 1912, Arizona restored the objectionable provision. [5]

TERRITORIAL GROWTH

COLONIAL PERIOD: 1775

Original Thirteen Colonies

Other British territories

UNITED STATES: 1790–1920

States

State claims

Special status areas

Territories

Unorganized territories

Claimed areas

Foreign areas

1803 Dates of territorial acquisitions
1805 Dates of initial territorial organization
(1809) Dates of latest change within given time period
1812 Dates of admission to the Union

Map scale 1:34,000,000

Compiled by H. George Stoll, Hammond Incorporated, 1967;
rev. by U.S. Geological Survey, 1970

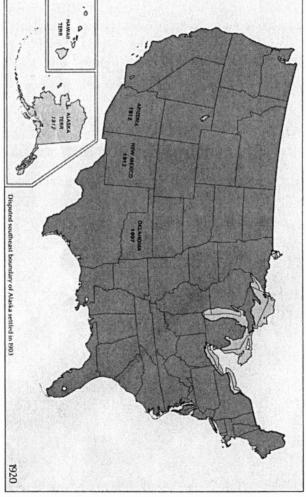

HAWAII
TERR.

ALASKA
TERR.
1912

ARIZONA
1912

NEW MEXICO
1912

OKLAHOMA
1907

Disputed southeast boundary of Alaska settled in 1903

1920

1912 HENRY FORD AND THE FIRST ASSEMBLY LINE

Henry Ford had been building the Model T Ford since 1908 when his engineers developed the first known assembly line. This very efficient method was described by Henry Ford himself:

> The first step forward in assembly came when we began taking the work to the men instead of the men to the work, we now have two general principles in all operations—that a man shall never have to take more than one step, if possibly it can be avoided, and that no man ever stoops over. [6]

The year 1912 saw parcel post established, civil government recognized in Alaska, and the drug label act adopted to prevent the adulteration of drugs. On June 10, 1912, the U.S. government adopted the eight-hour day for its employees.

Two amendments to the U.S. Constitution were enacted. The Sixteenth Amendment was adopted on February 25, 1913.

AMENDMENT XVI[7]

> The Congress shall have power to lay and collect taxes on income, from whatever source derived, without apportionment among the several states, and without regard to any census or enumeration.

The seventeenth amendment was ratified shortly after Taft left office on May 13, 1913:

AMENDMENT XVII[8]

> The Senate of the United States shall be composed of two Senators from each State, elected by the people thereof, for six years; and each Senator shall have one vote. The electors in each State shall have the qualifications requisite for electors of the most numerous branch of the State legislatures.

> When vacancies happen in the representation of any State in the Senate, the executive authority of such State shall issue writs of election to fill such vacancies. *Provided,* That the legislature of any State may empower the executive thereof to make temporary appointments until the people fill the vacancies by election as the legislature may direct.

> This amendment shall not be so construed as to effect the election or term of any Senator chosen before it becomes valid as part of the constitution.

On the international scene, Robert E. Peary reached the North Pole on April 6, 1909. Roald Amundsen, a Norwegian, reached the South Pole on December 16, 1911. One of the worst modern marine disasters was the sinking of the British White Star steamship, *Titanic,* on April 15, 1912. The largest passenger liner of its day, on her maiden voyage, struck an iceberg off Newfoundland and more than 1,500 lives were lost. [9]

When Roosevelt returned from Africa, he was so upset with what Taft had done to his friend, Pinchot, that he made a vow to run for president in 1912, In February 1912, he announced that he would accept the Republican nomination. He carried the preferential primaries in six states, but at the convention, the powers to be nominated Taft for a second term. Roosevelt left the convention, formed the Progressive Party with the logo of a Bull Moose, and campaigned with great vigor. [10]

On October 14, 1912, Roosevelt was campaigning and delivering a speech for the presidency in Milwaukee, Wisconsin, when he was shot in the chest by a New York saloonkeeper. Roosevelt completed the speech.

The Democrats nominated Thomas Woodrow Wilson after many ballots. With the Republicans helplessly split, Wilson won an easy victory. He won 435 electoral votes; Roosevelt got 88, and Taft only 8. Wilson's popular vote was 6,293,454; Roosevelt received 4,319,538 votes, and Taft got 3,484,980.

When Taft left Washington, he chose to teach. Appointed professor of law at Yale University, he taught until appointed by President Harding in 1921 as chief justice of the United States Supreme Court, something that he had always wanted. He served until 1930, the year that he died.

PART F

THE GREAT WAR AND THE ROARING TWENTIES
1913-1929

B orn in 1856, in Virginia, Woodrow Wilson experienced the devastation that prevailed in the Civil War. Well educated, he became a teacher and then president of Princeton University before becoming the governor of New Jersey.

A man with great ideas, he put many of them into practice. Nominated in 1912 for president of the United States, he campaigned on a platform of strengthening the antitrust laws, reorganizing the banking system, and reducing tariffs.

When elected, he became a hardworking president, calling a special session of Congress a little over a month after being inaugurated. Accomplishing most of his campaign promises, he soon faced international problems—first with Mexico and then keeping America neutral after the Great War started.

When German submarines sank American ships and a note trying Germany's promise to Mexico, Wilson was forced to declare war. Mobilization, both militarily and industrially, in a remarkable short period, made victory possible. Attempts at a lasting peace were unsuccessful, but not because Wilson didn't try.

Two amendments during Wilson's presidency were historic. Prohibiting the sale or manufacture of liquor caused more problems than they solved. The other amendment finally gave women the right to vote.

The election of 1920 returned the White House to the Republicans when Harding was elected as the country was looking for no foreign entanglements. The twenties, which lay ahead, brought forth both good times as well as scandals.

President Harding, elected in 1920, chose three outstanding cabinet members—Charles Evans Hughes, Andrew Mellon, and Herbert Hoover. Other choices turned out to create scandals that were just as bad as those in Grant's administration. When Harding died, Calvin Coolidge took over, and he attempted to seek world peace.

The twenties brought America into the modern age with rapid development of technology, including the radio, motion pictures with sound, and the automobile. They changed America in many ways, and the most significant advance in airplane history took place when a young man flew successfully across the Atlantic Ocean alone from New York to Paris.

It was a period of rapid change in many ways, and America was enjoying the Roaring Twenties. No one saw the problems that lay ahead.

CHAPTER XVIII

WOODROW WILSON, AMERICA'S FIRST WORLD LEADER

1856-1922 THE MAKING OF A PRESIDENT

Woodrow Wilson was fifty-six years old when he was inaugurated on March 4, 1913. Five other presidents were about the same age when they assumed the office: Washington, Jefferson, Madison, Monroe, and John Quincy Adams. At that stage in life, a person has had enough experience to be able to not only have seen much of the history of mankind but to also form thought-provoking as well as valid opinions of what is good and what is not.

Wilson came to the office of president with the greatest education of anyone who had ever held the office. His five volumes, *A History of the American People*, published the same year he became president of Princeton University in 1902, must have given him wonderful insight into the making of America.

He was born in Virginia in 1856, two years before Theodore Roosevelt was born. In his early years, Wilson was quite sickly, and after he entered Davidson College in 1873, he had to withdraw. He continued his education at home where his Presbyterian minister father's home teaching and extensive library made it possible for an excellent basic education. [1]

In 1875, he entered the College of New Jersey, which would change its name to Princeton. Majoring in history and literature, he received a bachelor of arts degree in 1879 and a master's degree in 1882. Studying law on his own, he earned a law degree from the University of Virginia. Not happy as a lawyer, he returned to school, this time to John Hopkins University in Baltimore, Maryland, and earned a Ph.D. in 1886. [2]

He married Ellen Louise Axson who was also born in Virginia. They had three daughters. Woodrow's first teaching assignment was at Bryn Mawr College in Pennsylvania in 1885. He next taught at Wesleyan College in Macon, Georgia, from 1888 to 1889. He then took a teaching position at Princeton University in the fall of 1890 until 1902 when he became president. [3]

As president of Princeton, he introduced many innovative changes, both in the curriculum and layout of buildings. His quadrangle concept of equal facilities for all students would be copied and used in many future universities. His eight year as chief administrator caught the attention of Democrat Party bosses. He was offered the candidacy of governor of New Jersey and readily accepted. He campaigned with new ideas—a progressive platform that rejected the political influence of the very bosses who had given him the nomination. He won the governorship with a large vote margin and immediately brought about reform by putting public utilities under state control, reorganizing and improving the state's school system and enacting antitrust legislation. [4]

His excellent speaking ability made him a good choice as a candidate for the president of the United States. He made a good showing at the Democrat convention in Baltimore but did not secure the nomination until William Jennings Bryan announced his support for Wilson. It took forty-six ballots before he won the nomination.[5] Thomas Marshall, governor of Indiana since 1909, was nominated as vice president and would serve with Wilson for both terms. [6]

Wilson campaigned on a platform of New Freedom, promising to strengthen anti-trust laws, reorganize the banking system, and reduce tariffs. He won the election of electoral votes easily with 82 percent of the electoral votes. His popular vote, like Lincoln's, was in the 40 percent range due to three candidates splitting the popular vote.

1913-1921 WOODROW WILSON TWENTY-EIGHTH PRESIDENT

On March 4, 1913 Woodrow Wilson swore to "preserve, protect, and defend the Constitution of the United States." [7] He then gave his inaugural address to the nation. His address has been compared to Jefferson's first inaugural and Lincoln's second inaugural addresses. [8]

The school teacher in Wilson, now president, was in a sense, lecturing the Congress when he so beautifully summarized the good of the past and condemned the bad. He lay out in specific terms how the best could be kept and the worst corrected:

> At last a vision has been vouchsafed us of our life as a whole. We see the bad with the good, the debased and decadent with the sound and vital. With this vision we approach new affairs. Our duty is to cleanse, to reconsider, to restore, to correct the evil without impairing the good, to purify and humanize every process of our common life without weakening or sentimentalizing it. There has been something crude and heartless and

unfeeling in our haste to succeed and be great. Our thoughts have been "Let every man look out for himself, let every generation look out for its self," while we reared giant machinery which made it impossible that any but those who stood at the levers of control should have a chance to look out for themselves. We had not forgotten our morals. We remembered well enough that we had set up a policy which was meant to serve the humblest as well as the most powerful, but with an eye single to the standards of justice and fair play, and remembered it with pride. But we were very heedless and in hurry to be great.[9]

He not only set the tone for change and improvement, he did not hesitate to list the wrongs and why they needed to be changed. He brought up many important areas that had been neglected far too long.

He said that tariffs should be reduced so that the country could become part of world commerce. He said that the banking and currency system needed to become more flexible. He took on the successful industrial system that had prevailed without regard to the need of the laboring force or depletion of the natural resources. He believed that agricultural reform was needed in terms of water and forest reclamation and renewal, and the waste connected with the mining industry needed correcting. [10]

While he praised the efficient production of industry, he felt that not enough thought had been given to the economy and costs of such endeavors. He believed that the government should be the safeguard of the health of a nation. Sanitary laws, food laws, and laws determining the conditions of labor where individuals could not determine for themselves needed to be strongly considered. [11]

He concluded his marvelous inaugural address with the following:

This is not a day of triumph; it is a day of dedication. Here muster, not the forces of party, but the forces of humanity. Men's hearts await upon us; men's lives hang in the balance; men's hopes call upon us to say what we will do. Who shall live up to this great trust? Who dares fail to try? I summon all honest men, all patriotic, all forward-looking men to my side. God helping me, I will not fail them, if they will but counsel and sustain me! [12]

WORDS INTO ACTION

Wilson wasted no time. He called a special session of Congress on April 15, a month and four days after his inauguration. Reviving the custom that had not been done since Jefferson was president, he addressed the Congress regarding the tariff revision he had campaigned on. [13]

When certain lobbyists attempted to stall the needed reform, he called a news conference, a first of its kind. He said, "I think the public ought to know the extraordinary exertions being made by the lobby in Washington to gain recognition for certain alterations of the tariff bill." [14]

He went on to blast the lobby for its shameful methods of spending large sums of money on paid advertisements to mislead the public. He challenged the Congress to join him in getting rid of the lobby. The bill, which became the Underwood Act, was passed on October 3, 1913, a relatively speedy process in terms of what it took to get a bill passed and signed.

The Underwood Act put raw wool, lumber, iron ore, and steel rails on the tariff free list. It lowered the duty tax on sugar and nine hundred other articles about 20 percent, established free trade with the Philippines, and provided for a graduated income tax. [15]

The next major concern that Wilson dealt with was the problem of banking and currency. The situation was corrected in a major way with the Glass-Owens Federal Reserve Act, passed in December 1913, providing for American currency to become more flexible. The act organized all national banks into twelve regional reserve banks under a Federal Reserve Board composed of the secretary of treasury, a comptroller of currency, and five members appointed by the president. Among other powers, it could transfer funds from one bank to another. It was the most important law that did away with the withholding of vast sums from circulation and instead allowed enough money to meet the needs of special areas. By keeping the banks under government control, it prevented the monopoly of currency by big banks or groups of banks. Later, it would be reinforced with the Rural Credit Act that allowed farmers to borrow money when needed. [16]

The Federal Trade Commission Act, passed in September 1913, established a five-member commission to keep an eye on all big corporations with the exception of banks and railroads. It published violations and abuses as well as enforced laws against unfair competition. [17]

Another important piece of legislation was the Clayton Antitrust Act, passed in 1914, helping the government close in on trusts, forbidding rebates, secret agreements, price privileges, and collusion between banks, railroads, and coal companies. [18]

A form of progress was shown when Gideon Sundback patented the *zipper* on April 28, 1913. He called it separated fasteners. On December 1, 1913, the first drive-in auto service station opened in Pittsburgh, Pennsylvania. On January 5, 1914, Henry Ford announced the adoption of a minimum wage of $5 per day, an eight-hour workday, and a profit-sharing plan.

In the latter part of July 1914, Woodrow Wilson's wife, Ellen Louise, became gravely ill and died on August 6 of a kidney ailment. Woodrow grieved in private and early the next year met Edith Galt, a widow whose husband had died in 1908. Edith and Woodrow were wed in December 1915. [19]

On July 14, 1914, Robert Goddard was granted a patent for a liquid fuel rocket. He was thirty years ahead of his time. On July 29, 1914, transcontinental telephone service began between New York and San Francisco. On August 15, 1914, the long-sought Panama Canal opened to limited use due to landslides. The formal opening would not be until July 12, 1920. [20]

WILSON IS FACED WITH INTERNATIONAL PROBLEMS WITH MEXICO

On April 9, 1914, several U.S. sailors were arrested by officers of President Huerta of Mexico. On April 20, Wilson asked Congress for authority to take whatever action was necessary. They gave overwhelming approval. On April 22, U.S. Marines landed at Vera Cruz, Mexico, and prevented German ships from unloading munitions. [21]

This brought the United States and Mexico to the brink of war, but three South American nations—Argentina, Brazil and Chile—volunteered to mediate the problem. Later, President Huerta fled to Europe, and Venustiano Carranza became president. Wilson supported Francisco "Pancho" Villa when Carranza rejected peace efforts, but when Villa raided Columbus, New Mexico, on March 9, 1916, Wilson sent Brigadier General John J. Pershing in pursuit of Villa. Pershing never found Villa when he invaded Mexico but managed to break up his guerrilla army. When peace was restored, Pershing was recalled. Mexico adopted a new constitution, and President Carranza had the job of hunting down Villa. [22]

The Adamson Act of 1916 was another success for the Wilson administration. This act made the eight hour day a normal thing for interstate railway employees which were a victory for the railroad unions. This was followed by the U.S. Employees Compensation Commission which administered benefits for Federal employees. [23]

WILSON'S ATTEMPT TO KEEP AMERICA NEUTRAL

On June 28, 1914, Archduke Francis Ferdinand, heir to the throne of Austria, was assassinated by a Bosnian revolutionary acting as an agent of the Serbian society called *Union or Death*. [24]

Austria made demands on Serbia. Russia backed Serbia when she did not comply with Austria's demands. On July 28, Austria declared war on Serbia. When Russia began mobilization, Germany declared war on Russia on August 1, 1914, and against France on August 3. The next day, Great Britain declared war on Germany. On August 6, Austria declared war on Russia; and on August 12, France and Great Britain declared war on Austria. By November of 1914, *eleven* European countries were at war. [25]

President Wilson made a proclamation of neutrality on August 4, 1914 and on August 18 made an appeal to the American people to be neutral not only in act but also in word and thought. [26]

On the same date that Wilson made a proclamation of neutrality, August 4, Germany initiated their planned offensive called the *Schiielffen Plan*. At night, they crossed the Belgium border and the war that would be given the name the *Great War* began in earnest. [27]

Germany's disregard of her pledge to the neutrality of Belgium in World War I and her military severity, which marked the invasion and the occupation of this little country, aroused the people of America and inspired this poem.

ABRAHAM LINCOLN WALKS AT MIDNIGHT[28]
In Springfield, Illinois
Vachel Lindsey

It is portentous, and a thing of state
That here at midnight, in our little town
A mourning figure walks, and will not rest.
Near the old court-house pacing up and down,

Or by his homestead, or in shadowed yards
He lingers where his children used to play,
Or through the market, on the well-worn stones
He stalks until the dawn-stars burn away,

A bronzed, lank man! His suit of ancient black,
A famous high top-hat and plain worn shawl
Make his the quaint great figure that men love,
The prairie-lawyer, master of us all.

He cannot sleep upon his hillside now,
He is among us—as in times before!
And we who toss and lie awake for long
Breathe deep, and start, to see him pass the door.

His head is bowed. He thinks on men and kings.
Yea, when the sick world cries, how can he sleep?
Too many peasants fight, they know not why,
Too many homesteads in black terror weep.

The sins of all the war-lords burn his heart.
He sees the dreadnaughts scouring every main.
He carries on his shawl-wrapped shoulders now
The bitterness, the folly and the pain.

He cannot rest until the spirit-dawn
Shall come;—the shining hope of Europe free;
The league of sober folk, the Workers' Earth,
Bringing long peace to Cornland, Alp and Sea.

It breaks his heart that kings must murder still,
That all his hours of travail here for men
Seem yet in vain. And who will bring white peace
That he may sleep upon his hill again.

On May 7, 1915, a German submarine torpedoed and sank the British steamship *Lusitania* with a loss of 1,198 passengers of which 139 were Americans. [29]

Wilson's note of protest was so mild that Secretary of State Williams Jennings Bryan resigned. When a stronger note was sent, Germany promised not to sink without warning and making provisions for the safety of noncombatants. This satisfied Wilson, and the submarine crisis came to an end for the year 1915. [30]

On January 15, 1915, the United States House of Representatives rejected a proposal to give the women the right to vote. They would have to wait another five and a half years for that right. On January 28 of that year, the United States, by an Act of Congress, created the Coast Guard. That same year saw the beginning of construction on the magnificent Lincoln Memorial by Daniel Chester French. It would be completed in 1922.

THE FLAG BY WOODROW WILSON

The things that that flag stands for were created by the experiences of a great people. Everything that it stands for was written by their lives. The flag is the embodiment, not of sentiment, but of history. It represents the experiences made by men and women, the experiences of those who do and live under the flag. (Address June 14, 1915)[31]

On January 28, 1916, Woodrow Wilson appointed Louis Brandeis to the United States Supreme Court, the first Jew to be appointed. On July 15 of that year the Pacific Aero Products Company was founded in Seattle, Washington. It would later change its name to the Boeing Company. And in New York City, Margaret Sanger opened the nation's first birth control clinic on October 16, 1916.

ELECTION OF 1916

The Republicans nominated Charles Evans Hughes who had served as governor of New York, as well as associate justice of the U.S. Supreme Court. The Democrats naturally nominated Wilson for a second term. He ran on the slogan, He Kept Us Out of War. The margin of victory was much narrower than 1912. Wilson won with 277 electoral votes to Hughes's 254. The popular vote also went to Wilson with 9,129,606 votes to Hughes's total of 8,538,221—difference of less than 600,000 votes.

In spite of Wilson's plea for Americans to be neutral in thought as well as words, most Americans felt a closer feeling for the Allies (England, France, and Russia), especially after the *Lusitania* was sunk. Wilson never gave up hope of bringing the war to a peaceful conclusion and spoke to that effect. His address on January 22, 1917—again was a memorable speech—to Congress was best summed up with the words in the speech, "peace without victory." It was a prelude to what would become Wilson's fourteen points for peace, including a league of nations. [32]

On February 5, 1917, Congress passed, over President Wilson's veto, an immigration act severely curtailing the influx of Asians.

THE ZIMMERMAN NOTE

Wilson's appeal for neutrality went for naught. A letter from the German foreign secretary, Arthur Zimmerman, to the German minister in Mexico was intercepted and decoded by the British Naval Intelligence Service, and they sent a copy to the United States' secretary of state. The letter, which received wide distribution in the American press, stated that if Mexico waged war against the United States, when Germany and Mexico won, Mexico would regain the lost territories of New Mexico, Texas, and Arizona. [33]

That letter, written on January 19, 1917, was released to the public on March 1. The mood of the country was in an uproar, and when three American ships were sunk by German submarines in the middle of March, Wilson had little chance of bringing about a peace without victory. [34]

Wilson went before a joint session of Congress on April 2, 1917, and gave an eloquent plea and advised "that the Congress declare the recent course of the Imperial German government to be in fact nothing less than war against the government and people of the United States . . . . The world must be made safe for democracy." [35]

Wilson remembered, in his youth, living in Georgia and the hardships and damage that resulted form the Civil War. He no doubt felt those fears when he closed his speech asking for war against Germany.

> It is distressing and oppressive duty, Gentlemen of the Congress, which I have performed in thus addressing you. There are, it may be, many months of fiery trial and sacrifice ahead of us. It is a fearful thing to lead this great peaceful people into war, into the most terrible and disastrous of all wars, civilization itself seeming to be in the balance. But the right is more precious than peace, and we shall fight for the things which we have always carried nearest our hearts—for democracy, for the right of

those who submit to authority to have a voice in their own Government, for the rights and liberties of small nations, for a universal dominion of right by such a concert of free people as shall bring peace and safety to all nations and make the world itself at last free. To such a task we can dedicate our lives and our fortunes, everything that we are and everything that we have, with the pride of those who know that the day has come when America is privileged to spend her blood and her might for the principles that gave her birth and happiness and the peace which she has treasured. God helping her, she can do no other.[36]

MOBILIZATION

While the United States was totally unprepared for war, organizing, preparing, and executing the needed parts of mobilization came about because the public answered President Wilson's "call to service."

Food, clothing, and coal for ships and factories as well as steel for arms, ammunition, and ships to carry the men and supplies across the Atlantic were gathered, harvested, mined, and manufactured with amazing speed.[37]

Complete cooperation was forthcoming in many forms. Manufacturing companies vied to outdo their rivals. War bond drives successfully helped the government pay for all the needed areas. The American people bought $3,000,000,000 in Liberty bonds.[38]

The Selective Service Act was passed on May 18, 1917. Less than a month later, on June 5, ten million men began registering for the draft. With this draft of men between the ages of twenty-one and forty-five, the army grew from 225,000 to 3,665,000 by the end of the war with over two million serving in Europe.[39]

The Germans were well aware of the potential that existed from the United States. They planned a spring offensive against the British and French before the United States could make a contribution. General John "Blackjack" Pershing was put in command of the American Expeditionary Forces (AEF). He was in France by June 13, 1917, and sent back word that 3,000,000 men would be needed. By June 26, a small contingent set foot in France.[40]

On July 4, 1917, Charles Stanton stood before the tomb of Lafayette in the Picpus Cemetery and said, "Lafayette, we are here".[41]

AMERICAN TROOPS BATTLE TOWARD VICTORY

At first American troops were used to fill in gaps of the Allies in the trenches where they had been battling for three long years. But when enough Americans arrived in 1918, the Americans were on their own.

On May 28, 1918, the American First Division of twenty-eight thousand men attacked the Germans and took Cantigny and held it in spite of three days of bombardment. A high-ranking German officer reported to his supreme command, "These men can fight." [42]

In the next five and a half months, the Americans won battle after battle. In June 1918, the marines won a victory at Belleau Wood, after a two-week battle. On July 15, Chateau-Thierry became the turning point of the war when the Third Division won a huge victory. On September 12 and 13, another victorious battle was won at Saint-Mihiel.

The Meuse-Argonne front was both at and in the forest. The Americans began their attack in the forest on September 26. In that battle, on October 8, 1918, army sergeant Alvin York killed 25 German soldiers and captured *132* others almost singlehandedly in the Argonne forest. He became the most decorated soldier of World War I. [43]

A method of warfare that had never been used before involved the airplane, invented only eleven years before the war started in 1914. Edward "Eddie" Rickenbacker, who was born in Columbus, Ohio, in 1890, went overseas with the American Expeditionary Force as a mechanical expert but transferred to aviation. He rose to command the Ninety-fourth Aero Squadron and shot down twenty-six enemy aircraft. He received the Distinguished Service Cross as well as the French medal, the Croix de Guerre. [44]

By November 4, there was a revolution in Germany. The kaiser, Germany's head of state, was unwilling to abdicate until the last moment. On November 8, the French general Foch put the written terms of the armistice in the hands of the German representative. The armistice was signed at 5:00 a.m. on November 11; and at 11:00 a.m., the "war to end all wars" was over. [45]

REQUIEM FOR A GENERATION

The exact total number of deaths from the needless killing in World War I will never really be known. It is estimated that over ten *million* deaths—mostly soldiers—perished as a result of modern warfare for which neither side was prepared.

Once it started, no nation would stop and consider any other possibilities. Methods of warfare had advanced beyond men's understanding of the consequences. The machine gun, the deadly accurate artillery, poisonous gas, even the invention of the tank, and the constant improvement of the airplane made warfare like none other in the history of mankind.

One battle lasted from February 21 to July 11, 1916! The French fell back to a line that almost reached Paris, except for a salient on the Meuse River near the town of Verdun. Here, the French made a stand with the challenge, "They shall not pass!" 350,000 Frenchmen paid with their lives. [46]

The Battle of the Somme took place just north and west of the river Somme, from July 1 to November 18, 1916. The British losses were over four hundred thousand men. While the French lost two hundred thousand. The German losses were between four hundred thousand and five hundred thousand. [47]

How are such devastating losses to be remembered and honored? The First World War produced some excellent authors and poets, and recognition of a few outstanding ones is but a small tribute to both them and to the men who gave their lives.

America came into the war late, but there were memorable men. Alfred Joyce Kilmer is best remembered for his poem "Trees" that he wrote in 1914. He also wrote a war poem, "The Peacemakers," before he, a sergeant in the infantry, was killed in action. Ernest Hemingway served with the Italian army and wrote his most memorable book, *Farewell to Arms*, a fictionalized version of wartime experiences. [48]

The English produced well-respected poets, such as Siegfried Sassoon who was wounded in the war and received both the Military Cross and the Distinguished Service Cross for bravery. Wilfred Owen, also an English poet, received the Military Cross for bravery and was killed in action. Another of the many English poets and authors was Rupert Brooke, who wrote the famous line in his memorable poem, "The Soldier," which he wrote in 1915 just before he died.[49]

THE SOLDIER[50]

If I should die, think only this of me:
That there's some corner of a foreign field
That is forever England. There shall be
In that rich earth a richer dust concealed;
A dust whom England bore, shaped, made aware,
Gave, once, her flowers to love, her ways to roam,
A body of England's breathing English air,
Washed by the rivers, blest by suns of home,
And think, this heart, all evil shed away,
A pulse in the eternal mind, no less
Gives somewhere back the thought of England given;
Her sights and sounds; dreams happy as her day;
And laughter, learnt of friends; and gentleness,
In hearts of peace, under an English heaven.

John McCrae, a Canadian physician and poet, wrote this memorable poem in 1915, during the Second Battle of Ypres.

IN FLANDERS FIELDS[51]

In Flanders fields the poppies blow
Between the crosses, row on row,
    That mark our place; and in the sky
    The larks, still bravely singing, fly
Scarce heard amid the guns below.

We are the dead. Short days ago
We lived, felt dawn, saw sunset glow,
    Loved and were loved, and now we lie
    In Flanders fields.

Take up the quarrel with the foe:
To you from falling hands we throw
    The torch; be yours to hold it high.
    If ye break faith with us who die
We shall not sleep, though poppies grow
    In Flanders fields.

The Germans produced a novelist who served in the German army from 1914 to 1918. His most memorable novel was the unforgettable *All Quiet on the Western Front*. This realistic account of the devastation of World War I and its effect on the German youth was translated into English, which became a best seller. It was dramatized as a U.S. film twice. The author, Erich Maria Remarque, sought refuge in the United States during World War II and then wrote *Arch of Triumph* in 1946. [52]

WILSON'S ATTEMPT FOR A JUST AND LASTING PEACE

President Wilson sailed for Paris, France, on December 4, 1918. He had his fourteen-point plan that would be too idealistic for the countries that had suffered for four years, and all he could salvage from his plan was the fourteenth point—A League of Nations.

"An association of nations formed under specific covenants to afford mutual guarantees of political independence and territorial integrity to great and small states alike." This was Wilson's dream—a league of nations—which was adopted by *all* of the countries in Europe. [53]

Wilson fought to have the League of Nations be a part of the peace treaty of Versailles, signed June 28, 1919. The league would start with most of the nations of the world—fifty-four in all. Germany was admitted into the league in 1926 but withdrew in 1935 as did Japan. The United States Constitution required two-thirds of the senators to concur on any treaty made, according to Article 2, Section 2. [54]

The treaty would come up for a vote in the latter part of 1919, so Wilson set out on September 4, 1919, on a speaking tour to gain support for his dream. Fate intervened when Wilson collapsed in Pueblo, Colorado, from exhaustion on September 25. He returned to Washington to recover but suffered a stroke on October 2. Unable to lobby the senators that he needed for a two-thirds majority, the treaty was defeated on November 19, 1919, on a vote of fifty-five in favor and thirty-nine opposed—nine short of the two-thirds needed. The opposition to the treaty was led by Senator Henry Cabot Lodge, a Republican. [55] The United States would never be a member of the league.

On February 16, 1919, the Grand Canyon National Park was established.

Two important amendments were ratified in Wilson's last two years. The Eighteenth Amendment was ratified on January 16, 1919.

AMENDMENT XVIII[56]

Section 1. After one year from the ratification of this article the manufacture, sale, or transportation of intoxicating liquor within, the importation thereof into, or the exportation thereof, from the United States and all territory subject to the jurisdiction thereof for beverage purposes is hereby prohibited.

Section 2. The Congress and the several States shall have concurrent power to enforce this article by appropriate legislation.

Section 3. This article shall be inoperative unless it shall have been ratified as an amendment to the Constitution by the legislatures of the several States, as provided in the Constitution, within seven years from the date of submission hereof to the States by Congress.

The Volstead Act, passed in October 1919 to enforce the Eighteenth Amendment, was passed over President Wilson's veto and became law. [57]

The Eighteenth Amendment was the only amendment ever to be repealed. It was the Twenty-first Amendment, passed on December 5, 1933, that brought back intoxicants.

AMENDMENT XXI[58]

Section 1. The eighteenth article of amendment to the Constitution of the United States is herby repealed.

Section 2. The transportation or importation into any State, Territory, or possession of the United States for delivery or use therein of intoxicating liquors, in violation of the laws thereof, is hereby prohibited.

Section 3. This article shall be inoperative unless it shall have been ratified as an amendment to the Constitution by conventions in the several States, as provided in the Constitution within seven years from the date of the submission hereof to the States by the Congress.

The Nineteenth Amendment was long overdue and was finally ratified on August 18, 1920, with Tennessee being the thirty-sixth state to ratify the amendment according to Article V of the Constitution of the United States. Elizabeth Stanton had finally been vindicated.

AMENDMENT XIX[59]

The right of citizens of the United States to vote shall not be denied or abridged by the United States or any State on account of sex.

The Congress shall have power to enforce this article by appropriate legislation.

President Wilson never fully recovered from his debilitating stroke, but that news was kept from the public. His wife, Edith, made many decisions regarding who he would see and which issues he would address. He believed the election of 1920 would be a referendum on the treaty and his vision of the League of Nations. [60]

The Republicans nominated Warren G. Harding for president and Calvin Coolidge for vice president. The Democrats nominated James M. Cox for president and Franklin Delano Roosevelt for vice president. Much more would be heard from this thirty-eight-year-old vice presidential candidate who had been serving as the assistant secretary of the United States Navy since 1913.

Three important actions took place just prior to the 1920 presidential election in November. On August 20, the first commercial radio station in Detroit began daily broadcasts. On September 5, airmail delivery began. And on October 21, the *World Series* was broadcast for the first time.

The vote for both electoral and popular votes was not even close. Harding received 404 electoral votes to 127 for Cox. The popular vote gave Harding 16,152,200 votes while Cox only got 9,147, 353 votes. Harding's popular vote was the highest percentage ever tabulated—64 percent. This was the first national election that women were allowed to participate in, but no record was kept of voting by gender, nor was it *ever* recorded by gender.

The people had spoken. They wanted to stay away from anything dealing with Europe. It ushered in a period of neutrality, isolation, and an era that would become know as the *Roaring Twenties.*

WILSON'S LEGACY LEFT A SMALL HOPE FOR A BETTER WORLD

The progress of mankind has had many, many advancements. At the same time, much of the progress has taken years, if not generations, to accomplish. No one knows how long man took to discover how to make and use fire.

One of the greatest accomplishments, Gutenberg's invention of movable type in 1454 came years after writing had been perfected. The idea of a democratic government was first tried to some degree in Greece in the fifth century BC. It did not become a reality until men in America made a declaration for their independence and then fought to make it come about.

Even then, their ideas were not perfect or complete. In 1776, they claimed all men were created equal, but it took until 1870 and the Fifteenth Amendment before the right to vote would not be denied on account of race, color, or previous servitude. It would be another fifty years before women has the same right to vote.

Woodrow Wilson had a dream that nations could live together forever in peace. His fourteen-point plan never really got off the ground, with the exception of the last point—a League of Nations. Unfortunately, his own country denied his dream of becoming a reality when the Senate voted not to join the League of Nations.

Where Wilson was willing to be more lenient on the countries that lost, England, France, and others wanted to exact crippling reparations. The Allies, with the exception of the United States, came to the peace table, bent on crushing their defeated foe. They wanted Germany's colonies in Africa, part of Germany returned to France and other parts to Poland. The United States wanted nothing from anyone, except the Virgin Islands that they had purchased for $25,000,000 from Denmark on August 4, 1916, and the treaty was ratified on January 17, 1917. [61]

While still president, Woodrow Wilson was awarded the Nobel Peace Prize for 1919, the first peace prize since 1913. He was the third American to receive the Nobel Peace Prize. Theodore Roosevelt was the first for his mediating the Russo-Japanese treaty in 1906. Second was Elihu Root who had been secretary of war under McKinley as well as Roosevelt, then secretary of state for Roosevelt as well as a senator from New York, devoting himself to the cause of international peace.

The severe penalties that the Allies put on Germany would come back to haunt them with the rise of Adolph Hitler in the 1930s. Only when World War II was concluded did Wilson's dream become a reality with the formation of the United Nations.

The lesson of treating defeated foes that Wilson had wanted at the end of World War I was not lost on the Allies at the end of World War II. Today, both Germany and Japan are democracies and have benefited from the conciliatory acts that the victorious Allies bestowed on them.

One might say that Woodrow Wilson was finally vindicated.

CHAPTER XIX

1920 PEACE, SCANDAL, AND THE ROARING TWENTIES

1865-1920 BACKGROUND OF WARREN G. HARDING

Harding was born in a farmhouse near Blooming Grove, Ohio on November 2, 1865, the first president to be born after the Civil War.

His father, a physician, purchased a local newspaper which Warren worked at—first just running errands but eventually learning how to set type. Attending a one-room school, he then went to Ohio Central College, graduating in 1882, trained as a teacher. When the family moved to Marion, Ohio, Harding went with them. He did not teach but sold insurance until he had enough money to purchase a struggling newspaper. About this time, he met Florence Kling, got married, and together they made the newspaper a prosperous enterprise.

He was elected to the Ohio State Senate in 1900 and served two terms. He next served as lieutenant governor. He ran for governor in 1910 but lost. In 1912, he gave the nominating speech for William Howard Taft, though Taft lost to Woodrow Wilson. In 1914, Harding was elected to the U.S. Senate and served for one term. In 1920, Harding's good friend, Harry Daugherty, convinced him to run for president. He would be up against two very popular candidates—Frank Lowden and Congressional Medal of Honor recipient, General Leonard Wood[1.]

Needing 493 votes for the Republican nomination, Harding could only muster 65 on the first ballot. Neither one of the other candidates could secure the needed number, but on the tenth ballot, Harding won the nomination. The convention nominated Calvin Coolidge, governor of Massachusetts, for vice president. Coolidge had gained national attention when he stood up to the American Federation of Labor president Samuel Gompers when Coolidge fired the Boston police, who were on strike, and called the state militia to maintain order. His telegram to Samuel Gompers was:

> There is no right to strike against the public safety by anybody, anywhere, anytime. [2]

THE ELECTION OF 1920

Harding hardly ever left his home during the campaigning, issuing statements from his front porch, while James Cox, his Democrat opponent toured the country. The Democrat's vice presidential candidate was Franklin Delano Roosevelt who had served as assistant secretary of the navy from 1913 to 1920. Much more would be heard from this aspiring young man.

Harding's slogans during the campaign were Back to Normalcy and No Entangling Alliances. The people were tired of the sacrifices they had made during the Great War and wanted peace and prosperity. Harding won with 404 electoral votes against Cox's 127. The popular vote was 16,162,200 for Harding and 9,147,353 for Cox. Receiving 64 percent of the popular vote for Harding was the largest percentage ever recorded.[3]

1921-1923 WARREN G. HARDING TWENTY-NINTH PRESTIENT

THREE OUTSTADING CHOICES

President Harding selected some outstanding men for his cabinet. Charles Evans Hughes had been governor of New York from 1907 to 1910 when he resigned to accept the position of associate justice of the U.S. Supreme Court, having been appointed by President Taft. In 1916, he ran for president of the United States against Roosevelt and Wilson. He served as secretary of state under Harding and Coolidge until 1925. In 1930, President Herbert Hoover appointed him chief justice of the United States Supreme Court and he served with distinction until he resigned in 1941.[4]

The second man who served in Harding's cabinet was Andrew Mellon, secretary of the treasury. He was well qualified for the position, having been president of the Mellon National Bank. He had developed coal, coke, and iron corporations and controlled the aluminum trust. One of the nation's leading financiers, he helped Harding in passing a federal budget bill in 1921, which led to dramatic savings for the government.[5]

The third outstanding choice was a man of worldly experience who had been to every continent, except Antarctica, as an engineer. At the outbreak of the World War, Herbert Hoover was appointed the chairman of American Relief Commission, helping those Americans stranded in Europe to reach America safely. During the war, he headed the U.S. Food Administration. After the war, he organized measures for countries faced with famine. [6]

Some of Hoover's major contributions as secretary of commerce included standardizing manufacturing products such as nuts, bolts, automobile tires, and even milk bottles. Putting together municipal building codes and introducing standardization in the building industry simplified many manufacturing steps. [7]

These three men, with outstanding backgrounds, would serve with distinction and go on to great accomplishments. One would become chief justice of the United States Supreme Court, a second would be appointed ambassador to Great Britain, and the third would become president of the United States.

Harding chose wisely in those three men. The same can not be said of some of his other cabinet choices.

TREATIES WITH RESERVATIONS

One of Harding's first official acts was to conclude treaties with Germany, Austria, and Hungary. This was done and ratified October 18, 1921. Parts of the Versailles Treaty were incorporated, but they were careful not to involve the United States in the League of Nations. [8]

On November 11, 1921, the Tomb of the Unknown Soldier, now known as the Tomb of the Unknowns, was dedicated on Arlington National Cemetery at an Armistice Day, now known as Veterans Day, ceremony. On February 8, 1922, President Harding had a radio installed in the White House.

A conference on the limitation of arms was held between November 12, 1921, and February 6, 1922. Harding sent his secretary of state, Charles Evans Hughes, which resulted in significant reduction in navies of Japan, France, England, and the United States. [9]

SCANDALS

Four of Harding's appointments were close friends of his. Harry Daugherty had encouraged Harding to run for president. Harding appointed him attorney general. Behind the scenes, Daugherty took bribes to grant immunity from prosecution to certain liquor dealers as well as sold paroles to wealthy federal prisoners. He was forced to resign. [10]

Harding's friend Charles Forbes had been appointed chief of the Veterans Bureau. He was found to be illegally selling government medical supplies to private people and taking kickbacks on new hospital contracts. When Harding confronted him, Forbes quickly resigned and sailed for Europe. When he returned, he was investigated, convicted, and sentenced to prison for two years. [11]

The worst scandal during the Harding administration was the one perpetuated by the secretary of the interior, Albert Fall. In 1922 he leased oil reserves illegally from two different places. One was in Elk Hill, California, and the other was in Teapot Dome, Wyoming. These had been established by President Wilson to be used by the navy in case of emergency. Fall was paid approximately $400,000 by two oil tycoons. The scandal also implicated the secretary of the navy Edwin Denby. [12]

In 1923 Albert Fall was convicted of bribery and conspiracy and sentenced to a year in prison and fined $100,000. Denby was found to be incompetent. [13]

President Harding and his wife, Florence, went on a nationwide speaking tour which took them to the Alaska Territory, a first for any president. When they returned to Seattle, Washington, Harding became very ill. His personal physician thought it was food poisoning and refused to let other doctors examine Harding. He continued his journey to San Francisco, California; there he died on August 2, 1923. [14]

His coffin was put aboard a special train that crossed the country to Washington. Thousands turned out to watch the train as it passed through their towns. It was greeted by Calvin Coolidge, who had been sworn in at 3:00 a.m. on August 3, 1923 by his father who was a notary public and a justice of peace. After he was sworn in, Coolidge went back to bed. [15]

President Harding only served for two years and five months, but in that short time he accomplished some positive things. Treaties with former enemies of the Great War and limitations of naval vessels for many of the major powers were to his credit. Unfortunately, he would be best remembered for the scandals that happened during his administration.

But something he could neither take credit for nor take the blame for was the beginning of the 1920s that has best been described as the *Roaring Twenties.*

MOVING INTO THE MODERN AGE

Before World War I, the United States was pretty much a rural country with cities growing larger every year. During the Great War, many attitudes changed. Women learned to work in munitions factories, worked on railroads in ever greater numbers, and became equal partners with men in 1920 with the passage of the Nineteenth Amendment on August 18.

Labor unions grew in number and strength with the demand for workers in so many different kinds of material, munitions, and other manufacturing positions. With no immigrants coming to America during the war, unemployment dropped from 15 percent to 2 percent.

One of the greatest changes was the migration of the blacks. In 1910, four out of five African Americans lived in the rural south. During the war, thousands migrated north to the big cities to get jobs in the factories that needed laborers. [16]

All this was a prelude to the next decade when some of the greatest changes in American history took place. And much, if not most of the changes were due to three factors—the radio, the movies, and the automobile.

THE RADIO

As early as 1911, the Boy Scouts of America manual had instructions on how to build a receiver. In 1919, broadcasting (a farm term meaning the act or process of scattering seeds) was little more than a hobby. In November 1920, Pittsburgh established the first commercial station—KDKA.

In the beginning of 1922, there were 28 broadcast stations. By the end of the year there were 570 stations, sharing only two radio frequencies. By the middle of the decade, the number of frequencies had expanded; and two networks, NBC (National Broadcasting Company) and CBS (Columbia Broadcasting System) provided needed programming like *The Maxwell House Hour* and *The General Motors Family Party*. Though the secretary of commerce, Herbert Hoover, was against it, advertising soon became a whole new industry, no longer limited to just the printed page. [17]

THE MOVIES

Until 1927, when *The Jazz Singer*, starring Al Jolson, brought sound to the films, silent movies were all people could enjoy, and enjoy they did. Movie stars like Charlie Chaplin, Douglas Fairbanks, Mary Pickford, Clara Bow, Joan Crawford, and especially Rudolph Valentino brought people to the theater every week. [18]

When sound came in (they were called talkies), movies became even more popular. People idolized the "stars" and emulated their dress and actions. When the actresses cut their hair, so did millions of American women. When the movie stars smoked, many took up the habit. Every town had a theater for movies. In the large cities, vaudeville acts were also included. It became the thing to do. Gather the family and head for the movies. It was the way of being entertained for over thirty years, until television came into each home, and people could watch a screen in the comfort of their own home.

THE AUTOMOBILE

Henry Ford's first car was successfully run in 1896. Twelve years later, he introduced the Model T Ford. By 1920, over eight million of these basic cars were on the roads that were so poorly constructed that the federal and state governments would have to spend millions to provide the necessary routes that people needed and demanded. In 1921, the national highway system was introduced. [19]

The car was the first major change in transportation for individuals since the invention of the bicycle in 1839. It provided people with an opportunity to see the country. The first shopping center opened in Kansas City, Missouri. in 1924. The first "mo-tel" (blend of motor and hotel) opened in San Luis Obispo, California, on December 12, 1925. It meant the growth of suburbs where people could live in their own houses and travel to the city for work. [20]

The automobile industry eventually provided jobs for one out of eight workers, including the petroleum, rubber, and steel industries. People no longer had to abide by train schedules to go from place to place. The automobile business was largely responsible for the five-day, forty-hour workweek. [21]

While Ford provided for the basics in terms of transportation, others were planning and working on a more elaborate concept. General Motors induced the public with fancier and more expensive cars. The Chevrolet competed with the Ford, but GM soon brought out other models with more to offer. The Pontiac was a step up from the *Chevy*, the Oldsmobile a step up from that; the Buick was more expensive; and then came the La Salle and the Cadillac.

Ford brought out the Model A in 1927 which became as big a seller as the Model T. Later, Ford would bring out the Mercury and Lincoln to compete with General Motors. Truly, the automobile changed America forever.

OTHER CHANGES IN THE TWENTIES

While the radio, movies, and automobile were the biggest changes that affected American life, there were other important inventions that helped to make women's work much easier. The electric iron replaced the flatiron that had to be heated over a stove. The electric washing machine did away with the scrubbing of clothes. The gas stove replaced the wood or coal-burning stove. The refrigerator replaced the ice box soon to be followed by the freezer, and central heating and indoor bathrooms became the norm. [22]

Prohibition became a means for illegal transportation of beer and liquor. Gangsters like Al Capone and George "Bugs" Moran became famous and made millions, illegally smuggling liquor into the country or brewing beer in secret.

New terms came into existence. A *speakeasy* was a private club that served intoxicants. Terms like *bootleg* (smugglers carried liquor in their boots) and *bathtub gin* (homemade brew) became part of the language. The twenties were also called the *jazz age*. It included the style of music that began in New Orleans and moved north with the migrating blacks. It came to Chicago, and a whole new sound was born. It inspired bands like Duke Ellington and Louis "Satchmo" Armstrong to bring a whole new sound to America. On February 14, 1924, the son of Russian Jewish immigrants, George Gershwin topped his musical career when his *Rhapsody in Blue* premiered in New York City. [23]

Women found a new freedom and were not afraid to express it. The dresses became shorter, and some bathing suits brought arrests for indecent exposure. The *Charleston* became the dance craze. Margaret Gorman won the Miss America beauty contest in 1921.

The twenties invented the term *sex appeal*. Women tried to achieve it by going to the neighborhood beauty parlor. In 1922, New York City had 750 beauty shops. By 1927, the city had *3,500* of them. [24]

The 1920s brought much good and some bad to the American scene. It was a great time to live—it was the *Roaring Twenties!*

CHAPTER XX

PROSPERITY, PEACE ATTEMPTS AND AIRPLANE HISTORY

1923-1929 CALIVIN COOLIDGE THIRTIETH PRESIDENT

C alvin Coolidge was born July 4, 1872, on a farm near Plymouth, Vermont. He lost his mother when he was twelve and his sister, Abigail, when she was only fifteen-three years younger than Calvin.

After schooling in Ludlow, a town ten miles from Plymouth, Calvin went to Amherst College. Upon graduating, he stayed in Northampton, Massachusetts, studying for the bar which he passed in 1897. He climbed the political ladder, first as a councilman then city solicitor followed by clerk of the General Court of Massachusetts then mayor of Northampton. Next he was elected to the senate of Massachusetts, then lieutenant governor and governor in 1918.

He met his wife, Grace Goodhue, while she was teaching the deaf in Northampton. They were married in 1905 and had two sons: John, who lived until the year 2000, and Calvin Jr., who died in 1924. [1]

He gained national recognition for his stand against Samuel Gompers regarding the policemen's strike in 1919 and was a unanimous choice for the vice presidential nomination at the 1920 Republican convention.

When Harding and he won the election, it was a contrast in personalities. Harding was outgoing and personable. Coolidge was shy, modest, and kept a low profile. When Harding died, Coolidge took command without hesitation. In his message to the nation in December 1923, he stated that he wanted to continue Harding's programs. This included keeping the tariff, reducing taxes, and was against soldiers' bonus. [2]

ELECTION OF 1924

Coolidge was nominated at the Republican convention without opposition. For vice president, the convention chose Charles Dawes who had been Harding's director of the Bureau of the Budget. Dawes would serve faithfully and well and received the Nobel Peace Prize in 1925 for his work in what was called the Dawes Plan. This plan rearranged the entire reparation schedule, extending time, and paring down the amounts due from Germany. [3]

The results of the election gave Coolidge 382 electoral votes to his Democrat opponent, John Davis's 136 electoral votes. Robert La Follette, a former governor of Wisconsin and a Republican senator, formed the Progressive Party but only garnered Wisconsin's 13 electoral votes. The popular vote gave Coolidge 15,725,016, Davis collecting 8,386,503, and La Follette 4,822,856.

THE MONKEY TRIAL

In May 1925, a trial was held in Dayton, Tennessee, that was labeled the *trial of the century*. A young high school biology teacher was arrested for using a textbook in his classroom that described evolution, which was in violation of state law.

The trial was broadcast countrywide (a first). Two giants opposed each other as lawyers for the prosecution and for the defense. William Jennings Bryan, a well-known politician, three times candidate for president of the United States, and a believer in the literal interpretation of the Bible, volunteered to work for the prosecution.

Clarence Darrow, a well-known and highly respected lawyer acted for the defense. Witnesses for both sides were called and questioned. On the ninth day, Darrow called Bryan to the stand as an expert on the Bible. When questioned, Bryan admitted that some Bible stories were illustrations rather that facts. Darrow was satisfied that he had made his point and pleaded his client guilty, and asked the case be closed. The judge agreed. This stopped Bryan from giving his closing arguments. He was apparently so brokenhearted that five days after the trial, on July 25, 1925, he died in his sleep. [4]

A RACE TO SAVE CHILDREN'S LIVES

In the winter of 1925, children in Nome, Alaska, were hit with diphtheria. The only antitoxin serum was in Anchorage. First by rail to Nenose, the serum was transported by an eighteen-team dogsled from there to Nome, in five and a half days. That trip normally took *twenty days!* The serum arrived in time to save the lives of the children. [5]

HISTORIC ACCOMPISHMENTS

On January 14, 1926, Chicago decided to build an airport at Cicero Avenue and Sixty-third Street. It was completed and dedicated on December 12, 1927. After World War II, it was renamed Midway Airport in honor of the battle of Midway—a decisive naval battle between the United States and Japan.

On August 6, 1926, Gertrude Ederle of New York became the first woman to swim the English Channel. It took her fourteen and a half hours. On January 7, 1927, commercial transatlantic telephone service was inaugurated between New York and London. On February 23, 1927 President Calvin Coolidge signed a bill creating the Federal Radio Commission—a forerunner of the Federal Communication Commission. And on May 4, 1927, the Academy of Motion Picture Arts and Science was founded.

1927 CHARLES LINDBERGH (1902-1974)

Charles Lindbergh was a twenty-five year-old airmail pilot when he flew between St. Louis and Chicago. After convincing some St. Louis businessmen to finance an attempt to fly nonstop from New York to Paris, he purchased a single-winged airplane from Ryan Aircraft in San Diego, and flew it across the country, setting a new transcontinental speed record.

Taking off at 7:52 a.m. on May 20, 1927, from Roosevelt Field on New York's Long Island, his flight took him up the coast of New England then Nova Scotia and over the island of Newfoundland. Out over the North Atlantic, he flew, dozed at times, ate his sandwich, and did his own navigation calculations.

Unknown to him, word by phone and radio brought word of his flight, and the French people flocked to Le Bourget Field outside of Paris. Flying over Ireland and then England, he approached France and found the Seine River, which he followed upstream to Paris and to history. It had taken him thirty-three and a half hours to reach Paris. [6]

He was interviewed by Edwin James of the *New York Times*.

> I saw a fleet of fishing boats . . . . I flew down almost touching the craft and yelled at them, asking if I was on the right road to Ireland.

> They just stared. Maybe they didn't hear me. Maybe I didn't hear them. Or maybe they thought I was a just a crazy fool . . . An hour later I saw land.

> At 10:24, the *Spirit of St. Louis* landed and lines of soldiers, ranks of policemen and stout steel fences went down before a mad rush as irresistible as the tide of the oceans.

"Well, I made it," smiled Lindbergh, as the white monoplane came to a halt in the middle of the field, and the first vanguard reached the plane." [7] (Lindbergh's own story in the *New York Times,* May 23, 1927.)

The significance of Lindbergh's accomplishment can best be appreciated and understood by what he did in a remarkably short period, from when an airplane was first flown—thanks to his courage and determination.

The Wright brothers' success on December 17, 1903 was the first step in a chronicle of historic events. Exactly twenty-three years, four months, and twenty-three days after their historic flights on the shores of the Atlantic Ocean, aviation advanced from its infancy to where a person could safely cross that ocean, a distance of just over 3,600 miles, in less than a day and a half.

Even more remarkable is the fact that Chuck Yeager, on October 13, 1947—twenty years, four months, and twenty-three days after Lindbergh's feat—was the first to fly faster than the *speed of sound*, something that some scientists said would never be done.

Twenty-one years, nine months, and seven days after Yeager's breakthrough, Neil Armstrong landed on the surface of the moon, July 20, 1969. He climbed down from the module Eagle; and as he stepped off the ladder, he summed up the history of sixty-five years, seven months, and three days of aviation progress with the never to be forgotten words, "That's one small step for man, one giant leap for mankind."

All four events—first flight ever, first across the ocean alone, first to break the sound barrier, and first to land on the moon—were done by Americans. These were just some of the great men in American history.

OTHER ACCOMPLISHMENTS IN THE LATE TWENTIES

On November 13, 1927, the Holland Tunnel under the Hudson River opened, linking New York City with New Jersey. On November 18, the first successful sound synchronized animated cartoon, Walt Disney's *Steamboat Willie,* starring Mickey Mouse, premiered in New York City. The next month, December 2, the Ford Motor Company unveiled its Model A, successor to the Model T. A year later, December 23, 1928, the National Broadcasting Company (NBC) established a permanent coast to coast radio hookup.

CALVIN COOLIDGE ATTEMPTS TO SEEK WORLD PEACE

The Dawes Plan was not the only attempt to secure a world free from war. Frank Kellogg, secretary of state in Coolidge's new administration, teamed up with French foreign minister, Aristide Briand, in a pact to eliminate war. They proposed an international agreement for the preservation of peace. The Kellogg Peace Plan passed, signed, and was accepted by first fifteen national powers and eventually by sixty-five nations. Passed on August 27, 1928, by nations, it was approved by the United States Senate on December 4, 1928. [8]

Unfortunately, the pact failed in preventing war as it did not address the actions to be taken in the event an aggressor nation invaded another as what happened when Germany invaded first Czechoslovakia, and then Poland, to start World War II. [9]

THE ELECTION OF 1928

Coolidge did not want to run in 1928 even though there was a demand for it. His name was placed in nomination at the Republican convention, but he simply said, "I do not choose to run for president." He gave his support to Herbert Hoover, his secretary of commerce, who had won the admiration of the public for his work as wartime food administrator. His opponent was Alfred E. Smith, former governor of New York and a Roman Catholic, the first ever to run for the presidency.

Once again, the people were satisfied with the peace and prosperity that had prevailed for the past ten years. Hoover won with 444 electoral votes to Smith's 87 votes. The popular vote gave Hoover 32,392,190 votes to Smith's 15,016,443 votes. The difference gave Hoover a 59 percent advantage, third highest in history so far. Only Harding's 64 percent and Theodore Roosevelt's 60 percent were higher. No one could predict what the future held for president-elect Herbert Clark Hoover.

LIBERTY AND INDEPENDENCE REVISITED

Just prior to the Battle of Lexington, Patrick Henry summed up the plight of the colonists with his appeal on March 23, 1775:

> What is it that the gentlemen wish? What would they have? Is life so dear, or peace so sweet, as to be purchased at the price of chains and slavery? Forbid it Almighty God! I know not what course others may take; but as for me, give me liberty or give me death!

Thomas Jefferson's plea to declare the cause of separation from Britain was best expressed in America's basic document:

> We hold these Truths to be self-evident, that all Men are created equal, that they are endowed by their Creator with unalienable Rights, that among these are Life, Liberty and the Pursuit of Happiness.

When the second war for independence from Britain—the War of 1812—was going badly for the Americans, Francis Scott Key, witnessing the bombardment of Ft. McHenry through the night from an enemy ship, saw in the dawn that:

> The Star-spangled Banner in triumph doth wave
> O'er the land of the free and the home of the brave.

In November 1863, a cemetery outside of Gettysburg, Pennsylvania, following a battle in July of that year which was decisive, was dedicated. As an afterthought, President Lincoln was asked to say a few words. How wrong he was when he said, "The world will little note, nor long remember what we say here." *No American* can ever forget the opening words of his Gettysburg Address:

> Four score and seven years ago, our fathers brought forth on this continent
> a new nation, conceived in liberty, and dedicated to the proposition that
> all men are created equal.

As the United States began to become a world power, Theodore Roosevelt, then vice president, expressed his country's position in dealing with foreign governments:

> There is a homely adage that runs, "Speak softly, but carry a big stick;
> you will go far." If the American nation will speak softly and yet build
> and keep at a pitch of the highest training a thoroughly efficient navy, the
> Monroe Doctrine will go far.

In 1927, there was a case before the United States Supreme Court in which associate justice, Louis Brandeis, summed up what Patrick Henry, Thomas Jefferson, Francis Scott Key, Abraham Lincoln, and Theodore Roosevelt were all talking about:

> Those who won our independence believed that the final end of the State
> was to make men free to develop their faculties; and that in its government
> the deliberate forces should prevail over the arbitrary. They valued liberty
> both as an end and as a means. They believed liberty to be the secret of
> happiness and courage to be the secret of liberty. (*Whitney v. California,*
> *274 U.D. 357, 375 [1927]*) [10]

No one could predict what lay ahead. No one could imagine the problems and needed solutions that the United States would face in the years ahead. It would be America's greatest challenge.

PART G

THE GREAT DEPRESSION AND WORLD WAR II
1929-1945

Herbert Hoover's Quaker upbringing and his vast experiences in helping others made him a wise choice to succeed Calvin Coolidge. In Hoover's inaugural address he saw a bright future for America.

Unfortunately, the high living of the 1920s gave way to a stock market collapse as a result of wild speculation by investors that thought the good times would go on forever.

A little over seven months after taking office, Hoover found the beginning of a depression that would make the so-called Panics of the nineteenth century look like child's play. When unemployment climbed to heights never before experienced, some people questioned whether democracy could really work. Anything Hoover tried could not save the country from the worst depression in its one-hundred and fifty year history.

When the 1932 election was held, people were ready for a change, and a distant cousin of Theodore Roosevelt was elected. A master politician from his experience as a State Senator, assistant secretary of the navy, and the governor of New York, Franklin Roosevelt was well prepared to take on the tough job of leading the country in the most desperate time in its history.

He set the tone for his plans in his inaugural address with " . . . the only thing we have to fear is fear itself." He turned words into action by first directing a *bank holiday,* and then getting Congress to pass needed legislation to aid the banks. Other programs were initiated and projects throughout the country gave many both jobs and hope.

The world situation had serious problems as well. Germany and Italy were controlled by dictators, as was Russia. Hitler's bold moves brought concessions from England and France, until Poland was invaded, and a world conflict was under way. Japan began her attempt to dominate the Far East, and that country's military leaders brought about Pearl Harbor.

The United States' involvement in World War II brought out the best in all of its citizens. Men volunteered and others accepted the military draft. Many women joined the various services, while others learned to do many different tasks that only men had done in the past.

Leaders emerged in a variety of ways and all worked for one goal—victory. When it came, the United States had lost a great leader in President Franklin Delano Roosevelt who died less than a month before victory in Europe. But the untried and mostly unknown vice president, Harry S. Truman, stepped up and successfully finished the job, making some tough decisions.

CHAPTER XXI

1929-1933 A DEPRESSION LIKE NONE OTHER

1874-1928 BACKGROUND OF HERBERT CLARK HOOVER

Herbert Hoover was born on August 10, 1874 on a farm near West Branch, Iowa. He was the first president born west of the Mississippi River. Orphaned at the age of ten, he was brought up a Quaker. His early childhood in a Quaker community influenced and gave him a sense of helping his fellow man that would be part of his life until the day he died.

With no parents, Hoover was sent to Oregon to live with an uncle. At the age of seventeen, he enrolled in a Californian university that had been founded only six years before by Leland Stanford, the Central Pacific railroad tycoon.

Working during the summer for the U.S. Geological Survey and studying mining in school, he graduated in 1895 with a degree in engineering. Working for a short time in California mines, he next jointed a London firm that sent him to Western Australia to develop mines.

This type of work kept him abroad for twenty years, but first he returned to California to marry Louise "Lou" Henry, a geology student he had met while at Stanford. His wife loved the outdoors, learning to hunt, fish, and ride horseback. After they were married, she converted to her husband's faith, and she became as conscientious in terms of helping others as her husband.

She joined him in his overseas adventures. When they left for China on the same day they were married, Lou began to learn Chinese.

Hoover's assignment in China was chief engineer of the Chinese Imperial Bureau of Mines. They were caught in Tianjin, China, during the Boxer Rebellion and survived. For protection, Lou carried a pistol.

In 1903, Hoover was appointed chief engineer for a London firm and traveled extensively in Asia, Africa, and North, and South America. They had two children, both boys, born in 1903 and 1907, named Herbert Charles and Allan Henry.

At the outbreak of World War I, Hoover was in London and was appointed chairman of the Commission for Relief in Belgium, which was in dire straits due to Germany's invasion of that small country. He set up a food distribution system that kept the people of Belgium from starvation.

When he was recognized for his efforts by the American press, Woodrow Wilson appointed him head of the U.S. Food Administration. He gained support to conserve food for the troops when the United States entered World War I.

After the war, Hoover founded the American Relief Administration and with the help of Congress, fought famine in Europe. He was proclaimed a hero by the millions in Europe. In 1921, President Harding appointed him secretary of commerce, a rather minor position when he took the job.

He performed important tasks, such as standardizing the production of manufactured goods. His work made it possible for the consumer to know what he was buying and to find the needed replacements when they were needed. What people take for granted today, he made possible.

When the Mississippi River flood caused extensive damage and hardships, President Coolidge asked for his help. In supervising relief efforts, he convinced business and industry leaders to lend their resources to help. Time and again, Hoover's Quaker upbringing showed in his sincere efforts to help those who could not do it for themselves.

When Coolidge pledged not to seek another term, the Republican Party encouraged Hoover to run, something that he had never done. His vice presidential running mate would be Charles Curtis, a man with Native American heritage. [1]

1929-1933 HERBERT HOOVER THIRTY-FIRST PRESIDENT

Hoover was administered the oath of office on March 4, 1929 by the chief justice of the Supreme Court, former President William Howard Taft. In his inaugural address, Hoover said:

I have no fears for the future of the country. It is bright with hope.

He had much to support his beliefs. Since the Great War, much had been accomplished. The automobile, the radio, and the movies typified the attitude that America could tackle anything and make it work.

There were some significant and historic events that took place during Hoover's one term as president.

On May 15, 1930 Ellen Church was the first airline stewardess, who went on duty aboard a United Airlines flight between San Francisco and Cheyenne, Wyoming.

In July of that year, Congress created the Veterans Administration, now called the Department of Veterans Affairs. In August, Captain Frank Hawks set an airspeed record by flying from Los Angeles to New York in eighteen hours and twenty-two minutes. And on October 9, 1930, Laura Ingalls became the first woman to fly across the country completing a nine-stop journey from Roosevelt Field in New York to Glendale, California. On December 6, 1930, Clarence Birdseye began selling packaged frozen food in Springfield, Massachusetts. And on March 3, 1931, the Star-Spangled Banner became our national anthem.

In 1931, Wiley Post and Harold Gatty took off for a flight around the world on July 23. They circled the globe, covering 15,400 miles in eight days, fifteen hours and fifty-one minutes. In 1933, Wiley Post did it again, alone, and broke his own record by a day. On October 5, 1931, Clyde Edward Pangborn and Hugh Herndon flew the first nonstop flight across the Pacific Ocean, landing in Washington State forty-one hours after leaving Japan.

On January 12, 1932, Hattie Caraway of Arkansas became the first woman elected to the United States Senate. On May 1, the Empire State Building was dedicated in New York City. It is one hundred stories high. And on March 20, Amelia Earhart took off from Newfoundland for Ireland to become the first woman to fly solo across the Atlantic Ocean. That same year, Charles and Ann Morrow Lindbergh's child was kidnapped.

CHANGING THE DATE OF ADMINISTERING THE OATH OF OFFICE

George Washington took the oath of office the first time on April 30, 1789. After that, all presidents took the oath on March 4 unless they had replaced a dead president. The exception was James Monroe's second term, which was administered on March 5, 1821, since March 4 was a Sunday. The reason for the delay from election day in November to March 4 was mostly because of the lack of good transportation.

Serious consideration was given to moving the date up for a couple of reasons. With a choice of trains, automobiles, and airplanes, elected officials could reach Washington in much less time. The other reason was to eliminate the lame-duck session of four months when outgoing senators and members of the House of Representatives could propose bills for consideration when they would not be serving in the next Congress.

The result of that decision was the Twentieth Amendment, which was ratified January 23, 1933. The first section covers the desired change:

AMENDMENT XX[2]

Section 1. The terms of the President and Vice President shall end at noon the 20th day of January, and the terms of Senators and Representatives at noon on the 3ʳᵈ day of January, of the years in which such terms would have ended if this article had not been ratified; and the terms of their successors shall begin.

On September 24, 1929, a brave lieutenant piloted a biplane over Mitchell Field in New York on the first *blind* or all-instrument flight ever. His name was James H. Doolittle. This daring aviator would go on to contribute much to aviation and to his country. He will be forever remembered as Lieutenant Colonel Jimmy Doolittle, the man who led B-25 Mitchell bombers off the deck of the U.S. aircraft carrier *Hornet* and bombed Tokyo, Japan. This next-to-impossible feat was accomplished on April 18, 1942, only four and a half months after the Japanese had bombed Pearl Harbor in Oahu, Hawaii, on December 7, 1941.

One month and five days after Doolittle's flight over New York, the bottom fell out of the American economy, and Hoover's prophesy of a bright tomorrow went down the drain. How could this happen? America had everything going its way. Economists to this day differ on the cause of the Great Depression, and it may well have been a number or a combination of factors.

CAUSES OF THE DEPRESSION

The 1920s made the stock market available to everyone. People borrowed and speculated. Easy credit made it easy to not only invest but also to produce goods—to the extent that more was produced than the public could purchase. Prosperity was being experienced by almost everyone—the exceptions were the farmers and the low-paid workers. Some economists believe one of the causes was that the high tariffs that the United States imposed on foreign goods forced other countries to do the same, which had the effect of slowing trade.

Dearborn, Michigan, is the site of the Ford Museum complex that Henry Ford established to exhibit and celebrates the many advancements that had taken place. Thomas Edison's Menlo Park laboratory and home had been relocated to the museum site, and President Hoover was attending the fiftieth anniversary of Edison's invention of the electric light on October 21, 1879. [3]

RESULTS OF THE DEPRESSION

As Hoover was returning from Michigan to Washington on Thursday, October 24, the value of stock began to fall at the New York Stock Exchange. By October 29, which would become known as *Black Tuesday*, over thirty *billion* dollars in stock value had been lost during the *crash* week. Banks began to close when people rushed to take out their money. In 1929, there were 659 bank closings. In 1930, there were 1,351 bank failures; the next year—1931-2,294 banks failed.

Unemployment in 1929 was 1,500,000. It jumped to 4,000,000 by 1930; and in 1932, 13,000,000 were out of work. That was almost a third of the workforce. The gross national product figure of $104 billion in 1929 fell to $58,500,000,000 by 1932. Automobile production dropped from 5,500,000 vehicles in 1929 to only 1,500,000 in 1932. [4]

RESPONSE TO THE DEPRESSION

At first, Hoover waited, believing that the stock market would correct itself. He encouraged state and local governments to help in the relief efforts, but they did not have the resources as their funds had dried up. Hoover worked tirelessly to find ways to get the country going again, but noting seemed to work. [5]

A moratorium of one year was put on war debts owed to the United States by European countries and eventually postponed forever. Only one country ever paid their war debt to the United States in full. That country was Finland. [6]

The 1930 midterm elections brought a majority of Democrats to Congress. With their help, Hoover was able to launch a program to stem unemployment. The federal treasury deficit in 1931 was $900,000,000. A year later the deficit was $2 *billion*. Taxes were raised on luxury items like automobiles and theater tickets. Bank checks and telephones were taxed. Income taxes were raised with surtax on million-dollar income. The revenue was inadequate. [7]

In 1932 Hoover proposed the Reconstruction Finance Corporation that allotted $2,000,000,000 for loans to banks, railroads, and other industries. It did not help much. [8]

One of the sad events during Hoover's last year in office was the march of World War I veterans to Washington, D.C., to ask for the bonus certificates they had received in 1925 to be redeemed for cash. By June of 1932, twenty thousand veterans had camped out in Washington. Congress passed a bill that they could redeem the certificates for from $225 to $400 per person. Hoover vetoed the bill. Most of the veterans went home—empty-handed. Some stayed in Washington because they no home to go back to. [9]

The election of 1932 had the Republicans nominating Hoover for a second term. The Democrats selected the governor of New York, Franklin Delano Roosevelt who had served as a New York State senator and as assistant secretary of the navy. He was a distant cousin of Theodore Roosevelt, the twenty-sixth president. Franklin won the election handily.

Roosevelt received 472 electoral votes to Hoover's 59 votes. The popular vote was 22,821,857 for Roosevelt and 15,761,845 for Hoover. The country was ready for a change.

HOOVER'S LIFE AFTER HE LEFT OFFICE

Hoover is often connected with the Great Depression. He did not cause it. He tried, unsuccessfully, to fix it, but to no avail. He probably accomplished more after he left the office of president. He established a library on *War, Revolution, and Peace* at his alma mater, Stanford University.

During World War II, he headed the Polish Relief Commission. As head of the Hoover Commission, he organized suggestions for the improvement of government practices, which were approved by Congress in 1947.

President Truman paid tribute to Hoover by signing a congressional resolution officially naming Boulder Dam the Hoover Dam, which had been completed in 1935. When he retired, he moved to the Waldorf Astoria Hotel where he personally answered as many as twenty thousand letters a month because he thought anybody who wrote him deserved an answer.

At 5:00 p.m. each day, he would stop and fix a one and a half martini for himself (his wife had died in 1944). He did not like olives and used little white onions instead. He called his drink a Gibson. [10]

AMERICA LOOKS FOR A NEEDED HERO

The great depression was a very dark period in the United States history. Not since the Civil War was the nation faced with so large a crisis. Lincoln had stated in his Gettysburg Address:

> Now we are engaged in a great civil war, testing whether that nation or
> any nation so conceived and so dedicated, can long endure.

Would the United States of America endure? Could it climb out of the depression and successfully fulfill the destiny that Lincoln had spoken of when he concluded his speech?

> That we here highly resolve that these dead shall not have died in vain—
> that this nation, under God, shall have new birth of freedom—and that
> government of the people, by the people, for the people shall not perish
> from the earth.

The country had endured for 150 years. Men like Washington and Jefferson had fought and governed through war and peace to make the United States a true land of the free and home of the brave. Lincoln and Grant had fought to preserve one nation. Katharine Lee Bates said it best:

O beautiful for heroes proved
In liberating strife,
Who more than self their country loved,
And mercy more than life!

What America needed was another hero. He came—not on a white horse but in a wheel chair. He would serve longer than any other president and died in office as commander in chief

CHAPTER XXII

ROOSEVELT ATTEMPTS TO GET AMERICA WORKING AGAIN

FIFTEEN PRESIDENTS FACE TRAGEDIES AND HARDSHIPS

Of the thirty-one presidents before Franklin Roosevelt, fourteen faced family tragedies. They all lost children. Four of the former presidents—Taylor, Pierce, Garfield, and McKinley—lost two children to early deaths. Hayes lost three. Nine of the fourteen lost children in their infancy: Jefferson, Monroe, Van Buren, Tyler, Taylor, Pierce, Hayes, Benjamin Harrison, and McKinley. The others—John Adams, William Henry Harrison, Taylor, Pierce, Lincoln, Hayes, and Arthur—lost children when they were four years of age or younger. Yet they all performed their tasks as president in a courageous manner. They all came into the presidency in relatively good health. They could walk to their assignments, climb into a carriage or automobile, board a ship, or ride a horse. That was not true of Franklin Delano Roosevelt.

1882-1923 BACKGROUND OF FRANKLIN DELANO ROOSEVELT

Roosevelt was born on the family estate at Hyde Park, New York, on January 30, 1882. After attending a prestigious preparatory school, Groton, he entered Harvard in 1900. Graduating in 1904, he stayed an extra year as editor in chief of the periodical, Harvard's *Crimson*. He then enrolled at Columbia University's law school.

While at Columbia, he married Anna Eleanor Roosevelt, the daughter of Theodore Roosevelt's brother on March 17, 1905. They would have six children between the years 1906 and 1916. One - Franklin Jr. died in infancy.

When he passed the examination for the bar, he stopped going to school. Joining a law firm, he became bored and wanted to run for a New York State Senate seat. The year was 1910, and the senate seat was in a heavily Republican district. But he would listen to people as often as he spoke and learned a great deal. This technique would be used the rest of his political life. He used his own money and his name recognition plus his interest in reform got him backing from the New York Democrats.

He won his first election and immediately began challenging legislation that favored business interest. He also championed women's right to vote. He backed Wilson for president in 1912, and when Wilson won, Roosevelt accepted a position of assistant secretary of the navy, the same job that his fifth cousin, Theodore Roosevelt, had held in 1898.

Roosevelt used the technique he had learned earlier of listening to others. He worked well with both admirals and the important men in business and industry. Negotiating government contracts, he wanted to expand the navy, anticipating the problems that were brewing in Europe. Living in Washington, this probably gave Roosevelt the ambition to move up the political ladder.

He ran for the U.S. Senate from New York in 1914, but lost—his first defeat. He continued to serve as assistant secretary for President Wilson until 1920. He was nominated for the vice presidency with James Cox as the presidential nominee from Ohio. They ran against Warren Harding and Calvin Coolidge and lost. People wanted to go back to normalcy and enjoy the good times.

Roosevelt went back to a law firm after the election, and then tragedy struck. Roosevelt was stricken with infantile paralysis (polio) in August 1921. Most men would have been happy to spend the rest of their lives attempting rehabilitation and living the life of ease.

Not Franklin Roosevelt. He sought different doctors' opinions, tried different medicines, and exercised. His early love of swimming led him to the mineral waters of Warm Springs, Georgia, where he could relax and hope for improvement. While it was enjoyable, it did not improve his mobility. However, he would return to Warm Springs many times over the next twenty-four years.

In 1924, seated in a wheelchair, he nominated Alfred Smith, governor of New York for the Democrat nomination for president. Al Smith lost the nomination to John Davis, from West Virginia. Davis lost to Coolidge; and four years later, Alfred Smith, a Roman Catholic, was nominated as the Democrat nominee for president. In 1928, Al Smith was opposed by Herbert Hoover who had gained world fame for his many accomplishments. The people wanted to keep the good times rolling, and Hoover won.

Roosevelt next ran for the governorship of New York. He won by appealing to the rural voters for his support of reforestation of overused land; he appealed to the workers by backing state-financed pensions, unemployment insurance, and regulating working hours. He also favored control of the energy industry. He won the election and used the technique of broadcasting his issues and program on the radio—he called them fireside chats.

271

When the Great Depression began in October 1929, Roosevelt remembered what he had learned earlier in his political career. He listened to people from all walks of life. He listened to people from the academic community; he listened to the workers and to those without jobs. He was not afraid to experiment, and he gained recognition, not only in New York, but nationwide.

In 1932, in the height of the Depression, he was one of the nominees for president at the Democrat Convention in Chicago. There were two major candidates, Roosevelt and John Nance Garner from Texas. Neither could gain a majority of the necessary votes. Roosevelt shrewdly offered Garner the position of vice president which Garner accepted.

They formed a formidable team, Garner appealing to the rural areas and Roosevelt favored in the northeast and larger cities. [1]

They won with a very large majority. Roosevelt and Garner received 472 electoral votes while Hoover and Charles Curtis (with Native American heritage) got only 59 electoral votes. The Democratic candidates received 22,821,857 popular votes, while the Republicans got 15,761,845 popular votes, a difference of over 7 million votes.

WHO WOULD WANT THIS JOB?

The country was in the greatest crisis since the Civil War. Millions had lost their jobs. Many could not find enough food to eat, clothes to wear, or a place to sleep. Quite a few left their families, wandering the country, looking for any kind of work. In the cities, some stood on the corner, selling apples.

Was this the end of an experiment called Democracy? In Italy, Benito Mussolini had marched on Rome with his Blackshirts in 1922, and became the dictator, replacing the monarchy.

In Russia, the country began a revolution in the middle of World War I that led to Vladimir Lenin bringing a Communist state into being, replacing centuries of rule under princes and tsars.

When Lenin died in 1924, Joseph Stalin, the general secretary of the Central Committee of the Communist Party, became the dictator. He literally eliminated any opposition by killing high-ranking army officers and millions of peasants in the Ukraine who only wanted to produce and eat the foot they had grown.

In Germany, the Weimar Republic was a disaster. Germany could not make the required reparation payments. In 1930, the Nationalist Socialist German Labor Party (Nazi), led by Adolf Hitler, gained seats in the Reichstag—Germany's parliament. By early 1933, Hitler was appointed chancellor by eighty-six-year-old President von Hindenburg, who died the next year. Hitler purged the other political parties; next, he suppressed freedom of the press and persecuted and ousted the Jews from various professions.

WAS THE PAST A PROLOGUE OR A PROMISE?

What had happened in America left some people wondering if there was a better way to govern. In 1776, Thomas Jefferson and fifty-five others signed America's first document:

> And for the support of this Declaration, with a firm Reliance on the Protection of Divine Providence, we mutually pledge to each other our Lives, our Fortunes, and our sacred honor.

James Madison, the father of the U.S. Constitution, said in the preamble:

> In order to form a more perfect Union, establish Justice, insure domestic tranquility, provide for the common defence, promote the general welfare, and secure the Blessings of Liberty to ourselves and our Posterity do ordain and establish this Constitution for the Untied States of America.

In 1814, Francis Scott Key, aboard a British warship that shelled Fort McHenry through the night, asked in the morning:

> Oh, say does that star spangled banner yet wave,
> O'er the land of the free and the home of the brave?

On a cold November day outside the town of Gettysburg, a cemetery was dedicated. As an afterthought, President Lincoln was asked to say a few words. He spoke for less than two minutes, and used only 276 words. He gave the country a challenge that would be a rallying cry to preserve the Union:

> It is for us, the living, rather to be dedicated here to the unfinished work which they who fought here have thus far so nobly advanced. It is rather for us to be here dedicated to the great task remaining before us—that from these honored dead we take increased devotion to that cause for which they gave the last full measure of devotion.

Were these just pretty words that were well said but did not mean much? Was this experiment that had lasted a little over 150 years about to end? Was there a hero like Washington or Lincoln who could lead the country from a world of chaos to a place in history where it would be respected and admired throughout the world?

The people had elected a person to lead them into the uncertain future and bring them out of the deep depression.

Could he do it? Could he lead them? Would they believe him? Would they follow him?

He could barely walk! But he had much more as the people would find out by what he said, by what he promised, and most important, by what he accomplished during his twelve years, one month and four days as president. He let nothing stand in his way to bring the country out of the Great Depression.

1933-1937 FRANKLIN DELANO ROOSEVELT THIRTY-SECOND PRESIDENT

On March 4, 1933, Franklin Roosevelt was sworn into office by chief justice of the Supreme Court, Charles Evans Hughes. Roosevelt's inaugural address was broadcasted over the radio, something that would be done from then on. Millions must have been listening and hoping for some words of encouragement. He began:

> President Hoover, Mr. Chief Justice, my friends: This is a day of national consecration, and I am certain, that my fellow-Americans expect that on my induction into the Presidency I will address them with a candor and a decision which the present situation of our nation impels.

> This is preeminently the time to speak the truth, the whole truth, frankly and boldly. Nor need we shrink from honestly facing conditions in our country today. This great nation will endure as it has endured, will revive and will prosper.

> So first of all let me assert my firm belief that the only thing we have to fear is fear itself. [2]

In January 1933, two months before the inauguration, the banks of Nevada were closed by the governor's proclamation. The next month, the State of Louisiana and the State of Michigan also closed their banks. By March 1, half the country had suspended banking. On March 1, the governor of New York shut banks in his state. The country was in a panic like none other it had ever experienced.

President Roosevelt wasted no time. On March 5, the day after he was sworn in, he declared a Bank Holiday that closed every bank in the country. This bold, decisive move saved the country. He called for a special session of Congress and got two bills passed quickly—the Banking Act that provided help to the banks and the Economy Act that sliced federal employees' salaries and reduced veterans' benefits, which gave financial relief to the tune of $500,000,000.

By allowing the sale of 3.2 beer, which was legal, they sought to take in $150,000,000 in revenue. This prompted the repeal of prohibition, and the Twenty-first Amendment was ratified in December of 1933. [3]

That was the beginning of Roosevelt's administration—bold, imaginative and decisive. In the next few years, so many different acts and programs were introduced that the media began referring to them by the first letter of the names.

ALPHABET SOUP

The FERA (Federal Emergency Relief Administration) created on May 12, 1933, was an expansion of the RFC (Reconstruction Finance Corporation) started under President Hoover. It appropriated $500,000,000 for food, clothing, shelter, and work.

The AAA—Agricultural Adjustment Act—also passed on May 12, provided for the reduction of cultivated land in order to regulate surpluses and help to raise farm prices.

The NIRA—National Industrial Recovery Act—was passed on June 16, 1933. It declared an emergency in unemployment and created the NRA—National Recovery Administration—that developed codes for reorganization and control of industry. The codes established the forty-hour week and a minimum *weekly* wage of between $12 and $15. It provided for collective bargaining, prohibited children under sixteen years of age from working, and required the books of businesses to be accessible. In 1935, the U.S. Supreme Court found the codes and monitoring practices so complicated that they unanimously voted the NRA unconstitutional.

The CWA—Civil Works Administration—was begun in November 1933 to create jobs for 4,000,000 men during the winter of 1933-34. Other organizations were created to also deal with unemployment. The WPA—Work Progress Administration—was designed to put as many as men as possible to work on road repairs and construction of schools, libraries, post offices, and even encouraged artists, musicians, and writers.

The CCC—Civilian Conservation Corps—created in March 1933 was extremely popular. Young men, eighteen to twenty-eight were placed in camps and put to work building wildlife preserves, national parks, erosion-control dams, as well as firebreaks. They planted trees and fought forest fires. When Roosevelt tried to reduce the program in July 1936, there was such an outcry that the program continued.

The TVA—Tennessee Valley Authority—was established in May 1933. Its main purpose was to develop and control the Tennessee River by building dams that gave electricity to people in seven states: Tennessee, Virginia, North Carolina, Georgia, Alabama, Kentucky, and Mississippi.

There were offshoots of these programs that helped millions. Roosevelt also wanted other changes that would benefit the country as well as help people and protect their investments. The FDIC—Federal Deposit Insurance Corporation—insured savings deposits. The SEC—Security Exchange Commission—was created to monitor the sale of stocks, something that was badly needed, especially after the 1929 *crash*.

The Social Security Act was created to provide for some assistance when people retired. They would contribute to the fund with a payroll tax that was automatically taken from their paychecks and matched by their employers. It became law on August 14, 1935.

The HOLC—Home Owners' Loan Corporation—helped home owners refinance to avoid defaulting on payments. The FHA—Federal Housing Authority—encouraged home ownership by guaranteeing loans made by banks up to 80 percent. The U.S. Housing Authority helped rebuild where slums existed and helped in low-cost housing.

The NLRA—National Labor Relations Act—gave workers the right to organize unions and to bargain collectively. The NLRB—National Labor Relations Board—was established to monitor relations between employers and workers.[4]

All of these emergency acts came about because of the need for action and because Roosevelt brought dedicated people into his cabinet. Four of his cabinet members served longer than any other—eleven or twelve years!

FOUR LONG-SERVING AND FAITHFUL CABINET MEMBERS

Cordell Hull had served in the Spanish-American War, the House of Representatives, and was elected to the Senate in 1931 when in 1933, Roosevelt asked him to become the secretary of state. He served until 1944.[5]

Henry Morgenthau, Jr., was a friend of Roosevelt's from their New York days together. In 1934, the secretary of the treasury, William Wooden, became ill, and Roosevelt asked his friend to take his place. He served until Roosevelt's death in 1945.

Harold Ickes, a graduate of the University of Chicago, was also active in the Republican Party. Roosevelt selected Ickes for the secretary of interior position. Also appointed administrator of public works, Ickes was responsible for spending billions of dollars on various-needed projects.[6]

The first woman to ever serve in a president's cabinet was Frances Perkins. Her long and faithful service was held during the entire time that Roosevelt was president, and then she worked with Harry Truman when Roosevelt died. Perkins was responsible for drafting important legislation including the Social Security Act and the Fair Labor Standards Act.[7]

There were, of course, others in the cabinet, but none served longer or more faithfully than those four. They truly helped get the new administration off to a good beginning—Roosevelt liked to refer to his programs as the New Deal.

All of this was a start to the country working its way out of the great depression. People began to have faith in their government with the many ways that were found to help people. Some interesting and far-reaching events took place during Roosevelt's first term.

On March 2, 1933, the movie *King Kong*, starring Fay Wray, had its premier in New York City. People loved it. In May 1933, the Century of Progress World's Fair opened on Chicago's lakefront, celebrating one hundred years of the city's existence. On June 5, the United States abandoned the gold standard. On July 22, Wiley Post completed the first solo flight around the world in seven days, eighteen hours and forty-five minutes. On December 5, national prohibition ended.

On October 17, 1933, a 1921 Nobel Prize winner for physics recipient chose the United States over other countries that offered him teaching posts. His property had been confiscated by the Nazi government of Germany. His name was Albert Einstein.[8]

On May 24, 1935, Major League Baseball's first night game was played in Cincinnati. The Reds defeated the Philadelphia Phillies 2-1. The very next day, May 25, Babe Ruth, playing for the Boston Braves in a game in Pittsburgh's Forbes Field, hit his 714th and the final home run of his career. The Boston Braves moved their franchise to Milwaukee, Wisconsin, and later moved it to Atlanta, Georgia. Here, Henry "Hank" Aaron broke Babe Ruth's record on April 8, 1974.

On June 10, 1935 William Wilson and Dr. Robert Smith founded Alcoholics Anonymous in Akron, Ohio, to help those people who were addicted. On November 22, 1935, a flying boat, the *China Clipper*, took off from Alameda, California, carrying more than one hundred thousand pieces of mail on the first transpacific airmail flight.

On August 9, 1936, Jesse Owens won his fourth gold medal at the Berlin Olympics, as the United States took first place in the 400-meter relay. On September 7, Boulder Dam, later named Hoover Dam, went into operation, creating Lake Mead as the dam began transmitting electricity to Los Angeles.

On December 30, 1936 the UAW (United Auto Workers) staged the first sit-down strike at the Fisher Body plant in Flint, Michigan. It ended on February 11, 1937, when General Motors agreed to recognize the United Auto Workers Union.

The country was a long ways from prosperity, but things were looking up. It made the election of 1936 the greatest one-sided victory since James Monroe's electoral win with all but one vote. Roosevelt received 523 electoral votes. The Republican candidate, Alfred Landon from Kansas, only got 8 electoral votes

1937-1941 ROOSEVELT'S SECOND ADMINISTRATION

The Twentieth Amendment went into effect, and Roosevelt began his second term on January 20, 1937. This meant no more holdovers—no "lame ducks." In February, Roosevelt wanted to add federal justices to those already appointed. It was seen very quickly that the purpose of packing the Supreme Court was a way of getting his programs a favorable backing, since he had to swallow the U.S. Supreme

Court's decision of finding the NRA unconstitutional. Efforts to get this approved by Congress failed.

In June 1937, and again in early 1938, two Supreme Court justices resigned, so Roosevelt was able to appoint two judges. Hugo Black, from Alabama, was a former member of the Ku Klux Klan. He was confirmed, after much controversy. Stanley Reed was appointed and confirmed the next year, but the confirmations left a bitter feeling toward Roosevelt's attempt to get around the Constitution.

A large part of Roosevelt's election margin of victory was because of the labor vote. When the Committee for Industrial Organization (CIO) engineered sit-down strikes in the automobile and steel industries, and the government stepped in to help arbitrate the settlements, the Department of Labor sided with the workers.

These bad feelings prevailed at the end of 1937 and the early part of 1938, bringing a recession, growing unemployment, and decreased production. These discouraging signs made for bad feelings between the administration and business leaders. The two sides blamed each other for the cause. It would take a war to bring the country out of this sad chapter of United States history.[9]

FOREIGN AFFAIRS OF THE THIRTIES

In November 1933, the United States recognized the new government of Russia, the Union of Soviet Socialist Republics. In 1934 the Tydings-McDuffie Act provided for the independence of the Philippines in ten years. That would be in the middle of World War II, but nobody realized it at the time.

The Civil War in Spain that started in July 1936, and the invasion of China by Japan a year later, July 1937, was of concern to the United States. Unlike the attempts made by the Kellogg Briand Pact to outlaw war, Congress took the opposite approach and sought neutrality, forbidding the shipment of arms to countries at war.

Italy invaded Ethiopia in 1935, and the only action the League of Nations took was to set sanctions (no importing of Italian goods). Italy's response was to leave the League of Nations. When the war ended in March 1936, with Italy occupying Ethiopia, the League of Nations dropped its sanctions.

In 1933, Germany withdrew from the League of Nations. On March 7, 1936, Adolph Hitler shocked the world by denouncing the Versailles Treaty's clause that provided for German disarmament. France, Great Britain, and Italy only put up a strong protest. The League of Nations did *nothing*. A year later on March 12 and 13, Germany invaded Austria. In September 1938, Germany annexed the Sudeten region of Czechoslovakia. Hitler had bluffed and acquired land without firing a shot. On November 9, 1938, Nazis looted and burned synagogues and Jewish-owned stores and houses in Germany and Austria in what became known as *Kristallnacht* (crystal night). Hitler's next objective was Poland, but first he had to make a nonaggression pact with Joseph Stalin.

Roosevelt had attempted to appeal to Germany, Poland, and Italy to discuss and arbitrate the problems between Germany and Poland. Hitler renewed his demands for a freehand in dealing with Poland regarding the Danzig corridor that had been given to Poland after World War I. When Poland would not back down to Hitler's demands, German troops invaded Poland on September 1, 1939.

Britain and France mobilized but were willing to negotiate if Germany withdrew from Poland. They refused, and Britain and France declared war on Germany September 3, 1939. World War II had begun.

UNITED STATES EVENTS LEADING UP TO WORLD WAR II

During Roosevelt's second term in office, a number of interesting as well as significant events took place. May 28, 1937 was the opening of the Golden Gate Bridge in California. Roosevelt pushed a button in Washington, D.C., signaling that traffic could cross. On October 27, 1938, DuPont gave a name to a newly developed synthetic yarn—they called it *nylon*. It would make possible stockings for the ladies; but more important, during World War II, thousands of parachutes would be made and used from it.

On June 12, 1939, the National Baseball Hall of Fame and Museum was dedicated in Cooperstown, New York. On June 28, 1939, Pan American Airways began Transatlantic service between New York and Portugal. It would only last a short time due to the coming conflict. On August 2, 1939, Albert Einstein sent a letter to President Roosevelt:

> Some recent work by E. Fermi and Léo Szilárd, which has been communicated to me in manuscript, leads me to expect the element of uranium may be turned into a new and important source of energy in the immediate future. Certain aspects of the situation which have arisen seem to call for watchfulness and, if necessary, quick action on the part of the Administration.[10]

Thanks to Einstein and Roosevelt, this letter resulted in the assignment of government funds for the development of the atomic bomb.

HITLER HAS ONLY ONE ENEMY TO DEFEAT IN ORDER TO RULE EUROPE

Great Britain had been struggling alone since the fall of France. Germany had swept through Poland as had Russia, and Poland was finished on September 29. Germany next invaded Norway on April 6, 1940 and captured it by April 30. On May 10, 1940, Germany invaded France by way of Belgium and Holland, as they had done in the First World War. By June 17, France asked for an armistice.

The only positive event was the successful evacuation of over 335,000 English and French troops from the beaches on the coast of France. This took place at the end of May 1940 and would always be remembered as the miracle of Dunkirk.

The Battle of France was over. Next would be the Battle of Britain, but before Germany could invade England, it had to destroy the Royal Air Force. That did not happen, and the tired and weary and outnumbered British fliers continued to battle Germany's Luftwaffe during the summer of 1940. On September 15, 1940, the tide turned as the Royal Air Force planes shot down *175* aircraft of the German Luftwaffe. Prime Minister Winston Churchill said it best:

> Never in the field of human conflict was so much owed by so many to so few.[11]

UNITED STATES REACTION TO THE WAR IN EUROPE

The United States amended the Neutrality Act of 1937, repealed the embargo on arms, and placed exports to belligerents on a cash-and-carry basis. That was in November 1939. In June of 1940, Congress passed the national defense tax bill that provided $994,300,000 for defense. In September the Selective Training and Service Act was passed, which meant all men between twenty-one and thirty-six were required to register for one year of training. By October 16, 16,400,000 were registered; and on October 29, the first peacetime draft lottery began. On November 15, 1940, the first 75,000 men were called to armed forces duty under peace time conscription. Seventy years earlier, Abraham Lincoln had asked for the same number of volunteers. On December 30, the Arroyo Seco Parkway, connecting Los Angeles and Pasadena, was opened. The Interstate Highway System was years away.

In November 1940, the Republicans went with Wendell Willkie who had been nominated over Thomas Dewey and Robert Taft, son of William Howard Taft, twenty-seventh president. The Democrats nominated President Roosevelt for a precedent-setting third term.

The results were not as huge a difference as in 1936, but they were significant. Roosevelt received 27,243,673 popular votes, almost the same as he had received in 1936. Wilkie received 22,304,755 popular votes. The Electoral College gave Roosevelt 449 votes while Wilkie received 82 votes.

In 1937, associate justice of the Supreme Court, Benjamin Cardoza, who had been appointed by President Hoover, stated in the case of *Palko v. Connecticut*:

> Freedom of expression is the matrix, the indispensable condition of nearly every other form of freedom.

Roosevelt must have read the court proceedings in that trial. Just prior to the end of Roosevelt's second term, on January 6, 1941, he gave his annual speech to

Congress. In the speech, he gave one of the greatest and yet succinct statements that expressed what America stood for:[12]

> In the future days, which we seek to make secure, we look forward to a world founded upon four essential human freedoms.
>
> The first is the freedom of speech and expression—everywhere in the world.
>
> The second is the freedom of every person to worship God in his own way—everywhere in the world.
>
> The third is freedom from want—which translated into world terms, means economic understandings which will secure to every nation a healthy peace time life for its inhabitants—everywhere in the world.
>
> The fourth is freedom from fear—which translated into world terms, means a world-wide reduction of armaments to such a point and in such a thorough fashion that no nation will be in a position to commit an act of physical aggression against any neighbor—anywhere in the world.

1941-1945 ROOSEVELT'S THIRD ADMINISTRATION

Roosevelt was given the oath of office on the Capitol steps on January 20, 1941. His vice president was Henry Wallace, son of Henry Wallace who had served as secretary of agriculture under President Harding.

On March 11, 1941, the Congress passed Roosevelt's Lend-Lease Act. This gave the president the power to provide both goods and services to countries whose defense he believed vital to the security of the United States.

In May, President Roosevelt proclaimed a state of national emergency. In June, the United States ordered German consulates throughout the country closed.

On July 26, General Douglas MacArthur was named commander of the U.S. forces in the Philippines. In August, aboard a British battleship, Roosevelt met with Britain's prime minister, Winston Churchill.

They proclaimed in a historic document, a statement of common aims. It was called the Atlantic Charter:[13]

1. Neither of their countries sought any territories.
2. They desired no territorial changes except by people freely expressed.
3. They respected the rights of all people to choose their own form of government.
4. They respected all countries the right to trade as the needs arose.

5. They wanted to secure improved labor standards, economic advancement, and social security.
6. They wanted to afford to all nations the means to dwell safely within their borders.
7. They wanted to assure travel on the high seas and oceans without hindrance.
8. And last, they wanted everyone to abandon the use of force.

Back in Washington four days later, Roosevelt signed a bill extending the length of service to eighteen months of the men who had been drafted earlier.

On December 2, 1941, President Roosevelt asked the government of Japan for a definition of its aims in Indochina.

Five days later, on December 7, their response was a surprise attack on the United States Naval Base in Pearl Harbor on Oahu, Hawaii. They also attacked the Philippines, Guam, Midway Island, Wake Island, Hong Kong, and Malaya.

War had come to America. Here was another challenge. How would the United States of America respond? Would it answer the call as it had in 1776, 1812, 1846, 1861, 1898, and 1917?

It had weathered the Great Depression. Now it must face a conflict that would determine the course of civilization for years, if not generations, to come.

CHAPTER XXIII

THEY ANSWERED THE CALL

Yesterday, December 7, 1941—a date which will live in infamy—the United States of America was suddenly and deliberately attacked by naval and air forces of the Empire of Japan.

As Commander-in-Chief of the Army and Navy, I have directed all measures be taken for our defense.

Always will we remember the character of the onslaught against us.

No matter how long it may take to overcome this premeditated invasion, the American people in their righteous might will win through to absolute victory.

With confidence in our armed forces—with the unbounded determination of our people—we will gain the inevitable triumph—so help us God.

I ask that the Congress declare that since the unprovoked and dastardly attack by Japan on Sunday, December seventh, a state of war has existed between the United States and the Japanese Empire.[1]

That message to the Congress on Monday, December 8, by President Roosevelt was probably heard by more Americans than any other previous message. The next day and the day after that, all week long and for many weeks to follow, thousands of young men lined up to volunteer for the army, the navy, the coast guard, or the marines. They didn't wait to be called. The minimum draft age at the time was twenty-one—later, in November 1942, it was lowered to eighteen. Men of all ages lined up at the recruiting offices across the country. They would accept "men"—boys still in high school aged seventeen—if they got their parents' *OK*. Those who had served in the CCC (Civilian Conservation Corps) or WPA (Work Progress Administration) more or less anticipated what was in store for them, having to work hard and take orders.

By the end of the war, nearly 16 million men would serve their country by either enlisting or being drafted. Of those nearly 16 million, 405,399 died in the service of their country—2.5 percent of the 16 million.[2]

The males were not the only ones that wanted to serve their country in uniform. About 330,000 women joined one of the five different women's corps. The army unit was called the Women's Army Corps—WACs; the navy had the initials WAVES which stood for Women Accepted for Volunteer Emergency Service. Only the Women's Marines served without initials. The SPARS represented the Coast Guard Women, and they used the Coast Guard motto, *Semper Paratus*—always ready. The Nurse Corps totaled *seventy-four thousand* commissioned officers. Five percent of all of the women served overseas with *thirty* being killed from enemy action.[3]

THE ESSENTIAL OF MODERN WARFARE

The Civil War tactics were not much different from those of the Roman legions. They marched abreast in long lines with their weapons. Their casualties were staggering.

The warfare used in World War I was not much different, with troops charging out of their trenches. The difference was the machine gun, which dealt tremendous deaths, to the charging soldiers. After the war, military leaders saw a need for a different strategy. The tank had been used late in the war, and large improvements were completed over the years between wars.

Germany led the way with their style of warfare. It was called *blitzkrieg*—a battle fought with great speed and force, usually with surprise and with close coordination of the ground forces with the air forces. They were successful in both Poland and France. They tried the same tactics when they invaded Russia in the summer of 1941. Time, weather, logistic problems, including extended lines of supply, and communication eventually caught up with them and contributed to the final defeat, but that was years away.

Land warfare would require large numbers of troops, armor, and most important, adequate supplies of gasoline, ordinance, food, and ammunition—all supplied by sufficient transportation.

Air warfare would be the right combination of fighters and bombers, again with the needed support—air fields, trained ground personnel, and sufficient supply of fuel and replacement parts.

The biggest change came in the methods of naval warfare. The last great naval battle of World War I was the Battle of Jutland fought off the coast of Denmark on

May 31 and June 1, 1916. Both Germany and the British each lost six capital ships, and both sides could see each other, even at a distance of six miles apart.

The Japanese changed all that with brilliant use of aircraft carriers guarded by both cruisers and destroyers. It would be *the* way naval engagements would be carried out throughout World War II, with a few exceptions.

There were basically three separate factors that would be the difference in winning the war—economic strength, well-planned military operations, and wise use of military intelligence.[4]

AMERICA'S ECONOMIC STRENGTH MAKES THE DIFFERENCE

Americans had invented the automobile and assembly line production. They also invented sewing machines, washing machines, the typewriter, and a host of useful mechanical devices. When asked to produce war goods—planes, tanks, ships, trucks, guns of all sorts, ammunition, communication equipment for a variety of tasks, and even nonperishable, and easily portable food—the American industries' know-how and ingenuity came through.

The only rifle available to the U.S. troops in 1941 was the Springfield rifle, a bolt-action, single-shot piece with a five-round clip. John Garand had developed a semiautomatic rifle that fired an eight-round clip by just pulling the trigger. It went into production and was used later in 1942. The marines did not receive this improved rifle until after their first invasion in August of 1942.

Another valuable weapon that was developed was the bazooka. This light portable shoulder weapon was capable of launching armor-piercing rockets and was very effective against tanks. The flamethrower came later in the war and was used to destroy enemy soldiers inside of caves or pillboxes—a very thick-walled enclosure used for defense.

The Wiley-Knight Automotive Company developed a small but very useful four-wheeled vehicle that had the title of general purpose, or GP for short. It didn't take the GIs (an acronym for government issue—a term that someone named all soldiers, marines, and sailors), long to refer to the vehicle as a jeep.

The Douglas Aircraft Company had developed an airplane that was used almost immediately—the two-engine DC-3. The Army Air Corps designated it C-47. The four-engine model was the C-54. These and many more articles of war were developed and used throughout the war by both the Americans and their allies.

To feed thousands of soldiers, marines, and others where food could not be served fresh, the C rations (canned food) and K rations (packaged meals) became the staple that GIs had to eat, frequently with distaste. Dehydrated food like potatoes, even milk, were other often used food items that left a lot to be desired.

America became the *arsenal of democracy*. The women of America proved that they could do any job anytime and anywhere. They came to work in record numbers.

They learned to weld; solder; measure with precision; and build planes, tanks, trucks, and ships. They did it gladly, knowing they were contributing to the war effort.[5]

Unemployment fell from 25 percent before Pearl Harbor to 1 percent during the war. Children became involved in many ways. They helped collect tin cans, wastepaper, aluminum, and bought war stamps to turn into war bonds. Everyone put up with rationing of meat, butter, sugar, coffee, shoes, and gasoline (mostly to save rubber tires that could not be manufactured because rubber plantations were in the hands of the enemy.)[6] Synthetic tires had yet to be invented.

Shortly after the war started and before the country was on a war footing in terms of production, President Roosevelt promised 50,000 planes a year. Most people thought he was crazy. By the end of 1942, the United States had produced 47,836 airplanes. The next year, the number jumped to 85,898 and the next year, 96,318. The year the war ended, the United States had made nearly 280,000 airplanes of every conceivable type[7]

On December 2, 1942 the first self-sustaining nuclear reaction was achieved by physicist Enrico Fermi and forty-two colleagues in a squash court under the grandstand of the University of Chicago's Stagg Field. It was the first step in producing an atomic bomb.

On October 26, 1944, Roosevelt announced with pride that:

> The production that has flowed from this country to all the battlefronts of the world has been due to the efforts of American business, American labor, and American farmers, working together as a patriotic team.[8]

SETBACKS

Because the United States Army was so small before the war—175,000 men—no offensive action could be taken. It would require time to train and equip enough men to take the fight to the enemy. Until that time, Japan and Germany were able to run roughshod over the world.

Germany had invaded the Soviet Union in the summer of 1941. They reached the suburbs of Moscow, but were stalled there by the extreme cold weather in the winter of 1941-1942.

Japan, on the other hand, had gone from one success to another. The first United States possession to fall was the island of Guam, which was used as a fuel stop for the transpacific Pan American clipper planes. It fell on December 10, 1941. On that same date, the Japanese air force sank two of Great Britain's largest naval vessels—the battleships *Prince of Wales* and the *Repulse*. They also attacked Clark Field in the Philippines, destroying most of the B-17 bombers. The blame for this negligence was thought, by some, to be the fault of General MacArthur who had ample warning following the attack on Pearl Harbor.

On December 11, a Japanese fleet bombarded Wake Island with the intention of capturing the small fueling station in short order. The U.S. Marines, part of a defensive battalion with 1,200 civilian workers who were preparing defensive positions, fought valiantly, sinking two Japanese ships. The enemy had to withdraw but returned in greater strength two weeks later. After fierce fighting, the marines were forced to surrender, the first time a U.S. Marine outfit *ever* had to do so.[9]

The Japanese made landings on the major islands of the Philippines between December 10 and December 22. By January 2, 1942, they had captured the capital, Manila. The American forces and the Filipinos fought a withdrawing action into the peninsula called Bataan. Here, fighting on half rations, they delayed the Japanese through the months of February and March. On April 8, General Wainwright ordered the withdrawal from Bataan to the island fortress of Corregidor. Here, the starving United States and Filipino forces held out until May 8 when fifteen thousand Americans and Filipino troops on Corregidor surrendered.[10]

General MacArthur had been ordered by President Roosevelt to go to Australia. He left Corregidor with his wife, his son, and his staff on March 11 by riding in torpedo patrol boats (PT boats), traveling at night to the southernmost island on Mindanao. From there they were flown to Australia where MacArthur proclaimed, "I came through, and I shall return." Those who were left to fight had a song that went:

> We're the battling bastards of Bataan;
> No mama, no papa, no Uncle Sam;
> No aunts, no uncles, no nephews, no nieces;
> No pills, no planes, no artillery pieces . . .
> And nobody gives a damn![11]

In the meantime, Japan continued winning battles wherever they went. Hong Kong fell on Christmas Day. Singapore—the British fortress of the Far East—had their guns pointed out to sea. The Japanese landed farther up the Malaya coast and drove down and captured Singapore on February 15, 1942.

With the newspapers and radio telling the American people of the continuous victories by the Japanese, there was a real fear that Japan would conquer anywhere they went. The people on the West Coast of the United States were even fearful of an invasion.

Politicians, led by California Governor Earl Warren, wanted the 127,000 Japanese living in the United States moved into the interior. Even though 60 percent of the Japanese were born in the United States, the demand was for *all* to be removed. On February 19, 1942, President Roosevelt signed an executive order, giving the military authority to relocate and intern Japanese Americans. They had to sell their homes at a great loss and lose everything they could not take with them to the internment camps. It was a sad day in American history.[12]

In December and January, Japan captured Borneo and its oil fields. In February, they took Sumatra, and in March Java. A small group of allied ships from America, Australia, and the Netherlands were destroyed in the three-day battle on February 27 through March 1. On April 1, Japanese forces invaded New Guinea, the second largest island on earth. (Greenland is first.) Their intentions were to capture Port Moresby, an Australian base on the southeast tip of New Guinea, and from there they could threaten Australia. To do so, they needed a naval task force to destroy the defending Australian air force.[13]

Prior to the war, the United States had deciphered the Japanese diplomatic code. The United States was able to "read" the encoded radio messages that Japan had been sending to Washington. On Oahu, Hawaii, Commander Joseph Rochefort was the chief cryptanalyst. Working night and day in the early months of the war, he was able to "break" some of Japan's military code and discovered that a naval task force was heading toward New Guinea and the Coral Sea. Admiral Nimitz, who had replaced Admiral Kimmel, using Rochefort's information sent two aircraft carriers to engage them in battle. The aircraft carriers *Hornet* and *Enterprise* had not returned from their surprise bombing of Tokyo on April 18, led by Lieutenant Colonel Doolittle. The carriers *Yorktown* and *Lexington* were sent under the command of Admiral Frank Fletcher.

The battle was the first time naval forces of both sides never saw each other's ships except through the aircraft that attacked each other's ships. The United States fought to a draw and lost the carrier *Lexington*; the *Yorktown* was damaged, but Japan lost a carrier and other naval vessels. More important, it forced Japan to reconsider the invasion of Australia and instead, concentrated on warfare in the Central Pacific.

Japan, humiliated by the bombing of their capital city, decided to force the United States to come out and fight by capturing Midway Island. Commander Rochefort had been working furiously on a small piece of code work that finally told him of Japan's plans for Midway. Nimitz didn't hesitate. He sent aircraft carriers *Hornet*, *Enterprise*, and the quickly repaired *Yorktown* to wait near Midway Island.

There, on June 3 through June 6, 1942, one of the major naval battles of *all* time took place, and the U.S. naval fliers bombed and sank *four* Japanese aircraft carriers. It slowed down the Japanese navy, but the Japanese army was still a formidable foe. The United States lost the aircraft carrier *Yorktown*.

During the spring of 1942, it was discovered that Japan was building an airbase on the southernmost island in the Solomon Island chain, Guadalcanal. If completed, it would provide an airbase for bombers that could cut the lifeline of supply ships coming from the Unites States, headed for Australia with much needed troops and supplies. A major decision, one that would have far-reaching consequences, had to be made and made fast.[14]

Was the United States prepared to go on the offensive? Was this the end of the set back? Time would tell.

UNITED STATES OFFENSE IN THE PACIFIC THEATER

In the summer of 1942, Japan attempted to capture Port Moresby by crossing the Owen Stanley Range of Mountains from the north side of New Guinea. The Australians stopped them, and it was rare good news to come out of the Southwest Pacific area.

When the powers in Washington found out about the Japanese building an airfield on Guadalcanal, Admiral King ordered Admiral Nimitz to send in the marines. Though weak due to limited training, Vice Admiral Ghormely executed the order. He sent the First Marine Division into Guadalcanal and two close islands, Tulagi and Gutava, under the command of Major General Vandergrift. They met little opposition on landing, and the fleeing Japanese had left large supplies of food as well as airfield equipment to build landing strips. The next few months were most decisive.

The Japanese navy scored victories over the American and Australian navies. They sank four cruisers and a destroyer as well as damaged another cruiser and two more destroyers without losing a ship in the battle. Admiral Fletcher made the decision to withdraw his fleet, including ships with badly needed supplies for the marines. The Japanese reinforced Guadalcanal shortly afterward, and the marines were left to fend for themselves. Five weeks into the fight for Guadalcanal, Admiral Ghormely advised General Vandergrift to consider either surrendering or abandoning his positions and fight a guerrilla style of warfare.[15]

Here began the longest and most deadly battle of the entire Pacific campaign. The United States Marines fought for over six months and not just the Japanese. They had to contend with a lack of food, malaria, mosquitoes, nightly bombing and constant rain. It is difficult—almost impossible—to picture what they went through. An epitaph on the grave of Pfc. Cameron of the United States Marines on Guadalcanal read:

> And when he goes to heaven
> To Saint Peter he will tell:
> Another Marine reporting, sir;
> I've served my time in hell.

For *six months*, the marines fought on land. The U.S. Marine air force took on the Japanese air force, and the two navies had seven major engagements. The U.S. Navy lost two carriers, seven cruisers, and fifteen other warships. A total of 134 aircrafts had been shot down, but some of the pilots bailed out and were rescued. The Japanese lost two battleships, one light carrier, four cruisers, seventeen other warships, and 1,300 irreplaceable aviators.[16]

Leaders were changed during those critical months. Admiral William "Bull" Halsey replaced Ghormaley, and Admiral Kincaid took over from Fletcher. Why was this battle which lasted so long and was fought so fiercely so important? The code breakers had discovered two important messages of the Japanese. One of the messages from Japanese Lieutenant General Harukichi Hyakutake to the commander of the Seventeenth Army read, "The operation to surround and recapture Guadalcanal will truly decide the fate of the control of the entire Pacific."[17]

The other message they decoded gave the exact itinerary of Admiral Yamamoto's visits to different battle areas. With that knowledge, the American army air force sent long-range P-38 Lightning fighters to the island of Bougainville and caught Yamamoto as he was about to land. He was killed, but the news was not released as it would have tipped off the Japanese that their code had been broken.

On February 9, 1943, the battle for Guadalcanal in the Southwest Pacific ended with an American victory. This battle, the first offensive move against the Japanese, began on August 7, 1942. It followed the Battle of Midway where the U.S. Navy had engaged a much larger naval force attempting to capture Midway Island. These two battles, one lasting only three days and the other lasting six months, were the turning points of the war, though the Japanese fought defensively until August 13, 1945, following the dropping of the second atomic bomb on Nagasaki.

There were many other battles in the Pacific theater. At Buna, New Guinea, MacArthur and the Australians destroyed the Japanese forces that had threatened Port Moresby. This baptism of fire for American soldiers was completed by September of 1943.

MacArthur's next objective was Lae, farther up the coast of New Guinea. Here he used paratroopers of the Eleventh Airborne. He then made a brilliant decision to *jump ahead* or skip areas of Japanese strongholds along the coast. The abandoned Japanese slowly starved. His next invasion was Hollandia in the Netherlands' part of New Guinea in April 1944. The islands of Biak and Morotai were taken in May and September of 1944. By October, MacArthur was ready to keep his promise and return to the Philippines.[18]

In the Solomon Island chain, the, marines took the Russell Islands in February 1943, New Georgia in June, Vella Lavella in August, Treasury Island in October, and Bougainville, the largest in the chain, in November 1943.[19]

In the central part of the Pacific under the command of Admiral Nimitz, when enough marines had been trained, he ordered invasions of Tarawa and Makin islands in November 1943. Starting in 1944, the following islands were invaded and captured: in January Kwajalein fell; in February Eniwetok. The Marianas were a group of three islands—Saipan was the toughest to take in June 1944, followed by Guam and Tinian in July. Tinian and Saipan would both be airbases from which B-29s would take off and bomb Japan. The Island of Palau was captured on September 15, 1944, just a month before MacArthur invaded the Philippines.[20]

Starting on June 19, 1944, the largest naval battle of the Pacific War took place. The Japanese fleet, sailing from the Philippines, consisted of nine aircraft carriers and other supporting vessels, including a large number of battle cruisers. A U.S.

submarine spotted the fleet and signaled the U.S. fleet under the command of Vice Admiral Marc Mitscher. Though the Japanese spotted the Americans first, Mitscher's naval air men were waiting for them. The air battle lasted all day, with the Japanese losing 350 planes to the United States losses of 30 aircraft. The battle was dubbed the Great Marianas Turkey Shoot. With daylight fading, the American pilots could hardly see the carriers to land. Admiral Mitscher ordered all ships to turn their lights on in spite of the danger of enemy submarines.[21]

On October 20, 1944 the U.S. Navy brought MacArthur's army to Leyte, one of the eastern Philippine islands. Three days later, the U.S. Navy destroyed a major portion of the Japanese navy in the Battle of Leyte Gulf. On July 5, 1945, the Philippines were back in United States' hands.

Iwo Jima was invaded on February 19, 1945, after weeks of shelling by the U.S. Navy, but it was still one of the bloodiest island fights of the entire war. On 23 February, members of the Fifth Marine Division planted a U.S. flag atop Mt. Suribachi. The act was caught on film and still pictures and became one of the most famous moments of World War II in the Pacific. Today, a statue of the men raising the flag, commemorating this heroic act, can be seen in Washington, D.C.

There were 20,965 casualties and of those, 6,821 brave marines gave their lives. Admiral Chester Nimitz spoke of this battle that lasted twenty-six days:

> Uncommon valor was a common virtue.

Iwo Jima, after it was secured, was used for emergency landings of B-29s that had bombed Japan. There were 24,761 crewmen saved by being able to land on this eight-square-mile island that was only 775 miles from Japan.[22] The last island to be invaded was done by both the army and the marines. It was Okinawa, only 350 miles from Japan. It started on April 1, 1945 and lasted to the end of June. Of the 100,000 Japanese soldiers on the island, only 7,500 were alive at the end to surrender.

ROOSEVELT PICKS MEN WHO KNOW HOW TO LEAD

President Roosevelt had picked leaders who proved their worth. His secretary of war Henry Stimson and secretary of navy William Frank Knox were both Republicans and did a superb job. General George C. Marshall was the chief of staff and was responsible for selection and, when necessary, discharging men under him. Admiral King had the same responsibility for the navy, which included the marines. General Hap Arnold, though part of the army, was in charge of the air force and developed an offensive weapon called daylight strategic precision bombing.

Roosevelt traveled overseas during the war on three different occasions to meet with other world leaders—Winston Churchill, Chinese leader Chiang Kai-shek, and Joseph Stalin—the Soviet leader. Roosevelt's first overseas journey was in January

1943. The American press, wanting to know where the president was, was given the reply: he was at the "White House."

When he returned from the overseas conference, the press wanted to know why they had been lied to regarding Roosevelt's location, and the response was, "We never lied to you. He was in Casablanca, under tight security. If you know your Spanish you know that *casa* means house and *blanca* means white."

UNITED STATES IN THE EUROPEAN THEATER

Hitler made his third mistake on December 10, 1941. Germany declared war on the United States. His first mistake was to allow 335,000 allied troops to be evacuated from Dunkirk in the last days of May 1940. He halted his tanks because Field Marshall Herman Goring wanted the glory of having his Luftwaffe finish the job. The RAF held off the German air force and allowed their escape. Those men who made it back to England would be the nucleus of a growing army that would someday recross the English Channel.

The second mistake was attacking Russia. At first successful, the German army soon bogged down in a war of attrition and eventually collapse from the weight of fighting a two front war.

The United States' response to Hitler's decision to declare war on the United States was swift. December 11, Roosevelt asked for a declaration of war against both Germany and Italy. Mussolini had followed Hitler and had declared war against the United States also. Roosevelt's request to Congress included the following:

> The long-known and the long-expected has thus taken place. The forces endeavoring to enslave the entire world now are moving towards this hemisphere.

> Never before has there been a greater challenge to life, liberty and civilization.

> I therefore request the Congress to recognize a state of war between the United States and Germany, and between the United States and Italy.[23]

The die was now cast. America was going to fight a two front war. Britain had been fighting Hitler for over two years, the Soviet Union for five and a half months. Now with the United States involved, there was a chance for civilization to survive.

While the Americans enlisted or were drafted and sent to the various army camps, naval stations, marine training centers, or air corps fields to train, Britain and Russia continued to fight the Germans and Italians on their respective fronts.

THE BRITISH CAMPAIGN IN AFRICA

In September 1940, Mussolini sent his army, headed by Marshall Graziani, to Libya and from there drove his army into Egypt. The British drove the Italians back to Libya. The Germans had defeated France, and Hitler could send troops to help his Axis partner. He sent Erwin Rommel, one of his best generals, with troops that became known as the *Afrika Korps.* On March 24, 1941, Rommel began his first offensive attack. He drove across Libya, bypassed Tobruk, and stopped before he could go into Egypt.

The British had captured the coding machine—an ultra—the Germans believed to be secure and unbreakable. With accurate knowledge, the RAF on the island of Malta—in the middle of the German's supply route—could bomb the slow-moving supply ships. Hitler thought of invading Malta, but when Rommel started his second offensive drive in May 1942, Hitler changed his mind.

Hitler had invaded Yugoslavia and then Greece. While he was eventually successful, he made the error of dividing his forces. He had the *Afrika Korps* attempt to take Egypt. He had troops fighting in the Balkans and the Island of Crete and was planning to invade Russia on June 22, 1941. His generals realized this military weakness but would never argue with their fuehrer.

Rommel was stopped at El Hammam, less than seventy miles from Cairo. People were ready to flee the capital of Egypt. Hitler ordered medals for the expected triumph. Mussolini planned to ride his favorite horse down the streets of Cairo.

Churchill went to Egypt in August 1942. He replaced General Auchinleck with General Alexander. General Gott was to take over the British Eighth Army, but was killed in an airplane crash. In his place they appointed Lieutenant General Bernard Montgomery. He was great at training troops and was very personable. His soldiers admired him. He had his faults, but results were what Churchill wanted.

When Montgomery felt they were ready, he started his offensive strike from where they had stopped Rommel—it was El Hamman, but also called El Alamein. The drive started on October 23, 1942, with great success. Rommel was back in Germany, resting in a sanatorium. His replacement in Africa had a heart attack and died. When Rommel got back to his *Afrika Korps,* he found disaster. Hitler gave orders to stand where they were, and if necessary, die. Rommel tried to comply, but later abandoned the order and retreated.[24]

Then on November 8, 1942, the United States Army landed in western North Africa. It was the Second front that Joseph Stalin wanted to take the pressure off his beleaguered armies. He really wanted an invasion of Europe, but this was what he got.

It is easy for historians, with 20/20 hindsight, to say that October and November were critical in World War II. The marines in the South Pacific were hanging on by the skin of their teeth in October 1942. The Germans were at the gates of Moscow and had all but eliminated the besieged city of Leningrad. They were about to capture Stalingrad and have all the oil they would need. Plans were being made to take Egypt and the Suez Canal. If Japan could conquer India, the Germans and Japanese could link up and rule the world.

But there would be two and a half more years of fighting and dying, and no one could predict what would happen. The United States' involvement in World War II obviously turned the tide, but not one fight, battle, or campaign made the difference. It had to be a combination of all of the countries that fought the Axis—Germany, Italy, and Japan. Together, the Allies turned the possibility of defeat into a victory for the people of the civilized world.

The U.S. "Arsenal of Democracy" made it possible to supply the allies with the needed tools for victory. The number of United States ships and men who manned them was a major factor. The freshly trained and superbly lead soldiers, sailors, marines, and airmen from the states were also a major contribution. How well did they do? Would there be setbacks? Could the untested Americans meet the necessary challenges before them? It is worthy of examination.

UNITED STATES INVOLVEMENT IN THE EUROPEAN THEATER

On November 8, 1942, the U.S. Army invaded three different locations in North Africa—Casablanca, along the Atlantic coast; Oran, on the Mediterranean coast; as was the third place, Algiers. It was not Eisenhower's first choice. Appointed by the chief of staff, General George C. Marshall, Ike, as he was called, was lieutenant colonel in 1940. He had served under MacArthur and had held important staff positions in Washington under Marshall. His greatest talents were his ability to get those of different persuasions to work together and his willingness to subordinate his ego for the greater good and his sense of what was important politically.[25]

Ike thought that with six months of intensive training and enough troops, France could be invaded. Churchill had seen the tragic consequences of the Dieppe Raid in August of 1942, which was a disaster. What they learned would be used in two years, but for now it was not at all practical. So Operation Torch was planned, approved, and carried out. It went smoothly at all three beaches. The problems came later when Rommel confronted the Americans for the first time in February 1943.

The American lieutenant general Lloyd Fredenhall made major mistakes at the battle area called Kasserine Pass in Tunisia. Eisenhower relieved him and appointed Major General George Patton. Patton's style of leadership made all the difference, and the American soldiers soon proved their worth. By May 7, 1943, when the Germans were pushed out of Africa, the GIs had learned to be crafty, competent, and courageous. They learned the art of camouflage, how to dig to stay safe and alive, and how to make patrolling pay off.[26]

On July 10, 1943, a combination of American and British infantry and paratroopers invaded the Island of Sicily and, by August 17, had taken the whole island. General Mark Clark, who had been training three divisions in Africa, sailed from there and on September 9 invaded Italy at Salarno, which was halfway up the coast. The Italians had quit the war, but the Germans put up stiff resistance to the point that General Mark Clark considered withdrawing his troops.[27]

The U.S. Air Force began bombing specific German targets and British and U.S. Navy destroyers and cruisers began providing shelling directed by artillery observers. This forced the Germans to withdraw farther up the coast to Naples. After that, the fighting was slow and progress even slower. The Americans finally got as far as Cassino by May 1944, and then they tried an end run around the Germans at Anzio. This almost became a disaster, but the U.S. prevailed and reached Rome on June 4, 1944. Italy had seen some of the hardest fighting up to that point.[28]

MEMORABLE AMERICANS

The Italian campaign bogged down from September 1943 to when U.S. forces finally reached Rome nine months later. But out of that part of the war came three individuals who left a mark that would be remembered for a long, long time.

Most war correspondents spent their time seeking information for stories to send back to the States by attaching themselves army or navy headquarters. Some went to the front lines, but none wrote about the war the way Ernie Pyle did. He wrote about the problems, concerns, and everyday happenings of the foot soldier in Italy. His columns were in many newspapers, and he gave the people back home a true picture of the situations that soldiers found themselves in. Near the end of the war in Europe, he went to the Pacific and, while there, was killed on a small island near Okinawa, called Ie Shiuma. He was buried there with this inscription on his grave:

At this spot the 77th Infantry Division lost a buddy, Ernie Pyle, 18 April 1945[29]

Another unforgettable character was Bill Mauldin, a cartoonist assigned to the Forty-fifth Infantry Division in Italy. His cartoons of Willie and Joe displayed the best picture of the many plights of the enlisted men. Some were very humorous and others told a story all their own with realistic portrayals how it really was over there and frequently in the front lines. Bill Mauldin's cartoons appeared both in the Forty-fifth Division's paper, but also in the army newspaper called *Stars and Stripes*. For his outstanding contribution, he was awarded the *Pulitzer Prize*.

The third person was a young man from Texas, named Audie Murphy. Assigned to the Thirty-sixth Infantry Division as a replacement, he fought in Africa, Italy, France, and Germany. He earned a battlefield commission and was awarded almost every medal that could be bestowed, including the Medal of Honor. After the war, he went to Hollywood and made movies. The first one was of his time in the army and called *To Hell and Back*.

OTHER HEROES

On February 3, 1943, the American troopship the *Dorchester* was hit by a torpedo in the North Atlantic. Four chaplains on board—a Catholic priest, a rabbi, and two Protestant ministers helped GIs and civilians on the sinking ship, distributing life jackets. When the supply ran out, they took off their own and gave them out—and went down with the sinking ship.

To land on the shores of foreign coasts in Europe and the many islands in the Pacific required *thousands* of special vessels. Andrew Higgins of New Orleans was responsible for designing and building four types of ships and boats that were used everywhere there was an invasion.

The largest vessel was the LST—landing ship, tank—that could run right up to the shore and discharge its cargo, either tanks, or trucks or Jeeps, with drivers all ready to run down the ramps that were dropped from the front of the ship. The next in size was the LCI—landing craft infantry—capable of running up to the shore and dropping down two ramps for the two hundred infantry or marines to run down and engage the enemy. The LCT—landing craft tank—could carry and discharge tanks or trucks loaded with soldiers. The smallest and best known of the four was the LCVP—landing craft for vehicles and personnel. These were the ones that transported troops who climbed down ropes from the side of the attack ships to be transported to the beach in waves—literally *hundreds* of them at one time.

What the enemy did not know was that the only *metal* on the LCVP was the ramp. The rest of the vessel was made of *plywood* and painted a metal gray. These LCVP were only thirty-six feet long and ten and a half feet wide, and could carry a platoon (about forty men) or a squad with a Jeep. Propelled by a diesel engine, twenty thousand of them were built. General Eisenhower said that the Higgins boats, as the GIs referred to them, won the war.[30]

THE SECOND FRONT COMES TO FRANCE

The largest and most famous invasion happened on June 6, 1944. It would have been impossible to have done it any sooner. The Dieppe Raid in 1942 was a disaster, but the military learned a great deal from it. The landing area had to be safe from enemy aircraft, so United States and British bombers pounded the enemy day and night. The fighter planes escorted the bombers as far as they could and continued to destroy the German Luftwaffe—bombers and fighters alike.

The actual planning had been going on for over two years, and when General Ike Eisenhower was appointed supreme Allied commander, he inherited the plans of what would be called Operation Overlord.[31]

The distance from England to France is only twenty miles between Dover and Pas-de-Calais. It was the logical place for the invasion. And that is exactly what the Allies wanted the Germans to think. To convince them that that was where it would take place, General Patton—in Germany's opinion, the best general that the Allies had—was given a "fake" army to be in charge of. Fake messages that could be heard across the English Channel were constantly sent regarding preparations, and orders were given between nonexisting outfits.

Hollywood artists and special effects personnel were employed to build fake but realistic-looking duplicates of airplanes, tanks and trucks. Some were made of rubber—blown up to look like the real thing.[32]

The planners thought of everything, but one thing they could not control was the weather. When the final date in early June was set, it was for a combination of reasons: warm weather, tides (low at dawn), and moonlight. June 5, 1944 was selected, but storms in the English Channel made it necessary to change the date.

The chief meteorologist, Group Captain Stagg, a Scotsman, predicted a thirty-six-hour relief from the storm. Not all of his fellow weathermen agreed, and when Ike confronted his staff, about half wanted to wait until another time. But Ike thought then decided and said, "OK, let's go."[33]

The greatest and largest undertaking began late at night on 5 June when paratroopers from the 82nd and 101st Airborne Divisions from the United States and the British 6th Airborne Gliders dropped behind enemy lines at strategic locations like the bridge nicknamed Pegasus, which was essential that it be captured so as to prevent German tanks in the Pas-de-Calais area from getting to the landing beaches in Normandy.

When the weather turned bad on June 4, and it looked like it would continue, Field Marshall Erwin Rommel drove to Germany to give his wife a pair of shoes for her birthday. When the invasion started on the morning of June 6, he was not available for immediate defensive decisions. When he did get back to Normandy, he realized he needed the Panzer Division's tanks and asked General Rundstedt, the overall general in charge, to ask Hitler for permission to transfer the tanks. The request was denied as Hitler thought the invasion at Normandy was a decoy and that the real invasion would come across from Dover. Once again, Hitler, who had only been a corporal in World War I, made the wrong decision.

Before the invasion started, Eisenhower issued two statements. The first was:

Soldiers, Sailors, and Airmen of the Allied Expeditionary Forces!

You are about to embark upon the Great Crusade, towards which we have striven these many months. The eyes or the world are upon you. The hopes and prayers of liberty-loving people everywhere march with you. In company with our brave Allies and brothers-in-arms on other fronts, you will bring about the destruction of the German war machine, the elimination of Nazi Tyranny over the oppressed people of Europe, and security for ourselves in a free world.

> I have full confidence in your courage, devotion to duty and skill in battle. We will accept nothing less than full Victory!
>
> Good luck! And let us all beseech the blessings of Almighty God upon this great and noble undertaking.

The other message was broadcast on June 6—D day.

> People of Western Europe: A landing was made this morning on the coast of France by troops of the Allied Expeditionary Force. This landing is part of the concerted United Nations plan for the liberation of Europe made in conjunction with our great Russian allies . . . I call upon all who love freedom to stand with us now. Together we shall achieve victory.[34]

The landings, both by air and by sea, were successful. The five landing beaches, named Utah, Omaha, Juno, Sword, and Gold were secured, although soldiers at Omaha had the most difficulty. Needed supplies were brought ashore, thanks to the ingenious devices called *Mulberry* Harbors. The huge cement structures were *floated* across the channel and then sunk to make harbors in deep-enough water in order to accommodate supply ships. Later, a cross-channel flexible pipe was laid that provided the needed gasoline.

While this historic invasion was being preformed, other events were taking place elsewhere. On June 22, 1944, President Roosevelt signed the Servicemen's Readjustment Act, better known as the GI Bill of Rights, authorizing a broad package of benefits for the World War II veterans. It would have far-reaching and beneficial results for years to come. On July 17, two wartime ammunition ships exploded in Port Chicago, California, near San Francisco, killing 322 black sailors assigned to the loading of the shells.

On August 21, the United States, Soviet Union, Britain, and China opened talks at Dumbarton Oaks in Washington that were to help pave the way to the establishment of the United Nations.

By the end of July, the Allies had enough men and material to break out of the beach area and proceed to move across France. On August 15, another invasion took place in the south of France, between Marseilles and Nice. With attacks from two different directions, the Germans fell back. When the Americans were close to Paris, Eisenhower ordered the U.S. troops to halt and allowed a French division the honor of liberating their capital.

The Allies moved quickly, and by September 1944, they were at the border of Germany. Unfortunately, there was just not enough gasoline for all units to keep the momentum going. Patton wanted Montgomery's fuel and vice versa. Montgomery proposed a plan to capture bridges leading into Germany. The airborne attack was named *Market Garden*. It started well, but soon bogged down, and many allied soldiers were killed or captured. Winter was coming; but the Allies needed to rest, recuperate, and replenish the men before they would have to go back into action.

Lack of good intelligence regarding the intentions of the Germans allowed them to prepare a counteroffensive in the middle of winter. On December 16, the Germans attacked through the Ardennes Forest. German's tanks swept through some of the recently replaced infantry divisions, like the 106th Division. The Germans were soon so deep into Allied lines that it became a salient that became known as the Battle of the Bulge. Divisions that were back near Paris, resting after many months in the front lines, were called up to help stem the advance of the Germans.

One of the divisions, the 101st Airborne, was sent to the very strategic town of Bastogne. They arrived, took up positions, and were shortly surrounded by German forces. The general of the division, Maxwell Taylor, was back in the States when it was called to assist. The deputy division commander was Brigadier General Anthony McAuliffe. The Germans sent a messenger to demand the surrender of the Allied forces within the town. General McAuliffe's reply to the demands will go down in history along with John Paul Jones's "I have not yet begun to fight," and Zachary Taylor's reply to Mexico's Santa Anna, "Tell him to go to hell." McAuliffe's reply to the German commander was much shorter. His one word-answer, "*Nuts*," bewildered the Germans, but every American soldier in Bastogne knew what it meant.

Eventually, the tide turned. The weather which had been so bad that airplanes could not be used to stop the Germans or resupply the surrounded troops finally cleared, and much needed supplies were dropped to the beleaguered troops. It was Hitler's last gamble, and it failed. By the end of January, the Americans and British were back where they had been on December 16. The Allies crossed the Rhine River and moved across Western Germany.

All this time, the Soviet armies had pushed the Germans back to their own borders, and it was just a matter of time before the Russians and Allies would meet. Berlin was a goal for both the United States as well as the Russians. General Eisenhower made the decision *not* to race his armies toward or into Berlin and allowed the Russians to do so. Criticized by some historians, Ike did the right thing. Russia lost 150,000 of their soldiers taking the capital.

TWO DEATHS

Two deaths in April were mourned. On April 30, 1945, Adolph Hitler committed suicide, eight days before Germany submitted to unconditional surrender on May 7, 1945. The war in Europe was over. The mourners included Hitler's remaining close friends.

The other death occurred on April 12. In Warm Springs, Georgia, President and Commander in Chief Franklin Delano Roosevelt complained of a headache and two hours later, died.

The nation and the people were stunned. Soldiers who fought for years broke down and cried when they heard the news. "He was the only president I ever knew" was a common remark that many young soldiers, sailors, airmen, and marines made.

One of America's best-loved and best-known authors and poets wrote a memorable poem on hearing of the president's death.

WHEN DEATH CAME APRIL TWELVE 1945[35]
Carl Sandburg

Can a bell ring in the heart
telling the time, telling a moment,
telling of a stillness come,
in the afternoon a stillness come
and now never come morning?

Now never again come morning,
say the tolling bells repeating it,
now on the earth is blossom days,
in earthy days and potato planting,
now to the stillness of the earth,
to the music of dust to dust
and the drop of ashes to ashes
he returns and it the time,
the afternoon time and never come morning,
the voice never again, the face never again.

A bell rings in the heart telling it
and the bell rings again and again
remembering what the first bell told,
the going away, the great heart still-
and they will go on remembering
and they is you and you and me and me.

And there will be roses and spring blooms
flung on the moving oblong box, emblems endless
from the frontline tanks nearing Berlin
        unseen flowers of regard to the Commander,
from battle stations over the South Pacific
        silent tokens saluting the Commander.

And the whitening bones of men at sea bottoms
or huddled and moldering men at Aachen,
    they may be murmuring,
    "Now he one of us,"
    one answering muffled drums
In the real and sphere of the shadow battalions.

Can a bell ring proud in the heart
    over a voice yet lingering,
    over a face past any forgetting,
    over a shadow alive and speaking,
over echoes and lights come keener, come deeper?

Can a bell ring in the heart
in time with the tall headlines,
the high fidelity transmitters,
the somber consoles rolling sorrow,
the choirs in ancient laments—chanting:
    "Dreamer, sleep deep,
    Toiler, sleep long,
    Fighter, be rested now,
    Commander, sweet good night."

It was a sad day for all people who loved freedom. Roosevelt had been instrumental in seeing that the United States would play a prominent role in securing freedom for so many people.

LEGACY OF A GREAT MAN

On January 6, 1941, the United States had not fully recovered from the Great Depression. In eleven months and one day, the United States would find itself in the greatest conflict in history.

On that day in January, before the Congress of the United States, President Roosevelt sought four freedoms: freedom of speech, freedom of worship, freedom from want, and freedom from fear. They had all been accomplished.

What a great legacy!

PART H

MEN WITH DECISIVE MINDED LEADERSHIP
1945-1963

With the war over in Europe in May 1945, no one could predict how long it would take to subdue Japan. Plans were in the works to invade the main southern island, Kyushu, in November 1945 and then the other main island, Honshu, in early 1946. This would give time to transport the American Armed Forces in Europe to the Far East. How many men would it take? How many would never come home? When would it end? The GIs in the Pacific theater had a saying, "the Golden Gate in '48." But once again, American greatness came through.

On July 16, 1945, the first ever atomic explosion took place in a desert in New Mexico. The years of planning since Albert Einstein had sent a letter to President Roosevelt in August of 1939 and millions of dollars in research and development were about to pay off.

A decision had to be made by President Truman. If he allowed the bomb to be dropped on Japan, it would save thousands of lives on *both* sides. After careful deliberation, he gave the go-ahead, and after practically obliterating two Japanese cities, the emperor of Japan overrode the military leaders of his devastated country, and the war ended on August 15, 1945.

Demobilization went smoothly, thanks to the GI Bill, and millions went to school—both colleges and trade schools. Others purchased homes or farms, and others started their own businesses. America was ready and anxious to enjoy the success in a peacetime setting. But not everything went so well overseas.

The Truman Doctrine and the Marshall Plan saved Europe from a Communist takeover. The Soviets, blocking entrance into Berlin, created the Berlin airlift. Then the Korean War began when Russian-backed North Korea invaded South Korea. It was the first test for the new United Nations, and the United States bore most of the fighting.

General Douglas MacArthur made brilliant military decisions but, politically, became a liability, and Truman had another tough decision to make.

When Eisenhower was elected in 1953, he was the first Republican to be elected and to serve two full terms since U. S. Grant. Eisenhower worked at ending the Korean War.

One of the most important medical breakthrough happened when the molecular structure, DNA, was discovered by three men, Crick, Wilkins, and Watson, on January 30, 1953.

Ike, as people loved to call him, saw some extremely important Supreme Court decisions handed down. First, it ruled that restaurants must serve all citizens in the District of Columbia, regardless of color. Then a series of decisions led to one of the most important decisions. In *Brown vs. the Board of Education*, the court said in effect, separate but equal was *not* the way to go in education.

Although there had been a number of civil rights acts passed over the years, the civil rights movement really got its start when a tired black woman refused to give up her seat on a bus in a town in Alabama.

In Eisenhower's second term, he forced the governor of Arkansas to allow black school children to integrate with whites. And he faced another monumental challenge when the Soviets were first to put up the world's first artificial satellite—Sputnik. As he did when the Battle of the Bulge happened in December 1944, he did not panic; but instead made decisions that led to the National Aeronautics and Space Agency—NASA, and its development would eventually make it possible to meet and pass the Soviets.

Ike also saw the last states—Alaska and Hawaii—join the Union. The many accomplishments in a relatively peaceful world would be capped with the introduction and beginning of the Interstate Highway System.

The third man with decisive-minded leadership following Truman and Eisenhower was JFK who would serve less than three years, but left a lasting impression with his speeches, his tough decisions, and his charisma.

Kennedy's inaugural address on January 20, 1961, was an electrifying speech to the nation and to the world. It would be compared with FDR's first inaugural address in 1933 and also with Lincoln's second inaugural address in 1865.

Kennedy asked, "What can you do for your country?" And when the Peace Corps was started, five thousand young men and women answered his question.

In April 1961, with the CIA backing, Cuban émigrés attempted to take over Cuba from Fidel Castro but would fail. Kennedy accepted the responsibility for the failure, but he did much better with other Latin American countries.

The Berlin wall went up in August 1961 and would remain for over twenty-eight years. But the greatest challenge Kennedy faced was in October 1962 when it was discovered that the Soviets were constructing ballistic missile launching pads in Cuba, only ninety miles from the shores of the United States of America.

After consulting with former President Eisenhower, Kennedy spoke to the nation explaining what the problem was and how he would handle it.

In February 1962, John Glenn became the first American to orbit the Earth, and he did this three times. A little over a year later, Gordon Cooper orbited the Earth twenty-two times before splashing down safely.

With a Democratic majority controlling both houses of Congress, most of Kennedy's programs became law. The one exception was civil rights. Martin Luther King, Jr., gave his memorable "I Have a Dream" speech the latter part of August 1963, on the steps of the Lincoln Memorial. It was the one hundredth anniversary of the Emancipation Proclamation.

In November 1963, President Kennedy was assassinated while riding in an open car in Dallas, Texas. America's thirty-fifth president was mourned like none other, since television captured it all for posterity.

CHAPTER XXIV

1945-1953 WHO THE HELL IS THIS GUY, TRUMAN?

Y our football team started the season on shaky ground. The quarterback is well-known after a couple of tough but successful seasons. Two other hopefuls had been the previous back-up quarterbacks, but they quit. You are now the only backup and you hardly know the plays.

Towards the end of the game—which your team is winning—the star quarterback is badly injured. Here is your chance to finish the game. How will you do?

This analogy is the story of Harry S. Truman, thirty-third president of the United States. He came into the awesome responsibility thrust upon him on April 12, 1945—a little less than three months after being inaugurated as the third vice president under President Roosevelt.

In November of 1944, very few men or women serving overseas had a chance to vote. They knew there was an election, just as there had been every four years for president. Many of the soldiers, sailors, airmen, and marine ages eighteen, nineteen, or twenty could not vote anyway. But they did know who had won the election—Roosevelt *again*. However that was the least of their concerns.

Those in Europe were fighting their way across France, and had yet to fight the Battle of the Bulge. Once that came and they recovered, they pushed their way into Germany; and by April 12, 1945, they knew the end of the war for them was just about over.

In the Pacific, the soldiers had gone ashore at Leyte in October 1944 and then invaded the major island of Luzon in January 1945. They captured the Philippine capital, Manila, two months later in March.

The army air force began bombing the homeland islands of Japan in November 1944. The U.S. Marines spent a month—February 19 to March 17, 1945—in a bloody battle to capture the island of Iwo Jima.

Both the marines and the army began the next to last invasion on Okinawa on April 1, 1945. This bloody battle lasted until June 21. The next invasion after that would be Japan itself, and no one wanted to even think about that.

So when they got the word about President Roosevelt's sudden death on April 12, many had never heard of the vice president. Those from the State of Missouri knew something about this man. But now the rest of the world would get to know the thirty-third president of the United States—Harry S. Truman.

1884-1945 BACKGROUND OF HARRY S. TRUMAN

When people learned about Harry Truman's background, it made it much easier to see and understand how he was able to take the job thrust upon him in the middle of the biggest war to ever be fought and make decisions almost immediately. These decisions would affect the United States and the world, then and now, in the near future, and for generations yet unborn.

Truman was born on May 8, 1884, in Lamar, Missouri. Only two years younger than FDR (Franklin Delano Roosevelt—as the press liked to refer to him), the Truman family of three children moved to Independence, Missouri, in 1890. He attended local public schools and, though severely nearsighted, enjoyed both reading and learning to play the piano. He especially liked to read biographies, histories, and stories about military battles. Little did he realize how important that would be.

He applied for entrance to West Point, but his eyesight put an end to that dream. He tried different odd jobs, which may have given him some insight into the struggles of the working man. He tried farming when his parents inherited one near Grandview, Missouri. At the same time he worked on the farm, he joined the National Guard and also the Kansas City's Democrat Party, which was run by Tom Pendergast, a political boss who gave workers jobs and helped elect politicians during the Great Depression. That helped him get a job as Postmaster at Grandview, Missouri.

When President Wilson asked Congress for a declaration of war, Truman's National Guard outfit was mobilized. After training at Fort Sill, Oklahoma, he returned to Missouri; and just as the soldiers did in the Civil War, through an election process, he was elected first lieutenant by the men in his outfit.

In 1918, his artillery outfit was sent to France. In March, he was promoted to the rank of captain and served with distinction. After the war, he returned to marry the girl he had known since fifth grade—Elizabeth (Bess) Virginia Wallace. He became part owner of a men's haberdashery. In 1922, with support from the Kansas City Democratic Party, he was elected supervisor of Jackson County roads and buildings. On this job, he not only improved roads but found ways of saving the county money.

When he lost the bid for reelection to a Ku Klux Klan supporter, he went back into the working world, including working at a bank. In 1926, with the blessing of

Tom Pendergast, he was elected to the job of supervisor of roads, buildings, and taxes. Tom Pendergast was a political boss that controlled Kansas City and Jackson County, Missouri. He gave jobs to workers during the Depression. He was later convicted of income tax evasion.

Taking the job seriously, Truman improved building construction systems, and even fired incompetent officials of Pendergast's political machine who were illegally taking tax money. Truman remained apart from Pendergast and was elected to the United States Senate in 1934.

In the Senate, he supported Franklin Roosevelt's New Deal and at the same time was cleared of any connection with the Pendergast crowd that was investigated and convicted.

In 1940, Truman ran for reelection against the governor of Missouri who had the backing of the Democratic Party. To battle him, Truman drove around the state and talked to the voters in plain language, which they liked, and he won the nomination and the election for a second term.

Starting in 1940, Truman investigated the waste that was being spent in military bases, and his committee ended up saving the country $15 *billion*. This brought him national attention during World War II, and when asked to be President Roosevelt's running mate, he told him to go to hell! He finally agreed and replaced Vice President Henry Wallace, who had replaced John Garner. Garner had not agreed with much of the New Deal, and Henry Wallace was considered a liability—some called him a socialist.[1]

Roosevelt's fourth inauguration took place on January 20, 1945. Eighty-three days later, Truman took the oath of office after being informed of Roosevelt's death by his wife, Eleanor Roosevelt.

People wondered who he was, especially the troops overseas. Even the Democratic Party bigwigs were not too sure and began planning on replacing him in the 1948 election. Would they be in for a surprise!

1945-1953 HARRY S. TRUMAN THIRTY-THIRD PRESIDENT

Truman met with members of the cabinet, and asked them to remain at their assigned posts. First Secretary of State James Byrnes, and then in more detail, Secretary of War Henry Stimson, informed Truman about the atomic bomb that they were attempting to construct in Los Alamos, New Mexico. Truman had never been informed about it at all.[2]

Less than a month after Roosevelt's death, the Germans accepted unconditional surrender. The terms of surrender were signed on May 7, 1945, and President Truman declared May 8 V-E (Victory in Europe) Day. It was also Truman's sixty-first birthday.

With the war over in Europe, the Soviet Union and the Allies took opposite approaches to securing the peace. The Soviets took anything of value from their zone of occupation. The Americans, remembering the harsh reparation that France and Britain had demanded after World War I, which had led to the rise of Hitler, took the opposite approach. They worked to rebuild, not just the buildings, but also the lives and the way the people would govern themselves.

As supreme commander, five-star General Dwight D. Eisenhower called in the German newspaper reporters and explained that he wanted a *free press*. He told them that if they did not like the way he was doing something, they were free to criticize. The reporters were dumbfounded. He told labor leaders that he wanted a free independent labor movement. He told the school teachers that they should teach that there are various view points on many subjects, and teachers and pupils must be free to explore the different points of view.[3]

The next month, June 1945, the final session of the conference to establish the United Nations was held. A year and a half later, on December 11, 1946, John D. Rockefeller would donate six blocks of Manhattan as a site for the United Nations Headquarters.

Truman addressed the conference group. With his sense of history, he must have been thinking of Woodrow Wilson's dream. Truman had no time for dreaming, he had too much to do.

In July and the early days of August, he met with Joseph Stalin, Winston Churchill, and Clement Atlee, Churchill's successor. At the meeting, President Truman proposed an international council to settle issues and to conduct trials against high-ranking Nazi officials for the war crimes they had committed, including the death camps that had been erected to eliminate all the Jews in Europe and others the Nazis considered undesirable.

While at the conference in Potsdam, Germany, Truman received important information. On July 16, 1945, the atomic age began when the first bomb ever built was tested in the desert near Alamogordo, New Mexico. It was an unqualified success. While at the Potsdam Conference, Truman issued a declaration on July 26, calling for Japan's unconditional surrender.

MAKING A TOUGH DECISION

When Truman returned to the United States, he had a major decision to make. He studied the casualty lists from Okinawa. The U.S. Army and Marines had been fighting from April 1 to June 22, and 12,520 soldiers and marines were killed and 36,680 were wounded.

The Japanese, fighting to practically the last man, lost 110,071. Only 7,500 surrendered, and most of those were either too wounded or too weak to do anything else.[4]

He knew about the Japanese unwillingness to surrender. He knew about the kamikaze attacks by willing Japanese pilots to take aloft obsolete airplanes and, if they avoided the antiaircraft fire, dive into American ships. He knew he was the last president since Theodore Roosevelt to have served in the army. His sense of history from all he had read would help him in making a decision regarding the atomic bomb.

He called in the military and civilian leaders to gain a perspective. Some thought the Japanese should be warned. Others felt it was too destructive or even uncivilized. When he asked for an estimate of casualties if he decided *not* to use the bomb, the military's best guess was five hundred thousand American lives would be lost forever.

Since Lieutent Colonel Jimmy Doolittle's raid in April of 1942, Japan had escaped any further bombing until November 1944. Later, on March 9 and 10, 1945, General Curtis LeMay sent 334 B-29 Superfortresses with 1,165 TONS of petroleum-based incendiaries to bomb Japan's most populated city—Tokyo. The results were 97,000 killed and 125,000 injured. Still, the Japanese would not think of surrendering.

With the war over in Europe, troop ships began bringing war-weary, but experienced soldiers to the Far East. Programs like ASTP (Army Specialized Training Program) back in the United States had been stopped, and the men going to college were sent to the Pacific theater. The overall commander for the invasion, General Douglas MacArthur, was planning to invade the southernmost Japanese island of Kyushu in November of 1945. From there his plan was to secure the island before invading Honshu, the island with Japan's capital—Tokyo.

Considering all factors, President Harry S. Truman made the decision of his life. He gave the go-ahead to drop the bomb.

AUGUST 6, 1945 DROPPING THE FIRST ATOMIC BOMB

One bomb weighing nine thousand pounds was aboard the B-29 Superfort *Enola Gay,* piloted by Colonel Paul Tibbetts, Jr. His copilot was Bob Lewis, the navigator was "Dutch" Van Kirk, Tom Ferebee was the bombardier, Bob Caron the tail gunner, and Morris Jepson was the engineer whose job it was to arm the bomb.

Little Boy, as the bomb was called, was released at 9:15 a.m. It exploded at the preset altitude of 1,890 feet. Bob Caron was the only one to see the incredible fireball. A giant mushroom cloud rose 45,000 feet. Hiroshima was obliterated.

"My God!" Bob Lewis wrote as the final entry in his log.

"I think this is the end of the war," Tibbett said to Lewis.

Three days later, a second bomb was dropped on Nagasaki. Less than a week later, Japan capitulated on August 14, 1945. World War II was over.[5]

First Announcement of the Atomic Bomb, August 6, 1945

Sixteen hours ago an American airplane dropped one bomb on Hiroshima . . . It is a harnessing of the basic power of the universe. The force from which the sun draws its power has been loosed against those who brought war to the Far East.[6]

With President Truman's announcement that Japan had accepted the terms of unconditional surrender, ending World War II, he proclaimed August 15 V-J Day. A week later, August 21, 1945, President Truman ended Lend-Lease aid to the Allies, a program under which the United States supplied Great Britain, the Soviet Union, China, France, and other Allied nations with vast amounts of war material between 1941 and 1945 in return for military bases in Newfoundland, Bermuda, and the British West Indies,

On board the Battleship USS *Missouri,* flagship of the Pacific Fleet, and obviously one of Truman's favorites, on September 2, 1945, Japan formally surrendered. Of the many flags that were hung aboard the ship that historic day was a United States flag with thirty-one stars. It had flown from the masthead of Commodore Matthew C. Perry's flagship when it entered Tokyo Bay in 1853, opening the door to Japan.[7]

DEMOBILIZATION

Over twelve million service men and women wanted only one thing, and one thing only: *to go home*

The leaders in Washington had been working on a fair and equitable system of demobilization for those who had served so faithfully. They considered four basic factors when devising a point system. For each month of service in the States, a person would receive one point; for each month served overseas, two points. If they were engaged in a battle or campaign, that was worth five points for each separate battle. If a soldier, sailor, airman, or marine was awarded a medal for wounds, or for heroism, he or she would earn five points for each.

If a person was drafted or enlisted in January 1942, was trained and sent overseas in either August (Guadalcanal) or November (North Africa), and lived throughout the entire war up to September 1945, that person earned ninety-one or ninety-two points. If they were in battles and received a medal, they had earned one hundred points or more.

With this table of points established, the decision was made that eighty-five points were needed to be sent home and honorably discharged. They got home in the fall and winter of 1945. After a period, the number was lowered to eighty points then seventy-five, and eventually to where anyone with two years of service was discharged. It was gradual and allowed the services to put new draftees into the spots that needed replacements. There were other concerns at home.

WHAT DO YOU DO WITH FIFTEEN MILLION EX-SERVICE PERSONNEL?

As the war drew to a close, and finally ended, there were articles in the newspapers and magazines regarding the returning service personnel. Some suggested that they would need rehabilitation before they could be turned loose on society. Some feared that they would not know how to act after being in combat. Other articles predicted vast unemployment and that America would be going back to a country in a state of depression.

When the Servicemen's Readjustment Act of 1944, better known as the GI Bill of Rights, was first being debated in Congress, there were serious concerns by those in academic circles that veterans would lower the standards in education. They would be so wrong, it was almost a joke.

Those educators did not seem to understand that because only 9 percent of the American population was enrolled in colleges in 1940 that anyone else was eligible. It wasn't that they didn't have the smarts; they just didn't have the money.

The GI Bill was introduced in Congress in January 1944. The main features were designed by the American Legion, which is also credited with overcoming objections by other organizations. After a nationwide campaign, it passed and was signed by President Roosevelt on June 22, 1944.

Basically, the GI Bill provided six different and equally important benefits. They were:

1. Education and training which included paying tuitions and a monthly stipend.
2. Loan guarantees for a home, farm, or business.
3. Unemployment pays of $20 a week for up to fifty-two weeks. The vets called it the 52-20 Club.
4. Job-finding assistance.
5. Top priority for building materials for VA hospitals.
6. Military review of dishonorable discharges.[8]

It is worthy of examination to see the results of the GI Bill.

HIGHER EDUCATION ENROLLMENT AND
BACHELOR DEGREES 1940-1950[9]

Year	Four-Year Enrollment	Percent of population	Bachelor Degrees Conferred
1940	1,494,000	9.1%	216,521
1942	1,404,000	8.4%	213,491
1944	1,159,000	6.8%	141,582
1946	2,078,000	12.5%	157,349
1948	2,403,000	14.7%	317,607
1950	2,281,000	14.2%	496,875

This is only part of the success as a result of the GI Bill. In the peak year of 1947, out of a veteran population of 15,440,000, some 7.8 million were trained, including:

> 2,230,000 in colleges
> 3,480,000 in other schools
> 1,400,000 in on-the-job training
> 690,000 in farm training

The total cost of the World War II education program was $14.5 billion. Millions, who would have flooded the labor market, instead opted for education, which reduced joblessness during the demobilization period. When the veterans did enter the job market, most were better prepared to contribute to society and to their growing families.[10]

More veterans were discharged in January 1946 than any other single month. By some coincidence, more babies were born in September 1946 than any other month. They needed a place to live and grow. This spawned a house-building boom in what were former cornfields, and suburban America would grow at an unprecedented pace. On February 21, 1947, Edwin Land unveiled his Polaroid Land Camera, which produced a black-and-white photograph in sixty seconds. Veterans could make a picture record of their growing families.

That same year, 1947, some significant events took place. On April 15, Jackie Robinson became the first black Major League player, making his debut with the Brooklyn Dodgers of the National League. Larry Doby was the first black to play in the American League, playing for the Cleveland Indians. On May 10, 1947, B. F. Goodrich of Akron, Ohio, announced development of the tubeless tire. On July 26, President Truman signed the National Security Act, creating the Department of Defense, the National Security Council, the CIA (Central Intelligence Agency), and the Joint Chiefs of Staff. On October 13, Captain (later Brigadier General) Chuck Yeager became the first person to fly faster than the speed of sound in a Bell X-1 rocket-powered research plane over Southern California.

Five years after the birth of a record number of babies, 1951, schools became overcrowded, and new schools were quickly constructed. It was a growing nation that had won the greatest war in history. Winning the peace was going to take longer than anybody could imagine.

WORKING FOR PEACE

A very important speech was made by Winston Churchill on March 5, 1946 at Westminster College in Fulton, Missouri. President Truman was in the audience. Churchill said that an *iron curtain* had descended on Europe from the Baltic to the Adriatic. The Soviet Union had taken control of many of the countries next to theirs. Bulgaria, Czechoslovakia, Hungary, Poland, and Romania had come under the domination of Communist Russia. Germany had been divided into separate zones, including Berlin. There was great concern that the Soviet Union would attempt to enslave all of Europe.[11]

When the Communists began a civil war in Greece, Truman took action. On March 12, 1947, in a message to Congress, he gave reasons for giving aid, both economically and militarily, to both Greece and Turkey. On May 22, the Congress appropriated $625 million for both. It would be known as the Truman Doctrine. But that was only the beginning of Truman's attempt to save Europe from Soviet domination.[12]

THE MARSHALL PLAN SAVES EUROPE

In 1945, chief of staff General George C. Marshall, now sixty-five years of age, retired from the army. In 1947, President Truman asked him to serve as secretary of state. It was a brilliant move. At a June commencement address that Secretary of State Marshall gave at Harvard University, he set forth the basic principles of American policy toward helping postwar Europe. On June 10, 1947, he said in part in a historic speech:

> Our policy is directed not against any country or doctrine, but against hunger, poverty, desperation and chaos. Its purpose should be revival of a working economy in the world, so as to permit the emergence of political and social conditions in which free institutions can exist.[13]

The European Recovery Plan, which became known as the Marshall Plan, cost the United States $12.5 billion over a four-year period, and it worked. Western Europe, including the American zone of Germany made remarkable progress in rebuilding their countries. Russia knew it had lost that battle, but it did not give up.[14]

On December 23, 1947, scientists of Bell Laboratories in New Jersey invented the point-contact transistor which paved the way for the era of miniaturized electronics.

IMPORTANT EVENTS OF 1948

On January 30, 1948, Orville Wright—American flight pioneer—died in Dayton, Ohio. Peter Goldmark of CBS demonstrated the long-playing record, which would begin a revolution in the recording industry.

On April 1, 1948, the Soviets began interfering with traffic going between Western Germany and Berlin, which was in the Soviet zone. On June 24 of that year, the Soviets stopped *all* rail, water, and road traffic, cutting off the American zone of Berlin from receiving badly needed items to survive.

American greatness once again answered the call. Employing hundreds of World War II cargo airplanes, they began flying needed food and even coal to the desperate citizens of Berlin. The airlift to circumvent the blockade became an international incident, with the Americans gaining positive publicity and the Russians berated throughout the free world. Having to admit defeat, the blockade was officially lifted on May 12, 1949—nearly a year later. There had been 277,264 flights by American airmen to save Berlin.

On the same date that the Soviets cut off transportation to Berlin, the United States passed the Selective Service Act of 1948 in order to maintain the necessary level of adequate armed strength.

The midterm election of 1946 had given the Republicans a majority in both the House of Representatives and the Senate. The Congress passed the Taft-Hartley Act, which restricted the many activities of unions. Truman vetoed the bill, but the Congress overrode his veto. Truman tried to put controls on rising prices, but that was also defeated.

The president was able, by executive order, to approve the desegregation of the armed services. By the time of the election of 1948, nobody gave President Truman a chance of being elected on his own. All the polls showed Thomas Dewey winning.

The Southern Democrats were so mad at Truman for calling an end to the *Jim Crow* state laws that maintained segregation, that he lost their support; and Strom Thurmond, governor of South Carolina, formed a States' Rights party. So Truman faced the fight of his political life.

He toured the country, and when election night was over, it was so close that the early edition of the *Chicago Tribune*'s headline read: DEWEY DEFEATS TRUMAN. The results were different. Truman received 24,105,695 popular votes and 303 electoral votes. Dewey received 22,969,176 votes and 89 electoral votes, while Thurmond got 1,169,021 votes and only 39 electoral votes. Pollsters were puzzled. How could this be? They searched for answers, and none could explain how Truman pulled the greatest election upset ever.

What the pollsters should have done was to ask some of the twelve to fifteen million ex-servicemen, many of whom went into the voting booth on that November day, and said, "Thanks, Harry, for dropping the bomb that probably saved my life," and pulled the lever, giving their vote to their former commander in chief.

That fall election also saw Maine Republican Margaret Chase Smith elected to the U.S. Senate, becoming the first woman to serve in both the House of Representatives and the U.S. Senate. She served in the Senate through 1973.

1949-1952 PRESIDENT TRUMAN'S OWN ADMINISTRATION

Truman's administration had the advantage of a majority of Democrats in both houses of Congress, thanks to the election of 1948. There were a number of legislative actions taken that would benefit the country. Truman wanted to increase public housing, which he did. Social Security was expanded, the minimum wage was increased, and stronger farm support was implemented.

The *cold war*, as it was called between the United States and Russia, continued. The airlift ended May 12. Investigations of possible Communist spies were conducted by the Un-American Activities Committee, which Richard Nixon led. In February, Senator Joe McCarthy made wild accusations that two hundred Communists had been employed by the federal government. None were ever found, and McCarthy was discredited after many months of hearings.[15]

On March 2, 1949, an American B-50 Superfortress, the *Liberty Lady II*, landed in Fort Worth, Texas, finishing the first nonstop around-the-world flight. A month later the NATO (North Atlantic Treaty Organization), designed to provide security to the democratic nations of the Atlantic community against possible overt action by Russia, was signed April 4, 1949.[16] In 1950, on May 1, poet Gwendolyn Brooks was the first African American person to win the Pulitzer Prize for her book, *Annie Allen*.

Architects and engineers had determined that the White House was in need of complete renovation. Truman agreed and moved to the Blair House during his term in office. On November 1, 1950, an assassination attempt was made on President Truman. It failed, but a Secret Service agent and one of the assassins were killed. The other assassin was captured and sentenced to be executed, but Truman commuted the sentence to life imprisonment. Twenty-nine years later, President Jimmy Carter set him free.[17]

KOREAN WAR

Following the defeat of Japan, General Douglas MacArthur had been appointed supreme commander for the Allied powers. He did not waste any time. In a series of decrees, he restored civil liberties, liberated political prisoners, dissolved the secret police, liberalized the educational curriculum, granted the right to vote to both men and women, encouraged the formation of labor unions, and abolished feudal land tenure. On January 1, 1946, Emperor Hirohito disclaimed the divinity that the people had bestowed on him.[18]

MacArthur enjoyed his roll of supreme commander, and the Japanese saw him as a savior. But that was not the problem. At the Potsdam Conference, it was decided to split Korea into two sections. The North would be under the control of the Soviets. The South would be under the *influence* of the United States, but they would quickly move to have self-rule. The Republic of Korea was proclaimed on August 15, 1948.[19]

The United Nations began preparing for a unification of the two Koreas when on June 25, 1950, the North Koreans attacked South Korea. Two days later, the UN Security Council called on all members of the United Nations to assist South Korea to repel the attack and restore peace.[20]

Two days later, President Truman responded with a statement on the Korean War. He appointed General MacArthur commander of the United Nations forces. The North Korean Army pushed down the large peninsula south and occupied almost all of South Korea except for a small perimeter at the southern end, around the town of Pusan. There the Americans and its United Nation allies held.

In a masterful stroke of what some thought was impossible, MacArthur launched an invasion at Inchon farther up the coast. They were able to surprise the North Koreans and, with fifteen other United Nations countries, drove the North Koreans back across the line that divided them—the 38th parallel.

When the UN forces went beyond the 38th parallel, the Chinese came into the war on the side of North Korea. When General MacArthur requested permission to extend the war into China, Truman refused the request. When MacArthur publicly attacked Truman's policy, the president had little choice but to relieve MacArthur of his command in April 1951.

MacArthur returned to the United States a hero. He addressed a joint session of Congress and ended his speech with:

*   *   *

> Old soldiers never die, they just fade away, and like the old soldier of the ballad, I now close my military career and just fade away—an old soldier who tried to do his duty as God gave him the light to see that duty. Good-bye.[21]

Lieutenant General Matthew Ridgeway replaced MacArthur, and the war dragged on until a truce was called on July 8, 1951. The truce only lasted a month before action resumed. Finally, on July 26, 1953, an armistice was signed. It was the first time that the United Nations had come to the aid of a country, and America had borne most of the fighting.

A number of other important events happened in 1951. January 1 saw David Dinkins sworn in as the first African-American mayor. On February 27, the Twenty-second Amendment, limiting presidents to two terms, was ratified. CBS transmitted the first commercial color telecast, a one-hour special broadcast from New York City to four other states on June 25. On August 21, construction of the first atomic-powered submarine was ordered. President Truman spoke to the nation from San Francisco in the first live coast-to-coast television broadcast on September 4. On November 10, coast-to-coast direct-dialing telephone service began between mayors of Englewood, New Jersey, and Alameda, California.

On July 25, 1952 Puerto Rico became a self-governing Commonwealth of the United States.

One of Truman's last acts was to try and stop a steel strike by directing his secretary of commerce to seize the mills to keep production going. The Supreme Court declared the seizure unconstitutional. Truman could have used the Taft-Hartley Act of 1947, which called for a cooling-off period so both labor and management could discuss their differences, but Truman hated to use the Republican sponsored bill.

Truman decided *not* to seek another term. That was still possible even though they had passed an amendment on February 27, 1951. The Twenty-second Amendment stated:

> But this Article shall not apply to any person holding the office of President when this Article was proposed by Congress

He had been president for almost eight years. He had performed in a courageous and admirable manner that few could have imagined.

He had big shoes to fill, following Roosevelt, but history will very likely grade him as one of the most decisive presidents.

CHAPTER XXV

DECISIVE MOMENTS IN AMERICAN HISTORY

When Columbus was looking for financial help and ships to get to the east by going west, he waited *seven years* in Spain to get an audience with King Ferdinand and Queen Isabella. So seventy days and seventy nights on the unexplored Atlantic was a drop in the bucket while sailing West and finally putting himself into history. What if he was not patient?

On June 11, 1776, the Continental Congress appointed a committee of five to draft a declaration. The committee selected John Adams and Thomas Jefferson. Adams persuaded Jefferson to write the draft. Jefferson agreed and brought forth the greatest document in American history, declaring the intentions of the oppressed colonists. What if Adams had decided to write the document?

When George Rogers Clark decided, in the middle of winter of 1779, to go from Kaskaskia to Vincennes and capture Lieutenant-Governor Hamilton and the outpost, it made it possible for the new United States to claim the territory that historians love to call the Old Northwest, stretching to the Mississippi River. What if Clark had decided to wait until spring when Hamilton wanted to recapture Kaskaskia?

When French Admiral de Grasse sailed from France on September 5, 1781, and reached Chesapeake Bay, and Generals Washington and de Rochambeau marched their troops to outside of Yorktown, they set up a siege; and British General Cornwallis was surrounded on land and sea. After three weeks, on October 19, he surrendered, ending the American Revolutionary War. What if the admiral had not sailed from France when he did?

In writing the Constitution, smaller states and larger states had different views of how they should be represented in the legislature. Connecticut solved the argument by proposing two legislatures, one based on population and the other with equal status for all states. What if Connecticut had not come up with that plan? Would there be a United States of America?

Meriwether Lewis and William Clark would not have succeeded if it was not for Sacagawea. She provided information and help that allowed the *Journey of Discovery* to buy horses and also purchase food as they were about to starve. What if Sacagawea had not been there?

On the night of September 13, 1814, an American aboard a British man-of-war was not allowed to leave while they bombarded the American Fort McHenry. In the morning, Francis Scott Key saw that the stars and stripes were still waving in the morning breeze. It inspired him to write a poem that became the American National Anthem. What would be our national anthem if Francis Scott Key had not been there on the morning of September 14, 1814?

On March 6, 1836, Mexican General Santa Anna issued the order to charge the Alamo in San Antonio, Texas. No quarters were given, and 187 Americans died as they fought 3,000 Mexicans. In the meantime, Sam Houston was training soldiers, and when he heard the news, Houston and his army chased and defeated Santa Anna at the Battle of San Jacinto on April 21, 1836. This victory allowed the establishment of the Republic of Texas, and on December 28, 1845, Texas became the twenty-eighth state of the Union. What if Santa Anna had allowed the Americans to surrender and leave the mission alive?

When Abraham Lincoln was nominated to run for the United States Senate in 1858, he challenged the incumbent Stephen Douglas to a series of debates throughout the State of Illinois. The results of the election showed that Lincoln received more votes than Douglas, but the United States Constitution, *at that time,* stated that the senators would be chosen by the state legislatures, and the Illinois General Assembly was ruled by the Democrats. That part of the U.S. Constitution was changed with the Seventeenth Amendment on April 8, 1913—fifty-five years later, and said, "Senators from each state (will be) elected by the people." What if the amendment had been ratified before 1858 and Lincoln would have been an Illinois Senator for at least six years?

When Ulysses S. Grant graduated from West Point in 1843, he served in the Mexican War. Following that, he married Julia Dent in 1848. When he was sent to California and separated from his love, he resigned. Together they tried farming, but failed at that. Then Grant tried selling firewood on the streets of St. Louis. Next he tried rent collecting, which he hated, and was *not* too proud to ask his successful father in Galena, Illinois, for a job. When thousands answered Lincoln's call for volunteers, Illinois Congressman Washburne asked Grant to take charge of enlistments and then to escort the volunteers to the capital, Springfield.

When Illinois Governor Yates needed someone to bring order out of chaos when thousand of volunteers came to Springfield, Grant's name was suggested. He did such a fine job that he was offered a commission. He took it and later captured two confederate strongholds and then won battles at Corinth and Shiloh. When Grant's opponents wanted him relieved because of the large number of casualties, Lincoln instead appointed him commander in chief. Grant then proceeded to fight Robert

E. Lee and the Confederate army and won the war. What if Lincoln had listened to those who wanted Grant dismissed?

Theodore Roosevelt was greatly admired by the people. But there were politicians, businessmen, and others who did not like his campaign to take on corrupt politicians. New York Senator Thomas Platt convinced the Republican Party to nominate Roosevelt for the national vice presidency when McKinley's vice president died.

At that time, the job of vice president was of no importance, and the position had no power. Six months after McKinley started his second term, he was assassinated. At first it was thought that he would recover, but a week later he died, and Theodore Roosevelt became the twenty-sixth president. What if McKinley had recovered?

Woodrow Wilson's dream was to have the United States be a part of the League of Nations. He toured the country hoping to sell his idea to the American public, but it was not to be. Without the United States as a member, the League of Nations did very little.

First Japan, then Italy, and finally Germany took advantage of the League's inability to enforce any rules. This led to World War II and the death of millions— some estimate fifty-six million military and civilian deaths. What if the U.S. Senate had voted to join the league in 1919 and had insisted that the league work for peace and not allow nations to prepare for war?

In 1920, Franklin Delano Roosevelt was nominated for the vice presidency on the Democratic ticket along with James Cox as the presidential nominee. They lost the election, and the next year Roosevelt was stricken with polio. At the age of thirty-nine, he could have decided to take it easy and retire. His family had plenty of money. What if he had chosen to do just that?

In 1942, the Japanese had conquered most of the islands in the Central Pacific. If they captured Midway Island, they could then launch attacks on Pearl Harbor, and the U.S. Navy would have to retreat to San Diego for safety.

Chief Cryptanalysis Commander Joseph Rochefort had been working *night and day* and came up with enough Japanese information that told that Japan intended to attack Midway. Admiral Nimitz sent the United States' remaining aircraft carriers to intercept in the hopes that by surprise, they could defeat a much-larger Japanese naval force. What if Commander Rochefort couldn't break the Japanese code?

American history is full of *what-ifs*. What really happened was that leaders with courage and the ability to lead took their rightful place and made the American nation great.

If we are lucky, such men come along in every generation. Such a man was the thirty-fourth president of the United States, Dwight David Eisenhower. He had been a great military leader in Europe during World War II. Americans love successful generals.

George Washington was the most revered, but there were others. William Henry Harrison had fought the Indians at Fallen Timbers under General Anthony

Wayne. He was also successful in the War of 1812 when he defeated the British at the Battle of the Thames, in Canada. Zachary Taylor was the hero in the Mexican War. Grant was the one who helped save the Union and was rewarded with two terms in the White House.

The Spanish-American War was so short that no general had time to be successful. But Theodore Roosevelt's charge up San Juan Hill in Cuba made him a national hero. The exception to having a general as president following a war was General John Pershing. After his success in World War I, he was promoted to general of the armies and served as chief of staff until 1924 when he retired.

What kind of president would Dwight D. Eisenhower make? It is worthwhile to examine his background, from childhood through his four years at West Point as well as his military career before he was selected to be the supreme commander of the Allied Forces in the European theater of operations.

CHAPTER XXVI

I LIKE IKE 1953-1961

1890-1942 PREPARATION OF A LEADER

Dwight David Eisenhower was born October 14, 1890 in Denison, Texas, one of seven brothers. The family moved to Abilene, Kansas, while Dwight was very young. He had a good basic rote learning education in the public schools. He enjoyed hunting, fishing, and playing cards. A very enthusiastic football player, he volunteered to play opposite a black when no one else would. In his freshman year, he scraped his knee which became so infected that the doctor wanted to amputate it. Dwight would not allow it and one of his brothers, Edgar, helped to keep the doctor away by sleeping in front of the entrance to Dwight's room.

He eventually recovered, but the two months' convalescence made him have to repeat his freshman year. While still in high school, he applied for both West Point and Annapolis. The navy rules would not accept anyone twenty years of age or older, so fate put him at West Point. He had no trouble with the entrance exams and started at West Point on June 12, 1911, when Plebes were to report.[1]

His four years at the military academy were a combination of lectures and being required to give exact answers. His experiences at Abilene gave him a good start on the rote style of teaching and learning. His family background helped him endure the Spartan life, and his family values were also an asset. His football experience helped him at West Point, and they won some early games. When they played Carlisle and Jim Thorpe, they were beaten 27-6. Later in the season, he twisted his knee and had to give up football. He became a cheerleader and then was asked to coach the junior varsity. These two experiences taught him organizational skills, competitiveness, enthusiasm, and the willingness to work hard.

He graduated in the class of 1915, in the middle of his class academically. When the doctors gave him an examination, they said it was doubtful he would be commissioned, and they first suggested the coast artillery. He instead chose the infantry and was stationed at San Antonio.[2] Assigned first to Fort Sam Houston, he met, courted and married Mamie Geneva Doud, who was called Mamie. Next he was stationed at Fort Oglethorpe, Georgia, to train officer candidates. He pestered the War Department for an overseas assignment, but they sent him to Fort Leavenworth, Kansas, where he learned about tanks. He next went to Fort George G. Meade, Maryland, to prepare a tank battalion for overseas. Thinking he was finally going to get to France, he was assigned to Camp Colt in Gettysburg, Pennsylvania.

On October 14, 1918, he was promoted to lieutenant colonel, and given orders to sail for France with his tank outfit. They were planning a spring offensive against the Germans in 1919. November 11, 1918, ended any hope of getting combat experience. What he gained instead were great organizational skills and the ability to get along with recruits, would-be officers, higher-ranking personnel, and civilians from all walks of life.[3]

Following World War I, the U.S. Army was quickly demobilized to about 130,000 men. Ike—his nickname since childhood—was reduced in the ranks to captain. In 1919, he was accompanying a convoy of trucks across the country to see how well it could be done. He took particular notice of the poor condition of the two lane highways all over the country.

In 1920, Ike met General Fox Conner, who had served as General Pershing's operation officer and was responsible for the AEF success in France. A brilliant man, after reading the Treaty of Versailles, he predicted another war in twenty years.

In 1922, Conner asked for Ike to serve in Panama with him, and Conner became Ike's mentor and a man Ike admired. He served in Panama three years and then was recommended for C&GS school (Command and General Staff school) at Fort Leavenworth. He studied their plans for the *next war*, and though he disagreed with much of them, he kept his mouth shut—another of Conner's earlier suggestions. Ike graduated first in the class, and then he was assigned to command a battalion at Fort Benning, Georgia. After a year, he was transferred to Washington, and so impressed Chief of Staff John Pershing that he was recommended for the Army War College. Following that, he was sent to France to serve on the Battlefield Monuments Commission then back to Washington to serve the assistant secretary of war. In 1930, during the Depression, General Douglas MacArthur was appointed chief of staff. MacArthur liked Ike and recommended him to serve under him in both Washington and the Philippines from 1935 to 1939.

After his tour in the Philippines, he was assigned to Fort Sam Houston, Texas, as the executive officer of the Fifteenth Infantry regiment of the Third Division in 1940. On March 11, he attained the rank of full colonel. Later, June 11, 1941, he became chief of staff of the division, and wrote the war plans for the maneuvers in Louisiana in August 1941. His plans worked so well that the Third Army won the maneuver war. When Pearl Harbor happened, Ike was called to Washington by chief of staff General George C. Marshall, a man Ike knew and respected.

Assuming that Marshall wanted to get Ike's ideas on the defense of the Philippines, he hopped a plane that was forced down because of weather, so he boarded a train for Washington, D.C.

When he arrived on December 14, General Marshall gave him a rundown of the situation in the Pacific, including the losses of ships, men, and material. Then he asked Eisenhower for his ideas of how to deal with the problems in the Pacific. Ike continued to work on war plans and took a quick trip to Britain to examine the possibilities on invading France.

When he returned, he submitted plans for the European theater of operations (ETO), and when he told General Marshall to read it very carefully, Marshall's reply was, "I certainly do want to read it. You may be the man to execute it. If that's the case, when can you leave?" Three days later, Marshall appointed Ike to command the ETO.[4]

Here was a man, at the age of fifty-two, who had been a major in the U.S. Army for sixteen years. He was a lieutenant colonel until 1940 and made full colonel in March. He met and worked for and with some of the smartest men in the military: Conner, Patton, MacArthur, and Marshall. He had gone to two of the army's most prestigious schools—C&GS and the Army War College. He had served faithfully and well in all of his assignments. He had good ideas and was not afraid to produce them. Most of all, he could get along with everyone and just as important, get everyone to do their best. In short, he had all the qualities of a *Leader.*

1942-1948 LEADING THE WAY TO VICTORY

The invasion of Africa by the Americans in November 1942 went very smoothly. When enough troops were put ashore, Ike had the army advanced toward Tunisia to meet up with British General Montgomery. The Americans were stopped and driven back from Kasserine Pass, and Eisenhower had to relieve the commanding general, Lieutenant General Lloyd Fredendall. By May 1943, the Americans were ready to invade Sicily. Patton and Montgomery attacked from two different directions, and Patton just barely beat Montgomery to Messina. When Patton visited an army field hospital, something he did quite often, he found a soldier without any wounds but scared to death. Patton accused him of cowardice, slapped him, and ordered him out of the hospital tent. When news reached the States, there were some who wanted Patton relieved. Taking a page from Lincoln, Ike would not listen and kept Patton on.

With Sicily secure, Italy came next. General Mark Clark was put in command, and Ike went to England to prepare for D day. *D day* is a term often used in military parlance to denote the day on which a combat attack or operation is to be initiated. The earliest use of the term was in World War I, in a field order directing the American Expeditionary Forces to attack on September 7, 1918 in the Saint-Mihiel Salient.

His years in the service, planning, training, executing orders, and learning to get along with superiors and being ever mindful of those in the enlisted ranks paid big dividends in planning the greatest invasion in history.

Ike cleverly used George Patton as a decoy to keep Germans off guard. He listened to those immediately under him and often took their advice. He made the decision to postpone, for one day, the invasion due to weather and then the night before visited the paratroopers who would be jumping in the early morning hours of June 6, 1944. He had prepared three announcements. One was to the Allied military personnel. The second was to the people of Europe, regarding his intentions. The third was a note that he never had to show. It said:

> Our landings . . . have failed . . . and I have withdrawn the troops. My decision to attack at this time and place was based upon the best information available. The troops, the air and the Navy did all that bravery and devotion to duty could do. If any blame or fault attached to the attempt it is mine alone.[5]

The landing was a success, and in July, Patton was turned loose with his tanks. After pushing the Germans back to the Rhine river, Patton and Montgomery bickered about who should get the much-needed gasoline. They did not like one another, and Ike had to work hard to get them to cooperate. Ike had constant problems with the British field marshall and could never get him, except once, to come to see him. Montgomery always told Ike to come to him.

The Allies' lack of good intelligence would be a problem. On December 16 at Versailles, outside of Paris, Eisenhower and his staff were holding a celebration. Ike's orderly, Sergeant McKeogh, was being married; Ike's driver, Second Lieutenant Kay Summersby, was to be awarded a British medal; and Ike had just been promoted to the newly established rank of general of the armies, giving him equal status with the rank of Field Marshall Montgomery. That same day, the Germans began a counteroffensive through the Ardennes—a forest between Luxembourg and France. When Ike heard the news, he saw it as an opportunity rather than a setback. He took control.

He ordered the two American paratrooper divisions who were recuperating from the Market Garden battle that Montgomery had planned but turned out to be a failure, to two different locations. The 82nd Division was sent to the northern edge of the German penetration, and the 101st Division was sent to Bastogne. These decisions were both timely and correct. Patton's Third Army immediately changed directions and started toward Bastogne.

When Montgomery demanded complete control of the ground forces, Ike was ready to fire him. Montgomery backed down and asked that Ike tear up his written order. Ike could be driven just so far. Once the skies cleared, the air force could drop badly needed ammunition and supplies, and the fighters and bombers could destroy the German tanks and infantry. It was one of Ike's greatest moments, and he finally got an admission from Montgomery that Ike had made the right decisions.[6]

The last few months of the war involved the question of who should capture Berlin. Ike asked Omar Bradley about casualties to take the German capital, and Bradley estimated one hundred thousand. Ike allowed the Russians to take Berlin and had to fight both Montgomery and Churchill that other places were more important, like saving Denmark from the Russians.

When Hitler killed himself on April 30, 1945, the end of the Second World War in Europe was in sight. A week later, May 7, General of the Armies Dwight David Eisenhower accepted the German's unconditional surrender from Generaloberst Alfred Jodl, the German chief of staff.

Ever since Eisenhower had been appointed supreme commander, it had been important that he keep the Combined Chiefs of Staff informed of the progress of the war. He would wire these reports to Washington.

What fancy words would come from the man whose efforts had saved Europe? Would they be eloquent and unforgettable? Would they go down in history books like Washington's farewell address or Lincoln's Emancipation Proclamation? After thanking everyone for their suggestions, he dictated the following:

> The mission of this Allied force was fulfilled at 0241 local time, May 7, 1945.[7]

What would Eisenhower do at the age of fifty-five? How could he do anything to top all that he had accomplished? He had much to consider.

While the war in the Pacific was still going, Ike gave a speech in London on June 12, 1945. It was well received, and it would be the first of many he would give the rest of his life. When he was sure all of the well-known generals that had helped him win the war had been sent home to be received by the admiring public, he returned and gave a speech to the joint session of Congress. There were many in the audience, both Republicans and Democrats, who saw a future president.

President Truman asked him to be chief of staff, the job that General Marshall had held during the war. He accepted and began December 3, 1945. He dealt with demobilization problems, gave more speeches, and met with many important civilians who wanted him to be CEO of their businesses.

He thought he might like to be head of a small college, but no offers came his way. When he was offered the presidency of Columbia University in New York City, he asked two people about it: his brother Milton who was president of Penn State, and President Truman. Both thought he should accept the position, and Truman said he would release him from the chief of staff position in early 1948.

After reading Ulysses Grant's *Memoirs,* he began writing his own. Using three secretaries and advice from two editors, he "wrote" his experiences into a best-selling book, *Crusade in Europe,* which was published in late 1948.[8]

Truman was reelected in a very close race with Tom Dewey. Ike remained president of Columbia for two years and supported Truman's decision to fight when North Korea invaded South Korea. Under constant pressure from both Democrats and Republicans to run for president, Ike would only consider running if the public demanded it. Truman asked him to run as a Democrat, but he chose instead the Republican Party.

Truman then selected Adlai Stevenson, governor of Illinois. The election was not even close. The Democrats had held the White House since 1933, nearly twenty years. But two slogans used by the Republicans helped swing the voting. One slogan was Had enough? and the second became a rallying cry with campaign banners and buttons claiming, I Like Ike.

Eisenhower received 33,778,964 popular votes to Stevenson's 27,314,992. Ike won 442 electoral votes, while Stevenson only got 89. The vice president elected with Ike was Richard Nixon, a navy veteran who had served in the Pacific theater. He was a member of the House of Representatives immediately after World War II and then a senator from California. Much more would be heard from this ambitious man in the future.

On January 20, 1953, Dwight D. Eisenhower became the oldest president since James Buchanan, who was sixty-five when he took office. No one had the experience that Eisenhower had lived through. Thirty-three years in the military, rising slowly but surely with growing confidence, worthwhile experiences, and a great personality, President Eisenhower was about to take on the biggest job of his life.

1953-1961 DWIGHT DAVID EISENHOWER THIRTY-FOURTH PRESIDENT

President Eisenhower kept a diary during his entire time in office. At the end of the first day in the Oval Office, he said he found the job to be fascinating, absorbing, challenging, and fulfilling.[9]

When he was supreme commander of the European theater of operations, he carefully selected good men and then let them do their job, not getting in the way or interfering unless absolutely necessary, such as firing Fredendall after the debacle at Kasserine Pass in Africa, keeping Patton when others wanted him sacked, and threatening Montgomery when he overstepped his authority.

Ike used the same plan of hiring good men and letting them do their job. Because he used this proven technique, he was often criticized as to not making any major decisions. Nothing could be farther from the truth. From the time he decided to run, he made carefully thought out plans, seeking advice from known experts, gathering the needed important information and then making decisions.

It had helped him climb the military ladder of success. He knew that this technique helped win the war. So why not apply it when he was president. There would always be one major stumbling block that he worked to overcome. Those in Washington, D.C. were not like his subordinates in the Army, where an order given was an order obeyed. Congressman, both in the House of Representatives and the U.S. Senate had two of their own priorities. One—get as much power as they can with any means available. Two—get reelected. In spite of this, Ike performed well for two terms. He saw that some major legislation was passed, major problems confronted, and major decisions made—all in the interest of a better America.

During Ike's eight years in the White House, the United States experienced peace as well as prosperity. The Housing Act was a compromise between the Republicans wanting to leave the problem to the housing industry and the Democrats wanting to give assistance in a very large and expansive manner. Ike sought the middle ground, and the housing boomed.[10]

When Ike turned down Truman's offer to run as a Democrat, Truman began criticizing Eisenhower at every turn. When Ike campaigned, he said he would go to Korea, planning to examine the problems that existed. Truman made fun of that approach, and when Eisenhower won the election in 1952, Truman said that Ike would not know how to be a good president. Truman would be proved wrong.

Ike's early years in Washington, working under MacArthur, attending Congressional hearings, and working on war plans prior to the U.S. entry into World War II gave him great insight into the workings of Washington. He was smart enough not to appoint any of his friends, civilian or military, to any important post such as cabinet member. He attacked problems with a military approach—get all the information (intelligence) you can, talk to experts in the particular field under investigation, and listen to all sides of an argument. Then make a decision and back it to the hilt. This approach served him well.

After he won the election, Ike flew to Korea on November 29, 1952. He spoke to all the military men connected with the war. He even sought MacArthur's council, but that proved to be worthless. When Ike became president, he had his secretary of state, John Foster Dulles, work hard at finally getting an armistice on July 26, 1953. Ike spoke to the nation on radio and television and greeted them with prayers of thanksgiving. He reminded the American people that:

> We have won an armistice on a single battlefield—not peace in the world.
> We may not now relax our guard nor cease our quest.

He then concluded his remarks with a quotation form Lincoln, "With malice towards none; with charity for all."[11]

There was no celebration or cheering crowds. But there was peace, and Ike would be forever remembered for bring an end to the first United Nations' action.

Two far-reaching and significant events occurred in 1953. On January 30, Francis H. Crick and Maurice Wilkins of Britain and American Dr. James D. Watson, aged twenty-five, discovered the molecular structure *deoxyribonucleic acid*, or for short, DNA. This building block of life, considered the most important scientific discovery of the twentieth century, would save lives in many different ways. For example, a person arrested for a crime they did not commit would be aided by DNA samples—when it could be shown that they were in no way connected with the crime.

The second far-reaching event was on June 8, 1953, when the U.S. Supreme Court ruled that restaurants in the District of Columbia could not refuse to serve blacks. Truman had ordered the armed forces to desegregate after World War II. During the Korean War, combat troops had been made up of both blacks and whites. It had shown that desegregation could work. The Supreme Court made an important ruling during the Korean War that would have a profound effect on civil rights.

A number of court cases dealing with school desegregation were brought out as early as 1931. One of the earliest was the case of *Alberto Alveres vs. Lemon Grove*—near San Diego. The court allowed Mexican Americans to return to the Lemon Grove School. In 1947, the U.S. Court of Appeals ruled that four schools in Orange County, California, could not put Mexican-American children in separate schools.

In 1949, with the NAACP's support, a class action lawsuit was brought against the Clarendon County School Board in South Carolina. The case of *Briggs vs. Elliott* was first of five cases later consolidated in the historic *Brown vs. Board of Education of Topeka*, Kansas.

On May 17, 1954, in a landmark ruling in the *Brown vs. Board of Education of Topeka*, Kansas, the Supreme Court said racial segregation of public schools was unconstitutional. Supreme Court Chief Justice Earl Warren stated:

> To separate (Negro children) from others of similar age and qualification solely because of their race generates a feeling of inferiority as to their status in a way unlikely ever to be undone . . . We conclude that in the field of public education the doctrine of "separate but equal" has no place. Separate educational facilities are inherently unequal.(Brown *v. Board of Education of Topeka*, Kansas)[12]

Robert Hutchins, president of the University of Chicago summed it up so well.

> Democracy . . . is the only form of government that is founded on the dignity of man, not the dignity of some men, or educated men or of white men, but of all men.[13](Democracy *and Human Nature*)

During the year 1954, a number of important and interesting events occurred. Eisenhower signed an order adding the words *under God* to the Pledge of Allegiance on June 14. On August 18, Assistant Secretary of Labor James Wilken became the first black to attend a cabinet meeting when he sat in for the secretary of labor James Mitchell. The *Tonight Show* premiered on September 27, with host Steve Allen.

The show is still running. Three days later, September 30, the first atomic-powered submarine, the *Nautilus,* was commissioned by the navy, thanks to Admiral Rickover. On November 12, Ellis Island was closed after processing twenty million U.S.-bound immigrants since its opening in 1892. And the first automatic toll collection booth went into service on the New Jersey Turnpike on November 10.

Senator Joseph McCarthy, a Republican from Wisconsin, was a constant thorn in Eisenhower's side. But Ike handled him the same way he handled Montgomery during the war—by ignoring him. Eventually McCarthy dug his own grave, so to speak, when he confronted Joseph Welch, the army counsel during the McCarthy—army hearings in the summer of 1954. McCarthy had made wild, unsubstantiated charges against Frederick Fisher, a member of Welch's law firm. Joseph Welch's retort was:

Have you no sense of decency, sir?

This was broadcast on television for all of America to see, and after that McCarthy, was never considered seriously again. McCarthy had been a problem that Ike was glad to see go away.

In 1954, Ike also worked hard to see that Social Security improve benefits and cover ten million *more* Americans. He had tried, unsuccessfully, in 1953, but with the midterm elections coming up, his proposals were more amenable to improving the system, and the bill was passed and signed.[14]

The year 1955 was marked by two important events—one was international the other dealt with something Eisenhower had dreamed of since 1919. The international problems dealt with China taking small islands near Formosa and threatening to invade others. The incident started in January and was not resolved until August 1. Eisenhower's Formosa's Doctrine was so vague (as Ike intended), that China did not dare to do anymore. Ike's handling of this crisis was *tour de force* and a great triumph for him and the world seeking peace.[15]

The other event was Eisenhower's desire to get an interstate highway built throughout the nation. When he had traveled the roads in an army convoy in 1919, he saw how poor the roads were. They had not improved much between cities, and he began his attempts to get federal backing. It would take four more years before serious construction began, and it was much needed in a country where nearly everyone owned a car and many had two cars in a family.

Other important events in 1955 included Jonas Salk, physician and researcher at the University of Pittsburg, working for four years and testing nearly two million children, was able to announce the success of the polio vaccination in April. The same month, Ray Kroc opened the first McDonald's fast food franchise in Des Plaines, Illinois, and changed the eating habits of the country. In July, Disneyland opened in Anaheim, California, and people rushed to this wonder playground for children and adults.

The most significant event in civil rights history took place on December 1, 1955. Rosa Parks, a hardworking black woman refused to yield her seat on a city bus to a white man in Montgomery, Alabama. Her arrest sparked a yearlong boycott of buses, and the Supreme Court struck down a law requiring blacks to sit at the rear of public buses.

Martin Luther King Jr. and his followers, including Jesse Jackson came later, but Rosa Parks was the first to take a stand, and her reason was, "I was not tired physically, or no more tired than I usually was at the end of a working day . . . . No, the only tired I was, was tired of giving in."

Much of the last part of 1955 was taken up with Eisenhower's heart attack that occurred in September. While he was recovering, there were many discussions on whether he would run for reelection in 1956 or whether they should pick another candidate. Finally, in March 1956, the doctors gave Ike a clean bill of health.

During 1956, a number of significant events happened. The Soviet Union proceeded to put down Hungary's attempt to become more of a democracy. At the Republican convention in San Francisco in August, Eisenhower was nominated for a second term with great acclaim. After much discussion during the early part of 1956, Richard Nixon was also renominated.

The Arab nations of Egypt, Syria, and Jordan had signed a pact. Their intentions were to eliminate the relatively new nation of Israel. When Israel attacked Egypt successfully, Eisenhower played a key role in the peaceful settlement.[16]

On November 13, 1956, the United States Supreme Court struck down laws calling for racial segregation of passengers on public buses.

The presidential election of 1956 was more one sided than Ike's first run for the office. Eisenhower received 35,581,003 popular votes to 25,738,765 for Stevenson. The electoral vote count was 457 for Ike and only 73 for Stevenson.

1957-1961 PRESIDENT EISHENHOWER'S SECOND TERM

Two major events dominated 1957. On September 4, Arkansas Governor Orval Faubus called out the National Guard to prevent nine black students from entering Central High School in Little Rock, Arkansas. Eisenhower was just starting his summer vacation at a naval base at Newport, Rhode Island, when he was informed of the governor's move. Faubus thought by sending a telegram to the president asking for his understanding and cooperation, he could sway Ike to his way of thinking. He didn't know Ike. Eisenhower gave a reply that made it perfectly clear where he stood. He said, "The federal Constitution will be upheld by me by every legal means at my command."[17]

After both sides argued, a meeting was arranged with Ike and Governor Faubus. After a twenty-minute discussion, Ike suggested that Faubus simply change the orders to the National Guard and allow the children into the school. The governor seemed to agree, but never gave the order.

When large crowds gathered, the mayor of Little Rock asked the president for the needed federal troops to maintain law and order. In a brilliant move, Ike nationalized the Arkansas Guard that Faubus had called out and also sent in the 101st Airborne Division. The nine students entered school, and a major step in American history had been taken. By October, Ike was able to withdraw the troops and integration had become a success.[18]

On October 4, 1957, the Soviet Republic launched the world's first artificial satellite into orbit around the Earth. They called it *Sputnik* (traveling companion), and it was the beginning of the space age. The American people were stunned. How could anybody be better or do something sooner than the United States of America? Some individuals wanted to lay the blame for the lack of progress on the American schools, but most politicians looked for other answers.

Each of the military services—army, navy and air force—vied for the money to build a workable satellite. When the Vanguard rocket blew up in December 1957, Eisenhower worked to create the National Aeronautic and Space Agency (NASA), giving this civilian agency enormous amount of money, personnel, and expertise. He signed the needed legislation on July 29. NASA wasted no time and continuously progressed bringing America into the space age.

During the years 1957 through 1959, some interesting as well as important events took place. In May 1957, the National League baseball approved the move of the Brooklyn Dodgers and New York Giants baseball teams to Los Angles and San Francisco, respectively. On July 16, Marine Major John Glenn established a transcontinental speed record, piloting a jet plane from California to New York in three hours, twenty-three minutes, and eight seconds. More would be heard from this man in the future.

On September 8, President Eisenhower signed into law the first civil rights bill since Reconstruction. That same month, the Miss America Pageant was shown on television for the first time. Lee Meriwether from California was declared the winner. And on December 16, the AFL-CIO voted to expel the International Brotherhood of Teamsters.

Also in 1958, transatlantic passenger jetliner service, which began as the British Overseas Airways Corporation (BOAC), began flights between New York City and London, England.

On January 3, 1959 Alaska become the forty-ninth state. On January 25, American Airlines opened the jet age in the United States with the first transcontinental flight of a Boeing 707. President Eisenhower joined Queen Elizabeth II in ceremonies opening the Saint Lawrence River on June 26. And on August 21, 1959, Hawaii became the fiftieth state in the Union.

In 1960, Ike's last year as president, the first two-way telephone conversation by satellite took place with the help of Echo 1, a balloon satellite on August 13. The next month, on September 24, the USS *Enterprise* also known as CVN-65—the first nuclear-powered aircraft carrier was launched at Newport News, Virginia.

THE RIGHT MAN IN THE RIGHT PLACE AT THE RIGHT TIME

President Eisenhower's eight years were successful because of his character, his vision, his military training, and his winning personality.

He handled each crisis without overacting. He prevented the chance of having to go to war with patience and skill. He cut taxes and increased defense spending. He had the unique ability, as Rudyard Kipling put it, to "keep his head when all about him were losing theirs." He was a magnificent leader for the people when they needed just his kind of leadership. Once again, America had chosen well.

CHAPTER XXVII

ASK NOT WHAT YOUR COUNTRY CAN DO FOR YOU

1917-1945 JOHN FITZGERALD KENNEDY'S VARIED EARLY EXPERIENCES

John F. Kennedy was born March 29, 1917 in Brookline, Massachusetts—one of nine children. His mother, Rose, was the daughter of a former Boston mayor, John Fitzgerald. His father, Joseph Kennedy came from a wealthy family, but he added to his own fortune by two lucky and shrewd moves.

He sold his investments in the stock market just before the crash in 1929. Anticipating the end of prohibition, he invested $100,000 in a company that imported Scotch whiskey and gin from Great Britain, eventually selling his interest for $8 million.

John F. Kennedy had private schooling, and when his father was appointed Ambassador to Great Britain, he joined him at the age of twenty. Here he met many important diplomats and political leaders, including Winston Churchill.

He attended the London School of Economics, and when World War II started in 1939, he returned to enroll at Harvard. While there, he wrote a book about the start of World War II, called *Why England Slept*. After starting graduate school at Stanford, in early 1941, he volunteered for military service.

At first rejected because of a football injury, he exercised and was accepted into the Navy. Having extensive sailing experience, he was commissioned and assigned as a commander of a motorized patrol boat (PT boat), the same type of vessel that MacArthur had used in his escape from the Philippines in March 1942.

In August 1943, while patrolling with other boats in the middle of the night, his patrol boat—PT-109—was cut in half by a Japanese destroyer. Two of his crew died, but Kennedy led the other ten to safety. While eight stayed on an obscure island, John and another crew member swam to other islands, eventually finding friendly natives. He wrote a message to the nearest Australian outpost on the only thing available, a coconut, and they were finally rescued. For his heroism, Lieutenant John F. Kennedy was awarded a U.S. Navy and Marine Corps medal.[1]

1945-1960 POLITICAL PREPARATION FOR THE PRESIDENCY

Jack—as he was called by his family and good friends—came back from the war as the oldest son. His older brother, Joseph Kennedy Jr. was killed on a flying mission in the European theater of operations, and had always thought he wanted to get into politics after the war. Jack decided to carry on his brother's dream, and after a short stint as a newspaper reporter, ran for the congressional seat being vacated by Congressman Curley of Boston.

After three terms in the House of Representatives, he then sought the senate seat held by Henry Cabot Lodge Jr., the grandson of then Senator Henry Cabot Lodge who opposed Woodrow Wilson in seeking confirmation of the Versailles Treaty. It was a close election in 1952, the year that Eisenhower was running for president, but Kennedy won the senate seat.[2]

Shortly after being sworn in as Massachusetts's junior senator, two things happened. He met and on September 12, 1953, married Jacqueline Lee Bouvier. The next year, Jack had operations on his back (the first was unsuccessful). While recovering, he and his good friend and advisor, Ted Sorenson, wrote *Profiles in Courage,* a story of eight U.S. senators who risked their political careers for unpopular causes. Thanks to his father's influence on Arthur Krock, the Pulitzer Prize Board displaced two other choices and gave the prize to Kennedy.[3]

In 1955 and again in 1956, Jackie Kennedy suffered miscarriages. Their daughter, Caroline, was born in 1957. At the Democrat Convention in the summer of 1956, Kennedy gave the nominating speech for Adlai Stevenson. It was so well received that his name was put in nomination for vice president. Instead, the convention chose Estes Kefauver. But that only whetted Kennedy's appetite. While he sought the reelection to the Senate in 1958, he was also having others work behind the scenes in preparation for a run for the presidency in 1960.

In the meantime, America was growing and changing. The veterans of World War II were having babies in record numbers. The population in 1940 was 132 million. By 1950, it had jumped to over 151 million, and by 1960 would reach nearly 180 million.

The beautiful music you could sing and dance to in the 1930s and 1940s gave way to rock and roll, and the youngsters in their teens went wild over a forty-year-old former truck driver named Elvis Presley. Hugh Hefner brought out a magazine that had no date on the cover because he wasn't sure there would be a second issue. He called it *Playboy.* On the cover he had a provocative picture of a girl named Norma

Jean Baker who had changed her name to Marilyn Monroe. When asked what she had on when she went to bed, she replied, "The radio."[4]

The one big stumbling block for John F. Kennedy in seeking the presidency was his religion. No Catholic had ever been elected, and the only one who had run, Al Smith of New York, had lost to Herbert Hoover in the election of 1928 by the fourth highest margin of difference. Only Harding, FDR, and Teddy Roosevelt had higher margins of victory. It would be an uphill battle, but Kennedy had already made a name for himself and was working hard in the U.S. Senate.

Appointed to the Foreign Relations Committee for which he was well qualified, he also served on the Committee on Improper Activities in Labor Management. His younger brother, Robert, served as counsel for that committee. When the state primaries began in early 1960, the key state was West Virginia, which was predominately Protestant. When he won that state primary, the rest was easy. He answered the media's concern about his religion in a sensible manner and won over the press of the country.

The national campaign would be a struggle right up to the day of voting. His opponent was Eisenhower's vice president, Richard Nixon. Kennedy and Nixon would battle it out on the campaign trail, but probably the deciding factor in the election was the debate that was held on television and radio. If you listened on radio, you believed that Nixon had won the debate. If you watched on TV, you were convinced that Kennedy had won.

The election was one of the closest races ever, with Kennedy winning the popular vote of 34,227,096 to Nixon's 34,107,647 votes, a difference of less than 120,000 votes. This gave Kennedy 50.1 percent of the popular votes, but he received 303 electoral votes to Nixon's 219. A new generation was about to take over. Kennedy set the tone of his administration with his inaugural address on January 20, 1961.

1961-1963 JOHN FITZGERALD KENNEDY THIRTY-FIFTH PRESIDENT

"We observe today not a victory of party but a celebration of freedom—symbolizing an end as well as a beginning—signifying renewal as well as change. For I have sworn before you and Almighty God the same solemn oath our forefathers proscribed nearly a century and three-quarters ago.

. . .

"We dare not forget today that we are the heirs of that first revolution. Let the word go forth from this time and place, to friends and foe alike, that the torch has been passed to a new generation of Americans—born in this century, tempered by war, disciplined by a hard and bitter peace, proud of our ancient heritage—and unwilling to witness or permit the slow undoing of those human rights to which this nation has always been committed, and to which we are committed today at home and around the world.

. . .

"Let every nation know, whether it wishes us well or ill, that we shall pay any price, bear any burden, meet any hardship, support any friend, oppose any foe to assure the survival and success of liberty.

. . .

" . . . to those nations who would make themselves our adversary, we offer not a pledge but a re quest: that both sides begin anew the quest for peace, before the dark powers of destruction unleashed by science engulf all humanity in planned or accidental destruction.

. . .

"So let us begin anew—remembering on both sides that civility is not a sign of weakness, and sincerity is always subject to proof. Let us never negotiate out of fear. But let us never fear to negotiate.

. . .

"Let both sides seek to invoke the wonder of science instead of its terror. Together let us explore the stars, conquer the deserts, eradicate disease, tap the ocean depths, and encourage the arts and commerce.

. . .

" . . . Since this country was founded, each generation of Americas has been summoned to give testimony to its national loyalty. The graves of young Americans who answered the call to service surround the globe.

. . .

"In the long history of the world, only a few generations have been granted the role of defending freedom in its hour of maximum danger . . . . And so, my fellow Americans: ask not what your country can do for you—ask what you can do for your country.

"My fellow citizens of the world: ask not what America will do for you, but what together we can do for the freedom of man.

"Finally, whether you are citizens of America or citizens of the world ask of us here the same high standards of strength and sacrifice which we ask of you. With a good conscience our only sure reward, with history the final judge of our deeds, let us go forth to lead the land we love, asking His blessing, and His help, but knowing that here on earth God's work must truly be our own."[5]

THE PEACE CORPS AND PROBLEMS WITH CUBA

One of President Kennedy's first programs was the Peace Corps. He selected Robert Sargent Shriver, his brother-in-law, as the first director. He built a very successful program that grew in two years from five hundred to five thousand volunteers that went to forty-six different countries. These highly motivated young men and women, acting as "ambassadors of peace," lived and worked with third world people, teaching basic educational, health, and safety programs. It was one of Kennedy's most successful ideas that had been originally proposed by Senator Hubert Humphrey in 1957.[6]

Fulgencio Batista was elected president of Cuba in 1940. After World War II, two other Cubans held that office. In 1952, Batista overthrew President Socarra, and proclaimed the title of Chief of State as well as Premier. He ruled with an iron hand until Fidel Castro overthrew the government in 1959, and relations with the U.S. grew from bad to worse. With sanctions imposed on Cuba, Castro became very friendly with the Soviet Union.[7]

On April 17, 1961, 1,600 Cuban émigrés stormed the coast of Cuba in the area called Bay of Pigs. This had the backing of the CIA (Central Intelligence Agency) and Kennedy's approval. The invasion was a disaster, and the invaders were quickly captured. The responsibility of the unsuccessful attempt was laid on Kennedy who did not approve of the use of U.S. Air Force as cover for the invasion. Kennedy accepted the responsibility for the failure, and when he consulted Eisenhower, Kennedy learned something.

Kennedy explained the planning, objective, and anticipated results to Ike. Ike asked him if he had consulted the people involved one at a time or in a group where people could give the pros and cons of the planned invasion. Kennedy admitted that he had not consulted in a group setting, the correct thing to do, and he thanked Ike for the military lesson.[8]

He had better luck in the Caribbean and in Latin America. He saw the need for economic aid and introduced a plan called the *Alliance for Progress,* which helped fund the economies of Latin American countries. It won support, and Kennedy was well received when he visited Columbia and Argentina in 1961 and Mexico in 1962.[9]

A number of interesting and in some cases, important events happened during 1961. On March 29, the Twenty-third Amendment was ratified. This gave the District of Columbia three electors in the Electoral College, which would be used in the next presidential election in 1964. [10]

On April 12, Major Yuri Gagarin of the Soviet Union became the first man to successfully orbit the earth in the space ship *Vostok I.* On May 5, Astronaut Alan Shepard, Jr., was the first American in space. It was only a fifteen-minute suborbital flight in a capsule launched from Cape Canaveral, Florida, but it was an important first step in the race with the Soviets.

This limited success in America's space effort encouraged President Kennedy to make a predictive hope. On May 25, in a forty-seven-minute address to a joint session of Congress, he announced a goal:

> I believe that this nation should commit itself, before the decade is out,
> to landing a man on the moon and returning him safely to the Earth. No
> single space project in this period will be more exciting, or more impressive
> to mankind, or more important for the long-range exploration of space;
> and none will be so difficult or expensive to accomplish.[11]

Many thought it would *never* be done. But NASA had been working at a feverish pitch, and it was successful on the next step. On November 29, 1961, at Cape Canaveral, a chimpanzee named *Enos,* was launched aboard the Mercury-Atlas 5 (MA-5) spacecraft, which orbited the Earth twice before returning safely to earth.

Germany was still divided in 1961. Since 1949 three million East Germans had fled to West Germany. With East Germany losing workers, they erected a wall. They said it was to keep the westerners out, but in reality, it was to keep the East Germans in. The wall went up in August 1961. Kennedy could not do much without going to war.[12]

When Babe Ruth hit sixty home runs in 1927, it was a record that some thought would never be broken. The baseball season had been expanded from 154 games to 162 games by 1961, when Roger Maris of the New York Yankees hit his sixty-first home run during the 162nd game on October 1.

On the last day of 1961, the Marshall Plan expired after distributing more than $12 billion in foreign aid. It had helped the western countries of Europe survive and withstand any take-over by the Soviet Union.

On February 20, 1962, those with television sets *throughout the entire world* saw Lieutenant Colonel John Glenn became the first American astronaut to successfully orbit the Earth. He circled it three times and splashed down in the ocean where he was picked up and returned to the United States a hero.[13]

On July 23, a Telstar communication satellite relayed the first live TV program from the United States to Europe. Many more satellites would follow, for weather observations, spying from the sky and a host of other uses.

On September 24, the U.S. Circuit Court of Appeals in New Orleans ordered the University of Mississippi to admit black applicant James Meredith, who, on his fourth try, was able to register on September 30.

On October 1, Johnny Carson succeeded Jack Parr, who had succeeded Steven Allen, as the regular host of the *Tonight Show*. Carson hosted the program for almost thirty years.

On October 15, 1962, a United States spy plane took pictures of ballistic missile launching pads being constructed in Cuba. Again, Kennedy consulted Eisenhower about different options: one, destruction of the missile sites by bombing; two, bombing and invading the island of Cuba; and three, setting up a blockade to stop delivery by ship of any missiles from Russia. Ike gave his opinion that blockage was the wisest choice. Some one suggested calling the plan something other than a blockade, which had a wartime connotation to it.

Kennedy went on television and explained the situation to the American people that he had ordered a "quarantine," and that U.S. Naval ships would stop and, if necessary, search any vessels coming to Cuba. It was a frightening time, and the chance of a nuclear war was never so close. But Kennedy held firm to his demands and finally, the Soviet leader, Chairman Nikita Khrushchev, backed down and said he would dismantle the launchpads if the United States would not invade Cuba. It was Kennedy's finest hour.[14]

The midterm elections of November 6 saw the Democrats gain a majority in both the House and the Senate. The House had 258 Democrats, while the Republicans had only 176. In the Senate, there were 67 Democrats and 33 Republicans. Whatever President Kennedy proposed for legislation would be passed with very little opposition, except civil rights, which would take longer.

1963 PROGRESS THEN TRAGEDY

The First Lady Jackie Kennedy won the hearts of the American people. She took over directing the restoration of the White House. She and Jack hosted informal parties that were the envy of those who were not invited. She set a trend in clothing and hairstyle such as the ever-famous pillbox hat. She was also well received overseas as she had studied abroad and could speak French and Spanish.

On May 15 and 16, L. Gordon Cooper, Jr., orbited the earth twenty-two times in the Mercury Capsule named *Faith*. On June 17, the Supreme Court ruled that local government could not require recitation of the Bible or in public schools.[15]

On June 26, President Kennedy visited West Berlin where he declared, "Ich bin ein Berliner" (I am a Berliner). The West Germans cheered. On July 1, the U.S. Post Office inaugurated the five-digit ZIP code.

In June, President Kennedy proposed a civil rights bill, but it would linger in Congress. James Meridith became the first black graduate from the University of Mississippi on the eighteenth. On August 28, over two hundred thousand people marched on Washington, D.C., for civil rights. They gathered in front of the Lincoln Memorial—a fitting place as it marked the one hundredth anniversary of the Emancipation Proclamation. At the end of the peaceful demonstration, the

Reverend Martin Luther King, Jr., gave a speech that ranks as one of the great speeches dealing with civil rights. He spoke not so much about the injustices that prevailed but instead invoked an image of what America could and should be:

> I have a dream that one day on the red hills of Georgia that sons of former slaves and sons of former slave owners will be able to sit down together at the table of brotherhood.
>
> I have a dream that my four little children will one day live in a nation where they will not be judged by the color of their skin, but by the content of their character.
>
> When we let freedom ring, when we let it ring in every village and hamlet, from every state and every city, we will be able to speed up that day when all God's Children, black men and white men, Jews and Gentiles, Protestants and Catholics, will be able to join hands and sing in the words of the old Negro spiritual, "Free at last! Free at last! Thank God Almighty, we are free at last!"[16]

President Kennedy was watching the demonstration on TV from the White House. When King finished, Kennedy was heard to remark, "That man is good."

From the 1962 Cuban missile crisis grew a feeling that something should be done to prevent the chances of a nuclear war. On June 10, Kennedy gave a commencement address at the American University in which he proposed discussion on a test ban treaty between the United States, the Soviets, and Great Britain. On September 24, 1963, the Senate approved the Nuclear Test Ban Treaty where the governments agreed to stop nuclear tests.[17]

RETROSPECTION

William Henry Harrison was elected in 1840. He died in office.
Abraham Lincoln was elected in 1860. He was assassinated.
James Garfield was elected in 1880. He was assassinated
William McKinley was reelected in 1900. He was assassinated.
Warren Harding was elected in 1920. He died in office.
Franklin D. Roosevelt was reelected in 1940. He died in office.
John F. Kennedy was elected in 1960. He was assassinated.

President Kennedy flew to Dallas, Texas, two days after his newborn son, two-day-old Patrick Kennedy, died. He went there to shore up his support from the state where his vice president Lyndon Johnson came from. The motorcade proceeded on a preplanned route, with the president and First Lady riding in the back of an open convertible. Also in the car were Texas governor John Connally and his wife. At about 12:30 in the afternoon, shots rang out, and President Kennedy was hit twice.

Immediately taken to the Parkland Hospital, he was pronounced dead shortly after 1:00 p.m., November 22, 1963. The country and the world had lost a champion. His body was flown back to Washington, D.C. Here, at the Capitol Rotunda, the coffin was visited by people throughout the night and day, paying their last respects.

The next day, the funeral procession to the Arlington National Cemetery was followed by dignitaries, heads of state, and diplomats representing ninety-two countries. It was watched on television by 93 percent of the American people and, thanks to Telstar, by untold millions overseas. It was a tragic day for Americans. They had lost someone who had so much to offer but did not get the time to do all that he wanted.

Vice President Lyndon Johnson took the oath of office aboard the plane returning Kennedy's body. Johnson authorized a committee to investigate the assassination. Chief Justice of the Supreme Court Earl Warren was appointed the chairman of the committee.

After exhaustive study, it was determined that one man had been responsible. Lee Harvey Oswald had been arrested and was being transferred from one jail to another when another man, Jack Ruby, in front of police and televisions cameras, shot Oswald who then died in the same hospital in which President Kennedy had died.

The Warren Commission issued a report that some thought was a cover-up for a conspiracy. Further investigation proved fruitless.

The year Kennedy was elected, there was a Broadway musical called *Camelot*. It was a story of the legendary King Arthur and the title song went, "Don't let it be forgot / That once there was a spot / That for one brief moment / That was known as Camelot."[18]

Many thought that best described the short but memorable two years, ten months, and two days of the thirty-fifth president of the United States.

PART I

JOHNSON, NIXON, AND FORD

The next three United States presidents had something in common. They all had early successes in their presidency. However, two of them had disastrous endings.

Lyndon Johnson wanted to run for president in 1960, but Kennedy beat him to it. Chosen as the Democratic vice presidential candidate, he worked diligently on the campaign, and they were successful. Johnson served faithfully and well as vice president. Put in charge of the new space program, he worked hard to make it a success.

When Kennedy was assassinated, Johnson took over running the government in a decisive manner. He appointed a commission to find the one or ones responsible for the assassination. In 1964, the twenty-fourth amendment—often called the poll tax amendment—was ratified. The poll tax was required for voting in parts of the United States that often disenfranchised poor people, especially the blacks in the South. Johnson signed the Civil Rights Act of 1964 on July 2, after a long delay.

Elected on his own in 1964, Johnson oversaw a number of important legislative acts that could have been his crowning achievement. However, he chose to accept a flimsy report on questionable action in the Gulf of Tonkin as fact and kept increasing the number of U.S. troops in Vietnam. This resulted in a higher number of casualties which led to war protests at home.

The assassination of Martin Luther King, Jr., produced many riots in the larger cities. When the polls showed his losing support, Johnson chose not to run, though eligible.

As president, Richard Nixon supported the development of the Environmental Protection Agency. He also nominated four people to the Supreme Court. Two major events happened in July of 1969. The space module Apollo 11 landed on the moon and Senator Edward Kennedy drove off a bridge in his home state of Massachusetts, killing his passenger Mary Jo Kopechne.

The twenty-sixth amendment was ratified in 1971. That same year, Nixon opened trade talks with China. His attempt to resolve the Vietnam War made his reelection in 1972 a landslide.

Other events with long-range impact in 1972 and 1973 included the Olympics in Munich, Germany where Arab terrorists killed eleven members of the Israeli Olympic team. Also the Supreme Court issued its decision on *Roe vs. Wade,* and the end of the Vietnam War was negotiated by Secretary of State Henry Kissinger.

In 1974, the hearings on the Watergate affair by the Judiciary Committee, which had begun earlier, drafted articles of impeachment against President Nixon.

On August 8, 1974, President Richard Nixon became the first president to resign from office.

Ford became the president and gave a speech that established his position by promising to be open and direct with the people. He quickly learned the necessary steps to being a leader, and he was encouraged by both the Congress and the people.

With Constitutional authority, Gerald Ford pardoned former President Richard Nixon. It was a heartwarming attempt to bring a closure to a sad part of American history.

CHAPTER XXVIII

FULFILLMENT THEN FAILURE

1908-1937 EARLY LIFE OF LYNDON BAINES JOHNSON

Lyndon Johnson was born on August 27, 1908 to Rebekah and Sam Johnson. He attended school in Johnson City, graduating at the age of sixteen from high school in May 1924. Instead of going to college, he and some friends went west where he performed farm chores like picking cotton. He returned to Johnson City and enrolled at Southwest State Texas Teachers College, but after a year needed money so he took a teaching position at the small town of Cotulla, Texas.

Only sixty miles from the Mexican border, his fifth, sixth, and seventh grade classes were mostly Mexicans. He was very strict and demanded that they speak only English. If he heard a boy speaking Spanish, he got paddled. If it was a girl, she got a tongue lashing. When he found out they were not getting enough to eat, he helped establish a free school-lunch program. His students thought he was great and were sorry to see him return to college. But these experiences of working with farmers and impoverished students gave him great insight and would be remembered when he became a congressman and president.[1]

After graduating from college in 1930, he got a teaching job at a Houston High School but also became interested in politics, campaigning for the local congressman Richard Kleberg, who won the election in 1932, the same year that Franklin Roosevelt won the White House. Kleberg asked Lyndon to be his secretary and come to Washington, D.C. After a little more than a year of teaching speech and debate, he resigned.[2]

Lyndon Johnson was about to find out how the other half lived. The train ride to Washington was just the beginning. Excellent food, pullman berths, and all you could drink. In Washington, he stayed at the Mayflower Hotel and lived the good life for four days. Then he had to seek a place to stay in Washington. A former girls school turned into a cheap hotel would be his home while learning the ropes of busy and bureaucratic Washington. His salary was $3,900 a year, twice what he had been making as a teacher, and he was lucky. By that time there were 10,000,000 people out of work in those dark days known as the Depression.[3]

Congressman Kleberg was very wealthy and spent little time in Washington, leaving the work to Lyndon. Johnson took on the task with a vengeance. A combination of on-the-job training and learning the tricks of the trade called politics, Lyndon worked tirelessly, seeking help and advice from all corners of the city. He learned how to answer the thousands of letters that came to the Congressional office. He learned how to make contacts with the important people. He met Claudia Alta Taylor who went by the nickname Lady Bird in 1934. He was so taken with this smart and pretty lady, he proposed on the first day they met. They were married shortly after and returned to Washington and found a place to live. Lady Bird taught herself to cook and entertain. Ever ambitious, Lyndon looked for a better opportunity.[4]

In June 1935, President Roosevelt established the National Youth Administration to help youngsters between sixteen and twenty-five get job training as well as jobs so they could stay in school. Johnson sought and got the job of Texas State Director. No one knew how to get started, but Lyndon worked seventeen hours a day, finding answers, solving problems, and providing jobs. It was one the most successful of NYAs national programs, and President Roosevelt recognized this up-and-coming young Democrat.[5]

In June 1937, Congressman James Buchanan of the Tenth District of Texas died. Lyndon wanted this seat and worked night and day, traveling to every town in the district, giving two hundred speeches in forty-two days. Some of his speeches were only five minutes, but it must have been effective. Considered an outsider with no chance of winning when the campaign started, he won with 28 percent of the votes against six other candidates. He received the congratulations of his victory in a hospital where two days before the election he had an emergency appendectomy.[6]

1937-1960 CONGRESSMAN, NAVAL SERVICE AND SENATE LEADER

From 1937 to 1942, Congressman Lyndon Johnson worked hard at supporting Roosevelt's New Deal. After Pearl Harbor, he joined the navy as a lieutenant commander. Sent to the Southwest Pacific, he spoke to General MacArthur, whom he came to admire. He wanted to see for himself the war firsthand and went in a B-26 bomber over part of New Guinea. The plane was attacked by Japanese Zeros, but the plane came back safely. He was the only member of the plane he rode in to receive a medal.[7]

After the war, he went back to Washington and served in the House of Representatives a total of twelve years, when in 1948, he was elected to the U.S.

Senate. He did a yeoman's job getting bills passed, first for Harry Truman and then as Senate leader, he helped President Eisenhower get the Civil Rights Bill passed, and raised the minimum wage. When the Russians sent up their satellite, *Sputnik,* he helped to get the National Aeronautic and Space Administration started and Eisenhower chose him to make a speech to the United Nations on the need for space to be an international cooperative effort.[8]

In 1960, he set his sights on the presidential election. He had tremendous experience, but he stepped into the campaign too late, as Kennedy had been planning and working for the same office for four years. When Kennedy won the nomination, he asked Johnson to be his vice presidential nominee. Every one was surprised when Johnson agreed and campaigned hard for the Democratic victory, which might not have been if Johnson had not been on the ticket, bringing in the much needed South.

1961-1963 A MOST UNHAPPY FELLA

As vice president, Johnson wanted important things to do and suggested a number of options. He wanted to supervise NASA, and he wanted the cabinet officers to send him copies of all important documents that they were sending to Kennedy. He put this in the form of a memo, and Kennedy ignored it.[9]

President Kennedy realized Johnson's need for recognition and saw his unhappiness at cabinet meetings. Someone suggested that he be sent overseas, and Kennedy agreed. In his nearly three years as vice president, Johnson spent two and a half months on trips to thirty-three different countries. They were mostly ceremonial, but he did meet heads of state. He went to Vietnam, but gave no indication of what should be done.

During the first two and a half years of his administration, Kennedy increased the number of military advisors sent to South Vietnam. President Eisenhower had sent seven hundred advisors; Kennedy increased the number of advisors to about sixteen thousand.[10]

When the East Germans erected the Berlin wall, Kennedy sent a reluctant Johnson to Germany. However, Johnson did a very good job of supporting the West Germans and assuring them of the U.S. desire to support and back them. Johnson was most effective and considered his mission a complete success.[11]

When Kennedy put Johnson in charge of the space program, LBJ took the bull by the horns. He brought in experts, including the German scientist Werner Van Braun. He contacted businessmen, the military and, of course, politicians. He got a commitment, and the space program began to show a real promise.[12]

An area that gave Johnson problems as well as cause for concern was the Committee on Equal Employment Opportunities. He tried to pass off this responsibility to the Secretary of Labor, but Kennedy would not allow it. Over the next two years, a little progress was made in giving blacks more jobs, but it did not satisfy those who wanted a comprehensive civil rights legislation that would challenge the "Jim Crow" segregation in the Southern states.[13]

When it came to fulfilling a campaign promise regarding Civil Rights, neither Kennedy nor Johnson pushed very hard to comply. Martin Luther King Jr. made an attempt in April 1963 to desegregate Birmingham, Alabama. He met with stiff resistance by the Birmingham police who beat the protesters with nightsticks, herding them into vans with electric cattle prods, snarling dogs, and high pressure water hoses. All this was seen across the country on television.

At the same time, Governor Wallace was denying blacks' entrance into the University of Alabama at Tuscaloosa. Finally, Kennedy asked for legislation to eliminate desegregation and discrimination. With a stubborn Congress controlled by Southern Democrats, the bill would not move forward for another year—1964.[1]

Lyndon Johnson and Robert Kennedy, President Kennedy's younger brother and attorney general, hated each other. Robert Kennedy believed Johnson was a constant liar; and when two of Johnson's close friends, Billie Sol Estes and Bobby Baker, were found guilty of fraud, theft, and corrupt dealings, Robert Kennedy was hoping to find a connection between them and Johnson so that Johnson could be replaced as vice presidential candidate for the 1964 election.[15]

By November 1963, Lyndon Johnson was miserable. He believed he was going to be replaced on the 1964 ticket. He had no power to do anything about it and was afraid he would be a forgotten man. Earlier, President Kennedy planned to come to Texas and, after discussing the pros and cons with both Johnson and Senator Yarborough, decided to come in the latter part of November. He first went to San Antonio on November 21 where he met Lyndon. After that, President and Mrs. Kennedy flew to Dallas the next day. Vice President Johnson and Senator Ralph Yarborough were in the fourth car of the procession.[16]

President Kennedy asked that the removable bulletproof top be taken off so that more people could see their president and First Lady, as well as their Governor John Connelly and his wife. The parade started at 12:30 p.m. Forty-five minutes later, the country had lost its thirty-fifth president, the fourth president, following Lincoln, Garfield, and McKinley to be assassinated.

Fearing a conspiracy, Johnson, along with Lady Bird, Jackie, and President Kennedy's coffin, were flown back to Washington aboard Air Force One. President Johnson was sworn into office aboard the plane as it flew into an unknown future.

1963-1969 LYNDON BAINES JOHNSON THIRTY-SIXTH PRESIDENT

On November 27, 1963, President Johnson addressed a joint session of Congress. His opening statement began:

All that I have I would have given gladly not to be standing here today.[17]

He appointed a commission to study the cause of the assassination and to find who might be responsible and to discover if there was a conspiracy. All sorts of speculations were soon to be considered, and possible suspects included Castro from Cuba, the Russians, and even the Mafia, CIA, and FBI. It took until 1964 for the Warren Commission to determine that both Lee Harvey Oswald, Kennedy's murderer, and Jack Ruby, who killed Oswald, acted alone.[18]

On January 23, 1964, the Twenty-fourth Amendment to the Constitution was ratified, eliminating the poll tax.

AMENDMENT XXIV[19]

Section 1. The right of citizens of the United States to vote in any primary or other election for the President or Vice President, for electors for President or Vice President, or for Senators or Representatives in Congress, shall not be denied or abridged by the United States or any State by reason of failure to pay any poll tax or other tax.

Section 2. The Congress shall have the power to enforce this article appropriate legislation.

A week later, January 30, the U.S. launched Ranger 6—an unmanned space craft carrying a TV camera. It crash-landed on the moon, as planned.

The "baby boomers," as they were called, born just after World War II, were in their teens in 1964. On February 12, they found a singing group to admire love and go crazy over. They came from England and were called the "Beatles." When introduced on Ed Sullivan's television show, over seventy million fans tuned in.[20] That same year, 1964, Sidney Poiter became the first black actor in a leading role to win an "Oscar" for *Lilies of the Field*.

President Johnson said he planned to continue Kennedy's goals and policies. The first and most important challenge was the Civil Rights Bill that President Kennedy and his brother, the attorney general, together had proposed. Although the Civil Rights Bill of 1957, under Eisenhower, was a start, this new bill of 1964 was far reaching and very inclusive.

It was signed on July 2 and included many factors. It insured voting rights for all, including those who did not pass a literacy test. It outlawed discrimination in employment as well as in education, housing, and public accommodations including travel, lodging, food, and service.[21]

It withstood a three-month filibuster and became the most far-reaching step to make sure that "all men are created equal" became a reality and that all had the unalienable rights like life, liberty, and the pursuit of happiness. It was Kennedy's dream, fulfilled by President Johnson.

1965-1969 PRESIDENT JOHNSON'S OWN TERM AS PRESIDENT

Johnson was nominated in 1964, with Hubert Humphrey of Minnesota as the vice president. They won the election easily, defeating Barry Goldwater from Arizona. Johnson received 43,167,895 popular votes to Goldwater's 27,175,770—a difference of 15,772,125 votes. Johnson also got a lopsided electoral vote margin with 486 electoral votes to 52, a 90 percent advantage.

Previous presidents like Roosevelt, Truman, and Kennedy each had a title for their overall administrative efforts. *New Deal* was Roosevelt's, *Fair Deal* was Truman's, and *New Frontier* was Kennedy's. Johnson chose the theme *Great Society* and proposed sweeping legislation that was aimed at eradicating poverty as well as a host of other bold moves.

PRESIDENT JOHNSON PRODUCES
MANY LEGISLATIVE IMPROVEMENTS

Lyndon Johnson had separate task forces study and brought recommendations to Congress. Johnson used his long-practiced skills he had developed as a congressman, senator, majority leader, and vice president. He brought business and labor leaders together as well as Democrats and Republicans. The results were outstanding.

The Economic Opportunity Act of 1964 established the Office of Equal Opportunity, which would oversee many new programs. In education, his Elementary and Secondary Education Act strengthened both rural and urban schools, providing special education for disabled as well as students with learning disabilities. Other programs in education included Head Start preschool programs as well as the Higher Education Act that provided funding to help colleges and universities expand to meet the needs of ever-increasing enrollments.

In health care legislation, Medicare was provided for the first time to the elderly, and Medicaid provided health care assistance to low-income Americans. All of this was provided under the Social Security Act of 1965.[22]

During Eisenhower's administration, the cabinet post of secretary of war and secretary of navy was combined into the secretary of defense. A new cabinet post was created named Health, Education, and Welfare in 1953, the first new post since Teddy Roosevelt had created the secretary of labor and commerce in 1903. In 1965, President Johnson reorganized an existing government agency into the Department of Housing and Urban Development.

Other legislation included the Fair Labor Standards Act that raised the minimum wage. An Immigration Reform Act eliminated the long-standing quota system. In 1967, Johnson signed the Water Quality Act and the Clean Air Act, a first step in protecting the environment.[23]

One of his last important pieces of legislation was the Fair Housing Act of 1968. This Act strengthened the Civil Rights Act by not allowing landlords, sellers, or real estate agents to refuse to rent or sell property because of race, religion, or ethnicity.

In 1965, many important events took place. On March 6, the first contingent of combat troops was sent by President Johnson to fight the Vietcong guerrillas in Vietnam. March 21 through March 25 was the historic march of three thousand blacks, led by the Reverend Martin Luther King, Jr., from Selma to Montgomery, Alabama.

On June 3, astronaut Edward White became the first American to walk in space during the Gemini 4 space mission.

If Johnson had done nothing further, he would have gone down as one of the great presidents. Unfortunately, he could not leave well enough alone. His foreign policy with regards to Vietnam and the consequences of his decisions were a complete failure.

VIETNAM—JOHNSON'S WATERLOO

When Johnson took over the presidency in November 1963, Kennedy had increased the number of military advisors from Eisenhower's initial seven hundred to about sixteen thousand. Johnson was reluctant to do anything about Vietnam, including discussing it until after the 1964 election. But at the end of July and the beginning of August, an incident took place in the Gulf of Tonkin that would have far-reaching and, in many people's minds, a decidedly tragic effect.

Three North Vietnam patrol boats were said to have attacked the USS *Maddox*, an American destroyer. The commander of the Maddox was not certain that weather effects on radar and overeager sonar men may have accounted for the report.[24]

Nevertheless, this incident was reported as factual by the commander of the Pacific Forces admiral Sharp in Honolulu. When Secretary of Defense Robert McNamara asked Sharp if there was any possibility there was no attack, Sharp's response was, "Yes, I would say there is a slight possibility."[25]

Nothing of consequence was done until after the November 1964 presidential election. Then over the next five years, more and more troops were sent to Vietnam. In February 1965, Vietcong attack on American military bases resulted in air strikes against North Vietnam.

As a result of this questionable battle in the Gulf of Tonkin, Johnson began committing more and more troops. In November 1965, there were 165,000 American troops in Vietnam. The number would reach over 500,000. As the number of soldiers increased, so did the casualties. In 1964, there were 164 American deaths. In 1965, there were 1,104 deaths; and in 1966, it increased to 5,008. The year 1967 saw 9,300 young Americans sacrifice their lives.[26] When the fighting stopped in 1973, 57,000 Americans had died.

There was a growing antiwar feeling when casualties increased with no sign of a successful conclusion in sight. Protest rallies increased, and a massive peace march took place in the nation's capital in 1967. Some who had registered for the draft, as they were suppose to, burned their draft cards or moved to Canada.

At home, the bad news started in January 1967, when astronauts Gus Grissom, Ed White, and Roger Chaffee died in a fire inside their Apollo 1 spacecraft during a ground test at Cape Kennedy, Florida.

Antiwar protests increased both in size and numbers. In spite of the Civil Rights legislation, riots occurred in cities. The Watts area riot of Los Angeles took place in 1965 and in Detroit in 1967. One good thing was the appointment of Thurgood Marshall to the U.S. Supreme Court in October 1967. He had argued successfully in the landmark case of *Brown vs. the Board of Education*, Topeka, Kansas. Marshall was the first black to be appointed to this top position.

On June 12, the Supreme Court struck down state laws banning interracial marriage.[27]

On December 3, 1967, Dr. Christian Barnard performed the first heart transplant in history. The patient lived eighteen days. Today, this procedure is both successful and frequently accomplished in many parts of the United States of America and the world.

The year 1968 was going to be a year of more violence, deaths, and a presidential convention in Chicago that turned ugly. More American soldiers died in 1968 and 1969 than in any other two-year period. The American public began to believe they had been misled by their government, and it was reflected in the number and intensity of the demonstrations.[28]

On April 4, 1968, Martin Luther King, Jr., was assassinated in Memphis, Tennessee. This provoked riots and fires in Harlem, Chicago, Detroit, Kansas City, Baltimore, and Atlanta. Not even Washington escaped, and when looters began pillaging the stores in Chicago, Mayor Daley gave orders to shoot to kill.[29]

The election process for president begins with primaries in different states at different times. Some begin as early as February. Polling showed that Johnson had lost some of his support, but polls also showed his winning by a large margin in the early primary in New Hampshire against a quiet, respected, and largely unknown Wisconsin senator by the name of Eugene McCarthy, who only had one issue. Stop the war! When the ballots were counted, Johnson received 49 percent, but McCarthy got 42 percent. It was a message for Johnson to do something. He stopped the bombing of North Vietnam.[30]

On March 16, Robert Kennedy announced his candidacy for president. Johnson believed he could still win the nomination and the election in November, but more polls showed him losing support throughout the country. So on March 31, when speaking about Vietnam, he ended his speech with:

> Accordingly, I shall not seek, and I will not accept, the nomination of my party for another term as your president.

But let men everywhere know, however, that a strong, a confident, and a vigilant America stands ready tonight to seek an honorable peace—and stands ready tonight to defend an honored cause—whatever the price, whatever the burden, whatever the sacrifices that duty may require.[31]

During April and May, Robert Kennedy's approval ratings kept going up. By June, when the California primary was held, it was all but certain that he had the Democratic nomination for president. The celebration of the California victory was being held in a hotel, and just after his victory speech, Robert Kennedy was shot by Sirhan Sirhan. This left the presidential nomination between Hubert Humphrey and Eugene McCarthy.

The Democratic convention was held in Chicago, and it was a disaster. The streets were filled with antiwar rioters, and the Chicago Police were shown on television beating the rioters. Senator Hubert Humphrey was nominated for president on the Democratic ticket, and Edmund Muskie would run as his vice presidential candidate.

Just before the election in November, Apollo 7, the first manned mission of the Apollo series, was launched with astronauts Wally Schirra, Don Eisle, and R. Walter Cunningham.

THE GOOD, THE BAD, AND THE BEAUTIFUL

Lyndon Johnson's failure to achieve any results in the Vietnam War far overshadowed his accomplishments in his programs to help the poor, the elderly, the minorities, and those that needed help in many different ways dealing with education.

His wife, Lady Bird, will be remembered for her efforts in getting the Highway Beautification Act of 1965 passed. It provided for limiting billboard advertising along the interstate highways that Eisenhower had initiated. She insisted that the beauty of the country be seen in the very best light.[32]

The war in Vietnam was still going on, and something had to be done. Could a new president solve the biggest problems the country faced since World War II? Could a new president bring the country, which had not been this divided since the Civil War, together again? Again, it would be a matter of wait and see.

CHAPTER XXIX

IF AT FIRST YOU DON'T SUCCEED, TRY, TRY AGAIN

1913-1968 EARLY LIFE, SCHOOLING, AND EXPERIENCES OF RICHARD NIXON

The election of 1960 between Richard Nixon and John Kennedy was closer in the popular vote count, percentagewise, than any other presidential election, with Kennedy winning by 119,429 votes, giving him 50.009 percent of the total vote of 68,334,763.

After serving as vice president under Dwight Eisenhower for eight years, Nixon must have felt frustrated but at the same time, determined. This determination came from a background of hard work in his youth, studying hard enough to win a scholarship to a well-respected law school, drive to succeed as a member of the House of Representatives as well as a senator from California.

Richard Milhous Nixon was born January 9, 1913, in Yorba Linda, California. The second of five sons, he was raised a Quaker and attended Whittier College, a Quaker school, during the Great Depression. Winning a scholarship to Duke's law school in 1937, he returned to California after graduating and married Thelma "Pat" Ryan on June 21, 1940. He worked for a well-established law firm in California until Pearl Harbor was bombed by the Japanese on December 7, 1941.[1]

He had an opportunity to go to Washington, D.C., and work for the OPA—Office of Price Administration. As a Quaker, he could have honestly avoided military service, but when informed that lawyers could get a navy commission, he enlisted and was sent to a ninety-day wonder camp. Both the army and the navy set up camps to train both enlisted men in the ranks and professional people from civilian life. After three months, they were made officers. Commissioned, he was sent to Ottumwa, Iowa, until the end of 1942. Next he was sent to New Caledonia in the Southwest Pacific.

Assigned to the Naval Air Transport Command, he worked on the airstrip. His next assignment was the island of Bougainville, which had been invaded earlier. He was very popular with his men.[2] Upon being discharged in 1946, he was approached to run for a congressional seat, and he agreed.

When World War II ended, a new type of conflict came into being. Tense times, failed diplomacy, and the Soviet Union's desire to dominate countries in Europe created what became known as the *cold war.*

Germany was divided into four zones—French, British, American, and Soviet. The old capital, Berlin, was in the Soviet zone and Berlin also was divided up. The first real challenge of the cold war was the Berlin blockade by the Soviets in June 1948, which lasted until May 1949. America spent time, money, and equipment, flying in needed supplies by airlift until the Russians realized the blockade was futile. In 1950, the Russians sent their army tanks into Hungary to stop the revolt by university students. In 1961, they erected the Berlin wall. By 1963, the Soviet influence had been brought to bear by communist takeover in Poland, Latvia, Lithuania, Estonia, Czechoslovakia, Hungary, Rumania, Bulgaria, and of course East Germany.

Truman had done his part with the Berlin Airlift, and the Truman Doctrine that had saved Greece and Turkey. Kennedy did nothing about the Berlin wall, and Johnson was too busy with Vietnam to do anything about the Soviet domination of Eastern Europe.

Communists were not looked upon with any favor. Anyone running for office suspected of having or showing sympathy to Communist Russia was not wanted, especially if they held a political office. Nixon used the technique of hinting about the Democratic candidate running for the same seat as some how connected. With that strategy, Nixon won the 1946 midterm election by fifteen thousand votes. Thus, Nixon began his political career as a member of the House of Representatives in January 1947.

He supported the Taft-Hartley Act that put certain restrictions on unions. He was a member of the House of Representatives' Un-American Activities Committee that investigated communism. He initiated the investigation of Alger Hiss, a high-ranking official of the State Department. Hiss was charged and brought to trial. The jury could not reach a verdict, but a second trial found him guilty.

Nixon won a Senate seat in much the same manner as he had won his first election, by tying the Democratic candidate, Helen Douglas, to being soft on communism. That was 1950, and two years later he was nominated as Eisenhower's vice presidential candidate. Eisenhower won elections in 1952 and 1956 by wide margins.

When Nixon ran for governor of California, he was defeated by Edmund Brown, Sr. Nixon blamed the media and said, "You won't have Nixon to kick around anymore." He moved to New York with his wife and two daughters.[3]

It looked like Nixon was on his way to the White House in 1960, but the first television debate ever was seen by millions. Nixon showed himself to be stiff, tired, and in need of a shave. Kennedy seemed relaxed, youthful, and with a sense of humor. Kennedy won, and Nixon would have to try again in the future.

VIETNAM BECOMES A FACTOR FOR NIXON

Kennedy increased the number of military advisors in Vietnam to nearly sixteen thousand. When Johnson took over after Kennedy's assassination, he brought in combat troops and increased their numbers following the election in 1964. By 1968, people were growing very tired of the Vietnam War and growing tired of Johnson handling of it. Meanwhile, Nixon was working hard by campaigning for nationwide Republican office holders and seekers since 1962.

Nixon won the Republican presidential nomination on the second ballot over Nelson Rockefeller and the recently elected governor of California, Ronald Reagan, at the 1968 Republican National convention in Miami, Florida. Spiro Agnew, former governor of Maryland, was nominated as his vice president. There were some antiwar demonstrators but nothing like the Democratic Convention held in Chicago where Hubert Humphrey, Johnson's vice president was nominated.

With the assassination of Martin Luther King, Jr., and Robert Kennedy in 1968, Nixon campaigned on the theme of Law and Order and appealed to the silent minority he labeled the Forgotten American.[4]

The election was close in the popular vote. Nixon received 31,710,470 votes, and the Democratic candidate, Hubert Humphrey, received 31, 209,677 votes. What made the difference was that Governor George Wallace of Alabama ran as an independent and picked up 9,893,952 votes. The electoral vote was not as close. Nixon received 301 votes, Humphrey 191, and George Wallace 46—all from the disgruntled Southern states. Nixon had finally made it.

1969-1974 RICHARD MILHOUS NIXON THIRTY-SEVENTH PRESIDENT

President Nixon's first year in office was filled with events of great importance, as well as others that would make the headlines of newspapers throughout the country. Nixon supported the development of the Environmental Protection Agency, a much-needed control to maintain environmental quality of the air, the water, the forests, and the wetlands of America. On June 9, the U.S. Senate confirmed Warren Burger to succeed Earl Warren as the chief justice of the U.S. Supreme Court. Nixon had the opportunity to nominate a total of four justices to the Supreme Court, most with conservative leanings.

He was faced with growing inflation and met it by imposing wage and price controls. Inflation continued until 1972.

On July 18, 1969, Senator Edward Kennedy, the last son of the Kennedy clan, in a car accident, lurched off a bridge on Chappaquiddick Island, Massachusetts, killing Mary Jo Kopenchne. He saved himself, walked home, changed clothes, and then reported the accident. After pleading guilty to leaving the scene of an accident, he was given a two-month suspended sentence.

ONE GIANT LEAP

In October 1957, the Soviet Union launched the first satellite ever to circumnavigate the earth. The United States was stunned. When John F. Kennedy became president, he promised that America would put a man on the moon safely and bring him home before the decade ended.

There were many different facets of America's commitment to explore space. The Mercury program put the first American in space when Alan Shepard went up 115 miles on May 5, 1961. Other programs followed including the Gemini and then the Apollo program with its ten successful missions.

On July 16, 1969, the *Apollo 11* was launched from the Kennedy Space Center, carrying Neil Armstrong, Edwin "Buzz" Aldrin, and Michael Collins. The *world* was watching on television, and at the launch site were thousands, including Charles Lindberg. Forty-two years earlier he made his historic airplane flight to Paris. Now the sixty-seven-year-old hero of the twenties was witnessing something no one could have dreamed possible in 1927.

Apollo 11's mission was to orbit the moon and deploy a landing craft, called Eagle, to the moon's surface. With Michael Collins piloting the command module, *Apollo* reached the moon and began its orbit. Neil Armstrong and Buzz Aldrin separated from the Apollo command module and landed on the surface of the Earth's moon.

The date on Earth was July 20, 1969. The astronauts' first message from their module on reaching the surface was, *"Houston, Tranquility Base here. The Eagle has landed."*

When Neil Armstrong stepped out of the Eagle, he climbed down a ladder toward the surface, *as the world watched*. The *world* heard him say, as he stepped on the moon's surface:

"That's one small step for man, one giant leap for mankind."[5]

Buzz Aldrin followed Armstrong down the ladder and the two bounded around due to the fact there is much less gravity on the moon. After collecting some samples of rocks, they climbed back into the Eagle. Could they blast off from the moon and make a rendezvous with the mother ship that Michael Collins was piloting? The world held their breath—they were 250,000 miles from Mother Earth.

They blasted off, made the rendezvous, and headed back to earth. On July 24, 1969, *Apollo 11* landed safely in the Pacific Ocean after completing the first lunar landing. President Kennedy's promise had become a reality. The U.S. was *the* leader in space exploration.

One other piece of good news happened in 1969. On November 10, the children's educational program, *Sesame Street*, made its debut on PBS (Public Broadcasting System). Many a child would learn their letters and their first words from this highly acclaimed program.

In 1970, events both bad and good happened. On May 4, the Ohio National Guard fired on a crowd of antiwar demonstrators at Kent State University, killing four students and wounding nine. On June 22, President Nixon signed a measure lowering the voting age from twenty-one to eighteen. It would become the Twenty-sixth Amendment when ratified on July 1, 1971.

AMENDMENT XXVI[6]

Section 1. The right of citizens of the United States, who are eighteen years of age or older, to vote shall not be denied or abridged by the United States or any State on account of age.

Section 2. The Congress shall have the power to enforce this article by appropriate legislation.

June 25, 1970 saw the American Medical Association vote to allow doctors to perform abortions for social and economic as well as medical reasons. And the second longest running prime time program (*60 Minutes* is the longest) began on Monday night, September 21, 1970 when the NFL *Monday Night Football* debuted on ABC. The announcers were Frank Gifford, former New York Giant star running back; Don Meredith, former Dallas Cowboys quarterback, and Howard Cossell. Cossell, not a football player, brought the layman's viewpoint to the game. Cleveland Browns defeated the New York Jets by a score of 31-21.

In 1971, *Apollo 14* successfully landed on the moon and explored for thirty-three hours in early February before heading back to earth safely. The previous attempt by *Apollo 13* almost ended in disaster, but the spaceship returned to earth safely after a major mishap while on the way to moon was temporarily fixed. On July 31, Apollo 15 astronauts took a six-and-a-half-hour ride on the moon in a specially designed vehicle.

Space exploration was becoming a common thing. Earth satellites were launched in 1971 to detect and map the world's resources. Also, space probes began to get a close-up look at Mars, Jupiter, and Mercury. Meanwhile, the war in Vietnam continued as did demonstrations of peace. Following the impressive but peaceful demonstration on October 15, 1969, called Moratorium Day, President Nixon gave an address on November 3. He laid out his hope for a peaceful solution but explained that the Vietcong (North Vietnam) were unwilling to negotiate. The war would drag on until 1973.

HISTORIC VISIT TO CHINA

When World War II ended in 1945, there was still a civil war in China between the Nationalists, commanded by General Chiang Kai-shek, and the Communists, commanded by Mao Tse-tung. This war raged off and on until April 1949 when the Nationalists were forced off the mainland and evacuated to Formosa, which was renamed Taiwan.

Since that time, the United States had very little to do with Communist China and supported the Taiwan government. In 1971, plans were made to open up talks with Communist China, and Nixon surprised everyone by opening trade talks. He visited China as well as the Soviet Union, hoping to ease tensions between the two superpowers.

These visits and his attempt to resolve the Vietnam War made the election of 1972 a landslide. Nixon received 47,108,459 votes to Senator George McGovern's 29,084,726 votes. This difference of 18,023,733 votes was the largest ever. The winning percentage was just under 62 percent, slightly less than Franklin Roosevelt's winning percentage in 1936. The Electoral College vote was 520 for Nixon, while McGovern got only 17. That was the good news. The next year, 1973, was one of the sorriest years, if not the saddest year in American history.

ONE RESIGNATION

Before Spiro Agnew was elected vice president, he had been governor of Maryland. He was accused of taking kickbacks in exchange for contracts as governor as well as vice president. He resigned as vice president and was convicted of income tax evasion. Placed on probation, he paid a fine of $10,000.[7]

President Nixon's troubles started on the night of June 17, 1972—a little over four-and-a-half months before the presidential election—when five men were caught in a burglary attempt in the office of the Democratic National Committee. The building was named Watergate.

By Nixon's own admission, he failed to take the matter seriously enough and do something about it. Had the break-in been dealt with at once, Nixon thinks his administration would have survived. Other investigative circumstances only added to the break-in probe.[8]

As newspaper and television reporters are inclined to do, under the protection of the First Amendment, they speculated on other connections dealing with the break-in without any proof to back up their speculations.

Those supposed speculations, or myths as Nixon called them, are dealt with in his own book, *In the Arena*. The myth that he ordered the break-in was never proved. He was accused of ordering payments to the Watergate defenders. While he discussed the options, he ruled out ever making a payment of any kind.

While others accused him of obstructing the investigation, he really invited cooperation from his staff. Nixon was accused of erasing tapes of conversations, which it turned out not to be true. Finally, accused of massive illegal wiretaps of many political opponents, such as friends of Mary Jo Kopechne who died from Kennedy's accident, and placing listening devices in senators' offices, none of which was ever proved. No evidence was presented to substantiate them. None of the charges were ever retracted by those who had made them.[9]

Other events were taking place during the time of the long-drawn-out Watergate investigation. In the summer of 1972, the Olympics were held in Munich, Germany. The good news was Mark Spitz, an American swimmer, earned a record *seven* Olympic gold medals, the last medal as part of the 400-meter relay team. At the same Olympics, eleven members of the Israel Olympic team were gunned down by Arab terrorists.

On January 22, 1973, the U.S. Supreme Court issued its landmark *Roe vs. Wade* decision on abortion. This decision would result in bitter feeling and violence that continues to this day.

Henry Kissinger had been appointed secretary of state, having served in the capacity of national security advisor. He worked diligently to seek an end to the Vietnam War. On January 23, 1973, President Nixon announced that an accord had been reached to end the war. For his service, Henry Kissinger received the Nobel Peace Prize along with the North Vietnam negotiator, Le Duc Tho. On March 29, 1973 the last U.S. combat troops left Vietnam—the nightmare was over.

On June 9, 1973, the horse Secretariat won the Belmont Stakes by the unbelievable margin of thirty-one-and-a-half lengths, becoming the first Triple Crown winner in twenty-five years. Earlier he had won the Kentucky Derby and the Preakness.

On October 6, Syria and Egypt attacked Israel. At first Israel lost ground but eventually defeated them in what became known as the Yom Kippur War. Because the United States supported Israel, the OPEC countries lowered their production of crude oil, creating long lines at the U.S. gas pumps. Gas stations were encouraged to limit customers to ten gallons. The oil embargo ended in March 1974.[10]

On October 17, Maynard Jackson was elected mayor of Atlanta, Georgia, the first black to lead a major city. On November 16, President Nixon signed the Alaskan pipeline bill, hailing it as the first step toward making the United States energy independent by 1980.

The year 1973 saw the introduction of laser scanning better known as bar coding. This method of labeling retail products, as well as other items proved to be a money and time saver. A bar code, technically called the Universal Product Code (UPC), was printed on number of different products, which contained eleven digits and lines and bars.

Store checkouts were speeded up when the bar was passed over a small window, or "beamed" by a hand-held *bar code reader*. The optical scanner "read" the sequence. This immediately told the cash register the cost at the same time showing the item and price on a screen as well as recording the fact for inventory in the store's computer. It proved to be a boon to retailers. Similar codes were developed for use in factories, warehouses, hospitals, and libraries.[11] The workplace was being modernized, and productivity was the result.

When Spiro Agnew resigned, the next in line for the position of vice president was the speaker of the House. But the Twenty-fifth Amendment passed in 1967 set forth the procedure for installing a new vice president.

XXV AMENDMENT[12]

Section 1. In the case of the removal of the President from office or of his death or resignation, the Vice President shall become President.

Section 2. Whenever there is a vacancy in the office of the Vice President, the President shall nominate a Vice President who shall take office upon confirmation by a majority vote of both Houses of Congress.

The remainder of the Twenty-fifth Amendment dealt with the steps to be taken in the event the president could no longer discharge the duties of the office.

Gerald Ford, a member of the House of Representatives, was the Republican minority leader since the Democrats controlled the Congress. He was sworn in as vice president on December 6, 1973.

The hearings on the Watergate affair dragged on into 1974. By the summer, the Judiciary Committee had drafted three articles of impeachment. The three articles were:

1. Obstruction of justice, making false or misleading statements to investigators, condoning counseling perjury.
2. Abuse of power, misusing the FBI, the IRS and the Secret Service, and maintaining an unlawful secret investigative unit (the Plumbers).
3. Failure to comply with Congressional subpoenas.[13]

After consulting with members of his staff as well as leaders of the Republican Party, Richard Nixon decided to resign. He spoke to the nation from the Oval Office on the evening of August 8, 1974. He began:

This is the thirty-seventh time I have spoken to you from this office. I have always tried to do what is best for the nation . . . In the past few days, however, it has become evident to me that I no longer have a strong enough political base in Congress to justify continuing that effort. I now believe that the Congressional purpose has been served, and there is no longer a need for the process to be prolonged . . . whatever the personal agony it would have involved, and my family unanimously urged me to do so. But the interest of the nation must always come before any personal consideration . . . because of the Watergate matter, I might not have the support of Congress that I would consider necessary to make the very difficult decisions and carry out the duties of this office in the way the interests of the nation require . . . Therefore, I shall resign the presidency effective at noon tomorrow.[14]

Gerald Ford was sworn in the next day, August 9, 1974. The book was closed on the political career of Richard Milhous Nixon.

WHAT GOES AROUND COMES AROUND

It is of some interest to note that a future president was asked his opinion regarding the possibility of impeaching President Nixon.

The following article by John Whitehead appeared in the *International Herald Tribune* on Friday, September 18, 1998.[15] Mr. Whitehead is speaking:

In February 1974, there was serious talk about impeaching President Nixon. While the people supported him a few months earlier, the polls now showed a significant number believed he should be impeached.

I asked Mr. Clinton what he thought. "I think that there's probable cause to believe that he's committed gross improprieties in office, if not criminal acts," Clinton said.

"The question of impeachment and removal are fundamentally political questions . . . If I were in Congress now I would think that the evidence for impeachment was very strong."

I then asked him what he thought the definition of impeachment should be. Clinton replied, "I think that the definition should include any criminal act plus willful failure of the president to fulfill his duty to uphold and execute the laws of the United States.

"(Another) factor that I think constitutes an impeachable offense would be the willful, reckless behavior in office; just totally incompetent conduct of the office and the disregard of the necessities that the office demands. Law and order for example."

When asked why he thought people were so hesitant about making a commitment toward impeachment, Mr. Clinton said, "I believe one major factor is that they fear the uncertainty that would ensue if the president is removed. It's the old problem of 'the devil you know is better than the one you don't.

"Congress has to serve as a limiting institution because Congress itself is needed to act as a strong and powerful brake on the abuse of power by the executive and administration.

"And it's very important to me that I attempt to aid the Congress in assuming its proper role in the constitutional frame work."

Like President Grant, the good things that had been accomplished overshadowed the scandals that prevailed in his administration.

Nixon had opened the door to China and had ended the Vietnam War that had claimed 57,000 American lives and wounded 150,000. While Nixon could not take credit for it, the successful landing on the moon and the safe return to Earth happened on his watch.

AMERICA IS TESTED ONE AGAIN

Eight presidents had died in office. Four had been assassinated and four had died from other causes. Still, the government continued in a smooth transition in each case. Another test would be to see if the United States of America could continue functioning after losing a president and vice president through resignations. Nothing like that had ever happened before.

What was needed was a president with honest down-to-earth values that could be used to reassure the American people that it could survive the most unpopular war in its history, as well as survive the first ever resignation of its president.

CHAPTER XXX

1974-1977 I HAVE NOT SOUGHT THIS ENORMOUS RESPONSIBILITY, BUT I WILL NOT SHIRK IT

1913-1945 THE MAKING OF A MAN

Leslie Lynch King was born on July 14, 1913 in Omaha, Nebraska, the same year as Richard Nixon. His parents were Dorothy Gardner King and Leslie King. Two years later, they were divorced, and Dorothy moved back to Grand Rapids, Michigan, with her two-year-old son to live with her parents.

Dorothy was in her early twenties and quite attractive. She met a young bachelor at a church social. Soon after, they were married. Formal adoption papers were taken out for the young Leslie, and Mr. and Mrs. Gerald Ford renamed their son Gerald R. Ford, Jr.[1]

Junie, his nickname (short for Junior), grew up in Grand Rapids and had three half-brothers much younger than he was. Junie played football: center on offense and roving linebacker on defense at South High School, which won the state championship in 1930.[2]

With the Depression making it tough for his family, Ford helped out working at the paint factory his father owned. He also worked part-time waiting on tables and washing dishes. One day, a man came into the restaurant and told Gerald Ford that he was his father. They went out to lunch, and then Ford went home and told his mother and stepfather. They had a long talk, and Jerry, as he was now called, learned a lot and grew up that night.[3]

With help from his high school coach, Clifford Gettings, and some Grand Rapids University of Michigan alumni, Jerry received a football scholarship. In 1931, the Depression meant his family did not have the money to help him; so the

Michigan football coach, Harry Kipke, found him a job at the university hospital in Ann Arbor, in the cafeteria.

Jerry Ford sat on the bench his first two years, while the first string center, Chuck Bernard—an all-American—helped Michigan win two Big Ten championships. In his senior year, Ford was the starting center, but the team lost most of previous players to graduation, and Michigan lost seven of the eight games.

The only game it did win was against Georgia Tech. In the 1934 game, Georgia Tech said it would not play if the Negro on Michigan University's team played. This made Jerry Ford so mad, he came close to taking himself out of the game. Growing up in Grand Rapids, he was a good friend with the son of a Negro chauffeur, and they enjoyed each other's company. Jerry did play in the game against Georgia Tech; and when one of the Georgia Tech players made a disparaging remark about Michigan's "nigger," Ford and another Michigan player hit him during a later play, and the player had to be carried off the field on a stretcher.[4]

Football taught Ford the value of both patience—waiting for his turn—and tolerance. These were lessons that Ford would use the rest of his life.

Upon graduation from Michigan in 1935, he was given the job of assistant coach at Yale University. He was able to combine his coaching job with attending law school part-time. It took him six years, but he graduated in the top third of his class. This was no small feat when he had never been a scholarly student in either high school or college.

Even more interesting is a partial list of some of his fellow law school students and friends. Potter Stewart and Byron White would both become United States Supreme Court justices. Peter Dominick would become Colorado's senator, Peter Frelinghuysen of New Jersey would become a member of the House of Representatives, J. Richardson Dilworth would become governor of Pennsylvania, Judge Morris Laker would become mayor of Philadelphia, R. Sargent Shriver would be President Kennedy's brother-in-law as well as director of the Office of Economic Opportunity (Peace Corps), and Cyrus R. Vance would be deputy secretary of defense and later secretary of state.

These men helped Ford broaden his horizons, and he never forgot what they taught him about global and national issues.[5]

Upon graduation from Yale Law School in June 1941, Ford returned to Grand Rapids to start a law practice with a good friend from his Michigan University days, Philip Buchen. It was a tough grind getting legal business; and after Pearl Harbor, Ford joined the navy on April 20, 1942. He was twenty-eight years old but still very fit and was assigned to physical training under former boxing champion Gene Tunney. Sent to the University of North Carolina to get aviation cadets in shape, he pestered his superiors in the navy for a combat assignment for a year and, in 1943, was assigned to gunnery training.

Following that, he was assigned to the light aircraft carrier—often called Jeep carriers—the USS *Monterey*. His ship participated in supporting invasions of the Gilbert Islands, Truk, Saipan Palau, the Philippines, Wake Island, and Okinawa. He experienced not only battle with the Japanese but also survived the typhoon of December 18, 1944. He earned ten battle stars, attained the rank of lieutenant commander and the highest marks obtainable for his service record.[6]

Following his discharge in January 1946, Ford joined the same law firm that his friend Philip Buchen had joined when Ford joined the navy. Philip had contracted polio as a youth and could not serve in the military. Shortly after starting work in Grand Rapids, Ford met Elizabeth (Betty) Bloomer Warren. She was young and attractive and in the middle of a divorce. She wouldn't date Jerry until the divorce was final, and then they hit it off. He proposed in February 1948, but would not get married until later as something had come up. That something turned out to be his decision to run for a seat in the House of Representatives. Jerry Ford campaigned like he did everything else—100 percent effort. They were married on October 15, 1948, and in November, Jerry won his first election. They moved to Washington, and Jerry Ford would be Michigan's representative from the Grand Rapids District for twelve consecutive terms—twenty-four years.[7]

A DEDICATED AND HONEST POLITICIAN

Congressman Gerald Ford worked at his job like he did everything else in his life—with dedication and hard work. He learned the art of political deal making and won the respect of his colleagues as an honest man. By 1953, he was a member of the Subcommittee on Defense as part of the powerful House Appropriations Committee. His naval military experience gave him real status, and he became an expert on military affairs.

Ten years later, he was chosen House Minority Leader. Rather than just criticize the Democratic programs, he sought alternatives. In November 1963, following President Kennedy's assassination, Lyndon Johnson appointed Ford as one of seven members of the Warren Commission to investigate the possibility of a conspiracy.

When he and Illinois Senator Everett Dirksen appeared on national television in a series of press conferences, he began to be noticed nationwide. The reporters called their press conference the Ev and Jerry Show.

At first, Ford supported President Johnson on the Vietnam War. But by 1967, he began to seriously question the strategy that was being employed and gave a speech entitled "Why Are We Pulling Our Punches in Vietnam?"[8]

The year 1968 saw the election of Richard Nixon as president and Spiro Agnew as vice president. Because the Democrats still had a majority in Congress, Ford remained Minority Leader in the House. Nixon and his new secretary of state Henry Kissinger worked at ending the Vietnam War. Four years later, Nixon won a landslide victory, but the Democrats still controlled both the Senate and the House of Representatives. Ford was now fifty-nine years old and, having been reelected twelve times, was giving serious consideration to retiring after his next term. Little did he realize the events that happened in 1973 would change his life.[9]

A STEP AWAY FROM THE WHITE HOUSE

Early in 1973, investigators turned up evidence that Spiro Agnew had been accepting bribes when he was Baltimore County executive and as governor of Maryland as well as vice president. As a result of the investigation, he was forced to resign on October 10, 1973.

Gerald Ford was nominated by Nixon to replace Agnew. This required approval of both Houses of Congress, according to the Twenty-fifth Amendment that had been ratified February 10, 1967. The Senate approved the nomination by a vote of 92 to 3 on November 27. The House of Representatives approved it by a vote of 387 to 35. Gerald R. Ford became the country's fortieth vice president on December 6, 1973.[10]

One of Vice President Ford's main tasks was to go on a nationwide tour to express his faith in President Nixon. By the middle of 1974, Ford had visited forty states and made hundreds of public appearances. The House Judiciary Committee voted for three articles of impeachment, and this forced Nixon to make a decision: be impeached followed by a trial by the United States Senate—which would require a two-thirds vote to convict—or resign from the presidency and save the country a lot of grief. Nixon consulted with his friends and then decided to resign. He said to Gerald Ford in their talk of over an hour, "I know you'll do well."[11]

1974-1976 GERALD RUDOLPH FORD THIRTY-EIGHTH PRESIDENT

Gerald Ford was sworn in by Chief Justice Warren Burger in the East Room of the White House at 12:05 p.m., August 9, 1974. He then gave a most difficult speech to the nation.

> I am acutely aware you have not elected me as your president by your ballots. I have not sought this enormous responsibility, but I will not shirk it.
>
> I believe that truth is the glue that holds government together, not only our government but civilization itself. That bond, though stained, is unbroken at home and abroad. In all my public and private acts as your President, I expect to follow my instincts of openness and candor with full confidence that honesty is always the best policy in the end. My fellow Americans,

our long nightmare is over. Our Constitution works; our great Republic is a government of law and not of men.

May our former president, who brought peace to millions, find it for himself.

I now solemnly reaffirm my promise I made to you last December 6: to uphold the Constitution, to do what is right as God gives me to see the right, and to do the very best I can for America . . . I will not let you down.[12]

On that same day, President Ford met with reporters and senior members of the White House staff. Over the next several days, he met with the Cabinet and asked them all to stay for continuity and stability. He dispatched personal messages to world leaders assuring them that American foreign policy would continue. Next he spoke before a joint session of Congress, asking for their cooperation and pledged that his administration would be free of illegal wiretapping and break-ins.

His fast pace surprised both Democrats and Republicans who thought he would take his time in leading the country. He met governors, mayors, county officials, members of the Black Caucus, and representatives from many women's groups.

He addressed the Veterans of Foreign Wars in Chicago, and thousands turned out in the streets to welcome him. On August 20, 1974, he announced his choice for vice president, Nelson Rockefeller of New York.

On August 28, he held his first news conference. Anticipating that their questions would be about the economy, the conflict in Cyprus, and the issue of possible amnesty for draft dodgers, he spent valuable time reviewing those items with members of his staff. Instead, many of the questions dealt with Watergate and Nixon's legal problems.

When asked if he was ruling out a pardon for Richard Nixon, he said no, as that was an option stated in Article II, Section 2 of the United States Constitution. Near the end of the news conference, he was asked if he planned to write a code of ethics for the executive branch to prevent future Watergates.

Ford's response was, "The code of ethics that will be followed will be the example that I set."[13]

PROBLEMS FOR A NEW PRESIDENT

Inflation that had started while Nixon was president was one of Ford's first problems to tackle. With Democratic-controlled Congress, he established the Council of Wage and Price Stability whose purpose was to expose any inflationary wage and price increases. Next, he proposed legislation to create public service jobs for those unemployed and to lower federal income taxes. Congress passed both of these.

A second major domestic problem was unemployment which reached 9 percent, the highest since before World War II. When inflation slowed down, and the economy started to pick up, unemployment dropped to 8 percent.[14]

Exactly one month after Ford was sworn in, he gave a speech that would pardon Richard Nixon. This pardon was welcomed by many but was also considered by some to be a deal that was made between Nixon and Ford. Parts of the speech are worth noting.

> Ladies and Gentlemen: I have come to a decision which I felt I should tell you and all of my fellow American citizens, as soon as I was certain in my own mind and in my own conscience that it is the right thing to do.

> As we are a nation under God, so I am sworn to uphold our laws with the help of God. And I have sought such guidance and searched my own conscience with special diligence to determine the right thing for me to do with respect to my predecessor in this place, Richard Nixon and his loyal wife and family.

> After years of bitter controversy and divisive national debate, I have been advised, and I am compelled to conclude that many months and perhaps years will have to pass before Richard Nixon could obtain a fair trial in any jurisdiction of the United States under governing decisions of the Supreme Court.

> . . .

> My conscience tells me clearly and certainly that I can not prolong the bad dreams that continue to reopen a chapter that is closed. My conscience tells me that only I, as President, have the constitutional powers to firmly shut and seal this book. My conscience tells me that it is my duty, not merely to proclaim domestic tranquility, but to use every means that I have to insure it.

> I do believe that the buck stops here, that I cannot rely upon public opinion polls to tell me what is right.

> I do believe that right makes might and that if I am wrong, ten angles swearing I was right would make no difference.

> I do believe with all my heart and mind and spirit, that I, not as President but as a humble servant of God will receive justice without mercy if I fail to show mercy.

Finally, I feel that Richard Nixon and his loved ones have suffered enough and will continue to suffer, no matter what I do, no matter what we as a great and good nation, can do together to make his goal of peace come true.

Now, therefore, I, Gerald R. Ford, President of the United States . . . . So grant a full, free and absolute pardon unto Richard Nixon for all offenses against the United States which he, Richard Nixon, has committed or may have committed or taken part in during the period from January 20, 1969 through August 9, 1974."[15]

This speech of explaining the pardon of Richard Nixon was one of Ford's greatest moments. America had always been a forgiving nation. Ulysses Grant had allowed the defeated Confederates to keep their weapons and their horses. Lincoln had said, "With malice towards none, with charity for all . . . let us strive . . . bind up the nation's wounds . . ." Wilson's attempt to preserve peace with charitable gestures failed, but Truman, Eisenhower, MacArthur, and Marshall did their part to make the world a better place for all. Unfortunately, this pardon would cost Ford his chance for reelection in 1976.

Also in 1974, a ruling in a court case of *Milleken vs. Bradley*, the U. S. Supreme Court stated that the white suburb of Detroit cannot be forced to integrate with predominantly minority city districts.

On July 5, 1975, Arthur Ashe defeated Jimmy Connors to become the first black tennis player to win the Wimbledon men's singles championship, the most prestigious tennis tournament of the four grand tournaments—the Australian Open, the French Open, the U.S. Open, and Wimbledon.

The remainder of Ford's term had many different problems. Two assassination attempts occurred in September 1975 while Ford was in California. One attempt was on September 5 and the other on September 22. Both attempts were by women, and both were sentenced to life imprisonment which was mandated by the law passed in 1965, following Kennedy's assassination.

In May 1975, Cambodian Communist troops seized the *Mayagüez*, a U.S. merchant ship in the Gulf of Thailand. The president quickly sent the marines into the area, and they recaptured the ship and rescued the crew.

Also in 1975, Ford and Kissinger helped Egypt and Israel settle a territorial dispute that would eventually lead to the Camp David Agreement in 1978, when Jimmy Carter was president. 1975 also saw the official end of the Vietnam War. On September 4, Jefferson County, Kentucky, became the first major metropolitan area to carry out court-ordered busing of children to achieve school desegregation.[16]

July 4, 1976 marked the two hundredth anniversary of the beginning of the United States of America. One hundred years earlier, the city of Philadelphia held the International Centennial Exposition where a young man had demonstrated his transmission of sound over an instrument he called a telephone. That same summer, colorful George Custer had made his "last stand."

John Adams had said that the Fourth of July should be celebrated with much pomp and ceremony. America did just that for five glorious days. Tall ships from thirty countries paraded in New York's harbor to say, "Happy Birthday, America."

Celebrations took place throughout the country with fireworks that John Adams would have thought just the thing. Gerald Ford took it all in with hundreds of thousands of fellow Americans, and it was one of his happiest moments.

BETTY FORD SETS A WONDERFUL EXAMPLE

Breast cancer with women had been around for unknown years, but it was not a topic for conversation. Betty Ford had surgery a month after her husband of twenty-seven years became president. Millions of Americans admired her courage to resume her busy schedule after she recovered. She worked at getting equal rights for women in the workplace. She raised four children that she could be proud of. After Jerry's defeat at the polls in 1976, Betty became addicted to drugs and alcohol. Her family's concern led her to place herself in the Long Beach Naval Hospital Alcohol and Drug Rehabilitation Center. Her public admission of her problem brought enormous support throughout the country. In 1982, the Betty Ford Center for drug and alcohol dependency was opened in Rancho Mirage, California.[17]

Both Jerry and Betty Ford had served their country proudly and well. They had helped to bring the United States together again.

PART J

CARTER HAD PROBLEMS AND REAGAN HAD SUCCESSES

Jimmy Carter was elected over Gerald Ford when the country had lost faith in the powers of Washington, D.C. The Vietnam War, followed by the Watergate scandal, helped an outsider, who portrayed a soft and calm manner, become the thirty-ninth president.

His success as governor of Georgia helped him in the beginning of his presidential administration. The Trans-Alaska oil pipeline was completed, and inflation rates came down. After his second year started, nothing went well. Russia invaded Afghanistan, inflation began a climb that was out of sight, and Iranians stormed the American Embassy, capturing all the Americans while the world watched as they were led out of the embassy blindfolded.

This brought his one term to a close when a popular former movie actor and governor of California soundly defeated him.

When America experienced its Great Depression of 1929, it looked for a leader. When inflation of the 1970s was higher than ever before, and the Soviet Union was controlling many countries, once again the American people looked for a leader to perform miracles both at home and abroad.

Taking office at the age of sixty-nine, Ronald Reagan moved decisively to create stability at home. Cutting taxes, firing air traffic controllers who illegally went on strike, stopping Communist involvement in the Western Hemisphere went a long way in winning over the American people. Speaking to the American people with conviction and purpose brought about his reelection in a record-breaking manner.

As Truman had done with his doctrine and the Marshall Plan, ordering the Berlin airlift, and stopping Communist expansion in Korea, Reagan worked to bring about a peaceful solution to the cold war. Turned down by Soviet leaders time after time, Reagan did not give up.

When Mikhail Gorbachev became leader of Russia, Reagan worked at getting open the lines of communication between them to solve the world tension. It took patience and time, and when he spoke at the Brandenburg Gate in Berlin, it was the beginning of the end of Soviet communism.

The Berlin wall came down, the Soviet Union became nonexistent, and the cold war came to an end. Reagan lived to the age of ninety-three, died peacefully, was honored by world leaders, and mourned by his countrymen. He came from humble beginnings, worked hard in all he did, and left the world a much richer place.

CHAPTER XXXI

THE HARD-LUCK PRESIDENCY OF JIMMY CARTER

1924-1976 PEANUT FARMER, NAVAL SERVICE, STATE SENATOR, GOVERNOR

James Earl Carter, Jr. would be known all his life as Jimmy. Born October 1, 1924 in Plains, Georgia, he had two sisters, Gloria and Ruth, and one brother, William, usually called Billy.

When Jimmy was four, the family moved to a peanut farm; and at a young age, he began to learn the peanut farm business. He attended public schools, favoring history, literature, and music.

He graduated from high school in 1941, and after attending Georgia Southwestern College, he next went to the Georgia Institute of Technology to improve his knowledge of mathematics. He was interested in attending the Naval Academy at Annapolis but needed the extra math instruction as he knew it would be a major part of the entrance exam. He entered the academy in 1943 and graduated three years later, ranking fifty-ninth in a class of 820.

He and Rosalyn Smith were married July 6, 1946, when she was only eighteen years of age. They would eventually have four children, the last—Amy Lynn—was born in 1967.

After graduating from Annapolis, Jimmy was assigned as an electronics instructor aboard two different battleships. The war was over, but the military was constantly upgrading new equipment. After his tour in battleships, he volunteered for submarine duty. He was with the group that helped develop the world's first nuclear submarine under Captain, later Admiral, Hyman Rickover. He stayed with this project until 1953.

Jimmy's father died, and he felt he should resign to help out the family in Plains, Georgia. He took over the farm, learning the business and improving production after studying modern farm techniques. The family business thrived under his management.

Carter disapproved of the segregation laws that existed in the 1950s. He refused to join a White Citizens' Council that was designed to preserve segregation. In 1962, he ran for a seat in the Georgia Senate. When he witnessed vote fraud in the primary and lost, he challenged the results and was declared the winner just before the general election. He won the seat and was reelected again in 1964.

In 1966, he ran for governor, but lost in the primary. For the next four years, he made 1,800 speeches all over the state. During the campaign, he opposed busing of students to achieve racial balance. This appealed to the conservative voters, and he was accused of appealing to the segregationists. He won the primary and easily defeated the Republican candidate in the general election.

ACCOMPLISHMENTS AS GOVERNOR

He spoke up for the poor, the weak, and the blacks. He reformed the many agencies that were doing duplicate work and combined three hundred state agencies and boards into just thirty agencies. He improved education by providing equal state aid for all school districts, regardless of wealth or lack of it. The selection procedure for judges was changed from politics to merit. He opened the door for blacks to be represented in major state agencies and boards. And he established a program to honor notable Georgians. Martin Luther King, Jr. was the first black nominated, and his picture was hung in the Georgia Capital in 1974.[1]

1974-1977 PLANNING A RUN FOR THE PRESIDENCY

During his term as governor, he decided that two important facts presented themselves that could serve him well. One, there were no other leading Democrats that might oppose him for the nomination of the presidency. Two, Gerald Ford had pardoned Richard Nixon, and this did not sit well with a lot of people.

In December 1974, he announced his candidacy for the presidency. He worked tirelessly along with his devoted wife, Rosalynn. He won the Iowa caucus—the first of many primaries. He next won in New Hampshire and the all-important state of Florida whose population made it the fourth largest in the nation.

His campaign theme of being from outside of the Washington inner circle appealed to those who had become disenchanted with the Nixon scandal and Ford's pardon. He professed to restore moral leadership to the presidency. He won the nomination with ease in New York City and then requested Senator Mondale of Minnesota to be his running mate.

Gerald Ford was nominated after a bitter fight with Ronald Reagan. Ford was nominated on the first ballot by a narrow margin and selected Robert Dole of Kansas as his running mate.[2]

In the campaign, Carter charged that Ford had done little to lower the 6 percent unemployment and promised to create jobs with federal spending. Ford countered that Carter's plan would bring a rise in inflation. Little did Ford realize how prophetic his claim would be. Carter pledged to consider pardons for the Vietnam War draft dodgers, and that appealed to a large group who had opposed the war.

The election was very close. Carter received 40,977,147 popular votes to Ford's 39,422,671—a percentage win of just fewer than 51 percent. The Electoral College votes for Carter were 297 to 240 for Ford. The swing came from the southern states that had voted for the Republicans before, but now they had a chance to vote for one of "their guys."[3]

1977-1981 JAMES EARL CARTER, JR. THIRTY-NINTH PRESIDENT

OFF TO A GOOD START

One of Carter's first decisions was to pardon draft dodgers of the Vietnam War. Many had burned their draft cards in a show of defiance or had moved to Canada. For those who had fought in World War II or Korea, it was a bitter pill to have to swallow as well as those who had lost loved ones in any of the conflicts, including the Vietnam War. But those who opposed the Vietnam conflict as well as those who fled their call to duty welcomed the pardon.

On a more positive note, Carter used his experience as Georgia's governor to eliminate and consolidate federal agencies. He also won congressional approval to lower federal income taxes. He proposed a Department of Energy, which Congress approved. The program to build the expensive B-1 bomber was halted, and further development of cruise missiles was conducted in its place.[4]

On May 31, 1977, the Trans-Alaska oil pipeline that Nixon had started in November 1973 was completed. In November, New Orleans elected its first African American mayor, Ernest Morial. When the slaves from Africa were brought over in the seventeenth and eighteenth centuries, their owners referred to them as Niggers. The abolitionists called them Negroes. During World War II, the term *colored troops* was used. It was probably Martin Luther King, Jr., who coined the term *black is beautiful*, which bestowed pride. Later the term *black* was dropped in favor of African Americans.

Each nationality that came to America over the years picked up nicknames, some of which were not very complimentary. The Germans are the largest nationality of Americans, and they were called Krauts or Hinnies. The Irish were looked down upon for years and called many different names, including Micks and Mackerel Snappers, the last referring to their Catholic practice of eating fish on Fridays. The English picked up the names Brits and Limeys. The Polish were often called Polacks, and many Hispanics that came from the Latin American countries were often called Spics. Italians picked up the nickname of Wops, Asians were called Slant Eyes, and American Indians went by the name of redskins.

Today, most Americans are just that—Americans—and nicknames no longer identify the millions and millions of loyal citizens of the United States. There is a good feeling among most people of the United States of America.

Most of the good things that took place during the Carter administration happened in his first year, with the economy showing improvement. The controversial events that took place after the first year would make people forget the good that he had accomplished.

In foreign affairs, he asked the Senate to ratify two treaties. One treaty would turn over the Panama Canal to Panama, if approved, on December 31, 1999. The Democratic-controlled Senate approved the treaty sixty-eight to thirty-two. Many questioned this move, but the second treaty gave the United States the right to defend the canal's neutrality. It was also approved.

THINGS BEGIN TO GO WRONG

The nation's economy had improved in 1977, but by 1978, inflation had become a major problem that would persist the rest of his term in office. Carter tried many things, from urging businesses to avoid price increases and labor to hold down wage demands, but nothing seemed to help. High import oil prices added fuel to the discontent, and it was reflected in the polls.

Inflation which had been called high by Carter before he was elected—6 to 8 percent—soared to 15 percent and would reach 21 percent. Unemployment was at an unacceptable level as were interest rates.

In 1978, Carter strengthened the ties between the U.S. and Communist China and established diplomatic relations in 1979. One of his biggest accomplishments was the peace treaty between Egypt and Israel that was finally signed. The idea had started with the Ford administration when Kissinger and Ford helped the two countries settle a territorial dispute.[5]

In 1978, the Supreme Court decided that colleges could take race into account but could not use quotas in granting admission. Alan Bakke, who had claimed he was denied admission into medical school because he was white, was admitted after the decision.

FROM BAD TO WORSE

In 1979, the bottom started to fall out. The Soviet Union invaded Afghanistan. Carter's answer was to not let the United States participate in the 1980 Olympics that were to be held in Moscow. Also in 1979, the government of Iran was overthrown; and the leader, the shah, Mohammed Reza Pahlavi, left Iran. When Carter approved his admittance into the United States for medical treatment, the Iranian revolutionaries stormed the United States Embassy in the capital, Tehran. They captured the U.S. employees and held them hostage for 444 days, demanding the return of the shah for trial in exchange for the U.S. prisoners.

Carter refused to comply with their demands and cut diplomatic relations. He authorized a rescue attempt; but this not only failed, but three of the eight helicopters broke down, a fourth crashed, and eight brave Americans died.

When the disposed shah died in July 1980, it was thought that the U.S. employees being held would be released, but the Iranians kept them for spite and a final insult.[6]

The American Broadcasting Corporation started a nightly newscast to follow the progress of the hostage problem, and called its program *Nightline*, hosted by Ted Koppel. The program still goes on.

In the summer of 1979, the movie star and legend, John Wayne, died in Los Angeles on June 11. Thanks to the marvels of television, video recordings, and the latest—DVDs, John Wayne can be seen and enjoyed by those who remember him as well as those born after he died.

In September of 1979, Carter granted clemency to four Puerto Rican nationalists imprisoned for the 1954 attack on the House of Representatives and a 1950 attempt on the life of President Harry Truman.

The polls showed Carter having very little support, and when the Democratic Convention was held in the summer of 1980, Edward (Ted) Kennedy was set to challenge him. His car accident where he drove off Chappaquiddick, Massachusetts bridge, that caused Mary Jo Kopechne's death was brought up after eleven years, and the convention renominated Jimmy Carter.

The Republicans nominated the governor of California who had served that State from 1967 to 1975. Ronald Reagan had fought with Gerald Ford for the nomination in 1976, but Reagan fell eighty votes short of getting the nomination at that convention. He planned for four years, when he sought the nomination in 1980.[7]

JIMMY CARTER AFTER HIS PRESIDENCY

When Jimmy Carter left the White House, he was only fifty-six years old. He wasted little time in keeping busy and productive. He founded a forum for discussion of national and international issues at Emory University in Atlanta. He wrote several books between 1982 and 1987. He had been asked to travel to North Korea to help reduce world tension, to Haiti to bring about a peaceful settlement, and to Cuba to try and improve relations between Cuba and the United States.

For his untiring efforts to find a peaceful solution in so many conflicts, he was awarded the Nobel Peace Prize for 2002.[8]

CHAPTER XXXII

"LIFE IS JUST ONE GRAND SWEET SONG, SO START THE MUSIC"

WHAT DID YOU DO BEFORE YOU BECAME PRESIDENT?

O f the thirty-nine presidents before Ronald Reagan, many had more than one career. On the other hand, some like William Henry Harrison, Ulysses Grant, and Dwight Eisenhower had only a military career prior to becoming president.

Martin Van Buren, John Tyler, James Polk, Franklin Pierce, James Buchanan, Grover Cleveland, and Calvin Coolidge were all lawyers. James Madison was a farmer, Herbert Hoover was a mining engineer, and Andrew Johnson was a tailor.

Abraham Lincoln and Benjamin Harrison were both lawyers, and then served in Congress—Lincoln in the House of Representatives, and Harrison in the Senate.

In all, there were twenty-three attorneys; twenty served in the military, ten were farmers or ranchers, eight were educators, and four were authors before they became president, five if you count Jefferson who authored the Declaration of Independence. But many wrote their memoirs or autobiography after they left office.

A few held three or more different types of positions before taking the oath of office. Washington was a surveyor and a planter as well as a general. John Adams was a farmer, an attorney, and a teacher. James Monroe was a farmer, an attorney, and served in the military. Teddy Roosevelt was a rancher, a soldier, a famous author, and governor of New York. Woodrow Wilson was a professor, an author, president of a university, and a governor. Warren Harding was an educator, an editor, and a publisher. Harry Truman was a farmer and a clerk before serving in the army during the First World War. He then served in the Senate before being selected as vice president. John Fitzgerald Kennedy was a journalist, an author, and a naval officer during World War II then served in the House of Representatives and later in the U.S. Senate—as did Lyndon Johnson and Richard Nixon.

Fourteen former presidents served as governors of their state. Andrew Jackson was governor of the Florida Territory before it became a state. All except Rutherford B. Hayes and Ronald Reagan served four years or less when they were governor. Hayes's three terms as governor of Ohio was from 1868 to 1877. Ronald Reagan served two full terms as governor of California, a period of eight years.

No one held more different jobs than Ronald Reagan. He was a lifeguard, a sports announcer, served as an officer in the army during World War II, an actor, president of the Screen Actors Guild, a television spokesman, a rancher, and governor of California before becoming the fortieth president of the United States.

When he graduated from Dixon High School in Illinois in 1928, he wrote in his yearbook, "Life is just one grand sweet song, so start the music." That pretty much was his guiding philosophy throughout his lifetime.

FROM TAMPICO TO HOLLYWOOD

Ronald Reagan's mother and father were as different as night and day. John Edward Reagan (everyone called him Jack) was of Irish descent, a Catholic, a born salesman with a gift of blarney and the charm of a leprechaun. Ronald said he could tell stories better than any one he ever knew.[1]

His mother, Nelle Wilson Reagan, who was of Scotch-English decent, expected to find the best in people, even among the prisoners of their local jail to whom she brought hot meals. A devout person, she never missed a Sunday at the Disciples of Christ Church.[2]

When Ronald was born on February 6, 1911, his father thought two things—he looked like a Dutchman, and thought he might grow up to be president some day.

Ronald believed that he inherited the best of qualities from each of them. From his father he learned about hard work, to be ambitious, and a "little something about telling a story." From his mother he learned the value of prayer and how to have dreams come true.[3]

Because his father was always looking for a better opportunity, the family, consisting of two boys—Neil, the oldest, and Ronald—moved frequently throughout Illinois. They lived in Chicago, Galesburg, Monmouth, then back to Tampico and finally Dixon.

It was in Dixon that Ronald Reagan continued his formal education that had started in Galesburg. He was nine years old when they moved to Dixon, and some of his happiest memories are of that place.

Dixon had the Rock River flowing through it, and Ronald found a whole new world. Hiking, fishing, skating in the winter, and swimming in the summer was a heaven on earth to him. He loved to read and devoured books on nature as well as other areas of interest like *Tarzan*, the Rover Boys series, and books about college life.[4]

His playmates were a mix of every type. His mother encouraged him to bring home black playmates. She lived the Golden Rule and passed it on to her sons.

When she told Ronald and his brother about her husband's addiction to alcohol, it helped him understand when he found his father dead drunk in the snow just outside their house one cold winter day. He dragged him into the house, put him to bed, and never mentioned it to anyone.[5]

He was very poor at baseball, always chosen last, and always striking out when at bat. In 1924 or 1925, the family went for a ride with their mother and father in the front seats. Ronald found a pair of his mother's glasses on the back seat, put them on, and a whole new world opened up. When he was tested, they found he was extremely nearsighted. When he wore heavy horned-rimmed glasses, the kids called him Four Eyes. The fact that he could see leaves on a tree, not just a blob of green, made it worth the kidding he learned to endure.[6]

Entertainment in the early twenties in small towns was usually made by those in town. Silent movies were the only outside diversion. Ronald's mother, who loved to act, encouraged Ronald to be part of the acts that were performed. At first he was reluctant, but seeing his brother Neil succeed, he finally relented. The people enjoyed what he said and laughed. It no doubt planted a seed in his desire to perform and please others.[7]

When Ronald entered Dixon High School in the fall of 1924, he wanted to play football badly. Only five-feet-three-inches high and weighing 108 pounds, he tried, but did not make the team. Working at a labor job the next summer, he saved money for college and also built up his small physique. In his sophomore year, there was a division for lighter players, and he loved to play in the line. In his junior year, he weighed over 160 and was five feet ten. He was on the varsity and, when given the chance, did well playing first string the rest of that year and all during his senior year.[8]

Another interesting chance came along when he was hired as a lifeguard at the Dixon local swimming area on the Rock River. Having taken lifesaving at the local YMCA, he was well qualified. He had this job that he called the best he ever had for seven summers. He kept a record, and at the end of the seventh summer, he had saved seventy-seven people, of which he was rightfully proud.[9]

Just about everyone remembers a teacher who had a great influence on their time in high school, and Ronald Reagan was no exception. He gives a great deal of credit to his teacher by the name of B. J. Frazer. He taught English and also was in charge of dramatics. Ronald learned a great deal about acting, and with success in football and life guarding in the summer, he began to lose shyness and was elected student body president.[10]

Ronald's choice of a college was an easy one. The girl he had been dating during high school was going to Eureka College, located 110 miles southeast of Dixon. He had made some money lifeguarding, but not enough for tuition, books, room, and board. He convinced the Eureka College president, Bert Wilson, and the football coach, Ralph McKinzie, to have half his tuition paid by a needy-student scholarship.

He earned his meals washing dishes at the Tau Kappa Epsilon fraternity house. He joined the TKEs.

A year before the Great Depression of 1929, the college of 250 students was going to have to cut some of the faculty and classes. When the students got wind of what was about to happen, they elected Reagan to represent the freshman on a committee that planned to meet with the trustees. Chosen to present the student committee's proposal for a strike, he was so persuasive, the entire student body agreed to strike. This brought the resignation of the president, and things went back to normal.

In his next year at Eureka College he got the football coach to get him a scholarship as before, and a job washing dishes in a girls' dormitory. His older brother Neil joined him at Eureka after he grew tired of manual labor.

The Great Depression hit the family hard. Jack Reagan lost his job in Dixon and could only find work in Springfield, the capital of Illinois. Ronald remembered the tough times and also recalled how everyone helped one another. His mother taught him the power of prayer, and he used it, even at football games, when he prayed that no one would be injured.[11]

Besides football at Eureka, Ronald helped start a swimming team and was not only the captain but also the coach of the team. His other love was acting that had started in high school. The English professor at Eureka, Ellen Marie Johnson, also taught dramatics. Ronald's role in the play, *Journey's End* came about because he had seen the play as a freshman. He did well in the part, and the college was invited, thanks to Miss Johnson, to a one-act play contest at Northwestern University and was in competition with schools like Princeton and Yale. Eureka placed second in the competition, and Ronald was one of three selected for individual honors. The head of Northwestern's Speech Department thought he should give serious consideration to acting, something he had dreamed about.[12]

He had majored in Economics but really wanted to do something in radio as it was the biggest means of entertainment besides the movies. He went to Chicago for interviews but met nothing but rejections. A program director at NBC suggested that he start out in the sticks. Her advice was taken to heart, and he returned to Dixon.

His next attempt was at radio stations in the tricities area of Davenport, Moline, and Rock Island. He was lucky to get a chance to try out at Station WOC in Davenport, Iowa, where he was told to broadcast an imaginary football game.

Taking a page from his own playing days, he described a game that Eureka won in the last minute. He did so well he was hired to do the Iowa-Minnesota game and got $5.

He did such a good job, he was hired at $10 a game for the rest of the season.

When the season was over, Reagan went back to Dixon. Here he had no job and watched his father—a staunch Democrat—handle the job of being in charge of the Works Progress Administration (WPA) for Dixon. He was impressed on how his dad handled the job of helping people who wanted to work, not receiving a hand out. But luck again rained down on Ronald Reagan. He got a call in February 1933 from Pete MacArthur of Station WOC. He was hired as an announcer for $100 a month. He did not do well at first, but worked hard on his delivery technique.

When Station WOC closed, he got a chance to work for Station WHO in Des Moines. This was one of only fifteen fifty thousand watts clear channel stations in America at that time. They needed someone to broadcast the famous Drake Relays. Reagan had run track in college and had no trouble with the assignment. He did so well, he was hired for the next four years. He covered football games, auto races, track tournaments, and swimming meets. He was making $75 a week and could help out his brother to finish college as well as his parents who appreciated his help.

Major league baseball games were often relayed by telegraph wire to radio stations like WHO in Des Moines. They would tap out in Morse code the pitch, where it was hit, and how the play went. Reagan would read the wire as it came across and broadcast the game as if he were in the stadium. One time the wire went "dead," and Reagan improvised for sometime with descriptions of foul balls. The wire was repaired and the game continued. Some thought the batter for the Cubs, Billy Jurges, had made a record for foul balls off pitcher, Dizzy Dean.[13]

Starting in 1935, Reagan went to California during the winter to learn more about the Chicago Cubs and the White Sox and to cover the spring training. Practice was cancelled when a large rain storm hit the Los Angeles area. Knowing about a group of singers—*the Oklahoma Outlaws*—that performed on a regular basis in Des Moines, Reagan traveled to Hollywood to watch them. The storm continued, and Reagan was unable to get back to Catalina Island where the Cubs played. He checked in to a hotel in Los Angeles and ran into a singer, Joy Hodges, who had worked for station WHO in Iowa. She was singing at the hotel, and when he spotted her at the restaurant, sent a note backstage. She joined him at dinner. He told her about his dream to be an actor, and Joy lined him up with an agent, Bill Meiklejohn—after telling Reagan to get rid of those horrible glasses.

His interview went well, and he next met a casting director for Warner Brothers studio. This led to a screen test and then he had to return to his job with the radio station. When he got back to Des Moines, he got a telegram.

WARNER OFFERS CONTRACT SEVEN YEARS STOP ONE YEAR
OPTION STOP STARTING $200 A WEEK STOP WHAT SHALL I DO
MEIKLEJOHN

He wired back as quickly as he could get to the Western Union:

SIGN BEFORE THEY CHANGE THEIR MINDS
DUTCH REAGAN

He had used that nickname as long as he could remember as his father called him the Dutchman when he was born; and when he was older, he liked being called Dutch rather than Ronald.[14]

HOLLYWOOD TO SACRAMENTO, CALIFORNIA

Becoming an actor and staying in the movie industry is two different things. Ronald Reagan's good looks, pleasant voice, and winning smile got him into the movies. But the character of his background made it possible for him to stay and succeed in a very competitive business.

His ability to think quickly on his feet came from his experience as a sports announcer. His ability to get along with all kinds of people came from watching his father work for the WPA (Works Progress Administration) and his mother's kindness to everyone. His ability to be persuasive came from his experience in getting into college as well as persuading the college trustees to keep the full program going. And most important, his acting ability came from his mother's insistence that he try out for local shows—and that led to falling in love with acting and pleasing others.

If anyone ever benefited from loving and dedicated parents and a world of experiences, it was Ronald Reagan. He never forgot that he came from humble, but proud beginnings. He helped his family when he could, and never forgot how much they had done for him. He appreciated his small-town roots and the chance to attend a very small college which gave him many opportunities to grow in a number of ways.

MOVIE CAREER

Ronald Reagan's career started on June 1, 1937. They sent him first to makeup where they changed his hairstyle. Next came wardrobe where he needed special shirts like James Cagney had. His large shoulders made his head seem small. Then publicity pondered changing his name. They didn't like Dutch, but when he told them his first name was Ronald, they thought that was just right.[15]

His first picture, *Love is in the Air,* got him good reviews, and his contract was extended. He was cast in B movies at first. These would not have leading Hollywood stars and were shown as a part of a double feature, something that was quite popular during the Depression. In the first year and a half he made thirteen pictures and invited his parents to move to California.[16]

Reagan had to join the Screen Actors Guild, which had won the right to be the actors' sole bargaining union after a five-year battle. He was leery at first of joining a union but soon found that it was backed by not only new actors like him but veterans as well. When he became a member of the board of directors to represent the younger and newer actors, he met stars like Cary Grant and Jimmy Cagney on the board. He became a firm believer in the actors' union.[17]

Being a sports enthusiast all his life, he knew a great deal about the famous Notre Dame coach, Knute Rockne, who died in a plane crash in 1931. He thought his life story would make a great movie and told movie star Pat O'Brien that he would make a great Knute Rockne. When the Warner Brothers Studio decided to make the film, he convinced them that he was perfect for the part of George Gipp, after he showed them a picture of himself in a Eureka College football uniform.

The movie was a tremendous success and is shown every fall at Notre Dame University in South Bend, Indiana. Reagan did not have a major role, but his unforgettable scene was when football player George Gipp was dying, and said to Rockne:

> Some day, when things are tough, and the breaks are going against the boys, ask them to go in there and win one for the Gipper. I don't know where I'll be, but I'll know about it, and I'll be happy.[18]

This one scene made Reagan a new star. He was put in A pictures—the first was *Santa Fe Trail* with Errol Flynn. The year was 1940, and he married movie actress Jane Wyman. They would have three children. Maureen was born in 1941. She died in 2001 of cancer. Their second child, Michael, was adopted in 1945. Their third child, Christina, was born in 1947 and only lived three days. The Reagans were divorced in 1948.

Ronald was able to purchase a home for his folks, and he got a job for his dad as his publicity secretary when Ronald started getting so much mail requesting autographed pictures.

One other memorable picture that Reagan made of over fifty pictures he was in was *Kings Row*. In one scene, he discovers that his legs have been amputated by a sadistic and vindictive surgeon, and he screams to his wife (Ann Sheridan):

> Randy, where's the rest of me?

It was so well done that they did not need a second "take." There was talk of a possible nomination for an Academy Award (Oscar), but James Cagney received it for his role as George M. Cohan in *Yankee Doodle Dandy.*[19]

Shortly after his success with his role in *Kings Row*, the Japanese bombed Pearl Harbor. As a reserve officer, he was subject to being called to active duty. When he took his physical exam, he passed, but with his sever nearsightedness, he would be restricted to duty in the continental United States. As one doctor said, if they sent him overseas, he'd shoot a general. Another doctor said, "Yes, and you'd miss him."[20]

ARMY SERVICE

Before he was to report to active duty, he completed a movie with Errol Flynn called *Desperate Journey,* a picture about RAF pilots shot down behind German lines, and their successful attempt to return to England.[21]

Reagan's first assignment as a second lieutenant was to serve as a liaison officer loading troops for shipment to the South Pacific. After a few months, he was transferred to the army air force intelligence in Los Angeles, California. Here his knowledge of the motion picture business was put to good use, making training films and documentaries. His movie contract gave him the advantage of being able to recruit movie directors to help make the training films that improved traditional methods of briefing officers prior to their mission.[22]

While assigned to this job, Reagan learned firsthand of the waste in the U.S. government due to bureaucracy. Because of the secret nature of the job they were doing for the air force, no civilians were hired. But midway through the war, they transferred over two hundred civilians to Reagan's base. Here he saw and experienced the inefficiency of the civil service. Incompetent workers could not be fired, only transferred and usually promoted. Supervisors were paid on how many workers were under them, so the workforce was never reduced.

During the war, a movie was made called *This is the Army.* Reagan was given a leave to star in the famous songwriter Irving Berlin's reprise of his World War I show called *Yip, Yip, Yaphank,* which had introduced the song "Over There," back in 1917. The movie was a huge moneymaker for the army relief, raising over $10 million.[23]

Reagan also saw films of the holocaust and the death camps that the Nazis had set up. He retained a copy and was able to show an unbelieving producer and his wife the film after the war. When the film ended, they sat in silence with tears in their eyes. Reagan ended his army career as a captain.[24]

THE SCREEN ACTORS GUILD EXPERIENCE

After the war, Reagan returned to making movies. The Communists were attempting to control the movie industry by invading and controlling the different unions. As a staunch supporter of the Screen Actors Guild, Reagan did his part in routing out the Communists. He became president of the guild and spoke out, defending the movie industry.[25]

Having been a New Deal Democrat during the Depression, he believed that the government could solve all the problems. But he began a transformation when he experienced the government's attempt to control everything. The civil service situation that he saw firsthand while in the Army and liberals denying that there were any problems with the Communists in the movie industry was the beginning of his seeing the Democratic Party in a new light.

He spoke on behalf of the Screen Actors Guild to the Congress's Un-American Activities Committee, defending his fellow actors. He was greatly disappointed when the committee accused some actors of communist actions without any proof. Again, he was beginning to question the motives of those in political power.[26]

His speeches began to take on a new tone, and the movie director, Mervyn LeRoy, asked Ronald to comfort a young actress who was being accused of being a Communist. Her name was Nancy Davis, but there was more than one Nancy Davis, and his research assured him that this one was not a Communist.

He volunteered to call her on the phone, but LeRoy thought she would feel better hearing the information in person, so Reagan took her to dinner. One thing led to another, and before long he proposed with, "Let's get married." Her response was, "Let's."

They were married on March 4, 1952 in a quiet ceremony with actor William Holden as his best man and Holden's wife, Ardis, as matron of honor. Reagan was forty-one, and Nancy was thirty-one. In Reagan's own words, he summed up how much Nancy meant to him.

> If ever God gave me evidence that He had a plan for me, it was the night
> Nancy came into my life.[27]

GENERAL ELECTRIC EXPERIENCE LEADS TO BIGGER THINGS

After they were married, Reagan became more selective of the roles he would accept. One picture he enjoyed making was *The Winning Team*, a movie on the life of Grover Cleveland Alexander, a great baseball pitcher. Nancy and Ronald had their first child, Patricia Ann, in the latter part of 1952.

Doing few films, Reagan even did a "gig" at the Last Frontier Hotel in Las Vegas for two weeks. He emceed a group called the Continentals. Television was becoming a growing industry in the 1950s, but actors shied away from taking part—it was considered the kiss of death. But Ronald did guest shots on TV, and this led to a big break for the Reagans.[28]

The General Electric Company proposed to make a weekly series of dramatic shows. Reagan would act in a few each year, but mostly he would host the show, introducing the drama about to be seen. He did the show for eight years, but did much more than that. General Electric had 139 plants throughout the country, and part of Reagan's contract called for him to visit the plants and give short talks about Hollywood and then meet the people in the factories. He would listen to their problems and soon realized that people were fed up with government controls imposed on them.

He began speaking less and less about Hollywood and more about how citizens should take an active part in their government. He did such a good job that he was asked to speak at local organizations like United Fund, chamber of commerce and state conventions of service organizations. In 1958, their son Ronald Prescott was born. Life was good for the Reagans.[29]

The income from General Electric allowed him to purchase a dream home overlooking the Pacific Ocean as well as a ranch north of Los Angeles in the Santa Monica mountains. Reagan had learned to ride horses back in Dixon and had promised himself if he ever got a chance, he would have a horse of his own.[30]

After the army, he asked his friend and actor Dan Dailey where he could buy a horse. Dan introduced him to a former captain in the Italian cavalry, Nino Pepitone, who owned thoroughbred horses. Nino taught Reagan things about riding and jumping, and Reagan fell in love with a horse. Reagan purchased Baby, a thoroughbred, and rode him in pictures that he was in. Later, with Nino's help, the Reagans went into the horse-breeding business. Another of his dreams came true.[31]

THE TURNING POINT IN RONALD REAGAN'S POLITICAL LIFE

By 1960, Ronald Reagan had reached a decision that was to affect his entire life. In 1952, he had hoped that Eisenhower would run as a Democrat for the presidency. He even wrote Ike a letter saying so. When Eisenhower finally decided to run as a Republican, Reagan showed the courage of his convictions and voted for him—a first for Reagan who had been a staunch liberal Democrat.[32]

In 1960, he campaigned for Richard Nixon. John Kennedy's father, Joseph Kennedy tried to persuade Reagan to vote for his son, but to no avail. He had read works of Thomas Jefferson, Franklin Roosevelt, and Woodrow Wilson. They all said that government should be limited, something that was not happening with the present Democratic Congress.[33]

By 1962, he had given hundreds of speeches in support of the Republican Party and in backing Richard Nixon for governor of California. When speaking in the Pacific Palisades, he was interrupted by a woman who asked if he was registered as a Republican. When he said no but intended to, she said, "I'm a registrar." She walked down the aisle, handed him a form, and he became a Republican. With that completed, he turned to the audience and said, "Now, where was I?"[34]

DECISION TO RUN FOR THE GOVENORSHIP OF CALIFORNIA

In 1964, Reagan was asked to be the cochairman of the Barry Goldwater presidential campaign in California. They asked him to give speeches like he had been doing, condemning the Democrats for their relentless expansion of the federal government with the fancy title of Great Society.

One speech at the Coconut Grove nightclub in front of eight hundred Republicans was so well received that a number of the big contributors to the Republican Party approached Reagan into taping the speech to be used late in the campaign. He agreed, and the speech was shown on October 12, 1964. The speech was extremely well received throughout the country, but Barry Goldwater lost the election to Lyndon Johnson.[35]

After the election, Reagan went back to work. This time he was the host of a TV series called *Death Valley Days*. When approached by important California Republicans to consider running for governor of California, his response was:

You're out of your minds.

But he did agree to give speeches to bring about party unity, something that was lacking in the Goldwater campaign. He gave speeches all over the state of California, and more and more people kept asking why he wouldn't run for governor. On January 4, 1966, he finally agreed to run for the office.[36]

After a bitter primary fight, he took his campaign to the people. His opponent, Governor Pat Brown, was seeking his third term, having beaten both Richard Nixon and Senator William Knowland in the two previous elections.

It often happened in Ronald Reagan's political life that people made the mistake of underestimating Reagan's ability. He was able to weather any storm and had the knack for saying the right thing at the right time.

Governor Pat Brown commissioned a TV commercial in which he told a group of small children, "I'm running against an actor, and you know who killed Abe Lincoln, don't you?" This went over like a lead balloon.[37]

When Pat Brown brought Senator Edward Kennedy to California to campaign, Kennedy spoke about Ronald. "Reagan has never held any political office before, and here he is seeking the top in government of California."

Reagan's response was, "I understand there's a senator from Massachusetts who's come to California, and he's concerned that I've never held office prior to seeking this job. Well, you know, come to think of it, the senator from Massachusetts never held *any* job before he became a senator."[38]

His opponent, Pat Brown, accused Reagan of not writing his own speeches, which was not true. Reagan suggested that he give a few opening remarks and then turn the event into a question and answer session. Maybe Reagan picked up that technique from reading how Teddy Roosevelt or Harry Truman campaigned. In any case, it was a marvelous way of involving people, and they grabbed the chance to voice their opinions, complaints, and ask questions; and Reagan showed how he had learned to think on his feet.

The mid 1960s saw the rise of burnings and student riots on college campuses. Many of the concerns and questions that Reagan had were about those problems. He responded that he thought students had no business being at the universities if they were unwilling to abide by the rules. If they refused to obey them, they should go somewhere else. The audience cheered when they heard his answer.

The other major problems in California at that time were that the people of that state paid the highest per capita tax, the state's crime rate was the highest, and that California had the most wasteful welfare program. Once again, Ronald Reagan—the former lifeguard, sports announcer, and movie star—was at the right place at the right time. He won the election with 58 percent of the votes to 42 percent for Governor Brown. Brown thought the conservatives and extremists had made the difference, but Reagan saw it in another way. The postwar baby boomers were of age to vote, and the middle of the road voters in both parties were fed up with the bureaucrats protecting their jobs with expensive programs. As Reagan noted in his autobiography, "There was unrest in the country, and it was spreading across the land like a prairie fire."[39]

1967-1976 GOVERNOR OF THE STATE OF CALIFORNIA

Governor Reagan wasted little time. Right after the election in November, a seasoned Republican legislator briefed Reagan. While Reagan knew the basics, this man told him about the political life in Sacramento. He explained the rules, procedure, and budget process and statuary powers of the governor. It was a crash course in government and was very helpful to the new governor.[40]

Prior to his inauguration on January 2, 1967, outgoing Governor Brown told Reagan to go to the Governors National Convention. Reagan appreciated this and met the governor of Ohio, Jim Rhodes. He explained to Reagan about using sharp businessmen to evaluate and make suggestions on improving state agencies. Reagan used his ideas.

Governor Reagan's financial advisor, Casper Weinberger, found that the state was spending more than it was taking in. He used this information and told the people in his inauguration address the problem and his plan to fix it. He was not afraid to meet problems head on.[41]

By setting good and realistic goals and appointing reliable and well-informed businesspeople to carry out programs to meet those goals, and at the same time staying out of their way so they could do their job, became Reagan's philosophy, policy, and management style while he was governor and would be used when he became president.

The first year as governor, Reagan had to raise taxes to pay for the deficit financing that had incurred from the previous administration. But in 1968, after much budget cutting and spending freeze, Casper Weinberger, the state finance director was able to report to Reagan a surplus in the budget of over $100 million. When Weinberger asked Reagan how he wanted to spend the surplus, Reagan responded, "I already know what I want to do with the money. Let's give it back to the people, give them a tax rebate."

"It's never been done," Cap said.

"You've never had an actor up here before, either," Reagan said.

The state legislature had to approve refunds, and Reagan's knowledge that they would rather spend than even think about returning the money to the people presented a dilemma. To thwart the legislature from finding out about the surplus and passing legislation against returning it, Reagan went on the air and told the Californians about the surplus and to expect a refund. When the legislature heard this, they went wild, but could do nothing but accept Reagan's promise.[42]

During his first term, the unrest on the college campuses continued. Student leaders from nine different University of California campuses asked to see Governor Reagan at the Capital. Reagan looked forward to the meeting. When he came into the room to meet them, they were dressed in worn T-shirts, and some were barefoot. Nobody stood up. Reagan listened as their spokesman began.

> Governor, we want to talk to you, but I think you should realize that it's impossible for you to understand us . . . You weren't raised in a time of instant communication or satellites and computer-solving problems in seconds . . . You didn't live in an age of space travel and journeys to the moon, of jet travel or high speed electronics . . .

While he paused to take a breath, Reagan said:

> *You're absolutely right. We didn't have those things when we were your age. We invented them . . .* [43]

Reagan's experience with blacks and Hispanics brought about an interesting meeting. Several black leaders in the San Francisco area wanted to talk to the governor about "treatment of blacks."

They came into the Governor's office ready to attack Reagan as a racist, but Reagan said,

> Look, are you aware that I've appointed more blacks to executive and policy-making positions in the state government than all the previous governors of California put together?

> "Yes," one said, "but why aren't you telling the people about it? How come you haven't bragged about it?"

Reagan went on to explain that he thought it was cheap politics to go out and "sing a song about it." He explained that he chose the best people for the job, not for their color. The black leaders left the meeting as friends of Ronald Reagan.[44]

This was but another example of how different Ronald Reagan was from the ordinary politician. He choose the best people, never his friends, and never worried about taking credit but instead, praised others for their accomplishments.

By the end of 1969, he decided to run for a second term. He ran against Jesse Unruh, the speaker of the California Assembly, a tax-and-spend liberal who had opposed Reagan's reforms. Ronald Reagan won a second term with 53 percent of the votes to 45 percent for Unruh. Reagan had his mandate to do something about the welfare programs that were costing the state a staggering amount of money and would eventually create a financial crisis.[45]

The Democrats' answer was to raise taxes, something Reagan was dead against. Those working in the welfare programs wanted to keep their lucrative jobs. Once again, Reagan went to the people to demand that the legislature do something. The people organized committees in all fifty-eight counties to apply pressure, urging the people to write their legislatures.

It worked so well that the new Democratic speaker, Bob Moretti, agreed to work together to solve the problem. By tightening standards and eliminating loopholes, they were able to reduce the welfare case loads from forty thousand a month to just eight thousand. By saving money, they were able to increase benefits for the really needy. During the 1973-74 recession, the new programs got seventy-six thousand people *off* the welfare rolls and into productive jobs. People wrote, thanking Reagan for restoring a sense of self-respect, and this reminded him of the satisfaction his father received during the Depression, helping others find jobs.

Governor Reagan left the State of California in a much a better state. Financially, the state government was less costly, more businesslike, and the quality of people hired for state positions was a big improvement. In eight years, Reagan used the line item veto 943 times and was never overridden by the legislature. Forty-two other states also have the line item veto, but the president of the United States does not. During his eight years, Reagan was able to announce four rebates of state taxes.

To show the difference in political thinking in California at that time, Reagan tells what happened after the fourth and largest rebate. The Democratic leader of the State Senate burst into his office and said, "Giving that money back to the people is an unnecessary expenditure of public funds."[46]

When Ronald Reagan ran for governor, he had to sell the family's ranch near Lake Malibu for tax purposes. After he left office in early 1975, a friend of his, Bill Wilson, took Ronald and Nancy up a long narrow winding road in the Santa Ynez Mountains, north of Santa Barbara. They fell in love with the ranch on seeing it and purchased the 688 acres called Tip Top. They changed the name to Rancho del Cielo—(Ranch in the Sky).

They slowly added to and improved on the small adobe house. They had six different trails that they could ride on their thoroughbreds, and life was both joyful and serene. Nancy had worked on a Foster Grandparents Program—older adults helping troubled children—and continued with it. Ronald wrote a newspaper column and had a regular radio spot to continue speaking about concerns he had about the country.

They also had a home in Pacific Palisades where they could see their grown children often. They enjoyed working on the new ranch in the sky and would have been content to spend the rest of their days in that manner. Reagan was nearing the age of sixty-five, and his life had been "one grand sweet song."

But he kept getting calls from many to consider running for president in 1976. Gerald Ford had given some indication of not running when he took over after Nixon resigned, but the taste of power changed his mind. Still others thought Reagan could do a better job. They were to have a great impact on getting Reagan once again to become involved in being a leader.[47]

CHAPTER XXXIII

MR. GORBACHEV, TEAR DOWN THIS WALL

ELECTIONS ARE SOMETIMES DECIDED BY UNUSUAL FACTORS

In the election of 1800, Thomas Jefferson and Aaron Burr received the same number of electoral votes—73. Because ten states cast their votes for Jefferson and four states for Burr, in accordance with the Twelfth Amendment, Jefferson became our third president.

In 1824, John Quincy Adams was selected over Andrew Jackson, when neither had a majority of the electoral votes, even though Jackson had won the popular vote.

Abraham Lincoln challenged Stephen Douglas in Freeport, Illinois, as part of the famous Lincoln-Douglas debates and asked Douglas:

> Can the people of a United States Territory, in any lawful way, against the wishes of any citizen of the United States, exclude slavery from its limits prior to the formation of a State Constitution?

Douglas's answer was yes, and it was published in many national newspapers, including those in the South. They did not like the answer, and in affect, this cost Douglas the election for president in 1860 where he had been considered the front-runner.

Rutherford B. Hayes was fortunate to win the election even though his opponent, Samuel Tilden, received nearly three hundred thousand more popular votes. Neither had the electoral votes until a commission awarded all the disputed electoral votes to Hayes, thanks to James A. Garfield who was the next president after Hayes.

Woodrow Wilson undoubtedly won the election of 1912 because Teddy Roosevelt entered the race as a third party. The election of 1948 between Harry

Truman, Thomas Dewey, and Strom Thurmond was one that had the pollsters wondering how Truman pulled off the upset of the century. It may well have been Truman's tough decision to drop the atomic bomb that ended World War II and probably save the lives of hundreds of thousands of GIs and millions of Japanese. Many grateful veterans voted for Harry.

Richard Nixon lost the election to John F. Kennedy by less than 120,000 votes out of over 68 million popular votes. The TV debates may have been a factor. No doubt he was bitter, but tried again in 1969, in the middle of the Vietnam War, which had become very unpopular. The riots in Chicago during the Democratic convention were seen nationwide on television. Nixon won, and the fact that George Wallace picked up nearly 10,000,000 popular votes assured Nixon of a victory.

The election of Ronald Reagan in 1980 had a most interesting history. People convinced Reagan to run in 1976. He campaigned extensively but made the mistake of leaving New Hampshire the day before the primary and left the wrong impression. Even though he won the primaries in a number of states, he lost the nomination at the convention to Gerald Ford by 80 votes.

This defeat made him more determined than ever. Jimmy Carter won the election, but his four years were filled with rising inflation, rising interest rates, and rising unemployment. When Carter allowed the shah of Iran to come to the United States for medical treatment after being deposed, the Iranian rebels stormed the American Embassy, and the bottom fell out for Jimmy Carter. A hostage crisis ensued.

In the Republican campaign, there were a number of candidates who wanted to be president. Bob Dole, Howard Baker, John Anderson, Phil Crane, John Connally, and George Bush all had distinguished service in American politics. By mid-February of 1980, the race had settled down to two people—Ronald Reagan and George Bush.

The *Nashua Telegraph* newspaper offered to sponsor a debate between just the two leading candidates, but when Bob Dole complained to the Federal Election Commission, the commission said that funding a debate was, in effect, making illegal campaign contributions to Bush and Reagan and would not allow the newspaper to pay for the air time.

Reagan suggested to the Bush camp that they split the cost of the debate, but Bush said no. Reagan decided to finance the debate himself—a few thousand dollars—and Bush agreed. Reagan invited the other Republican candidates to the debate, and when they all arrived at the high school gymnasium, there were only two chairs, but six candidates.

Bush's campaign manager protested and said George Bush would not participate if the others were allowed to enter the debate. After much discussion, and the audience getting impatient, Reagan decided to tell the audience what the delay was all about.

As Reagan approached the microphone, the editor of the *Nashua Telegraph,* Mr. Breen, shouted to the sound man, *"Turn Mr. Reagan's microphone off."*

Reagan did not like that one bit, with the editor acting like the *Nashua* paper was sponsoring the debate but not paying for it. Reagan spoke into the "mike" and said the first thing that came to his mind.

I'm paying for this microphone, Mr. Breen.

The audience roared their approval, and Reagan went on to win the debate, the New Hampshire primary, and the nomination.[1]

CHOOSING A VICE PRESIDENTAL CANDIDATE

When Reagan won the nomination as presidential candidate for the Republican Party in Detroit, his first big decision was to select a vice presidential candidate.

It was suggested that Gerald Ford be given consideration, and many thought this would be the perfect ticket. But then the Ford camp believed that Gerald Ford would have more authority than a vice president ever had. Reagan saw this as a copresidency and said it would not work. Gerald Ford himself realized the problems that would entail and agreed with Reagan and said he would abandon the idea of running as his vice president.

Time was short, and the delegates at the convention were waiting for Reagan's decision. After Ford left Reagan's suite, Ronald immediately called George Bush. It was a great choice.

George Bush had been a naval flier in World War II. From 1967 to 1977, he held important and varying positions that would give the Reagan-Bush ticket a perfect balance. George Bush had been a member of the House of Representatives from Texas for two terms. Following that, he was ambassador to the United Nations for two years when Nixon was president. In 1974, after Nixon resigned, President Ford offered George Bush a chance to be an envoy to China. Nixon had worked hard to get a working relationship with this Communist country, something that had not been done for over twenty years. Following that, Bush became director of the Central Intelligence Agency. With this kind of experience, Reagan knew he had found the right man.

"George, it seems to me that the fellow who came the closest and got the next most votes for president ought to be the logical choice for vice president. Will you take it?"

Immediately George Bush responded that he would be pleased to be on the ticket. His foreign policy experience and his appeal to the moderate part of the Republican Party made it a dream team.[2]

When the two—Reagan and Bush—came before the convention, the reception was a standing ovation, and the place went wild. After much celebrating, Ronald Reagan asked the delegates to join him in a silent prayer.

Ronald Reagan and George Bush had one goal—beating Jimmy Carter and Walter Mondale. The campaign would be very interesting. Reagan did not take Carter for granted—campaigning against an incumbent was something Reagan knew about. He had beaten Governor Brown fourteen years previously but knew this campaign would be tough and in some cases, mean. Reagan prepared himself by renting a place in Virginia in September. The fall of 1980 proved to be an exciting time.[3]

THE CAMPAIGN AND THE ELECTION OF 1980

Reagan had two great rules for himself when campaigning. One was called the Eleventh Commandment, which stated that when campaigning in primary elections, he would never speak ill of any Republican opponent. His other sense of fairness and good taste was when he would not bring up sensitive issues against a democratic opponent. Having been governor, he knew that important issues were sometimes being worked on, and it would be unfair to criticize their efforts. Such was the case with Iran seizing and kidnapping American Embassy officials and workers. But everything else was fair game.[4]

In 1976, when Jimmy Carter was challenging President Gerald Ford, Carter devised what he called the misery index. He added the rate of inflation and the unemployment and used the total—12 percent—to berate Ford's leadership.

By 1980, after four years of Carter's administration, the "misery index" was more that 20 percent; but for some reason, Carter never mentioned it.

In spite of the continued holding of American hostages and in spite of the growing unemployment, rising interest, and inflation rates, Ronald Reagan's biggest concern was the attitude that the country was in. Carter had told the nation not to expect so much, that we had to get by with less, and that the country was in a *malaise*—a vague sense of mental or moral ill-being.

To Reagan, this just did not fit with his philosophy of life. Being extremely nearsighted had not stopped him from succeeding. Being turned down in Chicago when he applied for a radio job didn't stop him. Working for General Electric and visiting their many plants gave him the opportunity to see the good throughout the country. His ability to turn California into a solvent state, take people off the welfare rolls, and return the taxpayers' money on four occasions had become part of Reagan's positive attitude about himself, his work—in the many different jobs he had held—and his feeling about the country that had given him so much. He had never forgotten his high school yearbook remark, "Life is just one grand sweet song, so start the music." He had a positive outlook all his life. What he wanted was to convey that same spirit to his campaign, and if he won, to the country.

Carter accused Reagan of being a racist and a warmonger. Reagan challenged Carter to a debate, but he refused—the first incumbent to do so since the debates began in 1960. Finally, Carter was forced to debate after much public pressure, and it was held one week before the election, on October 28. Carter's slow, Southern drawl was directly opposite from Reagan's quick, bright, and often humorous remarks.

When Carter claimed Reagan had opposed Medicare benefits for Social Security recipients (completely untrue), Reagan's response was, *"There you go again . . ."*

The audience loved Reagan's response. But the clincher was the closing statement that each candidate was allowed to make. When it was Reagan's turn, he asked the American people if they were better off now than they were four years ago. If so, to vote for Carter; if not, to vote for a change. It was a masterful stroke.

After one more week of campaigning, the Reagans returned to California. It had become a tradition to have dinner with close friends and then go to the Republican headquarters to wait for the results on the night of election day.

Reagan was in the shower late in the afternoon when his wife, Nancy, came in to tell him he had a phone call from Jimmy Carter. They had a phone in their bathroom, and Reagan picked it up and listened for a few minutes. He then said, "Thank you, Mr. President."

He hung up the phone and turned to Nancy and said, "He conceded. He said he wanted to congratulate me."

The voting polls in California would not close for another two hours, and he realized that he would be the next president of the United States.[5]

When the polls finally closed, the results showed Reagan had won the popular vote with 43,904,153 votes, while Carter received 35,483,883 votes and John Anderson, running on a National Unity ticket got 5,720,060 votes.

This gave Reagan 51.6 percent of the popular vote to 41.7 percent for Carter, and 6.7 percent for Anderson. The significant difference was in the Electoral College vote. Reagan was awarded 483 electoral votes, a 91 percent advantage over Carter, who only received 49 electoral votes. John Anderson did not receive any.

1981-1989 RONALD WILSON REAGAN FORTIETH PRESIDENT

Ronald Reagan took the oath of office on January 20, 1981. The inaugural ceremony was held on the west side of the Capitol for the first time. Here, Reagan could see the Washington Monument and the Lincoln and Jefferson memorials.

His hand was on his mother's bible and opened to the fourteenth verse of the seventh chapter of second Chronicles.

> If my people, which called by my name, shall humble themselves, and pray, and seek my face, and turn from their wicked ways; then will I hear from heaven, and will forgive their sin, and will heal their land.

Next to that passage, his mother had written, "A most wonderful verse for the healing of the nation."

His inaugural address spoke of the economic problems that the country faced, and he summed things up all up in one phrase.

"Government is not the solution to our problems; government is the problem."

Following the inauguration, they had lunch. Here, President Reagan was able to announce that the hostages from the American Embassy had been freed and were flying out. He gave credit to Carter. Another positive side of Reagan again showed.[6]

GETTING READY TO SOLVE MAJOR DOMESTIC PROBLEMS

He immediately started work on the double-digit inflation, the high unemployment, and the highest interest rates since the Civil War. While the people had voted in a Republican president and a Republican Senate, the House of Representatives was still controlled by the Democrats. And that part of Congress controlled the purse strings of the federal government, according to Sections 7 and 8 of Article I of the U.S. Constitution.

The president's first order of business was to lower the income tax rates, which were exceedingly high especially for the upper brackets. These high rates, in no small way, discouraged economic growth, held down employment growth, and brought about high interest rates.

He knew the Democratic House of Representatives would not agree to cutting taxes, but Reagan had been down that road before as governor of California. He did the same thing he had done then. In early February 1981, less than a month after becoming president, he went on national television.

He was straightforward when he spoke about the problems, and he proposed a solution by lowering taxes as John F. Kennedy had done when he was president and Regan had done when he was governor of California.

The Democrats did not like it when he called for a 30 percent tax cut over seven years. They also did not like Reagan launching a program under Vice President Bush's direction to reduce unnecessary government regulations that were stifling the economy.

When the Democrats proposed drastic cuts in military spending, Reagan said, "No!" He knew the Soviet Union was spending huge amounts of money on nuclear and conventional arms. He also knew the morale was low in the U.S. Armed Forces and wanted to increase military spending for the best equipment but also for deserved pay and allowance increases for the enlisted men and women.[7]

Other problems he worked on dealt with Communism's attempts to take over Latin American countries. His knowledge of their techniques came from his experience as president of the Screen Actors Guild. Reagan enlisted David Rockefeller to develop a plan to improve Latin American relations as well as their economy. It eventually worked, and Cuba remained the only communist country in the Western Hemisphere.[8]

The American auto industry suffered from Japan, sending its cars to the United States in larger and larger numbers. The previous oil embargo did not help. Reagan had the Secretary of Transportation Drew Lewis and later Secretary of State Alexander Haig work quietly behind the scenes to get the Japanese to voluntarily lower the number of imports, thereby eliminating the need for Congress to put on import limits.[9]

On March 28, with a little over two months as president, an attempt to assassinate Reagan was partly stopped. Reagan was shot, but he was immediately taken to George Washington University Hospital. He kept his sense of humor; and when he saw his wife, Nancy, he said, "Honey, I forgot to duck." Jack Dempsey had said that to his wife when he lost the boxing fight to Gene Tunney in 1926 in Chicago.

When a group of doctors and specialists told him they would have to operate, he told them, "I hope you are all Republicans." They answered with, "Today, Mr. President, we're all Republicans."[10]

Three days after he was released from the hospital, the space shuttle *Columbia* returned safely to Earth after its maiden voyage. Recuperating in the Lincoln Bedroom of the White House gave Reagan time to think about the problems the country faced. He knew what he wanted to do about the economy—lower taxes and eliminate duplicate programs and bureaucratic waste.

His experience as governor paid big dividends. He spoke to a joint session of Congress, which was televised throughout the nation. It was well received, but the Democrats used every procedural trick to try and block legislation. But Reagan had some tricks of his own. He flew to Chicago in early July 1981. He planned to speak at a fund-raiser for Governor Jim Thompson, but he also scheduled a speaking engagement in the Congressional District of Dan Rostenkowski, chairman of the powerful Ways and Means Committee. Reagan spoke to Rostenkowski's Democratic constituents that Dan had the fate of the tax-cut proposal in the palm of his hand. Part of his speech to them was:

> If all of you will join with your neighbor to send the same message to Washington, we'll have that tax cut and we'll have it this year.

When Reagan returned to Washington, he lobbied many Democratic congressmen, and on July 29, the House of Representatives voted 238 to 195 to pass the tax cuts. In *six months*, President Reagan had achieved a major victory on the biggest domestic issue. The Speaker of the House of Representatives, Tip O'Neill, called him and gave gracious congratulations.[11]

When Reagan was campaigning in the fall of 1980 for the presidency, he pledged that one of his first nominations to the U.S. Supreme Court would be a woman. He had expert help in compiling a list of qualified women, and when Justice Potter Stewart planned to retire, he nominated Sandra Day O'Connor of the Arizona Court of Appeals, and she was confirmed by the Senate on September

21, 1981, according to Section 2, Article II of the U.S. Constitution. There were no dissenting votes.[12]

Shortly after his decision to appoint Sandra Day O'Connor to the Supreme Court, another problem cropped up. He was informed by Drew Lewis, transportation secretary, that the Professional Air Traffic Controllers Organization (PATCO) was planning to strike. Their job was to manage the control towers and radar centers around the country.

President Reagan had been president of the Screen Actors Guild for six terms and had led that group in its first strike. He was the *first* president who was a *lifetime member* of the AFL-CIO Union, so he had a great appreciation for what unions tried to accomplish.

The PATCO salary demands were so high; it would cost the tax payers $700 million a year. He told his transportation secretary to inform the union that an illegal strike would not be tolerated. He took a page out of Calvin Coolidge's book, a former president that he admired. "There is no right to strike against the public safety by anybody, anywhere, at any time," then-governor of Massachusetts Coolidge had said to AFL President Samuel Gompers when he called a strike of the Boston Police.

Congress had passed a law forbidding strikes by government employees and the PATCO members had signed an agreement not to strike. Negotiations resumed for a time, but on August 3, 70 percent of the seventeen *thousand* air controllers went on strike.

The union leaders really believed that Reagan was bluffing or playing games. Reagan informed the FAA supervisors to maintain the safety of the airplanes and airways and, if necessary, reduce the number of flights. Then he called a press conference and told the reporters that if the striking air controllers did not report for work within forty-eight hours, their jobs would be terminated, which is exactly what happened.

Flights were reduced; the public understood the decision and for the most part agreed. Training a new bunch of controllers took time, but gradually, more and more flights were put in the air. Within two years, the air traffic control system was back to a normal schedule—safer and more efficient than ever.[13]

If the strike did nothing else, it convinced a lot of people that when President Ronald Reagan spoke, he meant what he said. The people who had voted for him were extremely pleased. His Democratic opponents also took notice. This determination to do the right thing, in spite of the opposition, would carry over in dealing with leaders of foreign countries.

WORKING TO ELIMINATE THE COLD WAR

The other big problem that faced Reagan and the United States, as well as the free world, was the desire of Communist Russia to dominate the world. Lenin had proposed it, and Stalin had attempted to carry it out. When he died in 1953, Georgi Malenkov became head of the Soviet government, but he only lasted two weeks before he was replaced by Nikita Khrushchev. Following Khrushchev came Leonid Brezhnev who was head of the Soviet Union when Reagan was elected in 1980.

The main problem with the Union of Soviet Socialist Republics was the nuclear arms race. Reagan believed it was crazy for two countries to keep building atomic bombs and missiles. Reagan's experience with the Communists dated back to when he was president of the Screen Actors Guild and his firsthand knowledge of their attempt to take over the various unions associated with Hollywood. He would not be fooled by them.

He tried to deal with Leonid Brezhnev and wrote a letter trying to get agreement on reducing the nuclear threat. This failed even though Reagan offered to stop the grain embargo that Carter had imposed when the Soviets invaded Afghanistan. The grain embargo had not been helpful to the American farmers, and Reagan saw the possibility of improving relations and helping the American farmers. Still, President Brezhnev would not agree to any arms reduction. This was the latter part of 1981.

When Brezhnev died on November 11, 1982, he was replaced with Yuri Andropov, former head of the Soviet secret police—the dreaded KGB. Andropov lasted a year and three months, dying in February 1983. He was replaced by Konstantin Chernenko, and he held the top position for a year and a month, dying on March 11, 1985. Three different Soviet leaders in four years. Ronald Reagan said to his wife, Nancy, "How am I supposed to get any place with the Russians, if they keep dying on me?"[14]

The next Russian leader was Mikhail Gorbachev. Once again, Reagan wrote a letter of condolence and again tried to get cooperation. This time, he got an encouraging reply. It was a start.

IMPORTANT EVENTS DURING PRESIDENT REAGAN'S FIRST TERM

On June 5, 1981, the Centers for Disease Control reported that five homosexuals in Los Angeles had come down with a rare kind of pneumonia—the first recognized cases of what later would become known as AIDS. On June 25 of that year, the Supreme Court ruled that the male-only military draft registration was constitutional.

On June 8, 1982, President Reagan became the first U.S. president to address the British parliament. This no doubt came about because of Reagan's close personal relationship with the prime minister, Margaret Thatcher. In 1980, before he ran for president, Governor Reagan made a trip to England. There he was introduced to the first woman to head the British Conservative Party. He planned to spend only a few minutes with her but ended up talking for almost two hours. He found her to be warm, feminine, gracious, and intelligent. At a reception that evening, an Englishman asked Reagan, "What do you think of our Mrs. Thatcher?"

Reagan's reply was, "I think she'd make a magnificent prime minister."

The Englishman looked at Reagan with disdain. "My dear fellow, a woman for prime minister?"

Reagan said, "England once had a queen named Victoria who did rather well."

"By jove," he said, "I'd forgotten that."[15]

President Reagan accomplished many things during his first term, but he was proudest of the economic recovery. The first phase of the tax cut he proposed shortly after his inauguration began to have an effect a year later—1982. Many jobs were created, unemployment went down, interest rates were reduced, and inflation was halted.[16]

On November 10, 1982, the Vietnam Memorial opened in Washington, D.C., On June 18, 1983, Astronaut Sally Ride became the first American woman in space, as she and four colleagues blasted off aboard the space shuttle *Challenger.* Exactly one hundred and ten years earlier, June 18, 1873, Susan B. Anthony had been fined $100 for trying to vote in the 1872 presidential election. As an advertising ad claimed, "You've come a long ways, baby." Four days later, the shuttle landed safely at Edwards Air Force Base in California.

On August 2, 1983, the House of Representatives voted 338-90, designating the third Monday in January as a federal holiday, honoring Martin Luther King, Jr. President Reagan signed the bill on November 2.

On Friday, October 21, 1983 Ronald and Nancy flew to Georgia for a weekend of golf at Augusta National Golf Course. The next morning, he was informed that the Organization of Eastern Caribbean States had asked the U.S. to intervene militarily in the island of Grenada, a small island ninety miles north of Venezuela.

Grenada's Prime Minister Bishop had been executed by leftist rebels. There were plans to build a suspiciously large airport so that other nearby islands could be invaded and taken over by those committed to Marxism. Reagan gave approval for an immediate invasion of the island that housed eight hundred American students attending medical school. The invasion was kept a secret from Congress, fearing leaks, and just before the marines and rangers landed, Reagan got a call from his friend, Margaret Thatcher, Britain's prime minister. She asked Reagan to call off the invasion, which he would not do.

He did inform leaders of Congress after the troops were well on their way. Nineteen hundred marines and rangers gained control of the airports and secured the college campus where the American students were housed.

To free the island from eventual Soviet takeover, nineteen Americans gave their lives and over a hundred were wounded. There were far more insurgents than had been reported. Instead of two hundred, they rounded up seven hundred well-trained Cuban warriors. They also found enough weapons and ammunition to equip thousands of terrorists. They also found documents proving that the

Soviet Union and Cuba were scheming to bring Communism to other Caribbean Islands.

Later, Reagan got a letter from a helicopter pilot explaining that Grenada produced half of the world's nutmeg. He went on to state that "you can't make eggnog without nutmeg, and without nutmeg you can't have Christmas. The Russians were trying to steal Christmas, and we stopped them," he said.

Reagan got his reward when he saw on television the American students arrive safely back on U.S. soil. Later, at the White House, the students embraced the soldiers and the marines who had rescued them, a big change from the treatment servicemen had received when they returned from Vietnam.[17]

Trouble often comes in bunches, and that was true about that weekend in Augusta, Georgia. Reagan was out playing golf when he was informed that an armed man had crashed a truck at the gate of the golf course and taken seven hostages. He wanted to speak to the president, but that was out of the question. Eventually, the gunman released the hostages and was arrested.[18]

That night, Reagan was asleep but was awakened at 2:30 a.m. He was informed that a suicide bomber had driven a truckload of dynamite past sentries and smashed into the U.S. Marine barracks at the Beirut Airport in Lebanon. Exactly 241 U.S. Marines were killed by the blast. Two minutes later, a second explosion was set off two miles away, killing fifty-eight French soldiers.

The problems in the Middle East were so mixed up that no one could figure out what to do. Syria was battling Lebanon, and all the Arab nations wanted to eliminate Israel, which the U.S. would defend if necessary. When Syria fired on a U.S. unarmed reconnaissance plane, Reagan responded with U.S. Navy aircraft taking out a dozen Syrian missile-launching and antiaircraft sites; and the battleship *New Jersey* fired its sixteen-inch guns. This brought on a new cease-fire, but it did not last; and in 1984, Reagan gave the order to pull out of Lebanon.[19]

On November 11, 1983, Reagan became the first U.S. chief executive to address the Diet, Japan's national legislature.

On October 11, 1984, space shuttle astronaut Kathryn Sullivan became the first American woman to perform a space walk.

OVERSEAS TRAVEL DURING PRESIDENT REAGAN'S FIRST TERM

In April 1984, the president and the First Lady, Nancy, flew to China for a six-day visit. President Reagan met with the different Chinese leaders, standing up to them when they made incorrect accusations. This brought greater respect, and the rest of the China trip was a pleasure. They had learned to eat with chopsticks and took former President Nixon's advice and didn't ask about the food.

They saw the Great Wall of China, just outside of Beijing, the capital of China. Next they flew to Xi'an, the ancient capital, and not too far away saw where archaeologists had unearthed hundreds of life-size terra-cotta warriors.

Their last days in China were spent in Shanghai. Here they toured a Chinese factory being modernized with U.S. technology, and they visited the Fudan University where Reagan made an address to the faculty (half of whom had attended school in America) and the students.[20] When it was opened to questions, Reagan's response to one question was, "You'd be surprised how much being a good actor pays off."[21]

Their next trip was a few weeks later when Reagan was to attend an economic summit in London. Before the summit, they traveled to Ireland where Reagan's ancestors had lived and his great-grandfather had journeyed to America in the middle 1800s.

The Irish government had dug into Reagan's genealogy and was able to introduce Ronald to some of his distant relatives, including one who resembled Ronald Reagan remarkably well.

Their next stop was the fortieth anniversary of the D day invasion by the fortieth president of the United States. The ceremony was held on the cliffs overlooking the English Channel, a place called Pointe du Hoc. It was here that 225 brave American Rangers scaled the cliffs during the early hours of June 6, 1944. One hundred died or were injured during the successful climb. Sixty-two of the 225 were present for the ceremony.

Next they went to Omaha Beach, the bloodiest of all the invasion beaches. Here President Reagan gave a short speech, which contained quotes from a letter Reagan had received from the daughter of a private who came ashore that fateful morning. He had told his family that he always wanted to go back and pay homage to his buddies that had died on that bloody day.

Unfortunately, Private Peter Zanatta died of cancer a few years before and was never able to fulfill his dream. President Reagan arranged for Peter Zanatta's family to be part of the delegation to honor those heroes.

President Reagan concluded his speech that day with these words:

> Through the words of his loving daughter, who is here with us today, a D day veteran has shown us the meaning of this day far better than any president can. It is enough for us to say about Private Zanatta and all the men of honor and courage who fought beside him four decades ago: We will always remember. We will always be proud. We will always be prepared, so we may always be free.[22]

THE CAMPAIGN AND THE ELECTION OF 1984

The growth of the economy and his appeal to the average American, plus his speeches, which always had a positive tone, helped to dub him the Great Communicator. Some believed he was born a gifted speaker. Nothing could be further from the truth.

As a young boy, Ronald Reagan had a feeling of insecurity and lack of confidence, due mostly to his poor eyesight. Shy, he hesitated to perform in the local Dixon drama presentations that were held in the early 1920s.[23]

When it was discovered that he was extremely nearsighted, things began to change. With eyeglasses, his confidence grew, and he tried out for football in his first year of high school. Weighing only 108 pounds, and being five feet three inches tall, he was cut from the team. Determined to make the team the next year, he worked all summer building up his body, working at a construction job. The next fall, he made the team, and his confidence grew even more.[24]

The Dixon High School hired a new English teacher who wore glasses as thick as Ronald's. B. J. Frazer taught English in a way that gave Ronald a chance to express himself in writing. Frazer recognized his talent and asked him to read some of his essays. They were humorous, and the class laughed. Ronald ate it up.

This led to trying his hand at acting, and he did well. His teacher, Frazer, gave him tips on acting, and he learned how to throw himself into a role.[25]

At Eureka College, Professor Ellen Marie Johnson was the drama teacher and furthered Ronald's education in acting and speaking. He became very good at memorizing scripts but had not gained experience in improvising or making off the cuff remarks.[26]

In fact, when working at radio station WOC in Davenport, Iowa, he was fired for a poor job of announcing. When rehired, he asked for help from Peter MacArthur, the program director that had hired him. Pete and others gave him a crash course in radio announcing. Ronald learned quickly and improved his rhythm and cadence—an important part of announcing—and also learned to put more emotion into his delivery.[27]

No doubt his years in Hollywood gave him plenty of experience in acting and having to memorize movie scripts; and following his movie career, he was hired by General Electric. He did not realize it at the time, but his eight years with them was to give him valuable speaking experience.

He hosted the television series, "The General Electric Theater." As part of his contract, he was asked to travel throughout the country to the 139 General Electric plants and give talks. He did so well, he was invited to speak to larger and larger groups. From local chamber of commerce meetings to eventually state conventions of service organizations, he perfected his delivery as well as his ability to think on his feet.

He did this for eight years and developed a style that was informative, easy to listen to, and at the same time humorous in just the right places. His formula was simple. He would start with a joke, and then tell the audience what he was going to tell them. Then he would tell them and then tell them what he had just told them.[28]

When he was governor of California, Reagan wrote his own speeches. When he was elected president he found it necessary to use speechwriters. He informed them about short sentences and not to use two syllable words if a one syllable word would do. And if you can, he told them, use an example.[29]

All this worked well during his first term as president. When he and George Bush were nominated for a second term in Dallas, Texas, he gave an acceptance speech that allowed him to show the difference between the Republicans and the Democrats. He said the choice was between a party of hope, confidence, and growth as opposed to the party of pessimism, fear, and limits.[30]

A serious problem arose during the first debate in early October in Louisville, Kentucky. Reagan had overtrained. His aides and speechwriters had filled him with so many details and facts that the debate was won by the Democratic nominee, Walter Mondale. Some in the press took this as an indication that maybe Reagan was too old to be president. One reporter thought the debate brought out what he called the senility factor.[31]

The second debate was two weeks later in Kansas City, Missouri. This time, Reagan didn't do much cramming. The panel of reporters took turns in asking the candidates questions. One panel reporter asked Reagan if age was going to be a handicap—it was a way of raising the question of Reagan's age of seventy-three. He was alluding, by inference, to the trouble Reagan had in the first debate.

Reagan's answer will go down in history as one of the most timely and clever responses in any presidential debate. His answer to the reporters question was:

> I am not going to exploit for political purposes my opponent's youth and inexperience.

The audience roared, and the TV cameras showed a shot of Mondale laughing.[32]

The results of the election were record breaking. President Reagan received 54,455,075 popular votes to Mondale's 37,577,185—a 59 percent advantage.

The Electoral College votes gave President Ronald Reagan a *record-breaking* 525 votes. Mondale could only win the state of Minnesota and the District of Columbia for a meager total of 13 electoral votes. Only John Quincy Adams's *one* electoral vote against James Monroe in 1820 and Alf Landon's *eight* electoral votes against Franklin Delano Roosevelt were less that Mondale's 13 electoral votes.

Following the election of 1984, Reagan received a very unusual message. Written in Russian on a fine piece of tissue paper was a message from ten women who were imprisoned in a Soviet forced-labor camp.

> Mr. President:
>
> We, women political prisoners of the Soviet Union, congratulate you on your reelection to the spot of president of the USA. We look with hope to your country which is on the road of FREEDOM and respect for HUMAN RIGHTS. We wish you success on this road.

This message and a poem had been smuggled out of the camp and then out of Russia and delivered to the offices of Radio Free Europe in Munich, Germany. The translation of the poem sent to President Reagan is as follows:

On the day of your election
There we were, in deep dejection,
In a filthy prison cell
Freezing cold and most unwell.
We did not have books or papers
Warming food or legal status,
Only frigid wind and stars
Through the naked window bars,
Like a breath of Dante's hell
As befits a prison cell.
And while others cast their ballots,
Partied, danced—we sat on pallets,
Vainly guessing (what a chore!)
How much more we had in store
Isolation, deprivation,
And what for?
Then a warder scurried up,
Threatened, lied to shut us up,
But by our calculation
Right across your mighty nation
States like Kansas, Illinois,
Gave us cause for lots of joy.
By "lights out" it was quite clear
You had nothing left to fear.
So we hunkered down to sleep
By the heater (minus heat)
Chilly drafts crept round the cell
And we sighed "We wish you well"
Mr. President.
The White House,
Coast to coast the USA
And those there, who're still awake
We're not sleeping, just like you,
All in goose-bumps, cold and blue,
Our teeth chattering in sorrow:
"Great October" day tomorrow!

Reagan asked himself how any government could stifle a people yearning for freedom by putting them in prison.[33]

It stiffened Reagan's resolve to deal with the Russians by not granting any concessions as the United States had done in the past.

1985-1989 PRESIDENT RONALD REAGAN'S SECOND TERM

The second term had plenty of challenges, problems, a tragedy, a celebration, and a triumph that would change the world. A problem that was as old as the Monroe Doctrine continued to plague Latin America. Communist Soviet Union was bent on controlling the countries in Central and South America. They had been thwarted in their attempt to take over the island of Grenada, but that did not stop them. Reagan's attempts to stop the Communist takeover of Latin American countries continued during his eight years.

In early 1985, Iran terrorists seized American hostages in Tehran, Iran. A secret deal, unknown to President Reagan, was set up to trade arms in exchange for release of the American hostages. The profits from the arms deal were to be used to help the Contras who were engaged in a struggle in Nicaragua battling the Communist-backed Sandinista forces.

When this deal was eventually uncovered, congressional hearings were held. National Security Advisor John Poindexter and Lieutenant Colonel Oliver North both admitted lying about the Iran-Contra deal and were indicted. Charges were dropped when Reagan's administration refused to release classified documents dealing with the arrangement.[34]

On June 14, 1985, TWA flight 847 was hijacked by terrorists, demanding the release of Shiite prisoners being held in Israeli jails. After seventeen days of negotiations, the hostages were released, with one exception. Navy diver Robert Stethem had been killed by the terrorists on the second day.[35]

Shortly after they were released, Ronald Reagan went for his yearly physical checkup. The doctors discovered possible cancerous polyps in his colon. Before they operated, Reagan signed a letter invoking the Twenty-fifth Amendment, making George Bush acting president during the time he was incapacitated. The operation was successful, and he reclaimed the presidency.[36]

On January 28, 1986, the space shuttle *Challenger* exploded seventy-three seconds after liftoff, killing all seven crew members, including Christa McAuliffe, a New Hampshire school teacher, the first teacher to be selected to go into space. When President Reagan met with the families at the Johnson Space Center in Houston, Texas, for a memorial service, for one of the few times in his life, Ronald Reagan found it difficult to say anything. They hugged one another, and all the families wanted the space program to continue.[37]

On April 9, 1986, Ronald Reagan was speaking to the American Society of Newspaper Editors in Washington, D.C., and made this observation:

I have always stated that the nearest thing to eternal life we'll ever see on this earth is a government program.[38]

On July 3, 1986, President Ronald Reagan presided over a gala ceremony in New York Harbor during which the renovated Statue of Liberty's torch was relighted.

THE LONG ROAD TO WINNING THE COLD WAR

In today's world with instant communication, cell phones, and television programs that solve mysteries, murders, and other problems in different settings in thirty or sixty minutes on a weekly basis, it has become the norm to expect events in the world to take less time and resolve themselves in a relatively short time. But the real world just doesn't work that way. Case in point is the so-called cold war that started in 1945 and continued for over forty-five years.

Major events in history come about in a variety of ways. The American Revolution started when the British were met at a small bridge near the town of Concord close to Boston. But there were many events that led up to that moment.

States' rights had been a rallying cry by the Southern states for years, but the firing on Fort Sumter in 1861 started the Civil War that claimed over six hundred thousand American lives.

The Monroe Doctrine of 1823 was put to the test when Spain declared war on the United States in 1898, and the Spanish-American War was the result.

The sinking of the British ship, *Lusitania,* in May 1915 was but one of the factors that led to the United States entering World War I.

The bombing of Pearl Harbor brought the United States into World War II that had been raging elsewhere for over two years.

The Korean War started when North Korea invaded South Korea, and the untested United Nations, led by the United States, stopped Communist aggression.

The Vietnam War was a slow buildup of first advisors and then United States troops partially due to a questionable Tonkin Gulf resolution.

But the longest conflict began in 1945 when two completely different types of government vied with one another on what system would prevail throughout the world. On the one hand, Communism attempted to reach out and grab control on every continent except for Australia and Antarctica.

Near the end of World War II in Europe, both the Allies and the Soviet Union were ready to launch a final offense to capture Berlin. Churchill wanted Eisenhower to proceed as did Montgomery. Ike, as supreme commander, consulted with his generals and decided to let the Soviets move in to take the capital of Germany.

The Russians lost 150,000 troops in their effort and later claimed half of Germany for their own, which included Berlin. But the German capital was divided into zones, occupied by four nations—the U.S., Great Britain, France, and the Soviet Union.

In the western part of Germany, elections were held, and the area was called the German Federal Republic. The Soviet's half of Germany was established and called the German Democratic Republic.

The Soviets plundered their half of Germany and took back to Russian everything of value that wasn't nailed down and, in many cases, removed the nails and took what they wanted. General Eisenhower and his successors took the opposite approach and helped the Germans rebuild not only their country but also their lives. You might say that was the beginning of what became known as the cold war.

Historians would explain it as a confrontation politically, ideologically, and economically between the Soviet Union and the United States and their allies.

By 1946, the Soviets had control either militarily or with Communist-controlled governments, of the satellite countries that extended from Finland in the north, down including Estonia, Latvia, Lithuania, Poland, Czechoslovakia, Hungary, Romania, Yugoslavia, and Albania.

Their next design was on taking control of Greece and Turkey. But President Truman, who had been at the Potsdam Conference in July and August of 1945, saw the Communists for what they were. He declared the United States foreign policy that the United States would act to prevent the overthrow of democratic institutions by any totalitarian government anywhere in the world.

It was really specifically aimed at Greece and Turkey. The Communists attempted to take Greece, but failed. The Truman Doctrine, as it would be called, gave military assistance and that was the first of many confrontations between the Soviet Union and the United States.

The United States did not simply sit back and react to Soviet advances. One of the greatest initiatives that were taken would become known as the Marshall Plan, proposed by the secretary of state and former general, George C. Marshall. His 1947 plan called for economic assistance to the tune of twelve and a half *billion* dollars over a four-year period. This greatly helped Western Germany and other Western European countries make remarkable progress in rebuilding their countries. The Soviets lost that battle but prepared itself for another confrontation.

In July 1948, the Soviets brought traffic to a halt and imposed a blockade of roads, rivers, and canals leading into Berlin, located in the Soviet Zone. The United States responded with the Berlin airlift that lasted until May 12, 1949 with over 275,000 flights of cargo planes, which brought needed food to the beleaguered Germans. That not only saved Berlin but the Soviets looked foolish in the eyes of the world.

The next attempt to expand their domination took place in Korea. Communist North Korea, with Soviet equipment and advisors, invaded South Korea in June 1950. The United States and their allies came to the aid of South Korea, and after three years of warfare which included the Communist Chinese, a cease-fire was declared in 1953, and nobody won. But once again, the advance of Communism was thwarted.

In 1956, the Soviet Union proceeded to put down a revolt in Hungary when students demonstrated a desire for democracy. In October 1957, a different form of confrontation took place. The Soviets put up the satellite, *Sputnik,* and were ready to claim outer space as their own. It took time and much expense, but over the next twelve years, the United States caught up with the Soviets and planted the U.S. Stars and Stripes on the moon in the name of peace on July 20, 1969.

During Eisenhower's presidency (1953-1961), Ike sent about seven hundred "advisors" to South Vietnam. Kennedy became president, and he increased the number to fifteen thousand advisors. When Lyndon Johnson won the election in 1964, he sent troops that eventually escalated the confrontation into the Vietnam War, and this conflict wasn't concluded until Nixon became president, and the United States finally pulled out with the last troops leaving in March 1973.

The United States did not lose the conflict in this Southeast Asian country. In the words of General William Westmoreland who commanded the U.S. forces from 1964 to 1968:

> By virtue of Vietnam, the U.S. held the line for 10 years and stopped the dominoes from falling.

In August 1961, the Soviets put up a wall dividing East Germany from the West. It would remain as a barrier to keep the East Germans from escaping to the West where it was economically a better place to live and work.

In October 1962, U.S. spy planes showed proof that ballistic missile launchpad were being constructed in Cuba, only ninety miles from the United States. President Kennedy stood up to the Soviet leader, Nikita Khrushchev, who eventually backed down and promised to remove the launchpads. America had never come closer to an atomic war than during that crisis, and John F. Kennedy will always be remembered for his tough stand.

A ray of hope emerged during President Gerald Ford's short time as president when he negotiated an arms-reduction agreement with the Soviet Union in 1974.

During Jimmy Carter's one term as president, he attempted to negotiate a strategic arms limitation treaty (SALT-II) with the Soviets, but when they invaded Afghanistan in December 1979, all talks were called off.

It seemed like very little progress had been made in thirty-four years (1945-1979) since the end of World War II. Would there *ever be peace* between two nations with so much power?

RONALD REAGAN AND MIKHAIL GORBECHEV EXCHANGE IDEAS

When Ronald Reagan took office in 1981, he attempted to meet and reason with the Soviet leaders, but with no success. President Reagan did not hold out much hope when the fourth Soviet leader assumed control on March 11, 1985, a few months short of forty years since the end of World War II in Europe. He had been rebuffed too many times.[39]

The year 1985 found Reagan corresponding with Mikhail Gorbachev on a regular basis. His first letter on March 12 expressed condolences on the death of Cherenkov and also suggested that Mikhail come to Washington.

Gorbachev's response was encouraging. He also wanted to meet Reagan, but not in the United States. His letter was more positive about the two systems of government reconciling their differences. Reagan at first didn't believe Gorbachev but was willing to work for a peaceful solution. Reagan believed that you bargain from a show of strength and worked to keep the MX program (Intercontinental ballistic missiles) as a way of pressuring Moscow when negotiations began in Geneva, Switzerland, later that year.[40]

That was encouraging, but an incident in East Germany, where an American Army officer was shot, brought forth another letter from Reagan. He protested the shooting, and Gorbachev issued orders that any further shooting was to stop.[41]

Further correspondence continued in June, September, and October, with each side explaining their side but at the same time listening to the other's side. The letters exchanged between Reagan and Gorbachev were frank but honest statements between both, and that was encouraging.

Prior to leaving for the summit at Geneva, Switzerland, Reagan spoke to the nation expressing hope of resolving the two nation's dilemma and promoting a lasting peace.

When Reagan left for Geneva, he brought with him a plan to live by during the summit. This plan was an old Russian adage:

Dovorey no provorey. (Trust, but verify.)[42]

The summit held formal meetings to discuss mutual concerns and problems. Reagan asked Gorbachev to meet on a one-to-one basis with only their interpreters. This was the beginning of a frank and honest exchange of ideas that would later lead to trusting one another and also the beginning of a true friendship.

It was at this first informal meeting that Reagan said to Gorbachev that they were two men, both from obscure rural hamlets with humble beginnings and were now leaders for two countries that could bring about World War III. Reagan added that they were the only two men in the world that could bring peace to the world.[43]

As Winston Churchill said on November 10, 1942, following the successful landing of American troops in North Africa and General Montgomery winning his way across North Africa to meet the Americans:

Now this is not the end. It is not even the beginning of the end. But it is, perhaps, the end of the beginning.[44]

The year 1986 found Reagan and Gorbachev exchanging letters following the summit in Geneva. Not much was accomplished. The United States had arrested and was holding a Russian spy named Gennadi Zakharov. In retaliation, the Russians arrested Nicolas Daniloff, a reporter for *U.S. News & World Report*. The two were eventually exchanged.[45]

In April, the leader of Libya, Muammar Quaddafi, ordered the firing of SAM (Surface-to-Air Missiles) at U.S naval aircraft many miles off the Libyan coast and had sent missile firing boats in the vicinity of the U.S. fleet that was practicing maneuvers. The United States responded by sinking the boats and knocking out the radar installations. Also that month, the nuclear reactor accident at Chernobyl, Russia, melted down, causing death, injury, and deformity.[46]

The United States received more and more evidence that the Soviet economy was in bad shape.[47] Mikhail Gorbachev suggested another summit, this time in Reykjavik, Iceland. The meeting was about reducing and eventually eliminating nuclear warheads of ballistic missiles. It looked like there was an agreement until Gorbachev said he would only approve the treaty if the SDI (Strategic Defense Initiative) were given up. The SDI had been an idea that a shield could be put in place to protect the United States from incoming ballistic missiles. It was still in the talking stage, but the Russians saw it as an offensive weapon rather than a defensive one. Reagan said he would never give up the idea, and the summit broke up.[48]

1987—A HISTORIC YEAR

On January 8, 1987, American Telephone and Telegraph settled the Justice Department antitrust lawsuit against it by agreeing to divest itself of the twenty-two Bell systems companies.

On March 28, 1987, when President Reagan was seventy-six years of age, he attended the annual Gridiron dinner, and in his speech said:

> It's true hard work never killed anybody, but I figure why take a chance.

This was in response that he was too old to be president.[49]

After another summit in Venice, Italy, President Reagan and the First Lady flew to West Berlin where he accepted an invitation to speak to an outdoor gathering at the Brandenburg Gate that divided West Berlin and East Berlin. The date was June 12, 1987. A West German official cautioned Reagan about what he would say, as the Soviets had listening devices that could eavesdrop on conversations. Ronald Reagan thought about history and spoke:

> Behind me stands a wall that encircles the free sectors of this city, part of
> a vast system of barriers that divide the entire continent of Europe.

From the Baltic, south those barriers cut across Germany in a gash of barbed wire, concrete, dog runs and guard towers.

Standing before the Brandenburg Gate, every man is a German, separated from his fellow men. Every man is a Berliner, forced to look upon a scar . . .

In this season of spring in 1945, the people of Berlin emerged from their air-raid shelters to find devastation. Thousands of miles away the people of the United States reached out to help. And in 1947, Secretary of State—as we have been told—George Marshall announced the creation of what would become known as the Marshall Plan. Speaking precisely forty years ago this month, he said, "Our policy is directed not against any country or doctrine, but against hunger, poverty, desperation, and chaos . . ."

In West Germany and here in Berlin, there took place an economic miracle . . . Your leader understood the practical importance of liberty—that just as truth can flourish only when the journalist is given freedom of speech, so prosperity can come about only when the farmer and businessman enjoy economic freedom.

Where four decades ago there was rubble, today in West Berlin there is the greatest industrial output of any city in Germany . . . Where city culture seemed to have been destroyed, today there are two great universities, orchestras and an opera, countless theaters, and museums. Where there was want, today there is abundance . . . From devastation, from utter ruin, you Berliners have, in freedom, rebuilt a city that once again ranks as one of the greatest on earth.

In the Communist world, we see failure, technological backwardness, declining standards of health, even want of the most basic kind—too little food . . . Freedom leads to prosperity. Freedom replaces the ancient hatred among the nations with comity and peace. Freedom is the victor. And now the Soviets themselves may, in a limited way, be coming to understand the importance of freedom. We hear much from Moscow about a new policy of reform and openness . . .

Are these the beginnings of profound changes in the Soviet state? Or are these token gestures, intended to raise false hopes in the West, or to strengthen the Soviet system without changing it? We welcome change and openness; for we believe that freedom and security go together, that the advance of human liberty can only strengthen the cause of peace.

There is one sign the Soviets can make that would be unmistakable, that would advance dramatically the cause of freedom and peace.

President Ronald Reagan—fortieth President of the United States—concluded his earth-shaking speech with these words:

> *General Secretary Gorbachev, if you seek peace, if you seek prosperity for the Soviet Union and Eastern Europe, if you seek liberalization: Come here to this gate! Mr. Gorbachev, open this gate! Mr. Gorbachev, TEAR DOWN THIS WALL!*[50]

Thomas Jefferson initiated the idea of the desire for freedom. Our Constitution guarantees that same freedom. The Monroe Doctrine assured the Western Hemisphere of the chance to gain and enjoy freedom. Lincoln made it possible for *all* Americans to have that same freedom. Woodrow Wilson's attempt to make the world safe for democracy was finally realized with the end of World War II, and the Marshall Plan made it possible for all countries to have freedom, except for the Union of Soviet Socialist Republics and the Eastern European countries they dominated.

Here was a seventy-six-year-old American telling the Soviets, that after over forty years of confrontations, to wake up and do the right thing. No one had ever said anything like it to the Soviet leaders before. Did it pay off? Read on, faithful reader.

The Soviet leader, Gorbachev, had announced a new program of *perestroika* and *glasnost*. While perestroika means renewal or renaissance, it came to mean an all-embracing modernization of the party and state. Glasnost means openness in economic and political decision making and open discussing of all questions and freedom of information.

He was serious about introducing major economic and political reform. There were to be free elections as well as political reform.

Seventy years after the Russian Revolution in 1917, Gorbachev made a blistering attack on Stalin and his ruthless slaughter of millions of Russian farmers in the Ukraine.[51]

October 1987 brought unforeseen problems to the United States. On October 19, the stock market had the largest one-day collapse of prices since 1914. That same month, it was discovered that a possible tumor had been located on the First Lady's left breast. She was operated on shortly, and it was successful. On October 26, Nancy Reagan's mother passed away in Phoenix.

The good news was that, in the words of George Schultz, secretary of state, he told President Reagan, "The Soviets blinked. Shevardnadze (president of the USSR), speaking for Gorbachev, is arriving Thursday for meeting on the INF (treaty) and plans for the summit."[52]

The summit was held in December. The Russians did not insist that Reagan drop his plans for the SDI. Under the agreement, 1,500 deployed Soviet nuclear warheads would be removed, and all Soviet ground-launched intermediate-range missiles in Europe, including the SS-20s, would be destroyed. On the United States side, all Pershing II and ground-launched missiles, with some four hundred deployed warheads, would be destroyed plus backup missiles on both sides. Part of the agreement called for permitted inspections to verify compliance. It was signed on December 8, 1987.[53] What a historic year!

The year 1988 was rather unremarkable. The stock market recovered, and the Iran-Contra scandal ended. On May 16, Surgeon General C. Everett Koop reported that nicotine was addictive in ways similar to heroine and cocaine. People who smoke could have told him that long before then.

On August 9, Reagan nominated Lauro Cavazos to be secretary of education. He would be the first Hispanic to serve in the president's cabinet.[54]

In November, George H.W. Bush was elected with 48,886,097 votes, while his opponent, Michael Dukakis received 41,809,074 votes. Bush's electoral votes were 426 to Dukakis's 111 electoral votes.

On November 9, 1989, nine months and nineteen days after leaving the presidency to the newly inaugurated George Bush, the Berlin Wall came tumbling down. A six-thousand-pound section of the wall would be sent to former President Ronald Reagan. It is on display at his presidential Library in California.

On October 3, 1990, East and West Germany were united once again. The cold war was over, and people could look back over the past forty-five years and see the many people who had contributed to this victory. As Margaret Thatcher explained, "President Reagan won the cold war without firing a shot."

On December 8, 1991, near Minsk, Russia, the presidents and prime ministers of Russia, Ukraine, and Belarus declared the USSR dissolved and found a Commonwealth of Independent States—CIS. On December 21, further agreement of eleven Soviet Republics agreed on formation of the Commonwealth of Independent States.

On December 31, 1991, the Soviet Union ceased to exist. When President Reagan gave his farewell address to the nation on January 11, 1989, he spoke words that summed it all up.

We meant to change a nation, and instead we changed a world.[55]

FREEDOM IS NOT FREE[56]

I watched the flag pass by one day.
It fluttered in the breeze,
A young Marine saluted it,
And then he stood at ease.

I looked at him in uniform
So young, so tall, so proud,
With hair cut square and eyes alert,
He'd stand out in any crowd.

I thought how many men like him
Had fallen through the years.
How many died on foreign soil?
How many mothers' tears?

How many pilots' planes shot down?
How many died at sea?
How many foxholes were soldiers' graves?
No, freedom is not free.

I heard the sound of "Taps" one night,
When everything was still.
I listened to the bugler play,
And felt a sudden chill.

I wondered just how many times
That "Taps" had meant "Amen",
When a flag has draped a coffin
Of a brother or a friend.

I thought of all the children,
Of the mothers and the wives,
Of fathers, son and husbands
With interrupted lives.

I thought about the graveyard
At the bottom of the sea.
Of unmarked graves in Arlington.
No, freedom is not free.
Cadet Major Kelly Strong
Air Force Junior ROTC
Homestead Senior High School
Homestead, Florida, 1988

A FINAL ANALYSIS

What final analysis can be said about American greatness? The Declaration of Independence was the beginning of a change in world history. It sought freedom from more than just the King of England. It sought freedom in thought as well as deed.

France followed suit by declaring its independence from the monarchy that had ruled France for generations. Later in the Western Hemisphere, countries, one by one, would gain their independence from the ruling countries in Europe.

After winning the struggle for independence, America hoped to put into effect the fulfillment of the dream for a government that would satisfy everyone. It was a start but left out the slaves and the women. Over a period and the Civil War, the "colored males" gained the right to vote. Fifty years later, women would be accorded the same right.

When the United States became recognized as a world power, it showed its determination in a number of ways. It challenged Spain and freed Cuba, the Philippines, and other islands.

World War I was a test for the United States. Originally neutral, it made the difference in the final determination to hopefully make the "world safe for democracy."

When the League of Nations failed, it brought about World War II. Again, the United States made the difference and gained the inventible victory, along with Great Britain and Russia.

With the GI Bill, more veterans entered college than ever before. This created a demand for higher education to provide for ever-increasing numbers, and today, college is considered as important and necessary as high school was before World War II.

Leaders like Truman, Eisenhower, Kennedy, and Reagan had the foresight and the courage to stand up for the rights of man, both here and abroad. They challenged the Communists in both word and deed. They helped to make the world safer for many people throughout the world.

Today there are more countries with a democratic form of government than ever before in the world, thanks to men of courage, and they came from the United States of America. Truly, it can be said, the world, as we know it, is because of American greatness.

EXPANDED TABLE OF CONTENTS

PART D *IMPREACHMENT, COMPLETING THE TRANSCONTINENTAL RAILROAD AND THE FIRST MAJOR SCANDALS* 1865-1877

CHAPTER XII 1865-1869 **ATTEMPTS AT RECONSTRUCTION**

PART I *JOHNSON, NIXON AND FORD 1963-1977*

CHAPTER XXVIII 1963-1969 **FULFILLMENT THEN FAILURE**

CHAPTER XXIX 1969-1974 **IF AT FIRST YOU DON'T SUCCEED, TRY, TRY AGAIN**

CHAPTER XXXIII 1981-1989 **MR. GORBACHEV,
TEAR DOWN THIS WALL**

APPENDIX

PRESIDENTIAL RESULTS OF ELECTORAL VOTES AND POPULAR VOTES

YEAR	PRESIDENTIAL CANDIDATES	ELECTORAL VOTES	PERCENT	POPULAR VOTES	PERCENT
1789	George Washington	69	100%	- a	-
1792	George Washington	132	100%	-	-
1796	John Adams	71	51%	-	-
	Thomas Jefferson	68	49%	-	-
1800	Thomas Jefferson	73	26.45%	-	-
	Aaron Burr	73	26.45%	-	
	John Adams	65	23.55%	-	-
	Charles Pinckney	64	23.19%	-	-
	John Jay	1			
1804	Thomas Jefferson	162	92%	-	-
	Charles Pinckney		14 8%	-	-
1808	James Madison	122	72%	-	-
	Charles Pinckney	47	28%	-	-
1812	James Madison	128	59%	-	-
	DeWitt Clinton	89	41%	-	-
1816	James Monroe	183	84%	-	-
	Rufus King	34	16%	-	-
1820	James Monroe	231	99.5%	-	-
	John Quincy Adams	1	.5%	-	-
1824	John Quincy Adams	84	32%	108,740	31%
	Andrew Jackson	99	38%	153,544	43%
	W.H. Crawford	41	16%	47,136	13%
	Henry Clay	37	14%	46,618	13%
		261	100%	356,038	100%
1828	Andrew Jackson	178	68%	647,231	56%
	John Quincy Adams	83	32%	509,097	44%
		261	100%	1,156,328	100%

YEAR	PRESIDENTIAL CANDIDATES	ELECTORAL VOTES	PERCENT	POPULAR VOTES	PERCENT
1832	Andrew Jackson	219	77%	687,507	56%
	Henry Clay	49	17%	530,189	44%
	Others	18	6%	unknown	-
		286	100%	1,217,696	100%
1836	Martin Van Buren	170	58%	762,678	51%
	William Henry Harrison	73	25%	550,816	37%
	Hugh Lawson	26	9%	146,107	9%
	Daniel Webster	14	5%	41,201	3%
	Willie Mangum	11	3%	unknown	
		294	100%	1,500,802	100%
1840	William Henry Harrison	234	80%	1,275,016	53%
	Martin Van Buren	60	20%	1,129,102	47%
		294	100%	2,404,178	100%

April 4, 1841-March 4, 1845 John Tyler served as president

YEAR	PRESIDENTIAL CANDIDATES	ELECTORAL VOTES	PERCENT	POPULAR VOTES	PERCENT
1844	James K. Polk	170	62%	1,337,243	51%
	Henry Clay	105	38%	1,299,062	49%
		275	100%	1,636,305	100%
1848	Zachary Taylor	163	56%	1,360,099	47%
	Lewis Cass	127	44%	1,220,544	43%
	Martin Van Buren	0	0%	291,263	10%
		290	100%	2,871,906	100%

July 9, 1850-March 4, 1853 Millard Fillmore served as president

YEAR	PRESIDENTIAL CANDIDATES	ELECTORAL VOTES	PERCENT	POPULAR VOTES	PERCENT
1852	Franklin Pierce	254	86%	1,601,474	54%
	Winfield Scott	42	14%	1,386,578	46%
		296	100%	2,988,052	100%
1856	James Buchanan	174	59%	1,838,169	45%
	John Fremont	114	39%	1,341,264	33%
	Millard Fillmore	8	2%	874,534	22%
		296	100%	4,053,967	100%

YEAR	PRESIDENTIAL CANDIDATES	ELECTORAL VOTES	PERCENT	POPULAR VOTES	PERCENT
1860	Abraham Lincoln	180	59%	1,866,452	40%
	John Breckinridge	72	24%	847,953	18%
	John Bell	39	13%	590,631	13%
	Stephen Douglas	12	4%	1,375,157	29%
		303	100%	4,680,193	100%
1864	Abraham Lincoln	212	91%	2,213,635	55%
	George McClellan	21	9%	1,805,237	45%
		233	100%	4,018,872	100%

April 15, 1865-March 9, 1869 Andrew Johnson served as president

YEAR	PRESIDENTIAL CANDIDATES	ELECTORAL VOTES	PERCENT	POPULAR VOTES	PERCENT
1868	Ulysses S. Grant	214	73%	3,012,833	53%
	Horatio Seymour	80	27%	2,703,249	47%
		294	100%	5,716,082	100%
1872	Ulysses S. Grant	286	82%	3,597,132	56%
	Horace Greeley (died after election)			2,834,079	44%
	Other Candidates	63	18%	35,097	0%
		349	100%	6,466,310	100%
1876	Rutherford B. Hayes	185	50.13%	4,036,298	48%
	Samuel Tilden	184	49.87%	4,300,590	52%
		369	100%	8,336,888	100%
1880	James Garfield	214	58%	4,454,416	50.05%
	Winfield Hancock	155	42%	4,444,952	49.95%
		369	100%	8,899,368	100%

September 20, 1881-March 4, 1885 Chester A. Arthur served as president

YEAR	PRESIDENTIAL CANDIDATES	ELECTORAL VOTES	PERCENT	POPULAR VOTES	PERCENT
1884	Grover Cleveland	219	55%	4,874,986	50.11%
	James Blaine	182	45%	4,851,981	49.89%
		401	100%	9,726,967	100%
1888	Benjamin Harrison	233	58%	5,444,337	49.56%
	Grover Cleveland	168	42%	5,540,309	50.44%
		401	100%	10,984,646	100%

YEAR	PRESIDENTIAL CANDIDATES	ELECTORAL VOTES	PERCENT	POPULAR VOTES	PERCENT
1892	Grover Cleveland	277	62%	5,556,918	47%
	Benjamin Harrison	145	33%	5,176,108	44%
	James Weaver	22	5%	1,041,028	9%
		444	100%	11,774,054	100%
1896	William McKinley	271	61%	7,104,779	52%
	William Jennings Bryan	176	39%	6,509,052	48%
		447	100%	13,613,831	100%
1900	William McKinley	292	65%	7,207,923	53%
	William Jennings Bryan	155	35%	6,358.138	47%
		447	100%	13,566,061	100%

September 14, 1901-March 4, 1905 Theodore Roosevelt served as president

YEAR	PRESIDENTIAL CANDIDATES	ELECTORAL VOTES	PERCENT	POPULAR VOTES	PERCENT
1904	Theodore Roosevelt	336	71%	7,623,486	60%
	Alton Parker	140	29%	5,077,911	40%
		476	100%	12,701,397	100%
1908	William Howard Taft	321	66%	7,678,908	54.5%
	William Jennings Bryan	162	34%	6,409,104	45.5%
		483	100%	14,088,012	100%
1912	Woodrow Wilson	435	82%	6,293,454	45%
	Theodore Roosevelt	88	17%	4,119,538	30%
	William Howard Taft	8	1%	3,484,980	25%
		531	100%	13,897,972	100%
1916	Woodrow Wilson	277	52%	9,129,606	52%
	Charles Evans Hughes	254	48%	8,538,221	48%
		531	100%	17,667,827	100%
1920	Warren Harding	404	76%	16,152,200	64%
	James Cox	127	24%	9,147,353	36%
		531	100%	25,299,553	100%

August 3, 1923-March 4, 1925 Calvin Coolidge served as president

YEAR	PRESIDENTIAL CANDIDATES	ELECTORAL VOTES	PERCENT	POPULAR VOTES	PERCENT
1924	Calvin Coolidge	382	72%	15,725,016	54%
	John Davis	136	26%	8,386,503	29%
	Robert La Follett	13	2%	4,822,856	17%
		531	100%	8,934,375	100%
1928	Herbert Hoover	444	84%	21,392,190	59%
	Alfred Smith	87	16%	15,016,443	41%
		531	100%	36,408,633	100%
1932	Franklin D. Roosevelt	472	89%	22,821,857	59%
	Herbert Hoover	59	11%	15,761,845	41%
		531	100%	38,583,702	100%
1936	Franklin D. Roosevelt	523	98%	27,476,673	62%
	Alfred Landon	8	2%	16,679,583	38%
		531	100%	44,156,256	100%
1940	Franklin D. Roosevelt	449	85%	27,243,466	55%
	Wendell Willkie	82	15%	22,304,755	45%
		531	100%	49,548,221	100%
1944	Franklin D. Roosevelt	432	81%	25,602,505	54%
	Thomas Dewey	99	19%	22,006,278	46%
		531	100%	47,608,783	100%

April 12, 1945-January 20, 1949 Harry S. Truman served as president

YEAR	PRESIDENTIAL CANDIDATES	ELECTORAL VOTES	PERCENT	POPULAR VOTES	PERCENT
1948	Harry S. Truman	303	57%	24,105,695	51%
	Thomas Dewey	189	36%	21,969,170	46.5%
	J. Strom Thurmond	39	7%	1,169,021	2.5%
		531	100%	47,243,886	100%
1952	Dwight D. Eisenhower	442	83%	33,778,964	55%
	Adlai Stevenson	89	17%	27,314,992	45%
		531	100%	61,093,956	100%

YEAR	PRESIDENTIAL CANDIDATES	ELECTORAL VOTES	PERCENT	POPULAR VOTES	PERCENT
1956	Dwight D. Eisenhower	457	86%	35,581,003	58%
	Adlai Stevenson	73	14%	25,738,765	42%
		530	100%	61,319,768	100%
1960	John F. Kennedy	303	58%	34,227,096	50.09%
	Richard M. Nixon	219	42%	34,107,647	49.91%
		522	100%	68,334,743	100%

November 22, 1963-January 20, 1965 Lyndon B. Johnson served as president

YEAR	PRESIDENTIAL CANDIDATES	ELECTORAL VOTES	PERCENT	POPULAR VOTES	PERCENT
1964	Lyndon B. Johnson	486	90%	43,167,895	61%
	Barry Goldwater	52	10%	27,175,770	39%
		538	100%	70,343, 100%	
1968	Richard M. Nixon	301	56%	31,710,470	43.5%
	Hubert Humphrey	191	35.5%	31,209,677	42.9%
	George Wallace	46	8.5%	9,893,952	13.6%
		538	100%	72,814,099	100%
1972	Richard M. Nixon	520	97%	47,198,459	62%
	George Mc Govern	17	3%	29,084,726	38%
		537	100%	76,193,185	100%

August 9, 1974-January 20, 1977 Gerald R. Ford served as president

YEAR	PRESIDENTIAL CANDIDATES	ELECTORAL VOTES	PERCENT	POPULAR VOTES	PERCENT
1976	Jimmy Carter	297	55%	40,108,459	51%
	Gerald R. Ford	240	45%	39,422,671	49%
		537	100%	79,531,130	100%
1980	Ronald Reagan	483	91%	43,904,153	51.6%
	Jimmy Carter	49	9%	35,483,883	41.7%
	John Anderson	0	0%	5,720,060	6.7%
		532	100%	85,108,096	100%
1984	Ronald Reagan	525	97.6%	54,455,075	59%
	Walter Mondale	13	2.4%	37,577,185	41%
		538	100%	92,032,260	100%

YEAR	PRESIDENTIAL CANDIDATES	ELECTORAL VOTES	PERCENT	POPULAR VOTES	PERCENT
1988	George H.W. Bush	426	79%	48,886,097	54%
	Michael Dukakis	111	21%	41,809,074	46%
		537	100%	90,695,171	100%
1992	William Clinton	370	69%	44,908,233	43.5%
	George H.W. Bush	168	31%	39,102,282	37.9%
	H. Ross Perot	0	0%	19,221,433	18.6%
		538	100%	103,231,948	100%
1996	William Clinton	379	70%	45,590,703	49.95%
	Robert Dole	159	30%	37,816,307	41.43%
	H. Ross Perot	0	0%	7,866,284	8.62%
		538	100%	91,273,294	100%
2000	George W. Bush	271	50.5%	50,456,160	48.2%
	Albert Gore	266	49.5%	50,996,064	48.7%
	Ralph Nadar	0	0%	2,883,000	2.7%
	Pat Buchanan	0	0%	449,000	.4%
		537	100%	104,784,224	100%
2004	George W. Bush	286	53%	59,017,382	51.57%
	John F; Kerry	252	47%	55,435,808	48.43%
	Ralph Nadar	0	0%	not sure	0%
		538	100%	114,453,190	100%

a Popular votes were not counted until 1824

PERSONAL FACTS ABOUT UNITED STATES PRESIDENTS

Name of President	Life Span	Years President	Military	Age	Times Married	Age Husband	Age Wife	No. of children
George Washington	1731-1799	1789-1797	Yes	57	1	27	27	2
John Adams	1735-1826	1797-1801	No	61	1	29	20	5
Thomas Jefferson	1743-1826	1801-1809	No	57	1	29	24	7
James Madison	1751-1836	1809-1817	No	57	1	43	26	1
James Monroe	1758-1831	1817-1825	Yes	58	1	28	18	3
John Quincy Adams	1767-1848	1825-1829	No	57	1	30	22	4
Andrew Jackson	1767-1848	1829-1837	Yes	61	1	24	24	1
Martin Van Buren	1782-1862	1837-1841	No	54	1	25	24	5
William Harrison	1773-1841	1841-	Yes	68	1	22	20	10
John Tyler	1790-1862	1841-1845	No	51	2	23;54	23;24	7;7
James K. Polk	1795-1849	1845-1849	No	49	1	29	21	0
Zachary Taylor	1784-1850	1849-1850	Yes	64	1	26	22	6
Millard Fillmore	1800-1874	1850-1853	No	50	2	26;58	28;45	2
Franklin Pierce	1804-1869	1853-1857	Yes	48	1	30	28	3
James Buchanan	1791-1868	1857-1861	No	65	0	-	-	0
Abraham Lincoln	1809-1865	1861-1865	Yes	52	1	33	24	4
Andrew Johnson	1808-1875	1865-1869	No	56	1	19	17	5
Ulysses S. Grant	1822-1885	1869-1877	Yes	46	1	26	22	4
Rutherford Hayes	1822-1893	1877-1881	Yes	54	1	30	21	8
James Garfield	1831-1881	1881-	Yes	49	1	27	26	7
Chester Arthur	1829-1886	1881-1885	No	51	1	30	22	3
Grover Cleveland	1837-1886	1885-89;93-97	No	47	1	49	22	5
Benjamin Harrison	1833-1901	1889-1893	Yes	55	2	20;63	21;38	2;1
William McKinley	1843-1901	1897-1901	Yes	54	1	28	24	2
Theodore Roosevelt	1858-1919	1901-1909	Yes	42	2	22;28	19;25	1;5
William H. Taft	1857-1930	1909-1913	No	51	1	29	25	3
Woodrow Wilson	1857-1924	1913-1921	No	56	2	29;59	25;43	3
Warren Harding	1865-1923	1921-1923	No	55	1	26	31	0
Calvin Coolidge	1872-1933	1923-1929	No	51	1	33	26	2
Herbert Hoover	1874-1964	1929-1933	No	54	1	25	24	2
Franklin Roosevelt	1882-1945	1933-1945	No	51	1	23	21	6
Harry S. Truman	1884-1972	1945-1953	Yes	60	1	35	34	1
Dwight Eisenhower	1890-1969	1953-1961	Yes	62	1	26	20	2
John F. Kennedy	1917-1963	1961-1963	Yes	43	1	36	34	3
Lyndon B. Johnson	1908-1973	1963-1969	Yes	55	1	26	22	2
Richard M. Nixon	1913-1994	1969-1974	Yes	56	1	27	28	2

Gerald R. Ford	1913-2007	1974-1977	Yes	61	1	35	30	4
Jimmy Carter	1924-	1977-1981	Yes	52	1	22	18	4
Ronald Reagan	1911-2004	1981-1989	Yes	69	2	29;41	26;31	2;3
George H.W. Bush	1924-	1989-1993	Yes	64	1	21	20	6
William Clinton	1946-	1993-2001	No	46	1	29	28	1
George W. Bush	1946-	2001-2008	Yes	54	1	31	31	2

ELECTIONS WITH WIDE ELECTORAL VOTE MARGINS

Year	Presidential Candidate	Percent Margin
1789	George Washington	100%
1792	George Washington	100%
1820	James Monroe	99.56%
1936	Franklin D. Roosevelt	98.49%
1984	Ronald Reagan	97.58%
1972	Richard M. Nixon	96.83%
1804	Thomas Jefferson	92.04%
1864	Abraham Lincoln	90.98%
1980	Ronald Reagan	90.78%
1964	Lyndon B. Johnson	90.33%
1932	Franklin D. Roosevelt	88.88%
1956	Dwight D. Eisenhower	86.22%
1852	Franklin Pierce	85.81%
1940	Franklin D. Roosevelt	84.55%
1816	James Monroe	84.33%
1928	Herbert Hoover	83.61%
1952	Dwight D. Eisenhower	83.23%
1872	Ulysses S. Grant	81.95%
1912	Woodrow Wilson	81.92%
1944	Franklin D. Roosevelt	81.00%
1840	William Henry Harrison	79.59%
1988	George Herbert Bush	79.32%
1832	Andrew Jackson	76.57%
1920	Warren Harding	76.08%
1868	Ulysses S. Grant	72.78%
1808	James Madison	72.18%
1924	Calvin Coolidge	71.94%
1904	Theodore Roosevelt	70.59%
1996	William Clinton	70.45%
1992	William Clinton	68.77%
1828	Andrew Jackson	68.20%
1908	William Howard Taft	66.46%
1900	William McKinley	65.32%
1892	Grover Cleveland	62.39%
1844	James K. Polk	61.82%
1896	William McKinley	60.63%

POPULAR VOTE MARGIN BY PER CENT

Year	Presidential Candidate	Percent Margin
1920	Warren G. Harding	64%
1936	Franklin D. Roosevelt	62%
1972	Richard M. Nixon	62%
1964	Lyndon B. Johnson	61%
1904	Theodore Roosevelt	60%
1928	Herbert Hoover	59%
1932	Franklin D. Roosevelt	59%
1984	Ronald Reagan	59%
1956	Dwight D. Eisenhower	58%
1872	Ulysses S. Grant	56%
1828; 1832	Andrew Jackson	56%
1864	Abraham Lincoln	55%
1952	Dwight D. Eisenhower	55%
1940	Franklin D. Roosevelt	55%
1908	William Howard Taft	54.5%
1988	George Herbert Bush	54%
1944	Franklin D. Roosevelt	54%
1852	Franklin Pierce	54%
1924	Calvin Coolidge	54%
1900	William McKinley	53%
1868	Ulysses S. Grant	53%
1840	William Henry Harrison	53%
1896	William McKinley	52%
1916	Woodrow Wilson	52%
1980	Ronald Reagan	51.6%
2004	George Walker Bush	51.57%
1948	Harry S. Truman	51.02%
1976	Jimmy Carter	50.96%
1960	John F. Kennedy	50.09%
1880	James Garfield	50.05%
1996	William Clinton	49.95%
1888	Benjamin Harrison	49.56%
1876	Rutherford B. Hayes	48.41%
2000	George Walker Bush	48.15%
1848	Zachary Taylor	47.35%

POPULAR VOTE MARGIN BY PER CENT (continued)

Year	Presidential Candidate	Percent Margin
1892	Grover Cleveland	47.19%
1856	James Buchanan	45.34%
1912	Woodrow Wilson	45.28%
1968	Richard M. Nixon	43.55%
1992	William Clinton	43.50%
1860	Abraham Lincoln	39.88%
1824	John Quincy Adams	30.54%

MARGIN OF VICTORY BY A MILLION OR MORE POPULAR VOTES

Year	Presidential Candidates	Margin over Rival
1972	Richard Nixon vs. George McGovern	18,023,733
1984	Ronald Reagan vs. Walter Mondale	16,877,890
1964	Lyndon B. Johnson vs. Barry Goldwater	15,992,125
1936	Franklin D. Roosevelt vs. Alfred Landon	10,797,090
1956	Dwight D. Eisenhower vs. Adlai Stevenson	9,842,238
1980	Ronald Reagan vs. Jimmy Carter and John Anderson	8,420,270
1996	William Clinton vs. Robert Dole and H. Ross Perot	7,774,396
1924	Calvin Coolidge vs. John Davis	7,338,513
1988	George Herbert Bush vs. Michael Dukakis	7,077,023
1932	Franklin D. Roosevelt vs. Herbert Hoover	7,060.012
1920	Warren Harding vs. James Cox	7,004,847
1952	Dwight D. Eisenhower vs. Adlai Stevenson	6,463,092
1928	Herbert Hoover vs. Alfred Smith	6,375,747
1992	William Clinton vs. George Herbert Bush and H. Ross Perot	5,805,951
1940	Franklin D. Roosevelt vs. Wendell Willkie	4,938,711
1944	Franklin D. Roosevelt vs. Thomas Dewey	3,596,227
2004	George Walker Bush vs. John F. Kerry and Ralph Nanda	3,581574
1904	Theodore Roosevelt vs. Alton Parker	2,545,575
1912	Woodrow Wilson vs. Theodore Roosevelt and William Taft	2,173,916
1948	Harry S. Truman vs. Thomas Dewey and Strom Thurmond	2,136,525
1976	Jimmy Carter vs. Gerald Ford	1,554,476
1908	William Howard Taft vs. William Jennings Bryan	1,269,804
1860	Abraham Lincoln vs. John Breckinridge, John Bell and Stephen Douglas	1,018,499

CLOSE ELECTIONS IN ELECTORAL VOTES
AND/OR POPULAR VOTES

Year	Candidates	Electoral Votes	Popular Votes
1796	John Adams	71	-
	vs.		
	Thomas Jefferson	68	-
1800	Thomas Jefferson	73	-
	vs.		
	Aaron Burr	73	-
1876	Rutherford B. Hayes	185	4,036,298
	vs.		
	Samuel Tilden	184	4,300,590
2000	George W. Bush	271	50,456,167
	vs.		
	Albert Gore	266	50,996,064
1916	Woodrow Wilson	277	9,129,606
	vs.		
	Charles Evans Hughes	254	8,538,221
2004	George W. Bush	286	59,017,382
	vs.		
	John F. Kerry	252	55,435,808
1844	James K. Polk	170	1,337,243
	vs.		
	Henry Clay	105	1,299,062
1880	James Garfield	214	4,454,416
	vs.		
	Winfield Hancock	155	4,444,952
1884	Grover Cleveland	219	4,874,986
	vs.		
	James Blaine	182	4,851,981

Year	Candidates	Electoral Votes	Popular Votes
1888	Benjamin Harrison vs.	233	5,444,337
	Grover Cleveland	168	5,540,309
1960	John F. Kennedy vs.	303	34,227,096
	Richard M. Nixon	219	34,107,647
1976	Jimmy Carter vs.	297	40,977,147
	Gerald Ford	240	39,422,671
1840	William Henry Harrison vs.	234	1,275,016
	Martin Van Buren	60	1,129,102

POPULATION GROWTH OF THE UNITED STATES
FROM 1790 TO 2000

Year	Population	Percent Increase
1790	3,929,219	
1800	5,308,483	35.1%
1810	7,239,881	36.4%
1820	9,638,453	33.15%
1830	12,866,020	33.5%
1840	17,069,453	32.7%
1850	23,292,856	35.9%
1860	31,443,325	35.6%
1870	39,818,449	26.6%
1880	50,189,209	26.0%
1890	62,979,766	25.5%
1900	76,212,168	21.0%
1910	92,228,496	21.0%
1920	106,021,537	15.0%
1930	123,202,624	16.2%
1940	132,164,569	7.3%
1950	151,325,758	14.5%
1960	179,323,175	18.5%
1970	203,320,031	13.4%
1980	226,542,199	11.4%
1990	248,718,302	9.8%
2000	281,422,509	13.1%

YEAR 2000 POPULATION BY ANCESTRY

ANCESTRY	POPULATION
GERMAN	42,885,000
IRISH	30,594,000
ENGLISH	24,515,000
ITALIAN	15,724,000
POLISH	8,977,000
FRENCH	8,325,000
SCOTTISH	4,891,000
TOTAL	135,911,000

YEAR 2000 POPULATION BY RACE

WHITE	228,104,000
BLACK	35,704,000
HISPANIC	35,306,000
ASIAN	10,589,000
TWO MORE MIXED RACES	3,898,000
AMERICAN INDIANS AND ALASKA NATIVES	2,644,000
NATIVE HAWAIIAN	464,000
TOTAL	281,422,000

NOTES

CHAPTER ONE DISCOVERIES AND EXPLORATION

1. Richard Webster, Managing Editor. *The Volume Library.* An Encyclopedia of Practical and Cultural Information. (New York: Educator's Association, Inc. 1944), p. 1479.
2. David Colbert, (ed.). *Eyewitness to America.* (New York: Pantheon Books, 1997), p. 4.
3. Helen Fern Daringer and Anne Thaxter Eaton. *The Poet's Craft.* (New York: World Book Company, 1935), pp. 67-68.
4. Webster. *The Volume Library.* p. 656.
5. *Ibid.*
6. *Ibid.*
7. *Ibid.,* p. 657.
8. *Ibid.*
9. *Ibid.*

CHAPTER TWO SPANISH AND FRENCH MISTAKES

1. Joseph S. Schlarman, Ph. D. *From Quebec to New Orleans; the story of the French In America . . . Fort de Chartes.* (Bellville, Illinois, Buechler Publishing Company. 1929). p. 42.

CHAPTER THREE ENGLISH COLONIZATION AND GROWING DISSATISFACTION

1. Webster. *The Volume Library.* p. 657.
2. *Ibid.*
3. *Ibid.,* p. 661.
4. Henry Steele Commager and Milton Cantor. *Documents of American History.* Volume I to 1898. (New Jersey: Prentice Hall, 1988), pp. 15-16.
5. The Colonial Williamsburg Foundation 2004 Calendar, Williamsburg, Virginia, 2003

6. Webster. *The Volume Library.* p. 59.
7. Commager. *Documents of American History.* p. 15.
8. Philip Van Doren Stern (ed.). *The Pocket Book of America.* (New York: Pocket Books, Inc., 1942). pp. 282-283.
9. Webster. *The Volume Library.* p. 658.
10. *Ibid.*
11. *Ibid.,* pp. 657-658.
12. *Ibid.*
13. *Ibid.*
14. *Ibid.*
15. *Ibid.*
16. *Ibid.,* p. 661.
17. *Ibid.,* p. 658.
18. Commager. *Documents of American History.* pp 31-32.
19. Webster. *The Volume Library.* p. 661.
20. *Ibid.*
21. Commager. *Documents of American History.* p. 37.
22. Webster. *The Volume Library.* p. 661.
23. Colbert. *Eyewitness to America.* pp. 41-44.
24. *Ibid.*
25. Commager. *Documents of American H9story.* pp. 43-45.
26. John Grafton. *The American Revolution.* Picture Source Book. (New York: Dover Publications, Inc., 1975), p. 13.
27. Webster. *The Volume Library.* p. 661.

CHAPTER FOUR. STEPS TO REBELLION

1. Duncan Emrich. *American Folk Poetry.* (Boston: Little, Brown and Company. 1974), p. 411.
2. Webster. *The Volume Library.* p. 662.
3. *Ibid.*
4. *Ibid.*
5. John Bartlett. *Familiar Quotations.* Fourteenth Edition. Emily Moison Beck, Editor. (Boston: Little, Brown and Company, 1968.) p. 464.
6. John Bartlett. *Familiar Quotations.* Fifteenth Edition. Pp. 419-420.
7. Webster. *The Volume Library.* p. 662.
8. Bartlett. *Familiar Quotations.* Fifteenth Edition. pp. 58-60.
9. Webster. *The Volume Library.* pp. 1443-44.
10. Bartlett. *Familiar Quotations.* p. 380.
11. Webster. *The Volume Library.* p. 664.
12. *Ibid.,* p. 1521.
13. Bartlett. *Familiar Quotations.* p. p. 465

14. William L. Langer. *An Encyclopedia of World History.* (Boston: Houghton Mifflin Company, 1968.) p. 552.

CHAPTER FIVE. THE WAR FOR INDEPENDENCE

1. Stern (ed.) *The Pocket book of America.* pp. 287-291.
2. Bartlett. *Familiar Quotations.* p. 455.
3. Stern (ed.) *The Pocket book of America.* pp. 286-287.
4. Bartlett. *Familiar Quotations.* p. 446.
5. Colbert. *Eyewitness to America.* pp. 79-81.
6. Webster. *The Volume Library.* p. 654.
7. Commager. *Documents of American History.* pp. 100-103.
8. Bartlett. *Familiar Quotations.* p. 423.
9. *Ibid.,* p. 461.
10. *Ibid.,* p. 484.
11. Bartlett, *Familiar Quotations.* Pp. 466-467.
12. Webster. *The Volume Library.* pp. 664; 667. Also: Phoebe Strong Cowen, *The The Herkimers and Schuylers.* An Historical Sketch of Two Families. (Albany, New York: Juel Munsell's Sons Publishers, 1903). pp. 32-33.
13. Stern. (ed.) *The Pocket Book of America.* p. 381.
14. Webster. *The Volume Library.* p. 1447.
15. *Ibid.,* p. 1573.
16. *Ibid.,* p. 1506.
17. *Ibid.,* p. 1512.
18. *Ibid.,* p. 1506.
19. *Ibid.,* p. 1537.
20. A.J. Langguth. *Patriots.* The Men Who Started the American Revolution, (New York: Simon and Schuster, 1988). p. 484
21. Webster. *The Volume Library.* p. 1477.
22. Bartlett. *Familiar Quotations.* p. 476.
23. Norman Forester (ed.). *American Poetry and Prose.* (Boston: Houghton Mifflin Company. 1947). p. 264.
24. Webster. *The Volume Library.* p. 1552.
25. Kenneth Seeman Giniger (ed.). *America, America, America.*(New York: Franklin Watts, 1957). p. 308

CHAPTER SIX STARTING A NEW NATION

1. Commager. *Documents of American History.* pp. 128-132.
2. *Ibid.,* pp. 132-134.
3. *Ibid.,* pp. 136-138.
4. *Ibid.,* p. 145.

5. In Philadelphia, a Mrs. Powell asked Dr. Franklin, "Well, Doctor what have we got a republic or a monarchy? A republic replied the Doctor if you can keep it." Recorded by James McHenry, one of Washington's aides, published in *American Historical Review,* XI (1906) 618. Cited in Bartlett's *Familiar Quotations. 16ᵗʰ Ed.* (Boston: Little, Brown and Company, 1992). p. 310.

6. *Webster's Seventh New Collegiate Dictionary.* (Springfield, Massachusetts. G & C Merriam Company, 1971). p. 668.

7. Commager. *Documents of American History.* p. 100-103.

8. John C. Bogle. *The Constitution of the United States.* (Philadelphia, Pennsylvania, National Constitution Center).

9. Commager. *Documents of American History.* p. 139.

10. *Ibid.,* p. 148.

11. *Ibid.,* p. 145.

12. *Ibid.,* p. 146.

13. Bartlett/ *Familiar Quotations.* p. 461.

14. Commager. *Documents of American History.* pp. 165-168

15. *Ibid.,* p. 146.

16. *Ibid.,* pp, 165-168.

17. *Ibid.,* pp. 169-175/

18. *Ibid.*

19. Bartlett. *Familiar Quotations.* p. 461

20. Emrich, (ed.). *American Folk Poetry.* p. 433. Composed by Stephen Foster.

21. Stern, (ed.) *The Pocket Book of America.*

CHAPTER SEVEN EXPANSION AND GROWTH

1. Commager. *Documetns of American History.* pp. 146-147.

2. Webster. *The Volume Library.* p. 670.

3. *Ibid., p.671.*

4. John P. Dunnell. *The Illinois and Michigan Canal and The Old Nortwest.* Unpublished Master's Thesis. (Normal: Illinois State University, 1955). p 28.

5. Ambrose, Stephen E. *Undaunted Courage.* (New York: Simon & Schuster, 1996). p. 68.

6. *Ibid., p.70.*

7. Reuben G. Thuwaites (ed.). *Jesuit Relations and Allied Documents.* (Cleveland: Burrows brothrs, 1903). XXII, p. 277.

8. Ambrose. *Undaunted Courage.* p. 76.

9. *Ibid.,* pp. 117-121.

10. Colbert, *Eyewitness to America,* p. 111.

11. *Ibid.,* p. 112.

12. Ambrose. *Undaunted Courage.* pp. 404-405.

13. Webster. *The Volume Library.* p. 671.

14. *Ibid.*

15. *Ibid.,* p. 672.

16. Emrich. (Ed,) *American Folk Poetry.* pp. 434-435.

17. Bartlett. *Familiar Quotations.* p. 553.

18. Webster. *The Volume Library.* p. 671.

19. Encyclopedia Britannica. *The* Annals *of America.* Vol. 4. 1797-1828. Chicago: Encyclopedia Britannica, Inc. 1976). Pp. 353-354.

20. *Ibid.*

21. Emrich. *American Folk Poetry.* pp. 439-440.

22. Dean Dorrell. *Eulogy for Nancy Hanks Lincoln.* Presented at the Boyhood National Memorial, February 10, 2002.

23. Commager. *Documents of American History.* p. 131,

24. Dunnell. *The Illinois and Michigan Canal and The Old Northwest.* pp. 20-21.

25. Webster. *The Volume Library.* p. 673.

26. Commager. *Documents of American History.* pp. 235-237.

27. Webster. *The Volume Library.* p. 673.

28. Langer (ed.). *An Encyclopedia of World History.* p. 812.

29. Webster. *The Volume Library.* p. 1320.

30. *Ibid.,* p. 1506.

31. Bartlett. *Familiar Quotation.* p. 616.

32. *Ibid.,* p. 10

33. Colbert. *Eyewitness to America.* pp. 149-151.

34. Webster. *The Volume Library.* p. 843.

35. Hazel Fellman (ed.). *The Best Loved Poems of the American People.* (New York: Garden City books, 1936). p. 432

36. Langer. *An Encyclopedia of World History.* p. 813.

37. Webster. *The Volume Library,* p. 1320.

38. *Ibid.,* p. 677.

39. *Ibid.,* p. 1320.

40. Commager. *Documents of American History.* pp. 311-312.

41. Gorton Carruth and Eugine Ehrlich (eds.). *The Harper Book of American Quotations.* (New York: Harper & Row, Publishers, 1988). p 204.

42. Bartlett. *Familiar Quotations.* _____

43. Howard Zinn. *A People's History of the United States.* (New York: Harper Colins Publisher 2003). p. 226.

44. Henry H. Hamilton. *The Epic of Chicago.* (Chicago: Willett, Clark and Company, 1932). p 251.

45. Dunnell. *The Illinois and Michigan Canal and The Old Northwest.* p. 86.

46. Commager. *Documents of American History.* pp. 315-317.

47. Horace Mann from *Common School Journal.*

CHAPTER EIGHT ATTEMPTS AT RECONCILIATION AND THE ROAD TO WAR

1. Emrich. *American Folk Poetry.* pp. 560-561.
2. Langer. *An Enclyclodedia of Word History.* p. 606.
3. Webster. *The Volume Library.* pp. 678-679.
4. Kenneth C. Davis. *Don't Know Much About the Civl War.*(New York: William Morrow and Company, Inc., 1996), pp. 178-180.
5. Webster. *The Volume Library.* p. 679.
6. *Ibid.*
7. Commager. *Documents of American History.* pp. 327-329.
8. Webster. *The Volume Library.* p. 679.
9. *Ibid.*
10. Commager. *Documents of American History.* pp. 329-331.
11. Allan Nevins. *Ordeal of the Union: A House Dividing 1852-1857.* New York: Charles Scriber's Sons, 1947). p. 450.
12. Webster. *The Volume Library.* p. 1578.
13. *Ibid.,* p. 1320.
14. *Ibid.,* p. 1467.
15. Commager. *Documents of American History.* pp. 339-345.
16. *Ibid.,* p. 147.
17. Bartlett. *Familiar Quotations.* p. 556., 1852
18. Zinn. *A People's History of the United States.* p. 383.
19. Webster. *The Volume Library.* p. 1543.
20. Bartlett. *Familiar Quotations.* p. 635.
21. Nevins. *The Emergence of Lincoln: Douglas, Buchanan, and Party Chaos.* 1857-1859. (New York: Charles Scribner's Sons, 1950). p. 356.
22. *Ibid.,* pp. 359-361.
23. Bartlett. *Familiar Qutatioins.* p. 635.
24. Nevins. *The Emerigence of Lincoln, 1857-1859.* pp. 374-376.
25. Bartlettt. *Familiar Quotations.* p. 635.
26. *Ibid.* p. 641.
27. Nevins. *The Emergence of Lincoln: 1857-1859.* pp. 378-390.
28. *Ibid.,* p. 381.
29. *Ibid.,* p. 382.
30. Nevins. *The Emergence of Lincoln: Proglogue to the Civil War.* 1859-1861 p.312.
31. *Ibid.*
32. Stephen E. Ambrose. *Nothing Like It in the World.* The Men Who Built the Transcontinental Railroad. 1863-1869. (New York: Simon & Schuster, 2000). p. 23.
33. Webster. *The Volume Library.* p. 1466.
34. Bartlett. *Familiar Quotations.* 16th Ed. p. 448
35. Nevins. *The Emergence of Lincoln: Prologue to the Civil War.* 1859-1861. p 222.

36. *Ibid.*, pp. 259-260.
37. Webster. *The Volume Library.* p. 1321.
38. Commager. *Documents of American History.* p. 372.
39. *Ibid.*, p. 369.
40. Langer. *The Encyclopedia of World History.* p. 816.
41. Commager. *Documents of American History.* pp. 385-388.
42. Alan Nevins. *The War For The Union: The Improvised War. 1861-1862.* (New York: Charles Scribner's Sons, 1959)., pp. 65; 70.

CHAPTER NINE THE FATE OF A NATION

1. Harry T. Williams. *Lincoln and His Generals.* (New York: Alfred A. Knopf, 1952), p. 3.
2. *Ibid.*, pp. 4-5.
3. Webster. *The Volume Library.* p. 681
4. Davis. *Don't Know Much About the Civil War.* pp. 178-180.
5. Langer. *An Encyclopedia of World History.* p. 817.
6. *Ibid.*
7. Davis. *Don't Know Much About the Civil War.*, pp, 153-156.
8. Williams. *Lincoln and His Generals.*, p. 16.
9. *Ibid.*, pp. 18-19.
10. *Ibid.* pp. 33-34.
11. Giniger. *America, America, America.* Pp. 84-86.
12. John Thompson. *America's Historic Trails.* (Washington, D.C.: National Geographic Society, 2001). pp. 144-146.
13. Webster. *The Volume Library.* p. 682.
14. Nancy Scott Anderson and Dwight Anderson. *The Generals. Ulysses S, Grant And Robert E. Lee.* (New York: Alfred A. Knopf. 1988). p. 192.
15. *Ibid.*

CHAPTER TEN THE TRANSCONTINENTAL RAILROAD—ONE OF THE GREATEST CHALLENGES PHASE ONE 1830-1862

1. Ambrose, *Nothing Like It in the World.*
2. Webster. *The Volume Library.* p. 1590.
3. Ambrose. *Nothing Like It in the World.* p. 35.
4. *Ibid.* pp. 51;55.
5. *Ibid.* pp. 43-45.
6. *Ibid.* pp. 47-50.
7. *Ibid.* p. 53.
8. Webster. *The Volume Library.* p. 1589.
9. Ambrose. *Nothing Like It in the World.* p.55.
10. *Ibid.* pp. 55-56.

11. *Ibid.* pp. 56-57.
12. *Ibid.* p. 58.
13. *Ibid.* p. 61.
14. *Ibid.*
15. *Ibid.,* pp. 66-67.
16. *Ibid.,* pp. 69-70.
17. *Ibid.,* pp. 75-76.
18. *Ibid.,* pp. 75-77.
19. *Ibid.,* pp. 80-81.
20. *Ibid.,* p.81.
21. *Ibid.,* pp. 32-32.
22. *Ibid.,* pp. 32-33.
23. *Ibid.,* pp. 33-34.
24. *Ibid.,* pp. 34-35.
25. *Ibid.,* pp. 38-39.
26. *Ibid.,* p. 84.
27. *Ibid.,* p. 85.
28. *Ibid.,* pp. 86-87.

CHAPTER ELEVEN THE BATTLES BEGIN

1.   Curt Johnson and Mark McLaughlin. *Civil War Battles.* (New York: The Fairfax Press, 1977) p. 39.
2.   *Ibid.*
3.   *Ibid.*
4.   Stern, (ed.). *The Pocket Book of America.* pp. 364-367.
5.   Williams. *Lincoln and His Generals.* p. 25.
6.   Langer. *An Encyclopedia of World History.* p. 817.
7.   *Ibid.* p. 830.
8.   Williams. *Lincoln and His Generals.* p. 25.
9.   Langer. *An Encyclopedia of World History.* p. 817.
10. *Ibid.*
11. Chester G. Hearn. *The Capture of New Orleans.* (Baton Rogue: Louisiana Stat University Press, 1995). Pp. 249-257.
12. Johnson and McLaughlin. *Civil War Battles.* p. 43.
13. Williams. *Lincoln and His Generals.* pp. 58-59.
14. Johnson and McLaughlin. *Civil War Battles.* p. 44.
15. *Ibid.*
16. *Ibid.*
17. *Ibid.*
18. *Ibid.,* pp. 47-50.
19. *Ibid.,* p. 49.

20. *Ibid.*, p. 46.

21. Giniger (ed). *America, America, America.* p. 96.

22. Alvin M. Josephy. *The Civil War in the American West.* (New York: Alfred A. Knopf, 1991). p. 4.

23. *Ibid.*, pp. 25-26.

24. *Ibid.*, p. 59.

25. *Ibid.*, pp. 65-75.

26. *Ibid.*, pp. 74-77.

27. *Ibid.*, p. 65.

28. *Ibid.*

29. *Ibid.*, pp. 91-92.

30. Commager. *Documents of American History.* p. 410.

31. *Ibid.*, p. 412.

32. Johnson and McLaughlin. *Civil War Battles.* p. 53.

33. *Ibid.*, p. 59.

34. *Ibid.*, p. 60.

35. Anderson. *The Generals. Ulysses S. Grant and Robert E. Lee.* pp. 10 ff.

36. *Ibid.*, pp. 21 ff.

37. Commager. *Documents of American History.* p. 417.

38. Johnson and McLaughlin. *Civil War Battles.* p. 69.

39. Emrich (ed). *American Folk Poetry.* pp. 451-452.

40. Commager. *Documents of American History.* p. 420.

41. Williams. *Lincoln and His Generals.* p. 199.

42. Curruth and Ehrlich. *The Harper Book of American Quotations.* p. 578.

43. Forester (ed). *American Poetry and Prose.* pp. 719-720.

44. Jill Canon. *Civil War Heroines.* (Santa Barbara, California: Bellerophon Books, 2000.)

45. *Ibid.*, p. 4.

46. *Ibid.*, p. 7.

47. *Ibid.*, p. 16.

48. *Ibid.*, p. 34.

49. *Ibid.*, p. 46.

50. *Ibid.*, p. 52.

51. *Ibid.*, p. 36.

52. *Ibid.*, p. 7.

53. *Ibid.*, p. 32.

54. *Ibid.*, p. 18.

55. *Ibid.* p. 34.

56. *Ibid.*, p. 10.

57. *Ibid.*, p.40.

58. Davis. *Don't Know Much About the Civil War.* p. 280.

59. Johnson and McLaughlin. *Civil War Battles.* p. 29.

60. *Ibid.*, pp. 80-81.

61. *Ibid.*, p. 85.

62. Williams. *Lincoln and His Generals.* pp. 262-263.

63. Johnson and McLaughlin. *Civil War Battles.* p. 91.

64. Williams. *Lincoln and His Generals.* pp. 226-227.

65. James F. Ruseling. *Men and Things I Saw in Civil War Days.* (New York: 1899). pp. 16-17, cited in Williams. *Lincoln and His Generals.* p. 272.

66. Johnson and McLaughlin. *Civil War Battles.* p. 97.

67. *Ibid.*, p. 103.

68. Commager. *Documents of American History.* pp. 428 f.

69. Williams. *Lincoln and His Generals.* p. 299.

70. Johnson and McLaughlin. *Civil War Battles.* p. 120.

71. Anderson. *The Generals. Ulysses S. Grant and Robert E. Lee.*, pp.361-362.

72. Williams. *Lincoln and His Generals.*, p. 306.

73. *Ibid.*, pp. 316-318.

74. Johnson and McLaughlin. *Civil War Battles.* p. 113.

75. Page Smith. *Trial By Fire. A People's History of the Civil War and Reconstruction.* (New York: McGraw Hill Book Company, 1982). p. 527

76 Johnson and McLaughlin. *Civil War Battles.* p. 123.

77. Davis. *Don't Know Much About the Civil War.* p. 442.

78. Commager. *Documents of American History.* p. 411.

79. Johnson and McLaughlin. *Civil War Battles.* p. 131.

80. *Ibid.*, p. 143.

81. *Ibid.*, p. 124.

82. Commager. *Documents of American History.* p. 443-443.

83. Johnson and McLaughlin. *Civil War Battles.* pp. 149-151.

84. *Ibid.*, pp. 156-158.

85. Bartlett. *Famous Quotations.* 15th Edition. P. 589.

86. Ulysses S. Grant. *Personal Memoirs of Ulysses S. Grant.* (New York: 1885-86). Cited in Kenneth Seeman Giniger (ed). *America, America, America.* pp. 102-105.

87. Hazel Fellman. *The Best Loved Poems of the American People.* pp. 433-434.

88. Allan Nevins. *The War for the Union: the Organized War to Victory: 1864-1865.* (New York: Charles Scribner's Sons, 1971). p. 322.

89. *Ibid.*, p. 323.

90. Stern. (ed.). *The Pocket Book of America.* pp. 308-309.

91. Louis Untermeyer (ed). *The Poems of William Cullen Bryant.* (NewYork: The Heritage Press, 1947). p. 151.

CHAPTER TWELVE ATTEMPTS AT RECONSTRUCTION

1. Langer. *An Encyclopedia of World History.* p. 821.

2. Commager. *Documents of American History.* p. 451-452.

3. Encyclopedia Britannica. *Annals of America*. Volume 9. pp. 593-594.
4. Commager. *Documents of American History*. pp. 458-460.
5. *Ibid.* p. 144.
6. *Ibid.* p. 147.
7. *Ibid.* p. 465-468.
8. Encyclopedia Britannica. *Annals of America*. Volume 10, pp. 21-23.
9. Commager. *Documents of American History*. p. 501.
10. *Ibid.*
11. *Ibid.*, pp. 499-500.
12. Webster. *The Volume Library*. p. 690.
13. *Ibid.*, p. 845.
14. Langer. *An Encyclopedia of World History*. p. 859
15. Commager. *Documents of American History*. p. 140.
16. Smith. *Trial by Fire*. pp. 702-703.
17. *Ibid.*, p. 783.
18. Commager. *Documents of American History*. p. 497-498.

CHAPTER THIRTEEN BUILDING AND COMPLETING THE TRANSCONTINENTIAL RAILROAD

1. Ambrose. *Nothing Like It in the World*. p. 98.
2. *Ibid.*, p. 36.
3. *Ibid.*
4. *Ibid.*, pp. 125-127.
5. *Ibid.*, p. 127.
6. *Ibid.*, pp. 74-75.
7. *Ibid.*, pp. 115-117.
8. *Ibid.*, p. 110.
9. *Ibid.*, pp. 122-124.
10. *Ibid.*, p. 147.
11. Bartlett. *Familiar Quotations*. 14th Edition. p. 30.
12. Ambrose. *Nothing Like It in the World*. p. 120.
13. *Ibid.*, p. 148.
14. *Ibid.*, p. 149.
15. *Ibid.*, p. 151.
16. *Ibid.*, p. 150.
17. *Ibid.*, p. 153.
18. *Ibid.*, p. 164.
19. *Ibid.*, p. 130.
20. *Ibid.*, p. 92.
21. *Ibid.*, p. 135.
22. *Ibid.*, p. 138.

23. *Ibid.*

24. *Ibid.*, pp. 138-139.

25. *Ibid.*, p. 167.

26. *Ibid.*, p. 140.

27. *Ibid.*, p. 171.

28. *Ibid.*

29. *Ibid.*, p. 172.

30. *Ibid.*, p. 173.

31. *Ibid.*, p. 174.

32. *Ibid.*, p. 176.

33. *Ibid.*, pp. 177-178.

34. *Ibid.*, p. 179.

35. *Ibid.*, p. 184.

36. *Ibid.*, p. 185

37. *Ibid.*, p. 191

38. *Ibid.*, p. 188.

39. *Ibid.*, p. 177.

40. *Ibid.*, p. 181.

41. Langer. *An Encyclopedia of World History.* p. 607.

42. Ambrose. *Nothing Like It in the World.* p. 193.

43. *Ibid.*, pp. 193-194.

44. *Ibid.*, p. 197.

45. *Ibid.*, pp. 199-200.

46. *Ibid.*, pp. 200-201.

47. *Ibid.*, p. 202.

48. *Ibid.*

49. *Ibid.*, pp. 203-204.

50. *Ibid.*, p. 207.

51. *Ibid.*, pp. 207-208.

52. *Ibid.*, pp. 208-211.

53. *Ibid.*, p. 212.

54. *Ibid.*, pp. 212-213.

55. *Ibid.*, p. 213.

56. Maury Klein. *Union Pacific.* Vol. 1 *Birth of a Railroad, 1862-1863.* Garden City, N.Y.: Doubleday,1987. Cited in Ambrose. *Nothing Like I In The World.* p. 216.

57. *Ibid.*

58. Ambrose. *Nothing Like It in the World.* p. 217.

59. *Ibid.*, p. 220.

60. *Ibid.*

61. *Ibid.*, p. 227.

62. *Ibid.*, p. 228.

63. *Ibid.*, p. 229.

64. *Ibid.*, p. 230.
65. *Ibid.*, pp. 231-232.
66. *Ibid.*, p. 233.
67. *Ibid.*, pp. 234-235.
68. *Ibid.*
69. *Ibid.*, pp. 238-239.
70. *Ibid.*, p. 239.
71. *Ibid.*, pp. 240-242.
72. *Ibid.*, p. 244.
73. *Ibid.*
74. *Ibid.*, p. 248.
75. *Ibid.*, p. 254.
76. *Ibid.*
77. *Ibid.*, p. 259.
78. *Ibid.*, p. 260.
79. *Ibid.* p. 265.
80. *Ibid.*, pp. 266-268.
81. *Ibid.*, p. 267.
82. *Ibid.*, pp. 268-269.
83. *Ibid.*, p. 273.
84. *Ibid.*
85. *Ibid.*, pp. 275-276.
86. *Ibid.*, pp. 278-279.
87. *Ibid.*, p. 284.
88. *Ibid.*, p. 286.
89. *Ibid.*, pp. 288.
90. *Ibid.*, p. 297.
91. *Ibid.*, p. 305.
92. *Ibid.*, p. 302.
93. *Ibid.*, p. 305.
94. *Ibid.*, p. 304.
95. *Ibid.*, p. 306.
96. *Ibid.*, p. 308.
97. *Ibid.*, p. 309/
98. *Ibid.*, p. 311.
99. *Ibid.*, p. 317.
100. *Ibid.*, p. 314.
101. *Ibid.*, p. 317.
102. *Ibid.*, pp. 290;295.
103. Webster. *The Volume Library.* p. 1603.
104. *Ibid.*, p. 1321.
105. *Ibid.*, p. 1537.

106. John W. Cunliffe, Karl Young and Mark Van Doren, Editors. *Century Reading in English Literature*. (New York: D. Appleton Company, Inc. 1940.) p. 968.

107. Langer. *An Encyclopedia of World History*. p.822,

108. Carruth and Ehrlich. *The Harper Book of American Quotations*. p. 299.

109. Ambrose. *Nothing Like It in the World*. p. 330.

110. *Ibid.*, p. 328.

111. *Ibid.*, p. 339.

112. *Ibid.*, pp. 346-350.

113. *Ibid.*, pp. 352.

114. *Ibid.*, pp. 359-360.

115. *Ibid.*, pp. 360-361.

116. *Ibid.*, pp. 361-362.

117. *Ibid.*, pp. 362-363.

118. *Ibid.*, pp. 364-365.

119. *Ibid.*, p. 366.

120. F.E. Shearer, Editor. *The Pacific Tourist*. An Illustrated Guide to the Pacific R.R.and California, and Pleasure Resorts Across the Continent. (New York: Adams and Bishop, Publishers, 1984.) pp. 181-185.

121. Emrich. *American Folk Poetry*. pp. 657-659. Professor Guy B. Johnson, author of *John Henry: Down a Negro Legend*. Chapel Hill, 1929, wrote: "I prefer to believe that (1) there was a Negro steel driver named John Henry at Big Bend Tunnel, that 2) he competed with a steam drill in a test of practicability of the device, and that (3) he probably died soon after the contest, perhaps from fever." The Big Bend Tunnel on the Chesapeake and Ohio Railroad, nine miles east of Hinton, West Virginia, was under construction from 1870 to 1872.

CHAPTER FOURTEEN FOR THE MOST PART, A SORRY CHAPTER IN OUR HISTORY

1. Johnson and McLaughlin. *Civil War Battles*. p. 46.

2. Bartlett. *Familiar Quotations*. 15th Edition. p. 589.

3. Ulysses S. Grant. *Personal Memoirs of Ulysses S. Grant*. Cited in Kenneth Giniger(ed,). *America, America, America*. pp. 102-105.

4. Commager. *Documents of American History*. Tenth Edition., pp. 460-461.

5. *Ibid.*, p. 507.

6. Ambrose. *Nothing Like It in the World*. p. 375.

7. *Ibid.*, p. 271.

8. Webster. *The Volume Library*. p. 1499.

9. *Ibid.*, p. 691.

10. Commager. *Documents of American History*. Tenth Edition., p.148.

11. Webster. *The Volume Library*. p.691.

12. *Ibid.*, pp. 609-610.

13. *Ibid.*, p. 692,

14. Ambrose. *Nothing Like It in the World.* p. 373.

15. *Ibid.*

16. Webster. *The Volume Library.* p. 692.

17. *Ibid.*, p. 1321.

18. Ambrose. *Nothing Like It in the World.* pp. 374-375.

19. Webster. *The Volume Library.* p. 692.

20. *Ibid.*, p. 693.

21. Commager. *Documents of American History.* Tenth Edition. p. 634.

22. Webster. *The Volume Library.* p. 1597.

23. *Ibid.*, p. 693.

24. *Ibid.*

25. *The Random House Encyclopedia:* Brothers Industry, 1993.

26. Webster. *The Volume Library.* p. 1459.

27. *Ibid.*, p. 1484.

28. Commager. *Documents of American History.* Tenth Edition. p. 545.

CHAPTER FIFTEEN HAYES, GARFIELD, ARTHUR, CLEVELAND, HARRISON AND CLEVELAND AGAIN

1. Commager. *Documents of American History.* p. 142.

2. Roger Matuz. Edited by Bill Harris. *The Presidents Fact Book.* (New York: BlackDog and Leventhal Publisher, 2004.) p. 308.

3. *Ibid.*, p. 314.

4. *Ibid.*, p. 316.

5. Zinn. *A Peoples' History of the United States.* p. 230.

6. *Ibid.*, p. 240.

7. *Ibid.*, pp. 245-250

8. Webster. *The Volume Library.* p. 693.

9. Zinn. *A Peoples' History of the United States.* p. 251

10. Bartlett. *Familiar Quotations.* p. 544.

11. *Ibid.*, p. 492.

12. Colbert. *Eyewitness to America.* pp. 280-281.

13. David McCullough. *The Path between the Seas.* (New York: Simon and Schuster,1977.) p. 1.

14. Matuz. *The Presidents Fact Book.* pp. 322-330.

15. Commager. *Documents of American History.* 16ᵗʰ Edition. pp. 561-563.

16. *Ibid.*, pp. 560-561.

17. Bartlett. *Familiar Qutations.* p. 492.

18. *Random House* Encyclopedia.

19. Webster. *The Volume Library.* p. 694.

20. *Encyclopedia Americana.* (Danbury Connecticut: Grolier Publishing Co. 2002.) pp. 568-569.

21. *Annals of America*. Volume 11, p. 107.

22. Webster. *The Volume Library*. p. 695.

23. *Ibid*.

24. Commager. *Documents of American History*. pp. 586-587.

25. Webster. *The Volume Library*. p. 695.

26. Matuz. *The Presidents Fact Book*. pp. 366-373.

27. *Statistical Abstract of the U.S.* 123rd Edition. Kathleen B. Cooper, Undersecretary of Economic Administration.

28. Langer. *An Encyclopedia of World History*. p. 825.

29. Webster. *The Volume Library*. p. 696.

30. Commager. *Documents of American History*. p. 605.

31. Webster. *The Volume Library*. pp. 606-607.

32. *Ibid*.

33. Matuz. *The Presidents Fact Book*. p. 360.

34. *Ibid.*, p. 350.

35. Stern. *The Pocketbook of America*. pp. 368-371.

36. *Ibid*.

37. William Rose Benet, Editor. *The Reader's Encyclopedia*. (New York: Thomas F. Crowell Company, 1948.)

CHAPTER SIXTEEN STEPS TO BECOMING A WORLD POWER

1. Webster. *The Volume Library*. p. 1549.

2. *Ibid.*, p. 697.

3. *Ibid.*, p. 1467.

4. Commager. *Documents of American History*. p.582.

5. Zinn. *A People's History of the United States*. p. 301

6. Bartlett. *Familiar Quotations*. 16th Edition, p. 538.

7. Commager. *Documents of American History*. Vol. II. Ninth Edition. p. 5-6.

8. Webster. *The Volume Library*. p. 698.

9. Benet. *The Reader's Emcyclopedia*.pp. 1232-1233.

10. Webster. *The Volume Library*. p. 698.

11. *Ibid*.

12. *Ibid*.

13. *Ibid*.

14. *Ibid*.

15. Samuel Gompers. Edited by Hayes Robbins. *Labor and the Common Welfare*. (Freeport, N.Y. Libraries Press, 1969.) p. 6.

16. *Ibid.*, p. 575.

17. Matuz. *The Presidents Fact Book*. pp. 388-389.

18. *Ibid.*, pp. 397-398.

19. *Ibid.*, pp. 398-403.

20. Webster. *The Volume Library.* p.699
21. *Ibid.*
22. *Ibid.,* p. 699.
23. *Ibid., p. 700.*
24. Bartlett. *Familiar Quotations.* p. 604.
25. Webster. *The Volume Library.* p. 699.
26. *Ibid.,* p. 700.
27. Matuz. *The Presidents Fact Book.* p. 406.
28. Webster. *The Volume Library.* p. 699.
29. Matuz. *The Presidents Fact Book.* p. 407.
30. Webster. *The Volume Library.* p. 699.

CHAPTER SEVENTEEN WILLIAM HOWARD TAFT TRUST-BUSTER

1. Webster. *The Volume Library.* p. 1592.
2. Commager. *Documents of American History.* pp. 54-55.
3. Webster. *The Volume Library.* p. 700.
4. *Ibid.*
5. Commager. *Documents of American History.* p. 62
6. Colbert. *Eyewitness to America.* p. 332.
7. Commager. *Documents of American History.* p. 814.
8. *Ibid.*
9. Webster. *The Volume Library.* p. 452.
10. *Ibid.,* p. 700.

CHAPTER EIGHTEEN WOODROW WILSON-AMERICA'S FIRST WORLD LEADER

1. Matuz. *The Presidents Fact Book.* pp. 435-436.
2. *Ibid.*
3. *Ibid.*
4. *Ibid.,* p. 437.
5. *Ibid.,* pp. 436-437.
6. Webster. *The Volume Library.,* p. 1552.
7. Commager. *Documents of American History.* p. 809.
8. *Ibid.,* pp. 82-84.
9. Commager. *Documents of American History.* p. 83.
10. *Ibid.* pp. 82-84.
11. *Ibid.*
12. *Ibid.*
13. *Ibid.,* p. 86.

14. *Ibid.*, p. 87.
15. Webster. *The Volume Library.* p. 701.
16. *Ibid.*
17. *Ibid.*
18. *Ibid.*
19. Matuz. *The Presidents Fact Book.* p. 442.
20. Langer. *An Encyclopedia of World History.* p. 856.
21. Commager. *Documents of American History.* p. 91.
22. Webster. *The Volume Library.* pp. 702-703/
23. *Ibid.*, p. 702.
24. Langer. *An Encyclopedia of World History.* p. 803.
25. *Ibid.*, pp. 804-805.
26. Webster. *The Volume Library.* p. 703.
27. Langer. *An Encyclopedia of World History.* p. 943.
28. Foerster. *American Prose and Poetry.* p. 1313.
29. Langer. *An Encyclopedia of World History.* p. 951.
30. *Ibid.*
31. Bartlett. *Familiar Quotations.* 15th Edition. P. 682.
32. Commager. *Documents of American History.* pp. 125-128.
33. *Ibid.*, p. 128.
34. Webster. *The Volume Library.* p. 703.
35. Commager. *Documents of American History.* p. 130.
36. *Ibid.*, p. 132.
37. Webster. *The Volume Library.* p. 703.
38. *Ibid.*, p. 704.
39. *Ibid.*
40. *Ibid.*
41. Bartlett. *Familiar Quotations.* 16th Edition. p. 580.
42. Webster. *The Volume Library.* p. 704.
43. *Ibid.*
44. *Ibid.*, p. 1577.
45. *Ibid.*, p. 704.
46. Langer. *An Encyclopedia of World History.* p. 959.
47. *Ibid.*
48. Benet. *The Reader's Encyclopedia.* pp. 585;483.
49. *Ibid.*, pp. 991;708.
50. Cunnliffe. *Century Readings in English Literature.* p. 1079.
51. Daringer. *The Poets Craft.* p. 267.
52. Benet. *The Reader's Encyclopedia.* p. 917.
53. Webster. *The Volume Library.* p. 706.
54. Commager. *Documents of American History.* p.809.
55. Matuz. *The Presidents Fact Book.* p. 447.

56. Commager. *Documents of American History.* p.814,

57. Webster. *The Volume Library.* p. 706.

58. Commager. *Documents of American History.* p.815.

59. *Ibid.,* pp. 814-815.

60. Matuz. *The Presidents Fact Book.* p. 447.

61. Langer. *An Encyclopedia of World History.* p. 1074.

CHAPTER NINETEEN PEACE, SCANDAL AND THE ROARDING TWENTIES

1. Matuz. *The Presidents Fact Book.* pp. 459-462.

2. *Ibid.,* p. 476.

3. Webster. *The Volume Library.* p. 707.

4. *Ibid.,* p. 1526.

5. *Ibid.,* p. 1554.

6. *Ibid.,* p. 1525.

7. Matuz. *The Presidents Fact Book.* p. 495.

8. Webster. *The Volume Library.* p. 707.

9. Commager. *Documents of American History.* pp. 181-183.

10. Matuz. *The Presidents Fact Book.* p. 465.

11. *Ibid.*

12. *Ibid.*

13. *Ibid.*

14. *Ibid.*

15. *Ibid.*

16. Peter Jennings and Todd Brewster. *The Century.* (New York: Doubleday, 1998.) p. 68.

17. *Ibid.,* pp. 109-111.

18. *Ibid.,* pp. 124-127.

19. *Ibid.,* pp. 103-107.

20. *Ibid.*

21. *Ibid.*

22. *Ibid.,* p. 113.

23. *Ibid.,* p. 132.

24. *Ibid.,* pp. 115-116.

CHAPTER TWENTY PROSPERITY, PEACE ATTEMPTS AND AVIATION HISTORY

1. Matuz. *The Presidents Fact Book.* p. 475

2. Webster. *The Volume Library.* p. 707.

3. *Ibid.,* p. 708.

4. Matuz. *The Presidents Fact Book.* p. 384.

5.   Thompson. *America's Historic Trails.* p. 168.
6.   Matuz. *The Presidents Fact Book.* p. 483.
7.   *New York Times.* May 23, 1927.
8.   Matuz. *The Presidents Fact Book.* p. 481.
9.   *Ibid.*
10. Bartlett. *Familiar Quotations.* p. 568.

CHAPTER TWENTY-ONE A DEPRESSION LIKE NONE OTHER

1.   Matuz. *The Presidents Fact Book.* pp. 491-495.
2.   Commager. *Documents of American History.* p. 815.
3.   Matuz, *The Presidents Fact Book.* p. 497.
4.   *Random House Encyclopedia.*
5.   Matuz. *The Presidents Fact Book.* pp. 497-498.
6.   Webster. *The Volume Library.* p. 709.
7.   *Ibid.*, p. 708-709.
8.   *Ibid.*, p. 709.
9.   Matuz. *The Presidents Fact Book.* p. 499.
10. *Ibid.*, p. 501.

CHAPTER TWENTY-TWO ROOSEVELT ATTEMPTS TO GET AMERICA WORKING AGAIN

1.   Matuz. *The Presidents Fact Book.* pp. 508-511.
2.   Commager. *Documents of American History.* p. 240.
3.   Webster. *The Volume Library.* pp. 709-710.
4.   Matuz. *The Presidents Fact Book.* pp. 514-515.
5.   Webster. *The Volume Library.* p. 1527.
6.   *Ibid.*, p. 1529.
7.   Matuz. *The Presidents Fact Book.* p. 516.
8.   Webster. *The Volume Library.* p. 149
9.   *Ibid.*, p. 711.
10. Bartlett. *Familiar Quotations.* pp. 635-636.
11. *Churchill.* Written and Edited by the Staff of the *New York Times.*
12. Commager. *Documents of American History.* pp. 446-449.
13. *Ibid.*, p. 451.

CHAPTER TWENTY-THREE THEY ANSWERED THE CALL

1.   Commager. *Documents of American History.* p. 451-452.
2.   Williamson Murry andAllan R. Millett. *A War to Be Won.* (Cambridge, Massachusetts: Harvard University Press, 2000.) p. 550.

3. *Ibid.*

4. *Ibid., p. ix.*

5. Stephen E. Ambrose. *New History of World War II.* (New York: Viking, 1968.) pp. 413-415/

6. *Ibid.*

7. Murry. *A War to Be Won.* p. 535.

8. Ambrose. *New History of World War II.* p. 426.

9. Murry. *A War to Be Won.* p. 179.

10. Ambrose. *New History of World War II.* P. 143.

11. *Ibid.*

12. *Ibid.,* p. 134.

13. *Ibid.,* pp. 144-145.

14. *Ibid.,* pp. 305-306.

15. Murry. *A War to Be Won.* p.211.

16. *Ibid.,* p. 215.

17. W.E.B. Griffin. *Line of Fire.* (New York: G.P. Putnam's Sons, 1992.) p. 166.

18. Ambrose. *New History of World War II.* pp. 334-335.

19. *Ibid.,* p. 319.

20. *Ibid.,* pp. 334-335.

21. *Ibid.,* p. 510.

22. *Ibid.,* pp. 565-566.

23. Commager. *Docuements of American History.* pp. 452-453.

24. Ambrose. *New History of World War II.* pp. 185-198.

25. *Ibid.,* p. 201.

26. *Ibid.,* p. 207.

27. *Ibid.,* pp. 342-343.

28. *Ibid.,* pp. 349-350.

29. *Ibid.,* pp. 369-370.

30. *Ibid.,* pp. 178-270/

31. *Ibid.,* p. 461.

32. *Ibid.,* p. 463.

33. *Ibid.,* pp. 470-471.

34. *Ibid.,* p. 468.

35. Sandburg, Carl. *The Complete Poems of Carl Sandburg.* pp. 637-638

CHAPTER TWENTY-FOUR WHO THE HELL IS THIS GUY TRUMAN?

1. Matuz. *The Presidents Fact Book.* pp. 534-537.

2. Ambrose. *New History of World War II.* p. 585.

3. *Ibid.,* pp. 600-601.

4. *Ibid.,* pp. 579-588.

5. Colbert. *Eyewitness to America*. pp. 434-437.

6. Matuz. *The Presidents Fact Book*. p. 551.

7. Admiral Stuart S. Murray. "A Harried Host on the Missouri"; in John T. Mason, Jr. *The Pacific War. Remembering An Oral History Collection*. (Annapolis: 1986) pp. 353-354, cited in Murray and Millett. *A War to Be Won*. p. 526.

8. *Department of Veterans Affairs*. http;//www.gibill.va.gov/education/GI-Bill. Htm. p.3.

9. Bureau of Census, 1975. U.S. Dept. of Commerce. *Historical Statistics of the U.S. Colonial time to 1970*. 1975

10. *Department of Veterans Affairs*. p. 4.

11. Jennings. *The Century*. p. 295.

12. Commager. *Documents of American History*. pp. 525-529.

13. *Ibid.*, pp. 532-534.

14. Matuz. *The Presidents Fact Book*. p. 541.

15. *Ibid.*, p. 544.

16. Commager. *Documents of American History*. Vol. II. Ninth Edition. P. 548.

17. Matuz. *The Presidents Fact Book*. pp. 544-545.

18. Langer. *An Encyclopedia of World History*. p. 1228.

19. *Ibid.*, p. 1286.

20. Commager. *Documents of American History*. pp. 553-554.

21. William Manchester. *American Caesar*, (Boston: Little, Brown and Company, 1978). p. 681.

CHAPTER TWENTY-SIX I LIKE IKE

1. Stephen E. Ambrose. *Eisenhower*. Volume One. (New York:Simon and Schuster, 1984.) pp. 18-42.

2. *Ibid.*, pp. 43-54.

3. *Ibid.*, pp. 55-66.

4. *Ibid.* pp. 67-153.

5. *Ibid.*, p. 309.

6. *Ibid.*, pp. 364-386.

7. *Ibid.*, pp. 387.-408.

8. *Ibid.*, p. 475,

9. Ambrose. *Eisenhower. The President*. Volume Two. p. 46

10. *Ibid.*, p. 158.

11. *Ibid.*, p. 106.

12. Commager. *Documents of American History*. Vol. II. Ninth Edition. P. 604.

13. Huntchins: On Democracy.

14. Ambrose. *Eisenhower. The President*. Vol. Two. p. 158.

15. *Ibid.*, p. 245.

16. Matuz. *The Presidents Fact Book*. p. 563.

17. Ambrose. *Eisenhower. The President*. Vol. Two. p. 414.

18. *Ibid.*, pp. 415-427.

CHAPTER TWENTY-SEVEN ASK NOT WHAT YOUR COUNTRY CAN DO FOR YOU

1. Matuz. *The Presidents Fact Book.* pp. 573-574.
2. *Ibid.*, pp. 574-575.
3. Sally Bedell Smith. *Grace and Power.* The Private World of the Kennedy White House. (New York: Random House, 2004.) p. 56.
4. Jennings and Brewster. *The Century.* pp. 346-347.
5. Commager. *Documents of American History.* Vol. II. Ninth Edition. pp. 654-656.
6. Smith. *Grace and Power.* pp. 177-179.
7. Langer. *An Encyclopedia of American History.* p. 1218.
8. Ambrose. *Eisenhower. The President.* Vol. 2. P. 656.
9. Matuz. *The Presidents Fact Book.* p. 581.
10. Commager. *Documents of American History.* Vol. II. Ninth Edition. p. 815.
11. David Bake. *Spaceflight and Rocketry.* (New York: Facts on File, Inc. 1996.) p. 119.
12. Jennings and Brewster. *The Century.* p. 307.
13. Langer. *An Encyclopedia of World History.* p. 1211.
14. Jennings and Brewster. *The Century.* pp, 373-375.
15. Commager. *Documents of American History.* Vol. II. Ninth Edition. pp. 678-680.
16. Bartlett. *Familiar Quotations.* p. 761.
17. Commager. *Documents of American History.* Vol. II. Ninth Edition. Pp. 678-681.
18. Matuz. *The Presidents Fact Book.* p. 587.

CHAPTER TWENTY-EIGHT FULFILLMENT THEN FAILURE

1. Robert Dallek. *Lone Star Rising.* Lyndon Johnson and His Times. 1908-1960. (New York: University Press, 1991.) pp. 30-81.
2. *Ibid.*, pp. 82-91.
3. *Ibid.*, pp. 93-95.
4. *Ibid.*, pp. 96-123.
5. *Ibid.*, pp. 125-144.
6. *Ibid.*, pp. 144-156.
7. *Ibid.*, pp. 236-240.
8. Matuz. *The Presidents Fact Book.* p. 599.
9. Robert Dullek. *Flawed Giant.* Lyndon Johnson and His Times.1961-1973. (New York: University Press, 1998.) pp. 8-9
10. *Ibid.*, p. 18
11. *Ibid.*, p. 20.
12. *Ibid.*, pp. 20-23.
13. *Ibid.*, pp. 23-30.

14. *Ibid.*, pp. 30-32.
15. *Ibid.*, pp. 33-43.
16. *Ibid.*, pp. 44-48.
17. *Ibid.*, p. 49.
18. *Ibid.*, pp. 49-51.
19. Commager. *Documents of American History.* Vol. II. Ninth Edition. p. 816.
20. Jennings and Brewster. *The Century.* pp. 391-392.
21. Commager. *Documents of American History.* Vol. II. Ninth Edition. pp. 687-688.
22. Matuz. *The Presidents Fact Book.* pp. 602-603.
23. *Ibid.*
24. Dullek. *Flawed Giant.* pp. 147-151-
25. *Ibid.*, p. 152.
26. Matuz. *The Presidents Fact Book.* p. 605.
27. *Ibid.*, p. 607.
28. *Ibid.*
29. Jennings and Brewster. *The Century.* pp. 409-4 11.
30. Dullek. *Flawed Giant.* pp. 527-528.
31. Commager. *Documents of American History.* Vol. II. Ninth Edition. p. 724.
32. Matuz. *The Presidents Fact Book.* p. 612

CHAPTER TWENTY-NINE IF AT FIRST YOU DON'T SUCCEED, TRY TRY AGAIN

1. Matuz. *The Presidents Fact Book.* p. 617.
2. Stephen E. Ambrose. *Nixon.* The Education of a Politician. 1913-1962. (New York: Simon and Schuster, 1987.) p. 101.
3. Matuz. *The Presidents Fact Book.* pp. 618-622.
4. *Ibid.*, p. 622.
5. Colbert. *Eyewitness to America.* pp. 508-509.
6. Commager. *Documents of American History.* Vol. II. Ninth Edition. p. 816.
7. Matuz. *The Presidents Fact Book.* p. 628.
8. Richard Nixon. *In The Arena.* (New York: Simon and Schuster, 1990.) p. 33.
9. *Ibid.*, pp. 33-37.
10. Stephen E. Ambrose. *Nixon.* Ruin and Recovery. 1973-1990. (New York: Simon and Schuster. 1991.) pp. 229-235.
11. Dale W. Jacobs. Editor in Chief. *The World book Encyclopedia.* Volume 2. (Chicago: Scott Fetzer Company, 20043.) p. 102.
12. Commager. *Documents of American History.* Vol. II. Ninth Editon. p. 816
13. Matuz. *The Presidents Fact Book.* p. 629.
14. Nixon. *In The Arena.* p. 430.
15. John W. Whitehead. "Clinton's Definition of Impeachment". *International Herald Tribune.* September 18, 1998.

CHAPTER THIRTY I HAVE NOT SOUGHT THIS ENORMOUS RESPONSIBILITY BUT I WILL NOT SHIRK IT

1. Jerald F. terHorst. *Gerald Ford and the Future of the Presidency.* (New York: The Third Press, Joseph Okpaku Publishing Company, Inc., 1974.) p. 28.
2. *Ibid.,* pp. 36-37.
3. *Ibid.,* pp. 38-40.
4. *Ibid.,* pp. 38-43.
5. *Ibid.,* pp. 43-44.
6. *Ibid.,* pp. 47-48.
7. *Ibid.,* pp. 49-51.
8. Jacobs. *The World Book Encyclopedia.* Vol. 7. p 375.
9. TerHorst. *Gerald Ford and the Future of the Presidency.* p. 136-137.
10. Jacobs. *The World Book Encyclopedia.* Vol. 7. p 376.
11. TerHorst. *Gerald Ford and the Future of the Presidency.* p. 185.
12. *Ibid.,* p. 188.
13. *Ibid.* p. 188-191/
14. Jacobs. *The World Book Encyclopedia.* Vol. 7. P. 378.
15. Matuz. *The Presidents Fact Book.* pp. 652-653.
16. Jacobs. *The World Book Encyclopedia.* Vol. 7. P. 378.
17. Matuz. *The Presidents Fact Book.* p. 651.

CHAPTER THIRTY-ONE THE HARD LUCK PRESIDENCY OF JIMMY CARTER

1. Jacobs. *The World Book Encyclopedia.* Vol. 4. Pp. 252-255.
2. *Ibid.,* pp. 255-256.
3. *Ibid.,* pp. 256-257.
4. *Ibid.,* p. 257
5. *Ibid.*
6. *Ibid.,* p. 259.
7. *Ibid.* pp. 258-259.
8. *Ibid.,* pp. 259-260.

CHAPTER THIRTY-TWO "LIFE IS JUST ONE GRAND SWEET SONG, SO LET THE MUSIC BEGIN"

1. Ronald Reagan. *An American Life.* (New York: Simon and Schuster, 1900.) p. 21.
2. *Ibid.,* p. 22.
3. *Ibid.,*
4. *Ibid.,* pp. 26-29.
5. *Ibid.,* pp. 33.

6. *Ibid.*, pp. 36-37.
7. *Ibid.*, p. 35.
8. *Ibid.*, pp. 38-40.
9. *Ibid.*, p. 40.
10. *Ibid.*, pp. 41-47.
11. *Ibid.*, pp. 44-56.
12. *Ibid.*, pp. 57-58.
13. *Ibid.*, pp. 62-74.
14. *Ibid.*, pp. 77-81.
15. *Ibid.*, pp. 82-84.
16. *Ibid.*, pp. 85-86.
17. *Ibid.*, pp. 89-90.
18. *Ibid.*, pp. 90-92.
19. *Ibid.*, pp. 92-96.
20. *Ibid.*, pp. 96-97.
21. *Ibid.*, p. 96.
22. *Ibid.*, p. 98.
23. *Ibid.*, p. 102.
24. *Ibid.*, pp. 99-100.
25. *Ibid.*, pp. 105-110.
26. *Ibid.*, p. 119.
27. *Ibid.*, pp. 120-123.
28. *Ibid.*, pp. 124-125.
29. *Ibid.*, pp. 126-129.
30. *Ibid.*, p. 131.
31. *Ibid.*, p. 130.
32. *Ibid.*, pp. 132-133.
33. *Ibid.*, p. 134.
34. *Ibid.*, p. 136.
35. *Ibid.*, pp. 138-143.
36. *Ibid.*, pp. 146-148.
37. *Ibid.*, p. 149.
38. *Ibid.*, p. 151.
39. *Ibid.*, pp. 152-154.
40. *Ibid.*, p. 156.
41. *Ibid.*, pp. 157-158.
42. *Ibid.*, p. 175.
43. *Ibid.*, p. 179.
44. *Ibid.*, pp. 183-184.
45. *Ibid.*, pp. 184-191.
46. *Ibid.*, pp. 189-191.
47. *Ibid.*, pp. 192-196.

CHAPTER THIRTY-THREE "MR. GORBACHEV, TEAR DOWN THIS WALL"

1. Reagan. *An American Life*. pp. 212-213.
2. *Ibid.*, pp. 215-216.
3. *Ibid.*, p. 216.
4. *Ibid.*, p. 218.
5. *Ibid.*, pp. 220-227.
6. *Ibid.*, pp. 226-227.
7. *Ibid.*, pp. 230-235.
8. *Ibid.*, pp. 237-240.
9. *Ibid.*, p. 241.
10. *Ibid.*, pp. 259-261.
11. *Ibid.*, pp. 285-289.
12. *Ibid.*, pp. 279-280.
13. *Ibid.*, pp. 282-283.
14. *Ibid.*, pp. 611.
15. *Ibid.*, p. 204.
16. *Ibid.*, p. 333.
17. *Ibid.*, pp. 447-457.
18. *Ibid.*, p. 452.
19. *Ibid.*, pp. 452-463.
20. *Ibid.*, pp. 368-372.
21. Lou Cannon. *President Reagan. The Role of a Lifetime.* (New York: Simon and Schuster, 1991.) p. 493.
22. Reagan. *An American Life*. pp. 373-376.
23. *Ibid.*, p. 35.
24. *Ibid.*, pp. 38-39.
25. *Ibid.*, pp. 41-42.
26. *Ibid.*, pp. 57-59.
27. *Ibid.*, pp. 70-71.
28. *Ibid.*, p. 247.
29. *Ibid.*, p. 246.
30. *Ibid.*, p. 326.
31. *Ibid.*, p. 328.
32. *Ibid.*, pp. 328-329.
33. *Ibid.*, pp. 606-607.
34. Matuz. *The Presidents Fact Book.* p. 684.
35. *Ibid., pp. 493-498.*
36. *Ibid.*, pp. 499-500.
37. *Ibid.*, pp. 403-404.
38. Cannon. *President Reagan. The Role of a Lifetime.* p. 88.

39. Reagan. *An American Life*. pp. 614-615.
40. *Ibid.*
41. *Ibid.*, pp. 615-616.
42. *Ibid.*, p. 633.
43. *Ibid.*, p. 636.
44. Churchill. *In Memoriam*. Written and Edited by the Staff of *The New York Times*. (New York: Bantam Books, 1965). P. 55.
45. Reagan. *An American Life*. pp. 672-674.
46. *Ibid.*, p. 664.
47. *Ibid.*, p. 660.
48. *Ibid.*, pp. 673-679.
49. Cannon. *President Reagan. The Role of a Lifetime*. p. 121.
50. Reagan. *An American Life*. pp. 681-683.
51. Mikhail Gorbachev. *Memoirs*. (New York: Doubleday, 1995.) pp. 718-722.
52. Reagan. *An American Life*. p. 686.
53. *Ibid.*, pp. 693-696.
54. *Ibid.*, pp. 699-700.
55. Cannon. *President Reagan. The Role of a Lifetime*. p. 792.
56. *Freedom Is Not Free by* Cadet Major Kelly Strong, Air Force Junior ROTC, Homestead Senior High School, Homestead, Florida. 1988.

BIBLIOGRAPHY

Allen, Gay Wilson and Walter B. Rideout. *American Poetry.* New York: Harper Row, 1965.

Ambrose, Stephen E. *Eisenhower.* Volume One. New York: Simon and Schuster, 1984.

—. *Eisenhower.* Volume Two. New York: Simon and Schuster, 1984.

—. *New History of World War II.* New York: Viking, 1966.

—. *Nixon. The Education of a Politician—1913-1962.* New York: Simon and Schuster, 1987.

—. *Nixon. Ruin and Recovery—1973-1990.* New York: Simon and Schuster, 1991.

—. *Nothing Like It in the World. The Men Who Built the Transcontinental Railroad 1863-1869.* New York: Simon and Schuster, 2000.

—. *Undaunted Courage.* New York: Simon and Schuster, 1996.

Anderson, Nancy Scott and Dwight Anderson. *The Generals. Ulysses S. Grant and Robert E. Lee.* New York: Alfred A. Knopf, 1988.

Baker, David. *Spaceflight and Rocketry. A Chronology.* New York: Fact on File, Inc., 1996

Bartlett, John. *Familiar Quotations.* A Collection of passages, phrases and proverbs Traced to their sources in ancient and modern literature. Fourteenth Edition. Boston: Little, Brown and Company, 1968.

—. *Familiar Quotations.* Fifteenth Edition. Boston: Little, Brown and Company, 1980.

—. *Familiar Quotations.* Sixteenth Edition. Boston: Little, Brown and Company, 2000.

Benet, William Rose. Editor. *The Reader's Encyclopedia.* New York: Thomas F. Crowell Company, 1948.

Bennett, Rose. Editor. *Visiting Our Past.* America's Historyland. Washington, D.C.: National Geographic Society, 1977.

Bogle, John C. *The Constitution of the United States.* Philadelphia, Pennsylvania: National Conference Center.

Bureau of Census, 1975. U. Department of Commerce. *Historical Statistics of the U.S. Colonial Times to 1970. 1975.*

Cannon, Lou. *President Reagan. The Role of a Lifetime.* New York: Simon and Schuster, 1991.

Canon, Jill. *Civil War Heroines.* Santa Barbara, California: Bellerphone Books, 2000.

Carey, John (Ed.). *Eyewitness to History.* Cambridge, Massachusetts: Harvard University Press, 1988.

Carruth, Gorton and Eugene Ehrlich. *The Harper Book of American Quotations.* New York: Harper & Row, Publishers, 1988.

Churchill. Written and Edited by the Staff of the *New York Times.* New York: Bantam Books, 1965.

Colbert, David. (Ed.). *Eyewitness to America.* New York: Pantheon Books, 1997. *The Colonial Williamsburg Calendar.* Williamsburg Foundation, 20004.

Commager, Henry Steel and Milton Cantor. *Documents of American History.* Volume I to 1898. Tenth Edition. Englewood Cliffs, New Jersey: Prentice Hall, 1988.

—. *Documents of American History.* Volume II. Since 1898. Englewood Cliffs, New Jersey: Prentice Hall, 1973.

Cooke, Alistair. *America.* New York: Alfred A. Knopf, 1973.

Cowen, Phoebe Strong. *The Herkimers and Schuylers.* An Historical Sketch of Two Families. Albany, New York: Juel Munsell's Sons Publishers, 1903.

Cunliffe, John W., Karl Young and Mark Van Doran, Editors. *Century Readings in English Literature.* New York: D. Appleton Century Company, Inc. 1946.

Dallek, Robert. *Lone Star Rising.* Lyndon Johnson and His Times. 1908-1960. New York: University Press, 1991.

—. *Flawed Giant.* Lyndon Johnson and His Times. 1960-1973. New York: University Press, 1998.

Daringer, Helen Fern and Anne Thazter Eaton. *The Poet's Craft.* New York: World Book Company. 1935.

Davis, Kenneth C. *Don't Know Much About the Civil War.* New York: William Morrow and Company, Inc. 1996.

Department of Veterans Affairs, http://www.gibill.va.gov.education/GI-Bill.jtm.

Dorrell, Dean. "Eulogy of Nancy Hanks Lincoln." Presented at the Boyhood National Memorial, February 2002.

Dunnell, John P., *The Illinois and Michigan Canal and the Old Northwest.* Unpublished Master's Thesis. Normal: Illinois State Normal University, 1955.

Emrich, Duncan. *American Folk Poetry.* Boston: Little, Brown and Co. 1974

Encyclopedia Americana. Danbury, Connecticut: Grolier Publishing Company, 2002.

Encyclopedia Britannica, Inc. *The Annals of America.* Volume 4, (1944). Chicago: Encyclopedia Britannica, Inc. 1976.

—. *The Annals of America,* Volume 8, (1852-1857). Chicago: Encyclopedia Britannica, Inc. 1976.

—. *The Annals of America,* Volume 9, (1858-1883). Chicago: Encyclopedia Britannica, Inc. 1976.

—. *The Annals of America,* Volume 11, (1884-1894). Chicago: Encyclopedia Britannica, Inc. 1976.

Fellman, Hazel (Ed.). *The Best Loved Poems of the American People.* New York: Garden City Books, 1936.

Forester, Norman. *American Poetry and Prose.* Boston: Houghton Mifflin Company, 1947.

Giniger, Kenneth Seeman. *America, America, America.* New York: Franklin Watts, 1957.

Gompers, Samuel. *Labor and the Common Welfare.* Editid by Hayes Robbins. Freeport, New York: Libraries Press. 1969.

Gorbachev, Mikhail. *Memoirs.* New York: Doubleday, 1995.

Gove, Philip B. Editor in Chief. *Webster's Seventh New Collegiate Dictionary.* Springfield, Massachusetts: G. & C. Merriam Company, 1971.

Grafton, John. *The American Revolution.* A Picture Source Book. New York: Dover Publication, Inc., 1975.

Grant, Ulysses S. Grant. *Personal Memoirs of Ulysses S. Grant.* New York: 1885-86.

Griffin, W.E.B. *Line of Fire.* New York: G.P. Putnam's Sons, 1992.

Hamilton, Henry. *The Epic of Chicago.* Chicago: Willett, Clark and Company, 1932.

Hearn, Chester, *The Capture of New Orleans.* Baton Rouge: Louisiana State UniversityPress, 1995.

Jacobs, Dale W. Editor-in-Chief. *The World Book Encyclopedia.* Volumes 2; 4; 7. Chicago: Scott Fetzer Company, 2003.

Jennings, Peter and Todd Brewster. *The Century.* New York: Doubleday, 1998.

Johnson, Curt and Mark McLaughlin. *Civil War Battles.* New York: Farfax Press, 1977.

Josephy, Alvin M. *The Civil War in the American West.* New York: Alfred A. Knopf, 1991.

Klein, Maury. *Union Pacific.* Vol I. Birth of a Railroad: 1862-66. Garden City, New York: Doubleday, 1987.

Langer, William L. (Ed.). *An Encyclopedia of World History.* Boston: Houghton Mifflin Company, 1968.

Langguth, A.J. *Patriots.* The Men Who Started the American Revolution. New York: Simon and Schuster, 1988.

Manchester, William. *American Caesar,* Boston: Little, Brown and Company, 1978.

Mason, John T. Jr. *The Pacific War. Remembering An Oral History Collection.* Annapolis, Naval Institute Press, 1986.

Matuz, Roger. Edited by Bill Harris. *The Presidents Fact Book*. New York: Black Dog & Leventhal Publishers, Inc. 2004.

McCullough, David. *The Path Between the Seas*. New York: Simon and Schuster, 1977.

Meltzer, Milton. *Milestones to American Liberty: The Foundations of the Republic*. New York: Thomas Y. Crowell Company, 1961.

Mudd, Roger. *American Heritage: Great Minds of History*. New York: Wiley and Sons, Inc. 1999.

Murray, Williamson and Allan R. Millett. *A War to be Won*. Cambridge, Massachusetts: Harvard University Press, 2000.

Murray, Stuart S. Admiral. "A Harried Host on the Missouri." in John Mason's *The Pacific War. Remembering An Oral History Collection*. Annapolis: Naval Insitutute Press, 1986.

Nevins, Allan. *Ordeal of the Union: A House Dividing 1852-1857*. New York; Charles Scribner's Sons, 1947.

—. *The Emergence of Lincoln, Douglas, Buchanan and Party Chaos, 1857-1859*. New York: Charles Scribner's Sons, 1950.

—. *The Emergence of Lincoln: Prologue to Civil War. 1959-1861*. New York: Charles Scribner's Sons, 1950.

—. *The War for the Union: The Improvised Warm 1861-1862*. New York: Charles Scribner's Sons, 1959.

—. *The War for the Union: War Becomes Revolution, 1862-1863*. New York: Charles Scribner's Sons, 1960.

—. *The War for the Union: The Organized War, 1863-1864*. New York: Charles Scribner's Sons, 1971.

—. *The War for the Union: The Organized War to Victory, 1864-1865*. New York: Charles Scribner's Sons, 1971. *New York Times*, May 23, 1927.

Nixon, Richard. *In the Arena*. New York: Simon and Schuster. 1990. *The Random House Encyclopedia*. Brother Floppy Disk developed and copyrighted 1992, Microlytics, Inc. erox Corp.

Reagan, Ronald. *An American Life*. The Autobiography. New York: Simon and Schuster, 1990.

Rusling, James F. *Men and Things I Saw in Civil War Days*. New York: 1899.

Sandburg, Carl. *The Complete Poems of Carl Sandburg*. San Diego, California: Harcourt, Inc., 1970.

Schlarman, Joseph H. *From Quebec to New Orleans: The Story of the French in America . . . Fort de Chartes*. Belleville, Illinois: Beuchler Publishing Company, 1929.

Shearer. F.E. Editor. *The Pacific Tourist*. An Illustrative Guide to the Pacific R.R. and California, and Pleasure Resorts Across the Continent. New York: Adams and Bishop, Publishers, 1884.

Smith, Page. *Trial by Fire.* A People's History of the Civil War and Reconstruction. New York: McGraw-Hill Book Company, 1982.

Smith, Sally Bedell. *Grace and Power.* The Private World of the Kennedy White House. New York: Random House, 2004.

Statistical Abstract of the U.S. 123rd Edition. Kathleen B. Cooper, Undersecretary of Economic Administration, 2000.

Stern, Philip Van Doren (Ed.). *The Pocket Book of America.* New York: Pocket Books, Inc., 1942.

TerHorst, Jerald F. *Gerald Ford and the Future of the Presidency.* New York: The Third Press, Joseph Okpaku Publishing Company, Inc. 1974.

Thompson, John. *America's Historic Trails.* Washington, D.C.: National Geographic Society, 2001.

Thuwaites, Reuben G. (Ed.). *Jesuit Relations and Allied Documents.* Cleveland: Burrows Brothers, 1903, XXIII.

Untermeyer, Louis (Ed.). *The Poems of William Cullen Bryant.* New York: The Heritage Press, 1947.

Webster, Richard, (Mng. Ed.). *The Volume Library.* An Encyclopedia of Practical and Cultural Information. Brief, Concise, Clear. Topically Arranged for Ready Reference and Home Study. New York: Educators Association, 1944.

Whitehead, John W. "Clinton's Definition of Impeachment." *International Herald Tribune.* September 18, 1998.

Williams, T. Harry. *Lincoln and His Generals.* Alfred A. Knopf. 1958.

Zinn, Howard. *A People's History of the United States.* 1492-Present. New York: Harper Collins, 2003.

INDEX